TOWARD A COGNITIVE SEMANTICS

Language, Speech, and Communication

Statistical Language Learning, Eugene Charniak, 1994

The Development of Speech Perception, edited by Judith Goodman and Howard C. Nusbaum, 1994

Construal, Lyn Frazier and Charles Clifton, Jr., 1995

The Generative Lexicon, James Pustejovsky, 1996

The Origins of Grammar: Evidence from Early Language Comprehension, Kathy Hirsh-Pasek and Roberta Michnick Golinkoff, 1996

Language and Space, edited by Paul Bloom, Mary A. Peterson, Lynn Nadel, and Merrill F. Garrett, 1996

Corpus Processing for Lexical Acquisition, edited by Branimir Boguraev and James Pustejovsky, 1996

Methods for Assessing Children's Syntax, edited by Dana McDaniel, Cecile McKee, and Helen Smith Cairns, 1996

The Balancing Act: Combining Symbolic and Statistical Approaches to Language, edited by Judith Klavans and Philip Resnik, 1996

The Discovery of Spoken Language, Peter W. Jusczyk, 1996

Lexical Competence, Diego Marconi, 1997

Finite-State Language Processing, edited by Emmanuel Roche and Yves Schabes, 1997

Children with Specific Language Impairment, Laurence B. Leonard, 1997

Type-Logical Semantics, Bob Carpenter, 1997

Statistical Methods for Speech Recognition, Frederick Jelinek, 1997

WordNet: An Electronic Lexical Database, Christiane Fellbaum, 1998

WordNet 1.6 CD-ROM, edited by Christiane Fellbaum, 1998

Investigations in Universal Grammar: A Guide to Experiments on the Acquisition of Syntax and Semantics, Stephen Crain and Rosalind Thornton, 1998

A Prosodic Model of Sign Language Phonology, Diane Brentari, 1998

Language Form and Language Function, Frederick J. Newmeyer, 1998

Semantics and Syntax in Lexical Functional Grammar: The Resource Logic Approach, edited by Mary Dalrymple, 1998

Understanding Language Understanding: Computational Models of Reading, edited by Ashwin Ram and Kenneth Moorman, 1999

The Syntactic Process, Mark Steedman, 2000

Toward a Cognitive Semantics, Volume I: Concept Structuring Systems, Leonard Talmy, 2000

Toward a Cognitive Semantics, Volume II: Typology and Process in Concept Structuring, Leonard Talmy, 2000

TOWARD A COGNITIVE SEMANTICS

VOLUME II: TYPOLOGY AND PROCESS IN CONCEPT STRUCTURING

Leonard Talmy

The MIT Press
Cambridge, Massachusetts
London, England

Second printing, 2001
© 2000 Massachusetts Institute of Technology

This book was set in Times New Roman by Asco Typesetters, Hong Kong and was printed and bound in the United States of America.

Library of Congress Cataloging-in-Publication Data

Talmy, Leonard.
  Toward a cognitive semantics / Leonard Talmy.
     p.   cm. — (Language, speech, and communication)
  Includes bibliographical references and index.
  Contents: v. 1. Concept structuring systems — v. 2. Typology and process in concept structuring.
  ISBN 0-262-20120-8 (V. I, hc : alk. paper)
  ISBN 0-262-20121-6 (V. II, hc : alk. paper)
  1. Cognitive grammar. 2. Semantics—Psychological aspects. 3. Concepts.
I. Title. II. Series.
P165.T35   2000
415—dc21   99-40217
                                                             CIP

For Theodore Kompanetz

Contents

Introduction

The linguistic representation of conceptual structure is the central concern of this volume and of its companion volume. While such conceptual organization in language had once been insufficiently addressed, attention to it has been increasing over the last two to three decades. The growing research in this relatively recent linguistic domain—which has generally come to be known as cognitive linguistics—has developed into an alternative approach to the study of language that now complements other approaches. The work gathered in the present pair of volumes has been a part of this growth of research and has helped to foster it. Under the common title *Toward a Cognitive Semantics*, these volumes include most of my published material up to the present. Further, this material has been wholly revised, extended, augmented by unpublished material, and thematically organized. Under its individual title *Concept Structuring Systems*, volume I highlights the material that demonstrates the fundamental systems by which language shapes concepts. And under the individual title of *Typology and Process in Concept Structuring*, the present volume, volume II, highlights the material on typologies according to which concepts are structured and processes by which they are structured.

The nature and necessity of cognitive linguistics are perhaps best characterized at the outset. To this end, I consider cognitive linguistics within a larger framework of approaches to the analysis of language. For a heuristic comparison, one can select three such approaches that address the content-related portion of language (here setting phonology aside). With simple labels, these three approaches can be designated as the formal, the psychological and the conceptual. Particular research traditions have largely based themselves within one of these approaches, while aiming—with greater or lesser success—to address the concerns of the other two approaches. These relationships suggest the following sketch.

The formal approach basically addresses the structural patterns exhibited by the overt aspect of linguistic forms, largely abstracted away from or regarded as autonomous from any associated meaning. This approach thus includes the study of morphological, syntactic, and lexical structure. For one prominent example, the tradition of generative grammar over the past four decades has, of course, centered itself within this formal approach. But its relations to the other two approaches have remained limited. It has all along referred to the importance of relating its grammatical component to a semantic component, and there has indeed been much good work on aspects of meaning, but this enterprise has generally not addressed the overall conceptual organization of language. The formal semantics that has been adopted within the generative tradition has generally included only enough about meaning to correlate with the formal categories and operations that the main body of the tradition has focused on. And the reach of generative linguistics to psychology has largely considered only the kinds of cognitive structure and processing that might be needed to account for its formal categories and operations.

The second approach, the psychological, looks at language from the perspective of relatively general cognitive systems. Thus, the field of psychology has a long tradition of examining language from the perspective of perception, memory, attention, and reasoning. Further, it has in part addressed the concerns of the two other approaches of the present heuristic comparison. Thus, it has probed language both for its formal properties and for its conceptual properties. The latter kind of investigation has included analyses of semantic memory, the associativity of concepts, the structure of categories, inference generation, and contextual knowledge. But these studies have largely remained within certain circumscribed areas. Thus, the psychological tradition has insufficiently considered the kinds of structural categories that are central to the conceptual approach, as these are characterized next. And it has insufficiently considered the global integrated system of schematic structures with which language organizes conceptual content that it expresses—itself perhaps the main target of the conceptual approach.

The third approach to language considered here, the conceptual approach, is concerned with the patterns in which and the processes by which conceptual content is organized in language. Since the term "structure" will be used to refer both to patterns and to processes, the conceptual approach can more simply be said to address how language structures conceptual content. The relatively recent tradition of cognitive linguistics has centered itself within this approach. It has thus addressed the structuring within language of such basic conceptual categories as those of space and time, scenes and events, entities and processes, motion and location, and force and causation. It has also addressed the linguistic structuring of basic ideational and affective categories attributed to cognitive agents, such as attention and perspective, volition and intention, and expectation and affect. It addresses the semantic structure of morphological and lexical forms, as well as of syntactic patterns. And it addresses the interrelationships of conceptual structures, such as those in metaphoric mapping, those within a semantic frame, those between text and context, and those in the grouping of conceptual categories into large structuring systems. Overall, and perhaps above all, cognitive linguistics seeks to ascertain the global integrated system of conceptual structuring in language.

Cognitive linguistics, further, addresses the concerns of the other two approaches to language. First, it examines the formal properties of language from its conceptual perspective. Thus, it seeks to account for grammatical structure in terms of the functions this serves in the representation of conceptual structure.

Second, as one of its most distinguishing characteristics, cognitive linguistics aims to relate its findings to the cognitive structures that concern the psychological approach. It seeks both to help account for the behavior of conceptual phenomena within language in terms of those psychological structures, and at the same time, to help work out some of the properties of those structures themselves on the basis of its detailed understanding of how language realizes them. Thus, the tradition of cognitive linguistics is working to determine the more general cognitive structures pertaining to conceptual content that will encompass both the cognitive structures known from psychology and those known from linguistics. It is this trajectory toward unification with the psychological that motivates the term "cognitive" within the name of this linguistic tradition. The word "toward" in the title of this volume and of its companion in fact refers to the long-range form of this trajectory that I see for our research tradition: to integrate the linguistic and the psychological perspectives on cognitive organization in a unified understanding of human conceptual structure.

The appeal that cognitive linguistics makes to psychological structure is also what distinguishes it from the tradition of semantics in general. Like cognitive linguistics, the tradition of semantics, after all, has as its subject the patterns in which conceptual content is structured in language. But unlike cognitive linguistics, it has not systematically sought to relate its findings to more general cognitive categories and processes.

In terms of this sketch, then, cognitive linguistics can be seen as complementary to other linguistic approaches. Because it has directly engaged a domain of linguistic phenomena that the other approaches had addressed either insufficiently or indirectly, its growth can be regarded as a necessary development for our understanding of language.

Although the term "cognitive linguistics" is by now well established as the name for the research tradition just described, I will refer at least to my own body of work as "cognitive semantics." The word "semantics" in the new term has the advantage of indicating the particular approach, the conceptual, within which this research is based and from which it considers the concerns of other approaches to language. The word provides this indication because, as noted earlier, semantics is specifically concerned with the conceptual organization of language.[1]

This usage calls for further comment on my view of semantics. Semantics simply pertains to conceptual content as it is organized by language. Hence, the word "semantic" simply refers to the specifically linguistic form of the more generic notion "conceptual." Thus, general conception—that is, thought—includes linguistic meaning within its greater compass. And while linguistic meaning—whether that expressible by an individual language or by language in general—apparently involves a selection from or constraints on general conception, it is qualitatively of a piece with it. Thus, research on cognitive semantics is research on conceptual content and its organization in language and, hence, on the nature of conceptual content and organization in general. In this formulation, conceptual content is understood to encompass not just ideational content but any experiential content, including affect and perception.

The issue of methodology is raised by the fact that cognitive semantics centers its research on conceptual organization, hence, on content experienced in consciousness. That is, for cognitive semantics, the main object of study itself is qualitative mental phenomena as they exist in awareness. Cognitive semantics is thus a branch of phenomenology, specifically, the phenomenology of conceptual content and its structure in language. What methodology, then, can address such a research target? As matters stand, the only instrumentality that can access the phenomenological content and structure of consciousness is that of introspection.

As is the case with any cognitive system, different aspects of the semantic system differ in their degree of accessibility to consciousness. For example, one might be strongly aware of any particular meaning of a word one has heard, while having only slight or no awareness of, say, the extent of that word's range of polysemy or homonymy. Thus, these two different semantic aspects of a word—its current particular meaning and its range of meaning—differ in their access to consciousness. In general, those aspects of the semantic system that are more accessible to consciousness are more amenable to direct assessment by the method of introspection. In a complementary fashion, those aspects that are less accessible to consciousness can to that degree be ascertained only through the conventional nondirect methods of analysis, such as comparison and abstraction. Even in this latter case, though, an investigator must still start with the original conceptual content that itself can be accessed only through introspection. For one must begin by comparing such conscious contents in order to abstract from their patterns less conscious aspects of structure.

Like any method in a scientific endeavor, introspection must be employed with rigor. For example, it must include such procedures as the controlled manipulation of the linguistic material whose meanings are being assessed. Further, the findings resulting from introspection must be correlated with those resulting from other methodologies. Such other methodologies include the analysis of introspective reports by others, the analysis of discourse and corpora, crosslinguistic and diachronic analysis, the assessment of context and of cultural structure, the observational and experimental techniques of psycholinguistics, the impairment studies of neuropsychology, and the instrumental probes of neuroscience. With respect to this last methodology, perhaps in the long run, the neuro-scientific understanding of brain function will account for the findings of introspection. Even then, though, introspection will still be needed to ensure that the neuroscientific description of the brain is, in its account, in fact addressing what is otherwise known to be subjectively present in the mind. Thus, introspection will continue to be the method needed to probe the subjective contents of consciousness.

The method of introspection can be justified in much the same way as the methods settled on by any science. In any science, a researcher must go to where the relevant data under study are to be found. For example, if one's area of scientific study is geology, one must go examine the earth. Here, "going to where the data are" entails physical travel to terrestrial sites. In the same way, if one's area of scientific study is linguistic mean-ing, one must go to where meaning is located. And meaning is located in conscious experience. In the case of such subjective data, "going" to their location consists of introspection.

But while the use of introspection may call for specific justification in cognitive semantics, it is already a necessary component in most of linguistics, even apart from semantics. Thus, the formal linguistic study of syntax ultimately depends on a tissue of judgments made by individuals as to the grammaticality or the logical-inferential properties of sentences. Such judgments are purely the product of introspection.

More generally, in fact, much of human psychological theory rests on a presumption of some form of consciousness or the efficacy of introspection, whether so articulated or not. The typical psychological subject is assumed to understand the instructions for an experiment and to willingly try to perform in accordance with that understanding. Such understanding and endeavor are consciousness-related phenomena.

Consciousness is thus often a necessary concomitant at the subject end within the cognitive sciences. But in addition, one can argue, it is also necessary at the researcher end in *any* scientific endeavor, however much this endeavor is regarded as objective. Thus, even in the most technical scientific experiments, after all the displays have appeared on monitor screens, all the printouts have emerged, and all the gauges have shown particular values, some researcher will still have to assess such registrations and apprehend their import in her consciousness. Dennett (1991) has attempted to put phenomenology itself on a scientifically objective basis with his idea of heterophenomenology. This involves individuals putting their putative experiences in a written form, which can then be treated like any other object in the world. But, from the present perspective, this move omits one crucial point: someone with his own phenomenology still must then read the transcripts to apprehend their import in turn, or else they will remain just a pattern of marks on paper (or of states in a computer).

All in all, then, the use of introspection must be recognized as an appropriate and arguably necessary methodology in cognitive science, together with the other generally accepted methodologies.

Turning to the structure and content of the present volume and its companion, these volumes include most of my work on cognitive semantics and related areas of cognitive science, spanning the last two decades or so. Further, all the papers in the volumes have been revised and updated. Almost all the papers have been expanded, with their analyses extended. For most of the papers, these changes have been extensive, with several papers having been wholly rewritten. In addition, previously unpublished work has been added to the published. Due to these revisions, expansions, and additions, a high proportion of the material in the two volumes is new.[2]

The changes in and the arrangement of the material have yielded a more integrated pair of volumes. Thus, the revised papers more clearly present their ideas as cohering within a single theoretical framework, and they now share a uniform terminology. And the papers, now chapters, have been sequenced not in chronological order, but rather in accordance with their subject matter.

Thus, in volume I, the chapter in part 1 establishes the theoretical orientation of both volumes in terms of conceptual structure, and it introduces the notion of extensive and integrated "schematic systems." The remaining three parts of volume I include chapters on three such schematic systems. In volume II, the chapters in part 1 examine the typological patterns that certain conceptual structures map onto. The work here mostly addresses event structure, and so it in part expands the examined scope of semantic structure from aspects of events to whole events. Next, while the preceding chapters had treated both static and dynamic cognitive processes, the chapters in part 2 step beyond that to focus on online interactive processing of multiple factors. The chapters in part 3 extend the conceptually and cognitively oriented analyses that had been applied to language in the preceding chapters to other cognitive systems, namely, to the cognitive systems that underlie culture and narrative. In fact, the last section of the final chapter on narrative structure presents in a more general form the same kind of conceptual structures that were introduced in chapter 1 of volume I. It can thus be seen that the arrangement of the chapters through the two volumes generally follows a trajectory from the more core aspects of conceptual structure in language to conceptual structure in nonlinguistic cognitive systems.

Each volume of the pair superimposes its own thematic organization on this overall sequence. Volume I sets forth the pattern of concept-structuring systems in language and examines several such schematic systems in detail. In particular, the schematic system of "configurational structure" is treated in chapters 2 and 3, that of the "distribution of attention" is treated in chapters 4 to 6 and that of "force and causation" is treated in chapters 7 and 8. Together, all such schematic systems constitute the fundamental conceptual structuring system of language, and the organizing aegis of volume I is the outlining of this fundamental system.

Volume II furthers the analysis of concept structuring in language by examining its relation to typology and process. It sets forth typologies acccording to which concepts are structured and processes by which they are structured. Cognitive process can be heuristically understood to operate over three time scales. The short-term scale is that of current online processing. The mid-term scale occurs developmentally over some period of an individual's lifetime. The long-term scale occurs across the succession of an individual's momentary judgments that cumulatively—and in interaction with those of others—realize the maintenance or gradual change of various aspects of language and culture. In chapters 1 to 4, typological patterns are understood to involve this third long-term scale of process. These chapters thus treat a language's selection and maintenance of one typological category out of a small universally available set as well as the diachronic shift from one such category to another. At this time scale, chapter 4 also treats the process of hybridization that a language can manifest in a diachronic shift between two language types. Chapter 7 treats the mid-term scale of process in positing a cognitive system that governs a child's acquisition of cultural patterns. The short-term scale of process is treated in chapters 5 and 6, which, respectively, describe online resolutions to semantic conflicts and to the co-constraints of a current set of communicative goals and means. The short-term scale is further treated in chapter 8, which outlines the cognitive factors by which a producer or a recipient of a narrative structures and integrates the whole of that narrative.

It may be useful to present an outline of the themes that characterize my work and of the development they went through—as well as of where these themes first appeared and where they appear in the two volumes. Overall, this body of work from its outset has centered on semantic/ conceptual structure, examining the form and processes of this structure. All the particular concerns that were listed earlier as objects of study for cognitive linguistics have in fact been central themes throughout my own work. Some specifics follow. References to previously published papers will be marked with "T-", and references to chapters in volumes I and II will be marked with "I-" and "II-".

One theme that has continued from my dissertation on is the examination of event structure. One type of event structure to which I have given much attention pertains to motion. In my analysis, the general form of such a structure consists of a basic "Motion event"—that is, an event of motion or location—together with a "Co-event" that relates to it as its

Manner or Cause, all within a larger "Motion situation." Such an analysis first appeared in my dissertation, T-1972, and was developed further in T-1985b—which appears now in chapters II-1 and II-2 in a much expanded form.

As a concomitant to this study of Motion events, much research was done on the general schematic structuring of space and of time, as well as of the objects and processes that occur therein. In its most direct treatment, the analysis of spatial structure first appeared in T-1972/1975b and was further developed in T-1983—a revision of which now appears in chapter I-3. And direct analysis of temporal structure first appeared in T-1977/1978c and was developed in T-1988b—now revised as chapter I-1. It should be noted that some aspects of the way language conceptually structures Motion events in space and time appear in virtually every chapter. For example, fictive conceptualizations of Motion are described in chapter I-2, while selected windows of attention upon different phases of a Motion event are described in chapter I-4.

The Motion situation and the event complex that it comprises were subsequently generalized. This generalization involved the notion of a "framing event" to which the co-event relates, now within a larger "macro-event." This macro-event now encompasses not only a Motion situation but also situations of "temporal contouring," state change, "action correlating," and "realization." This generalization was first described in T-1991, which in expanded form now appears as chapter II-3. Further, while it was earlier seen that a co-event could relate to a Motion event as its Manner or Cause, the number of distinct relations that a co-event can bear to a framing event—what I term "support relations" —is now understood to be much greater, as shown both in chapter II-1 and in chapter II-3.

Another type of event structure that has been much analyzed in my work pertains to causation. In particular, this analysis is based on the notion of a causing event relating to a caused event within a larger causative situation. But the analysis has further aimed to identify the conceptual primitives that underlie such causative situations, both over a range of types and from the most basic to the very elaborate. Among such variants, a causative situation can include "agency," a cognitive category that then criterially depends on the distinct concepts of "intention" and "volition." This analysis of causation again first appeared in T-1972, and it was developed further in T-1976b, which now appears in a much revised form as chapter I-8. Further perspectives on linguistic causation appeared in T-1985b (chapter II-1) and in T-1996b (chapter I-4). The former of these two works describes the lexicalization patterns that represent the interaction of different causative types with different aspect types, as well as discussing how grammatical devices permit conversions between these types. The latter work describes the linguistic windowing of attention over a causal chain and, specifically, how the medial portion of such a chain is regularly omitted from attention in what appears to be a linguistic correlate of a general attentional pattern.

Much like the generalization of the Motion situation to the macro-event, the event structure complex involving causation was generalized to one involving "force dynamics." Force dynamics covers the range of relations that one entity can bear to another with respect to force. This range includes one entity's intrinsic force tendency, a second entity's opposition to that tendency, the first entity's resistance to such opposition, and the second entity's overcoming of such resistance. It further includes the presence, absence, imposition, or removal of blockage to one entity's intrinsic force tendency by a second entity. In force dynamics, causation thus now appears within a larger conceptual framework in systematic relationship to such other concepts as permitting and preventing, helping and hindering. Force dynamics had some roots in T-1972, was developed further in T-1976b (now chapter I-8), and became greatly elaborated in T-1985a/1988a (now somewhat further expanded as chapter I-7).

As can be seen from the preceding, a principal concern of mine has been with the structure of an event complex that consists of constituent events in a particular relationship. Thus, as just discussed, in a Motion situation and its generalization to a macro-event, a co-event can bear any of a set of support relations to the framing event. And in a causative situation and its generalization to a force dynamic situation, one component relates to another component with respect to force, including the case where the two components are themselves events. In a similar way, I examined the structure of an event complex in two further respects: the Figure-Ground relations and the subordinate/coordinate relations that can hold between constituent events. While Figure-Ground relations were addressed for the case of physical elements in T-1972, they were later generalized to apply to any type of entity, including events, thus applying to the case where one event relates as Figure to another event as Ground within a larger event complex. This generalization first appeared in T-1975a/1978a—now revised as chapter I-5 (see below for more on Figure and Ground). And the subordinate or coordinate relations that one event can bear to another within a larger event complex were analyzed into a large set of "cross-event relations," including ones that are temporal, conditional, reason based, concessive, additive, and substitutional. This further treatment of the structure of event complexes appeared in T-1978b—now wholly rewritten as chapter I-6.

A major concomitant of this work on event complexes has been concern with the patterns of the overt linguistic representation of such complexes. Thus, much attention has been paid to the syntactic representation of events with a Figure-Ground or a subordination/coordination relationship, as seen in chapters I-5 and I-6. Of special interest, though, has been the circumstance in which a complex structure at the conceptual level— say, a pair of constituent events and the relation between them—is expressed by a unitary syntactic constituent, such as by a single clause. Such telescoped representation was termed "conflation." Such conflation of a complex conceptual structure into a single clause occurs extensively in the representation of the Motion situation and of the causative situation. Analysis of the conflation patterns for such situations first appeared in T-1972, was elaborated in T-1976b, 1985b, and 1991, and now appears mainly in chapter I-8 for causation and in chapters II-1 to II-3 for Motion and its generalizations.

In thus relating the conceptual level to the formal level, I have especially examined certain patterns. These are the specific patterns in which particular semantic constituents within the conceptual complex are represented by particular syntactic constituents within a sentence. These are patterns, in other words, of what shows up where. Such "meaning-form mappings" have been represented notationally and/or diagrammatically in my work for all the event types just indicated—that is, for those involving Figure/Ground, subordination/coordination, causation, and Motion. In the case of the Motion situation in particular, it was found that different languages characteristically employ different meaning-form mappings and can be placed into a typological classification on this basis (see below for more on typologies and universals).

This perspective of meaning-form mapping went further to inform most of my work on lexical semantics. To be sure, this work has included much on the semantic infrastructure of individual morphemes. But mostly it has addressed the systematic patterns in which meanings of certain categories appear alone or are combined together in morphemes of certain classes. (Combinations of meanings in a morpheme were also called "conflation," in a parallel usage of this term.) I have treated lexical semantics of the latter kind as an integral part of the meaning-form mappings that pertain to whole conceptual complexes represented over whole sentences. Thus, in my analysis, the lexicalization pattern exhibited by a class of morphemes correlates with the syntactic pattern of the sentence structure in which that class of morphemes fits. The development and the locations of my work on meaning-form mappings and on systematic lexical semantics are the same as those last cited above.

Work on all the preceding issues led to the notion of schematic systems. To begin with, observation of the conceptual structuring of space and of time—especially of the parallelisms between them—engendered the idea that these two forms of structuring could be combined into a single more general schematic system, that of "configurational structure." It further appeared that this schematic system of configurational structure also encompasses the linguistic representation of more domains than just those of space and time, such as the domain of qualitative properties.

Then, in addition to that of configurational structure, further large schematic systems were identified. In fact, the general picture emerged that all of the conceptual structuring that linguistic forms effect can be comprehended under a certain number of such large schematic systems. Thus, much as certain linguistic forms in a portion of discourse organize a referent situation in terms of configurational structure, so other linguistic forms specify where one is to locate one's perspective point from which to regard the now structured referent situation. Such specifications constitute a second schematic system, that of "location of perspective point." Still further linguistic forms specify the particular distribution of attention that one is to direct over the structured situation from one's adopted perspective point. Such specifications, then, constitute a third large schematic system, that of "distribution of attention." A fourth large schematic system of "force dynamics" pertains to the linguistic representation of force interactions and causal relations occurring between certain entities within the structured situation. These four schematic systems of configuration, perspective, attention, and force are the main systems that my work has elaborated so far, but there are further schematic systems that future work will endeavor to detail. The idea of such schematic systems was first articulated in T-1983, was developed further in T-1988b, and now informs the organization of chapter I-1, as well as of volume I's parts 2 to 4.

More closely regarded, the schematic system of attention can be seen to cover several different patterns of attentional distribution that have been separately elaborated in my work. One of these can be called the "center-periphery" pattern. A case of this pattern is "Figure-Ground" organization, whose original description in my work represented an early attempt to unify psychological and linguistic categories. In Figure-Ground organization, the entity that functions as the Figure of a situation attracts focal attention and is the entity whose characteristics and fate are of concern. The Ground entity is in the periphery of attention and functions as a reference entity used to characterize the Figural properties of concern. Figure-Ground organization was first investigated in T-1972 for objects relating to each other in Motion or causative situations, and, as noted earlier, was extended to the interrelationship of constituent events within a larger event complex in T-1975a/1978a as well as T-1978b (chapters I-5 and I-6). The center-periphery pattern was later seen to operate as well in the domain of force interactions in the form of two further thematic roles, the "Agonist" and the "Antagonist." These have appeared as cited above for force dynamics.

Other patterns of attentional distribution have also been investigated. Thus, in the pattern termed "level of attention," linguistic forms direct one's greatest attention either to a level of the component elements making up some aspect of a referent situation, or to the level of the whole that encompasses those components. This pattern was set forth in T-1978c/ 1988b and appears now in chapter I-1. A third pattern of attentional structure is the "windowing" of attention. In this pattern, linguistic forms can differentially direct greatest attention to, withdraw attention from, particular portions of a referent situation. This pattern was first presented in T-1996b and appears now in chapter I-4.

In addition to treating all the preceding conceptual domains and concept-structuring systems, my work sets forth certain fundamental organizing principles that are in effect across these domains and systems. One of these principles is the centrality of schematic structure. This is the idea that the structural specifications of linguistic forms are regularly conceptualized in terms of abstracted, idealized, and often virtually geometric delineations in particular relationships with each other. T-1972 included descriptions of such schemas for paths of motion through space and for causal interactions. It also included the representation of schemas by diagrams whose structurally relevant components are labeled. Those diagrams were used to represent the schematic structure of a set of causing events expressed by Atsugewi satellites; they are reproduced in chapter II-2. While appeal to schematic structure appears in most of my papers, it perhaps reached its most developed form for representing configurational structure in T-1977 and T-1983 (now revised as chapters I-1 and I-3) and for representing force dynamic structure in T-1985a/1988a (now revised as chapter I-7).

A second organizing principle is that the closed-class system of language is its most fundamental and comprehensive conceptual structuring system. That is, collectively, the meanings of the closed-class forms of languages structure conceptual content in general—and do so within the more particular schematic systems otherwise examined separately. This study of the overall system can be called "closed-class semantics" or the "semantics of grammar." The idea of pitching such a study at the superordinate level that comprehends all closed-class forms first appeared in my work in T-1978c and was greatly developed in T-1988b, now revised as chapter I-1.

A third organizing principle pertaining to the conceptual structuring systems of language is that, in general, the same ideational complex can be represented in terms of alternative conceptualizations. Thus, a speaker can generally select one or another of such conceptualizations as the one she will use to represent the ideational complex that she currently wants to communicate. I termed this cognitive capacity to construe an ideational complex in a range of ways the principle of "conceptual alternativity." The idea of a systematic choice among alternatives of conceptualization was first articulated in my work in the succession of papers T-1977/T-1978c/T-1988b, now revised as chapter I-1. The idea was extended to other semantic domains in T-1983, now revised as chapter I-3, as well as in T-1996b, now revised as chapter I-4.

A fourth organizing principle is a parallelism between the linguistic representation of spatial structure and that of temporal structure. Many of the same forms of conceptual structuring are evident in both space and time, in both things and processes, and, accordingly, in the referents of both the linguistic forms that prototypically represent these, namely, nouns and verbs. The articulation of this parallelism first appeared in T-1977; it was developed further in T-1978c and still further in T-1988b (now revised as chapter I-1).

Finally, language has certain pervasive properties that my work treats at length. First, one such property is cognitive dynamism, including the system of processes that manipulate otherwise static conceptual structures in language. As discussed earlier, the work in volume II covers the long-term scale of process that pertains to typological maintenance and change, the mid-term scale that pertains to developmental change, and the short-term scale of online cognitive processing. With respect to this short-term type of process, my earliest treatment of it was in T-1976b and T-1977, now revised as chapters II-5 and II-6. The first of these works deals with the simultaneous occurrence of different communicative goals in a speaker and the cognitive processes by which they are concurrently satisfied through the communicative means available. The second work deals with the semantic conflicts that can occur between the specifications of two forms together in the same portion of discourse, and the array of cognitive processes by which the conflicts are reconciled. These processes include "shifting," "blending," "juxtaposing," "juggling," and "blocking." In addition, T-1978c/1988b—now revised as chapter I-1—developed the idea that closed-class forms trigger cognitive operations that manipulate conceptual structures. Subsequently, in T-1983—now revised as chapter I-3—section 4 deals with the cognitive processes by which the finite, indeed relatively small, inventory of morphemes in a language can be deployed so as to represent, at least potentially, the open-ended range of the contents of consciousness. And T-1995b, now revised as chapter II-8, outlines the conceptual parameters and strata that must be interactively deployed for an individual to be the producer or the understander of a narrative. In addition to such processual forms of cognitive dynamism, the bias of language toward conceptual dynamism—that is, the propensity to represent an otherwise static concept in terms of action—was demonstrated in T-1996a, now revised as chapter I-2.

Second, the typological and universal properties of language have been treated extensively in my work. In fact, my papers have presented virtually no phenomenon in any particular language for its own sake, but only insofar as it illuminates a typological or universalist issue. Most of my typological findings are presented in chapters 1 to 4 of volume II, which represent revisions of T-1982, T-1985b, T-1987, and T-1991, while some further typological observations are made in chapter 6 of volume I, a revision of T-1978b. Chapter II-2 specifically lists a large set of typological and universal factors observable in lexical patterns. Essentially all the rest is universalist in orientation. Further, though, even the typological analyses have a universalist underpinning. Thus, in my analyses of them, the alternatives within each proposed typology are simply different permutations of the elements within a single basic pattern that is itself universal. Hence, the overarching trajectory of this body of work has been to ascertain the universal properties of conceptual organization in language.

In the exploration of one further pervasive property of language—and beyond—an organizing perspective that has been progressively developing over my work and that will inform much of my future work can be called the "overlapping systems model" of cognitive organization. In this model, human cognition comprehends certain relatively distinct major cognitive systems. These appear to include language, perception, reasoning, affect, attention, memory, cultural structure, and motor control. The general finding is that each cognitive system has some structural properties that may be uniquely its own, some further structural properties that it shares with only one or a few other cognitive systems, and some fundamental structural properties that it has in common with all other cognitive systems. These have been termed "systems" because the structural overlaps across them suggest a cognitive organization other than the autonomy of Fodorian "modules."

To date, my work has examined similarities and dissimilarities of structure—in particular of conceptual structure—between language and each of several other major or lesser cognitive systems. These have been visual perception, kinesthetic perception, attention, understanding/reasoning, pattern integration (as in narrative), cultural structure, affect, and motor control. It has also examined structural properties common to all these systems.

Three of my recent papers have made major forays into other cognitive systems. T-1996a (chapter I-2) closely examines visual perception for its parallels to semantic structure. It also generalizes the traditionally distinguished systems of "perception" and of "conception" into a single unified cognitive system of "ception." T-1995a (chapter II-7) proposes that humans have a cognitive system that has evolved to acquire, manifest, and transmit cultural structure in a way comparable to that of the presumed cognitive system for language. And T-1995b (chapter II-8) proposes that humans have a cognitive system for interconnecting an assembly of mental experiences so as to form them into a single overall conceptual pattern. In particular, this system can integrate a sequence of experiences that are cognized over time into a single pattern understood as a story, a history, or a life—that is, generically, as a narrative. In its "Parameters" section, further, this last work contains the most extensive identification and analysis I have made to date of the foundational structural properties common to all the cognitive systems. This analysis is presented primarily with reference to the proposed cognitive system that underlies the structure of narrative, but the analysis is intended to be quite general across the whole range of cognitive systems.

The following is a guide to the chapters that compare the conceptual structure of language with that of another cognitive system or with all other cognitive systems in accordance with the overlapping systems model of cognitive organization. Comparisons of language structure to the structure in visual perception appear in chapters I-1 to I-3. Comparisons of language structure to the structure of kinesthetic perception appear in chapter I-7. Comparisons of language structure to the attentional system appear in chapters I-4 to I-6. Comparisons of language structure to the structure of the understanding/reasoning system appear in chapters I-1 and I-7. Comparisons of language structure to the pattern integrating system that underlies narrative appear in chapter II-8. Comparisons of language structure to the structure of the cognitive culture system appear in chapters I-2 and II-7. Comparisons of language structure to the structure of the affect system appear in chapter I-1. And an analysis of the structuring principles that seem to run in common through all the cognitive systems appears in chapter II-8.

In all, I see the work in the present pair of volumes as joining with that of other cognitive linguists, as well as with that of other cognitive scientists, in a collective enterprise. The ultimate aim of this enterprise is to understand the general character of conceptual structure in human cognition.

Several formatting conventions are followed in this volume. In the sections where they are characterized, newly introduced terms appear in semibold. Linguistic forms are cited in italics. Italics are also used to indicate emphasis. Single quotes enclose any cited semantic element. For instance, they enclose the literal gloss of a non-English form. Double quotes enclose a casual or colloquial English translation of a non-English form (as well as being used for their ordinary functions).

I would like to thank the National Science Foundation and the American Council of Learned Societies for their support in the preparation of this volume during my 1996–97 sabbatical year.

I am greatly indebted to the people who have helped in the development of the ideas in this volume, both through their work and through our discussions. I will thank them individually in the separate chapters. But here I will give my special thanks to Stacy Krainz and Kean Kaufmann, without whose counsel and assistance this volume could not have been completed.

I have dedicated this volume and its companion to the memory of the psychologist Theodore Kompanetz, my friend and mentor—and a world genius who, unfortunately for the world, did not put in writing any of the sweep and depth of his understanding.

Notes

1. For me, the addition of the word "cognitive" to that of "semantics" in this term for my work is in fact redundant, since semantics is intrinsically cognitive. The added qualifying word—apart from marking the trajectory toward the psychological approach that is missing from traditional semantics—is needed due to the existence of alternative views of meaning as independent of mind.

2. The only published paper not included is Talmy 1975b. It was omitted because most of the material in it was treated in a more developed form in subsequent papers. Its still useful parts have been incorporated into several of the present revised chapters.

As for my dissertation, Talmy 1972, the only portion of it that appears here close to its original form is the description of Atsugewi forms in chapter 2 of volume II. Certain other portions of the dissertation are represented in more developed form in a number of the chapters in the two volumes. Note, though, that some portions of the dissertation are unrepresented here for reasons of space but are still worth consulting. They discuss material not otherwise addressed, or discuss the material in a way or in a degree of detail not represented here. As one example, the dissertation's section 10.4 on "alpha-, beta-, and gamma-order" lays out a crosslinguistic paradigm for valence permutations.

PART 1

TYPOLOGICAL PATTERNS IN THE REPRESENTATION OF EVENT STRUCTURE

Chapter 1

Lexicalization Patterns

1 INTRODUCTION

This study addresses the systematic relations in language between meaning and surface expression.[1] (The word "surface" throughout this chapter simply indicates overt linguistic forms, not any derivational theory.) Our approach to this has several aspects. First, we assume we can isolate elements separately within the domain of meaning and within the domain of surface expression. These are semantic elements like 'Motion', 'Path', 'Figure', 'Ground', 'Manner', and 'Cause', and surface elements like verb, adposition, subordinate clause, and what we will characterize as **satellite**. Second, we examine which semantic elements are expressed by which surface elements. This relationship is largely not one-to-one. A combination of semantic elements can be expressed by a single surface element, or a single semantic element by a combination of surface elements. Or again, semantic elements of different types can be expressed by the same type of surface element, as well as the same type by several different ones. We find here a range of universal principles and typological patterns as well as forms of diachronic category shift or maintenance across the typological patterns.

We do not look at every case of semantic-to-surface association, but only at ones that constitute a pervasive pattern, either within a language or across languages. Our particular concern is to understand how such patterns compare across languages. That is, for a particular semantic domain, we ask if languages exhibit a wide variety of patterns, a comparatively small number of patterns (a typology), or a single pattern (a universal). We will be interested primarily in the last two cases, as well as in the case where a pattern appears in no languages (universal exclusion). We will also address diachronic shifts from one typological pattern to another, as well as the cognitive underpinnings of these patterns (both treated further in chapter II-4). Our approach can be summarized as in this procedural outline:

(1) ("entities" = elements, relations, and structures: both particular cases and categories of these)
    a. Determine various semantic entities in a language.
    b. Determine various surface entities in the language.
    c. Observe which (a) entities are expressed by which (b) entities—in what combinations and with what relationships—noting any patterns.
    d. Compare (c)-type patterns across different languages, noting any metapatterns.
    e. Compare (c)-type patterns across different stages of a single language, noting any shifts or nonshifts that accord with a (d)-type metapattern.
    f. Consider the cognitive processes and structures that might give rise to the phenomena observed in (a) through (e).

This outline sketches the broad project of exploring meaning-surface relations. But our present undertaking is narrower in several ways. First, there are two directions for exploring meaning-surface relations, both of them fruitful. One direction is to hold a particular semantic entity constant and observe the surface entities in which it can appear. For example, one could observe that the semantic element 'negative' shows up in English as a verb-complex adverb (will *not* go), as an adjective (*no* money), as an adjectival derivational affix (*un*kind), and as a verbal incorporated feature (*doubt*); in Atsugewi as a verb requiring an infinitive complement (mit^{h}i:p 'to not'); and in some languages as a verbal inflection. The other direction is to hold constant a selected surface entity and to observe which semantic entities are variously expressed in it. While chapter II-3 follows the former direction, the present chapter explores in only this second direction.

Within this limitation, we narrow our concerns still further. One can examine lexemes consisting of different numbers of morphemes for the meanings that appear in them. At the low end of the scale are the "zero" forms. Thus, by one interpretation, there is a missing verbal expression in English constructions like *I feel like [having] a milk shake* and *I hope for [there to be] peace*, or in German ones like *Wo wollen Sie denn hin [gehen/fahren/...]?"* 'Where do you want to go?'. One might conclude that such missing verbal meanings come from a small set, with members like 'have', 'be', and 'go'.[2] Alternatively, one could investigate the meanings expressed by surface complexes. A comparatively lengthy construction might encode a single semantic element. Consider the approximate semantic equivalence of the construction *be of interest to* and the simple verb *interest*, or of *carry out an investigation into* and *investigate*. However, this study looks only at the mid-portion of this range: single morphemes and, to a lesser extent, words composed of root and derivational morphemes.

In particular, we will investigate one type of open-class element, the verb root, the topic of section 2, and one type of closed-class element, the **satellite**, defined and treated in section 3. These two surface types are vehicles for roughly the same set of semantic categories.[3] The aim in these two sections is to set forth a class of substantial meaning-in-form language patterns, and to describe the typological and universal principles that they embody. Section 4 looks at the effect of these patterns on semantic salience in the complex composed of both verb and satellites together. And the conclusion in section 5 argues the advantages of the approach adopted here. The present chapter fits this volume's overall purview by examining the conceptual structure of certain semantic domains; the typological patterns in which this conceptual structure is parceled out in the morphosyntactic structures of different languages; and the cognitive processes that support this typology and that lead diachronically to category shift or maintenance within the typology.

1.1   Characteristics of Lexicalization

We outline now some general characteristics of lexicalization, as part of this study's theoretical context. A meaning can be considered associated with surface forms mainly by three processes: lexicalization, deletion (or zero), and interpretation. We can contrast these three in an example where no one process clearly applies best. Consider the phrase *what pressure* (as in *What pressure was exerted?*), which asks 'what *degree of* pressure'—unlike the more usual *what color*, which asks for a particular identity among alternatives. How does the 'degree' meaning arise? One way we could account for it is by lexicalization—that is, the direct association of certain semantic components with a particular morpheme. By this interpretation, *pressure* here differs from the usual usage by incorporating an additional meaning component: $pressure_2 = degree\ of\ pressure_1$ (or, alternatively, there is a special *what* here: $what_1\ degree\ of$). Or we could assume that some constituent like *degree of* has been deleted from the middle of the phrase (or that a zero form with the meaning 'degree of' now resides there). Or else, we could rely on a process of semantic interpretation, based on present context and general knowledge, to provide us with the 'degree' meaning.[4]

In general, we assume here that lexicalization is involved where a particular meaning component is found to be in regular association with a particular morpheme. More broadly, the study of lexicalization must also address the case where a *set* of meaning components, bearing particular relations to each other, is in association with a morpheme, making up the whole of the morpheme's meaning. In the clearest case, one morpheme's semantic makeup is equivalent to that of a set of other morphemes in a syntactic construction, where each of the latter morphemes has one of the original morpheme's meaning components. A familiar example here is the approximate semantic equivalence between *kill* and *make die*. However, such clear cases are only occasional: it would be unwise to base an approach to lexicalization on semantic equivalences solely between morphemes that are *extant* in a language. What if English had no word *die*? We would still want to be able to say that *kill* incorporates the meaning component 'cause'. As a case in point, this is exactly what we would want to say for the verb (to) *poison* 'kill/harm with poison', which in fact lacks a noncausative counterpart that means 'die/become harmed from poison' (*They poisoned him with hemlock. | *He poisoned from the hemlock*).

To this end, we can establish a new notion, that of a morpheme's *usage*: a particular selection of its semantic and syntactic properties. We can then point to usage equivalences between morphemes, even ones with different core meanings and even across different languages.

To consider one example, there is a usage equivalence between *kill* and *make appear*. *Kill* includes in its meaning the notion 'Agent action on Patient' ('causative') and, syntactically, it takes an Agent subject and Patient object. This usage is equivalent to that of *make*, which incorporates the notion 'Agent-to-Patient relation', in construction with *appear*, which incorporates the notion 'Patient acting alone' ('noncausative') and takes a Patient subject. Such relationships can be represented, for cases involving both lexical (*L*) and grammatical (*G*) morphemes, as in (2).

(2) usage of L_2 = usage of L_1 in construction with G
    (e.g., L_2 = kill, L_1 = appear, and G = make)

We can say here that L_2 incorporates the meaning of G and that L_1 either does not incorporate it or incorporates a meaning complementary to it. In the special case where a single morpheme can function equally as L_1 or L_2, we can say that it has a range of usages. For example, there is a usage equivalence between break$_2$ and make break$_1$, as seen in *I broke the vase* and *I made the vase break*, so that *break* can be said to have a usage range covering both the causative and the noncausative. An equivalent way of characterizing such a usage range is as in (3). As an example of this, the causative/noncausative usage range of *break* equals the causative usage of *kill* plus the noncausative usage of *appear*.

(3) usage range of   usage of   usage of
$$L_3 \quad = \quad L_2 \quad + \quad L_1$$
where L_2 and L_1 are related as in (2)

One terminological note: We will refer to the meaning-in-form relation with three terms. They are "lexicalization" from McCawley (e.g., 1968); "incorporation" as used by Gruber (1965); and "conflation," a term coined for this purpose by the author (Talmy 1972) and that has now gained general currency. These terms have different emphases and connotations that will become clear as they are used below, but all refer to the representation of meanings in surface forms.

1.2   Sketch of a Motion Event

A number of the patterns looked at below are part of a single larger system for the expression of motion and location. We will here provide a sketch of this system. Additional analysis appears in chapters I-2 and I-3 as well as in Talmy (1975b).

To begin with, we treat a situation containing motion and the continuation of a stationary location alike as a **Motion event** (with a capital M). The basic Motion event consists of one object (the **Figure**) moving or located with respect to another object (the reference object or **Ground**). It is analyzed as having four components: besides **Figure** and **Ground**, there are **Path** and **Motion**. The **Path** (with a capital P) is the path followed or site occupied by the Figure object with respect to the Ground object. The component of **Motion** (with a capital M) refers to the presence per se of motion or locatedness in the event. Only these two motive states are structurally distinguished by language. We will represent motion by the form **MOVE** and location by BE$_{LOC}$ (a mnemonic for 'be located').[5] The Motion component refers to the occurrence (MOVE) or nonoccurrence (BE$_{LOC}$) specifically of **translational motion**. This is motion in which the location of the Figure changes in the time period under consideration. It thus does not refer to all the types of motion that a Figure could exhibit, in particular excluding "self-contained motion" like rotation, oscillation, or dilation, itself treated below. In addition to these internal components, a Motion event can be associated with an external **Co-event** that most often bears the relation of Manner or of Cause to it. All these semantic entities can be seen in the sentences in (4).

(4)		*Manner*	*Cause*
	a. *Motion*	The pencil rolled off the table.	The pencil blew off the table.
	b. *Location*	The pencil lay on the table.	The pencil stuck on the table (after I glued it).

In all four sentences, *the pencil* functions as the Figure and *the table* as the Ground. *Off* and *on* express Paths (respectively, a path and a site). The verbs in the top sentences express motion, while those in the bottom ones express location. In addition to these states of Motion, a Manner is expressed in *rolled* and *lay*, while a Cause is expressed in *blew* and *stuck*.

The terms **Figure** and **Ground** were taken from Gestalt psychology, but Talmy (1972) gave them a distinct semantic interpretation that is continued here. The Figure is a moving or conceptually movable object whose path or site is at issue. The Ground is a reference frame, or a reference object stationary within a reference frame, with respect to which the Figure's path or site is characterized.

These notions of Figure and Ground have several advantages over Fillmore's (e.g., 1977) system of cases. The comparison is set forth in detail in chapter I-5, but some major differences can be indicated here. The notion of Ground captures the commonality—namely, function as reference object—that runs across all of Fillmore's separate cases "Location," "Source," "Goal," and "Path." In Fillmore's system, these four cases have nothing to indicate their commonality as against, say, "Instrument," "Patient," and "Agent." Further, Fillmore's system has nothing to indicate the commonality of its Source, Goal, and Path cases as against Location, a distinction captured in our system by the MOVE/ BE_{LOC} opposition within the Motion component. Moreover, the fact that these Fillmorean cases incorporate path notions in addition to their reference to a Ground object—for example, a 'from' notion in Source and a 'to' notion in Goal—opens the door to adding a new case for every newly recognized path notion, with possibly adverse consequences for universality claims. Our system, by abstracting away all notions of path into a separate Path component, allows for the representation of semantic complexes with both universal and language-particular portions.[6]

2   THE VERB

In this study of the verb, we look mainly at the verb root alone. This is because the main concern here is with the kinds of lexicalization that involve a single morpheme, and because in this way we are able to compare lexicalization patterns across languages with very different word structure. For example, the verb root in Chinese generally stands alone as an entire word, whereas in Atsugewi it is surrounded by many affixes that all together make up a polysynthetic verbal word. But these two languages are on a par with respect to their verb roots.

Presented first are the three typologically principal lexicalization types for verb roots. In most cases, a language uses only one of these types for the verb in its most characteristic expression of Motion. Here, "characteristic" means that (1) it is *colloquial* in style, rather than literary, stilted, and so on; (2) it is *frequent* in occurrence in speech, rather than only occasional; (3) it is *pervasive*, rather than limited—that is, a wide range of semantic notions are expressed in this type.

2.1   Motion + Co-Event

In a Motion-sentence pattern characteristic of one group of languages, the verb expresses at once both the fact of Motion and a Co-event,[7] usually either the manner or the cause of the Motion. A language of this type has a whole series of verbs in common use that express motion occurring in various manners or by various causes. There may also be a series of verbs expressing location with various Manners or Causes, but they are apparently always much fewer. The meaning-to-form relationship here can be represented as in the accompanying diagram. Language families or languages that seem to be of this type are Indo-European (except for post-Latin Romance languages), Finno-Ugric, Chinese, Ojibwa, and Warlbiri. English is a perfect example of the type.

(5) *English expressions of Motion with conflated Manner or Cause*
   BE$_{LOC}$ + Manner
   a.   The lamp *stood/lay/leaned* on the table.
   b.   The rope *hung* across the canyon from two hooks.

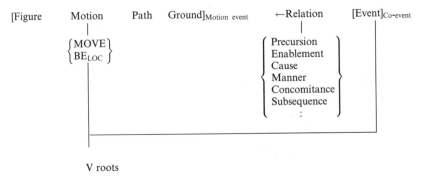

V roots

Co-event conflated in the Motion verb

MOVE + Manner

Nonagentive

c. The rock *slid/rolled/bounced* down the hill.

d. The gate *swung/creaked* shut on its rusty hinges.

e. Smoke *swirled/rushed* through the opening.

Agentive

f. I *slid/rolled/bounced* the keg into the storeroom.

g. I *twisted/popped* the cork out of the bottle.

Self-agentive

h. I *ran/limped/jumped/stumbled/rushed/groped my way* down the stairs.

i. She *wore* a green dress to the party.

MOVE + Cause

Nonagentive

j. The napkin *blew* off the table.

k. The bone *pulled* loose from its socket.

l. The water *boiled* down to the midline of the pot.

Agentive

m. I *pushed/threw/kicked* the keg into the storeroom.

n. I *blew/flicked* the ant off my plate.

o. I *chopped/sawed* the tree down to the ground at the base.

p. I *knocked/pounded/hammered* the nail into the board with a mallet.

Here, the assessment of whether it is Manner or Cause that is conflated in the verb is based on whether the verb's basic reference is to what the Figure does or to what the Agent or Instrument does. For example, in 'I rolled the keg ...', *rolled* basically refers to what the keg did and so expresses Manner, whereas in 'I pushed the keg ...', *pushed* refers to what I did, and so gives the Cause of the event.

To a speaker of a language like English, such sentences may seem so straightforward that they offer little to ponder. How else might such propositions be colloquially expressed? But in fact there are languages with very different patterns of expression. Even a language as seemingly kindred as Spanish *can express virtually none* of the above sentences in the way that English does, as is demonstrated below.

2.1.1 The Pattern Underlying Co-Event Conflation We can indicate the type of conflation pattern involved here with a construction that represents the separate semantic components individually—that is, that decomposes or "unpacks" the sentences. The Manner or Cause notion conflated in the verb is then best represented by a separate subordinate clause standing for a Co-event. In this construction, the relation that the Co-event bears to the main Motion event is then indicated by a form like WITH-THE-MANNER-OF or WITH-THE-CAUSE-OF. Such a form represents a deep or mid-level morpheme (see below) that functions semantically like the subordinating preposition or conjunction of a complex sentence. Thus, the form WITH-THE-CAUSE-OF functions like the English subordinator *by* in an agentive construction (as in *I moved the keg into the storeroom by kicking it*), or like the subordinators *from* or *as a result of* in a nonagentive construction (as in *The napkin came off the table from/as a result of the wind blowing on it*). Although they are otherwise awkward, these forms have the advantage that they mnemonically suggest their intended semantic content; that they exhibit the same form across differences of agentive and nonagentive usage; and that their consistent pattern allows the easy introduction of further such forms, a number of which appear later. Also in the constructions below, the subscript "$_A$" is placed before a verb to indicate that the verb is agentive (thus, $_A$MOVE = CAUSE to MOVE). And the form GO is used to represent self-agentive motion.

(6) *Unconflated paraphrases of English Motion expressions*
   BE_{LOC} + Manner
   a'. The lamp lay on the table. = [the lamp WAS_{LOC} on the table]
       WITH-THE-MANNER-OF [the lamp lay there]
   b'. The rope hung across the canyon from two hooks. =
       [the rope WAS_{LOC} (EXTENDED) across the canyon]
       WITH-THE-MANNER-OF [the rope hung from two hooks]

MOVE + Manner

Nonagentive

c′. The rock rolled down the hill. = [the rock MOVED down the hill] WITH-THE-MANNER-OF [the rock rolled]

d′. The gate swung shut on its rusty hinges. = [the gate MOVED shut (= the gate shut)] WITH-THE-MANNER-OF [the gate swung on its rusty hinges]

Agentive

f′. I bounced the keg into the storeroom. = I $_A$MOVED the keg into the storeroom] WITH-THE-MANNER-OF [I bounced the keg]

Self-agentive

h′. I ran down the stairs. = [I WENT down the stairs] WITH-THE-MANNER-OF [I ran]

MOVE + Cause

Nonagentive

j′. The napkin blew off the table. = [the napkin MOVED off the table] WITH-THE-CAUSE-OF [(something) blew on the napkin]

k′. The bone pulled loose from its socket. = [the bone MOVED loose from its socket] WITH-THE-CAUSE-OF [(something) pulled on the bone]

Agentive

m′. I kicked the keg into the storeroom. = [I $_A$MOVED the keg into the storeroom] WITH-THE-CAUSE-OF [I kicked the keg]

o′. I chopped the tree down to the ground at the base. = [I $_A$MOVED the tree down to the ground] WITH-THE-CAUSE-OF [I chopped on the tree at the base]

Note that many of the decompositional constructions here may relate more directly to sentences without conflation, which can therefore paraphrase the original conflational sentences, as in (7).

(7) c″. The rock rolled down the hill.
       The rock went down the hill, rolling in the process/the while.

    j″. The napkin blew off the table.
       The napkin moved off the table from (the wind) blowing on it.

    m″. I kicked the keg into the storeroom.
       I moved the keg into the storeroom by kicking it.

2.1.2 Properties of Co-Event Conflation We here examine certain properties of the relation that the Co-event bears to the main Motion event within a larger Motion situation.

2.1.2.1 Two Verb Usages In the above examples, the same verb form appears in the subordinate clause of the unpacked construction as in the single clause of the integrated sentence. On the conflational account put forward here, the former use of the verb form is more basic, and the latter use incorporates this former use, in its particular relation to the Motion event, together with an additional semantic component of Motion. An English-type language will generally have a regular pattern of such "lexical doublets."

Thus, in its basic usage the verb *float* refers to the buoyancy relation between an object and a medium, as seen in (8).

(8) The craft floated on a cushion of air.

Given the subscript "1" to mark this usage, the verb can also appear in a subordinate clause, next to a main clause referring to motion.

(9) The craft moved into the hangar, floating$_1$ on a cushion of air.

But the same verb form has a second usage that includes the idea of motion together with that of buoyancy. The verb in this usage—here marked with the subscript "2"—can appear in a one-clause sentence that is virtually equivalent to the preceding two-clause sentence.

(10) The craft floated$_2$ into the hangar on a cushion of air.

Accordingly, the relationship between the two meanings of *float* can be represented in isolation as

(11) MOVE WITH-THE-MANNER-OF [floating$_1$] → float$_2$
  or MOVE [floating$_1$ (the while)] → float$_2$

and can be represented within the larger sentence as in (12).

(12) The craft MOVED [floating$_1$ (the while)] into the hangar on a cushion of air
$$\downarrow$$
  floated$_2$

The same pair of usages can be seen in an agentive verb such as *kick*. In its basic usage, here again marked with the subscript "1," this verb refers to an agent's impacting his or her foot into some object, but presupposes nothing about that object's moving. This is obvious when that object is understood in fact to be fixed in place.

(13) I kicked$_1$ the wall with my left foot.

Again, this verb can be used in a subordinate clause alongside an independent reference to motion, as in (14a). And again, it has a second usage, marked with the subscript "2," that now incorporates this reference to motion, together with the basic meaning of *kick$_1$* in its causal relation to this motion, as seen in (14b).

(14) a. I $_A$MOVED the ball across the field, by kicking$_1$ it with my left
        foot

    b. I $_A$MOVED [by kicking$_1$] the ball across the field with my left foot
        $\downarrow$
        kicked$_2$

We can note that Mandarin, for one, is of the same typological category as English in that it conflates the Co-event in its verb. But the parallel goes further. It also has the same double usage for a single verb form.

(15) a. Wǒ yòng   zuó jiǎo tī$_1$ le   yī xià   qiáng
        I   use(-ing) left foot kick PERF one stroke wall
        'I kicked the wall with my left foot.'

    b. Wǒ yòng   zuó jiǎo bǎ   qiú tī$_2$ guò le   cāo-chǎng
        I   use(-ing) left foot D.O. ball kick across PERF field
        'I kicked the ball across the field with my left foot.'

2.1.2.2   The Lexicalization Account   Certain evidence may support the proposal of two distinctly lexicalized usages for a verb like *float* or *kick*. To begin with, such a verb in its second usage co-occurs with two constituents of certain semantically different types, while the verb in its first usage co-occurs with only one of these constituents. Thus, *float* in (12) occurs with the directional constituent *into the hangar* and the locative constituent *on a cushion of air*. Our interpretation is that the verb conflates within itself two separate concepts, one of motion and one of situated relationship, that, respectively, are in semantic association with the two constituents. In its first usage, though, *float* lacks an incorporated concept of motion, and so occurs only with the locative constituent. Similarly, *kick* in its second usage may incorporate both a concept of caused motion and a concept of body-part impact that associate, respectively, with a directional constituent (here, *across the field*) and a body-part-naming constituent (*with my left foot*), whereas *kick* in its first usage associates only with the latter type of constituent.[8]

We can further support the idea that the two usages of a verb like *float* each represent two distinct lexicalizations by showing verbs that have only the one or the other of these usages. To illustrate with this verb itself, note in (16) that the verbal form *be afloat* can occur in the same semantic and syntactic contexts as *float₁*, but not in those of *float₂*.

(16) a. The craft floated₁/was afloat on a cushion of air.
     b. The craft floated₂/*was afloat into the hangar on a cushion of air.

Further, verbs that are otherwise comparable to *float*—and that they might have been expected to exhibit its same two usages—in fact have only one or the other of them. Thus, *lie*, as used in (17a), is semantically much like *float₁* in referring to the support relation between one object and another—rather than buoyancy of an object in a medium, the relationship here is one of a linear object in roughly horizontal contact along its length with a firm undersurface. But it cannot also be used in a motion-incorporating sense like *float₂*, as seen in (17b), which attempts to express the pen's moving down the incline while in lengthwise contact with it. Conversely, *drift* and *glide* only express motion through space, in the way that *float₂* does, as seen in (18b). They cannot also be used in a nonmotion sense, as attempted in (18a).

(17) a. The pen lay on the plank.
     b. *The pen lay quickly down along the incline.

(18) a. *The canoe drifted/glided on that spot of the lake for an hour.
     b. The canoe drifted/glided halfway across the lake.

Comparably for agentive forms, *throw* is semantically much like *kick₂* in referring to a distinct motion event caused by a prior body action, as seen in (20b). But it has no usage parallel to *kick₁* referring to the body action alone—that is, to swinging an object around with one's arm without releasing it into a separate path, as seen in (20a). Complementarily *swing* itself is generally restricted to this latter sense, parallel to *kick₁*, as seen in (19a), but cannot be used in a sentence like that in (19b) to express consequent motion through space.

(19) a. I swung the ball with my left hand.
     b. *I swung the ball across the field with my left hand.

(20) a. *I threw the ball with my left hand without releasing it.
     b. I threw the ball across the field with my left hand.

All these forms fit—and can further illustrate—the lexicalization formulas of (2) and (3). When plugged into (2), the forms immediately above exhibit not only usage equivalence but also semantic equivalence. Thus, the usage and meaning of *throw* (L_2) is the same as that of *swing* (L_1) when this form is in construction with the largely grammatical sequence (G) *cause to move by* ... *-ing* ('throw' = 'cause to move by swinging'). And as for *kick*, this form is seen to possess a range of usages because it can be plugged into *both* sides of formula (2): $kick_2 = $ *cause to move by* $kicking_1$; or, equivalently by formula (3), *kick* (L_3) has usages equaling the usage of *throw* (L_2) taken together with the usage of *swing* (L_1).[9]

Further support for the idea of separate lexicalization for distinct usages comes from historical changes in word meaning. For example, in their traditional use the verbs *hold* and *carry* formed a near-perfect suppletive pair, differing only in that *carry* additionally incorporated a Motion event while *hold* did not.

(21)   *Without motion*   *With motion*

    a.   I held the box as I lay on   *I held the box to my neighbor's
        the bed.   house.

    b.   *I carried the box as I lay   I carried the box to my
        on the bed.   neighbor's house.

Currently, though, *carry* in some contexts—those where motion has just occurred or is about to occur—can also be used in a locative sense: *I stood at the front door carrying the box.* Such a partial extension from the original motion usage into the domain of locative usage would seem better handled by an account based on lexicalization than by one based on constructions.

The usage relationships posited here are accorded some psychological reality by data on children's errors. Bowerman (1981) documents a stage in English acquisition where children become "aware" of motion conflation in verbs and then overextend the pattern. Thus, verbs that in adult English, idiosyncratically, cannot be used with an incorporated motion meaning become so used by children, as (22) suggests.

(22) a. Don't hug me off my chair (= by hugging move me off).

    b. When you get to her [a doll], you catch her off (on a merry-go-round with a doll, wants a friend standing nearby to remove the doll on the next spinaround).

    c. I'll jump that down (about to jump onto a mat floating atop the tub water and force it down to the bottom).

Note that while the *carry* example extended a motion usage to a locative usage, these children's examples have gone in the opposite direction.

In all the preceding, where we have treated the second usage of a verb —the usage that occurs within the more complex single-clause sentence— as a lexicalization of additional components conflated into it, Aske (1989) and Goldberg (1995) treat it as the original simplex verb and treat the additional complexities of the surrounding construction as the source of the additional meanings. Perhaps the evidence adduced above can be largely reconstrued to serve as well for this constructional position. In the end, the important thing is that we correctly identify the semantic components and their interrelationships, whether these are seen as involving lexical conflation or constructions. However, either approach should aim to be consistent in its treatment of any pairing of usages. For example, our lexicalization approach should—and does—treat intransitive *break* and transitive *break* as distinct lexical items, the latter item incorporating the meaning of the former item together with a component of causation. Many of the same arguments adduced for the two usages of verbs like *float* apply as well to verbs like *break*. Thus, transitive *break* has a greater number of internal components that associate with a greater number of arguments in the sentence. Some verbs comparable to *break* occur only in the intransitive usage, like *collapse*, or only in the transitive usage, like *demolish*. Historical change has extended some one-usage verbs to a double usage. And children make the error of extending a one-usage verb into the other usage. Correlatively, a constructionist approach should claim that no distinct lexical item for transitive *break* exists in English. Rather, it should treat the transitive causative usage of *break* as consisting of intransitive *break* in interaction with the structure of the surrounding sentence, since that would parallel its treatment of Motion-Manner verbs like *float$_2$*.[10]

2.1.2.3 Translational and Self-Contained Motion

When the motion complex expressed by a sentence can be analyzed into a Motion event and a Co-event of Manner, certain further properties can be observed. The Motion event abstracts from the complex the main translational motion that the Figure exhibits, while the Co-event, if it too involves Motion, abstracts from the complex an event of "self-contained Motion." In translational motion, an object's basic location shifts from one point to another in space. In self-contained Motion, an object keeps its same basic, or "average," location. Self-contained Motion generally consists of oscillation, rotation, dilation (expansion or contraction), wiggle, local wander, or rest. Thus, the Motion complex expressed by (23a) can be analyzed as in (23b) into a Motion event of pure translation, which the deep verb MOVE uniquely refers to, and a Co-event of Manner that represents an event of oscillatory or rotational self-contained Motion. (And, as seen below, a language like Spanish regularly represents such a Co-event with its own verb in a separate gerundive clause.) These two types of self-contained Motion are represented in isolation by the sentences in (23c).[11]

(23) a. The ball bounced/rolled down the hall.
      b. [the ball MOVED down the hall] WITH-THE-MANNER-OF
          [the ball bounced/rolled]
      c. The ball bounced up and down on the same floor tile. / The log rolled over and over in the water.

The cognitive correlate of this linguistic phenomenon is that we apparently conceptualize, and perhaps perceive, certain complex motions as a composite of two abstractably distinct schematic patterns of simpler motion. For example, we may conceptualize, and perceive, the complex motion of a ball describing a succession of gradually diminishing parabolic arcs through a hallway as consisting of two superimposed or fused—but otherwise distinct—schematized motions: motion forward along a horizontal straight line and motion iteratively up and down along a vertical straight line. The componential separation of Motion event and Manner Co-event that we have established for the linguistic structure underlying Motion thus reflects this process of separation that our cognition performs.

This analysis of a Motion complex into a main Motion event and a Co-event raises an issue of **conceptual separability**: how cleanly the complex can be partitioned into autonomous component events. The separation can be quite clean, as in partitioning the motion complex in the "hovercraft" example into a translational schema ([the craft MOVED into the hangar]) and an autonomous component of self-contained Motion of the rest type ([the craft floated on a cushion of air]). Separation is a bit more difficult in the case of the ball bouncing down the hall, since the pure self-contained bouncing motion would take place in a straight vertical line, whereas in the full motion complex, it has blended with the forward motion to yield a parabolic resultant. Separation is still more difficult in the case of the ball rolling down the hall, since the component of rotation that one conceptually abstracts out is not wholly independent, but rather must take place in the right direction and at the right speed so as to correlate with the forward translational motion. The separation becomes fully problematic with cases like a canoe gliding across a lake or a book sliding down an incline, since it is not clear what candidate for an autonomous Co-event might be left after one has conceptually subtracted the event of translational motion from gliding or sliding. After all, the Manner of, say, *slide* includes a component of friction, or rubbing, between contacting surfaces of the Figure and Ground objects, but such friction can in fact exist only in the course of the Figure's translational motion, and so could not be adduced independently of it.

It might thus be argued that Manner should not be treated as some separate event that bears a relation to some simplified main event, but, at most, only as an aspect of a complex event, on the grounds that in reality some putative Manners cannot exist in isolation. Cognitively, however, linguistic structure attests that we at least conceptualize Manner regularly as a separate event. In a similar way, it is attested by linguistic structure itself—from the fact that certain forms of aspect can be expressed by main verbs, as in *I started/continued/stopped/finished sweeping*—that the "temporal contour" of a process can be abstracted off from the remainder of that process for conceptualization as a separate process in its own right (see chapter II-3).

2.1.3   Extensions of the Co-Event Conflation Pattern   In the languages that have it, the pattern seen so far for Co-event conflation normally applies far beyond the expression of simple Motion. We here consider five such extensions of the pattern. Again, virtually none of these extensions can be expressed as such in languages like Spanish. In the examples that follow, *F* stands for Figure; *G* for Ground; *A* for Agent; *(to) AGENT* for (to) cause agentively; $_A$MOVE for agentively cause to MOVE; and capital-letter words for deep or mid-level morphemes. The following characterization of such morphemes holds throughout this chapter (indeed, throughout this volume).

Neither a deep nor a mid-level morpheme has explicit form as an overt morpheme. A **deep morpheme** represents a concept that is believed to be both fundamental and universal in the semantic organization of language. A **mid-level morpheme** represents a particular conceptual complex that consists of a deep-morphemic concept together with certain additional semantic material, and that is recurrent in the semantic organization of a particular language, though it is often also to be found in many other languages. Thus, a deep or mid-level morpheme represents a single specific meaning that is inferred to function structurally in the semantic organization of a language or of language in general. The precise details of such a meaning—as with the meaning of any surface lexical morpheme—can be progressively more finely determined through linguistic investigation. The meanings of the deep and mid-level morphemes posited here are, to be sure, not all greatly detailed in this way below, but they are at least characterized schematically.

Lacking overt form, a deep or mid-level morpheme could be represented by any convenient symbol. But our practice has been to use a surface word, written in capitals, that is suggestive of the morpheme's meaning. However, it is to be emphasized that deep and mid-level morphemes are entities distinct from and in principle not to be identified with the surface words chosen to designate them. Thus, below, the mid-level verb GO—which is intended to refer solely to an Agent's volitionally self-propelled motion, apart from any notion of deixis—is not to be identified with the English lexical verb *go*, which does incorporate deixis and has a wide range of disparate usages.

More specifically, GO represents a semantic complex in which an animate entity volitionally and intentionally causes the translocation of its whole body through space via internal (neuromuscular) control or the results thereof (as in driving a vehicle). Within this complex, the object that exhibits the pure translocational concept of the simplex MOVE verb is the body of the animate entity. The distinction between the self-agentive motion of GO and the autonomous motion of MOVE has been rigorously maintained in the author's work, although often disregarded elsewhere. However, it is true that languages represent self-agentive and autonomous motion largely with the same syntactic constructions and often with the same lexical forms. An example is, in fact, the surface English verb *go*, as seen in *The plumber/The rain went into the kitchen.*

Comparably to GO, the mid-level verb PUT is here intended to designate a certain concept that plays a structural role in the semantic organization of English (as well as many other languages). The concept is as follows: an Agent's controlledly moving an object through body part movements but without whole-body translocation. PUT thus at least covers the range of English *put* (*I put the book in the box*), *take* (*I took the book out of the box*), *pick* (*I picked the book up off the floor*), and *move* (*I moved the book three inches to the left*). PUT is accordingly not to be identified with the English lexical verb *put*.

2.1.3.1 *Conflation onto Mid-Level Verbs Based on BE$_{LOC}$ or MOVE*

For the first extension, we note that material from the Co-event can conflate not only onto the two deep verbs BE$_{LOC}$ and MOVE (or with their agentive counterparts), but also onto certain mid-level verbs based on those deep verbs. Three examples of such mid-level verbs that take Co-event conflation are shown in (24), and a number of further examples appear in (25) and (26).

(24) *Mid-level verbs that take Co-event conflation*

a. COVER: [F] BE$_{LOC}$ all-over [G]

[paint COVERED the rug] WITH-THE-MANNER-OF [the paint was in streaks/dots]

Paint streaked/dotted the rug.

b. GIVE: [A$_1$] $_A$MOVE [F] into the GRASP of [A$_2$]

[I GAVE him another beer] WITH-THE-MANNER-OF [I slid the beer]

I slid him another beer.

c. PUT: [A] controlledly $_A$MOVE [F] by limb motion but without body translocation

[I PUT the hay up onto/down off of the truck] WITH-THE-CAUSE-OF [I forked the hay]

I forked the hay up onto/down off of the truck.

(*I forked the hay to my neighbor's house down the block* shows that *fork* is based on PUT, not on $_A$MOVE.)

2.1.3.2 *Conflation onto Combinations of MOVE with Matrix Verbs*

We have previously seen that the Co-event can conflate with the agentive form of MOVE, which has been represented as $_A$MOVE. This agentive form can be best understood as deriving from the combination of MOVE and a causative matrix verb that can be represented as "(to) AGENT." Thus, (to) $_A$MOVE derives from (to) AGENT to MOVE. The second extension of the present pattern is that the Co-event can also conflate with combinations of MOVE and matrix verbs other then (to) AGENT, or indeed with nestings of such combinations. These other matrix verbs can include further causative verbs, like "(to) INDUCE" (see section 2.6 for a range of deep causative verbs) or verbs of attempting, like "(to) AIM." The deep verb INDUCE is intended to represent in its pure and abstracted form the concept of 'caused agency', as described in detail in chapter I-8. The deep verb AIM is intended to represent the intention of an Agent to cause some circumstance, where the outcome is moot. The examples in (25) demonstrate a nested succession of such combinations based on the self-agentive verb "GO" (itself based on MOVE, as just noted above).

(25) a. GO: [A] AGENT himself [i.e., his whole body, = F] to MOVE

   [the child WENT down the hallway] WITH-THE-MANNER-OF [the child hopped]

   The child hopped down the hallway.
   Similarly: I ran into the house.

   b. GET: [A₁] INDUCE [A₂] to GO

   [I GOT him out of his hiding place] WITH-THE-CAUSE-OF [I lured/scared him]

   I lured/scared him out of his hiding place.
   Similarly: I talked him down off the ledge. / I prodded the cattle into the pen. / They smoked the bear out of its den.

   c. URGE: [A₁] AIM to GET [A₂] = [A₁] AIM to INDUCE [A₂] to GO

   [I URGED her away from the building] WITH-THE-CAUSE-OF [I waved at her]

   I waved her away from the building.
   Similarly: I beckoned him toward me. / I called him over to us.

The (b) and the (c) types of conflation must be distinguished because the (b) type presupposes the occurrence of the motion event, which therefore cannot be denied—*They lured/scared/smoked/prodded/talked him out, *but he didn't budge*—whereas the (c) type, with its incorporated notion of 'aiming/attempting', only implicates the occurrence of the motion event, which is therefore defeasible—*They waved/beckoned/called him over, but he didn't budge.*

2.1.3.3 *Conflation onto Metaphorically Extended MOVE*   The third extension of the present pattern is that the Co-event can conflate with METAPHORIC EXTENSIONS of MOVE—which are here represented by the deep verb within quotes: "MOVE"—or with mid-level morphemes built on "MOVE". One type of such metaphoric extension is from motion to change of state, the only type we illustrate here.[12] Some surface constructions for change of state in English are patterned like motion constructions, so that the form "MOVE" can be readily used in their underlying representations (see (26a) and (26d)). To represent change of state constructions with an adjective, though, we use the more suggestive forms BECOME for the nonagentive and MAKE$_1$ for the agentive (see (26b) and (26e)). And in some constructions, the change of state pertains to coming into existence, a semantic complex that we represent with the mid-level verb FORM in the nonagentive and with the verb MAKE$_2$ in the agentive (see (26c) and (26f)).

(26) *Motion-like change of state constructions*
   Nonagentive
   a. "MOVE": [F] MOVE metaphorically (i.e., change state)

   [he "MOVED" to death] WITH-THE-CAUSE-OF [he choked on a bone]

   (He died from choking on a bone.—or:)
   He choked to death on a bone.

   b. BECOME: "MOVE" in the environment: __Adjective

   [the shirt BECAME dry] WITH-THE-CAUSE-OF [the shirt flapped in the wind]

   (The shirt dried from flapping in the wind.—or:)
   The shirt flapped dry in the wind.
   Similarly: The tinman rusted stiff. / The coat has worn thin in spots. / The twig froze stuck to the window.

   c. FORM: [F] "MOVE" into EXISTENCE (cf. the phrase *come into existence*)

   [a hole FORMED in the table] WITH-THE-CAUSE-OF [a cigarette burned the table]

   A hole burned in the table from the cigarette.

   Agentive
   d. "$_A$MOVE": [A] AGENT [F] to "MOVE"

   [I "$_A$MOVED" him to death] WITH-THE-CAUSE-OF [I choked him]

   (I killed him by choking him.—or:)
   I choked him to death.
   Similarly: I rocked/sang the baby to sleep.

   e. $_A$BECOME = MAKE$_1$: "$_A$MOVE" in the environment: __Adjective

[I MADE$_1$ the fence blue] WITH-THE-CAUSE-OF [I painted the fence]

I painted the fence blue.

f. $_A$FORM = MAKE$_2$: [A] AGENT [F] to "MOVE" into EXISTENCE (cf. the phrase *bring into existence*)

[I MADE$_2$ the cake out of fresh ingredients] WITH-THE-CAUSE-OF [I baked the ingredients]

I baked a cake out of fresh ingredients.
Similarly: I knitted a sweater out of spun wool. / I hacked a path through the jungle. / The mouse chewed a hole through the wall.

2.1.3.4 Conflation across the Various Relations of the Co-event to the Motion Event   The fourth extension of the present pattern is that the relation borne by the Co-event to the Motion event with which it conflates need not be limited to that of either Manner or Cause, but can in fact range over a sizable set of alternatives. Selected from this larger set, eight of these relations are presented here. These are roughly sequenced according to the temporal relationship of the Co-event to the Motion event, beginning with the Co-event taking place beforehand and ending with its occurring afterward. This range of conflation generally works for both nonagentive and agentive cases, and examples of both types are given where feasible.[13]

In the first relation, **Precursion**, the Co-event precedes the main Motion event but does not cause or assist its occurrence. The Motion event would proceed much the same if the Co-event had not occurred. Thus, in the first example of (27a), some glass could have fallen over the carpet without having first splintered. The splintering of the glass preceded but did not cause the motion of the glass onto the carpet. Likewise, in the second example of (27a), my grinding the caraway seeds preceded but did not cause its entering the test tube—the researcher could have simply poured or dropped the seeds in instead.

(27) a. *Precursion*

    i. [glass MOVED onto the carpet] WITH-THE-PRECURSION-OF [the glass splintered]

       Glass splintered onto the carpet.

    ii. [the researcher $_A$MOVED the caraway seeds into the test tube] WITH-THE-PRECURSION-OF [the researcher ground the caraway seeds]

       The researcher ground the caraway seeds into the test tube.

Note that languages can differ in their constraints on the semantic closeness that the Co-event must bear to the main Motion event when it bears
a relation of Precursion to it. English generally requires that the Co-event
precede the Motion event directly and be conceptually associated with it
as part of a single activity. Thus, if the second example above is to be used
felicitously, the researcher could not, say, have used a mortar and pestle
to grind the seeds on an earlier occasion and then later poured the
grounds out of the mortar into the test tube, but would rather have to
hold the mortar over the test tube so that each portion of seeds ground by
the pestle drops immediately into the test tube. Further, grinding the seeds
and getting them into the test tube cannot be considered anything but an
integrated event. But Atsugewi permits a Co-event of Precursion to precede the Motion event by any interval and to bear no canonical relation
to it. Examples of this are given under the "Usage 3" headings in section
4.2.4 of chapter II-2. An example from that section can be sketched here
to highlight its contrast with English. Consider the verb root -miǎ'-,
whose meaning can be loosely rendered in English as 'for an architectural
structure to deintegrate (lose its structural integrity)'. This verb root can,
for example, take the Path + Ground suffix that means 'down into a
volume enclosure in the ground', while also taking the Cause prefix that
means 'as a result of the wind blowing on it'. The resulting verb could
refer to a situation in which a house collapsed down into the cellar from
the wind. Here, the verb root refers to a Co-event of deintegration that is
simply in a temporally concurrent Manner relation to the main event
involving a downward motion. But the same verb root can take a different
affix set: the Path + Ground suffix meaning 'up', together with a Cause
prefix meaning 'as a result of an Agent's whole body acting on it'. The
resulting verb can be used to refer to a situation in which a boy crawling
under the pile of boards from a house that had previously collapsed lifted
them up with his body as he stood. Here, the verb root refers to a Co-
event of architectural deintegration that can have occurred indefinitely
long before the main event involving an upward motion and that bears no
particular canonic association with that later event. Thus, this verb can
express Precursion of the temporally and associatively decoupled type
that English precludes.

In the **Enablement** relation, the Co-event directly precedes the main
Motion event and enables the occurrence of an event that causes the
Motion but does not itself cause this Motion. Thus, in the first example of
(27b), your reaching to or grabbing the bottle does not cause the bottle to

move off the shelf. Rather, it enables you to subsequently keep the bottle in your grip as you move your arm back from the shelf, which *is* the event that does cause the bottle's motion. Likewise, in the second example of (27b), my gathering up jelly beans into a scoop does not cause them to move into the sack. But it does enable them next to be lifted to the sack and sluiced off the scoop, which then does cause them to enter the sack.

(27) b. *Enablement*

 i. [could you $_A$MOVE that bottle down off the shelf] WITH-THE-ENABLEMENT-OF [you reach to/grab the bottle]

 Could you reach/grab that bottle down off the shelf?

 ii. [I $_A$MOVED jellybeans into her sack] WITH-THE-ENABLEMENT-OF [I scooped up the jellybeans]

 I scooped jellybeans up into her sack.

 In the relation of **reverse enablement**, the Co-event named by the verb is an event that has previously taken place and that now gets undone. This new event, in turn, enables the main Motion event named by the satellite. This latter relation of enablement is the same as that just described. Thus, in the first example of (27c), I first undo a prior event of tying—that is, I untie the sack. This enables me to open the sack. Note that this event of opening is not caused by the act of untying, which is thus only an enablement, but by an act of pulling on the mouth of the sack with my fingers.[14]

(27) c. *Reverse enablement*

 i. [I $_A$MOVED the sack TO AN-OPEN-CONFORMATION] WITH-THE-ENABLING-REVERSAL-OF [(someone) had tied the sack]

 Ich habe den Sack aufgebunden.
 I   have the sack open-tied
 "I untied the sack and opened it."

 ii. [I $_A$MOVED the dog TO FREENESS] WITH-THE-ENABLING-REVERSAL-OF [(someone) had chained the dog]

 Ich habe den Hund losgekettet.
 I   have the dog   free-chained
 "I set the dog free by unchaining it."

 In the Cause relation, much discussed earlier, the Co-event can precede the main Motion event in the case of **onset causation**, or it can co-occur with the main Motion event in the case of **extended causation** (see chapters I-7 and I-8). And it is construed as bringing about the occurrence of this Motion. That is, the Motion event would not take place if the Co-event did not occur.

(27) d. *Cause*
    Onset

     i.   [our tent MOVED down into the gully] WITH-THE-ONSET-CAUSE-OF [a gust of wind blew on the tent]

         Our tent blew down into the gully from a gust of wind.

     ii. [I $_A$MOVED the puck across the ice] WITH-THE-ONSET-CAUSE-OF [I batted the puck]

         I batted the puck across the ice.

    Extended

     iii. [the water MOVED down to the midline of the pot] WITH-THE-EXTENDED-CAUSE-OF [the water boiled]

         The water boiled down to the midline of the pot.

     iv. [I $_A$MOVED the toothpaste out of the tube] WITH-THE-EXTENDED-CAUSE-OF [I squeezed on the toothpaste/ tube]

         I squeezed the toothpaste out of the tube.

In the Manner relation, also much discussed, the Co-event co-occurs with the Motion event and is conceptualized as an additional activity that the Figure of the Motion event exhibits—an activity that directly pertains to the Motion event but that is distinct from it. In this conceptualization, the Co-event can "pertain" to the Motion event in several ways, such as by interacting with it, affecting it, or being able to manifest itself only in the course of it. Thus, the Co-event can consist of a pattern of motion by the Figure—specifically, a so-conceivedly abstractable type of self-contained motion—that coalesces with the Figure's translational motion to form a more complex envelope of movement, as in the case of a ball bouncing or rolling down a hall. Or the Co-event can be a conceptually abstractable activity by the Figure that could exist only in association with translational motion by the Figure, as in the case of a canoe gliding through water, of a book sliding down an incline, or of a baby crawling across the floor.

(27) e. *Manner*

    i. [the top MOVED past the lamp] WITH-THE-MANNER-OF [the top spun]

       The top spun past the lamp.

    ii. [the frond MOVED into its sheath] WITH-THE-MANNER-OF [the frond curled up]

       The frond curled up into its sheath.

    iii. [I $_A$MOVED the mug along the counter] WITH-THE-MANNER-OF [I slid the mug]

       I slid the mug along the counter.

The **Concomitance** relation is like Manner in that in it, the Co-event co-occurs with the main Motion event and is an activity that the Figure of the Motion event additionally exhibits. But here, this activity does not in itself pertain to the concurrent Motion, in the sense of "pertain" just described, and could just as readily take place by itself (although the presumed difference between Manner and Concomitance may have the character more of a gradient than of a sharp division). Thus, in the first example of (27f), the woman could wear a green dress whether or not she goes to a party, and without any effect on her path to one. The concomitance relation is not robustly represented in English (thus, speakers differ on their acceptance of the second example below). But it is readily available in some languages, like Atsugewi. This language, for example, can say the equivalent of "The baby cried along after its mother" to mean "The baby followed along after its mother, crying as it went."

(27) f. *Concomitance*

    i. [she WENT to the party] WITH-THE-CONCOMITANCE-OF [she wore a green dress]

       She wore a green dress to the party.

    ii. [I WENT past the graveyard] WITH-THE-CONCOMITANCE-OF [I whistled]

       I whistled past the graveyard.

       cf. I read comics all the way to New York.

In the relation of **Concurrent Result**, the Co-event results from—that is, is caused by—the main Motion event, and would not otherwise occur. It takes place concurrently with, or during some portion of, the Motion event. The Figure of the Co-event here may be the same as that of the Motion event, but it need not be. Thus, in the second example of (27g), the water splashes as a result of and concurrently with the rocket's motion into it.

(27) g. *Concurrent result*

    i. [the door MOVED TO A-POSITION-ACROSS-AN-OPENING] WITH-THE-CONCURRENT-RESULT-OF [the door slammed]

    The door slammed shut.

    ii. [the rocket MOVED into the water] WITH-THE-CONCURRENT-RESULT-OF [the water splashed]

    The rocket splashed into the water.

Finally, in the **Subsequence** relation, the Co-event takes place directly after the main Motion event, and is enabled by, is caused by, or is the purpose of that Motion event. In fact, Subsequence may better be considered a cover term for a small set of such finer relations that will need to be structurally distinguished.[15]

(27) h. *Subsequence (including Consequence/Purpose)*

    i. [I will GO down to your office] WITH-THE-SUBSEQUENCE-OF [I will stop at your office]

    I'll stop down at your office (on my way out of the building).

    ii. [I will GO in (to the kitchen)] WITH-THE-SUBSEQUENCE-OF [I will look at the stew cooking on the stove]

    I'll look in at the stew cooking on the stove.

    iii. [they $_A$MOVED the prisoner into his cell] WITH-THE-SUBSEQUENCE-OF [they locked the cell]

    They locked the prisoner into his cell.

    (with PLACE: [A] PUT [F] TO [G])

    iv. [I PLACED the painting down on the table] WITH-THE-SUBSEQUENCE-OF [the painting lay (there)]

    I laid the painting down on the table.
    Similarly: I stood/leaned/hung the painting on the chair/ against the door/on the wall.
    Comparably: I sat down on the chair.

2.1.3.5 Multiple Conflation   The final extension of the present pattern is that Co-event conflation is not limited to occurring just once within a two-clause structure but can in fact take place n times within a structure containing $n + 1$ clauses. By one approach, it can be theorized that such a structure arrays these clauses in a hierarchical embedding, and that conflation occurs successively, beginning with the lowest pair of related clauses. The examples below, though, simply present the clauses of these structures in sequence. The first example below exhibits a triplet of forms, extended beyond the doublets seen earlier. Thus, the most basic of the forms, *reach*$_1$ refers to extending a limb along its axis toward an object; *reach*$_2$ refers to moving an object by one's grip on it after having thus reached toward it; and *reach*$_3$ refers to giving the object thus moved and thus reached toward.

(28) a. [could you GIVE me the flour]
WITH-THE-ENABLEMENT-OF [you $_A$MOVE the flour down off the shelf], WITH-THE-ENABLEMENT-OF [you reach$_1$ to it with your free hand]?
$\Rightarrow$ [could you GIVE me the flour,]
WITH-THE-ENABLEMENT-OF [you reach$_2$ the flour down off that shelf with your free hand?]
$\Rightarrow$ Could you reach$_3$ me the flour down off that shelf with your free hand?
Similarly: [I $_A$MOVED a path through the jungle]
WITH-THE-ENABLEMENT-OF [I $_A$FORMED a path
($\Longrightarrow$ *out*)]
WITH-THE-CAUSE-OF [I $_A$MOVED STUFF away]
WITH-THE-CAUSE-OF [I hacked at the STUFF with my machete]
$\Rightarrow$ I hacked out a path through the jungle with my machete.
   b. [the prisoner SENT a message to his confederate]
WITH-THE-MANNER-OF [the prisoner $_A$MOVED the message along the water pipes]
WITH-THE-ENABLEMENT-OF [the prisoner $_A$FORMED the message ($\Longrightarrow$ *out*)]
WITH-THE-CAUSE-OF [the prisoner tapped on the water pipes]
$\Rightarrow$ The prisoner tapped out a message along the water pipes to his confederate.

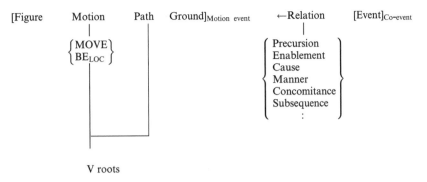

V roots

Path conflated in the Motion verb

2.2 Motion + Path

In the second typological pattern for the expression of motion, the verb root at once expresses both the fact of Motion and the Path. If a Co-event of Manner or Cause is expressed in the same sentence, it must be as an independent, usually adverbial or gerundive type constituent. In many languages—for example, Spanish—such a constituent can be stylistically awkward, so that information about Manner or Cause is often either established in the surrounding discourse or omitted altogether. In any case, it is not indicated by the main verb root itself. Rather, languages of this type have a whole series of surface verbs that express motion along various paths. This conflation pattern can be represented schematically as in the accompanying diagram.

2.2.1 The Pattern Underlying Path-Event Conflation   Language families or languages that seem to be of this type are Romance, Semitic, Japanese, Korean, Turkish, Tamil, Polynesian, Nez Perce, and Caddo. Spanish is a perfect example of the type. We draw on it for illustration, first with nonagentive sentences, and point out how pervasive the system is here.[16]

(29) *Spanish expressions of Motion (nonagentive) with conflation of Path*
    a. La botella entró   a la cueva (flotando)
        the bottle MOVED-in to the cave (floating)
        "The bottle floated into the cave."
    b. La botella salió   de la cueva (flotando)
        the bottle MOVED-out from the cave (floating)
        "The bottle floated out of the cave."

    c. La botella pasó   por la piedra (flotando)
        the bottle MOVED-by past the rock   (floating)
        "The bottle floated past the rock."

    d. La botella pasó   por   el tubo (flotando)
        the bottle MOVED-through through the pipe (floating)
        "The bottle floated through the pipe."

    e. El globo subió   por   la chimenea (flotando)
        the balloon MOVED-up through the chimney (floating)
        "The balloon floated up the chimney."

    f. El globo bajó   por   la chimenea (flotando)
        the balloon MOVED-down through the chimney (floating)
        "The balloon floated down the chimney."

    g. La botella se fué   de la orilla (flotando)
        the bottle MOVED-away from the bank (floating)
        "The bottle floated away from the bank."

    h. La botella volvió   a la orilla (flotando)
        the bottle MOVED-back to the bank (floating)
        "The bottle floated back to the bank."

    i. La botella le   dió vuelta a la isla   (flotando)
        the bottle to-it gave turn   to the island (floating)
                (= 'MOVED around')
        "The bottle floated around the island."

    j. La botella cruzó   el canal (flotando)
        the bottle MOVED-across the canal (floating)
        "The bottle floated across the canal."

    k. La botella iba   por el canal (flotando)
        the bottle MOVED-along along the canal (floating)
        "The bottle floated along the canal."

    l. La botella andaba   en el canal (flotando)
        the bottle MOVED-about in the canal (floating)
        "The bottle floated around the canal."

    m. Las dos botellas se juntaron   (flotando)
        the two bottles MOVED-together (floating)
        "The two bottles floated together."

    n. La dos botellas se separaron   (flotando)
        the two bottles MOVED-apart (floating)
        "The two bottles floated apart."

Further Spanish nonagentive verbs that manifest this Path conflating pattern are *avanzar* 'MOVE ahead/forward', *regresar* 'MOVE in the reverse direction', *acercarse* 'MOVE closer to (approach)', *llegar* 'MOVE to the point of (arrive at)', *seguir* 'MOVE along after (follow)'.

In its agentive forms as well, Spanish shows the same pattern of conflating Path in the verb. Again, Manner or Cause, if present, is expressed in an independent constituent. We can see this for Manner:

(30) *Spanish expressions of Motion (agentive) with conflation of Path*

    a. Metí   el barril a la bodega   rodándolo
       I-$_A$MOVED-in the keg   to the storeroom rolling-it
       "I rolled the keg into the storeroom."

    b. Saqué   el corcho de   la botella retorciéndolo
       I-$_A$MOVED-out the cork   from the bottle twisting-it
       Retorcí el corcho y lo saqué   de la botella
       I-twisted the cork   and it I-$_A$MOVED-out from the bottle
       "I twisted the cork out of the bottle."

And we can see it for Cause:

    c. Tumbé el   árbol serruchándolo// a hachazos/ con una hacha
       I-felled the tree   sawing-it//   by ax-chops/ with an ax
       "I sawed//chopped the tree down."

    d. Quité   el papel del   paquete cortándolo
       I-$_A$MOVED-off the paper from-the package cutting-it
       "I cut the wrapper off the package."

One category of agentive motion can be represented by the mid-level verb PUT. In this type, an Agent moves a Figure by the motion of some body part(s) (or an instrument held thereby) in steady contact with the Figure, but without the translocation of the Agent's whole body.[17] As before with simple MOVE, Spanish conflates PUT with different Path notions to yield a series of different verb forms with the separate indication of distinctions of path, as seen in table 1.1.

Notice that English does use different verb forms here, *put* and *take*, in correlation with the general path notions 'to' and 'from' in a way that suggests the Spanish type of Path incorporation. And this may be the best interpretation. But an alternative view is that these are simply suppletive forms of the single more general and nondirectional PUT notion, where the specific form that is to appear at the surface is determined completely by the particular Path particle and/or preposition present. In expressing this notion, English uses *put* in conjunction with a 'to'-type preposition (*I put the dish into/onto the stove*); *take* with a 'from'-type preposition

Table 1.1
Spanish 'putting' verbs, differing according to distinctions of Path (A = Agent,
F = Figure object, G = Ground object)

A poner F en G	A put F onto G
A meter F a G	A put F into G
A subir F a G	A put F up (on)to G
A juntar F_1 y F_2	A put F_1 and F_2 together
A quitar F de G	A take F off G
A sacar F de G	A take F out of G
A bajar F de G	A take F down from G
A separar F_1 y F_2	A take F_1 and F_2 apart

except when *up* is present (*I took the dish off/out of the stove*), *pick* with a 'from'-type preposition in the presence of *up* (*I picked the dish up off the chair*); and *move* with an 'along'-type preposition (*I moved the dish further down the ledge*).

As further evidence for the interpretation of their purely formal character, these distinctions of verb form are effaced when there is Manner conflation. Thus, beside a different-verb pair of sentences such as *I put the cork into/took the cork out of the bottle* is the same-verb pair *I twisted the cork into/out of the bottle*, where the Manner verb *twist* supplants both *put* and *take*. Comparably, beside *I put the hay up onto/took the hay down off the platform* is *I forked the hay up onto/down off the platform*. Thus, it can be seen that any Path information borne by the English PUT verbs is less than and no different from that expressed by the particles and prepositions occurring in the same sentence and, accordingly, they can be readily supplanted under the Manner conflation typical of English.

On the other hand, the Spanish PUT verbs express the bulk of Path distinctions—the only prepositions used with this subsystem are *a, de,* and *en*—and so are central, unsupplanted fixtures in the Spanish sentence, as is typical for *that* language.

English does have a number of verbs that genuinely incorporate Path, as in the Spanish conflation type. Important examples are *enter, exit, ascend, descend, cross, pass, circle, advance, proceed, approach, arrive, depart, return, join, separate, part, rise, leave, near, follow.* And these verbs even call for a Spanish-type pattern for the rest of the sentence. Thus, any Manner notion must be expressed in a separate constituent. For example, a sentence like *The rock slid past our tent* exhibits the basic English pattern with a Manner-incorporating verb and a Path preposition, but the use of a Path-incorporating verb requires that any expression of Manner occur in a separate constituent (where it is rather awkward), as seen in *The rock passed our tent in its slide/in sliding.* These verbs (and the sentence pattern they call for) are not the most characteristic type in English, however, and many are not the most colloquial alternatives available. And, significantly, the great majority—here, all but the last four verbs listed—are not even original English forms but rather are borrowings from Romance, where they are the native type. By contrast, German, which has borrowed much less from Romance languages, lacks verb roots that might correspond to most of the Path verbs in the list.

2.2.2 Components of Path   Although Path has so far been treated as a simplex constituent, it is better understood as comprising several structurally distinct components. The three main components for spoken languages are the Vector, the Conformation, and the Deictic (though sign languages may additionally have Contour and Direction).

The Vector comprises the basic types of arrival, traversal, and departure that a Figural schema can execute with respect to a Ground schema. These Vector forms are part of a small set of **Motion-aspect formulas** that are quite possibly universal. These formulas are given in (31), with the Vectors shown as deep prepositions written in capitals.[18] In these formulas, the Figure and the Ground appear as highly abstracted and fundamental schemas. The **fundamental Figure schema** appears first—here, always as "a point." A **fundamental Ground schema**—a member of a very small set—follows the Vector. Each formula is exemplified with a sentence whose more specific spatial reference is based on the formula.

(31) a. A point BE_{LOC} AT a point, for a bounded extent of time.
         The napkin lay on the bed/in the box for three hours.
     b. A point MOVE TO a point, at a point of time.
         The napkin blew onto the bed/into the box at exactly 3:05.
     c. A point MOVE FROM a point, at a point of time.
         The napkin blew off the bed/out of the box at exactly 3:05.
     d. A point MOVE VIA a point, at a point of time.
         The ball rolled across the crack/past the lamp at exactly 3:05.
     e. A point MOVE ALONG an unbounded extent, for a bounded extent of time.

The ball rolled down the slope/along the ledge/around the tree for 10 seconds.

e′. A point MOVE TOWARD a point, for a bounded extent of time.

The ball rolled toward the lamp for 10 seconds.

e″. A point MOVE AWAY-FROM a point, for a bounded extent of time.

The ball rolled away from the lamp for 10 seconds.

f. A point MOVE ALENGTH a bounded extent, in a bounded extent of time.

The ball rolled across the rug/through the tube in 10 seconds.
The ball rolled 20 feet in 10 seconds.

f′. A point MOVE FROM-TO a point-pair, in a bounded extent of time.

The ball rolled from the lamp to the door/from one side of the rug to the other in 10 seconds.

g. A point MOVE ALONG-TO an extent bounded at a terminating point, at a point of time/in a bounded extent of time.

The car reached the house at 3:05/in three hours.

h. A point MOVE FROM-ALONG an extent bounded at a beginning point, since a point of time/for a bounded extent of time.

The car has been driving from Chicago since 12:05/for three hours.

The Conformation component of the Path is a geometric complex that relates the fundamental Ground schema within a Motion-aspect formula to the schema for a full Ground object. Each language lexicalizes its own set of such geometric complexes. To illustrate, the fundamental Ground schema in (32a) to (32c) is 'a point'. To this fundamental Ground schema, English can add, for example, the particular Conformation notion: 'which is of the inside of [an enclosure]'. Or it can add another particular Conformation notion: 'which is of the surface of [a volume]'. In each such Conformation, the schema for the full Ground object is indicated in brackets. For felicity, it must be easy to geometrically idealize any full Ground object that is in reference down to this indicated schema—as, say, in referring to a box for 'an enclosure' or a bed for 'a volume'. For the three formulas of (32a) to (32c), then, the combination of the Vector and the fundamental Ground schema with these Conformations is as shown in (32).

(32) a. AT a point which is of the inside of [an enclosure] = *in* [an enclosure]

AT a point which is of the surface of [a volume] = *on* [a volume]

b. TO a point which is of the inside of [an enclosure] = *in(to)* [an enclosure]

TO a point which is of the surface of [a volume] = *on(to)* [a volume]

c. FROM a point which is of the inside of [an enclosure] = *out of* [an enclosure]

FROM a point which is of the surface of [a volume] = *off (of)* [a volume].

The full formulas of (32a) to (32c) together with the 'inside' Conformation are shown in (33a) along with sentences built on the entire complexes. The comparable presentation for the 'surface' comformation appears in (33b).

(33) a. i. A point BE_{LOC} AT a point which is of the inside of an enclosure for a bounded extent of time.
The ball was in the box for three hours.

ii. A point MOVE TO a point which is of the inside of an enclosure at a point of time.
The ball rolled into the box at exactly 3:05.

iii. A point MOVE FROM a point which is of the inside of an enclosure at a point of time.
The ball rolled out of the box at exactly 3:05.

b. i. A point BE_{LOC} AT a point which is of the surface of a volume for a bounded extent of time.
The napkin lay on the bed for three hours.

ii. A point MOVE TO a point which is of the surface of a volume at a point of time.
The napkin blew onto the bed at exactly 3:05.

iii. A point MOVE FROM a point which is of the surface of a volume at a point of time.
The napkin blew off of the bed at exactly 3:05.

Comparably, the Vector plus the fundamental Ground schema of (31d), "VIA a point," can be combined with the Conformation 'which is to one side of [a point]' to yield *past* (*The ball rolled past the lamp at exactly 3:05*). It can also be combined with the Conformation 'which is (one of the points) of [a line]' to yield *across* (*The ball rolled across the crack at exactly 3:05*). And it can be combined with the Conformation 'which is (one of the points) of [a plane]' to yield *through* (*The ball sailed through the pane of glass at exactly 3:05*).

In a similar way, the Vector and the fundamental Ground schema of (31e), "ALONG an unbounded extent," can be combined with the Conformation 'which is to one side of and parallel to [an unbounded extent]' to yield *alongside* (I walked alongside the base of the cliff for an hour). And the Vector plus the fundamental Ground schema of (31f), "ALENGTH a bounded extent," can be combined with the Conformation 'which is coterminous and coaxial with [a bounded cylinder]' to yield *through* (*I walked through the tunnel in 10 minutes*). (A much expanded and more detailed presentation of such structures appears in the appendix to chapter I-3.)

With the Vector and the Conformation components of Path thus distinguished, we can characterize the Spanish pattern for representing a Motion event more precisely. The verb root conflates together Fact-of-Motion and the Vector and Conformation components of the Path constituent. The preposition that can occur with a Ground nominal represents the Vector alone. Thus, in the form "F *salir de* G," the verb means 'MOVE FROM a point of the inside (of an enclosure)', while the preposition simply represents the Vector 'FROM'. Comparably, in the form "F *pasar por* G," the verb means 'MOVE VIA a point that is to one side (of a point)', while the preposition represents solely the Vector 'VIA'.

In languages that include it in their characteristic representation of Motion events, the Deictic component of Path typically has only the two member notions 'toward the speaker' and 'in a direction other than toward the speaker'.[19] Languages with a Path conflating verb system can differ in their treatment of the Deictic. Spanish largely classes its Deictic verbs—*venir* 'come' and *ir* 'go'—together with its "Conformation verbs" (a term for the verbs that incorporate Fact-of-Motion + Vector + Conformation)—for example, *entrar* 'enter'. Thus, in a typical motion sentence, the main verb slot will be occupied by one or the other of these Path verb types, while any gerundive verb form will express Manner.[20]

Like Spanish, Korean can occupy its main verb slot with either type of Path verb—that is, with a Conformation verb or a deictic verb—and accompany this with a gerundive constituent of Manner. But unlike Spanish, Korean can represent both Path components concurrently in nonagentive sentences (Choi and Bowerman 1991). In this case, the Deictic verb is the main verb, the Conformation verb appears in a gerundive constituent, and a Manner verb can still appear in a further gerundive constituent. Thus, Korean is a characteristically Path verb type of language, but it structurally distinguishes the Deictic component from the Conformation component of Path and accords it higher priority when both components are present.

2.3   Motion + Figure

In the third major typological pattern for the expression of Motion, the verb expresses the fact of Motion together with the Figure. Languages with this as their characteristic pattern have a whole series of surface verbs that express various kinds of objects or materials as moving or located. This conflation type can be represented schematically as in the accompanying diagram.

This pattern can first be illustrated close to home, for English does have a few forms that conform to it. Thus, the nonagentive verb (to) *rain* refers to rain moving, and the agentive verb (to) *spit* refers to causing spit to move, as seen in (34).

(34) a. It *rained* in through the bedroom window.   Nonagentive
      b. I *spat* into the cuspidor.   Agentive

But in the languages for which this pattern is characteristic, there are scores of Motion + Figure verbs with the most colloquial and extensive of

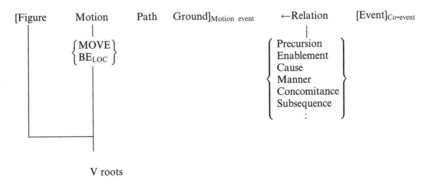

Figure conflated in the Motion verb

usages. Atsugewi, a Hokan language of northern California, is an example par excellence of this type. The verb roots in (35) are just a sampling.

(35) *Atsugewi verb roots of motion with conflated Figure*

-lup-	'for a small shiny spherical object (e.g., a round candy, an eyeball, a hailstone) to move/be-located'
-ṭ-	'for a smallish planar object that can be functionally affixed (e.g., a stamp, a clothing patch, a button, a shingle, a cradle's sunshade) to move/be-located'
-caq-	'for a slimy lumpish object (e.g., a toad, a cow dropping) to move/be-located'
-swal-	'for a limp linear object suspended by one end (e.g., a shirt on a clothesline, a hanging dead rabbit, a flaccid penis) to move/be-located'
-qput-	'for loose dry dirt to move/be-located'
-staq̓-	'for runny icky material (e.g., mud, manure, rotten tomatoes, guts, chewed gum) to move/be-located'

These verb roots can also have an agentive meaning. For example, -staq̓- has the further meaning option: '(for an Agent) to move runny icky material'. Thus, such verb roots typically function equally in the expression of events of location, of nonagentive motion, and of agentive motion. Each of these usages is now exemplified with -staq̓- here in referring to guts (an instance of 'runny icky material'). Each example gives both the morphophonemic and the phonetic form (the superscript vowel represents a special morphophoneme of this language). (Note that an independent nominal for 'guts' could be included along with the verb, thus providing a separate reference to the Figure entity beside the one already provided by the verb root.)

(36) *Atsugewi expressions of motion with conflated Figure*

    a. *Locative suffix*   -ik·   'on the ground'

       Cause prefix   uh-   'from "gravity" (an object's own weight) acting on it'

       Inflectional affix set   '- w- -ᵃ   '3rd person–subject; factual mood'

/'-w-uh-staq̓-ik·-ᵃ/ ⇒ [ẇostaq̓ík·a]

Literal: 'Runny icky material is located on the ground from its own weight acting on it.'

Instantiated: "Guts are lying on the ground."

b. *Directional suffix*   -ičt   'into liquid'

Cause prefix   ca-   'from the wind blowing on the Figure'

Inflectional affix set   '- w- -ª   '3rd person–subject, factual mood'

/'-w-ca-staq̇-ičt-ª/ ⇒ [čwastaq̇íčta]

Literal: 'Runny icky material moved into liquid from the wind blowing on it.'

Instantiated: "The guts blew into the creek."

c. *Directional suffix*   -cis   'into fire'

Cause prefix   cu-   'from a linear object, moving axially, acting on the Figure.'

Inflectional affix set   s- '- w- -ª   'I–subject (3rd person–object), factual mood'

/s-'-w-cu-staq̇-cis-ª/ ⇒ [sčustáq̇cʰa]

Literal: 'I caused it that runny icky material move into fire by acting on it with a linear object moving axially.'

Instantiated: "I prodded the guts into the fire with a stick."

Atsugewi's pattern of conflating the Figure with Motion extends to such Figural objects as body parts and garments. Note that the usual English construction for referring to body-part control involves expressing the body part as the direct-object nominal of a verb of maneuvering, as in *I laid my head on the pillow/pulled my arm back out of the cage/put my ear against the wall/stuck my tongue out.* There is only an occasional verb root for body-part motion, which then usually involves additional semantic constraints—for example, *step*, 'controlledly ₐMOVE one of one's feet while standing on the other', as in *I stepped into the puddle/over the crack.* But in Atsugewi, the regular pattern involves a verb root that refers to a particular body part as moving or located and that can take the full range of directional suffixes. Similarly, instead of such English constructions as *I have a hat on/put my shirt on/took my shoes off/put a coat on her,* Atsugewi has verb roots that refer to a particular garment moved or located for wear that takes affixes indicating whether the garment is on, or is put on or taken off oneself or someone else.[21]

Table 1.2
Three main typological categories for Motion verbs

Language/language family	The particular components of a Motion event characteristically represented in the verb root
Romance Semitic Polynesian Nez Perce Caddo Japanese Korean	Motion + Path
Indo-European (not Romance) Chinese Finno-Ugric Ojibwa Warlpiri	Motion + Co-event
Atsugewi (and apparently most northern Hokan) Navaho	Motion + Figure

2.4   A Typology for Motion Verbs

The three conflation patterns for Motion verbs discussed so far are apparently the main ones found across languages. But other patterns occur or, in some cases, fail to occur. This range is discussed here.

2.4.1   Motion + Co-Event, Path, or Figure   The three main conflation patterns for Motion verbs that languages exhibit are summarized in table 1.2. Subcategorization of these three types, based on where the remaining components of a Motion event are expressed in a sentence, is treated later.

2.4.2   Motion + Ground   The typology just presented raises questions about the nonoccurring combinatory possibilities. It can be seen that one Motion-event component, the Ground, does not by itself conflate with the Motion verb to form any language's core system for expressing Motion. Conflations of this sort may not even form any minor systems.

Sporadic instances of such a conflation do occur, however, and can provide an idea of what a larger system might be like. The verb root *-plane* in the English verbs *emplane* and *deplane* can be taken to mean 'move with respect to an airplane'—that is, to specify a particular Ground object plus the fact of Motion, without any indication of Path. It is the separate prefixal morphemes here that specify particular Paths. What a full system of this sort would have to include is the provision for expressing many further Paths and Grounds. Thus, in addition to the forms just seen with prefixal *em-* and *de-*, we might expect such a system to contain *circumplane,* 'move around an airplane', and *transplane,* 'move through an airplane'. And there should be many further verb roots participating in this system, say, *(to) house* 'move with respect to a house' (*I enhoused/dehoused/circumhoused*), and *(to) liquid,* 'move with respect to liquid' (*The penguin will enliquid/deliquid/transliquid*). But such systems are not to be found.

It is not clear why the Ground component should be so disfavored. One might first speculate that, in discourse, the Ground object of a situation is the most unvarying component and therefore the one least needing specification. But on further consideration, the Figure would seem to be even more constant—since a discourse often tracks the same Figure object moving progressively with respect to a succession of Ground objects—yet it forms the basis for a major typological system. One might next speculate that the Ground object is the component least salient or accessible to identification. But there seems nothing more obscure about airplanes, houses, and liquids (to pick some likely Ground objects) than, say, about notions of Path, which do form the basis for a major typological system.

Explanation may next be sought in a concept of hierarchy: the different conflation types seem to be ranked in their prevalence among the world's languages, with conflation of Path apparently as the most extensively represented, of Co-event next, and of Figure least so. It may therefore be the case that Ground conflation is also a possibility, but one so unlikely that it has not yet been instantiated in any language that has come to attention. However, while great disparity of prevalence for the different conflation types would be most significant if proved by further investigation, it would then itself require explanation, so that the present mystery would only have moved down a level.

2.4.3 Motion + Two Semantic Components There are further combinatorial possibilities to be considered. Among these: *two* components of a Motion event conflating with fact-of-Motion in the verb root. Minor systems of such conflation do exist. For example, the Ground *and* Path together are conflated with Motion in a minor system of agentive verbs in English, with forms like *shelve* '$_A$MOVE onto a shelf' (*I shelved the books*) and *box* '$_A$MOVE into a box' (*I boxed the apples*).[22] Another minor system of agentive verbs in English conflates the Figure and Path together with Motion: *powder* '$_A$MOVE facial powder onto' (*She powdered her nose*), *scale* '$_A$MOVE the scales off of' (*I scaled the fish*).

Conflation systems of this multicomponent sort apparently never form a language's major system for expressing Motion. The reason for such a prohibition seems straightforward for any system that would undertake to make relatively fine semantic distinctions: it would require an enormous lexicon. There would have to be a distinct lexical verb for each fine-grained semantic combination. For example, beside *box* meaning 'put into a box', there would have to be, say, a verb *foo* 'take out of a box', a verb *baz* 'move around a box', and so on, and further verbs for the myriad of Ground objects other than a box. Such a system would not be feasible for language, whose organization relies less on large numbers of distinct elements and more on combinatorial devices that operate with a smaller set of elements.

However, one can imagine another kind of multicomponent conflational system, one with fairly broadband references and hence fewer total elements, acting as a kind of classificatory system, that contained verbs with meanings like 'move to a round object', 'move from a round object', 'move through/past a round object', 'move to a linear object', 'move from a linear object', and so forth. A system such as this would indeed be feasible for language, yet also seems unrealized, and an explanation here, too, must be awaited.

2.4.4 Motion + No Further Semantic Component Another combinatorial possibility is that the verb root expresses the Motion component alone, without the conflation of any other component of the Motion event. This pattern does occur, perhaps with some frequency, in representing the locative type of Motion event. In a language with this arrangement, a single verb form represents the deep verb BE$_{LOC}$ and does not conflate with various Paths, Figures, or Co-events. Spanish has this arrangement: the verb *estar* 'to be located' is followed by various locative prepositions or prepositional complexes that represent the site, but it does not have a set of distinct verb roots that conflate BE_{LOC} with various sites to yield such meanings as 'to be in', 'to be on', 'to be under'.[23]

For the representation of the motion type of a Motion event, Atsugewi does in fact have a minor system with a nonconflated verb. A verb root consisting of the vowel *i-* that directly takes any of the Path + Ground suffixes can be interpreted as expressing the 'MOVE' notion in isolation. However, this form is not the main way that Motion is expressed in Atsugewi (although it is not fully clear when its use is called for).

If indeed the pattern with lack of conflation occurs rarely or never as the main system of a language, one explanation may be its relative inefficiency. The pattern calls for the re-expression of the same morpheme with the same fixed meaning—whether 'MOVE' alone or '$MOVE/BE_{LOC}$'— for every reference to a Motion event. Yet this one fixed meaning can readily be gotten from the other represented components of the Motion event, as is demonstrated by the fact that the previously described major systems for expressing a Motion event in fact lack any morpheme to represent the Motion component alone.

2.4.5   Motion + A Minimally Differentiated Semantic Component   Certain major systems do exist, however, that, in effect, approach the zero-conflation type. These are systems in which Motion does conflate with another component of the Motion event, but where only two or three distinctions pertaining to that component are represented, rather than a great many distinctions, as we have seen previously.

Thus, Southwest Pomo conflates MOVE with the Figure, but not with that aspect of the Figure that pertains to the type of object or material that it is, as in Atsugewi, but rather with the numerosity of the Figure, and here it marks only three distinctions. Specifically, the Southwest Pomo verb roots *-w/-ʔda/-pʰil* mean, respectively, 'for one/two or three/ several together ... to move', and these three roots appear recurrently in verbs referring to Motion events. Any representation of the Figure's object type or material characteristics takes place not in the verb root but in the subject nominal.

In a comparable way, it appears that Hindi, in its expression of non-agentive motion, conflates MOVE with Path, but only with the deictic portion of Path, not with the portion that pertains to geometric configurations. And here, only the two-valued 'hither/thither' distinction within deixis is conflated with MOVE so as to yield two verb roots—essentially, 'come' and 'go'—that appear recurrently in constructions representing non-agentive motion events. The Conformation portion of Path is expressed in a separate Path satellite or prepositional complex.

Finally, in Supalla's (1982) analysis, the main system in American Sign Language for representing Motion events has at its core a small set of hand movement types that can be regarded as the counterpart of verb roots. These hand movements represent a component of the Path constituent that does not seem to receive distinct structural recognition as a Path component in any spoken language. This component can be termed the 'Contour' and consists of certain distinctions in the shape of the Path described by a Figure. Supalla distinguishes seven Path Contours in all, and three for cases of actual motion: straight line, curve, and circle.

As the dominant hand moves to trace out a Path-Contour, it may concurrently represent other components of the Path—namely, the Vector, Conformation, Deictic, and Direction of the Path—as well as a certain set of Manners. In addition, the hand's shape concurrently represents the classificatory category of the Figure and, potentially also, certain aspects of an Instrument or Agent. These further semantic representations behave analogously to separate satellite classes accompanying the verb root in a spoken language. The central observation here, though, is that in the main system for representing Motion events in ASL, the verb root equivalent incorporates the Path, as in Spanish, but it incorporates only the Contour component of Path and then marks only three distinctions within that component.

2.4.6 Split System of Conflation   So far, we have mostly treated a language in terms of having a characteristic conflation type, sometimes along with some minor systems and occasional forms of a different conflation type. Alternatively, though, a language can characteristically employ one conflation type for one type of Motion event, and characteristically employ a different conflation type for another type of Motion event. This can be called a "split" or "complementary" system of conflation.

As suggested earlier, Spanish has such a split system with respect to state of Motion. For a locative situation with an underlying BE_{LOC}, Spanish characteristically uses the zero-conflation pattern. But for an event of actual motion with an underlying MOVE, we have seen Spanish characteristically to use Path conflation.[24] Even within this MOVE type, though, a further split can be seen. Aske (1989) and Slobin and Hoiting (1994) have observed that motion events whose paths are conceptualized as crossing a boundary—as would be typical for 'into' and 'out of'—are the ones that are represented with the Path conflation pattern. But motion events with a path conceptualized as not crossing a boundary—as would be typical for 'from', 'to', and 'toward'—are characteristically represented with the Co-event conflation pattern, just like English, as in *Corrí de mi casa a la escuela*, 'I ran from my house to the school'.

A different split pattern occurs in Emai (Schaefer 1988). Emai has an extensive set of Path verbs, much like Spanish, but in a Motion sentence, it generally uses this set only for self-agentive motion. It instead uses a main verb with Co-event conflation for nonagentive and agentive motion. It can use this latter conflation type for self-agentive motion as well, if the Manner is other than that of 'walking'.[25]

Tzeltal exhibits yet another split pattern, in fact employing each of the three main conflation types for separate types of Motion event. Like Atsugewi, this language has a large set of verb roots in which the Figure is conflated. These "positional roots" largely distinguish Figure objects in terms of their disposition: their form, orientation, and arrangement relative to other objects. Unlike Atsugewi, though, when applying them to a Motion event, Tzeltal uses these roots for only one circumstance: where the Figure is or ends up supported at some location. The stative form of the roots refers to a locative situation, having the sense 'for a Figure with X disposition to be at a particular supportive location'. The inchoative form of the roots, the "assumptive," refers to the arrival at a supportive location of a Figure that has X disposition or that acquires it in the process. And the agentive form of the roots, the "depositive," refers to an Agent's placing at a supportive location a Figure that has X disposition or that acquires it in the process, where the Agent controls this motion—that is, holds the Figure with body part or instrument.

In addition, though, like Spanish, Tzeltal has a set of Path-conflating verb roots—the "movement verbs"—that are used for two further types of Motion event. The nonagentive form of the verbs is used for autonomous Figural motion, thus having the sense '(for a Figure) to MOVE along X Path'. The agentive form of the verbs is used for controlled agentive motion, thus having the sense '(for an Agent) to $_A$MOVE (the Figure) along X Path while holding (it)'.

Finally, like English, Tzeltal uses Co-event-conflating verbs in construction with the "directional" form of the Path verbs—which here, then, function like Path satellites. This construction covers much the same range of usages as the English construction—for example, the counterparts of an agentive noncontrolled Cause type like "I kicked it in," of an agentive controlled Cause type like "I carried it in," of a self-agentive Manner type like "I ran out," and of a nonagentive Manner type like "It fell down" (though this is the least well-represented type). Although the situations that the last three of these types refer to can largely also be represented by the path-verb construction, the first type can only be represented by the present construction.[26]

2.4.7 Parallel System of Conflation In a split system, a language uses different conflation types for different types of Motion event. But in a parallel system of conflation, a language can use different conflation types with roughly comparable colloquiality in the representation of the *same* type of Motion event. English would exemplify a parallel-type system if its Path verb-based constructions were as colloquial as its Co-event verb-based constructions—for example, if *The bottle exited the cave floating* were as colloquial as *The bottle floated out of the cave*. But this is not the case, so that English has been classed as being characteristically of the Co-event conflation type. On the other hand, modern Greek does exemplify the parallel system of conflation in using exactly the two types of conflation just cited with comparable colloquiality to represent most events of autonomous or self-agentive motion. Thus, for most Path notions, Greek has both a Path satellite for use with a Manner-Cause verb, and a Path verb that can be accompanied by a Manner/Cause gerund. In (37), we illustrate this for the Path notion 'in(to)'.[27]

(37) a. etreksa mesa (s-to   spiti)
        I-ran   in   (to-the house [ACC])
        "I ran in (-to the house)."
     b. bika   (trekhondas) (s-to   spiti)
        I-entered (running)   (to-the house [ACC])
        "I entered (the house) (running)."

A sampling of parallel Path satellite and Path verb constructions in Greek follows, using the notation of section 3.

(38) [*se* 'at/to'; *apo* 'from'; V_C = the Co-event verb; V_{MC} = verb
     conflating MOVE + Co-event]

into	F V$_{MC}$ ◄mesa	F beno (se + ACC> G)
	(se + ACC> G)	(V$_C$-GER)
out (of)	F V$_{MC}$ ◄ekso	F vgheno (apo + ACC> G)
	(apo + ACC> G)	(V$_C$-GER)
up (along)	F V$_{MC}$ ◄pano	F anaveno (se + ACC> G)
	(se + ACC> G)	(V$_C$-GER)
down (along)	F V$_{MC}$ ◄kato	F kataveno (apo + ACC>
		G) (V$_C$-GER)
back (to)	F V$_{MC}$ ◄piso	F ghirizo (se + ACC> G)
	(se + ACC> G)	(V$_C$-GER)

2.4.8 Intermixed System of Conflation In principle, a language might exhibit no consistent pattern of conflation for some type of Motion event, but rather intermix different forms of conflation for the various members of that Motion event type. As will be seen in section 2.7.1, Latin appears to intermix different lexicalization patterns in its expression of change of state. But no language has come to attention in which some characteristic conflation pattern has not emerged for each semantically distinguishable type of Motion event. What such an intermixed system might look like can be readily imagined. Consider that for some Path notions, Greek does not have parallel constructions, but either a Path verb or a Path satellite alone. Thus, 'across' and 'past' can be expressed only with Path verbs (*dhiaskhizo* and *perno*), while 'around' can be expressed only with a Path satellite (◄*ghiro*). If the remainder of the Path notions were also expressed by either the one or the other conflation form without any principled semantic basis—instead of the actually occurring pattern of doublets for the majority of the Path notions—then Greek would be an example of an intermixed system of conflation.

2.5 Aspect

In addition to the Motion typology we have just seen, languages form a typology according to their characteristic way of expressing (change of) state. This is a domain that involves aspect and causation and their interaction, as addressed in this and the next two sections. "Aspect" can be characterized as the 'pattern of distribution of action through time'. The term "action" as used here applies to a static condition—the continuance of a location or state—as well as to motion or change. The accompanying figure shows some of the aspect types lexicalized in verb roots, with nonagentive and agentive English verbs exemplifying each.

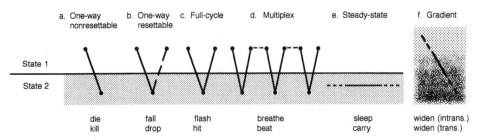

Various grammatical tests demonstrate the distinctness of these types and of the verb roots incorporating them. The resettable type of a one-way verb is distinguished from the nonresettable type by its compatibility with iterative expressions, as in *He fell three times*. The nonresettable verbs cannot occur here: **He died three times*. This same one-way form is distinguished from a full-cycle form by its ability to occur with expressions of reversal, as in *He fell and then got up*, which the latter cannot do: **The beacon flashed and then went off*. A gradient verb can appear with adverbs of augmentation, as in *The river progressively widened*, unlike a steady-state verb: **She progressively slept*. And so on.

Sometimes all that distinguishes two verb forms that otherwise have the same core meaning is a difference in incorporated aspect. In certain sectors of their usage, this is the case with *learn*, which (for many speakers though not all) incorporates a completive aspect, and *study*, which is steady-state. The semantically comparable verb *teach* has a lexicalization range covering both of these aspect types, as (39) shows.

(39)   *Completive aspect*   *Steady-state aspect*
        We learned/*studied French in   We *learned/studied French for
        three years.   two years.
        She taught us French in three   She taught us French for two
        years.   years.

Lexicalized aspect figures in the analysis of a language in several ways. First, aspect generally seems to be part of the intrinsic meaning of verb roots.[28] It is doubtful that any verb root can have a meaning wholly neutral with respect to aspect—even in languages where the root is always surrounded by aspect-specifying inflections.

Second, a verb root's intrinsic aspect determines how it interacts with grammatical elements that also have aspectual meaning. Many of the latter appear only with verb roots of a particular aspect type, operating on them to yield a different aspect type as a resultant. For example, in English the grammatical form *keep -ing* operates on a one-cycle verb of the (c) type to yield a multiplex aspectual meaning of the (d) type. This shift takes place for *flash* in *The beacon kept flashing*. Similarly, we can make the reverse change from the (d) type to the (c) type with the abstract grammatical form V_{dummy} *a* [__ + Deriv]$_N$—that is, by using a construction that has the verb root in a derived nominal form. This is what happens to the verb root *breathe* (with an inherent multiplex meaning) in the sentence *She took a breath* (with a 'once only' meaning).[29]

Third, different languages have different patterns of aspect incorporation in their verbs. For example, we will see in section 2.7 how verbs referring to states are lexicalized in some languages with the (b) "one-way" aspect-type—with the sense of entering into the states—while for the same states other languages will use the (e) "steady-state" aspect type.

Fourth, verb roots' aspect incorporation can correlate with surrounding factors. For example, it seems generally that a language with a ready inflection indicating 'multiplexity' has few verb roots like English *beat, wag, flap, breathe* with inherent multiplex aspect. Rather, the verb roots by themselves refer to one cycle's worth of the action, and take the inflection to signal multiplexity. One language apparently like this is Hopi (Whorf 1956), and another is American Sign Language (Elissa Newport, personal communication).

2.6 Causation

By one analysis, quite a few distinct types of causation are lexicalized in verbs (see chapter II-6). The number is appreciably greater than the usually recognized two-way distinction between 'noncausative' and 'causative'. Some verbs incorporate only one causation type, while others demonstrate a range of incorporations. A number of such types are listed below, in order of increasing complexity or deviation from the basic (except for the interposed type of (40g)). All but two of these types can be illustrated with the verb *break*. Other verbs are given to illustrate types (40h) and (40i). Most of these types are here named for the kind of element that acts as the verbal subject.

(40) *Different types of causative meaning incorporated in the verb root*
   a. The vase broke.   Autonomous event (not causative)

   b. The vase broke from a ball's rolling into it.   Resulting-event causation

c. A ball's rolling into it broke the vase.	Causing-event causation
d. A ball broke the vase (in rolling into it).	Instrument causation
e. I broke the vase in rolling a ball into it.	Author causation (i.e., with result unintended)
f. I broke the vase by rolling a ball into it.	Agent causation (i.e., with result intended)
g. I broke my arm when I fell (= My arm broke [on me]...).	Undergoer situation (not causative)
h. I walked to the store.	Self-agentive causation
i. I sent him to the store.	Inducive causation (caused agency)

Previous linguistic treatments (e.g., McCawley 1968) have represented their incorporated causative element by the capitalized form "CAUSE." Since more distinctions are recognized here, more representational forms are needed.[30]

(41) a. ... broke ...   = ... broke ...
     b. ... RESULTED-to-break ...   = ... $_R$broke ...
     c. ... EVENTed-to-break ...   = ... $_E$broke ...
     d. ... INSTRUMENTed-to-break ... = ... $_I$broke ...
     e. ... AUTHORed-to-break ...   = ... $_{Au}$broke ...
     f. ... AGENTed-to-break ...   = ... $_A$broke ...
     g. ... UNDERWENT-to-break ...   = ... $_U$broke ...

The autonomous (40a) type presents an event occurring in and of itself, without implying that there is a cause. Such causes as there may be fall outside of attention.[31]

In the (40b) "resulting-event causation" type, on the other hand, this main event has resulted from another event and would not otherwise have occurred. The causing event can be expressed not only by a full clause, as in (40b) and again in (42a) below, but also by a verb-derived nominal, as in (42b), or by what can be termed an "action noun," as in (42c). A standard noun as in (42d), however, will not do.

(42) The window cracked
     a.   from a ball's sailing into it   Nominalized clause
     b.   from the pressure/bump of a branch   Verb-derived nominal
          against it

> c. from the wind/a fire/the rain   Action noun
> d. *from a ball   Standard noun

The clause-like behavior of action nouns can be attributed to their being in fact conflations of full clauses. Thus, the examples in (42c) might be considered to have internal semantic structures equivalent to the clauses in (43).

(43) a. wind   'air's blowing [on the Figure]'
     b. rain   'rainwater's falling [on the Figure]'
     c. fire   'flames acting [on the Figure]'

Such semantic conflation, taking place in the noun, exemplifies lexicalization in a grammatical category other than the verb root and the satellite, the ones addressed in this chapter. (For further examples, involving conflation in subordinating and coordinating conjunctions and in certain adverb classes, see chapter I-6.)

Perhaps most verbs that are lexicalized to express either the autonomous or the resulting-event type of causation can also express the other type. English verbs whose range includes both these causation types but no others are *die, fall, drift, disappear, sleep.* English appears to lexically distinguish these two causation types only in the stative with the verbs *be* and *stay*, as (44) suggests.

(44) a. The pen was on the incline.   Autonomous situation
     b. The pen *was/stayed on the incline   Resulting-event causation
        from a lever pressing against it.

While the (40b) type focuses on the main event as *resulting* from another event, the (40c) "causing-event" type focuses on the latter (now the subject) as *causing* the main event.[32] And the instrumental (40d) type focuses on just that object within the causing event that actually *impinges* on the affected elements of the resulting event.[33] English has very few verbs that incorporate the (c) or (d) types without also incorporating the (e) and (f) types. One example, though, is *erode*, as in *The river's rushing along it/The river/?*The scientists eroded that section of land.* Further, there may be no verbs that are lexicalized only for the (c) or the (d) type without also being able to express the other type.

In both author (40e) and agent (40f) causation, an animate being wills a bodily action that leads (through a variously sized chain of causal events) to the main event referred to.[34] In the author type, the being intends all these events except the final one; in the agent type, the final one, too, is intended. English verbs associated with the author type and only slightly or not at all with the agentive are *spill, drop, knock (down)*, and bimorphemic *mislay*. Strictly agentive verbs are *murder, throw, persecute*.

The Undergoer in the (40g) type is like an Author in that he does not intend the event mentioned. But he also has not intentionally undertaken any actions that culminate in that event. Rather, the event is conceived of as occurring independently of the Undergoer but as affecting his subjective state, usually adversely. Many languages express the Undergoer in an oblique constituent, as does Spanish.

(45) a. Se me quebró el brazo.
     'The arm broke itself [to] me.' = 'I broke my arm.'
    b. Se me perdió la pluma.
     'The pen lost itself [to] me.' = 'I lost my pen.'

English does have this construction (with *on*: My arm broke on me). But it also has verbs that allow the Undergoer as subject, as seen in: I *broke* my arm, I *caught* my sweater on a nail, I *developed* a wart in my ear. And English also has verbs that require the Undergoer as subject, like *lose* and *forget*. We can contrast the agent, author, and undergoer types with the three verbs in *I hid/mislaid/lost my pen somewhere in the kitchen*. These verbs all have a similar core meaning, one involving an object's becoming not findable. But each incorporates a different causation type:

$$(46) \begin{Bmatrix} \text{to AGENT} \\ \text{to AUTHOR} \\ \text{to UNDERGO} \end{Bmatrix} \text{ that NP become not findable}$$

$$(\text{approx.} = \begin{Bmatrix} \text{to } hide \\ \text{to } mislay \\ \text{to } lose \end{Bmatrix} \text{NP})$$

The self-agentive (40h) type is like the agentive except that the animate being's bodily action is itself the final and relevant event, not just an earlier event in a causal sequence. Often, the whole body is moved through space as a Figure. In their usual usage, the English verbs *go, walk, run, jump, trudge, recline, crouch*, and so on incorporate this type. The verb *roll* can incorporate several different causation types, among them the self-agentive, and so permits a contrastive example.

(47) a. The log rolled across the field.   Autonomous event
    b. The boy rolled the log across the field.   Agent causation
    c. The boy rolled across the field on   Self-agentive causation
       purpose.

In the inducive (40i) type, something (whether a thing, an event, or another Agent) induces an Agent to intentionally carry out an act.[35] For most inducive verbs, the agentively performed act that is induced is in fact a self-agentive type of act, in particular, an act of 'going'. For example, the verb in *I lured him out of his hiding place* means 'by luring, to INDUCE to GO'. Atypically, *sic/set ... on*, as in *I sicced/set the dogs on the intruder*, mean 'by issuing directions, to INDUCE to attack', and so refer to a self-agentive act of attacking rather than of going. Some English verbs that incorporate only the inducive type (at least, in one sector of their usage) are *send, drive (off), chase (away), smoke (out), lure, attract, repel, sic ... on*. The verb *set ... upon* has a range that permits a contrastive example.[36]

(48) a. The dogs set upon us.   Self-agentive causation
     b. He set the dogs upon us.   Inducive causation (caused agency)

Our method for distinguishing causation types rests on finding verbs that incorporate only one type or that have ranges differing by only one type (or, at least, ranges that overlap in enough different ways). For example, we can try to use each of the verbs *die, kill, murder* in every one of the causative types listed in (40).

(49) a. He died/*killed/*murdered yesterday (i.e., 'He underwent death').
     b. He died/*killed/*murdered from a car hitting him.
     c. A car's hitting him *died/killed/*murdered him.
     d. A car *died/killed/*murdered him (in hitting him).
     e. She unintentionally *died/killed/*murdered him.
     f. She *died/killed/murdered him in order to be rid of him.
     g. He *died/*killed/*murdered his plants (i.e., 'His plants died on him').
     h. He *died/*killed/*murdered (i.e., 'He killed himself by internal will').
     i. She *died/*killed/*murdered him (i.e., 'She induced him to kill [others]').

From (49) we can derive the summary in table 1.3, where we see just the acceptable usages.

The different acceptability patterns here help determine which of the posited causative types are structurally distinguished by language. Thus, we have here established the following: The agentive (f) is a type by itself —it alone accommodates *murder*. And there are at least distinctions between the (a/b) set of types—*die* but not *kill* ranges over these; the (c/d/e)

Table 1.3
Acceptable types of causative usage: *die*, *kill* and *murder*

	die	kill	murder
a	√		
b	√		
c		√	
d		√	
e		√	
f		√	√
g			
h			
i			

set of types—*kill*'s range minus the agentive (f), which was already isolated; and the (g/h/i) set of types—suiting none of the verbs. We can
now seek cases that exhibit distinctions within these clusters of types. As
already seen, the (a) and (b) types are distinguished, at least in the stative,
by English *be* and *stay*. And we have already seen that the (e) author type
of causation is selectively lexicalized in such verbs as *mislay*, thus sepa-
rating the (e) type from the (c)-(d)-(e) cluster of types. The (g) type can be
separated out by the fact that it alone accommodates the verb *lose* (in its
'not findable' sense), as we could demonstrate with an array of sentences
like that above. Besides, (g) has already been distinguished from (h) and
(i) in that *break* can incorporate it but not the latter two types. These
latter two types themselves are distinguished in that only (h) accommodates *trudge* and only (i) accommodates *sic ... on*. It is, however, quite
possible that no verbs distinguish between the (c) and (d) causation types,
even crosslinguistically, so that these would have to be merged.

We can establish more conclusively that a verb incorporates a particular causation type by using special test frames. For example, here are two
sets of frames that can test for author- and agent-type incorporation in
English verbs:

(50) a. *S author-causative*
         S accidentally
         S in (+ Cause clause)
         S ... too ...
         may S!

b. *S agent-causative*
   S intentionally
   S in order that . . .
   NP intend to S
   NP$_1$ persuade NP$_2$ to S
   S!

When placed in these frames, the verbs *mislay* and *hide* show complementary acceptability patterns. In this way each verb is shown to incorporate the one but not the other of the two causation types tested for.

(51) a. I accidentally mislaid/*hid my pen somewhere in the kitchen.
      I mislaid/*hid the pen in putting it in some obscure place.
      May you mislay/*hide your pen!
     b. I intentionally *mislaid/hid my pen somewhere in the kitchen.
      I *mislaid/hid the pen so that it would never be seen again.
      I intend to *mislay/hide my pen somewhere in the kitchen.
      She persuaded me to *mislay/hide my pen.
      *Mislay/Hide your pen somewhere in the kitchen!

What might be seen as a problem for this demonstration—the fact that *mislay* is bimorphemic, with its prefix explicitly expressing unintentionality—can be avoided by replacing the *mislay/hide* pair in the demonstration with the pair *spill/pour* with largely the same results. This new pair has the additional advantage that it allows illustration of the 'S . . . too . . .' frame, which *mislay/hide* do not easily fit: I spilled/*poured the milk by opening the spout too wide.

Note that the same test frames employed in the preceding demonstration can also be used with verbs like *break*, which can incorporate any of a range of causative types, to select out one particular causative reading. For example, *break* is interpretable only as an author type verb in (52a) and only as an agent type in (52b).

(52) a. I broke the window by pressing against it *too* hard.
     b. I broke the window *in order* to let the gas escape.

Further evidence that verbs have different causative lexicalizations is that they take different grammatical augments to indicate a shift in causation type. Table 1.4 shows a sample from English of such augments and the shifts they mediate. In (53) each shift is illustrated with a verb that is lexicalized solely in the starting-point causative type and that is placed with the relevant grammatical shifters in a clause. Accompanying this, for

Table 1.4
Lexicalized causation types shifted by grammatical elements

	autonomous	agentive	self-agentive	undergoer	inducive
a	V ⟶	make V			
b	V ⟶		make REFL V		
c	{V or V} ⟶			have V	
d		V ⟶	V REFL		
e		{V or V} ⟶			have V

Note: (a)–(e) correspond to (a)–(e) in (53).

comparison, is a causatively equivalent clause with an unaugmented verb (in italics) lexicalized solely in the causation type at the end of the shift. Thus, (53a) shows *disappear*, which is solely autonomous (*The stone disappeared/*The witch disappeared the stone*), rendered agentive by the augment *make*, and thereby equivalent to the unaugmented *obliterate*, which itself is solely agentive (*I obliterated the stone/*The stone obliterated*).[37]

(53) a. The witch made the stone disappear.
   Cf. The witch *obliterated* the stone.

b. He made himself disappear.
   Cf. He *scrammed*.

c. You might have your toy sailboat drift off.
   Cf. You might *lose* your toy sailboat.

   You might have your wallet (get) stolen in the crowd.
   Cf. You might *lose* your wallet in the crowd.

d. She dragged herself to work.
   Cf. She *trudged* to work.

e. I had the maid go to the store.
   Cf. I *sent* the maid to the store.

   I had the dog attack the stranger.
   Cf. I *sicced* the dog on the stranger.

We can observe causative lexicalization patterns at different levels of linguistic organization. At the level of individual lexical items, a verb's particular range of lexicalizations can often be explained on the basis of its core meaning alone. For example, the basic referent of *break* can apply to a person's body part but not to his whole body (*I broke his arm/*I broke him*) and, accordingly, the verb lacks a self-agentive usage (**I broke,* in the sense 'I broke myself/my body'). Similarly, *erode* resists agentive usage because an agent cannot generally marshal the instrumentalities of erosion. On the other hand, it seems purely arbitrary that *poison* has an agentive but not an autonomous usage (*He poisoned her with toadstools/*She poisoned after eating toadstools*) while *drown* has both (*He drowned her/She drowned*), or that *conceal* has an agentive but not a self-agentive usage (*I concealed her/*She concealed in the bushes*) while *hide* has both (*I hid her/She hid in the bushes.*) But motivated or idiosyncratic, all these lexicalization patterns are associated with particular lexical items.

Patterns also operate at the level of a whole semantic category. For example, virtually all English verbs that refer to death without expressing its cause (in contrast, for example, to *drown*) observe the basic causative/noncausative distinction—that is, are lexicalized for either the noncausative (40a/b) types or the (40c–e) causative types but not for both. The pattern applies to both simplex and complex expressions, as (54) shows.

(54) Noncausative   Causative

die	kick off	kill	exterminate
expire	kick the bucket	slay	off
decease	bite the dust	dispatch	waste
perish	give up the ghost	murder	knock/bump off
croak	meet one's end	liquidate	rub out
pass away	breathe one's last	assassinate	do in
		slaughter	do away with

By contrast, almost all English verbs expressing the material disruption of an object—for example, *break, crack, snap, burst, bust, smash, shatter, shred, rip, tear*—apply equally in both noncausative and causative cases (*The balloon burst/I burst the balloon*). There are not many more exceptions than *collapse*, lacking an agentive usage (**I collapsed the shed*), and *demolish*, lacking the autonomous usage (**The shed demolished*).

Different languages often exhibit different lexicalization patterns for a particular semantic category. For example, verbs referring to states are mostly lexicalized in the autonomous type in Japanese but are mostly agentive in Spanish. Japanese adds an inflection to its verbs to express the corresponding agentive, while Spanish adds its reflexive clitics (here serving not in a "reflexive" but in a "de-agentivizing" function) to express the autonomous. We can illustrate these complementary patterns with the verbs for 'open'.

(55) *Japanese*
    a. Doa ga   aita
       door SUBJ open (PAST)
       "The door opened."
    b. Kare wa doa o   aketa
       he   TOP door OBJ open (CAUS PAST)
       "He opened the door."
Spanish
    c. Abrió   la puerta
       he-opened the door
       "He opened the door."
    d. La puerta se   abrió
       the door REFL opened
       "The door opened."

Finally, at the broadest scope, some lexicalization patterns affect the whole lexicon of a language. One example is that in Japanese the causing-event (40c) and instrument (40d) causation types are barely represented at all. Thus, verbs otherwise corresponding to our *kill* and *break* cannot be used (without extreme awkwardness) with the causing event or Instrument as subject. To express these constituents, one must use the (40b) resulting-event causation type instead.

2.7   Interaction of Aspect and Causation

Different verb roots incorporate different combinations of aspectual and causative types. One might at first expect a language to have a roughly equal distribution of the combinations over its lexicon and to have grammatical elements that bring about a semantic shift from each such combination to any other. But we find two limiting factors. First, not all aspect-causative combinations are relevant to every semantic domain. For example, in many languages the semantic domain of 'states' seems to involve only (or mainly) the three aspect-causative types listed in (56) (cf. Chafe 1970).

(56) a. Being in a state   Stative
     b. Entering into a state   Inchoative
     c. Putting into a state   Agentive

Second, even for such a smaller set, the relevant verbs in a language generally are not evenly lexicalized over the different types. For example, for the expression of 'states', there are languages in which the verb roots are preponderantly lexicalized in only the (a) or only the (b) or only the (c) type. In other languages, such verb roots show a small range of lexicalizations, either over the (a/b) types or over the (b/c) types. There are also languages in which the same verb root is used equivalently for all three aspect-causative types. Sometimes a language's roots exhibit different patterns for different categories within the 'states' domain. Wherever the verb roots are restricted in their aspect-causative ranges, there are generally grammatical devices for getting to the remaining types. But because of all these limitations, the number of devices required can be quite small.

We first demonstrate these lexicalization patterns for one category of states, that of 'postures': postures or orientations that are assumed by the human body or by objects treated as comparable to the body.[38] We can use English here to illustrate the pattern of lexicalization largely limited to the 'being-in-a-state' type. This is seen in verbs like *lie, sit, stand, lean, kneel, squat, crouch, bend, bow*, etc.[39] These verbs must generally take on additional elements for the other aspect-causative types to be conveyed. For example, *lie* by itself refers to being in the lying posture. The verb must be augmented by a satellite—yielding the form *lie down*—to signify getting into the posture. And it must be further augmented by an agentive derivation—*lay down*—to refer to putting into the lying posture,[40] as (57) illustrates.

(57) a. She lay there all during the program.
　　 b. She lay down there when the program began.
　　 c. He laid her down there when the program began.

Unlike English, Japanese is a language where posture verbs are generally lexicalized in the 'getting into a state' type, with the other types derived therefrom. For example, the basic meaning of *tatu* is 'to stand up' (comparable to the English verb *arise*). When this verb is grammatically augmented by the *-te iru* form, whose meaning can be rendered as 'to be (in the state of) having [Ved]', the resultant meaning is 'to be in a standing posture'. And when the verb is augmented by the agentive or by the inducive suffix, yielding the forms *tateru* and *tataseru*, the resultant meanings are 'to put into a standing posture' a thing or a person, respectively. To illustrate:

(58) a. Boku wa　tatta
　　　　 I　　 TOP arose
　　　　 "I stood up."

    b. Boku wa   tatte   ita
       I   TOP having-arisen was
       "I was standing."
    c. Hon o   tateta
       book OBJ AGENTED-to-arise
       "I stood the book up."
    d. Kodomo o   tataseta
       child   OBJ INDUCED-to-arise
       "I stood the child up."

Exemplifying the third pattern, Spanish lexicalizes posture notions in the agentive 'putting-into-a-state' type, the other types being derived therefrom. For example, the verb *acostar* is inherently transitive, with the meaning 'to lay (someone) down'. To it must be added the reflexive morpheme, giving *acostarse*, to get the meaning 'to lie down'.[41] And for the steady-state meaning 'to lie', the verb must be suffixed with the past participle ending and put in construction with the verb 'to be': *estar acostado*.[42]

(59) a. Acosté   el niño
       I-laid-down the child
       "I laid the child down."
    b. Me   acosté
       myself I-laid-down
       "I lay down."
    c. Estaba acostado
       I-was   laid-down
       "I lay (there)."

These typological findings can be represented together in a single schematic matrix, as in table 1.5.

Table 1.5
Lexicalization patterns for verbs of posture (V = verb root, SAT = satellite, PP = past participle inflection)

	be in a posture	get into a posture	put into a posture
English	V ⟶	V + SAT ⟶	V + CAUS + SAT
Japanese	'be' + V + PP ⟵	V ⟶	V + CAUS
Spanish	'be' + V + PP ⟵	V + REFL ⟵	V

For each class of language, table 1.5 shows the aspect-causative type of the verb in which postural notions are generally lexicalized, and the patterns by which the other types are derived therefrom.

Other languages have other means for deriving the nonbasic aspect-causative types from the favored one. For example, German is like English in having the stative type as basic for posture notions, as with verbs like *liegen* 'lie' and *sitzen* 'sit'. But it does not derive the inchoative 'getting-into-a-state' type directly from this. Rather, it first derives the agentive 'putting-into-a-state' type, with verbal forms like *legen* and *setzen*. And from this, in the manner of Spanish, it uses the reflexive to get back to the inchoative, with forms like *sich legen* and *sich setzen*. Schematically:

(60) *German*

$$\text{V} \longrightarrow \text{V} + \text{CAUS}$$
$$\text{V} + \text{CAUS} + \text{REFL} \longleftarrow\rfloor$$

In the preceding lexicalization patterns, the verb root incorporated only one aspect-causative type. There are further patterns in which the same verb form serves equally for two types, while grammatical augmentation is required for the third. In one pattern of this sort, the 'being-in-a-state' and the 'getting into-a-state' types are represented by the same lexical form, but an augmented form is used for the 'putting-into-a-state' type. The verb root in a pattern like this may be thought to capture a factor common to the two types it represents, namely, the involvement of only a single participant (note that the unrepresented 'putting-into-a-state' type, requiring an agent, involves two participants). By one analysis, modern literary Arabic exemplifies this pattern for posture notions (but see below for an alternative interpretation), as in the following root referring to 'sleeping' or 'lying'.

(61) a. Nām-a   t-ṭifl-u   ʕalā   s-sarīr
$\begin{Bmatrix}\text{was-lying}\\\text{lay-down}\end{Bmatrix}$-he   the-child-NOM $\begin{Bmatrix}\text{on}\\\text{onto}\end{Bmatrix}$ the-bed

"The child was lying on the bed." / "The child lay down onto the bed."

b. Anam-tu   t-ṭifl-a   ʕalā   s-sarīr
laid-down-I the-child-ACC on(to) the-bed

"I laid the child down onto the bed."

In another pattern, the same verb root is used to express both the inchoative 'entering-into-a-state' and the agentive 'putting-into-a-state' types, while a different formulation is required for the stative 'being-in-a-state' type. The common factor captured by the verb with two usages in this pattern would seem to be 'change-of-state'. In familiar languages, there are no apparent instances of this as the predominant pattern for verbs expressing postures. But if we switch here to another category of states, that of 'conditions' (further treated below), the pattern can be exemplified by English. Here, for instance, the verb *freeze* lexicalizes the condition of 'frozenness' together with either the agentive or the inchoative type. For the stative type, however, the grammatical form *be* + 'past-participle-inflection' must be added, yielding *be frozen*, as in (62).

(62) a. The water was frozen.
    b. The water froze.
    c. I froze the water.

The remaining possible two-way pattern—where the verb root would be used for both the stative and the agentive types, but not the inchoative—does not appear to have any realization. One reason for such a gap may be that these two types do not share a factor that is common to them both while absent from the inchoative.

Consideration of these two-way cases next brings us to the pattern where the same verb root is used, without any grammatical augment, for all three aspect-causative types. In fact, this pattern seems to be the one English posture verbs are moving toward in a process of change going on now. Thus, as noted earlier, it is somewhat forced for modern English to interpret posture verbs as pure statives, with augmentation required for the other aspect-causative types. For one thing, marking of an agentive-nonagentive distinction has in many dialects all but disappeared colloquially, with forms like *lay* or *sit* serving for both meanings. For another, the satellite can often appear in stative usages as well. Thus, the combination of verb + satellite can to a large degree be used equally for all three aspect-causative types, as (63) illustrates.

(63) a. He lay down/stood up all during the show.
    b. He lay down/stood up when the show began.
    c. She laid him down/stood him up on the bed.

Nevertheless, a distinction in the use of forms does still hold to this extent: the satellite seems somewhat awkward in some stative expressions, for example in *He lay (?down) there for hours.* And the verb without satellite may be somewhat awkward in colloquial speech for the agentive usage: *?She laid/stood the child on the bed.*

This same lexicalization pattern occurs without qualification in English for several individual verbs of other 'state' categories. One clear example is *hide*, a 'position' verb, as (64) shows.[43]

(64) a. He hid in the attic for an hour.   Being in a position

    b. He hid in the attic when the sheriff   Getting into a position
       arrived.

    c. I hid him in the attic when the sheriff   Putting into a position
       arrived.

We can point to one further lexicalization pattern. Here, the verb root is always accompanied by morphemes with their own aspect-causative meanings, making it difficult to determine whether the verb root itself incorporates any aspect-causative type of its own. Perhaps it does not, and the conclusion to be drawn is that such a verb refers solely to a particular state, abstracted away from all notions of aspect and causation, and that it requires augmentation for *every* aspect-causative indication. If so, then the morphemes that express this augmentation can themselves exhibit some of the same patterns of incorporation as seen earlier for verb roots. Thus, in some cases, there would be distinct morphemes for each of the aspect-causative types. In other cases, a single set of forms would serve for some pair of aspect-causative types, with another set for the third. This latter pattern can be exemplified by Atsugewi. Here, a verb root referring to posture is always surrounded by aspect-causation indicating affixes. And among these, generally, one set serves for both the 'getting-into-a-state' and the 'putting-into-a-state' meanings, while a different set is required for 'being-in-a-state'. This is illustrated in (65).

(65) a. *Verb root*   -it^u-   'for a linear object to be
                                              in//move into/out of/while
                                            in a lying posture'

       Directional suffix   -miċ   'down onto the ground'
       Inflectional affix set   s- w- '- -^{a} 'I–subject (3rd person–
                                            object), factual mood'

    /s-'-w-it^u-miċ-^{a}/ ⇒ [sẇit^{h}miċ]

    "I lay down onto the ground." / "I laid it down onto the ground."

    b. *Verb root*   -it^u-   as for (a) above
       Locative suffix   -ak·   'on the ground'
       Inflectional affix set   s- '- w- -^{a} 'I–subject (3rd person–
                                                   object), factual mood'

/s-'-w-it^u-ak·-^{a}/ $\Rightarrow$ [sẃit·ák·a]

"I was lying on the ground."

Arabic forms like those cited earlier have an alternative analysis that places them at this point of the exposition. The verb root can be taken to be a consonantal form that—like the Atsugewi root—names the state alone and always takes different interposed vowel sequences as grammatical augmentations. These grammatical elements, then, follow a pattern complementary to that of Atsugewi: one vowel sequence handles both the stative and the inchoative, while another handles the agentive.

2.7.1 Consistency of Patterns within a Language Lexicalization patterns for aspect-causative types exhibit different degrees of pervasiveness in a language, first in the degree to which a pattern predominates *within* a semantic category. For example, posture notions in English are largely consistent in their stative lexicalization, with perhaps only inchoative *arise* falling outside this pattern. By contrast, posture notions in Latin show up in verbs of a variety of lexicalization types. Each type of verb employs different means to yield other aspect-causative meanings (e.g., stative *sedere* 'to sit' takes a prefixal satellite to yield the inchoative *considere* 'to sit down', while agentive *inclinare* 'to lean (something) against' takes the reflexive to yield the inchoative *se inclinare* 'to lean (oneself) against'); see (66).

(66) | Stative | | Inchoative | | Agentive | |
|---|---|---|---|---|---|
| stare | 'stand' | surgere | 'stand up' | ponere | 'lay, set' |
| sedere | 'sit' | locare | 'set, lay' | | |
| iacere | 'lie' | inflectere | 'bow, bend' | | |
| cubare | 'lie' | inclinare | 'lean' | | |

Second, a pattern in a language that predominates within one category of a semantic domain may or may not do so *across* the categories. As already seen, English is inconsistent in this way because its posture verbs are generally lexicalized in the stative, while its condition verbs have the two aspect-causative meanings other than stative.

Table 1.6
Lexicalization patterns for Latin verbs of condition (V = verb root, PP = past participle inflection)

	be in a condition	enter into a condition	put into a condition
Independent	V	V + INCHOATIVE	V + CAUS
Dependent	'be' + V + PP	V + MEDIOPASSIVE	V
Examples			
Independent	patere	patescere	patefacere
	'to be open'	'to open (intr.)'	'to open (tr.)'
Dependent	fractus esse	frangi	frangere
	'to be broken'	'to break (intr.)'	'to break (tr.)'

Latin also exhibits different patterns across categories. To show this, we first point out that what has so far been considered the single category of "conditions" is better understood as comprising two separate categories. One of these is "independent conditions": conditions that objects are conceived of as occurring in naturally. The other category is that of "dependent conditions": conditions conceived of as not original for objects, ones that objects must be brought into by external forces. In many languages, independent conditions are frequently lexicalized in adjectives. In Latin they are, too, but they also frequently appear in verbs. Here they are generally lexicalized in the 'being-in-a-state' type, with the other types derived therefrom. Dependent conditions, on the other hand, are generally lexicalized in verbs in the agentive, and these follow the Spanish pattern for derivation (except that instead of the reflexive, the mediopassive inflections are used). A schematic representation is given in table 1.6.

The other languages we have looked at in this section show greater consistency across categories. They have the same lexicalization patterns for their verbs of condition as they do for their verbs of posture. We illustrate this extension of the patterns first for Japanese (67a) and Spanish (67b). Compare (58) and (59) with the following:

(67) a. *Japanese*

    i. Mizu   ga   kootte ita
       water SUBJ frozen be (PAST)
       "The water was frozen."

    ii. Mizu   ga   kootta
       water SUBJ freeze (PAST)
       "The water froze."

        iii. Mizu o   koorasita
            water OBJ freeze (CAUSE PAST)
            "I froze the water."

    b. *Spanish*
        i. El agua estaba helada
            the water was   frozen
            "The water was frozen."
        ii. El agua se   heló
            the water REFL froze
            "The water froze."
        iii. Helé   el agua
            I-froze the water
            "I froze the water."

Comparably, Arabic verbs referring to conditions are lexicalized like posture verbs, with the stative and the inchoative using the same form. Compare (61) with (68).

(68) a. ʕAmiy-a   ṭ-ṭifl-u
       { was-blind   } -he the-boy-NOM
       { became-blind }
       "The boy was/became blind."
   b. Aʕmay-tu   ṭ-ṭifl-a
       made-blind-I the-boy-ACC
       "I blinded the boy."

2.7.2 Other Aspect-Causative Types There are aspect-causative types other than the three listed in (56) that might seem quite relevant to notions of states. These would involve the transition from being in a state to not being in that state. Such a transition could apply to both the non-agentive and the agentive, as seen in (69).

(69) b′. exiting from a state
     c′. removing from a state

However, such types of 'state departure' seem to be under a universal constraint excluding them from at least one type of lexicalization: a verb root can refer to both state location and state entry, but it cannot refer to either of these and also to state departure. Thus, the Arabic verb form for 'be/become blind' cannot also mean 'cease being blind'. Likewise, the English *hide*, as in *He hid*, can refer to 'being in hiding' or 'going into hiding', but not also to 'coming out of hiding'. Further, by one interpretation, even for a verb root that is lexicalized not for a range of senses but only for a single change-of-state sense, that sense is always state entry, not state departure. Thus, by this interpretation, the basic sense of English *die* is not 'leave death' or 'become not alive', but rather 'enter death' or 'become dead'—as is indeed suggested by the fact that this verb is etymologically related not to adjectival or nominal *live/life* but to *dead/death*.

In addition, state departure—though not excluded from them—seems quite underrepresented among grammatical devices that interact with verb roots. For example, English *hide* cannot be used with departure-indicating satellites or prepositions, either in the postposed location

(70) a. *He hid out of the attic. = He came out of the attic, where he had been hiding.
   b. *I hid him out of the attic. = I got him out of the attic, where he had been hiding.

or prefixally:[44]

(71) a. *He unhid from the attic.
   b. *I unhid him from the attic.

Comparably, adjectives of condition have ready adjunct verbs or verb-forming affixes to express state location and state entry but, in English and many other languages, not state departure.[45]

(72) be-in-a-state:
   be sick
   enter-into-a-state: exit-from-a-state:
   get sick   **lose* sick*
   sick*en*   **de*sick*
   put-into-a-state: remove-from-a-state:
   make (someone) sick   **break* (someone) sick*
   sick*en* (someone)   **de*sick (someone)*

American Sign Language is similarly constrained. Thus, its signs for conditions (like 'sick') can generally be executed with a number of distinct movement patterns indicating different aspects ('be sick', 'be sick for a long time', 'stay sick', 'become sick', 'become thoroughly sick', 'repeatedly become sick', 'be prone to becoming sick', and so on), but state departure is not among these (*'cease being sick'). The idea must be expressed with a combination of two signs ('be sick' + 'finish').

To be sure, English does have *un-* and *de-/dis-* for use with some position and condition verbs (*unload, decentralize*). But their use is limited, and it is also largely secondary in that the forms indicate *reversal* of state entry rather than state departure directly. Thus, *central* must first add *-ize* indicating state entry before it can add *de-*; there is no **decentral*.

The distinct treatment that languages accord state departure as against state location and state entry often shows up as well in their adpositional systems expressing Path. For example, the same morpheme expresses 'at' and 'to' but a different one expresses 'from' in French *à/à/de*, Japanese *ni/ni/kara* (though *e* is also used for the 'to' meaning alone), and Atsugewi *-i?/-i?/-uk·a*. English exhibits this pattern in some of its prepositional and relative-interrogative forms, as the sentences in (73) illustrate.

(73) a. She was *behind* the barn.   *Where* was she?
    b. She went *behind* the barn.   *Where* did she go?
    c. She came *from behind* the barn.   *Where* did she come *from*?

It is not clear why there should be this avoidance of expressing state departure. But in any case, among grammatical elements it is only a tendency, not an absolute. In Atsugewi, verb roots referring to postures and positions (and apparently also conditions) regularly take grammatical elements that indicate state departure, at least in the agentive. We exemplify this with the verb root used previously in (65).

(74) *Verb root*   -it^u-   'for a linear object to be in//
    move into/out of/while in-a
    lying posture'

    Directional suffix   -ič   'up off something'
    Inflectional affix set   s- w- '- -^{a} 'I–subject (3rd person–object),
    factual mood'

/s-'-w-it^u-ič-^{a}/ ⇒ [sẃit·úč]

"I picked it up off the ground, where it had been lying."

2.8 Personation

As a contrast with the earlier section on causation, we introduce here a semantic category that in most previous treatments has been incorrectly merged with that of causativity. For actions of certain types, approximately the same actional content is manifested whether one or two participants are involved. For example, whether John shaves himself or shaves me, the action still involves one hand moving one razor over one face. The only relevant difference here is whether the hand and the face belong to the same body. The distinction here is not one of different causation types. Among causation types, an increase in participants brings along with it an increment in actional content, as in going from the autonomous *The snow melted* to the agentive *John melted the snow*, which indicates an additional action complex on the part of John. Involved here, rather, is a new parameter, one that we will call **personation**, pertaining to the role structure ascribed to an action. An action complex of certain kinds can be taken to manifest either locally, in the body and movements of a single actor (the *monadic* personation type), or distributively, with an actor's body acting on that of a further participant (the *dyadic* personation type).

A verb root can be lexicalized for just one personation type (either one), taking grammatical augmentation to express the opposite type, or it can range over both types. Languages exhibit different patterns, with a bias toward one or another type of lexicalization. Consider, for example, the category of actions involving the use of hands or handled materials on a body. French, for one language, apparently must lexicalize such actions in the dyadic personation type, as actions performed on a *different* person's body. For the case of action on an actor's *own* body, grammatical derivation must be employed—here, the reflexive.

(75) a. Je raserai   Jean
       I will-shave, John
       "I will shave John."
    b. Je me   raserai
       I myself will-shave
       "I will shave."

English, too, has many verbs with this personation type; (76) provides examples.

(76) a. I cut/bandaged/tickled John.
    b. I cut/bandaged/tickled $\left\{ \begin{array}{l} \text{myself} \\ \text{*}\text{–}\phi \end{array} \right\}$.

But there is a sizable group of English verbs whose simplest form can—in addition to being used to refer to action on another person's body—also express the Agent acting on his own body. This kind of verb thus has a range of incorporations that includes not only the dyadic personation type, but the monadic type as well, as (77) shows.

(77) a. I shaved.
    b. I washed.
    c. I soaped up.
    d. I bathed.
    e. I showered.
    f. I scratched (too hard)/Don't scratch!
    g. I buttoned up.
    h. I dressed.
    i. I undressed.
    j. I changed.

As discussed in note 4, there is no reason to assume that these verbs incorporate any *reflexive* meaning in conjunction with some basically other-directed sense. It is quite possible to regard these verbs simply as expressing actions that manifest directly in the actor's own person. In having such a group of forms, English distinguishes itself from French, which must use the reflexive with all the corresponding verb forms (except, as in (78e) and (78j), where the concept is expressed with a verb + noun construction).

(78) a. se raser
    b. se laver
    c. se savonner
    d. se baigner
    e. ... (prendre une douche)
    f. se gratter
    g. se boutonner
    h. s'habiller
    i. se déshabiller
    j. ... (changer de vêtements)

As already noted, English verbs of the type in (77) generally can also express the dyadic personation type (e.g., *I shaved him*), and so cover the range of lexicalization types. But Atsugewi has a group of verbs like those in (77) that refer only to the monadic type. To express the dyadic type, these verbs must add an inflectional element—usually the benefactive suffix *-iray*. With this set of forms, Atsugewi behaves in a way quite complementary to that of French. One example:

(79) a. *Cause prefix +*
   Verb root   cu-sṗaí-   'comb the hair'
   Inflectional affix set   s- '- w- -ᵃ   'I–subject'

   /s-'-w-cu-sṗaí-ᵃ/ ⇒ [sċuspáíᵃ]

   "I combed my hair."

   b. *Cause prefix +*
   Verb root   cu-sṗaí-   'comb the hair'
   Benefactive suffix   -iray   'for another'
   Inflectional affix set   m- w- -isahk   'I–subject, thee–object,
                                                    factual mood'

   /m-w-cu-sṗaí-iray-isahk/ ⇒ [mcusṗaíəré·sahki]

   "I combed your hair."

American Sign Language appears to lexicalize exclusively in the monadic personation type for referring to a certain class of actions, those that in any way involve the torso. Signs for such actions intrinsically refer to them as a person would perform them on herself. These signs must be augmented by additional gestures (such as a shift in body direction) in order to indicate that the actions are performed on someone else. For example, a signer can assert that she had put on earrings by (among other gestures) bringing her two hands toward her ears. However, to assert that she had put the earrings on her mother (who has been "set up" at a certain point of nearby space), she cannot simply move her hands outward toward where her mother's ears would be. Rather, she only begins by moving her hands outward, but then shifts her body direction slightly and adopts a distinct facial expression—indicating that her torso is now representing that of her mother—and curves her hands back around, moving them again to her own ears. That is, an additional gestural complex is necessary to indicate that the referent action is to be understood as other-directed.

Note that actions lacking physical contact can also be lexicalized with different personations. For example, the English verb *get* (in the sense of 'go and bring back') is basically monadic, as seen in (80a), but can add a benefactive expression for the dyadic, as in (80b). Complementarily, *serve* is basically dyadic, as in (80d), but can add a reflexive for the monadic type, as in (80c). The reflexive here signals only this change in personation type, for it lacks the literal interpretation it has in *I shaved John/I shaved myself*.

(80) *Monadic*   *Dyadic*
   a. I got some dessert from the → b. I got some dessert from
       kitchen.   the kitchen for Sue.
   c. I served myself some dessert ← d. I served (Sue) some
       from the kitchen.   dessert from the kitchen.

The semantic category of personation can be conceptualized schematically. Consider an ideational complex to which the category of personation might be applied. In a sentence that refers to such a complex, the predicate (typically a verb) by itself refers literally to a specific portion of the complex, a portion here called an "action." And the subject nominal of the sentence generally refers to an actor within the complex (typically an Agent) that is responsible for the action. As discussed in chapters I-4 and I-8, an unbroken causal linkage is generally conceptualized as progressing—spatially, in the typical case of a physical referent—from the actor to the action that she is responsible for. Accordingly, one can conceptualize an "envelope" enclosing the actor and the action, as well as all causal activity connecting the two.

The schematic conceptualization proposed here is that if the action within the envelope affects some entity outside the envelope, then the ideational complex is understood as dyadic and the sentence that represents it will prototypically be syntactically transitive. But if the envelope encloses all of the ideational complex—apart from any incidental elements that are understood as unaffected by the action within the envelope—then the ideational complex is understood as monadic and the sentence that represents it will prototypically be syntactically intransitive. Accordingly, the schematic envelope proposed here can be termed the **personation envelope** or the **transitivity envelope**.[46]

The accompanying figure represents the two schematic situations just outlined. In (Aa), representing the sentence *The girl is beating the drum*, the envelope encloses 'the girl' as the actor and 'beating' as the action but excludes 'the drum'. This is because the verb *beat* by itself merely implies the presence of a further affected object, but literally refers only to the action that could affect such an object. And this verb is appropriately transitive, requiring the presence of a direct object nominal referring to the affected object. However, in (Ab), representing the sentence *The girl is drumming*, the envelope encloses not only 'the girl' as actor and 'beating' as an activity, but also 'a drum' as an object. This is because the action that the verb *drum* literally refers to includes within its unified compass

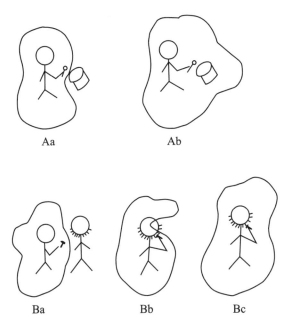

Aa   Ab

Ba   Bb   Bc

components both of a dynamic activity and of engaged physical material. And the verb is appropriately intransitive.

The same schematization can be carried over to the earlier issues involving the reflexive, as represented in part B of the figure. Here, (Ba), representing the sentence *I shaved him*, represents a particular ideational complex as involving basic dyadicity and transitive syntax. The schematic envelope encloses the actor 'I' and the action of 'shaving'—that is, of removing beard by running a razor over a face. But it excludes an affected object 'him', whose face it is that receives the razor action. In (Bb), representing the sentence *I shaved myself*, the envelope again encloses both the actor 'I' and the action of 'shaving', but now it excludes the actor's 'face', treating it as an external affected object. In effect, therefore, this case differs from the preceding one only in that the reflexive here indicates that the face acted on by the razor belongs to the same actor whose arm wields the razor, rather than to a different individual. A situation like this might be called **reflexively dyadic** in personation type. While the verb *shave* here is still transitive, one might want to refer to its syntax distinctively as being **reflexively transitive**. But in (Bc), representing the sentence *I shaved*, the envelope now encloses the whole of the complex in which 'I', as actor, perform the activity of 'shaving' on the 'face' of the same actor,

'I'. This ideational complex is thus here being conceptualized as monadic. The verb *shave* here can be understood as being basically intransitive and as having a literal semantic reference to an action that encompasses both a razor-wielding hand and a beard-bearing face that belong to the same individual.

2.9 Valence

We saw in the sections on causation and personation that patterns in the number and types of arguments adjoining a verb can form the basis for typologies. We now see that the same is true for patterns in the salience accorded such arguments.

2.9.1 General Considerations

In conceptualizing an event that involves several different entities in distinct roles, one is able to direct greater attention to some one of these entities than to the others or, perhaps, to adopt its actual perspective point. A secondary degree of attention or perspective taking, further, can be accorded to some second entity. Such cognitive forms of focusing in are indicated linguistically by a variety of devices. One device is to make the focused element the grammatical sub- ject—or, for assigning secondary focus to an additional element, to make that the direct object. (Within the scope of our description, it will suffice to adopt simple notions of the grammatical relations "subject" and "direct object," and to associate these with the case markings "nominative" and "accusative" in the languages that have these.) Now, a lexical verb that refers to a multiroled event can have built-in constraints on its freedom to assign focus. It can be limited to taking only a particular one of the ele- ment types as subject (or direct object), and so lexicalizes focus on that element type. In other instances a single verb can accommodate different element types in the focus position, and so has a range of lexicalizations. Such focusing properties are here called the **valence** of a verb. Tradition- ally, the term valence has been used to refer (either solely or additionally) to the *number* of distinct element types occurring in association with a verb. In this chapter, the issue of element number arises only in the treatment of causation and personation. Valence here is used just for the particular case assignment(s) that a verb exhibits, given a fixed number of certain types of elements in association with it.

The notion of incorporated valence can be effectively demonstrated where there are two verbs whose subject limitations together equal the range of subject possibilities of a third verb. This is the case with *emanate* and *emit* on the one hand and *radiate* on the other. All three of these verbs refer to roughly the same event, an event having both a Figure element and a Ground element. But *emanate* requires the Figure as subject, while *emit* requires the Ground as subject—as contrasted with *radiate*, which accommodates either. Thus, *emanate* incorporates focus on the Figure (the radiation) and *emit* does this for the Ground (the radiator), while *radiate* can incorporate either focus.

(81) *Valence properties for* emanate, emit, *and* radiate

Figure as subject	*Ground as subject*
Light emanates from the sun.	*The sun emanates light.
*Light emits from the sun.	The sun emits light.
Light radiates from the sun.	The sun radiates light.

We can demonstrate a similar relationship with an agentive example. *Steal, rob,* and *rip off* all refer to the same event and take nominals for the Agent, Figure, and Ground roles.[47] All give the Agent primary focus as subject. But for secondary focus as direct object, *steal* selects the Figure (the possessions) while *rob* selects the Ground (the possessor). *Rip off* accommodates either.

(82) *Valence properties for* steal, rob, *and* rip off

Figure as direct object	*Ground as direct object*
I stole his money from him.	*I stole him of his money.
*I robbed his money from him.	I robbed him of his money.
I ripped his money off from him.	I ripped him off (?of his money).

Some verbs—*suffuse* and *drain* are examples—can accommodate their nominals in either the basic Figure-above-Ground precedence or the inverted Ground-above-Figure precedence in both the nonagentive and the agentive. Under inversion, the Figure acquires one of two "demotion particles." It acquires *of* when there is an underlying 'from'-type Path, as with *drain*, and it acquires *with* for other Path types, as with *suffuse* (some languages use different cases for this). Thus, the full array of these two verbs' forms in effect constitutes a paradigm against which other verbs, more limited in one respect or another, can be compared. See (83).

(83) a. *Valence patterns for a non-'from'-type Path (F = Figure, G = Ground, A = Agent)*

	Nonagentive	*Agentive*
Basic	Perfume (F) suffused	I (A) suffused perfume
precedence	through the room (G).	(F) through the room (G).
Inverted	The room (G) suffused	I (A) suffused the room
precedence	with perfume (F).	(G) with perfume (F).

b. *Valence patterns for a 'from'-type Path*

	Nonagentive	*Agentive*
Basic	The gasoline (F) drained	I (A) drained the gasoline
precedence	from the fuel tank (G).	(F) from the fuel tank (G).
Inverted	The fuel tank (G)	I (A) drained the fuel tank
precedence	drained of gasoline (F).	(G) of gasoline (F).

(The word *slowly* can be inserted in the preceding sentences for smoother reading.)

Actually, this paradigm is abridged from a still larger one (see Talmy 1972: 301–375) that distinguishes three Figure-Ground precedence relations: the basic format with Figure above Ground in the case hierarchy, that with Figure demotion alone, and that with Figure demoted and Ground promoted. Perhaps no single verb exhibits all the forms, but a pair of verbs can serve to illustrate (see Fillmore 1977, Hook 1983).

(84)

	Nonagentive	*Agentive*
Basic	The bees swarmed in the	I pounded my shoe on
precedence	garden.	the table.
With Figure	It swarmed with bees in	I pounded with my shoe
demoted	the garden.	on the table.
With Ground	The garden swarmed	I pounded the table with
promoted	with bees.	my shoe.

Note that the *with* appearing here as a demotion particle and still marking the Figure becomes the *with* that marks the Instrument when a sentence of the present sort is embedded in a causative matrix (see note 31). Thus, the sentence in (85a) can be embedded as in (85b) to yield (85c).

(85) a. I kicked the ball (G) with my left foot (F).
[<I kicked my left foot (F) into the ball (G)]
   b. I MOVED the ball (F_2) across the field (G_2) by kicking it (G_1) with my left foot (F_1).
   c. I kicked the ball (F) across the field (G) with my left foot $(F_2 \Rightarrow I)$.

In the same way as with aspect and causation, a language can have grammatical devices for use with a verb of one valence type in order to express a different type. German has this arrangement for cases of the preceding sort. Its prefix *be-* can indicate a shift in secondary focus from the Figure onto the Ground, as (86) suggests.

(86) a. Ich raubte ihm   seine   Tasche
        I   stole   him(DAT) his(ACC) wallet
        "I stole his wallet from him."   Figure as direct object
     b. Ich *beraubte*   ihn   seiner   Tasche
        I   SHIFT-stole him(ACC) his(GEN) wallet
        "I robbed him of his wallet."   Ground as direct object[48]

Where a language, as here, has a grammatical device for getting to a particular valence type, it might tend to have relatively few verb roots lexicalized in that type. In fact German appears to have fewer verb roots like our *rob* and *pelt*, roots that intrinsically take the Ground as direct object, using instead its complexes of Figure-taking root plus valence shifter, like *be-raub(en)* and *be-werf(en)*. The two languages contrast in a similar way in what can be called verbs of giving, this time as to how they indicate focus on (and, hence, the point of view of) the giver or the receiver. Both languages do have cases where the distinction is indicated by distinct verb roots of complementary valence type, as (87) illustrates.

(87) give   teach   get (in the sense of 'receive')   learn
     geben   lehren   kriegen   lernen

But in other cases, English has two verb roots where German has only one, one lexicalized with focus on the receiver. A prefix *ver-* reverses the perspective to the giver's point of view, see (88).

(88) sell   bequeath   lend
     *ver*kaufen   *ver*erben   *ver*leihen   *ver*borgen

     buy   inherit   borrow
     kaufen   erben   leihen   borgen

This shift in perspective is illustrated in (89).

(89) a. Ich kaufte das Haus von ihm
        I   bought the house from him
        "I bought the house from him."
     b. Er *ver*kaufte   mir   das Haus
        he bought(REVERSE) me(DAT) the house
        "He sold me the house."

2.9.2 Valence in Verbs of Affect   Consider verbs of affect with respect to valence. These verbs generally require either the Stimulus or the Experiencer of an affective event as the subject.[49] Accordingly, they incorporate focus on either the qualities of the Stimulus or the state of the Experiencer. Compare this lexicalization difference in *frighten* and *fear* (illustrated in (90)), which refer to roughly the same affective situation.[50]

(90) a. That frightens me.   Stimulus as subject
     b. I fear that.   Experiencer as subject

For verbs lexicalized in either valence type, there are grammatical, or grammatical-derivational, means for getting to the opposite type. Thus, a verb with a Stimulus subject can generally be placed in the construction "BE V-en P" (not a passive: the preposition P can be other words than *by*) to bring the Experiencer into subject position. And a verb with an Experiencer subject can often figure in the construction "BE V-Adj to," which places the Stimulus as subject. See table 1.7.

While possibly all languages have some verbs of each valence type, they differ as to which type predominates. In this respect, English seems to favor lexicalizing the Stimulus as subject.[51] While some of its most colloquial verbs (*like, want*) have the Experiencer as subject, the bulk of its vocabulary items for affect focus on the Stimulus, as we see in table 1.8.[52]

By contrast with English, Atsugewi roots appear to have Experiencer subjects almost exclusively. Virtually every affect-expressing verb (as well as adjectives in construction with 'be') elicited in fieldwork was lexicalized with an Experiencer subject. To express a Stimulus subject, these forms take the suffix *-ahẇ*. For one example see table 1.9.[53]

Table 1.7
Derivational patterns for affect verbs focused on the Stimulus or the Experiencer

Stimulus as subject	⇒	*Experiencer as subject*
It frightens me		I am frightened of it
It pleases me		I am pleased with it
It interests me		I am interested in it
Experiencer as subject	⇒	*Stimulus as subject*
I fear it		It is fearful to me
I like it		It is likable to me
I loathe it		It is loathsome to me

Table 1.8
Affect verbs in English

Stimulus as subject					
please	key up	astonish	annoy	incense	worry
satisfy	turn on	awe	bother	infuriate	concern
gratify	interest	wow	irk	outrage	trouble
comfort	engage	confuse	bug	miff	distress
soothe	captivate	puzzle	vex	put out	upset
calm	intrigue	perplex	pique	disgruntle	disturb
charm	fascinate	mystify	peeve	frustrate	disconcert
amuse	beguile	baffle	nettle	chagrin	unsettle
cheer	entrance	bewilder	irritate	embarrass	shake up
tickle	bewitch	boggle	provoke	abash	discombobulate
delight	tantalize	stupefy	gall	cow	frighten
thrill	matter to	dumbfound	aggravate	shame	scare
transport	bore	flabbergast	grate on	humiliate	alarm
move	surprise	shock	piss off	disgust	grieve
stir	startle	dismay	exasperate	gross out	hurt
arouse	amaze	appall	anger	revolt	pain
excite	astound	horrify	rile		torment
Experiencer as subject					
like	marvel over	want	lust for	abhor	worry about
enjoy	wonder at	feel like	crave	deplore	grieve over
care for	trust	desire	need	anger over	sorrow over
fancy	respect	prefer	covet	fume over	regret
	esteem	wish for	envy	seethe over	rue
relish	admire	hope for	dislike	gloat over	hurt from
love	appreciate	hanker after	resent	distrust	ache from
adore	value	hunger for	hate	fear	suffer from
delight in	prize	thirst for	detest	dread	bear
thrill to	cherish	long for	despise		stand
exult over	revere	yearn for	loathe		tolerate

Table 1.9
Derivation of Experiencer-subject verb roots to Stimulus-subject in Atsugewi

Experiencer as subject		
verb root:	-lay-	'to consider as good'
Cause prefix:	sa-	'by vision'
derivational suffix:	-im	(no specific meaning: occurs here idiomatically)
inflectional affix-set:	s- '-w- -ᵃ	'I—subject, 3rd person object'
/s-'-w-sa-lay-im-ᵃ/ ⇒ [sẃsal·ayíw]		
"I find it beautiful"		
Derived to; Stimulus as subject		
verb root:	-lay-	'to consider as good'
Cause prefix:	sa-	'by vision'
valence-shifting suffix:	-ahẃ	'from Stimulus to Experiencer'
inflectional affix-set:	'- w- -ᵃ	'3rd person subject'
/'-w-sa-lay-ahẃ-ᵃ/ ⇒ [ẃsal·ayáhẃa]		
"It is beautiful"		

It may be that the boundaries of the 'affect' category here are too encompassive or misdrawn for good comparative assessments. There may be smaller categories following more 'natural' divisions that reveal more about semantic organization. For example, a 'desiderative' category might well be separated out by itself: *all* the English verbs of 'wanting' listed in table 1.8 have Experiencer subjects, and this arrangement might be widespread, if not universal. Thus, although colloquial expressions with the opposite valence occur in other languages

(91) a. *Yiddish*

    Mir   vilt   zikh esn

    me-to wants self to-eat

   b. *Samoan*

    'Ua sau   ('iate a'u) le fia 'ia

    ASP come (to me) the want (to)eat

    "A desire for eating has come on me (I feel like eating)."

they are derived constructions based on verb roots with *Experiencer* subjects. (However, Kaluli of New Guinea may possibly be a language in which all mental verbs—including those of 'wanting' and 'knowing'—put the Experiencer in the surface case that identifies it as the affected argument (Bambi Schieffelin, personal communication).) Perhaps, too, one

Table 1.10
'Cognitive' Verbs

Stimulus as subject				
strike	occur to			
seem to	dawn on			
remind ... of				
Experiencer as subject				
know	think	consider	remember	learn
realize	feel	suspect	forget	discover
believe	doubt	imagine	wonder about	find out

should separate out an 'assessment' category for notions like 'esteem', 'value', 'prize'; in table 1.8 the English verbs for these notions again all require Experiencer subjects. We had already separated out a 'cognitive' category for the more intellective mental processes. Verbs of this category were excluded from the affect list above, and again English seems to favor Experiencer as subject for them, as shown in table 1.10.

A single semantic-cognitive principle might account for all these correlations between category of mental event and lexicalization tendency: Subjecthood, perhaps because of its frequent association with agency, may tend to confer on any semantic category expressed in it some initiatory or instigative characteristics. Accordingly, with Stimulus as subject, an external object or event (the stimulus) may be felt to act on an Experiencer so as to engender within him or her a particular mental event. Conversely, with Experiencer as subject, the mental event may be felt to arise autonomously and to direct itself outward toward a selected object. For example, a mental event of 'wanting' might be psychologically experienced across cultures as a self-originating event, and so, by this principle, have a preponderant tendency across languages to correlate with Experiencer subjecthood.

3   SATELLITES

In section 2, we have examined a connected set of semantic categories that appear lexicalized in an open-class type of surface element, the verb root. Here, to demonstrate the parallelism and to augment earlier typologies, we will examine roughly the same set of semantic categories, but now lexicalized in a closed-class type of surface element. This is an element that has not been generally recognized as such in the linguistic literature. We term it the **satellite to the verb**—or simply, the **satellite**, abbreviated "Sat." It is the grammatical category of any constituent other than a noun-phrase or prepositional-phrase complement that is in a sister relation to the verb root. It relates to the verb root as a dependent to a head. The satellite, which can be either a bound affix or a free word, is thus intended to encompass all of the following grammatical forms, which traditionally have been largely treated independently of each other: English verb particles, German separable and inseparable verb prefixes, Latin or Russian verb prefixes, Chinese verb complements, Lahu nonhead "versatile verbs" (see Matisoff 1973), Caddo incorporated nouns, and Atsugewi polysynthetic affixes around the verb root. A set of forms that can function as satellites in a language often overlaps partially, but not wholly, with a set of forms in another grammatical category in that language, generally the category of prepositions, verbs, or nouns. Thus, English satellites largely overlap with prepositions—but *together, apart,* and *forth,* for example, serve only as satellites, while *of, from,* and *toward* serve only as prepositions. In a similar way, Mandarin satellites largely overlap with verb roots. And in Caddo, the satellites of one type largely overlap with noun roots. One justification for recognizing the satellite as a grammatical category is that it captures an observable commonality, both syntactic and semantic, across all these forms—for example, its common function across one typological category of languages as the characteristic site in construction with the verb for the expression of Path or, more generally, of the "core schema" (chapter II-3).

There is some indeterminacy as to exactly which kinds of constituents found in construction with a verb root merit satellite designation. Clearest are the forms named earlier, such as English verb particles, Latin verb prefixes, Chinese resultative complements, and the noninflectional affixes in the Atsugewi polysynthetic verb. Seemingly also deserving satellite status are such compounding forms as the first element in English *(to) test-drive.* Probably meriting satellite status are incorporated nouns, like those in the Caddo polysynthetic verb, while pronominal clitics like those in French may merit the designation less, and full noun phrases are entirely excluded. It is uncertain what status should be accorded such verb-phrase forms as inflections, an auxiliary, a negative element, a closed-class particle like English *only* or *even,* or a free adverb semantically related to the verb root. It is further not clear whether this indeterminacy is due to the present theory's early stage of development or to a clinelike character for the satellite category.

A verb root together with its satellites forms a constituent in its own right, the **verb complex**, also not generally recognized. It is this constituent as a whole that relates to such other constituents as a direct object noun phrase.

The satellite is easily illustrated in English. It can take the form of either a free word or an affix (satellites are marked here by the symbol ◄ that, in effect, "points" from the satellite to its head, the verb root).

(92) a. *Satellite*   ◄over   ◄mis-
     b. *Verb complex*   start ◄over   fire ◄mis-
     c. *Example sentence* The record started   The engine misfired.
                          over.

As many as four such satellites can appear together in a verb complex, as in (93). (Here, *right*—belonging to a morpheme set that also includes *way* and *just*—is semantically dependent on the following satellite as its modifier, but it fills a syntactic slot and behaves phonologically like a prototypical satellite.)

(93) Come ◄right ◄back ◄down ◄out from up in there!
     (said, for example, by a parent to a child in a treehouse)

The term traditionally applied to the above element in English is "verb particle" (see Fraser 1976). The term **satellite** has been introduced to capture the commonality between such particles and comparable forms in other languages. Within Indo-European, such forms include the "separable" and "inseparable" prefixes of German and the verb prefixes of Latin and Russian, as shown in table 1.11.

Another kind of satellite is the second element of a verb compound in Chinese, called by some the "resultative complement." Another example is any nonhead word in the lengthy verbal sequences typical of Tibeto-Burman languages. In the case of Lahu, Matisoff (1973) has called any such word a "versatile verb." A third example is any of the noninflectional affixes on the verb root in the Atsugewi "polysynthetic verb."[54] We now examine a range of types of semantic material that appear in satellites.

3.1 Path

The satellites in English are mostly involved in the expressions of Path. Generally, the Path is expressed fully by the combination of a satellite and a preposition, as in (94a). But usually the satellite can also appear alone, as in (94b). The ellipsis of the prepositional phrase here generally requires

Table 1.11
Satellites as verb prefixes in German, Latin, and Russian

	A. German	
	"separable" prefix	*"inseparable" prefix*
satellite	◄entzwei	◄zer-
verb complex	brechen ◄entzwei (entzweibrechen)	brechen ◄zer- (zerbrechen)
ex. sentence	Der Tisch brach entzwei "The table broke in two"	Der Tisch zerbrach "The table broke to pieces"
	B. Latin	C. Russian
	prefixes	*prefixes*
satellite	◄in-	◄v-
verb complex	volare ◄in- (involare)	letet' ◄v- (vletet')
ex. sentence	Avis involavit "The bird flew in"	Ptica vletela "The bird flew in"

that its nominal be either a deictic or an anaphoric pronoun (i.e., that the Ground object be uniquely identifiable by the hearer).[55]

(94) a. I ran *out of* the house.
    b. (After rifling through the house,) I ran *out* [i.e., ... of it].

Some symbolism here can help represent the semantic and grammatical situation. The symbol > is placed after a preposition, in effect pointing toward its nominal object. Thus this symbol, together with ◄, encloses the full surface expression (the satellite plus preposition) that specifies Path, as illustrated in (95a). For a still finer representation, parentheses are used to mark off the portion that can be optionally omitted, and *F* and *G* indicate the locations of the nominals that function as Figure and Ground, as shown in (95b).

(95) a. ◄out of>
    b. F ... ◄out (of> G)

English has quite a few Path satellites. Some are presented in the sentences in (96), here without any final Ground-containing phrase.

(96) *Some Path satellites in English*

I ran *in*$_1$.	He ran *across*.	It flew *up*$_1$.
I ran *out*$_1$.	He ran *along*.	It flew *down*.
I climbed *on*.	He ran *through*.	I went *above*.
I stepped *off*$_1$.	He ran *past/by*.	I went *below*.
He drove *off*$_2$.	She came *over*$_1$.	I ran *up*$_2$ (to her).

I stepped *aside*.	It toppled *over₂*.	She followed along *after* (us).
She came *forth*.	She spun *around₁*.	They slammed *together*.
She walked *away*.	She walked *around₂*.	They rolled *apart*.
He went *ahead*.	She walked (all)	It shrank *in₂*.
He came *back*.	*about*.	It spread *out₂*.

In addition, English has a number of Path satellites that would not be generally recognized as such—that is, as being in the same semantic category as those of (96).

(97) *More Path satellites in English*

F . . .	◄loose	(from> G)	The bone pulled loose (from its socket).
F . . .	◄free	(from> G)	The coin melted free (from the ice).
F . . .	◄clear	(of> G)	She swam clear (of the oncoming ship).
F . . .	◄stuck	(to> G)	The twig froze stuck (to the window).
F . . .	◄fast	(to> G)	The glaze baked fast (to the clay).
F . . .	◄un-	(from> G)	The bolt must have unscrewed (from the plate).
F . . .	◄over-	∅> G	The eaves of the roof over-hung the garden.
F . . .	◄under-	∅> G	Gold leaf underlay the enamel.
G . . .	◄full	(of> F)	The tub quickly poured full (of hot water).

The languages in most branches of Indo-European have Path systems that are homologous with the one just seen for English. That is, they also use a satellite and a preposition, with the prepositional phrase generally omissible. This is illustrated in (98) and (99) for Russian (see Talmy 1975b for an extensive treatment of such forms in this language).[56]

(98) *Some Path expressions in Russian*

F . . .	◄v- v + ACC>	'into'
F . . .	◄vy- iz + GEN>	'out of'
F . . .	◄pere- čerez + ACC>	'across'

F . . .	◄pod- pod + ACC> 'to under'
F . . .	◄pod- k + DAT> 'up to'
F . . .	◄ob- ob + ACC> 'to against'
F . . .	◄ot- ot + GEN> 'off a ways from'
F . . .	◄na- na + ACC> 'onto'
F . . .	◄s- s + GEN> 'off of'
F . . .	◄pro- mimo + GEN> 'past'
F . . .	◄za- za + ACC> 'to behind/beyond'
F . . .	◄pri- k + DAT> 'into arrival at'
F . . .	◄do- do + GEN> 'all the way to'
F . . .	◄iz- iz + GEN> '(issuing) forth from'

(99) a. Ja vbežal (v   dom)
    I in-ran (into house(ACC))
    "I ran in (-to the house)."

   b. Ja vybežal (iz   doma)
    I out-ran (out of house(GEN))
    "I ran out (of the house)."

We want to emphasize for all these Path examples that satellites should be well distinguished from prepositions. No confusion can occur in most Indo-European languages, where the two forms have quite distinct positional and grammatical characteristics. For example, in Latin, Classical Greek, and Russian (see (98) and (99)), the satellite is bound prefixally to the verb, while the preposition accompanies the noun (wherever it turns up in the sentence) and governs its case. Even where a satellite and a preposition with the same phonetic shape are both used together in a sentence to express a particular Path notion—as often happens in Latin, Greek, and Russian (again, see (98) and (99))—the two occurrences are still formally distinct. However, a problem arises for English, which, perhaps alone among Indo-European languages, has come to regularly position satellite and preposition next to each other in a sentence. Nevertheless, there are still ways in which the two kinds of forms—satellites and prepositions—distinguish themselves.

To begin with, the two classes of forms do not have identical memberships: there are forms with only one function or the other. Thus, as already noted, *together, apart, away, back*, and *forth* are satellites that never act as prepositions, while *of, at, from*, and *toward* are prepositions that never act as satellites.[57] Furthermore, forms serving in both functions often have different senses in each. Thus, *to* as a preposition (*I went to the store*) is

different from *to* as a satellite (*I came to*), and satellite *over* in its sense of
'rotation around a horizontal axis' (*It fell/toppled/turned/flipped over*)
does not have a close semantic counterpart in prepositional *over* with its
'above' or 'covering' senses (*over the treetop, over the wall*).

Next, there are differences in properties. First, with regard to phrase
structure and co-occurrence, a satellite is in construction with the verb,
while a preposition is in construction with an object nominal. Consistent
with this fact, when a Ground nominal is omitted—as it generally may be
when its referent is known or inferable—the preposition that would have
appeared with that nominal is also omitted, while the satellite remains.
Consider, for example, the sentence *He was sitting in his room and then
suddenly ran out (of it)*. If the *it* is omitted, the preposition *of* that is in
construction with it must also be omitted. But the satellite *out*, which is in
construction with the verb *ran*, stays in place. Moreover, a sentence can
contain a satellite in construction with the verb with no notion of any
object nominal, even an omitted one, as in *The log burned up*. But a
preposition always involves some object nominal—though this might
have been moved or omitted, as in *This bed was slept in*, or *This bed is
good to sleep in*.

Second, with regard to positional properties, a preposition precedes its
nominal (unless this has been moved or omitted), as in (100a). But a free
satellite (i.e., one not prefixal to the verb) has these more complex characteristics: It precedes a preposition if one is present, as in (100b). It either
precedes or follows a full NP that lacks a preposition, as in (100c), though
it tends to follow the NP if that location places it directly before a subsequent preposition, as in (100d). And it must follow a pronominal NP that
lacks a preposition, as in (100e).

(100) a.   I ran from the house/it.
      b.   I ran away from the house/it.
      c.   I dragged away the trash. / I dragged the trash away.
      d.   ?I dragged away the trash from the house. / I dragged the trash
           away from the house.
      e.   *I dragged away it (from the house). / I dragged it (away from
           the house).

Third, with regard to stress, in the unmarked case and with only pronominal objects (which are more diagnostic than nonpronominal objects),
a preposition is unstressed and a satellite is stressed, as can be determined
for the sentences in (100). In fact, in a sentence whose NPs are all prono-

minal, a satellite—or the final satellite if there are more than one—is generally the most heavily stressed word of all, as in *I dragged him away from it*, or in *You come right back down <u>out</u> from up in there*.

Finally, the English Path system has a special feature. There are a number of forms like *past* that behave like ordinary satellites when there is no final nominal, as in (101a), but that, if there is a final nominal, even a pronominal one, appear directly before it and get heavy stress. That is, they have the prepositioning property of a preposition but the stress of a satellite.

(101) a. (I saw him on the corner but) I just drove *pást*.
     b. I drove *pást* him.

Because of its distinct dual behavior, the latter usage of a form like *past* can be considered to exemplify a new (and perhaps rare) grammatical category—a coalesced version of a satellite plus a preposition that could be termed a **satellite preposition** or "satprep"—as suggested symbolically in (102a). Alternatively, it can be considered an ordinary satellite that happens to be coupled with a zero preposition, as suggested in (102b).

(102) a. F ... ◄past> G
     b. F ... ◄past ∅> G

Examples of other satpreps in English are *through*, as in *The sword ran through him*, and *up*, as in *I climbed up it*. Indeed, despite its apparent bimorphemic origin, the form *into* now acts like a satprep that is phonologically distinct from the combination of the satellite *in* followed by the preposition *to*, as seen in *The bee's sting went into him*, versus *Carrying the breakfast tray, the butler went in to him*. On the same phonological basis, *out of* also behaves like a single satprep unit, by contrast with the sequence *out from*, as in *She ran out-of it* versus *She ran out from behind it*. Perhaps English has developed the satprep form because it has come to regularly juxtapose its inherited satellite and preposition forms. But, as will shortly be seen, Mandarin, for one other language, also exhibits a homolog of the satprep. A summary of the various satellite and preposition distinctions in English is given in (103).

(103) a. *Preposition + NP*   (Mary invited me to her party.) I went to it.
     b. *Satellite*   (I heard music on the second floor.) I went úp.

c. *Satellite +* (There was a door set in the wall.) I went
   preposition + NP úp to it.
d. *Satprep + NP* (There was a stairway to the second
   floor.) I went úp it.
e. *Satellite + NP* (They wanted the phone on the second
   floor.) I took it úp.

Mandarin Chinese has Path satellites and constructions that are entirely homologous with those of English. A number of these satellites are listed in (104) (they variously may, cannot, or must be further followed by the satellite for 'hither' or for 'thither').

(104) ◄qù   'thither'   ◄guò   'across/past'
      ◄lái   'hither'   ◄qǐ   'up off'
      ◄shàng 'up'   ◄diào 'off (He ran *off*)'
      ◄xià   'down'   ◄zǒu   'away'
      ◄jìn   'in'   ◄huí   'back'
      ◄chū   'out'   ◄lǒng 'together'
      ◄dào   'all the way (to)'   ◄kāi   'apart/free'
      ◄dǎo   'atopple (i.e., pivotally over)' ◄sàn 'ascatter'

These satellites participate in Path expressions of either the coalesced or the uncoalesced type. The only apparent difference from English is an order distinction: the object of the coalesced form follows the verb complex, whereas the prepositional phrase of the uncoalesced form precedes it (as is general with prepositional phrases of any kind). Some satellites can participate in both constructions. One of these is the satellite meaning 'past', which we see in (105) and (106) in two different sentences that receive the same translation in English.

(105) F ... ◄guò (-∅> G-biān) (coalescence of satellite and preposition)
            past   side
      Píng-zi piāo guò shí-tóu páng-biān
      bottle float past rock('s)   side
      'The bottle floated past the rock.'

(106) F ... ◄guò (cóng> G-biān) (the uncoalesced form with both a
            past from   side   satellite and a preposition)
      Píng-zi cóng shí-tóu páng-biān piāo guò
      bottle from rock('s)   side float past
      'The bottle floated past the rock.'

3.2 Path + Ground

In a conflation pattern distinct from the preceding one, a satellite can express at once both a particular Path and the kind of object acting as Ground for the Path. Satellites of this sort seem to be rare in the languages of the world. However, they constitute a major type in certain Amerindian languages. English does have a few examples, which can serve to introduce the type. One is the form *home* in its use as a satellite, where it has the meaning 'to his/her/ ... home'. Another is the form *shut*, also in its satellite use, where it means 'to (a position) across its/ ... associated opening'. These forms are illustrated in (107) in sentences, optionally followed by prepositional phrases that amplify the meanings already present in them.

(107) a. She drove *home* (to her cottage in the suburbs).
       b. The gate swung *shut* (across the entryway).

The reason it can be concluded that such satellites incorporate a Ground in addition to a Path is that they are informationally complete with respect to that Ground, rather than anaphoric or deictic. Accordingly, a discourse can readily begin with their use, as in *The President swung the White House gate shut and drove home.* By contrast, a Path satellite is informationally complete with respect to the Path, but it only indicates a type of Ground and, by itself, can only be anaphoric or deictic with respect to any particular instantiation of such a Ground. Thus, while English *in* indicates an enclosure as Ground, it cannot by itself refer to a particular enclosure, as seen in *The President drove in.* For that, it must be accompanied by some explicit reference to the Ground object, as in *The President drove into a courtyard.*

Atsugewi is one language that has such Path + Ground satellites as a major system.[58] It has some 50 forms of this sort. We can illustrate the system by listing the 14 or so separate satellites that together are roughly equivalent to the English use of *into* with different particular nominals. (A plus sign here indicates that the satellite must be followed by one of -*im*/-*ik·*, 'hither'/'thither'.)

(108) *Path + Ground satellites in Atsugewi*

-ict	'into a liquid'
-cis	'into a fire'
-isp -u· +	'into an aggregate' (e.g., bushes, a crowd, a rib cage)
-wam	'down into a gravitic container' (e.g., a basket, a cupped hand, a pocket, a lake basin)

-wamm	'into an areal enclosure (e.g., a corral, a field, the area occupied by a pool of water)
-ipsnᵘ +	'(horizontally) into a volume enclosure' (e.g., a house, an oven, a crevice, a deer's stomach)
-tip -u· +	'down into a (large) volume enclosure in the ground' (e.g., a cellar, a deer-trapping pit)
-ikn +	'over-the-rim into a volume enclosure' (e.g., a gopher hole, a mouth)
-ikc	'into a passageway so as to cause blockage' (e.g., in choking, shutting, walling off)
-iksᵘ +	'into a corner' (e.g., a room corner, the wall-floor edge)
-mik·	'into the face/eye (or onto the head) of someone'
-mic	'down into (or onto) the ground'
-cisᵘ +	'down into (or onto) an object above the ground' (e.g., the top of a tree stump)
-iks	'horizontally into (or onto) an object above the ground' (e.g., the side of tree trunk)

Instances of the use of this satellite system can be seen in the Atsugewi examples appearing earlier—(36a) to (36c), (65a), (65b), and (74). Two further examples are given in (109).

(109) a. *Verb root*   -st aq-   'for runny icky material to move/be located'

    Directional suffix   -ipsnᵘ   'into a volume enclosure'

    Deictic suffix   -ik·   'hither'

    Cause prefix   ma-   'from a person's foot/feet acting on (the Figure)'

    Inflectional affix set '- w- -ᵃ   '3rd person–subject, factual mood'

/'-w-ma-staq-ipsnᵘ-ik·-ᵃ/ ⇒ [ma·staqipsnuk·a]

Literal: 'He caused it that runny icky material move hither into a volume enclosure by acting on it with his feet.'

Instantiated: "He tracked up the house (coming in with muddy feet)."

    b. *Verb root*   -lup-   'for a small shiny spherical object to move/be located'

Directional suffix	-mik·	'into the face/eye(s) of someone'
Instrumental prefix	phu-	'from the mouth—working egressively—acting on (the Figure)'
Inflectional affix set	m- w- -ᵃ	'thou–subject, 3rd person–object, factual mood'

/m-w-phu-lup-mik·-ᵃ ⇒ [mphol·úpʰmik·a]

Literal: 'You caused it that a small shiny spherical object move into his face by acting on it with your mouth working egressively.'

Instantiated: "You spat your candy-ball into his face."

3.3 Patient: (Figure/)Ground

Another type of satellite is one that indicates the Patient of an event being referred to. Such satellites constitute a major system, for example, in "noun-incorporating" Amerindian languages. These languages include an affixal form of the satellite within their polysynthetic verb. Caddo is a case in point. Here, the satellite gives a typically more generic identification of the Patient. The sentence may also contain an independent nominal that gives a typically more specific identification of the same Patient, but the satellite must be present in any case. Here first are some nonmotion examples, with (110a) showing the Patient as subject in a nonagentive sentence, and (110b) and (110c) showing it as direct object in agentive sentences.

(110) a. ʔínikuʔ hák-*nisah*-ni-káh-saʔ ⇒ [ʔínikuʔ háhnisánkáhsaʔ]
church PROG-house-burn-PROG
Literally: 'The church is house-burning (i.e., building-burning).'
Loosely: "The church is burning."

b. cú·cuʔ *kan*-yi-daʔk-ah ⇒ [cú·cuʔ kanidaʔkah]
milk   liquid-find-PAST
Literally: 'He liquid-found the milk.'
Loosely: "He found the milk."

c. widiš *dáʔn*-yi-daʔk-ah ⇒ [widiš dânnidaʔkah]
salt   powder-find-PAST
Literally: 'He powder-found the salt.'
Loosely: "He found the salt."

Without the independent noun, the last example would work as in (111).

(111) *dáʔn*-yi-daʔk-ah 'He powder-found it.' / 'He found it (something powdery).'

In Caddo's general pattern for expressing Motion, the verb root indicates fact-of-Motion together with Path, in the manner of Spanish. The incorporated noun can under limited conditions—it is not yet clear what these are—indicate the Figure, as in the following locative example.

(112) yak-čah-yih   *nisah*-ya-ʔah ⇒ [dahčahih tisáyʔah]
      woods-edge-LOC house-be-TNS
      Literally: 'At woods edge it-house-is.'
      Loosely: "The house is at the edge of the woods."

Usually, the incorporated noun indicates the Ground:

(113) a. wá·kas na-*yawat*-yá-ynik-ah ⇒ [wá·kas táywacáynikah]
         cattle   PL-water-enter-PAST
         Literally: 'Cattle water-entered.'
         Loosely: "The cattle went into the water."
      b. *nisah*-nt-káy-watak-ah ⇒ [tisánčáywakkah]
         house-penetrate/traverse-PAST
         Literally: 'He-house-traversed.'
         Loosely: "He went through the house."

3.4 Manner

An uncommon type of satellite is one expressing Manner. An extensive system of such satellites is found in Nez Perce, another polysynthetic language of North America (see Aoki 1970). In Motion sentences, the verb root in this language is like that of Spanish: it expresses Motion + Path. But at the same time, a prefix adjoining the root specifies the particular Manner in which the Motion is executed. An example of this arrangement is given in (114).

(114) /hi-   ququ·-   láhsa -e/ ⇒ [hiqqoláhsaya]
      3rd person galloping go-up PAST
      Literally: 'He/she ascended galloping.'
      Loosely: "He galloped uphill."

We list a selection of Nez Perce Manner prefixes in (115). Note that this prefix system includes not only types of locomotive manners but extends as well to types of Concomitance, both of affect ('in anger') and of activity ('on the warpath').

(115) *Nez Perce Manner prefixes*

ʔipsqi-	'walking'
wilé·-	'running'
wat-	'wading'
siwi-	'swimming-on-surface'
tukʷe-	'swimming-within-liquid'
we·-	'flying'
tu·k̓e-	'using a cane'
ceptukte-	'crawling'
tuk̓weme	'(snake) slithering'
wu·l-	'(animal) walking/(human) riding (on animal at a walk)'
quqú·-	'(animal) galloping/(human) galloping (on animal)'
tiq̓e-	'(heavier object) floating-by-updraft/wafting/gliding'
ʔiyé·-	'(lighter object) floating-by-intrinsic-buoyancy'
wis-	'traveling with one's belongings'
kipi-	'tracking'
tiw̓ek-	'pursuing (someone: D.O.)'
cú·-	'(plurality) in single file'
til-	'on the warpath/to fight'
qisim-	'in anger'

Assuming that polysynthetic forms arise through boundary and sound changes among concatenated words, one can imagine how a Nez Perce-type system could have developed from a Spanish type. Originally independent words referring to Manner came regularly to stand next to the verb and then became affixal (and in most cases also lost their usage elsewhere in the sentence). Indeed, one can imagine how Spanish might evolve in the direction of Nez Perce. The preferred position for Manner-expressing gerunds in Spanish is already one immediately following the Path verb, as in (116).

(116) Entró   corriendo/volando/nadando/ ... a la cueva
      he-entered running   flying   swimming   to the cave

Such gerunds might in time evolve into a closed-class system of fixed postposed satellites, and perhaps even further into suffixes on the verb. One could thus imagine the few kinds of changes that would turn the Spanish system for expressing Motion into a homolog of the Nez Perce system.

3.5   Cause

A kind of satellite found in a number of languages, at least in the Americas, has traditionally been described as expressing "Instrument." However, these forms seem more to express the whole of a Cause event. This is because, at least in the familiar cases, not only the *kind* of instrumental object that is involved is indicated, but also the *way* in which this object has acted on a Patient (to cause an effect). That is, a satellite of this sort is equivalent to a whole subordinate clause expressing causation in English. In particular, a satellite occurring in a nonagentive verb complex is equivalent to a *from*-clause, as in (to take an actual example in translation): 'The sack burst *from a long thin object poking endwise into it'*. And, the same satellite occurring in an agentive verb complex is equivalent to a *by*-clause, as in 'I burst the sack *by poking a long thin object endwise into it'*.

Perhaps the greatest elaboration of this satellite type occurs in the Hokan languages of northern California, with Atsugewi having some 30 forms. Here, most verb roots must take one or another of the Cause satellites, so that there is obligatory indication of the cause of the action expressed by the verb root (some verb roots cannot take these satellites, but they are in the minority). The full set of these satellites subdivides the semantic domain of possible causes fairly exhaustively. That is, any perceived or conceived causal condition will likely be covered by one or another of the satellites. The majority of the Atsugewi Cause satellites —those in commonest use—are listed in (117). They are grouped according to the kind of instrumentality they specify. As in other Hokan languages, they appear as short prefixes immediately preceding the verb root. Instances of these satellites in use in a verb have appeared in examples (36a) to (36c) as well as in (109a) and (109b). In addition, section 4 of chapter II-2 presents the Cause satellites with elaborated semantic descriptions and as used within numerous examples of verbs.

(117) *Atsugewi Cause satellites (P = the Patient, E = the Experiencer)*
      Natural forces
      ◄ca-   'from the wind blowing on P'
      ◄cu-   'from flowing liquid acting on P' (e.g., a river on a bank)
      ◄ka-   'from the rain acting on P'
      ◄ra-   'from a substance exerting steady pressure on P' (e.g., gas in the stomach)

◄uh-   'from the weight of a substance bearing down on P'
         (e.g., snow on a limb)
◄miw-   'from heat/fire acting on P'

Objects in action

◄cu-   'from a linear object acting axially on P' (e.g., as in
         poking, prodding, pool-cueing, piercing, propping)
◄uh-   'from a linear object acting circumpivotally (swinging)
         on P' (as in pounding, chopping, batting)
◄ra-   a. 'from a linear object acting obliquely on P' (as in
            digging, sewing, poling, leaning)
         b. 'from a linear/planar object acting laterally along the
            surface of P' (as in raking, sweeping, scraping,
            plowing, whittling, smoothing, vising)
◄ta-   'from a linear object acting within a liquid P'
         (as in stirring, paddling)
◄ka-   'from a linear object moving rotationally into P'
         (as in boring)
◄mi-   'from a knife cutting into P'
◄ru-   'from a (flexible) linear object pulling on or inward upon
         P' (as in dragging, suspending, girding, binding)

Body parts in action

◄tu-   'from the hand(s)—moving centripetally—acting on P'
         (as in choking, pinching)
◄ci-   'from the hand(s)—moving manipulatively—acting on
         P'
◄ma-   'from the foot/feet acting on P'
◄ti-   'from the buttocks acting on P'
◄wi-   'from the teeth acting on P'
◄pri-   'from the mouth—working ingressively—acting on P'
         (as in sucking, swallowing)
◄phu-   'from the mouth—working egressively—acting on P'
         (as in spitting, blowing)
◄pu-   'from the lips acting on P'
◄hi-   'from any other body part (e.g., head, shoulder) or the
         whole body acting on P'

Sensations

◄sa-   'from the visual aspect of an object acting on E'
◄ka-   'from the auditory aspect of an object acting on E'
◄tu-   'from the feel of an object acting on E'
◄pri-   'from the taste/smell of an object acting on E'

Table 1.12
Typology of Motion verbs and their satellites

Language/language family	The particular components of a Motion event characteristically represented in the:	
	Verb root	Satellite
A. Romance Semitic Polynesian	Motion + Path	A. ∅
B. Nez Perce		B. Manner
C. Caddo		C. (Figure/)Ground [Patient]
Indo-European (not Romance) Chinese	Motion + Co-event	Path
Atsugewi (most northern Hokan)	Motion + Figure	Path + Ground and Cause

3.6   Motion-Related Satellites: Extending the Motion Typology

Table 1.2 (section 2.4) showed the three major categories into which languages fall in their treatment of Motion. The typology was based on which component of a Motion event is characteristically expressed in the verb root (together with 'fact of Motion', which always appears there). For each such language type, the next issue is where the remaining components of the Motion event are located. The satellite is the most diagnostic syntactic constituent to look at after the verb, and so we can make a revealing subcategorization by seeing which Motion components characteristically appear in the satellites that accompany the verb (see table 1.12).[59]

3.6.1   Verb-Framed and Satellite-Framed Systems   As noted, the typology summarized in this table is based on looking at selected syntactic constituents—first the verb root and then the satellite—to see which components of a Motion event characteristically show up in them. But a complementary typology could be based on looking at selected components of a Motion event to see which syntactic constituents they characteristically show up in. This latter approach is adopted in chapter II-3. As observed there, the typologically most diagnostic component to follow is the Path. Path appears in the verb root in "verb-framed" languages such as Spanish, and it appears in the satellite in "satellite-framed" languages such as English and Atsugewi. Further, as a major generalization over the typology that has been treated in the present chapter, where Path appears, there, too, appear four other kinds of semantic constituents: aspect, state change, action correlation, and realization.

3.6.2 Typological Shift and Maintenance   Tracing the route by which a language shifts its typological pattern for the expression of Motion events—or indeed, maintains its pattern while other changes are ongoing —can be a rich research area for diachronic linguistics. We can suggest some processes here.

Consider first some forms of change and maintenance within Indo-European. For their characteristic representation of Motion events, Latin, classical Greek, and Proto-Germanic all exhibited the presumably Indo-European pattern of using Co-event-conflating verb roots together with Path satellites that formed prefixes on the verb roots. Perhaps because of phonological changes that rendered the Path prefixes less distinct from each other and from the verb roots, all three languages apparently became unable to maintain their inherited pattern. Both Germanic and Greek proceeded to develop a new set of Path satellites that largely supplanted the prior set. In German, for example, a few of the original Path satellites continue on as "inseparable prefixes," while the new set comprises the much more numerous "separable prefixes." This development of a fresh Path satellite system permitted the maintenance of the inherited pattern for representing Motion events with Co-event verb conflation.

The languages arising from Latin, on the other hand, each developed a new system of Path-conflating verbs, rather than reestablishing the Path satellite system. In this process, each of the daughter languages formed its set of Path verbs in its own way by variously coining new verbs or shifting the semantics of inherited verbs so as to fill out the basic directional grid of the new Path verb system. At the same time, these languages may have undergone the complementary change of advancing their gerundive constructions for the expression of Manner and Cause. The factors that may have tilted one language toward reestablishing its typological category and another language toward shifting to another category must yet be discerned.[60]

From its classical to its contemporary form, Chinese appears to have undergone a typological shift in a direction just the reverse of that exhibited by the Romance languages: from a Path-conflation pattern to a Co-event-conflation pattern (see Li 1993). Classical Chinese had a full set of

Path verbs used as main verbs in the representation of Motion events. Through the development of a serial verb construction, these Path verbs have progressively come to have their main occurrence as second-position elements following a Manner/Cause-conflating verb. While the serial verb interpretation is still available, these second-position elements appear to have been incrementally turning into a system of Path satellites following a Manner/Cause main verb. Favoring this reinterpretation is the fact that some of the morphemes with clear Path senses in second position have become less colloquial or obsolescent or obsolete as main verbs, or that in their usage as a main verb, they have meanings only partially or meta-phorically related to their second-position Path sense.

3.6.3 Cognitive Underpinnings of Typological Shift and Maintenance

Section 2.4 and section 3 up to the present point have outlined the cross-linguistic range of meaning-form patterns for expressing a Motion situation. This range has been seen to constitute a structured typology: it includes some alternative patterns with perhaps equal priority of occurrence, it includes some patterns hierarchically ranked in priority, and it excludes some patterns. Although this typological structuring among patterns must have its basis in human cognitive organization, exactly how it is based there is not clear. It might be an innate part of the language system in our cognition, or it might arise secondarily as a consequence of other cognitive properties or from the effects of external exigencies on cognition. Whatever its exact basis, this typological structure is largely responsible for the long-range diachronic maintenance of a pattern or shift from one pattern to another in a language.

This long-range effect is the cumulative result of speakers' numerous moment-to-moment "choices" in expression. Speakers opt among alternatives of expression through cognitive processing that accords with their cognitively based structural typology. Such choices sometimes yield nonce forms, innovative expressions, and constructions that "push the envelope" of the language's current structure. In such novel formations, speakers may tend to shift more easily among equally ranked patterns, to shift toward a more highly ranked pattern or to maintain an already highly ranked one, and to avoid excluded patterns. Of course, momentary speaker choices and their cumulative diachronic effect respond not only to cognitively based typological structure, but also to other cognitive structures pertinent to language. The latter might include a requirement for an adequate number of lexical distinctions within certain semantic areas (such as that of Paths undertaken with respect to Ground objects), or a tendency toward maintaining the overall semantic organization of the language (see chapter II-4). Further, speaker choices arise not only in a direct way from such typological and other cognitive structures, but also indirectly from exposure to other speakers' choices (themselves arising from the counterpart cognitive structures within the other speakers). That is, the diachronic effect actually arises cumulatively from two forms of cognitive processing, one responding to typological structure and the other to interpersonal interaction.

In sum, the diachronic maintenance or change of universals and typologies of concept structuring in language results cumulatively from ongoing cognitive processes in correlation with relatively stable structures in cognition. Considerations like the preceding and their future elaboration may eventually help unify our understanding of concept structuring, typology (in the general sense that includes universality), and process (in the general sense that includes structure) in the cognitive organization of language.

3.7   Aspect

Many languages have satellites that express aspect. Frequently, these satellites do not indicate purely 'the distribution pattern of action through time' (as aspect was characterized earlier). This purer form is mixed with, or shades off into, indications of manner, quantity, intention, and other factors. Accordingly, a liberal interpretation is given to aspect in the examples below. In this way, we can present together many of the forms that seem to be treated by a language as belonging to the same group. The demonstration can begin with English. Though this language is not usually thought of as expressing aspect in its satellites (as, say, Russian is), it is in fact a fully adequate example.

(118) *English aspect satellites (V = do the action of the verb)*

◄re-/◄over   'V again/anew'
                          When it got to the end, the record automatically
                          restarted/started over from the beginning.

◄on   'continue Ving without stopping'
                          We talked/worded on into the night.
                          'resume where one had left off in Ving'
                          She stopped at the gas station first, and then she
                          drove on from there.
                          'go ahead and V against opposition'

He was asked to stay on the other side of the door, but adamant, he barged on in.

◀away   'continue Ving (with dedication/abandon)'
They worked away on their papers.
They gossiped away about all their neighbors.
'feel free to embark on and continue Ving'
'Would you like me to read you some of my poetry?' 'Read away!'

◀along   'proceed in the process of Ving'
We were talking along about our work when the door suddenly burst open.

◀off   'V all in sequence/progressively'
I read/checked off the names on the list.
All the koalas in this area have died off.

◀up   'V all the way into a different (a nonintegral/denatured) state'
The log burned up in two hours (cf. The log burned for one hour before I put it out).
The dog chewed the mat up in 20 minutes (cf. The dog chewed on the mat for 10 minutes before I took it away).

◀back   'V in reciprocation for being Ved'
He had teased her, so she teased him back.

Other languages have forms comparable to those of English, though often with different, or more varied meanings. Russian is a case in point. In addition to several forms like those in the English list, Russian has (at least) the following (some of the examples are from Wolkonsky and Poltoratzky 1961).

(119) *Russian aspect satellites*

◀po-   'V for a while'
Ja poguljal
I "po"-strolled
"I strolled about for a while."
Xočets'a   poletat' na samolëte
wants-REFL "po"-fly on airplane
"I'd like to fly for a while on a plane (i.e., take a short flight)."

◄pere-   'V every now and then'
               Perepadajut doždi
               "pere"-fall   rains (N)
               "Rains fall (It rains) every now and then."

◄za-   'start Ving'
               Kapli doždja   zapadali odna za   drugoj
               drops rain-GEN "za"-fell one   after another
               "Drops of rain began to fall one after
               another."

◄raz- + REFL   'burst out Ving'
               Ona rasplakalas'
               she   "raz"-cried-REFL
               "She burst out crying."

◄pro-/◄pere-   'complete the process of Ving'
               Pivo perebrodilo
               beer "pere"-fermented
               "The beer has finished fermenting."

◄po-   'V as one complete act'
               On eë   poceloval
               he   her "po"-kissed
               "He kissed her" (vs. was kissing, kept kissing,
               used to kiss).

◄na- + REFL   'V to satiation'
               On naels'a
               he   "na"-ate-REFL
               "He ate his fill."

◄s-   'V and de-V as one complete cycle' [only with
               motion verbs]
               Ja sletal   v odin mig   na   počtu
               I   "s"-flew in one moment to the post office
               "I got to the post office and back in no time."

Within its affixal verb complex, Atsugewi has certain locations for a group of aspect-related satellites. These are semantically of two kinds, indicating what can be called 'primary' and 'secondary' aspectual notions. The primary kind indicates how the action of the verb root is distributed with respect to the general flow of time. The secondary kind indicate how the action is distributed with respect to another ongoing event, namely

Table 1.13
Atsugewi aspect satellites' meanings

V's action is related to:	
the general temporal flow	*an ongoing locomotory event*
almost V	go and V
still V	go Ving along
V repeatedly	come Ving along
V again/back, reV	V in passing
start Ving	V going along with someone
finish Ving	V coming along with someone
V as a norm	V in following along after someone
V awhile/stay awhile and V	V in going to meet someone
V in a hurry/hurry up and V	
V a little bit/spottily/cutely	

one of moving along (see Wilkins' (1991) "associated motion"). In translation, these forms can be represented as in table 1.13. We can illustrate the second satellite type as in (120).

(120) *Verb root*   acp-   'for contained solid material to
                                        move/be located'

       Secondary aspect   -ikc   'to a position blocking passage',
       suffix   hence: 'in going to meet (and
                                         give to) someone approaching'

       Inflectional affix set s- '- w- -ᵃ   'I–subject (3rd person–object),
                                          factual mood'

       Independent noun   taki̇·   'acorn(s)'
       Nominal marker   c

/s-'-w-acp-ikc-ᵃ c taki̇·/ ⇒ [sẁacpík̔ʰca c taʔk̕í·]

Literally: 'I caused it that contained solid material—namely, acorns—move, in going to meet (and give it to) someone approaching.'

Loosely: "I carried out the basket full of acorns to meet him with, as he approached."[61]

3.8 Valence

In section 2.9 we saw satellites (German *be-* and *ver-*, Atsugewi *-ahẇ*) involved solely with valence: they signaled shifts for the incorporated valence requirements of verb roots. There are also satellites that basically refer to other notions, such as Path, but themselves incorporate valence requirements. When these are used with verbs that have no competing requirements, they determine the grammatical relations of the surrounding nominals. We look at this situation now.

3.8.1 Satellites Determining the Figure-Ground Precedence Pattern of the Verb Consider the Path satellites (or satellite + preposition combinations) referring to surfaces in (121).

(121) a. Water poured *onto* the table.   'to a point of the surface of'
      b. Water poured *all over* the table.   'to all points of the
                                                              surface of'

These satellites require the Ground nominal as prepositional object and (in these nonagentive sentences) the Figure nominal as subject. The same holds for the satellite that refers to interiors in the following case.

(122) a. Water poured *into* the tub.   'to a point/some points of the
                                                            inside of'

However, English has no form comparable to *all over* for interiors, as (122b) suggests.

(122) b. *Water poured all into/? the tub.   'to all points of the
                                                              inside of'

A new locution must be resorted to. This locution, moreover, differs from the others in that it has the reverse valence requirements: the Figure as prepositional object and the Ground (in nonagentive sentences) as subject.

(123) The tub poured *full of* water.

By the opposite token, the satellite for surfaces does not allow this reverse valence arrangement, as (124) indicates.

(124) *The table poured all over with/of water.

This same pattern applies as well to agentive sentences, except that what was the subject nominal is now the direct object.

(125) *'surfaces'*
      a. I poured water onto the table.
      b. I poured water all over the table.
         (*I poured the table all over with/of water.)

'interiors'

   c. I poured water into the tub.

     (*I poured water all into the tub.)

   d. I poured the tub full of water.

Using the earlier notation, the valence requirements of these satellites can be represented as in (126).

(126) a. F ... ◄on (-to> G)

     b. F ... ◄all-over (∅> G)

     c. F ... ◄in (-to> G)

     d. F ... ◄full (-of> F)

With the concept of a precedence hierarchy among grammatical relations that places subject and direct object above prepositional object, we can say that in English the notion of a 'filled surface' expressed in a satellite requires the basic Figure-above-Ground, or F-G, precedence, while the notion of a 'filled interior' requires the reverse Ground-above-Figure, or G-F, precedence.

In many languages, certain notions expressed in satellites require one or the other of these same precedence patterns. For example, in Russian, the notion 'into' can only be in the basic F-G precedence pattern, as seen in (127).

(127) a. Ja v-lil   vodu   v stakan

        I in-poured water(ACC) in glass(ACC)

        "I poured water into the glass."

     b. *Ja v-lil   stakan   vodoj

        I in-poured glass(ACC) water(INSTR)

        *"I poured the glass in with water."

By contrast, the notion 'all around' (i.e., 'to all points of the surrounding surface of') requires the reversed G-F precedence pattern:

(128) a. *Ja ob-lil   vodu   na/? sabaku

        I circum-poured water(ACC) on   dog(ACC)

        *"I poured water all round the dog."

     b. Ja ob-lil   sabaku   vodoj

        I circum-poured dog(ACC) water(INSTR)

        "I poured the dog round with water."

Accordingly, these satellites can be represented notationally as in (129).

(129) a. F ... ◄v- (v + ACC> G)

     b. G ... ◄ob- (∅ + INSTR> F)

Outside Indo-European, Atsugewi exhibits similar cases of Path satellites requiring either basic F-G or reversed G-F precedence. Two such satellites, respectively, are -cis 'into a fire' and -mik· 'into someone's face' (represented in (130) as *afire* and *aface*).

(130) a. /acʰ   ∅-   s-'-i:-ᵃ   s-'-w-ra+pĺ-cis-ᵃ   c   ahw̓-i?/

       water OBJ- TOPICALIZER   INFL-pour-afire   NP fire-to

       ⇒ [ʔácʰ·i se· sw̓lapʰĺicʰ·a c ʔahw̓í?]

       'I-poured-afire water (D.O.) (F) campfire-to (G)'

       "I threw water over the campfire."

     b. /acʰ- aʔ   t-   s-'-i:-ᵃ   s-'-w-ra+pĺ-mik·-ᵃ c   aw̓tih/

       water-with NONOBJ- TOPICALIZER INFL-pour-aface   NP man

       ⇒ [ʔacʰ·ʔá cʰe· sw̓lapʰĺim·ik·a c ʔáw̓te]

       'I-poured-aface man (D.O.) (G) water-with (F)'

       "I threw water into the man's face" ("I threw the man aface with water").

In some cases, a Path satellite can be used with either valence precedence. English *through* works this way in usages like the examples in (131).

(131) (*it* = 'my sword')

     a. I (A) ran it (F) *through* him (G).

     b. I (A) ran him (G) *through* with it (F).

Of these two usages of *through*, the former is actually a satellite preposition. Both usages would appear in our formula representation as in (132).[62]

(132) a. F ... ◄through> G

     b. G ... ◄through (with> F)

In other cases, there are two satellites, with the same meaning and sometimes with similar forms, that act as a complementary pair in handling either valence precedence. The Yiddish separable verb prefixes for directional 'in', *arayn-* and *ayn-*, work as in (133) (see chapter II-5).

(133) a. F ... ◄arayn- (in> G) '(directional) in F-G'

       G ... ◄ayn- (mit> F) '(directional) in G-F'

b. Ikh hob nishtvilndik arayn-geshtokhn a dorn (F) in   ferd (G)
   I   have accidentally in(F-G)-stuck   a thorn   in-the horse
   "I stuck a thorn into the horse."

c. Ikh hob nishtvilndik ayn-geshtokhn dos ferd (G) mit a dorn (F)
   I   have accidentally in (G-F)-stuck the horse   with a thorn
   "I stuck the horse (in) with a thorn."

3.8.2 Satellites Requiring Direct Object to Indicate 'Bounded Path'
Several Indo-European languages have the same pattern for distinguishing between bounded and unbounded Paths through the use of two parallel constructions. These constructions differ with respect to a valence-controlling satellite. When the Path is bounded and is completed 'in' a quantity of time, the verb has a Path satellite that requires the Ground as direct object. For the corresponding unbounded Path that lasts 'for' a quantity of time, there is no Path satellite at all but rather a Path preposition that takes the Ground as prepositional object. Russian exhibits this pattern. The satellites illustrated here are *ob-* 'circum-', present in (134ai) but not (134aii), *pro-* 'length-', present in (134bi) but not (134bii), and *pere-* 'cross-', present in (134ci) but not (134cii).

(134) a. i. Satelit   obletel   zemlju   (za 3 časa)
              satellite(NOM) circum-flew earth(ACC) in 3 hours
              "The satellite flew around the earth in 3 hours—i.e., made one complete circuit."

         ii. Satelit   letel   vokrug zemli   (3 d'na)
              satellite(NOM) flew-along around earth(GEN) for 3 days
              "The satellite flew around the earth for 3 days."

       b. i. On probežal (vsju) ulicu   (za 30 minut)
              he length-ran all   street(ACC)   in 30 minutes
              "He ran the length of the (whole) street in 30 minutes."

         ii. On bežal   po   ulice   (20 minut)
              he ran-along along street(DAT) for 20 minutes
              "He ran along the street for 20 minutes."

       c. i. On perebežal ulicu   (za 5 sekund)
              he cross-ran street(ACC)   in 5 seconds
              "He ran across the street in 5 seconds."

         ii. On bežal   čerez ulicu   (2 sekundy) i   potom ostanovils'a
              he ran-along across street(ACC) for 2 seconds and then   stopped
              "He ran across the street for 2 seconds and then stopped."

A comparable pattern may exist in German, though presently with varying degrees of colloquiality. In this pattern, the inseparable form of a Path satellite is used for the transitive construction. The satellites illustrated here are inseparable *über-* 'cross-' and *durch-* 'through-', present in (135a) but not (135b).

(135) a. Er überschwamm/durchschwamm den Fluss   in 10 Minuten.
         he over-swam/through-swam   the river(ACC) in 10 minutes
         "He swam across/through the river in 10 minutes."
      b. Er schwamm schon 10 Minuten (über/durch den Fluss),   als   das Boot kam.
         he swam   already 10 minutes over/through the river (ACC), when the boat came
         'He had been swimming (across/through the river) for 10 minutes when the boat came.'

The question of universality must be asked with regard to satellite valence distinctions like those we have seen. For example, in Indo-European languages, satellites expressing a 'full interior' seem without exception to require the reversed G-F precedence pattern, and satellites expressing bounded Paths largely tend to require the Ground as direct object. Are these and comparable patterns language-particular, family-wide, or universal?

4 SALIENCE IN THE VERB COMPLEX

A theoretical perspective that encompasses both sections 2 and 3 pertains to *salience*—specifically, the degree to which a component of meaning, due to its type of linguistic representation, emerges into the foreground of attention or, on the contrary, forms part of the semantic background where it attracts little direct attention (see chapter I-4). With regard to such salience, there appears to be an initial universal principle. Other things being equal (such as a constituent's degree of stress or its position in the sentence), a semantic component is backgrounded by expression in the main verb root or in any closed-class element, including a satellite—hence, anywhere in the main verb complex. Elsewhere, though, it is fore-grounded. This can be called the principle of **backgrounding according to constituent type**.

For example, the first two sentences in (136) are virtually equivalent in the total information that they convey. But they differ in that the fact of the use of an aircraft as transport is foregrounded in (136a) due to its representation by an adverb phrase and the noun that it contains, whereas it is an incidental piece of background information in (136b), where it is conflated within the main verb.

(136) a. I went by plane to Hawaii last month.
      b. I flew to Hawaii last month.
      c. I went to Hawaii last month.

The following second principle appears to serve as a companion to the preceding principle. A concept or a category of concepts tends to be expressed more readily where it is backgrounded. That is, speakers tend to opt for its expression over its omission more often where it can be referred to in a backgrounded way than where it can only be referred to in a foregrounded way. And it tends to be stylistically more colloquial, or less awkward, where it can be backgrounded than where it must be foregrounded. This can be called the principle of **ready expression under backgrounding**. For instance, a Manner concept—such as, the use of aeronautic transport, as in the preceding example—is probably expressed more readily—that is, is expressed more frequently and colloquially—when represented in a backgrounding constituent, like the main verb of (136b), than when represented in a foregrounding constituent, like the adverb phrase of (136a).

This second principle itself has a companion: Where a concept is backgrounded and thus is readily expressed, its informational content can be included in a sentence with apparently low cognitive cost—specifically, without much additional speaker effort or hearer attention. This third principle can be called **low cognitive cost of extra information under backgrounding**. Thus, (136b), in addition to expressing the same informational content as (136c), including the specific concept of translocation, adds to this the fact that this translocation was accomplished through the use of aeronautic transport. But this additional concept is included, as it were, "for free," in that (136b) can apparently be said as readily, and with as little speaker or hearer effort, as the less informative sentence in (136c). Finally, a consequence of the third principle is that a language can casually and comfortably pack more information into a sentence where it can express that information in a backgrounded fashion than can another language—or another sector of usage within the same language—that does not permit the backgrounded expression of such information. This can be called the principle of **ready inclusion of extra information under backgrounding**.

This fourth principle can be demonstrated with respect to the present issue of differential salience across different language types, as well as across different sectors of a single language. Languages may be quite comparable in the informational content that they can express. But a way that languages genuinely differ is in the amount and the types of information that can be expressed in a backgrounded way. English and

Spanish can be contrasted in this regard. English, with its particular verb-conflation pattern and its multiple satellite capability, can convey in a backgrounded fashion the Manner or Cause of an event and up to three components of a Path complex, as in (137).

(137) The man ran back down into the cellar.

In this rather ordinary sentence, English has backgrounded—and hence, by the fourth principle, been readily able to pack in—all of the information that the man's trip to the cellar was accomplished at a run (*ran*), that he had already been in the cellar once recently so that this was a return trip (*back*), that his trip began at a point higher than the cellar so that he had to descend (*down*), and that the cellar formed an enclosure that his trip originated outside of (*in-*). Spanish, by contrast, with its different verb-conflation pattern and almost no productive satellites, can background only one of the four English components, using its main verb for the purpose; any other expressed component is forced into the foreground in a gerundive or prepositional phrase. Again by the fourth principle, such foregrounded information is not readily included and, in fact, an attempted inclusion of all of it in a single sentence can be unacceptably awkward. Thus, in the present case, Spanish can comfortably express either the Manner alone, as in (138a), or one of the Path notions together with a gerundively expressed Manner, as in (138b) to (138d). For acceptable style, further components must either be omitted and left for possible inference, or established elsewhere in the discourse:

(138) *Spanish sentences closest to information-packed English sentence of (137)*

    a. El hombre corrió a -l   sótano
       the man   ran   to-the cellar
       "The man ran to the cellar."

    b. El hombre volvió   a -l   sótano corriendo
       the man   went-back to-the cellar   running
       "The man returned to the cellar at a run."

    c. El hombre bajó   a -l   sótano corriendo
       the man   went-down to-the cellar   running
       "The man descended to the cellar at a run."

    d. El hombre entró   a -l   sótano corriendo
       the man   went-in to-the cellar   running
       "The man entered the cellar at a run."

In comparing texts written in satellite-framed languages like English and in verb-framed languages like Spanish, Slobin (1996) documents an additional difference between the two language types other than where they locate their expression of Path and Manner. As already observed in Talmy (1985b), Slobin verifies that in sentences representing Motion, English expresses Manner liberally, while Spanish does so only sparingly.[63] While he seeks a cause for this difference in the fact that English characteristically represents Manner in the main verb while Spanish does so in a gerundive constituent, he does not say why this fact should lead to the observed effect. On the contrary, it might be argued that in principle the two languages should be equivalent in their behavior, since both language types express Manner and Path in the verb and in a nonverbal constituent, but simply do so in opposite ways.

We would hold that the first two principles posited at the beginning of this section are required to explain the difference in behavior between English and Spanish. In English, both Manner and Path are characteristically expressed in backgrounding constituents: the main verb root and the closed-class satellite. It should be expected therefore that both of these semantic categories will be readily included in a sentence—and that is what is found. But characteristically in Spanish, only Path is expressed in a backgrounding constituent, the main verb root, whereas Manner is expressed in a foregrounding constituent, a gerundive or an adverb phrase. It would thus be expected that the expression of Path is readily included in a sentence, while that of Manner is not—and, again, that is what is found. One test for this account would be the behavior of a verb-framed language that expresses Manner not in a gerundive or an adverb phrase but in a genuine closed-class satellite. Such a language would then be expected to include the expression of Manner in a sentence as readily as that of Path, unlike the verb-framed languages that Slobin has examined. An example of such a language is Nez Perce, as discussed in section 3.4. But it remains to examine texts from this language, or a comparable one, with an eye toward testing the prediction of ready Manner expression.

While the kind of contrast exemplified so far in this section has been at the level of a general pattern difference between two languages, the same kind of contrast can be observed at the level of individual morphemes, even between such similarly patterned languages as Russian and English. For example, Russian has a Path satellite + preposition complex, ◂*pri-*

$k + \text{DAT}>$ 'into arrival at', that characterizes the Ground as an intended destination. English lacks this and, to render it, must resort to the Spanish pattern of expression using a Path-incorporating verb *(arrive)*. As seen in the illustration in (139b), English, as usual with this nonnative conflation type, exhibits awkwardness at further expressing the Manner component. As a baseline for comparison, (139a) illustrates the usual Russian-English parallelism. Here, both languages represent the Path concept 'to a point adjacent to but not touching' with a satellite + preposition complex: Russian ◂*pod-* $k + \text{DAT}>$, and English ◂*up to*>.

(139) a. *Russian* On pod-bežal k vorotam
           he up.to-ran to gates(DAT)
        English "He ran up to the gate."
     b. *Russian* On pri-bežal   k vorotam
           he into.arrival-ran to gates(DAT)
        English "He arrived at the gate at a run."

In this example, English shows how different sectors of usage within a single language—even where this involves only different individual concepts to be expressed—can behave differently with respect to the two principles set forth at the beginning of this section. Thus, Manner (here, 'running') can be expressed readily in a backgrounding constituent (the main verb) when in conjunction with the 'up to' Path notion. But it is forced into a foregrounding constituent (here, an adverb phrase) when in conjunction with the 'arrival' path notion, and so can be expressed only at greater cognitive cost.

At the general level again, we can extend the contrast between languages as to the quantity and types of information that they characteristically background, for as English is to Spanish, so Atsugewi is to English. Like English, Atsugewi can represent both Cause and Path in a backgrounded way in its verb complex. But further, it can backgroundedly represent the Figure and the Ground in its verb complex (as has already been shown). Take for example the polysynthetic form in (36b), approximately represented in (140) with its morphemes glossed and separated by dashes.

(140) (it)—from-wind-blowing—icky-matter-moved—into-liquid—Factual
         Cause . . . .]   Figure . . . .]   Path + Ground

We can try to match English sentences to this form in either of two ways: by achieving equivalence either in informational content or in backgroundedness. To achieve informational equivalence, the English sentence must include full independent noun phrases to express the additional two components that it cannot background—that is, the Figure and the Ground. These NPs can be accurate indicators of the Atsugewi referents, like the forms *some icky matter* and *some liquid* in (141a). Or, to equal the original form in colloquialness, the NPs can provide more specific indications that would be pertinent to a particular referent situation, like the forms *the guts* and *the creek* in (141b). Either way, the mere use of such NPs draws foregrounded attention to their contents. The representation of Cause and Path is not here at issue between the two languages, since both employ their means for backgrounding these components. Atsugewi backgrounds Cause in its Cause satellite and Path in its Path + Ground satellite, while English backgrounds Cause in the verb root (*blow*) and Path in its Path satellite (*in(to)*).

(141) a. Some icky matter blew into some liquid.
      b. The guts blew into the creek.

If, on the other hand, the English sentence is to achieve equivalence to the Atsugewi form in *backgroundedness* of information, then it must drop the full NPs or change them to pronouns, as in (142).

(142) It blew in.

Such equivalence in backgrounding, however, is only gained at the cost of forfeiting information, for the original Atsugewi form additionally indicates that the 'it' is an icky one and the entry is a liquid one. Thus, due to the quantity and semantic character of its satellites, as well as the semantic character of its verb root, Atsugewi can, with relatively fine differentiation, express more of the components of a Motion event at a backgrounded level of attention than English is able to do.[64]

5 CONCLUSION

The principal result of this chapter has been the demonstration that semantic elements and surface elements relate to each other in specific patterns, both typological and universal. The particular contributions of our approach have included the following.

First, the chapter has demonstrated the existence and nature of certain semantic categories such as 'Motion event', 'Figure', 'Ground', 'Path', 'Co-event', 'Precursion', 'Enablement', 'Cause', 'Manner', 'Personation', and so on, as well as syntactic categories such as 'verb complex', 'satellite', and 'satellite preposition'.

Second, most previous typological and universal work has treated languages' lexical elements as atomic givens, without involving the semantic components that comprise them. Accordingly, such studies have been limited to treating the properties that such whole forms can manifest, in particular, word order, grammatical relations, and case roles. On the other hand, most work on semantic decomposition has not involved crosslinguistic comparison. The present study has united both concerns. It has determined certain semantic components that comprise morphemes and assessed the crosslinguistic differences and commonalities that these exhibit in their patterns of surface occurrence. Thus, instead of determining the order and roles of words, this study has addressed semantic components, as they appear at the surface, and has determined their presence, their site (i.e., their "host" constituent or grammatical relation), and their combination within a site.

Third, this method of componential crosslinguistic comparison permits observations not otherwise feasible. Section 4 demonstrated this for the issue of information's "salience." Former studies of salience have been limited to considering only whole lexical items and, hence, only their relative order and syntactic roles—and, appropriate to these alone, have arrived at such notions as topic, comment, focus, and old and new information for comparison across languages. But the present method can, in addition, compare the foregrounding or backgrounding of incorporated semantic components according to the type of surface site in which they show up. It can then compare the systemic consequence of each language's selection of such incorporations.

Fourth, our tracing of surface occurrence patterns has extended beyond treating a single semantic component at a time, to treating a concurrent set of components (as with those comprising a Motion event and its Co-event). Thus, the issue for us has not just taken the form: semantic component 'a' shows up in surface constituent 'x' in language '1' and shows up in constituent 'y' in language '2'. Rather, the issue has also taken the form: with semantic component 'a' showing up in constituent 'x' in language '1', the syntagmatically related components 'b' and 'c' show up in that language in constituents 'y' and 'z', whereas language '2' exhibits a different surface arrangement of the same full component set. That is, this study has been concerned with whole-system properties of semantic-surface relations.

Fifth, the meaning-form patterns revealed by the present approach can be seen to exhibit certain diachronic shifts or nonshifts in the history of a language. We can trace the ways in which the semantic componential makeup of certain classes of morphemes in the language changes in correlation with alterations in the syntactic patterns that bring the morphemes together in sentences.

Finally, the present approach suggests cognitive structures and processes that underlie the newly posited semantic and syntactic categories, the semantic composition of morphemes and its correlation with syntactic structure, the typologies and universals of meaning-form correlations, and the shifts that these undergo.

Notes

1. This chapter is a much revised and expanded version of Talmy (1985b). The compendium of meaning-form associations that had been included in Talmy (1985b) now appears, somewhat revised, in chapter II-2, together with further analyses of material otherwise presented in the present chapter.

Grateful acknowledgement is here extended to several people for their native-speaker help with languages cited in this chapter: to Selina LaMarr for Atsugewi (the language of the author's fieldwork studies), to Mauricio Mixco and Carmen Silva for Spanish, to Matt Shibatani and to Yoshio and Naomi Miyake for Japanese, to Vicky Shu and Teresa Chen for Mandarin, to Luise Hathaway, Ariel Bloch, and Wolf Wölck for German, to Esther Talmy and Simon Karlinsky for Russian, to Tedi Kompanetz for French, to Soteria Svorou for Greek, to Gabriele Pallotti for Italian, and to Ted Supalla for American Sign Language.

In addition, thanks go to several people for data from their work on other languages: to Haruo Aoki for Nez Perce, to Ariel Bloch for Arabic, to Wallace Chafe for Caddo, to Donna Gerdts for Halkomelem, to Terry Kaufman for Tzeltal, to Robert Oswalt for Southwest Pomo, to Ronald Schaefer for Emai, to Martin Schwartz for Greek, to Bradd Shore for Samoan, and to Elissa Newport and Ursula Bellugi for American Sign Language—as well as to several others whose personal communications are acknowledged in the text. The author has supplied the Yiddish forms, while the Latin data are from dictionaries. Special thanks go to Tim Shopen for his invaluable editorial work with earlier drafts of this chapter. And thanks as well to Melissa Bowerman, Dan Slobin, Johanna Nichols, Joan Bybee, Ed Hernandez, Eric Pederson, and Kean Kaufmann for fruitful discussions.

2. A zero form in a language can represent a meaning not expressed by any actual lexical item. For example, no German verb has the general 'go' meaning of the zero form cited. *Gehen* refers to walking, so that one could not ask *Wo wollen Sie denn hingehen?* of a swimmer.

3. Chapter I-1 argues that the referents of the closed-class forms of a language constitute its basic conceptual structuring system. Accordingly, the significance of the fact that the set of semantic categories presented here are also expressed by the

closed-class satellite form is that these categories are therefore part of the basic structuring system of a language.

4. Apart from these three processes, an analyst can sometimes invoke what we might term *semantic resegmentation*. Consider the case of *shave* as used in (vi):

(i)   I cut John.

(ii)   I shaved John.

(iii) I cut myself.

(iv)   I shaved myself.

(v)   *I cut.

(vi)   I shaved.

We could believe that a reflexive meaning component is present in (vi) due to any of the three processes just described: because it is lexicalized in the verb, deleted from the sentence, or to be inferred by pragmatics. However, we only need to assume that a reflexive meaning is present if we consider this usage to be derived from that in (ii)/(iv). We could, alternatively, conclude that the (vi) usage is itself basic and refers directly to a particular action pattern involving a single person, with no reflexive meaning at all.

5. These forms express universal semantic elements and should not be identified with the English surface verbs used to represent them. They are written in capitals to underscore this distinction.

6. Our Figure is essentially the same as Gruber's (1965) "theme," but Gruber, like Fillmore, did not abstract out a semantic form like our Ground. Langacker's (1987) "trajector" and "landmark" are highly comparable to our Figure and Ground and, specifically, his landmark has the same abstractive advantages that Ground does over the systems of Gruber and Fillmore.

7. The term **Co-event** is now used as a replacement for the term "supporting event" that was employed in Talmy (1991).

8. This proposed association between a component incorporated in the verb and an external constituent can be lexicosyntactic as well as semantic. For example, in its basic usage, the intransitive verb *choke* in English distinctively requires the preposition *on* in the constituent that names the object that causes obstruction, as in (a), unlike many other languages, which require an instrumental *with*-type preposition. But this lexicosyntactic requirement for *on* is retained in the second usage of *choke* that additionally incorporates a change-of-state concept of 'becoming', as in (b). Our interpretation is that this second usage derives from the first usage, where the peculiar prepositional requirement is based. These relationships are shown explicitly in (26a).

(a) He choked on a bone.

(b) He choked to death on a bone.

9. In the verbs treated so far that exhibit both type 1 and type 2 usages—like *float* or *kick*—the type 1 usage has been lexically basic, while the type 2 usage is built on that by the addition of a component of translational motion. In this regard consider the two verbs *jump* and *run*, which can both refer to propelling one's

body through pedal launches. *Jump* appears to behave as just described with respect to basicness. Used without further spatial reference, as in *I jumped*, it exhibits a type 1 usage, referring solely to an act of pedally launching oneself into the air (and perhaps also returning to the ground). In turn, it can add an increment of translational motion in a type 2 usage, as in *I jumped along the hallway*. By contrast, *run* appears to be basically lexicalized in the type 2 usage since, when used without further spatial reference, as in *I ran*, the only interpretation is that I moved along through space, propelling myself through alternating pedal launches. To obtain a type 1 sense, one must add a phrase like that in *I ran in place*. This type 1 sense would seem to be derived from the type 2 sense by a semantic process of "cutting back" on the basic meaning—what is termed "resection" in chapter II-3.

10. As with many alternative linguistic descriptions, each of the present two approaches handles some aspects of language better and some worse. To illustrate the latter, this chapter's lexical analysis strains our intuition when it treats the three uses of *reach* in (28) as distinct lexicalizations. On the other hand, the construction analysis cannot easily account for verbs like *lie* in (17) that refuse occurrence in a motion construction, nor verbs like *glide* in (18) that require a motion construction. Here, nothing is saved with a construction analysis since the individual lexical verbs would in any case need to be marked as to which constructions they can occur in. Further, nothing in the construction analysis explains why English cannot use the motion construction to represent reverse enablement as German can (see (27c)), nor the under-fulfillment, over-fulfillment, and anti-fulfillment relations as Mandarin can (see II-3 (51)–(53)), nor a relation like that in 'He sat/lay to the hospital' to mean "He drove/rode lying on a stretcher to the hospital" as Arrerndte can (David Wilkins, personal communication).

11. To be sure, under a finer granularity, self-contained Motion resolves into translational motion. Thus, in the upward phase of its bounce cycle, the ball translates from the floor to a point in midair. And in the course of half a rotation, a point on the log translates from one end to the other of an arc. But such local translations cancel each other out within the broader scope of a coarser granularity.

12. As shown at length in chapter II-3, three further metaphoric extensions are from motion to "temporal contouring," to "action correlating," and to "realization."

13. In chapter II-3, the relations that a Co-event can bear to a main event are termed "support relations," and they are treated there in a much broader theoretical context. In addition, a distinct set of semantic relationships between a Co-event verb and a framing satellite are described in section 7 of chapter II-3. Included among those relationships—which, unlike the ones here, are borne by the satellite to the verb—are confirmation, fulfillment, underfulfillment, overfulfillment, and antifulfillment.

14. Reverse enablement does not exist as a construction type in English. What might at first be taken to exemplify this type, verbs with the prefixal satellite *un-*, in fact do not do so. Rather, the satellite *un-*, as in *untie*, directly refers to the

process of reversal per se. It does not refer to the main Motion event, as does the German satellite *auf-* '[MOVE] to an open conformation'.

15. As an index of their generality, the different types of Co-event relations are found as well in verbs not based on a Motion event. Purpose, for example, is conflated in the English verbs *wash* and *rinse* (see chapter II-3). These verbs, beyond referring to certain actions involving the use of liquid, indicate that such actions are undertaken *in order to* remove dirt or soap. Evidence for such an incorporation is that the verbs are virtually unable to appear in contexts that pragmatically conflict with Purpose

(i) I washed/rinsed the shirt in tap water/*in dirty ink.

whereas otherwise comparable verbs like *soak* and *flush*, which seem not to express any Purpose beyond the performance of the main action, *can* appear there:

(ii) I soaked the shirt in dirty ink/I flushed dirty ink through the shirt.

Further, Cause and Manner can be conflated as well in verbs that do not participate in the Motion system. For example, the English verb *clench* expresses (in one area of its usage) the curling together of the fingers of a hand specifically caused by internal (neuromotor) activity. No other cause can be compatibly expressed in conjunction with this verb:

(iii) a. My hand clenched into a fist from a muscle spasm/*from the wind blowing on it.
       b. I/*He clenched my hand into a fist.

By contrast, *curl up* expresses a main action similar to that of *clench*, but it incorporates no restrictions as to the cause of the action:

(iv) a. My hand curled up into a fist from a muscle spasm/from the wind blowing on it.
      b. I/He curled my hand up into a fist.

16. In more colloquial usage, the gerundive *flotando* would generally occur immediately after the verb, but for clarity it is here placed finally—also a possible, if more awkward, location.

Whether in a generic or polysemous way, the Spanish preposition *por* covers a range of Path types, each here glossed with its closest distinct English form.

17. The same semantic complex except with translocation of the Agent's body can be represented by the mid-level verb CARRY, which underlies the English verbs *carry, take*, and *bring*.

18. As with any deep morpheme, the form used to represent a particular deep preposition is not to be identified with any English lexical item. Several of the forms are in fact devised. Thus, ALENGTH is used to represent the basic concept of a path with full span over a bounded extent. Note that it may be necessary to subdivide the Vectors To and From into two types, one involving the concept of a discrete translocation and the other involving the concept of progression along a linear trajectory.

19. The Deictic is thus just a special choice of Vector, Conformation, and Ground, not a semantically distinct factor, but its recurrence across languages earns it structural status.

20. An exception to this characterization of Spanish is a somewhat limited construction, exemplified by *Venía/Iba entrando a la casa*, 'He was coming/going into the house'.

21. Chapter II-4 shows that Atsugewi presents a wholly different partitioning of semantic space—that one is on a different semantic landscape—than that of, say, familiar European languages. For example, Atsugewi wholly lacks verbs of 'object maneuvering' like English *hold, put* (in), *take* (out); *have, give* (to), *take* (from); *carry, bring* (to), *take* (to); *throw, kick, bat* (away); *push, pull* (along). The components of the semantic material expressed by such verbs are in Atsugewi variously omitted, or apportioned out over different constituent types, or expressed by the construction.

22. In English, the particular Paths occurring in this system appear to be virtually limited to the contact-forming 'into/onto' type. Exceptional, thus, is *quarry* '$_A$MOVE out of a quarry', as in *We quarried the granite*, and the verb *mine* with a similar sense, as in *We mined the bauxite*.

23. It may be a general tendency that languages with Path conflation for motion do not extend this conflation type to the locative and, like Spanish, there employ zero conflation. But this pattern is not universal. Halkomelem, a Salish language of Canada (Gerdts 1988), does indeed have a set of verb roots that conflate BE_{LOC} with particular sites.

And though perhaps rarely forming a characteristic system, the verbal expression of location + site is clearly under no prohibitory constraint. English, for one, has a number of incidental instances of such conflation—for example, *surround* ('be around'), *top* ('be atop'), *flank* ('be beside'), *adjoin, span, line, fill*, as in *A ditch surrounded the field, A cherry topped the dessert, Clothing filled the hamper*. It is just that such verbs seldom constitute the colloquial system for locative expression.

24. English is more consistent than Spanish—that is, has less of a split system than Spanish—in that it extends its pattern of Co-event conflation for motion events to locative situations as well. This is seen in constructions like *The painting lay on/stood on/leaned against the table*, although, like Spanish, English also has the zero-conflation construction with *be*, as in *The painting was on/against the table*.

25. In Emai, a path is construed as being either of two main types: a linear progression along a trajectory, or a discrete translocation to or from a point. After a Co-event-conflating main verb, the trajectory type of path is represented by one of the Path verbs, now serving as a satellite rather than as a main verb. The translocation type of path is represented by a system of nonverbal locative markers.

26. Position verbs can also occur in construction with the directionals. For example, the assumptive form of the verb referring to a 'crooked Figure' together with the directional for 'down' can mean 'after falling, for an object that is already crooked or that has become crooked in the process of falling to come to rest on a surface'. Note that Atsugewi has a semantically and syntactically comparable construction, as detailed in section 4.2.4 of chapter II-2. The main difference is

that the Tzeltal position verbs include the semantic component of 'coming to rest on a surface' in these constructions, whereas in Atsugewi, the verb roots that refer to (change of) shape lack such a component, and so enter constructions representing a greater range of translational events.

27. Here and in the other forms, there may tend to be this distinction between the two constructions: the Path verb suggest progression along a trajectory that leads to the Figure's final location, while the Path satellites suggest only its arrival at that final location. If such a semantic distinction does prove correct, it may be adjudged that Greek here does not have a parallel system after all, but rather a split system.

28. This is not to imply that a verb root always has exactly one basic aspect. A verb root can show a certain range of aspect, each manifesting in a different context. Thus, English *kneel* is one-way in *She knelt when the bell rang* and is steady-state in *She knelt there for a minute*.

29. These two grammatical forms—*keep -ing* and V_{dummy} *a [__ + Deriv]$_N$*—may be thought to trigger certain cognitive processes. Respectively, these are **multi-plexing** and **unit excerpting**. Such processes are discussed in chapter I-1.

30. Our representation of the self-agentive and the inducive types was shown in section 2.1.3.2.

31. Not only intransitive sentences can be autonomous. For example, *An acorn hit the plate* is autonomous. The requirement, rather, is that the sentence must not express a cause (as does *An acorn broke the plate*).

32. Arguments are given in chapters I-6 and II-6 why the resulting-event (b) form should be considered semantically more basic than the causing-event (c) form.

33. This impinging object is the Figure within the causing event, but it is the Instrument with respect to the overall cause-effect situation. That is, for this author "Instrument" is not a basic notion, as it is, say, for Fillmore (1977). It is a derived notion, to be characterized in terms of other, more basic notions: the Instrument of a cause-effect sequence is the Figure of the causing event.

34. The act of will is the first link in the causal chain. Through internal (neuro-motor) activity, it brings about the movement of the body. Note that such bodily motion, even when not referred to, is a necessary link for a final physical event. Thus, while *Sue burnt the leaves* only mentions Sue as the initiator and the leaves' burning as the final event, we must infer not only that fire was the immediate Instrument but also that Sue (due to her will) acted physically to marshal it. The typical omission of explicit reference to all the causal subevents in the chain between an initiator and a final subevent are treated at length in chapter I-4.

35. To describe this more analytically: something acts on a sentient entity, causing within it the intention to carry out an act. The intention in turn leads to its actually carrying out the act, in the usual manner of agency. Thus, the entity is caused to act as an Agent. Thus, another good term for the "inducive" is "caused agency" (other treatments use the term "instigative"). See chapter I-8.

36. A semantic and constructional parallelism can be observed here. Shifting one's attention from an autonomous construction to a homologous agentive construction (as from *The ball rolled away* to *I rolled the ball away*) involves a shift from an intransitive to a transitive, and the semantic addition of agency. Similarly, going from a self-agentive construction to a homologous inducive construction (as from *The horse walked away* to *I walked the horse away*) involves a shift from intransitive to transitive and the addition of a further agency. The following sentences illustrate all four constructions while using the same participants:

(i)   Inducive: They sent the drunk out of the bar.

(ii) Self-agentive: The drunk went out of the bar.

(iii) Agentive: They threw the drunk out of the bar.

(iv) Autonomous: The drunk sailed out of the bar.

The semantic character of the former relationship seems to get imputed to the latter relationship. Thus, we tend to understand a self-agentive event as occurring in and of itself, and to take the inducer of an inducive event as directly bringing about the final event without the intermediary volition of the actor. This semantic imposition is termed the cognitive process of "physicalization" in chapter I-7, and the backgrounding of the intermediary agent in the inducive is treated at length in chapter I-4.

37. Verbs that range over two lexicalization types can be used either with or without a grammatical augment for the *same* meaning. We see this for *hide* over the agentive and self-agentive types, and for *set . . . upon* over the self-agentive and inducive types:

(i)   She hid herself behind the bushes = She hid behind the bushes

(ii) He had his dogs set upon (i.e., fall upon) us = He set his dogs upon us

38. For these, the three aspect-causative types we have noted for verbs of state have the following particular manifestation: (1) a body or object is in a posture noncausatively, or else an animate being self-agentively maintains its body in the posture; (2) a body or object comes into a posture noncausatively, or else an animate being self-agentively gets its body into the posture; (3) an agent puts a body other than its own, or some other object, into a posture.

39. The stative usage of the last two verbs here may not be immediately obvious. It can be seen in the following:

(i)   She bent over the rare flower for a full minute.

(ii) He bowed before his queen for a long minute.

40. The pattern we are concerned with here held better in older forms of English. Thus, the idea of agent derivation for the verb is quite questionable for modern English. But enough of the pattern remains to serve as illustration and to represent languages that do have such forms clearly. Among these latter are apparently many Uto-Aztecan languages (Wick Miller, personal communication) and Halkomelem.

41. This use of the reflexive is a special grammatical device, not a semantically motivated one, because there is no way to construe the normal meaning of the reflexive in this context. Normally, the reflexive entails that exactly what one would do to another, one does to oneself. In the present case, what one does to another is to place one's arms around his or her body, lift, and set down. But that is clearly not what one does with oneself. The movement is accomplished, rather, by internal—that is, neuromuscular—activity.

42. This suffix in Spanish generally incorporates a passive meaning (unlike the otherwise comparable Japanese *-te*, which has no voice characteristics). However, the present construction, as in *estaba acostado*—which might be taken literally as 'I was laid-down'—will generally be understood with a nonpassive reading, as in the sentence gloss 'I lay (there)'.

43. The postures category treated in the preceding is mostly nonrelational. One can largely determine a body's configuration by observing it alone. But the 'positions' category is relational. It involves the position assumed by one object with respect to another (especially where the latter provides support). Some position notions that are frequently found lexicalized in verbs across languages are 'lie on', 'stand on', 'lean against', 'hang from', 'stick out of', 'stick/adhere to', 'float on (surface)', 'float/be suspended in (medium)', 'be lodged in', '(clothes) be on', 'hide/ be hidden (from view) + Loc. The postures and positions categories may have no clear boundary between them or may overlap. But these heuristic classes, in some version, do seem to be treated differently in many languages.

44. English may have a few instances where a lexical item, unlike *hide*, can participate in expressions for all three state relations, including state departure:

(i)   She *stood* there speaking.

(ii) She *stood up* to speak.

(iii) She *stood down* when she had finished speaking.

45. Constructions with *stop*—for instance, *stop being sick* and *stop someone from being sick*—are not counted because, in them, *stop* operates on an already verbal construction with *be*, rather than directly on the adjective *sick* itself.

46. The qualifier "prototypical" has here been applied to the syntactic form of a sentence because of certain hedges that one might want to allow for. For example, the sentence *I took a nap* is formally transitive (and for some speakers can passivize, as in *Naps are taken by the schoolchildren in the afternoon*). But some might still want to treat this sentence as intransitive, both on semantic grounds and on the basis of its kinship to the formally intransitive sentence *I napped*. In the other direction, the sentence *I pounded on the table* is formally intransitive. But some might still want to treat it as transitive, both on the semantic grounds that it refers to an affected object outside the actor and on the basis of its kinship with the formally transitive sentence *I pounded the table*. The semantic basis of such alternative judgments is precisely addressed by the personation envelope.

47. For this section, the earlier limitation to single-morpheme verbs has been relaxed. Considered here, thus, are a lexical complex like *rip off* and, later, a mor-

phemically complex verb like *frighten*. This is feasible because valence properties can inhere in morphemic complexes of this sort as well as in single roots.

48. The final genitive expression here would now be only literary. However, other verbs take a colloquial *mit* phrase containing the Figure:

(i) a. Ich warf faule Äpfel auf ihn.
    "I threw rotten apples at him."
b. Ich bewarf ihn mit faulen Äpfeln.
    "I pelted him with rotten apples."

(ii) a. Ich schenkte ihm das Fahrrad.
    "I "presented" the bicycle to him."
b. Ich beschenkte ihn mit dem Fahrrad.
    "I "presented" him with the bicycle."

49. In the official terminology adopted in the present work—used, for example, in chapter I-2—the two main entities in an experiential situation are the "Experiencer" and the "Experienced." The Experiencer can emit a "Probe" toward the Experienced, while the Experienced can emit a "Stimulus" toward the Experiencer. In this section, though, for ease in distinguishing the two main experiential entities at a glance, we loosely use the word "Stimulus" in place of "Experienced."

50. The two valence types here pertain not only to verbs but also to adjectival and larger constructions that express affect. Thus, the expressions italicized in (i) can be used only with the case-frame surround shown for them:

(i) a. *Stimulus as subject*
    That *is odd to* me.
    That *is of importance to* me.
    That *got the goat of me* → *got my goat*.
b. *Experiencer as subject*
    I *am glad about* that.
    I *am in fear of* that.
    I *flew off the handle over* that.

51. English used to favor Stimulus-subject even more than it does now, but a number of verbs have shifted their valence type. For example, the affect verbs *rue* and *like*—as well as the sensation verb *hunger* and the cognition verb *think*—used to take the Experiencer as grammatical object but now take it as subject.

52. These lists avoid verbs that refer more to an affect-related action than to the affect itself. For example, *quake* and *rant*—candidates for the Experiencer-subject group—really refer directly to the subject's overt actions, and only imply his or her accompanying affect of fear or anger. Similarly, *harass* and *placate*—potentially Stimulus-subject verbs—refer more to the activities of an external Agent than to the resultant state of irritation or calm in the Experiencer.

53. This arrangement applies as well to verbs of sensation. Thus, 'be cold' is lexicalized from the point of view of the Experiencer feeling the sensation. *-Ahẃ* is added for the perspective of the Stimulus object rendering the sensation:

(i) *Verb root*   -yi:sḱap-   'feel cold'
    Inflectional affix set   s- '- w- -ᵃ   'I–subject, factual mood'
    /s-'-w-yi:sḱap-ᵃ/ ⇒ [sẇye·sḱápʰ]
    "I am cold (i.e., feel cold)."

(ii) *Verb root*   -yi:sḱap-   'feel cold'
     Valence-shifting suffix -ahẇ   'from Stimulus to Experiencer'
     Inflectional affix set   '- w- -ᵃ   '3rd person–subject', factual mood'
     /'-w-yi:sḱap-ahẇ-ᵃ ⇒ [ẇye·sḱapáhẇa]
     "It is cold (i.e., to the touch)."

54. There appears to be a universal tendency toward satellite formation: elements with certain types of meaning tend to leave the locations in a sentence where they perhaps logically belong and move into the verb complex. This tendency, whose extreme expression is polysynthesis, is also regularly evident in smaller degrees. A familiar example is that of quantifier floats. Examples in English are the "floats" of negative and other emphatic modifiers on nouns that parallel quantifier floats:

(i)   **Not* JOAN hit him ⇒ JOAN did*n't* hit him.

(ii) *Even* JOAN hit him ⇒ JOAN *even* hit him.

(iii) Joan gave him *only* ONE ⇒ Joan *only* gave him ONE.

55. Some Path expressions generally do not permit omissions of this sort. Such is the case with *into* in the sense of 'collision' and also with *up to* in the sense of 'approach' (although some contexts do allow *up* alone):

(i)   It was too dark to see the tree, so he walked into it (*... walked in).

(ii) When I saw Joan on the corner, I walked up to her (*... walked up) (but acceptable is: When I saw Joan on the corner, I walked up and said "Hi").

56. When they do not take a Path satellite, Russian verbs of motion exist in pairs of distinct forms, traditionally termed the "determinate" form and the "indeterminate" form. Examples of such paired forms are 'walk': *idti/xodit*'; 'drive': *yexat'/yezdit*'; and 'run': *bežat'/begat*'. Semantically, each form of a pair has a cluster of usages distinct from that of the other form. But it may be adjudged that the main semantic tendency of the determinate cluster is comparable to the meaning of the English satellite *along*, as in *I walked along*, and that of the indeterminate form is comparable to the meaning of the English satellite *about* (in the sense of 'all about/all around'), as in *I walked about*. It can also be observed that the set of prefixal Path satellites in Russian lacks forms semantically comparable to these two English satellites. Accordingly, one interpretation of the motion verb pairs in Russian is that they represent the conflation of a deep MOVE or GO verb with a deep satellite ALONG or ABOUT (as well as with a Manner event). Such verb pairs are thus, in effect, suppletive extensions of the prefixal Path satellites.

57. There is some dialectal variation. For example, *with* is only a preposition in some dialects, but in others it is also a satellite, as in *Can I come with?* or *I'll take it with*.

58. Judging from their distribution, satellites of this type seem to be an areal phenomenon rather than a genetic one. Thus, Atsugewi and Klamath, neighbor-

ing but unrelated languages, both have extensive suffixal systems of these satellites. But the Pomo languages, related to Atsugewi and sharing with it the extensive instrumental prefix system (see section 3.5), quite lack Path + Ground satellites.

59. This typology has served in several other lines of research—for example, that seen in Choi and Bowerman (1991) and that in Berman and Slobin (1994). Slobin (1996) has uncovered correlates of the present sentence-level typology within larger stretches of discourse.

60. Gabriele Pallotti (personal communication) reports that southern Italian dialects have a Path conflation pattern, that northern dialects have a Co-event conflation pattern, and that central dialects, including standard Italian, have both patterns in parallel, with discourse factors determining the pattern used. Thus, Neapolitan has *ascire, trasere, sagliere, scinnere* 'exit, enter, ascend, descend', but forms like **'nna fuori* 'go out' are impossible. In Northern Italy, the opposite holds. The Bolognese dialect, for example, has *ander fora, ander dainter, ander so, ander zo* 'go out, go in, go up, go down'. But there are no verbs with the meanings 'exit, enter, ascend, descend'. And standard Italian has both patterns. Thus, it has *uscire, entrare, salire, scendere* 'exit, enter, ascend, descend', and *andare fuori/dentro/su/giú* 'go out/in/up/down'. Further, both these patterns represent Manner in their usual respective way. Thus, Manner appears as a separate gerund in the Path conflating forms—for example, *é uscita/entrata/salita/scesa correndo* 'she entered/exited/ascended/descended while running'. And Manner appears in the main verb in the Coevent-conflating forms—for instance, *é corsa fuori/dentro/su/giú* 'she ran out/in/up/down'.

What remains to be determined diachronically is whether the Co-event conflation pattern in the northern and central dialects was retained from Latin and accompanied by the development of a new Path satellite system, or whether the Co-event conflation pattern is a later development (in effect, a return to the Latin pattern), accompanied by the loss of the Path conflation system in the northern dialects. In either case, the processes of the Co-event-conflating Germanic languages just to the north may have been an influencing factor.

61. Though this may remove some of Atsugewi's mystique, notice that the German satellite *entgegen-* also has the 'in going to meet' meaning, as in *entgegenlaufen* 'run to meet'. And Latin *ob-* parallels Atsugewi *-ikc* still further in having both the 'meeting' and the 'passage-blocking' meanings, as in *occurrere* 'run to meet' and *obstruere* 'build so as to block off'.

62. Such formulas might usually present a satellite construction in a nonagentive format. But they are readily adapted to an agentive presentation:

(i)   A ... F ◂through> G

(ii) A ... G ◂through (with> F)

Such finer formulations can be useful in representing language particularities. Thus, English in fact lacks the (132b) construction and only has its agentive (ii) counterpart.

63. Slobin (1996) has further observed that verb-framed languages like Spanish not only express Manner less readily than satellite-framed languages like English, but that they also have fewer distinct lexical verbs for expressing distinctions of Manner. The four principles posited here do not account for this phenomenon, so further explanation must be sought.

64. The Atsugewi polysynthetic verb can background still more: Deixis and four additional nominal roles—Agent, Inducer, Companion, and Beneficiary. However, Deixis is distinguished only as between 'hither' and 'hence', and the nominal roles only as to person and number or, in certain circumstances, merely their presence in the referent situation. (See Talmy 1972.)

Chapter 2

Surveying Lexicalization Patterns

1 INTRODUCTION

Using different perspectives and scopes, the three sections that follow in this chapter survey the material that was presented in chapter II-1.[1] The first two sections below employ a crosslinguistic scope, while the last section surveys material within a single language. In particular, section 2 tabularizes and augments the meaning-form associations described in chapter II-1. An analysis of this sort will be necessary for the goal within cognitive semantics of determining the patterns in which conceptual content is structured for the language system. Section 3 summarizes the typological and universal findings of chapter II-1. This summary, containing 67 entries, sets forth the findings in that chapter as a significant contribution to typological and universalist research. And section 4 lays out and exemplifies the system of Cause and related satellites in Atsugewi, which played a major role in the development of the theoretical framework of chapter II-1. This comprehensive treatment may be especially useful since a morphological system of this sort is relatively rare in the languages of the world.

2 COMPENDIUM OF MEANING-FORM ASSOCIATIONS

The investigation of meaning-form associations carried out in chapter II-1 is only a beginning. Among further endeavors, it calls for a thorough crosslinguistic determination of which semantic categories are represented with what frequencies by which surface constituents. For cognitive linguistics, the purpose of this endeavor will be to let us discern the patterns in which conceptual content is structured by the language system. The fine-grained cataloging thus called for is initiated here in a more modest

Table 2.1
Which semantic categories are expressed by which verb-complex elements

Semantic categories	Expressed within the verb-complex by		
	Verb root	Satellite	Inflections
A. Main event			
1. main action/state	+	[+/−]	−
B. Co-event			
2. Cause	+(M)	+	[±]
3. Manner	+(M)	+	−
4. Precursion, Enablement, …	+(M)	(+)	−
5. Result	−	[−/+]	−
C. Components of a Motion event			
6. Figure	+(M)	+	[−]
7. Path	+(M)	+	−
8. Ground alone	(+)	+	[−]
7 + 8. Path + Ground	+(M)	+	−
D. Essential qualities of the event (and of its participants)			
9. *hedging	−	[−]	−
10. ×degree of realization	[−]	(+)	−
11. polarity	+	+	+
12. phase	+	+	[±]
13. aspect	+	+	+
14. ×rate	[−]	[±]	−
15. causativity	+	+	−
16. personation	+	+	[±]

17. number in an actor	+	[±]	+
18. distribution of an actor	+	+	[−]
19. *symmetry/*color . . . of an actor	−	−	−
E. Incidental qualities of the event or its participants			
20. *relation to comparable events	−	−	−
21. ×locale (qualitative spatial setting)	[±]	(+)	−
22. ×period (qualitative temporal setting)	(+)	(+)	−
23. ×status of the actors	(+)	−	−
24. gender/class of an actor	[−]	+	+
F. Relations of the referent event or its participants to the speech event or its participants			
25. path deixis (deictic spatial direction)	+(M)	+	−
26. *site deixis (deictic spatial location)	[−]	[−]	[−]
27. tense (deictic temporal location)	−	[−]	+
28. person	−	[±]	+
−relations to the speaker's cognitive state (namely, to the speaker's−)			
29. valence/voice (−attention)	+	+	+
30. factivity/evidentiality (−knowledge)	(+)/+	+	+
31. attitude (−attitude)	+	+	−
32. mood (−intent)	−	+	+
−relations to the speaker-hearer interaction			
33. speech-act type	(+)	+	+
G. Qualities of the speech event			
34. status of the interlocutors	[±]	+	+
H. Factors pertaining neither to the referent event nor to the speech event			
35. *speaker's state of mind, *yesterday's weather, . . . ,	−	−	−

format in table 2.1 and in the annotations that follow in section 2.2. Included here are the meaning-form occurrence patterns presented in chapter II-1. But these are here augmented so as to further include a number of additional semantic categories as well as one additional verb-complex constituent beyond the verb root and satellite, namely, verbal inflections.

While the table's indications are based only on the author's linguistic experience and must be amplified by a thorough cross-language survey, such a survey might nevertheless lead to very few major upsets. For if a language comes to attention with a meaning-form association formerly thought nonexistent, that association will likely be rare. If the table's discrete plus/minus indications are then simply converted to frequency indications, these will exhibit roughly the same pattern as before.

Given such an array, the major issue to be addressed next, of course, is whether the array shows any regular patterns and, if so, what factors might explain them. The data at hand here suggest only partial regularities and, in fact, there are exceptions to every explanatory factor considered. (See Bybee 1980, 1985, for work on related issues.) However, answers may emerge in the future as more pieces come into place

- with the inspection of more languages
- with a more principled determination of which surface forms are to be considered satellites and how these are to be distinguished from other verb-complex constituents
- with the inclusion of the remaining verb-complex constituents such as adverbial particles and auxiliaries (some of table 2.1's semantic categories that are not represented in the root, satellite, or inflections—for example, 'hedging' and 'spatial location'—*are* in fact represented in other verb-complex constituents)
- with the consideration of further semantic categories and the remaining sentence constituents

2.1   Table of Semantic Categories and Their Expression

Symbols used in Table 2.1

+   This semantic category shows up in this surface constituent either in many languages or with great elaboration in at least a few languages.

(+)   This category shows up in this constituent in only a few languages, and there with little elaboration.

–   This category does not show up in this constituent in any languages known to the author, and may possibly never do so.

+/–   This category shows up in this constituent in one capacity or by one interpretation, but not another, as explained in the annotations that follow.

[ ]   There is some question about this assignment of + or –, as explained in the annotations that follow.

×   This category has only slight representation in the verb-complex constituents treated here.

*   This category is possibly never expressed in the verb-complex constituents treated here.

(M)   This category can join alone with the 'fact-of-Motion' category in the verb root and there forms an elaborated system for the expression of Motion events. (The category may also be able to show up in the verb root in other capacities.)

2.2 Brief Descriptions and Illustrations of Semantic Categories

In the following annotations, (a), (b), and (c) refer to the categories' occurrence in verb roots, satellites, or inflections, respectively.

1. *Main Action/State.*
   a. This semantic category—which includes motion and locatedness—is the one most identified with the verb root. It is joined there by the other categories given a "+" in column (a). Thus, in *kill*, agent causativity (no. 15) joins the main action of 'dying' and, in *lie*, a Manner notion (no. 3), 'with a horizontal supported posture', joins the main state of 'being located'.
   b. But there may be an exception to the preceding. By the interpretation favored here for the resultative construction in Indo-European and Chinese languages, the satellite presents its expression of a resulting event as the main action or state, while the verb root, generally expressing a cause, presents this as a subordinate event. Thus, we consider English *melt/rust/rot away* to be best interpreted as meaning 'disappear [= ◀away] by melting/rusting/rotting' and German *sich er-kämpfen/-streiken* as meaning 'obtain [= ◀er-] (e.g., territory, wages) by battling/striking'. The alternative interpretation would consider the Result expressed by the satellite as the subordinate event

and the verb's Cause as the main one, with the reading of (say) *rust away* then taken to be 'rust with the result of disappearing'.

c. This category is not indicated by inflections.

2. *Cause*. This category refers to the qualitatively different kinds of causing events such as can be expressed by an English subordinate *from-* or *by*-clause. It is distinguished from causativity (no. 15), which corresponds to a superordinate clause of the type "NP CAUSES S."

   a. Cause is regularly incorporated in the verb roots of most Indo-European languages expressing either motion or other action. Thus, English *blow* in *The napkin blew off the table* means 'move from (due to) the air blowing on [it]'.

   b. Atsugewi has some two dozen prefixal satellites expressing cause, for example *ca-* 'from the wind blowing on [it]'.

   c. Causing-event types are generally not expressed in inflections. However, by one analysis, the distinct agentive and inducive inflections of some languages (e.g., Japanese) do indicate different causing events of the types: '[the Agent CAUSES S] by acting physically' versus '... by inducing another Agent (to act physically)'.

3. *Manner*. Manner refers to a subsidiary action or state that a Patient manifests concurrently with its main action or state.

   a. It is regularly incorporated in most Indo-European languages' verbs of Motion (as well as other kinds of action), as in English *float* in *The balloon floated into the church*, which means 'move, floating in the process'.

   b. Nez Perce has over two dozen prefixal satellites indicating Manner—for example, *ʔiyé·* 'floating in the process'.

   c. Manner is not indicated inflectionally.

4. *Precursion, Enablement, ...* In addition to a relation of Cause or of Manner, an associated event can bear any of a number of further relations to a main event. The additional relations discussed in the text are Precursion, Enablement, Concomitance, Consequence, and Purpose.

   a. In English, a Co-event with each of the relations cited above can be conflated with the verb in a Motion event. Thus, we have Precursion in *Glass splintered over the food*, Enablement in *I grabbed the bottle down off the shelf*, Concomitance in *She wore a green dress to the party*, Consequence in *They locked the prisoner into his cell*, and Purpose in *I'll stop down at your office on the way out of the building*. Events with these relations can also conflate with non-Motion-event verbs. Thus, Purpose is incorporated in *wash* 'apply liquid to, in order to clean' and in *hunt (I hunted deer)* 'search for, etc., in order to capture'.

  b. Purpose is expressed in 'benefactive' satellites (for example the Atsugewi suffix *-iray*), which have the meaning 'in order to benefit/give [it] to [the actor named by the direct object nominal]'.

  c. The relations from Precursion through Purpose are seemingly not expressed inflectionally.

5. *Result*. A causing event (no. 2) always has a resulting event paired with it because the two are conceived in terms of a single larger causal interaction.

  a. When both a causing event and a resulting event are expressed together in a verb root, as they can be, the question here is, which of them is taken as the main event and which as the subordinate event? Thus, in *I kicked the ball along the path*, does *kick* mean 'move by booting' with the Result as main event and Cause as subordinate, or instead 'boot with the result of moving', with the reverse ascriptions? We favor the former interpretation (the same as in no. 2). Thus, it may be that Result never incorporates in a verb root as a subordinate event (hence the "−" in table 2.1 in the (a) column), but only as a main event.

  b. In the resultative construction, Result *is* expressed in the satellite, in many languages with numerous distinctions. However, by the interpretation favored here and already discussed in no. 1(b), it appears there not as a subordinate event but as the main event. Our conclusion is that *all* incorporation of Result, whether in verb root or satellite, is as main event.

  c. Result is not expressed inflectionally.

6. *Figure*. The Figure is the salient moving or stationary object in a Motion event whose path or site is the relevant issue.

  a. It is systematically incorporated in Atsugewi's motion verb roots—for example, in *-i-* 'for a smallish planar object (shingle, button, stamp, etc.) to move/be located'. The occasional English examples include *rain (It rained in through the window)* 'for rain(drops) to fall'.

b. A set of Atsugewi prefixes, overlapping with the causal set, indicates Figures. A set of Caddo prefixes indicates Patient, which sometimes coincides with a Motion event's Figure.

c. Inflections do not represent the Figure qua Figure, but they can indicate properties of subject and object—grammatical roles in which the Figure often occurs.

7. *Path*. This category refers to the variety of paths followed or sites occupied by the Figure object in a Motion event.

a. It is a regular component in the Motion-verb systems of many language families—for example, Polynesian, Semitic, and Romance —as in forms like Spanish *entrar* 'move in', *salir* 'move out', *subir* 'move up', *bajar* 'move down', *pasar* 'move past/ through'.

b. Path is the main category expressed by the satellites of most Indo-European languages outside of Romance, as in English with forms like *in, out, up, down, past, through*.

c. Path is not indicated inflectionally.

8. *Ground*. The Ground is the reference object in a Motion event, with respect to which the Figure's path/site is characterized.

a. The Ground does not appear alone with the (fact of) Motion component in any language's most characteristic Motion verb-root system, but only in occasional forms, like English *(de-/em-)plane*, or in combination with additional components (see following paragraph 7 + 8).

b. A set of Atsugewi prefixes, overlapping with that for Causes, indicates various body-part Grounds—for example 'finger' or 'buttocks' as when used with a verb root meaning 'get a splinter'. A set of Caddo prefixes indicates Patient, which often coincides with a Motion event's Ground.

c. Inflections do not represent a Ground object per se but only insofar as it serves as a grammatical subject or object.

7 + 8. *Path + Ground*. The combination of Path and Ground is privileged in that it occurs more than other combinations of Motion event components (except for those with the 'fact of Motion' component itself) and certainly more than the Ground alone.

a. Many languages have a series of verb roots in which this combination joins with 'MOVE'—for example, English *berth* *(The ship berthed)* 'move into a berth' or causative *box* (I boxed the apples) 'cause-to-move into a box'.

b. Atsugewi has a major system of suffixal satellites that express some two-score instances of the Path + Ground combination—for example, *-ict* 'into a liquid'. English has a few examples, such as *aloft* 'into the air', *apart (They moved apart)* 'away from each other', and *home (I drove home)* 'to one's home'.

c. Inflections do not represent this combination.

9. *Hedging.* Among other functions, hedges qualify the categoriality of a linguistic element's referent. They are mostly indicated around verbs by adverbs or special expressions, like those in *He sort of danced/She danced after a fashion.*

a,b,c. However common they may be in that form, they are seemingly not incorporated in verb roots nor expressed by satellites or inflections. As possible exceptions, one may wish to consider as hedges such diminutivizing verb satellites as Atsugewi *-inkiy*, which changes 'to rain' into 'to drizzle'; or Yiddish *unter-*, which in *unter-ganvenen* changes 'to steal' into 'to pilfer a bit every now and then'.

10. *Degree of Realization.* This category divides a referent action or state—almost anywhere along its semantic continuum—into a more central core of essential aspects and a periphery of commonly associated aspects, and indicates that only one or the other of these is realized. Languages regularly indicate this with adverbs or particles near the verb—for example, English *almost* and *(just) barely*. Thus, *I almost ate it* can suggest lifting an item to the mouth and perhaps even inserting and chewing it but excludes at least the essential aspect of swallowing it. Conversely, *I just barely ate it* suggests getting an item down the gullet but without the usually attendant gusto in chewing and tasting.

a. It is doubtful that a genuine sense of 'almost' or 'barely' is ever really incorporated in a verb root. But perhaps coming close are forms like *falter* and *teeter*, as in *He teetered on the cliff edge*, which suggests 'almost falling'.

b. Atsugewi has a suffixal satellite *-iwt*, which indicates 'almost' in all the customary senses. It is the only such form known to the author.

c. This category is apparently not indicated inflectionally.

11. *Polarity.* Polarity is the positive or negative status of an event's existence.

a. Verb roots can incorporate polarity of two types. One type pertains to the root's own referent action/state—for example, as in English *hit* or *miss* (= not hit) *the target*. The other type pertains to the action/state of a complement clause. In the latter type, incorporated polarity has some of the same syntactic consequences as independent polarity elements (like *not*)—for instance, in requiring either *some* or *any:*

I managed to/ordered him to/suspect I'll -see someone/*anyone.
I failed to/forbade him to/doubt I'll -see anyone/*someone.

b. Cheyenne indicates the negative with a prefix *saa-* in its polyaffixal verb (Dan Alford, personal communication).

c. Some languages incorporate positive and negative in two distinct sets of inflections that otherwise indicate tense, mood, person, and so on. Thus, in one part of its verb paradigm, Tamil has separate positive and negative inflections for the future neuter.

12. *Phase.* Distinguished from aspect because of its different behavior, the category of 'phase' refers to changes in the status of an event's existence. The main member notions for any type of event are 'starting', 'continuing', and 'stopping'. Bounded events also have the phase notions of 'inaugurating' and 'finishing'. To exemplify the two notions of termination, *I stopped reading the book* refers to a change from reading to not reading at any point in the book, while *I finished reading the book* refers to reading *all* of the book, and only then not reading.

a. Phase notions can be incorporated in verb roots or collocations, as in *strike up* 'initiate the playing of [a tune]'—and, by one interpretation, also in *reach* (e.g., *reach the border*) 'finish going toward', *shut up* 'stop talking', and *halt* 'stop moving'. Phase notions can also appear as the sole meaning of a verb without the incorporation of further semantic referents, as in English *start, stop, finish.* Strikingly, the particular phase concept of 'stopping' can appear only in verbs—whether alone or with other semantic material—not as an auxiliary, satellite, or inflection.

b. Phase notions other than 'stopping' can be expressed by satellites. For example, 'finishing' is expressed by German *fertig-*, as in *fertig-bauen/-essen* 'finish building/eating' (or, more literally, 'build/eat to completion'). The concept of 'inaugurating' is expressed by German *an-*, as in *an-spielen* 'open play (e.g., at cards)' or *an-schneiden* 'make the initial cut in'. And 'starting' in the specific sense of 'bursting out' is expressed by Yiddish *tse* (+ *zikh*), as in *tse-lakh zikh* 'burst out laughing'.

c. Depending on the interpretation, phase either is or is not expressed in inflections. Thus, a preterite inflection seems to indicate stopping or finishing in conjunction with an unbounded or bounded event, as in *She slept/She dressed*. But it may be better interpreted as being basically a tense/aspect indicator, 'wholly occurring before now', that merely *implies* cessation. There is also the "inchoative" inflectional indication of 'entry into a state'—that is, 'becoming'—but it is not clear whether this should be classed together with 'starting'.

13. *Aspect.* Aspect is the pattern of distribution through time of an action or state.

   a. It is regularly incorporated in verb roots—for example, in English *hit*—which can refer to a single impact, as against *beat*, which indicates an iteration.

   b. It also appears frequently in satellites, as in the Russian prefixal system for indicating perfective/imperfective distinctions.

   c. It appears regularly in inflections as well, as in the Spanish conjugational forms indicating the preterite and imperfect.

14. *Rate.* Rate refers to whether an action or motion takes place faster or slower relative to some norm.

   a. Though some verb roots obviously indicate different rates of speed—for instance, the range from slow to neutral to fast is seen in the English verbs *trudge, walk, run* or *nibble, eat, bolt* (one's food)—languages seem to include them haphazardly and in conjunction with further semantic differences, rather than base a regular system of lexical distinctions on rate alone.

   b. Satellites generally appear not to indicate rate, with some potential exceptions: an Atsugewi suffix *-iskur*—which has the same form as an independent verb 'to hurry' and, with a verb root, was in elicitation always translated as 'hurry up and V'—might actually or additionally there mean 'V quickly'. Dyirbal (Dixon 1972) has a suffix *-nbal/-galiy* said to mean 'quickly' but only as part of a semantic range that also includes 'repeatedly', 'start', and 'do a bit more'. We have heard one report that Yana may have had affixes with precisely the meanings 'quickly' and 'slowly'.

   c. Rate is not indicated inflectionally.

15. *Causativity.* With the notions in this category, an event is conceived either as occurring by itself or as resulting from another event, where this latter event is either initiated by an agent or not, and such an agent is either intentional or not.

    a. Causative notions are regularly incorporated in verb roots. Thus, English *die* indicates only an event of death itself, while *murder* indicates that an intentional agent has initiated an action that has caused that event.

    b. As an example for satellites, the Yiddish prefix *far-* can be combined with a comparative adjective in a verb formation meaning 'to cause to become (more) [Adj]', as in *far-besern* 'to improve (transitive)', from *beser* 'better'. If the reflexive *zikh* can be considered a satellite, then it too is an example, for it changes a causative form into a noncausative: *farbesern zikh* 'to improve (intransitive)'.

    c. In Japanese, separate inflections indicate agent causation, inducive causation, and decausitivization.

16. *Personation.* Personation refers to the configuration of participants that an action is conceived to be associated with.

    a. Different languages' verb roots tend to incorporate different personation types. Thus, typical for French, the verb for 'comb the hair', *peign-*, intrinsically refers to one's doing the action to another (dyadic). The corresponding Atsugewi verb, *cu-spal̓*, refers to one's manifesting the action in oneself (monadic).

    b. Satellites can reverse a root's personation type. The Atsugewi benefactive suffix makes the 'comb' verb dyadic, and the French reflexive—considered here as a satellite—converts its verb to monadic.

    c. Inflections otherwise involved with causativity may also serve in switching personation types.

17. *Number in an Actor.* This is the numerosity of the participants—from one to many—behaving as any single argument of an event. It is listed under category "D" as an essential aspect of an event because such numerosity affects how the event is manifested.

    a. Many Amerindian languages have distinct roots for an action manifested by different numbers of Patients. Thus, the Southwest Pomo verb roots *-w/-ʔda/-pʰil* mean, respectively, 'for one/two or three/several together ... to go'. It is a possible universal that the Patient is the only semantic role characterized for number in the verb root.

    b. It is not clear whether satellites indicate number. The closest case known to the author is an Atsugewi dual verb clitic, *-hiy*.

    c. Inflections in many languages indicate the number of the subject nominal and sometimes also of the direct object nominal. Interestingly, inflectional indications of number seem always to be linked to a particular *syntactic* role, such as subject or object, while those in the verb root correlate instead with a *semantic* role, the Patient.

18. *Distribution of an Actor.* This refers to the arrangement of multiple Patients—whether they form an aggregate or a linear distribution in space and/or time (in the latter case correlating with aspect).

    a. Different distributions are incorporated systematically in certain Southwest Pomo roots: *-pʰil/-hayom* 'for several together/separately to go', *-hsa/-ʔkoy* 'act on objects as a group/one after another'.

    b. The Atsugewi suffix *-ayw* indicates 'one after another' for multiple Patients. Though less freely usable, the English satellite *off* can do the same: *read off/check off* (items on a list), (animals) *die off*.

    c. There is some indeterminacy as to whether a type of affix like Atsugewi's *-ayw* might not be better considered inflectional. Other than this, though, inflections seem not to indicate distribution.

19. *Symmetry, Color of an Actor.* Many characteristics of an event's participants are not marked anywhere in the verb complex, even though they seem as reasonable (from an a priori perspective) as the qualities that *are* marked. Thus, while an argument's numerosity and distribution can be marked, there will be no marking for its color or whether it has a symmetrical arrangement, even though these very qualities are important in other cognitive systems, such as visual perception.

20. *Relation to Comparable Events.* Many adverbial or particle forms indicate whether an action or state has occurred alone, or in addition to, or in place of another one of a comparable category, like the forms in English *He only danced/also danced/even danced/danced instead.* These notions, however, seem never to be expressed as satellites or inflections, or incorporated in the verb root.

21. *Locale* (qualitative spatial setting). This category pertains to the type of area or physical setting in which an event takes place.
    a. This category is not obviously conflated in verb roots. To exhibit it, a language would need to have distinct verb roots with meanings like 'to eat indoors' and 'to eat outdoors', or like 'to perish at sea' and 'to perish on land'.
    b. Kwakiutl has a small set of verb suffixes with meanings like 'in the house' and 'on the beach'. Klamath's locative suffixes may be an additional example, though these seem really more to indicate Ground than locale—that is, to indicate something more like *She hit him in the nose* (Ground) than *She hit him in the kitchen* (locale). The satellites in English *eat in/eat out* (suggested by Martin Schwartz) are perhaps a real, if limited, example.
    c. Locale is not expressed inflectionally.

22. *Period* (qualitative temporal setting). This category locates an event within a particular time period, especially a cyclic one.
    a. There may be small systems of verb roots differing principally as to temporal setting. Thus, English *to breakfast, brunch, lunch, sup/dine* could be interpreted as meaning 'to eat in the morning/late morning/midday/evening'.
    b. Yandruwandha verbs optionally take the suffixal satellites *-thalka* 'in the morning', *-nhina* 'by day', or *-yukarra* 'at night' (Bernard Comrie, public presentation). It is possible that only the day's cycle is ever thus represented and not, say, that of the month or year.
    c. Inflections appear not to indicate this category.

23. *Status of the Actors.* This refers to either absolute or relative social characteristics of the animate participants in a referent event (and does not pertain to the interlocutors of the speech event, which is treated below).
    a. Japanese verbs of giving differ according to the relative social rank of the giver and the receiver, and so incorporate status.
    b,c. Actors' status does not seem to appear in satellites or inflections.

24. *Gender/Class of an Actor.* This refers to category memberships based on sex or other characteristics and associated either with an event's actors themselves or with the nouns that refer to them.
    a. It appears that no verb roots are lexicalized specifically for use with nouns of a particular *grammatical* gender or class. Thus, for

example, Spanish could not have two different verbs for 'to fall', one for use with feminine-noun subjects and the other with masculines. While there do exist verb roots associated with nouns of a particular *semantic* gender (or various other properties), for example roots referring to pregnancy, the association seems less one of systematic categorial distinctions involving selectional features or the like than a matter of individual pragmatic applicability. Thus if a man were in fact to become pregnant, one could simply proceed to say 'The man is pregnant'.

b. The grammatical class of the subject and at times also the direct object noun is marked by affixal satellites in Bantu languages.

c. The subject's grammatical gender is indicated in the inflections in all Hebrew tenses and in the Russian past tense forms—for example, in *Pes layal/Sabaka layala* 'The hound barked/The dog barked'.

25. *Path Deixis* (deictic spatial direction). This refers to whether the Figure in a Motion event is moving toward the speaker or in some other direction.

a. It is found incorporated in verb roots, such as English *come/go* and *bring/take*.

b. It is frequently marked by satellites, like the pair in Atsugewi, *-ik·/-im*, and in Mandarin, ... *lái/* ... *qù*.

c. It is not marked inflectionally.

26. *Site Deixis* (deictic spatial location). This category would characterize the location of an event's occurrence with respect to the speaker or hearer (e.g., near or away from one or the other, in or out of their range of vision). It is readily indicated by adverbs or particles, such as English *here* and *there*. But it appears not to occur otherwise in the verb complex. As possible exceptions: We have heard a report that some Northwest Coast Amerindian languages have distinct verb roots meaning 'to be here' and 'to be there'. And the evidential satellites or inflections for visual versus other-sensory information, in Wintu as well as other languages, might be used for inferences about spatial deixis.

27. *Tense* (deictic temporal location). Like the preceding category, but for time instead of space, tense characterizes the temporal location of an event with respect to the moment of the speaker-hearer interaction.

a. By our interpretation, tense is not incorporated in verb roots. We consider a possible candidate such as English *went* not as a conflation of semantic 'go' + 'past' but as a suppletive form standing in the place of the morphemes *go* and *-ed*. The reason is that *went* can only appear in environments where other verb roots are followed by *-ed*. And if *went* genuinely incorporated a past sense, one might expect it to be used as well in expressions like **I am wenting* to mean 'I was going', or **I will went* to mean 'I will have gone'.

b,c. Tense is marked by affixes and particles (as well as auxiliaries) in many languages. It is not clear that any of these should be taken to be satellites; the affixes among them would normally be taken to be inflections.

28. *Person.* Person refers to the relation between an actor in a referent event and a participant in the speech event (i.e., the speaker or hearer). Thus, in English, if an actor is the same individual as the speaker, the form *I* is used; if the same as the hearer, *you*; and if neither, *he/she/it* or a full nominal is used.

a. No verb roots appear to be specific to a particular person. Distinct forms like English *am/is* invite the same objection as was raised for *went* above. Japanese verbs of giving, sometimes suggested as incorporating person, seem rather to basically indicate relative status, which in turn has certain canonic associations with personal arrangements. (Note that some *noun* roots do incorporate person—for example, the distinct Kikuyu nouns for 'my father', 'your father', and 'his father'.)

b. If clitics like Spanish *me/te* can be construed as satellites, this part of speech can be given a plus for person.

c. Person is notably indicated by inflections.

29. *Valence/Voice.* This category refers to the particular distribution of attention and perspective point that the speaker assigns to the different actors in an event when this factor is associated with the grammatical relations of the nouns referring to the actors. The two traditional terms for this category differ only in that 'voice' refers to the assignment when it is marked by inflections or auxiliaries and 'valence' otherwise.

a. The category is often incorporated in verb roots, like English *sell* and *buy*, which place the main perspective point at the giver and the receiver, respectively, for the same event.

b. The German satellite *ver-* redirects the main perspective onto the giver in an exchange, as in *ver-kaufen* 'sell' (vs. *kaufen* 'buy').

c. The category is frequently marked by inflections, as in Latin *emere* 'to buy' and *emi* 'to be bought'.

30. *Factivity/Evidentiality.* This category distinguishes the speaker's belief in, versus ignorance of, an event's truth. The two traditional terms, factivity and evidence, differ only as to whether this category is indicated in the verb root itself or outside it.

a. Only rarely, it seems, does a verb root indicate a speaker's state of knowledge as to its own referent event. One example might be English *be*, indicating speaker's certainty of a copular attribution, and *seem*, indicating uncertainty, as in *She was/seemed sad.* But many verbs do indicate state of knowledge pertaining to a *complement* event, as in *Jan (i) realized/(ii) concluded that she'd won:* (i) the speaker believes the winning to be factual, (ii) the speaker is noncommittal about its actuality.

b. Wintu has a set of 'evidential' suffixes, probably to be taken as satellites, that indicate whether the speaker knows for sure or infers an event, as well as the evidence by which he arrived at his knowledge or supposition (Schlicter 1986).

c. In Atsugewi, there are two distinct inflectional sets for the 'factual' and the 'inferential'.

31. *Attitude.* The category here is the speaker's attitude toward the referent event.

a. Attitude is incorporated in verb roots. For example, the verbs in *They raided/marauded the village* refer to roughly the same objective event, but *maraud* additionally indicates the speaker's attitude of disapproval toward the event. The negative attitudinal content of *traipse*, as compared (say) with *walk*, is evident from the leadingness of this question by a trial attorney: *Did you confirm that Ms. Burnett was traipsing around the restaurant?*

b. The Atsugewi suffixal satellite *-inkiy* indicates the speaker's 'cute' regard for the event. For example, with a root 'flap', it could be used to speak of baby ducklings moving their wings about.

c. Attitude seems not to be indicated inflectionally.

32. *Mood.* Mood refers to a speaker's feelings or intentions with respect to the actualization of an event. It includes a neutral regard, a wish for

(something unrealizable), a hope for (something realizable), a desire to (realize something), and an attempt at (realizing something).

    a.   It appears that no verb roots have an intrinsic mood to them. It might at first be thought that a verb like *want*, as in *She wants to go*, is desiderative, but it really only refers to the *actor's* desire, not to that of the speaker, whose mood toward this event is here neutral.

    b,c.   Many languages have affixes—whether taken as satellites or inflections—that indicate mood under terms like indicative, subjunctive, optative, desiderative, conative.

33. *Speech-Act Type.* This category indicates the speaker's intentions with respect to the hearer in referring to an event.

    a.   The vast majority of verb roots are neutral with respect to speech-event type. But a few verbs do incorporate a particular type—for example, the Halkomelem roots meaning 'to be where' and 'to go whither' are solely interrogative. And mainly imperative are the English forms *beware*, the collocation *be advised* (which does accommodate modals, but only with an imperative sense: *You should/*can be advised that ...*), and perhaps forms like *whoa, giddiyap, scat.*

    b,c.   The category is often marked by satellites and inflections. For example, Atsugewi has distinct inflectional paradigms for these speech-act types: declarative (I tell you that ...), interrogative (I ask you whether ...), imperative (I direct you to ...), admonitive (I caution you lest ...).

34. *Status of the Interlocutors.* Status is the same here as in no. 23 but refers to the participants of the speech event rather than to the actors of a referent event.

    a.   The Japanese verbs of giving do not really fit here; they basically indicate the actors' status, and it is only incidental if some of the actors turn out also to be participants in the speech event. However, some of Samoan's distinct status-level verbs (e.g., those for eating) may well have usages sensitive solely to who it is that is speaking and being addressed.

    b.   Satellites and clitics are used by a number of languages to indicate the absolute or relative gender (men's and women's speech) and status of the interlocutors.

c. Inflections for second person in many European languages distinguish degrees of formality that are partly based on relative status.

35. *Speaker's State of Mind,* ... It seems that no markers or incorporations indicate notions unrelated to either the referent event or the speech event. If they existed, one might encounter cases like *The chair broke-ka* meaning 'The chair broke and I'm currently bored' or 'The chair broke and it was raining yesterday'.

3 COMPENDIUM OF TYPOLOGIES AND UNIVERSALS

In this section, we abstract out and organize the typological and universal findings discussed in chapter II-1. Our classification of the different types of typologies and universals, set forth next, builds on Greenberg 1963.

3.1 The Different Types of Typological and Universal Principles, and the Symbols Used to Represent Them

A = a principle of analysis

T = a typology, involving any factor by which languages differ from each other

   +T = preponderant tendency across languages, involving a factor that holds for most languages, though not for all

   −T = a crosslinguistic rarity, involving a factor that holds for few languages, though not for none

+U = a positive universal, involving a factor that holds either characteristically or without exception within every language

−U = a negative universal (universal exclusion), involving a factor that holds only uncharacteristically or not at all within every language

U′ = an integrated property of universal grammar—that is, of language in general—summed over different language types, involving a factor that *may* occur (is not excluded from occurring) in any language

Statements of the **U′**-type and statements of the **T**-type are interconvertible, incorporating equivalences of the following form:

U′: "Language displays property P" (i.e., manifests it at least in part, though not uniformly)

⟺ **T:** "Some languages have property P and some do not"

> = a relative principle, involving a factor that pertains only to a set of languages already possessing a particular other factor; hence:

>U = an implicational universal

>T = a subtypology

/ = a principle involving two factors of different "universality" types

In brackets, we indicate the sections or other locations where each finding is described. In 1 to 58, the brackets refer to locations in chapter II-1; 59 to 67 refer to table 2.1.

3.2   Typological and Universal Principles Involving:

3.2.1   Properties of Language Organization

1. **+U:** Language distinguishes the two levels of meaning and of surface form. There are properties pertaining to each level independently, and also to their interrelations (including properties of lexicalization). [1]

2. **A:** Within a language, a property or pattern is "characteristic" if it is colloquial, frequent, and pervasive. [2]

3. **A/U, T:** Morphemes' "usages" or "usage ranges"—a particular subset of their semantic and syntactic properties, wholly exclusive of their core meanings—relate them to each other in systematic patterns within the same language and across languages, even where there is no common core meaning. [1.1]

4. **+U:** For any semantic category of "grammatical"-type meaning (e.g., aspect, causativity) incorporated within lexical items in a language, two kinds of lexical items generally occur: those that incorporate only a single value of the category, and those that can express some range of the category's values. [1.1, 2.5, note 25, 2.6, 2.8, 2.9]

3.2.2   Properties of Semantic Organization

5. **U′/+U:** Language distinguishes the following semantic categories (as determined in the present study): Motion event; (fact of) Motion, Figure, Ground, Path; Vector, Conformation, Deictic (and Contour, Direction); Co-event; Precursion, Enablement, Cause, Manner, Concomitance, Subsequence (Result or Purpose); causativity, agency,

intention, volition, inducement, undergoerhood; personation, primary/
secondary focus (as for valence); and aspect; as well as the remaining
categories listed in table 2.1 (except nos. 19 and 35). Many of these
categories have systematic realization in every language. [body of
text]

6. **+U:** A state of locatedness is conceived and subdivided into
   components in the same way as an event of translational movement.
   (The term "Motion event" is here used for both.) [1.2]

7. **+U:** A Motion event has four components: Figure, Motion, Path, and
   Ground. [1.2]

8. **+U:** Regularly in association with a Motion event is a conceptually
   separable Co-event. The Co-event bears a semantic relation to the
   Motion event, oftenest that of Manner or Cause, but also Precursion,
   Enablement, Concomitance, and Subsequence. [1.2, 2.1]

9. **+U:** Languages distinguish between translational and self-contained
   Motion. The latter encompasses oscillation, rotation, dilation (expan-
   sion/contraction), wiggle, local wander, and rest. Languages generally
   analyze a complex movement into a combination of these two types.
   [2.1.2.3]

10. **+U:** Some 10 seemingly universal "motion-aspect" formulas consti-
    tute the semantic cores of all Motion events. [2.2.2]

11. **U':** The semantic category of causativity encompasses more and finer
    distinctions than the generally recognized causative/noncausative op-
    position. Within the causative are at least the resulting-event, causing-
    event, instrument, author, agent, self-agent, and inducive types, and
    within the noncausative are the autonomous and the undergoer types.
    [2.6]

12. **+U:** Semantic properties involving the different causation types in-
    clude the following:
    a. An event can be conceptualized as independent of any causal
       connections (the autonomous type). [2.6]
    b. An agent's intention can extend over different lengths of a causal
       sequence (the author type vs. the agent type). [2.6]
    c. Agency involves one event of intention, one of volition, and, in the
       physical realm, one of body(-part) motion. [note 31]

    d. Body motion can be the end goal of agency (the self-agentive type). [2.6]

    e. Agency can itself be externally caused (the inducive type). [2.6]

    f. The Instrument is a derived notion: the Figure of a causing event is the Instrument within the whole causal sequence. [note 30]

    g. The self-agentive type tends to become conceptualized as the autonomous type and, in a parallel way, the inducive type tends to become conceptualized as the simple agentive type. [note 33]

13. **−T:** Ordinary aspect involves the temporal distribution of an action considered directly with respect to the background temporal flow. In addition, a few languages have systematic indication of a secondary aspectlike phenomenon: an action's temporal distribution considered with respect to a separately occurring event of locomotion (executed by the same actor). [3.7]

3.2.3 Properties of Surface Forms

14. **U′:** Language distinguishes at the surface two underrecognized grammatical categories: the verb "satellite" and the "verb complex." The verb root together with all satellites that are present constitute the verb complex. [3]

15. **T:** Some languages have full systems of satellites, while other languages have virtually no satellites. [3, 4]

16. **U′:** Languages have a recurrent tendency to exhibit "satellite formation." By this process, certain morphemes or morpheme classes—especially ones with a more grammatical-type meaning—move into a satellite relation with the verb. They leave their original locations in the sentence, where they had been in construction with other elements, perhaps more logically so. Quantifier float is one example of the process. Polysynthesis is its greatest realization. [note 50]

17. **+U:** In a Motion-event sentence, if the Ground nominal is an anaphoric or deictic pronoun, it can generally be omitted. Any Path-indicating adposition with that pronoun must then also be omitted, whereas any Path-indicating satellites must remain. [3.1]

18. **> −T:** Languages having both satellites and adpositions generally keep them formally distinct. English and Mandarin seem to have in addition a rare part of speech—the "satellite preposition"—that coalesces the two forms. [3.1]

3.2.4   Properties of the Relations Between the Semantic and the Surface Levels

19. **+U/A:** Elements at the semantic and at the surface levels of language do not necessarily correspond one-to-one. Theories of lexicalization have described the following types of semantic-surface relations (i.e., lexicalization types), categorized by the quantities of elements involved.

At the semantic level	*At the surface level*
a. no semantic content	1. no surface element
b. a single semantic element	2. a single morpheme
c. a combination of semantic elements	3. a combination of morphemes

Types of semantic-surface correspondence	*Yielding at the surface*
a-1	
a-2/a-3	a "dummy" element/expression
b-1/c-1	a "zero" form or a deleted underlying form
b-2	a simplex morpheme (the prototypical form)
b-3	an idiom or collocation (or a discontinuous form)
c-2	conflation (or a portmanteau)
c-3	conflation occurring over a collocation

[In the last case, the elements of (c) must not correspond one-one with the elements of (3).] [1–1.1]

20. **A:** In addition to the preceding lexicalization types, there are two further ways to account for a semantic component assumed to be present at the surface (aside from syntactic-structural meanings):

    a. It arises by semantic/pragmatic interpretation in accordance with the context and general knowledge. [1.1]

    b. It is not really present after all, once the referent situation is viewed from an alternative perspective by the process of "semantic resegmentation." [note 4]

21. **+U:** A zero form can behave exactly like a normal morpheme, with its own precise meaning (or meaning range) and syntactic properties. [note 2]

22. **+U:** Languages possess a "shifter" type of closed-class element. When used with a lexical item that incorporates notion A of a particular semantic category (e.g., of aspect, causation, or valence), it shifts notion A to notion B within the same category. [2.5, table 1.4, 2.7, 2.8]

23. **>U/+T:** A language's possession of a productively occurring shifter that changes notion A to notion B tends to correlate with a comparative lack in that language of lexical items that incorporate notion B. [2.5, 2.9.1]

24. **A:** The verb root, since it is a single morpheme, is a surface form relevant to the comparison of lexicalization patterns across languages; the whole verb is not, because it can contain varying numbers of affixes. [2]

25. **+U:** The 'fact-of-Motion' component of a Motion event always appears in the verb root. [2.1–2.4]

26. **T:** In its most characteristic expression of a Motion event, a language will usually conflate in the verb root, together with 'fact of Motion', one of these three semantic components: the Figure, or the Path, or the Co-event. [2.1–2.4]

27. **−U:** In its most characteristic expression of a Motion event, no language conflates the Ground component with 'fact of Motion' in the verb root. But this form of conflation can occur as a minor pattern. [2.4.2]

28. **−U:** In its most characteristic expression of a Motion event, no language combines *two* of the Figure, Path, Ground, and Co-event components to conflate in the verb root with 'fact of Motion'. But this form of conflation can occur as a minor pattern. [2.4.3]

29. **−U:** In its most characteristic expression of a Motion event, no language conflates *none* of the other Motion-related components together with 'fact of Motion' in the verb root—that is, 'fact of Motion' does not characteristically appear alone in the verb root. However, this form of nonconflation may occur as a minor system or as one branch

of a split system (here, typically, in the expression of location events). [2.4.4]

30. **−T:** In its most characteristic expression of a Motion event, a language can approach the "zero-conflation" pattern in that—although it does incorporate one of the three main Motion-related components with 'fact of Motion'—it distinguishes only some two or three senses of that component, rather than the at least dozens of distinctions otherwise typically found. [2.4.5]

31. **T:** In its most characteristic expression of a Motion event, a language can conflate one of the three main Motion-related components in the verb root together with 'fact of Motion' for one category of Motion event, conflate another such component for another category of Motion event, and even conflate the third such component with yet another category of Motion event. This is a "split" or "complementary" system of conflation. [2.4.6]

32. **−T:** In its most characteristic expression of a Motion event, a language can conflate one of the three main Motion-related components together with 'fact of Motion' in one series of verb roots, and conflate another such component with 'fact of Motion' in another series of verb roots, where both of these series are equally colloquial and pertain to the same categories of Motion event. This is a "parallel" system of conflation. [2.4.7]

33. **−U?:** Possibly no language fails to have a most characteristic pattern for the expression of a Motion event, instead variously conflating the three main Motion-related components together with 'fact of Motion' in its different verb roots. This would be an "intermixed" system of conflation. [2.4.8]

34. **> +U/ >T:** Languages of the Figure- or the Co-event-conflating type apply their conflation pattern to the expression of both motion and location. Some languages of the Path-conflating type apparently also do so. But most languages of the Path-conflating type apply their conflation pattern only to the case of motion. [2.1–2.3]

35. **> +U:** Languages of the Co-event-conflating type have a system of polysemous verbs—lexical doublets—with one usage expressing a Co-event referent alone and the other expressing the Co-event conflated with Motion. Verbs with only one or the other usage, as well as

suppletive pairs with complementary usages, generally also occur. Further conflation of this sort with an additional Motion clause can yield lexical triplets (and so on). [2.1]

36. **>T:** Languages of the Path-conflating type can either class together the Deictic component and the Conformation component of Path, or they can treat these two components as structurally distinct and accord priority to one of them. [2.2.2]

37. **>T:** With a particular Motion component characteristically conflated in the verb root, languages form subtypologies on the basis of which of the remaining components appear in the satellite. [2.6]

38. **−U:** No language's verb roots apparently distinguish systematically between the "autonomous" and the "resulting-event" types of causation, although they do do so in occasional instances. [2.6]

39. **−U:** No language's verb roots appear to distinguish between the "causing-event" type and the "instrument" type of causation. [2.6]

40. **>+U:** In a language having them, the verb roots that express the "causing-event" or "instrument" type of causation can generally also express the "author" and "agent" types. [2.6]

41. **T:** Languages differ as to the extensiveness shown by a favored lexicalization pattern (e.g., one involving lexicalized causation, aspect-causation, or valence), both with respect to a particular semantic category and across semantic categories. [2.6 (end), 2.7.1, 2.9.1]

42. **T:** Languages differ as to the type of aspect that they characteristically incorporate in the verb roots that express certain semantic domains. [2.5]

43. **T:** In the main, a language will characteristically conflate in a verb root, together with a 'state' notion, one of these three aspect-causative types: the stative, the inchoative, or the agentive. But in some languages, the same verb root characteristically ranges over the expression of a particular pair of these types. And in some languages, the same verb root can range over the expression of all three of the types, but whether this is ever the characteristic pattern or always only a minor pattern remains to be determined. Finally, by one interpretation, in some languages, the root expresses the 'state' alone, incorporating none of the three aspect-causative types, with accom-

panying morphemes supplying the expression of those types. By another interpretation, though, such verb roots—in fact, all verb roots—incorporate an aspect-causative component (or a range thereof) and do not present their core referent abstracted away from properties of temporal distribution or causality. [2.5, 2.7]

44. **+U/>T:** In all the preceding cases, the aspect-causative type(s) that are not expressed by the root are indicated by accompanying morphemes. In the case of 'state-alone' roots, these additional morphemes themselves either indicate each of the three aspect-causative types separately, or they use one form to indicate a pair of the types and another form for the remaining type. [2.7]

45. **>T:** Languages that are typologically alike in characteristically incorporating a particular one of the three aspect-causative types, in their 'state' verb roots, can form a subtypology by differing in their patterns for deriving the remaining aspect-causative types. [table 1.5 and example (60)]

46. **−U:** Where the same verb root—or nonroot morphemic material— expresses a pair of the three main aspect-causative types, this pair can be either stative + inchoative or inchoative + agentive, but it cannot be stative + agentive. [2.7]

47. **−U:** A verb root can refer to both state location and state entry, but it cannot refer to one or both of these and also to state departure. Possibly, no verb root in fact ever lexicalizes the notion of leaving a state. (Thus, a verb 'die' should be interpreted to mean 'enter death', not 'leave life': in any language, the verb could be cognate with the former noun but not with the latter.) [2.7.2]

48. **−U:** As to their quantity of forms and usages in any language, the grammatical elements and derivational patterns that indicate 'state entry' generally exceed, and may equal, but are never fewer than those indicating 'state departure'. That is, 'state entry' is unmarked relative to 'state departure'. [2.7.2]

49. **T:** In each language, person-involved actions are characteristically lexicalized in verb roots either in the monadic personation type, or in the dyadic personation type, or in a form covering both types. [2.8]

50. **+U:** The valence with which a mental event is lexicalized in a verb root may correlate universally with a particular cognitive-linguistic

principle: When it is the subject, the Experiencer is conceptualized as initiatory in the mental event, whereas when it is not the subject, the Experiencer is conceptualized as reactive in the event. [2.9.2]

51. **T:** Languages differ as to whether predominance is given to the Experiencer as subject or as nonsubject in the lexicalization of valence for mental events and, accordingly, whether the conception of the Experiencer predominates as initiatory or as reactive. [2.9.2]

52. **+T:** Preponderantly, verbs that express certain subcategories of mental events—among them, 'wanting' and 'valuing'—lexicalize the valence so that the Experiencer appears as syntactic subject, functioning in an initiator role. [2.9.2]

53. **+U:** Universally, the Figure is higher than the Ground on a hierarchy of semantic roles. One consequence is that, in every language, the basic "precedence" pattern is for the Figure-expressing nominal to appear higher than the Ground-expressing nominal in the hierarchy of grammatical relations: subject, object, oblique. [2.9, 3.8]

54. **U′:** Either basic or inverted Figure-Ground precedence can be required by a particular lexical item or a particular semantic notion. A requirement of the semantic type can hold over a whole language, over a whole language family, or in some cases perhaps also universally. [2.9, 3.8]

55. **U′:** Often, within a language or across languages, the same semantic element can be represented at the surface with different degrees of salience—that is, more foregrounded or backgrounded. [4]

56. **+U:** Other things being equal, a semantic element is backgrounded in its salience by being expressed in the main verb root or in any closed-class element (including a satellite—hence, anywhere in the verb complex). Elsewhere it is foregrounded. [4]

57. **T:** Languages differ greatly as to the quantity and types of semantic elements that they can express at a backgrounded level of salience. [4]

58. **+U/T:** A greater "cost" attaches to a notion's foregrounded, as against backgrounded, expression within a sentence, due to its greater claim on space, attention, and canons of style. Accordingly, a language tends more often to omit a notion requiring foregrounded expression, leaving it to be inferred from context if possible. Consequently, a language with greater provision for backgrounding regu-

larly expresses more information explicitly than a language with lesser provision. [4]

59. **+U:** By one interpretation, all incorporation of Result, whether in verb root or in satellite, is as main event, not as subordinate event. [section 2.2, descriptions 1 and 5]

60. **−U:** Unlike the other Phase notions, that of 'stopping' does not appear in closed-class elements (such as verbal auxiliaries, satellites, or inflections). (See principles 47–48 about the restrictions on 'state-departure'.) [section 2.2, description 12]

61. **>+U/−U:** 'Number', when appearing in verb inflections, refers to the grammatical subject or object, whereas when incorporated in the verb root, it refers to the semantic Patient—and apparently to no other semantic roles. [section 2.2, description 17]

62. **−U:** Only a limited and small set of semantic categories can appear in the verb complex to qualify the participants in a referent event—mainly 'person', 'number', 'distribution', 'status', 'gender/class'. All other semantic categories, such as 'color', are excluded. [table 2.1]

63. **U′:** For our three verb-complex constituents—the verb root, satellite, and inflections—semantic categories with generally clear representation in all three are 'polarity', 'phase', 'aspect', 'causativity', 'personation', 'number', 'valence/voice', 'factivity/evidence', 'speech-act type', 'status of interlocutors'. [table 2.1]

64. **−U:** Semantic categories excluded from the verb root but not from inflections are 'gender/class of an actor', 'tense', 'person', 'mood'. [table 2.1]

65. **−U:** Semantic categories excluded from verb inflections but not from the root are the main action or state (including 'Result'), Motion event components, and Co-event (table 2.1, nos. 1–8), as well as 'distribution of a (multiple) actor', 'status of the actors', '(deictic) Direction', 'speaker's attitude'. [table 2.1]

66. **U′:** Whereas many semantic categories can appear either in the verb root or in verb inflections but not in both, most of these same categories *can* appear in the satellite. [table 2.1]

67. **−U:** Although readily occurring elsewhere in the verb complex—for example, as particle words—the semantic categories of 'hedging',

'rate', 'relation to comparable events', 'spatial setting', and '(deictic) spatial location' are at best only marginally expressed in the verb root, satellite, or inflections. And the categories of 'degree of realization', 'status of actors', and 'temporal setting' are only rarely expressed there. [table 2.1]

4   ATSUGEWI CAUSE SATELLITES AND POLYSYNTHETIC VERBS

In this section, we set forth and exemplify the system of Cause and related satellites in Atsugewi. In particular, section 4.1 contains a fairly thorough listing of the shapes and meanings of Atsugewi's system of Cause and related satellites. Forms as yet poorly attested are marked with an asterisk. Section 4.2 presents a number of examples of full polysynthetic verbs in Atsugewi, arranged by the semantic type of the verb root. The numbers accompanying the forms in section 4.1 will be used as indices by which they will be referred to in the examples of section 4.2. We include this detailed description of the Cause satellites first because of their intrinsic semantic interest—this morphological category is relatively rare in the languages of the world. Second, it is presented because of their significance for the crosslinguistic typology of the representation of Motion and other events that was presented in chapter II-1. Further, examples of the multiaffixal verbs are presented to provide a broader sense of the patterns in which the components of a polysynthetic form combine their individual meanings into a unified semantic structure.

4.1   Cause and Related Satellites

Atsugewi has a set of prefixal Cause satellites that immediately precede the verb root. These satellites refer to a causal event that includes an Instrument. These satellites are presented in section 4.1.1. In an additional usage, this same set of satellites can refer to a Motion event that includes a Figure. This usage is described in section 4.1.2. Finally, Atsugewi also has a set of Figure/Ground satellites. This set largely overlaps the set of Cause satellites, sharing forms with the same shape and related meanings. But each set has some unshared forms. The Figure/Ground satellites are presented in section 4.1.3.

4.1.1   Cause Satellites   As discussed in section 2.5 of chapter II-1, the Atsugewi Cause satellites generally express a particular kind of instrumentality acting in a particular way on the Figure or Patient so as to

bring about the event expressed by the verb root. In the terms of chapter
II-1 and of chapter II-3, a satellite of this type represents a Co-event
that bears the relation of Cause to the framing event. In the terms of
chapter I-4, it represents the penultimate subevent in a causal chain—that
is, the immediate cause of the final result in the chain.

Only satellite 25 for 'heat/fire' has distinct forms for nonagentive and
agentive usages. The remaining Cause satelllites can mostly occur in
either usage. Accordingly, when occurring in a nonagentive verb, they can
best be glossed in English with a clause that begins with *as a result of* or
from. But when occurring in an agentive verb, they are best glossed with a
clause that begins with *by*. For uniformity, though, all the glosses are in
the form of a clause beginning with *as a result of*. The satellites are
grouped below by the type of instrumentality and event that they specify.

4.1.1.1   Type: Generic or Noncausal

0. i-/a-

   'as a result of something/nothing acting on the Figure' (used—though
   only infrequently—where the event of the verb root is conceptualized
   as uncaused, or where more specific indication of Cause is undesirable)

4.1.1.2   Type: 'As a Result of a Body-Part Acting on the Figure'   The
satellites here prototypically refer to body parts of humans. They can also
refer to the body parts of animals, in accordance with analogies to the
human parts. These analogies have some flexibility, so that, for example,
what English refers to as the 'leg' of a chicken could be covered either by
ma- (3) for 'leg' or by *ci-* (2) for 'hand'. The satellites refer only to inalien-
ably possessed parts of a body that are activated neuromuscularly, not to
severed body parts.

As can be seen, two satellites can refer to the same body part engaged
in different kinds of actions. Thus, *tu-* (1) and *ci-* (2) both refer to the
hands, but acting centripetally as against manipulatively, while *pri-* (6)
and *phu-* (7) both refer to the mouth, but acting ingressively as against
egressively. Otherwise, though, a satellite covers reference to a wide range
of actions by the body part. In particular, it can cover onset causation,
when the body part comes into contact with a Figure (as when a foot
kicks a rock across a field), as well as extended causation, when the body
part stays in contact with a Figure (as when a foot slides a rock across a
field). When a satellite below appears in an agentive verb form, the satellite might accordingly be best represented by any of a range of verbs in a

by-clause, as in 'by hitting, throwing, holding, carrying, putting, taking the Figure (with one's hands, feet, teeth, etc.)'.

1. tu-
   'as a result of the hand/hands of an entity—working centripetally—that is, ward upon itself/toward each other—acting on the Figure' [e.g., by grasping, catching, squeezing, strangling]

2. ci-
   'as a result of the hand/hands of an entity—working manipulatively (other than as for *tu*-)—acting on the Figure'

3. ma-
   'as a result of the foot/feet or leg/legs of an entity acting on the Figure'

4. ti-
   'as a result of the buttocks/pelvic region of an entity acting on the Figure'

5. wi-
   'as a result of the teeth of an entity acting on the Figure'

6. pri-
   'as a result of the mouth-interior of an entity—working ingressively—acting on the Figure' [e.g., by sucking in]

7. phu-
   'as a result of the mouth-interior of an entity—working egressively—acting on the Figure' [e.g., by spitting out]

8. *pu-
   'as a result of the mouth-exterior/lips of an entity acting on the Figure'

9. hi-
   'from the whole/unspecific part/specific part not treated by another satellite—of the body of an entity acting on the Figure'

10.–15.
   'as a result of the arm of a person acting on the Figure'
   [The arm of an entity is treated as a linear object. In accordance with its particular manner of acting on the Figure, it is specified by one or another of those satellites—(10) to (15) in the following section—which specify linear objects acting in various ways on a Figure.]

4.1.1.3 Type: 'As a Result of a Geometric Object Acting on the Figure'
Each of the satellites listed here can have up to three specific types of us-

age. These usages are defined individually and given separate diagrams. The three usages are indicated generically in (1). As discussed in chapter I-5, a "meta-Figure" in a "self-referencing" event is an object that moves with respect to itself or holds a shape characterized with respect to itself.

(1) *When containing a "geometric" Cause satellite, the verb can express*
   a. *A translational motion event*
   'a Figure MOVE + Path + Ground as a result of the Instrument acting on it'
   b. *A self-referencing motion event*
   'a meta-Figure MOVE into/out of a SHAPE [or: "MOVE" into/ out of a STATE] as a result of the Instrument acting on it'
   c. *A translational or self-referencing locative event*
   'a Figure BE_{LOC}/$REMAIN_{LOC}$ + Path (site) + Ground as a result of the Instrument acting on it'
   'a meta-Figure BE_{LOC}/$REMAIN_{LOC}$ in a SHAPE [or: "BE"/ "REMAIN" in a STATE] as a result of the Instrument acting on it'

Some (a)-type definitions below contain the alternative forms "onto/while contacting." These forms refer, respectively, to onset causation and extended causation (see chapter I-7). Two diagrams are then given for the two cases. And some (b)-type definitions include the alternative forms "onto/into" to indicate that the Instrument may merely come into contact with the meta-Figure or may additionally penetrate it. Again, two different diagrams are provided. Note that in all the definitions, the particular part of the geometric Instrumental object that makes contact with the Figure or meta-Figure is specified within brackets. In the diagrams, "I" labels the Instrument, "F" labels the Figure, and "f" labels the meta-Figure.

10. uh-
   Note: Here, "kinemically" means that the object flies freely along its trajectory without continuing causal control. And "circumpivotally" means that the linear object swings through an arc about a pivot point.
   a. 'as a result of a linear object kinemically moving circumpivotally [with one end] onto/while contacting the Figure' [e.g., by batting/ by throwing]

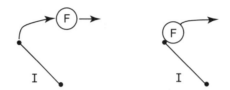

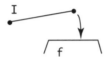 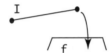

b. 'as a result of a linear object kinetically moving circumpivotally [with one end] onto/into the meta-Figure' [e.g., by pounding/by chopping]

11. cu-

   a. 'as a result of a linear object moving axially [with one end] perpendicularly onto/while contacting the Figure' [e.g., by prodding, striking with a pool cue/by pushing steadily with a stick]

   b. 'as a result of a linear object moving axially [with one end] perpendicularly onto/into the meta-Figure' [e.g., by poking/by piercing, skewering]

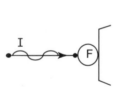 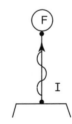

   c. 'as a result of a linear object pressing axially [with one end] perpendicularly on the Figure' [e.g., by holding pinned against a wall, by supporting with a cane]

12A. ra-

    a. 'as a result of a linear object moving axially [with one end] obliquely while contacting the Figure' [e.g., by thrusting up at an angle]

    b. 'as a result of a linear object moving axially [with one end] obliquely onto/into the meta-Figure' [e.g., by digging, awling, sewing]

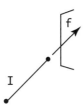

    c. 'as a result of a linear object pressing axially [with one end] obliquely on the Figure' [e.g., by propping, leaning, poling]

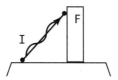

12B. ra-

    a. 'as a result of a linear/planar object moving laterally [with one end/edge] along a surface while contacting the Figure' [e.g., by raking, sweeping, scraping off]

b. 'as a result of a linear/planar object moving laterally [with one end/edge] over/through the meta-Figure (a surface)' [e.g., by smoothing over/by whittling, plowing]

c. 'as a result of a linear/planar object pressing laterally [with its side] on the Figure, meta-Figure' [e.g., by gripping in a vise, hugging, being pinned down by a log]

12C. ra-

b. 'as a result of a planar object moving in its own plane [with one edge] into the meta-Figure' [e.g., by scoring, slicing, sawing]

12D. ra-

a. 'as a result of a circular object moving rotationally (i.e., rolling) [with its perimeter] along a surface while contacting the Figure' [e.g., by carting, driving]

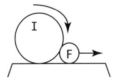

b. 'as a result of a circular/cylindrical object moving rotationally (i.e., rolling) [with its perimeter] along a surface over the meta-

Figure' [e.g., by flattening with a rolling pin or a steamroller, by getting run over]

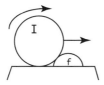

13. ta-

    a. 'as a result of a linear object moving laterally [with one end] through liquid while contacting the Figure [e.g., by paddling (a hot cooking rock around in soup to cook it)]

    b. 'as a result of a linear object moving laterally [with one end] through the meta-Figure (a liquid)' [e.g., by stirring]

Note: ra- (12Ba,b) is usually used instead of *ta-*

14. *ka-

    b. 'as a result of a linear object moving with axial spin [with one end] into the meta-Figure' [e.g., by boring]

Note: ra- (12Ab) has been found instead of *ka-* for 'by screw-driving'

15A. ru-

    a. 'as a result of a (flexible) linear object moving axially with axial tension (i.e., pulling) [with one end] while contacting the Figure' [e.g., by pulling on with a rope, by contracting one's muscle]

    c. 'as a result of a (flexible) linear object pulling axially [with one end] on the Figure' [e.g., by suspending with a cord]

15B. ru-

    c. 'as a result of a (flexible) linear object (under axial tension) pressing laterally [with its side] circumferentially in on the Figure, meta-Figure' [e.g., by binding, girding]

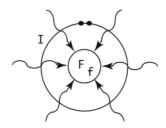

16. mi-

    b. 'as a result of a knife cutting [with its edge] into the meta-Figure'
    Note: ra- (12Cb) may be used instead of *mi-*

4.1.1.4   Type: 'As a Result of a Free-Flying Object Acting on the Figure'

17. uh-

'as a result of a free-flying object [other than that specified by *phu-* (18)] kinemically sailing/falling onto the Figure' [e.g., as a result of being hit by a hailstone or by a thrown, kicked, batted object]

18. phu-

'as a result of matter, propelled by the mouth working egressively [= *phu-* (7)] kinemically sailing onto the Figure' [e.g., as a result of being hit by blown breath, spit, spat-out object]

4.1.1.5 Type: 'As a Result of a Substance/Energy Acting on the Figure'

19. ca-

    'as a result of the wind blowing on the Figure'

20. cu-

    'as a result of flowing liquid acting on the Figure'

21. ka-

    'as a result of falling rain acting on the Figure'

22. ra-

    'as a result of a substance exerting a steady push/pressure on the
    Figure' [e.g., as a result of pressure from gas in one's stomach, ice fog
    under the soil]

23. ru-

    'as a result of a substance exerting a steady pull on the Figure' [e.g.,
    as a result of the pull from a stream on an anchored cloth]

24. uh-

    a. 'as a result of the weight of a substance bearing down on the
       Figure' [e.g., as a result of snow weighing down a limb]
    b. 'as a result of gravity/the Figure's own weight acting on the
       Figure' [e.g., by falling]

25. miw-

    'as a result of heat/fire acting on the Figure'
    mu:-
    'by the Agent's applying heat/fire to the Figure'

26. *wu:-

    'as a result of light shining on the Figure'

4.1.1.6 Type: 'As a Result of a Sensible Aspect of an Object, Event Acting on the Experiencer'

The satellites in this set often occur with verb roots that specify an emotive or cognitive state. A verb containing such a satellite and root generally exhibits the semantic pattern represented in (2).

(2) *When containing a "sensory" Cause satellite and a "cognitive" root, the verb can express*
    'an Experiencer come into/be in the specified affective/cognitive state
    of mind as a result of a sensible aspect of an object/event acting on
    the Experiencer'

27. sa-/su-/si-/siw-
'as a result of the visual aspect of an object, event acting on the Experiencer'

28. ka-/ku-/ki-/kiw-
'as a result of the auditory aspect of an event acting on the Experiencer'

29. tu-
'as a result of the feel of an object acting on the Experiencer'

30. pri-
'as a result of the smell/taste of an object acting on the Experiencer'

31. tu-
'as a result of the taste of an object acting on the Experiencer'

4.1.2 Cause Satellites Used as Motion-Event Satellites In the prototypical verb of Atsugewi, the root refers to the main Motion event, in which a particular kind of Figure moves or is located. And the Cause satellite refers to an event in which a particular kind of entity, functioning as an Instrument, acts in a particular way on the Figure, thereby causing its motion or location.

In addition, though, any of the Cause satellites in the preceding section can also be used to refer to a Motion event. In this case, the same entity that before functioned as an Instrument now functions as a Figure. And this entity acts in the same way as before, but now does so on a Ground object.

In the case where the verb root already refers to a particular kind of Figure object as moving, the shifted satellite simply provides an additional characterization of that same Figure object, as well as an additional characterization of the way this object moves. In the case where the verb root is nonprototypical and makes no reference to the Figure, the satellite provides the only characterization of the Figure and its movement within the verb.

To illustrate the shift in usage, the previously presented Cause satellite *ra-*, 12Ab, is repeated in (3a), though now with its object marked as functioning as the Instrument. And (3b) gives the meaning of the same satellite in its shifted usage.

(3) ra-
a. 'as a result of a linear object, as Instrument, moving axially [with one end] obliquely into the meta-Figure'

b. 'with a linear object, as Figure, moving axially [with one end] obliquely into the Ground'

4.1.3 Figure/Ground Satellites Atsugewi has a set of Figure/Ground satellites that occupies the same verb slot as the Cause satellites and that partially overlaps that set, with the common forms having the same shape and related meanings. When occurring in a Motion verb, a satellite of this type indicates the kind of Figure or Ground entity involved. It thus provides an independent specification of the Figure or Ground, alongside any that may be provided by the verb root or an external nominal.

4.1.3.1 Type: 'A Body Part'

32. tu-

    the hand(s), arm(s)

33. ma-

    the foot (feet), leg(s)

34. ti-

    the buttocks

35. wi-

    the teeth

36. pu-

    the mouth, a mouth-shaped object [e.g., a flower]

37. ce-

    the eye(s), an eye-shaped object [e.g., a button, a hailstone]

38. hi-

    the whole/specific part not treated by another prefix/unspecific part—of the body

4.1.3.2 Type: 'A Geometric Object'

39. uh-

    a linear/planar object in kinemic swinging motion [e.g., a pendulum]

40. cu-

    a linear/planar object moving/sticking perpendicularly into a surface [e.g., a car in collision/the sunshade on a cradleboard]

41. pa-
    a linear object sticking perpendicularly out from a surface [e.g., an erect penis, the target stick in the game of horseshoes]

42. ra-
    a linear/planar object sticking obliquely into/against/out of a surface [e.g., a leaning cradleboard, a shingle]

43. ih-/uh-
    a planar object lying flush against a surface [e.g., a spread-out blanket, a board nailed to the wall]

44. ru-
    a (flexible) linear object attached at one or both ends and involved with suspension/tension [e.g., sinew, a belt, an unerect penis, an icicle]

45. cri-
    a set of linear objects parallelly together [e.g., hairs in a plait, stalks in a sheaf, sticks in a bundle]

46. cu-
    material tightly packed in a space [e.g., caulking material]

4.1.3.3   Type: 'A Free-Flying Object'

47. uh-
    a kinemically free-flying object

4.1.3.4   Type: 'A Substance/Energy'

48. ca-
    wind

49. cu-
    flowing liquid

50. ka-
    rain

51. uh-
    a weightful substance/object, a load

52. miw-
    heat/fire

53. wu:-/ma:-
    light

4.2   Examples of Atsugewi Polysynthetic Verbs

This section presents a number of Atsugewi polysynthetic verbs. These are grouped in accordance with the semantic type of the verb root they contain. Each of the numbered examples in this section begins with the presentation of a single verb root. This root is then followed by several different sets of affixes, lettered (a), (b), and so on, with which it can occur to form a polysynthetic verb. Relative to those in chapter I-1, the Atsugewi examples here are presented in a more formal format with the following features:

• The meaning of the root is always represented in a nonagentive form even though the root is to appear underneath in an example with an agentive interpretation.

• Likewise, the meaning of a Cause satellite is represented in a nonagentive 'as a result of' form, even though the satellite is to appear in an example with an agentive interpretation.

• Each prefixal satellite is followed by a parenthesized number that refers to its listing in section 4.1. In a few examples, the prefixal satellite might have either—or perhaps both—of two different polysemous readings. In that case, both readings and their numbered listings in section 4.1 are provided.

• Where the definition of a prefixal satellite in section 4.1 has included alternative wordings, the definition here usually contains only the alternative relevant to the particular example in which the satellite is to appear. And the definition given for any other affix in an example is generally only the one sense out of its polysemous range that is relevant to that example.

• The inflectional affixes that appear fore and aft on an Atsugewi verb for the most part do not separately represent the subject and the direct object, or person and number and mood. Rather, they must be taken together as a set that represents a particular complex of values for those categories. The definition for each inflectional affix-set shows in order: the personal surface subject, the personal surface object, the mood. The third person in Atsugewi is not distinguished for number or other categories, and so is here represented simply by a "3." An affix set that can represent a transitive with third-person direct object can also represent an intransitive with no object. Accordingly, its direct object is indicated as "(3)."

• To the right of the inflectional affix set, the particular semantic causative type expressed by the example is indicated by one of the following terms: nonagentive, self-agentive, agentive, and undergoer. The affix set is not provided with this information within its definition because, for the most part, it and the rest of the morphemes in the verb do not distinguish between these causative types and in fact can be used for all of them.

• Under each set of affixes with which the root can occur to form a polysynthetic verb, this verb is shown in both morphophonemic and broad-phonetic form.

• For some examples, a literal translation is then given—that is, a part-for-part rendering into English of the verb's morphemes and their structural interrelations.

• For all examples, there is then given an "instantiated" translation—that is, an English sentence suggested by the native speaker that often contains particular referents not specifically implied by the Atsugewi verb, but that depicts a situation to which the Atsugewi verb could be used to refer.

The following symbols are used in the presentation of the examples:

R:	root
CI:	a Cause prefixal satellite—that is, one expressing a Cause event with an Instrument
CI → MF:	a Cause prefixal satellite that has semantically shifted to express a Motion event with a Figure
F:	a Figure prefixal satellite
G:	a Ground prefixal satellite
PG:	a Path + Ground suffixal satellite(s)
Px:	other prefix
Sx:	other suffix
Ax:	the inflectional affix set

The following phonological symbols are used:

• A colon (:) following a vowel lengthens it and, if the vowel is a high vowel (i/u), lowers it to a mid-vowel (e/o).

• An apostrophe alone in a space (') glottalizes any immediately following consonants. (This form by itself is the phonological shape of a particular inflectional morpheme.)

• A superscript "a" or "u" (^{a}/^{u}) changes a following /i/ to [a] or [u]; or, when final, it becomes an [a] or [u] if it directly follows the verb-initial syllable or any consonant cluster, but otherwise is zero.

4.2.1   Root Type: 'Figure + Motion'

---

1. R: -swal-
   'for a flexible (not stiff/resilient) linear object, especially one
   suspended from one end, to move/be-located'

---

a. CI: ca- (19)   'as a result of the wind blowing on the Figure'
    PG: -mič   'down onto the surface of the ground'
    Ax: '- w- - ª   '3, (3), factual'—nonagentive

/'-w-ca-swal-mič-ª/ ⇒ [čwaswálmič]

Literal: 'flexible linear objects suspended from one end moved down
to the surface of the ground as a result of the wind blowing on it'
Instantiated: "The clothes blew down from the clothesline."

b. CI: ra- (12Ba)   'as a result of a linear object moving laterally
                            [with one end] along a surface while contact-
                            ing the Figure'
   PG: -im   'thither'
   Ax: '- -a: '2s, (3), imperative'—agentive

/'-ra-swal-im-a:/ ⇒ [łaswalʔwá·]

Literal: 'you AGENT it that a flexible linear object moves thither by
moving a linear object laterally [with one end] along a surface while
contacting it!'
Instantiated: "Slide that dead snake away with this stick."

c. CI: tu- (1)   'as a result of the hand of a person, working in
                            upon itself, acting on the Figure'
   PG: -ič   'up'
   Ax: s- '- w- - ª   '1s, (3), factual'—agentive

/s-'-w-tu-swal-ič-ª/ ⇒ [stuswalíč]

Literal: 'I AGENTed it that a flexible linear object moved up by
acting on it with my hand, working in upon itself'
Instantiated: "I picked up the rag."

d. CI: uh- (10a)   'as a result of a linear object kinemically
                            moving circumpivotally [with one end] while
                            contacting the Figure'
   PG: -ičt   'into a liquid'
   Ax: '- w- - ª   '3, (3), factual'—agentive

/'-w-uh-swal-ič-ᵃ/ ⇒ [ẁoswalíčta]

Literal: 'she AGENTed it that flexible linear object's material moved into a liquid by moving a linear object circumpivotally [with one end] while contacting it'

Instantiated: "She threw the clothes into the laundry tub."

e. CI: ti- (4)   'as a result of the buttocks/pelvic region of a person acting on the Figure'

PG: -ič   'up'

Ax: n- w- - ᵃ   '3, (3), evidential'—agentive

/n-w-ti-swal-ič-ᵃ/ ⇒ [ntwiswalíč]

Literal: 'he evidently AGENTed it that flexible linear objects suspended from one end are located up by acting on them with his pelvic region'

Instantiated: "I see where he's carrying the rabbits he killed hung from his belt."

f. Px: p-   'mis-, mal-'

F: ru- (44)   'a flexible linear object attached at one end and involved with suspension, tension'

PG: -iǩs   'at the lateral surface of a solid'

Ax: '- w- - ᵃ   '3, (3), factual'—undergoer

/'-w-p-ru-swal-iǩs-ᵃ/ ⇒ [p̓luswalíǩsa]

Literal: 'he UNDERWENT it that a flexible linear object suspended from one end—which was a flexible linear object attached at one end and involved with tension—was mal-located at the lateral surface of a solid'

Instantiated: "His penis stayed limp (on him), he couldn't get an erection."

---

2. R: -staǧ-
'for runny, "icky" material to move/be-located'

---

a. CI: ca- (19)   'as a result of the wind blowing on the Figure'

PG: -ič̓t   'into liquid'

Ax: '- w- - ᵃ   '3, (3), factual'—nonagentive

/'-w-ca-staq̓-ič̓t-ᵃ/ ⇒ [č̓wastaq̓ič̓ta]

Literal: 'runny icky material moved into liquid as a result of the wind blowing on it'

Instantiated: "The guts that were lying on the bank blew into the river."

b. CI: ci- (2)   'as a result of the hands of a person, working manipulatively, acting on the Figure'

   PG: -ik̓s   'horizontally onto the lateral surface of a solid'

   Ax: s- ' - w- - ᵃ   '1s, (3), factual'—agentive

/s-'-w-ci-sta̓q̓-ik̓s-ᵃ/ ⇒ [sċwasta̓q̓ík̓sa]

Instantiated: "I patted some mud against the wall."

c. CI: uh- (10a)   'as a result of a linear object kinemically moving circumpivotally [with one end] while contacting the Figure' 'dually together'

   PG: -i·w

   Ax: same as for (b)

/s-'-w-uh-sta̓q̓-i·w-ᵃ/ ⇒ [swosta̓q̓í·wa]

Instantiated: "I slammed together the hunks of clay I held in either hand."

d. CI: ra- (12Aa)   'as a result of a linear object moving axially [with one end] obliquely while contacting the Figure'

   PG: -im   'thither'

   Ax: same as for (b)

/s-'-w-ra-sta̓q̓-im-ᵃ/ ⇒ [swrasta̓q̓íw]

Instantiated: "I slung away the rotten tomatoes, sluicing them off the pan they were in."

e. Px: :-   'augmentative' [here used idiomatically]

   CI: pri- (6)   'as a result of the mouth-interior of a person, working ingressively, acting on the Figure'

   PG: -iċ   'up'

   Ax: same as for (b)

/s-'-w-:-pri-sta̓q̓-iċ-ᵃ/ ⇒ [spre·sta̓q̓iċ]

Instantiated: "I picked up in my mouth the already-chewed gum from where it was stuck."

f. CI: ma- (3)   'as a result of the feet of a person acting on the Figure'

    PG: -ipsn^u 'into a volumetric enclosure'
            -im   'thither'

    Ax: same as for (b)

/s-'-w-ma-staq̇-ipsn^u-im-^{a}/ ⇒ [śma·staq̇ípsnu]

Literal: 'I AGENTed it that runny icky material moved thither into a volumetric enclosure by acting on it with my feet'

Instantiated: "I tracked the house up (with the manure I'd stepped in)."

g. *With a metathesized form of the root: -q̇st^{-a}-*

    CI: phu- (7)   'as a result of the mouth-interior of a person, working egressively, acting on the Figure'

    PG: -mik·   'onto a head, into a face, into an eye'

    Ax: same as for (b)

/s-'-w-phu-q̇st^{-a}-mik·-^{a}/ ⇒ [sṗhoq̇stím·ik·a]

Literal: 'I AGENTed it that runny icky material moved into a face by acting on it with my mouth interior working egressively'

Instantiated: "I spat in his face."

---

3. R: -lup-
    'for a small shiny spherical object to move/be located'

---

a. CI: cu- (11a)   'as a result of a linear object moving axially [with one end] perpendicularly onto the Figure'
                                       'out of a snug enclosure/a socket; into detach-
    PG: -hiy-ik·   ment from moorings'
    Ax: s- '- w- - ^{a} '1s, (3), factual'—agentive

/s-'-w-cu-lup-hiy-ik·-^{a}/ ⇒ [sćul·up^{h}yik·a]

Literal: 'I AGENTed it on him that a small shiny spherical object move out of its moorings, by axially moving a linear object [with one end] perpendicularly onto it'

Instantiated: "I poked his eye out with a stick."

b. CI: pri- (6)   'as a result of the mouth-interior of a
                                  person, working ingressively, acting on
                                  the Figure'
   PG: -nikiy   'all about, here and there, back and forth'
   Ax: same as for (a)

/s-'-w-pri-lup-nikiy-ᵃ/ ⇒ [sṗlil·upʰnika·]

Instantiated: "I rolled the round candy around in my mouth."

c. CI: phu- (7)   'as a result of the mouth-interior of a person,
                                  working egressively, acting on the Figure'
   PG: -im   'thither'
   Ax: same as (a)

/s-'-w-phu-lup-im-ᵃ/ ⇒ [sṗhol·upíw]

Instantiated: "I spat out the round candy."

---

4. R: -hmuṗ-
   'for a cover for a horizontal surface to move/be-located vertically
   with respect to that surface' [*Note:* A different root treats a cover that
   moves horizontally with respect to its surface, e.g., slipping/sliding
   over it.]

---

a. CI: uh- (10a)   'as a result of a linear object kinemically
                                  moving circumpivotally [with one end] while
                                  contacting the Figure'
   PG: -cam   'to a position athwart a fire site'
   Ax: s- '- w- - ᵃ   '1s, (3), factual'—agentive

/s-'-w-uh-hmuṗ-caw-ᵃ/ ⇒ [sẇohmúṗcaw]

Instantiated: "I threw a blanket over the fire."

b. CI: ra- (12Aa)   'as a result of a linear object moving
                                  axially [with one end] obliquely while
                                  contacting the Figure'
   PG: -mik·   'onto a head, into a face, into an eye'
   Ax: same as for (a)

/s-'-w-ra-hmuṗ-mik·-ᵃ/ ⇒ [sẇrahmúṗmik·a]

Instantiated: "I slung the blanket up over his head."

c. CI: ci- (2)   'as a result of the hands of a person, working
                               manipulatively, acting on the Figure'
   PG: -pik-ayw   'around'
   Ax: same as (a)

/s-'-w-ci-hmup̓-pik-ayw-ᵃ/ ⇒ [sċwehmúp̓pʰkaywa]

Instantiated: "I tucked the kids in."

d. F: uh- (51)   'a weightful/resting substance/object'
   PG: -cisᵘ   'down onto the upper surface of a solid'
           -ak·   'locative'
   Ax: s- '- w- - ᵃ   '1s, (3), factual'—undergoer

/s-'-w-uh-hmup̓-cisᵘ-ak·-ᵃ/ ⇒ [sẅohmúp̓cʰak·a]

Literal: 'I UNDERGO it that a cover for a horizontal surface—
which is an object resting on something—is located [having moved]
down onto the upper surface of a solid [and now] locatively situated'
Instantiated: "I have a cap on."

---

5. R: -ṭ-
'for a (smallish) planar object to move/be-located, thereby becoming/
remaining/ceasing to be functionally attached'

---

a. CI → MF: cu- (11a)   'with a linear object, as Figure, moving
                               axially [with one end] perpendicularly
                               onto the Ground'
   PG: -mik·   'onto a head, into a face, into an eye'
   Ax: s- '- w- - ᵃ   '1s, (3), factual'—agentive

/s-'-w-cu-ṭ-mik·-ᵃ/ ⇒ [sċutmík·a]

Literal: 'I AGENTed it that a smallish planar object, as Figure,
moved into attachment onto (a location at) a head, with a linear
object, also the Figure, moving axially [with one end] perpendicularly
onto the Ground'
Instantiated: "I stuck the sunshade onto the cradleboard."

b. CI → MF: ra- (12Ab)   'with a linear object, as Figure,
                               moving axially [with one end]
                               obliquely onto the Ground'
   PG: -wi·sᵘ   'to all over a surface'
               -ik·   'hither'
   Ax: same as for (a)

/s-'-w-ra-ṭ -wi·sᵘ-ik·-ᵃ/ ⇒ [sẅraṭwí·suk·a]

Instantiated: "I shingled the roof."

c. F: uh- (43)   'a planar object lying flush against a
                               surface'
   PG: -a·sẏ   'multiply together'
   Ax: same as for (a)

/s-'-w-uh-ṫ-a·sẏ-ᵃ/ ⇒ [sẇohṫá·sẏa]

Instantiated: "I patched a hole in the wall with boards."

d. Px: p-   'back, reflexive'
   F: ce- (37)   'eye, eye-shaped object'
   PG: -i·w   'dually together'
   PG: -ihiy   'on one's body'
   Ax: same as (a)

/s-'-w-p-ce-ṫ-i·w-ihiy-ᵃ/ ⇒ [sṗċeṫ·í·wehè·]

Literal: 'I AGENTed it that smallish planar objects—which were
eye-shaped objects—to come dually together back to me on my body
so as to become attached'
Instantiated: "I buttoned up."

4.2.2   Root Type: Motion + Path + Ground

---

6. R: -spaq̇-
   'to move into, through mud'

---

a. CI → MF: ra- (12Bb)   'with a linear object, as Figure, moving
                                    laterally [with one end] through the
                                    Ground'
   Ax: s- '- w- - ᵃ   '1s, (3), factual'—agentive

/s-'-w-ra-spaq̇-ᵃ/ ⇒ [sẇraspáq̇]

Literal: 'I AGENTed it that [a Figure] move through mud, as
Ground, with a linear object, as Figure, moving laterally with one
end through the Ground'
Instantiated: "I worked the stick around in the mud."

b. CI: uh- (10a)   'as a result of a linear object
                                    kinemically moving
                                    circumpivotally [with one end]
                                    while contacting the Figure'

or

CI → MF: uh- (17)   'with a free-flying object, as
                                Figure, sailing/falling onto the
                                Ground'
PG: -im   'thither'
Ax: same as for (a)

/s-'-w-uh-sṗaq̓-im-ᵃ/ ⇒ [sẇospaq̓íw]

Instantiated: "I threw the apple into the mud puddle."

c. CI → MF: tu- (1)   'with the hand(s) of a person, as
                                  Figure, (working centripetally),
                                  acting on the Ground'
   PG: -im   'thither'
   Ax: same as for (a)

/s-'-w-tu-sṗaq̓-im-ᵃ/ ⇒ [stusṗaq̓íw]

Instantiated: "I stuck my hand into the mud."

d. CI → MF: ma- (3)   'with the foot of a person, as Figure,
                                  acting on the Ground'
   PG: -tip -u·   'into a pit'
                 -im   'thither'
   Ax: s- '- w- - ᵃ   '1s, (3), factual'—nonagentive

/s-'-w-ma-sṗaq̓-tip-u·-im-a/ ⇒ [sṁa·sṗáq̓tʰpu·ma]

Instantiated: "I stepped into a deep mudhole."

---

7. R: -kʰok-
'to move into contact with a big stomach'

---

a. CI → MF: hi- (9)   'with the body of a person, as Figure,
                                  acting on the Ground'
   Ax: s- '- w- - ᵃ   '1s, (3), factual'—nonundergoer

/s-'-w-hi-kʰok-ᵃ/ ⇒ [sẇhekʰ·ókʰ]

Literal: 'I UNDERWENT it that [a Figure] moved into contact with
a big stomach, as Ground, with my body, as the Figure, acting on the
Ground'

Instantiated: "I bumped into his protruding belly."

b. CI → MF: uh- (10a)   'with a linear object, as Figure, kinetically moving circumpivotally [with one end] onto the Ground'

PG: -wam-im   'into someone's body'

Ax: s- '- w- - ᵃ   '1s, (3), factual'—agentive

/s-'-w-uh-kʰok-wam-im-ᵃ/ ⇒ [sẁohkʰokúʔṃaw]

Instantiated: "I hit him in his big stomach with my fist."

c. CI → MF: tu- (1)   'with the hands of a person, as Figure, working toward each other, acting on the Ground'

Ax: same as for (b)

/s-'-w-tu-kʰok-ᵃ/ ⇒ [stúkʰ·ókʰ]

Instantiated: "I grasped his protruding belly between my hands." / "I played with the deer's stomach (that was lying on the ground)."

4.2.3   Root Type: Figure + Motion + Path + Ground

8. R: -luc-
'for the natural surface growth on a (once-)living object to come detached from (part of) that object'

a. CI: ra- (12Ba)   'as a result of a planar object moving laterally [with one edge] along a surface while contacting the Figure'

Ax: s- '- w- - ᵃ   '1s, (3), factual'—agentive

/s-'-w-ra-luc-ᵃ/ ⇒ [sẁlal·úcʰ]

Instantiated: "I scraped the fur off the hide."

b. CI: ru- (15Aa)   'as a result of a linear object moving with axial tension [with one end] while contacting the Figure'

Ax: same as for (a)

/s-'-w-ru-luc-ᵃ/ ⇒ [sẁlul·úcʰ]

Instantiated: "I pulled a handful of hair out of his head."

c. CI: mu:- (25)   'by the AGENT's applying heat/fire to the Figure'

Ax: same as for (a)

/s-'-w-mu:-luc-ᵃ/ ⇒ [sṁo·lúcʰ]

Instantiated: "I burned the quills off the porcupine." / "I scalded the feathers off the chicken."

d. CI: wi- (5)   'as a result of the teeth of a person acting
                                       on the Figure'

   Ax: same as for (a)

/s-'-w-wi-luc-ᵃ/ ⇒ [sẁe·lúcʰ]

Instantiated: "I slid the bark off a willow twig, holding one end in my teeth."

e. CI: ma- (3)   'as a result of the foot of a person acting
                                       on the Figure'

   Ax: same as for (a)

/s-'-w-ma-luc-ᵃ/ ⇒ [sṁa·lúcʰ]

Instantiated: "I skinned the rabbit by accidentally stepping on it."

f. G: ti- (34)   'the buttocks'
   Ax: s- '- w- - ᵃ '1s, (3), factual'—undergoer

/s-'-w-ti-luc-ᵃ/ ⇒ [stẁil·úcʰ]

Literal: 'I UNDERWENT it that natural surface-growth came detached from a living object—which was buttocks'
Instantiated: "I skinned my behind when I fell."

g. G: hi- (38)   'a specific part of the body not treated by
                                       another satellite'

   Ax: same as for (f)

/s-'-w-hi-luc-ᵃ/ ⇒ [sẁhel·úcʰ]

Instantiated: "I scraped some hair off my head when I fell."

---

9. R: -skit-
   'for (soft) material to snag on/get lodged in an object'

---

a. CI: cu- (20)   'as a result of flowing liquid acting on the Figure'
   Ax: '- w- - ᵃ   '3, (3), factual'—nonagentive

/'-w-cu-skit-ᵃ/ ⇒ [ċuskítʰ]

Instantiated: "Some brush that was borne along by the stream got snagged on a limb that was jutting up."

b. CI → MF: uh- (17) 'with a kinemically free-flying object, as Figure, sailing/falling onto the Ground'

Ax: '- w- - ᵃ '3, (3), factual'—nonagentive

/'-w-uh-skit-ᵃ/ ⇒ [ẇoskítʰ]

Instantiated: "A ball sailing through the air got caught in the tree."

c. Px: p- 'mis-, mal-'

CI: ra- (12Bb) 'as a result of a linear object moving laterally [with one end] over the meta-Figure (a surface)'

& G: ra- (42) '(one end of) a linear object sticking obliquely out of a surface'

Ax: s- '- w- - ᵃ '1s, (3), factual'—undergoer

/s-'-w-p-ra-skit-ᵃ/ ⇒ [sṗraskítʰ]

Literal: 'I UNDERWENT it that soft material, as Figure, snagged on an object, as Ground—which was (one end of) a linear object obliquely sticking out of a surface—as a result of that linear object, as Instrument, moving laterally [with one end] over the Ground [a surface]'

Instantiated: "I caught my shirt on a nail."

d. CI: wi- (5) 'as a result of the teeth of a person acting on the Figure'

& G: wi- (35) 'the teeth'

PG: -im 'into one's body'

Ax: same as for (c)

/s-'-w-wi-skit-im-ᵃ/ ⇒ [sẇe·skitíw]

Instantiated: "I got a piece of food caught in my teeth."

e. CI: uh- (10a) 'as a result of a linear object kinemically moving circumpivotally [with one end] onto the Figure'

& G: uh- (39) '(one end of) a linear object in swinging motion'

Ax: '- w- - ᵃ '3, (3), factual'—undergoer

/'-w-uh-skit-ᵃ/ ⇒ [ẇoskítʰ]

Instantiated: "The chicken pecking at the bone got a piece of meat caught in its bill."

---

10. R: -m̓ur-
  'for fluid to come out of a biologic membranous sac'

---

a. CI: hi- (9)   'as a result of the whole body of an entity acting
                             on the Figure'
   PG: -ik·   'hither'
   Ax: '- w- - ᵃ   '3, (3), factual'—nonagentive

/'-w-hi-m̓ur-ik·-ᵃ/ ⇒ [ẇhe?m̓urík·a]

Instantiated: "The cow's birth sac (amnion) burst from the baby calf
inside."

b. CI: tu- (1)   'as a result of the hand of a person, working in
                             upon itself, acting on the Figure'
   Ax: s- '- w- - ᵃ   '1s, (3), factual'—agentive

/s-'-w-tu-m̓ur-ᵃ/ ⇒ [st̓u?m̓úrᵘ]

Instantiated: "I made the milk squirt out of the cow's teat by
squeezing it in my hand."

c. CI: ci- (2)   'as a result of the hands of a person, working
                             manipulatively, acting on the Figure'
   Sx: -cic   'go and'
   Ax: s- '-   '1s, (3), intentive'—agentive

/s-'-ci-m̓ur-cic/ ⇒ [sĉi?m̓úrᵘcicʰ]

Instantiated: "I'll go milk the cow."

d. CI: ra- (12Bc)   'as a result of a linear object pressing
                             laterally [with its side] on the Figure'
   PG: -im   'thither'
   Ax: same as for (b)

/s-'-w-ra-m̓ur-im-ᵃ/ ⇒ [sẇra?m̓uríw]

Instantiated: "I made the milk squirt out by pressing against the
cow's udder with a stick."

e. CI: pri- (6)   'as a result of the mouth-interior of a person,
                             working ingressively, acting on the Figure'
   PG: -ik·   'hither'
   Ax: '- w- - ᵃ   '3, (3), factual'—agentive

/'-w-pri-m̓ur-ik·-ᵃ/ ⇒ [ṗri?m̓urík·a]

Instantiated: "He sucked on the woman's breasts to start the milk flow."

f. CI: phu- (7)   'as a result of the mouth-interior of a person, working egressively, acting on the Figure'
   PG: -im   'thither'
   Ax: same as for (e)

/'-w-phu-m̊ur-im-ᵃ/ ⇒ [ṗhoʔm̥uríw]

Instantiated: "The doctor sucked the matter out of the boil and spat it out."

---

11. R: -sćak̇-
    'for a sharp-pointed linear object to move axially with its point into the substance of yielding material'

---

a. CI → MF: cu- (11b)   'with a linear object, as Figure, moving axially [with one end] perpendicularly into the meta-Ground'
   Ax: s- '- w- - ᵃ   '1s, (3), factual'—agentive

/s-'-w-cu-sćak̇-ᵃ/ ⇒ [sćusćák̇]

Instantiated: "I skewered the piece of meat with a fork."

b. CI: uh- (10a)   'as a result of a linear object kinemically moving circumpivotally [with one end] while contacting the Figure'
   PG: -cisᵘ   'down into-the-substance-of a solid resting on the ground'
           -im   'thither'
   Ax: same as for (a)

/s-'-w-uh-sćak̇-cisᵘ-im-ᵃ/ ⇒ [sẇosćák̇cʰu]

Instantiated: "I swung the pickax down into the tree stump."

c. CI: same as for (b)
   PG: -mik·   'onto a head, into a face, into an eye'
   Ax: same as for (a)

/s-'-w-uh-sćak̇-mik·-ᵃ/ ⇒ [sẇosćák̇mik·a]

Instantiated: "I threw a nail into his eye."

d. Px: p-   'mis-, mal-'
   G: tu- (32)   'the hand(s), arm(s)'
   PG: -im   'into one's body'
   Ax: s- '- w- - ᵃ   '1s, (3), factual'—undergoer

/s-'-w-p-tu-sčak̓-im-ᵃ/ ⇒ [sp̓tusčak̓íw]

Literal: 'I UNDERWENT it that the end of a sharp-pointed linear object mal-moved axially into the substance of yielding material—which was a hand—into my body'

Instantiated: "I got a thorn stuck in my finger."

e. Px: :-   'augmentative' [here used idiomatically]
   G: ti- (34)   'the buttocks'
   PG: same as for (d)
   Ax: same as for (d)

/s-'-w-:-ti-sčak̓-im-ᵃ/ ⇒ [stwe·sčak̓íw]

Instantiated: "I got a splinter stuck in my behind."

---

12. R: -puq-
   'for dust to move off a surface (into a cloud)'

---

a. CI: ma- (3)   'as a result of the feet of a person acting on the Figure'
   Ax: s- '- w- - ᵃ   '1s, (3), factual'—agentive

/s-'-w-ma-puq-ᵃ/ ⇒ [sm̓a·póqʰ]

Instantiated: "I kicked up the dirt as I walked along."

b. CI: ra- (12Ba)   'as a result of a planar object moving laterally [with one edge] along a surface while contacting the Figure'
   Ax: same as for (a)

/s-'-w-ra-puq-ᵃ/ ⇒ [sẘrap·óqʰ]

Instantiated: "I swept the dust up into a cloud."

c. CI: uh- (10a)   'as a result of a linear object kinemically moving circumpivotally [with one end] while contacting the Figure'
   Ax: same as for (a)

/s-'-w-uh-puq-ᵃ/ ⇒ [sẁohpóqʰ]

Instantiated: "I shook out the blanket."

d. CI: phu- (18)   'as a result of matter propelled by the mouth working egressively sailing into the Figure'

PG: -uww   'off from over a surface'

    -ihiy   'on one's body'

Ax: same as for (a)

/s-'-w-phu-puq-uww-ihiy-ᵃ/ ⇒ [sṗhop·oqúw·ehè·]

Instantiated: "I blew the dust off my clothes."

e. CI: i- (0)   'as a result of anything/nothing acting on the Figure'

PG: -asẁ   'all about within itself' [e.g., hair tousling about, clothes flapping about]

Ax: '- w- - ᵃ   '3, (3), factual'—nonagentive

/'-w-i-puq-asẁ-ᵃ/ ⇒ [ẁip·oqásẁa]

Instantiated: "There's dust swirling about over the road (where the horses had ridden past)."

---

13. R: -hapuk-

'for a body part (or a perceptual sense) to fail in an attempt to secure an object (or a sensible aspect thereof) because either the object or the body part passed to one side of the other'

This R occurs idiomatically with

Px: :-Sx: -miċ

a. CI → MF: tu- (1)   'with the hands of a person, as Figure, working toward each other, acting on the Ground'

Ax: s- '- w- - ᵃ   '1s, (3), factual'—undergoer

/s-'-w-:-tu-hapuk-miċ-ᵃ/ ⇒ [sṫo·hapúkʰmiċ]

Literal: 'I UNDERWENT it that a body part, as Figure, failed in an attempt to secure an object, as Ground, where my hands, as the Figure, working toward each other, were to act on the Ground, because my hands and the object passed to one side of each other'

Instantiated: "I missed catching the ball."

b. CI → MF: ma- (3)   'with the foot of a person, as
                                  Figure, acting on the Ground'

Ax: same as for (a)

/s-'-w-:-ma-hapuk-mič-ᵃ/ ⇒ [sm̓a·hapúkʰmič]

Instantiated: "I missed a step as I was walking down the stairs."

c. CI → MF: ti- (4)   'with the buttocks of a person, as
                                  Figure, acting on the Ground'

Ax: same as for (a)

/s-'-w-:-ti-hapuk-mič-ᵃ/ ⇒ [sʼtwe·hapúkʰmič]

Instantiated: "As I bent to sit down, I got the chair pulled out from under me."

d. CI → MF: si- (27)   'with the vision of an Experiencer,
                                  as Figure, acting on a Ground'

Ax: same as for (a)

/s-'-w-:-si-hapuk-mič-ᵃ/ ⇒ [sẁse·hapúkʰmič]

Instantiated: "I looked over too late to catch sight of that deer."

4.2.4   Root Type: Meta-Figure + Motion + Path + Meta-Ground   In its basic usage, a verb root of this type refers to a particular kind of object moving in a particular way relative to itself—that is, as a meta-Figure moving with respect to itself as meta-Ground. Hence, it refers to a particular kind of object shifting from one kind of configuration to another. In this usage, a Cause satellite refers to the cause of the configurational shift, while any Path + Ground satellite refers to the spatial characteristics of the shift.

In addition, though, a verb root of this type can participate in two further usages. In one usage, the particular object that the root refers to acts as a Figure that executes translational Motion, while at the same time it acts as the meta-Figure that undergoes its configurational shift. In the third usage, the object again executes translational Motion, but it has already shifted into its final configuration. In these latter two usages, the Cause satellite and the Path + Ground satellite both pertain to the translational motion. The three usages can be summarized as follows.

Usage 1: for the object (as meta-Figure) to shift from its initial configuration to its final one

Usage 2: for the object (as Figure) to move + Path + Ground, while the object (as meta-Figure) shifts from its initial configuration to its final one

Usage 3: for the object (as Figure) to move + Path + Ground, after the object (as meta-Figure) has shifted from its initial configuration to its final one

---

14. R: -miq̓-

Usage 1: 'for an architectural structure to shift from intactness to a lack of structural integrity'

a. CI: uh- (24b)   'as a result of gravity/the Figure's own weight acting on the Figure'
    PG: -tip -asw̓   'apart'
    Ax: n- w- - ᵃ   '3, (3), evidential'—nonagentive

/n-w-uh-miq̓-tip-asw̓-ᵃ/ ⇒ [nohméq̓tʰpasẁa]

Instantiated: "The house fell apart."

b. CI: ci- (2)   'as a result of the hands of a person, working manipulatively, acting on the Figure'
    PG: -ikc -ik -ayw   'into fragments'
    Ax: s- '- w- - ᵃ   '1s, (3), factual'—agentive

/s-'-w-ci-miq̓-ikc-ik-ayw-ᵃ/ ⇒ [sċwim·eq̓íkʰcikaywa]

Instantiated: "I tore the house to pieces, demolished the house."

Usage 2: 'for (part of) an architectural structure to move, thereby shifting from intactness to a lack of structural integrity'

a. CI: miw- (25)   'as a result of heat/fire acting on the Figure'
    PG: -miċ   'down onto the surface of the ground'
    Ax: n- w- - ᵃ   '3, (3), evidential'—nonagentive

/n-w-miw-miq̓-miċ-ᵃ/ ⇒ [nᵊmwewméq̓miċ]

Instantiated: "The house burnt down to the ground."

b. CI: cu- (20)   'as a result of flowing liquid acting on the Figure'
    PG: same as for (a)
    Ax: same as for (a)

/n-w-cu-miq̓-miċ-ᵃ/ ⇒ [ṇcum·eq̓miċ]

Instantiated: "The house collapsed from the flood."

c. CI: uh- (24b) 'as a result of gravity/the Figure's own weight acting on the Figure'

PG: -tip -u· 'down into a pit in the ground'

-im 'thither'

Ax: same as for (a)

/n-w-uh-miq̓-tip-u·-im-ᵃ/ ⇒ [nohméq̓tʰpu·ma]

Instantiated: "The house fell all the way down into the cellar."

d. CI: ca- (19) 'as a result of the wind blowing on the Figure'

PG: -uww -ay 'off from over a surface'

Ax: n- w- - ᵃ '3, (3), evidential'—nonagentive

/n-w-ca-miq̓-uww-ay-ᵃ/ ⇒ [n̩cwam·eq̓úw·e·]

Instantiated: "The roof blew off the house."

e. CI: ma- (3) 'as a result of the foot of a person acting on the Figure'

PG: -taw 'out of an enclosure'

Ax: s- '- w- - ᵃ '1s, (3), factual'—agentive

/s-'-w-ma-miq̓-taw-ᵃ/ ⇒ [sm̩a·méq̓ta·]

Instantiated: "I kicked the door out off its hinges."

Usage 3: 'for an architectural structure to move, having already shifted from intactness to a lack of structural integrity'

a. CI: hi- (9) 'as a result of the whole body of a person acting on the Figure'

PG: -ic̓w 'up'

Ax: '- w- - ᵃ '3, (3), factual'—agentive

/'-w-hi-miq̓-ic̓w-ᵃ/ ⇒ [w̓hem·eq̓íc̓wa]

Instantiated: "The kid crawling under the pile of boards from the collapsed house lifted them up as he stood."

---

15. R: -n̓uq̓-

Usage 1: 'for a live articulated object to shift by bending at its articulations from an extended conformation into a folded-together shape'

a. F: tu- (32) 'the hand(s), arm(s)'

PG: -a·sy̓ 'multiply together/into an accumulation'

Ax: s- '- w- - ᵃ '1s, (3), factual'—agentive

/s-'-w-tu-n̓uq̓-a·sẏ-ª/ ⇒ [st̓uʔn̥oq̓á·sẏa]

Instantiated: "I made a fist."

b. CI: ci- (2)   'as a result of the hands of a
                                                 person, working manipu-
                                                 latively, acting on the Figure'
    Optional PG: -a·sẏ   'multiply together/into an
                                                 accumulation'
    Ax: same as for (a)

/s-'-w-ci-n̓uq̓ (-a·sẏ)-ª/ ⇒ [sċwiʔn̥óq̓] [sċwiʔn̥oq̓á·sẏa]

Instantiated: "I doubled the cat up (by drawing its limbs together)."

Usage 2: 'for a live articulated object to move, shifting from an extended
conformation into a folded-together shape in the process'

a. Px: p-   'back, reflexive'
    F: tu- (32)   'the hand(s), arm(s)'
    PG: -a·sẏ   'multiply together/into an accumulation'
    PG: -ihiy   'on one's body'
    Ax: s- '- w- - ª   '1s, (3), factual'—agentive

/s-'-w-p-tu-n̓uq̓-a·sẏ-ihiy-ª/ ⇒ [sp̓tuʔn̥oq̓á·sẏehe·]

Literal: 'I AGENTed it that a live articulated object, as Figure—
which was my arms—moved multiply together back onto my body,
shifting from an extended conformation into a folded-together shape
in the process'

Instantiated: "I folded my arms across my chest."

b. CI: ma- (3)   'as a result of the foot of a person acting
                           on the Figure'
    PG: -miċ   'down onto the surface of the ground'
    Ax: same as for (a)

/s-'-w-ma-n̓uq̓-miċ-ª/ ⇒ [sm̓aʔn̥óq̓miċ]

Instantiated: "As he was sitting there, I bent his head down to the
ground with my foot."

c. CI: ma- (3)   'as a result of the foot of a person acting
                           on the Figure'
    PG: -iċt   'into a liquid'
    Ax: same as for (a)

/s-'-w-ma-n̓uq̓-iċt-ª/ ⇒ [sm̓aʔn̥oq̓íċta]

Instantiated: "I shoved the reluctant cat into the water with my foot, getting him doubled up as I did so."

Usage 3: 'for a live articulated object to move, having already shifted from an extended conformation into a folded-together shape'

a. CI: ci- (2)   'as a result of the hands of a person, working manipulatively, acting on the Figure'

   PG: -wam   'into a gravitic container'

   Ax: s- '- w- - ᵃ   '1s, (3), factual'—agentive

/s-'-w-ci-n̂uq̓-wam-ᵃ/ ⇒ [sċwi?ŋoq̓ú?m̥a]

Instantiated: "I stuck the doubled-up cat into the basket."

---

16. R: -caqih-

Usage 1: 'for the leg set on a creature to shift from a closed to an open conformation'

a. CI: ci- (2)   'as a result of the hands of a person, working manipulatively, acting on the Figure'

   PG: -tip -asw̓   'apart'

   Ax: s- '- w- - ᵃ   '1s, (3), factual'—agentive

/s-'-w-ci-caqih-tip-asw̓-ᵃ/ ⇒ [sċwic·aqéhtʰpasw̓a]

Instantiated: "I spread his legs apart with my hands."

b. F: ma- (33)   'feet, legs'

        or ti- (34)   'buttocks'

   PG: same as for (a)

   Ax: s- '- w- - ᵃ   '1s, (3), factual'—self-agentive

/s-'-w-ma-caqih-tip-asw̓-ᵃ/ ⇒ [sm̓a·caqéhtʰpasw̓a]

or /s-'-w-ti-caqih-tip-asw̓-ᵃ/ ⇒ [st̓wic·aqéhtʰpasw̓a]

Instantiated: "I spread my legs apart."

Usage 2: 'for the leg set on a creature to move, shifting from a closed to an open conformation in the process'

a. F: uh- (51)   'a weightful substance/object, a load'

   PG: -ikn   'to a position over/astraddle an edge'

         -ik·   'hither'

         -ihiy   'on one's body'

   Ax: s- '- w- - ᵃ   '1s, (3), factual'—agentive

/s-'-w-uh-caqih-ikn-ik·-ihiy-ᵃ/ ⇒ [sẇohcaqékʰnikèh·e]

Literal: 'I AGENTed it that a creature's leg set—which was a weightful object/a load—moved to a position astraddle an edge hither on my body, shifting from a closed to an open conformation in the process'

Instantiated: "I set him up on my back with his legs over my shoulders so I could carry him someplace."

Periphrastic usage: in construction with the verb *i*, 'to go', as second element taking all affixation.

a. PG: -im   'thither'
   Sx: -ak   'continuative'
   Ax: '- w- - ᵃ   '3, (3), factual'—self-agentive

/-caqih'-w-i-im-ak-ᵃ/ ⇒ [caqéhẇì?m̩akʰ]

Instantiated: "The frog went jumping along."

4.2.5   Root Type: Takes Sensory Prefixes

17. R: -lay-

   'for a person to come into/be in a pleased state of mind'

This root occurs idiomatically with the suffix

Sx: -im

and will here be presented with the same affix set:

Ax: s- '- w- - ᵃ   '1s, (3), factual'

a. CI: sa- (27)   'as a result of the visual aspect of an object acting on the Experiencer'

/s-'-w-sa-lay-im-ᵃ/ ⇒ [sᵊsal·ayíw]

Instantiated: "I find it good-looking, pretty/I like it (e.g., a picture)."

b. CI: ka- (28)   'as a result of the auditory aspect of an event acting on the Experiencer'

/s-'-w-ka-lay-im-ᵃ/ ⇒ [sḱwal·ayíw]

Instantiated: "I find it good-sounding/I like it (e.g., the singing)."

c. CI: pri- (30)   'as a result of the smell/taste of an object acting on the Experiencer'

/s-'-w-pri-lay-im-ᵃ/ ⇒ [spĺil·ayíw]

Instantiated: "I find it good-smelling, good-tasting/I like it (e.g., the flower)."

d. CI: tu- (31)   'as a result of the taste of a body acting on the Experiencer'

/s-'-w-tu-lay-im-ᵃ/ ⇒ [stúl·ayíw]

Instantiated: "I find it good-tasting, tasty/I like it (e.g., the food)."

Notes

1. This chapter brings together three separately completed analyses of material otherwise presented in chapter II-1. Section 2 below is a modestly revised version of the compendium of meaning-form associations that first appeared in Talmy 1985b. Section 3 is a moderately revised version of the compendium of typologies and universals that otherwise appeared only as a working paper, Talmy 1987. And section 4, which presents Atsugewi's Cause satellites and many examples of its polysynthetic verbs, is a moderate revision of a section in my dissertation, Talmy 1972:407–467, not previously published. The acknowledgments for the present chapter are the same as for chapter II-1.

Chapter 3

A Typology of Event Integration

1 INTRODUCTION

Three basic findings converge in this study.[1] The first finding is that, in the underlying conceptual organization of language, there is a certain type of event complex, what we term the "macro-event," that is fundamental and pervasive. On the one hand, the macro-event can be conceptualized as composed of two simpler events and the relation between them. But the macro-event is—perhaps universally—also amenable to conceptualization as a single fused event and, accordingly, to expression by a single clause. Substantively, a macro-event consists of a pair of cross-related Figure-Ground events, as this was described in chapter I-6. Talmy (1972, 1985b) had further described such an event complex and its "conflation" into a single clause in the expression of Motion. But it is now possible to demonstrate the existence of a generic category of such event complexes that extends well beyond the case of Motion alone. And it is possible to characterize the general structure of this event complex in rather precise terms.

The second finding, just alluded to, is that the macro-event pertains not just to Motion, but to as many as five otherwise quite distinct types of event. Talmy (1985b) had already seen that "change of state," as an event type, bears a linguistic parallel to Motion. But it is now evident that there are three further types of event with parallel semantic and syntactic properties. These are events of "temporal contouring," "action correlating," and "realization." Of these further types, action correlating is newly introduced here. Temporal contouring and realization have been discussed previously but not as types of events or even as events per se.

The third finding is that languages fall into two typological categories on the basis of where they characteristically express the schematic core of the event complex—in the verb or in a satellite to the verb. This typology formed part of the typology for Motion set forth in Talmy 1985b. But it is now apparent that it extends as well to all five types of events that the macro-event pertains to and, indeed, constitutes the main evidence for grouping the five event types together.

For an immediate idea of the kind of phenomenon to be treated, the English sentences in (1) illustrate macro-events with each of their five types of events in turn. And they illustrate the typological category in which the schematic core of the event type is expressed by a satellite.

(1) *The satellite (in italics) expresses*
    a. *the path in an event of motion*
       The ball rolled *in*.
    b. *the aspect in an event of temporal contouring*
       They talked *on*.
    c. *the changed property in an event of state change*
       The candle blew *out*.
    d. *the correlation in an event of action correlating*
       She sang *along*.
    e. *the fulfillment or confirmation in an event of realization*
       The police hunted the fugitive *down*.

Thus, in (1a), the satellite *in* indicates that the ball entered something while rolling. The *on* in (1b) indicates that "they" continued in their process of talking. The *out* in (1c) indicates that the candle became extinguished as a result of something blowing on it. The *along* in (1d) indicates that "she" joined or accompanied another person, where her singing duplicated or complemented that person's own musical activity. And the *down* in (1e) indicates that the police fulfilled their intention of capturing the fugitive, which was the goal of their engaging in the hunting activity.

Further display of concrete examples such as these is delayed until section 2, since the task of section 1 is to set forth the theoretical framework and parameters that the remainder of this study's analysis will depend on.

2 THE MACRO-EVENT

We begin the formal analysis with a characterization of the macro-event.

2.1 An Event in General

We first address the nature of an event in general, as a basis for characterizing the macro-event.

2.1.1 Conceptualization of an Event By the operation of very general cognitive processes that can be termed **conceptual partitioning** and the **ascription of entityhood**, the human mind in perception or conception can extend a boundary around a portion of what would otherwise be a continuum, whether of space, time, or other qualitative domain, and ascribe to the excerpted contents within the boundary the property of being a single unit entity. Among various alternatives, one category of such an entity is perceived or conceptualized as an **event**. This is a type of entity that includes within its boundary a continuous correlation between at least some portion of its identifying qualitative domain and some portion of the so-conceived temporal continuum—that is, of the progression of time. Such a correlation may rest on a primitive phenomenological experience that can be characterized as **dynamism**—a fundamental property or principle of activeness in the world. This experience is probably both foundational and universal in human cognition.

2.1.2 Event Complexes An entity that can be cognized as an event can also be conceptualized as having a particular type of internal structure and degree of structural complexity. Such structural properties can be reflected by properties of the syntactic forms that can represent the event. At one end of the range of such properties, a **unitary event** is one that can be represented by a single syntactic clause and that, under a current conceptualization, consists of components that are considered not to constitute events in their own right. For the phenomenon treated here, we need to consider only one type of event higher on the scale. This event can in many languages be syntactically represented by—to use the traditional terminology—a complex sentence consisting of a main clause and a subordinate clause that has a subordinating conjunction. We can adapt this syntactic terminology to characterize the conceptualization of an event represented by a formal structure of this sort. Thus, such an event can be called a **complex event**. It is in turn partitioned into a **main event** and a **subordinate event**—themselves conceptualized as unitary events in the simplest case—together with the relation that the subordinate event bears to the main event (see chapter I-6).

2.1.3 Conceptual Integration of Events A general cognitive process appears to be at work in language whereby an event that under a more analytic conceptualization would be understood as complex and represented by a multiclause syntactic structure can be alternatively conceptualized as unitary and represented by a single clause. This process of reconceptualization involves the conceptual integration or conflation of events and will here be termed **event integration**. This chapter mainly addresses event integration with respect to the macro-event. But event integration—or, at least, its syntactic counterpart—has been well addressed in the literature with respect to concepts like "clause union," especially in relation to agentive causation. We briefly sketch the semantics of agentive event integration here for two reasons. First, it can serve as a more familiar model for the subsequent treatment of macro-event integration. Second, Agent-initiated causal events leading up to a macro-event are themselves frequently included within macro-event integration, and so play a role in the full description of the latter (as discussed later).

One seemingly universal instantiation of event integration pertains to agentive causation. Conceived more analytically, such causation consists of a causal chain in which an agent's action initiates a succession of events that lead to the final event under consideration. The Agent has volitionally performed the initiating action and has a scope of intention that extends over the whole sequence. Such a complex of distinct events can be syntactically represented by a complex of distinct clauses. But the same body of content can also be conceptually integrated so as to be experienced as a unitary event and, correspondingly, to be represented syntactically by a single clause. Thus, a particular agentive referent can be conceptualized as a causal sequence of separate events and be so represented syntactically, as in (2a), or it can be reconceived as a neounitary event expressed monoclausally as in (2b).

(2) a. The aerial toppled because I did something to it [e.g., because I threw a rock at it].
    b. I toppled the aerial.

2.2 Composition of the Macro-Event

Though the macro-event has already been referred to and illustrated, we here begin a more formal characterization of it.

2.2.1 The Macro-Event as a Conceptual Integration of a Complex Event

A crosslinguistic comparison strongly suggests that there is a fundamental and recurrent category of complex event that is prone to conceptual integration and representation by a single clause, a type here termed a **macro-event**. Thus, on the one hand, the macro-event is expressed by a single clause and is regularly conceptualized as a unitary event. On the other hand, a closer syntactic and semantic analysis of such single clauses shows that their conceptual structure and content closely resemble that of a complex event of a certain class and, indeed, they can often be alternatively expressed by complex sentences.

The difference in conceptualization can be illustrated for a case of nonagentive causation. The complex sentence in (3a) represents part for part the main event, subordinating relation, and subordinate event of a complex event. This can be contrasted with the single-clause sentence in (3b), which expresses virtually the same contents with the same structuring and interrelation of components but which presents this complex as a unitary event—that is, as a macro-event.

(3) a. The candle went out because something blew on it.
    b. The candle blew out.

The category of complex event amenable to conceptual integration as a macro-event is greatly constrained. In the appropriate complex event, the main and subordinate events must be of certain distinct classes, and these events must bear certain relations to the whole complex and to each other. These properties are addressed at length in this chapter. More generally, one of the major concerns is the cognitive issue of event cohesion or fusion. This concern, with respect to conceptual content, pertains to the amount of it, the kinds of it, and the relations among different portions of it that can or must be present together in consciousness to permit the experiencing of that content as a single coherent unit of eventhood. As will be seen below, languages differ as to the maximum amount of conceptual content of a particular kind and organization that can be packaged colloquially within a single clause and hence readily experienced as a single macro-event. Much of this broader concern, though, must await further treatment.

2.2.2 The Framing Event   Within the macro-event, we first examine the properties of the main event as a unitary event considered by itself. This main event will later be termed a "framing event" for the properties it has in relation to the remainder of the macro-event, but we will use this term here as well. The framing event constitutes a particular event schema, one that can be applied to several different conceptual domains. At present, the framing event can be seen to schematize five different domains—a finding based on their comparable semantic and syntactic treatment across languages. These five types include an event of Motion or location in space, an event of contouring in time (aspect), an event of change or constancy among states, an event of correlation among actions, and an event of fulfillment or confirmation in the domain of realization.

We now examine the internal structure of the framing event. The framing event consists of four components. The first component is a **figural entity**. The figural entity is generally the component on which attention or concern is currently most centered. Its condition is conceptualized as a variable the particular value of which is the relevant issue. The second component is a **ground entity**. This component is conceptualized as a reference entity, with respect to which the condition of the figural entity is characterized. The third component is a process by which the figural entity either makes a transition or stays fixed with respect to the ground entity. This will be called the **activating process**, because it is the component conceived as contributing the factor of dynamism to the event. The activating process generally has only two values: **transition** and **fixity**. Thus, for example, in the domain of "Motion," these two values are realized as 'motion' and 'stationariness,' while in the domain of "state change," they are realized as 'change' and 'stasis'. Finally, the fourth component is an **association function** that sets the figural entity into a particular relationship with the ground entity.

The four components that make up a framing event generally differ in their distinctiveness in the referential context. It can be observed that the figural entity is generally set by context, and that the activating process generally has either of only two values. Accordingly, it is another portion of the event that most determines its particular character and that distinguishes it from other framing events. This portion is the particular association with a particular ground entity that the figural entity has entered into. Thus, either the association function alone or the association function together with the ground entity can be considered the schematic core of the framing event. This will be called the **core schema**. It will be seen to figure crucially in the syntactic mappings described below.

To help clarify it, this general characterization can be particularized for an event of motion in space. Here, both the figural entity and the ground entity are each a physical *object*. The activating process, here of the transition type, constitutes *motion*. And the association function that relates the figural entity to the ground entity constitutes the *path*. The core schema here will then be either the path alone or the path together with the ground object.

In addition to its autonomous properties, the main event has certain properties with respect to the rest of the macro-event. Relative to the whole, the main event provides or determines certain overarching patterns. Thus, the main event can be said to perform a *framing* function in relation to the macro-event. Hence, our term for it is the **framing event**.

In this way, the framing event provides for the whole macro-event the overarching conceptual framework or reference frame within which the other included activities are conceived of as taking place. The framing event thus determines at least the overall temporal framework and thereby determines the aspect of the sentence that expresses the macro-event. It also generally determines the overall spatial framework where a physical setting is involved—or some analogous reference frame where another conceptual domain is involved. Further, the framing event determines all or most of the argument structure and semantic character of the arguments overall within the macro-event, as well as determining all or most of the syntactic complement structure in the sentence that expresses the macro-event. In addition, the framing event constitutes the central import or main point—or what will here be termed the **upshot**—relative to the whole macro-event. That is to say, it is the framing event that is asserted in a positive declarative sentence, that is denied under negation, that is demanded in an imperative, and that is asked about in an interrogative.

Within the macro-event, the main event can also manifest certain framing functions relative to the subordinate event. First, the framing event can anchor the subordinate event within, or link that event to, the overarching conceptual framework that it determines. Second, the framing event can bear to the subordinate event the relation of "structurer" in a cognitive process of conceptual structuring. In particular here, the framing event can act as an abstract structure conceptually imposed on the subordinate event acting as a "substrate."

Generally in this relationship, the semantic character of the framing event is more that of an abstract schema, while that of the subordinate event tends to be more substantive or perceptually palpable. For this reason, the content of the subordinate event is often more vivid than that of the framing event and thus might draw much or at times even more attention to itself; in this respect it might seem semantically more primary than the framing event. Nevertheless, it is the framing event that frames, shapes, provides the upshot, and is determinative of the further factors outlined above.

2.2.3   The Co-Event   As to its intrinsic properties, the kind of event that constitutes the subordinate event within a macro-event is probably most frequently and perhaps prototypically an aspectually unbounded activity. But other event types do occur. For that reason, no single semantic characterization can yet be given for the subordinate event considered autonomously. But for its relative roles, the subordinate event can be held to constitute an event of **circumstance** in relation to the macro-event as a whole and to perform functions of **support** in relation to the framing event. In these supporting functions, the subordinate event can be seen to fill in, elaborate, add to, or motivate the framing event. The degree of its parity with the framing event can vary. This can range from an ancillary status, as in its lesser capacity to determine the conceptual structure of the whole macro-event. And it can range up to a peer status, as in its contribution to informational content. To highlight this functional range, we will term it a **co-event**, since "co-" ranges from subordinateness, as in "co-pilot," to coequality, as in "co-author." The term "Co-event" was already introduced in chapter II-1, but since it was more specialized there—considered only in relation to a Motion event—it was capitalized. Here, the lowercase "co-event" relates generally to any type of framing event.

Generically, the co-event bears a support relation to the framing event. In any given usage, however, this general support relation is particularized as one out of a certain set of specific relations. These include Precursion, Enablement, Cause, Manner, Concomitance, Purpose, and Constitutiveness. The most frequent among these are Cause and Manner.

There is of course a correspondence between the particular function that the framing event performs with respect to the co-event, and the particular support relation that the co-event bears to the framing event. Thus, when the framing event acts as a substrate shaper with respect to the co-event, the latter will generally bear a Constitutive relation to the former. And when the framing event serves to anchor the co-event within its framework, the co-event usually has a Manner or Concomitance relation to the framing event.

2.2.4   Summarizing the Components of the Macro-Event   In sum, the macro-event is a complex event that can be conceptually integrated into a unitary event expressable in some languages by a single clause. It is composed of a co-event, a framing event, and the support relation that the co-event bears to the framing event. The framing event serves to sche-

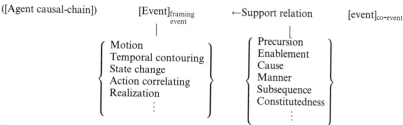

Conceptual structure of the macro-event

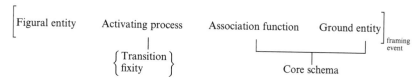

Conceptual structure of the framing event

matize a conceptual domain. It is composed of four components: a figural entity, an activating process, an association function, and a ground entity. The activating process can constitute either a transition or fixity. Either the association function alone or that together with the ground entity constitutes the core schema. In addition, the macro-event may include an Agent-initiated causal chain of events that in turn causes either or both of the framing event and the co-event. The two accompanying figures diagram these components and their relations. They also show the known conceptual domains that the framing event can schematize, as well as some particular forms of the support relation.

2.3 Mappings of the Macro-Event onto Syntactic Structures

With the macro-event now characterized semantically, we examine its syntactic realizations.

2.3.1 The Typology of Verb-Framed and Satellite-Framed Languages

The existence of the macro-event as a cognitive unit and its specific conceptual structuring may be universals of linguistic organization. But the world's languages generally seem to divide into a two-category typology on the basis of the characteristic pattern in which the conceptual structure of the macro-event is mapped onto syntactic structure. To characterize it initially in broad strokes, the typology consists of whether the core schema is expressed by the main verb or by the satellite.

As treated in chapter II-1, the **satellite to the verb**—or simply, the **satellite**, abbreviated Sat—is the grammatical category of any constituent other than a nominal or prepositional-phrase complement that is in a sister relation to the verb root. The satellite, which can be either a bound affix or a free word, is thus intended to encompass all of the following grammatical forms: English verb particles, German separable and inseparable verb prefixes, Latin or Russian verb prefixes, Chinese verb complements, Lahu nonhead "versatile verbs," Caddo incorporated nouns, and Atsugewi polysynthetic affixes around the verb root. The rationale for recognizing the satellite as a grammatical category is that it captures an observable commonality, both syntactic and semantic, across all these forms. For example, it is the characteristic site for the expression of the core schema across one typological category of languages.

Languages that characteristically map the core schema into the verb will be said to have a **framing verb** and to be **verb-framed** languages. Included among such languages are Romance, Semitic, Japanese, Tamil, Polynesian, Bantu, some branches of Mayan, Nez Perce, and Caddo. On the other hand, languages that characteristically map the core schema onto the satellite will be said to have a **framing satellite** and to be **satellite-framed** languages. Included among them are most Indo-European minus Romance, Finno-Ugric, Chinese, Ojibwa, and Warlpiri. Although the core schema in satellite-framed languages is largely expressed by the satellite alone, it is also often expressed by the combination of a satellite plus a presposition, or sometimes by a preposition alone. Such a "preposition" itself can consist not only of a free adposition, but also of a nominal inflection, or sometimes of a construction containing a "locative noun." Note that the core schema generally appears alone in the satellite (or associated constituent) in satellite-framed languages, but appears conflated together with the activating process in the verb of verb-framed languages.

With the schematic core of the framing event located either in the verb or in the satellite, one must observe where in each case the co-event appears. Languages with a framing satellite regularly map the co-event into the main verb, which can thus be called a **co-event verb**. On the other hand, languages with a framing verb map the co-event either onto a satellite or into an adjunct, typically an adpositional phrase or a gerundive-type constituent. Such forms are accordingly called a **co-event satellite**, a **co-event gerundive**, and so on. The accompanying figures diagram these relationships.

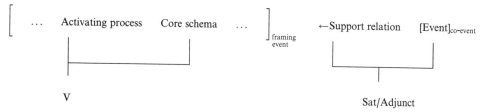

Syntactic mapping of macro-event in verb-framed languages

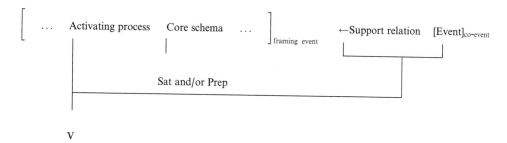

Syntactic mapping of macro-event in satellite-framed languages

2.3.2 Introductory Illustration For an introductory illustration of these relationships, we contrast English, a basically satellite-framed language, though not the most thoroughgoing example of the type, and Spanish, a verb-framed language. Consider first a nonagentive sentence with a motion-type framing event. In the English *The bottle floated out*, the satellite *out* expresses the core schema—here, the path—while the verb *float* expresses the co-event, which here bears the support relation of Manner to the framing event. By contrast, in the closest Spanish counterpart, *La botella salió flotando* 'The bottle exited floating', the verb *salir* 'to exit' expresses the core schema—again, the path—while the gerundive form *flotando* 'floating' expresses the co-event of Manner.

Comparably for an agentive sentence with a state-change type of framing event, in the English *I blew out the candle*, the satellite *out* expresses the core schema of the framing event—transition to a new state, that of being extinguished—while the verb *blow* expresses the co-event, one with the relation of Cause to the framing event. But in the closest Spanish counterparts, *Apagué la vela de un soplido/soplándola*, 'I extinguished the candle with a blow/blowing-it', the main verb expresses the transition to a new state while the adjunct, either the prepositional phrase or the gerundive, expresses the co-event of Cause.

2.3.3   The Co-Event Constituent in Verb-Framed Languages   In verb-framed languages, the constituent that expresses the co-event exhibits a certain characteristic. The degree of its syntactic integration into the main clause of the sentence can range over a gradient. The least integrated end of the gradient is represented, for example, in Spanish and Japanese. Thus, certain end-of-sentence gerundives in Spanish and certain *-te* constructions in Japanese—in both cases, expressing a co-event—may be interpreted syntactically as adverbial subordinate clauses. They do not function as satellites. By this interpretation, the overall construction is a complex sentence composed of two clauses and could therefore not represent a macro-event. A Spanish example is given in (4a).

But both languages also have constructions in which a verb (sometimes with additional constituents) referring to the co-event is in direct construction with the main verb—that is, with the framing verb (see Aske 1989, Matsumoto 1991). With this syntactic pattern, the whole sentence now can be interpreted as a single clause, and hence as representing a macro-event. A Spanish example appears in (4b). The gerundive verb here may nevertheless be considered to represent only a midway integration into the framing clause because its gerundive grammatical form still points to a separate-clause origin.

(4) a. La botella salió de la cueva flotando.
        'The bottle exited from the cave, floating.'
    b. La botella salió flotando de la cueva.
        'The bottle exited floating from the cave.'

Nez Perce (see chapter II-1) is at the most integrated end of the gradient. In this language, the constituent that expresses the co-event is a monomorpheme prefixed to the co-event verb. That is, it is an unmistakable satellite, and the whole sentence is now also unmistakably a single clause. This type of satellite can be termed a **co-event satellite**.

2.4   The Complementarity of Two Typological Perspectives

The basis for the typology presented in this chapter is complementary to the basis for the typology developed in chapter II-1. As was noted in the introduction to that chapter, one can fruitfully trace the relations between elements of meaning and elements of expression in either of two ways. One can fix one's attention on a particular constituent type and observe which semantic component comes to be expressed in it in different languages. Or one can attend to a particular semantic component and observe which constituent type it comes to be expressed in in different languages. Thus, chapter II-1 held constant a particular element of expression—the verb root—and observed which different types of semantic elements were characteristically represented there in different languages. To simplify matters, the basic finding was that languages mainly fall into three categories on the basis of whether they characteristically place the Co-event, the Path, or the Figure in the verb root.

The complementary procedure is adopted in the present chapter. Here, we hold constant a particular semantic element—the Path, or, more generally, the core schema—and observe the different formal elements in which it is expressed in different languages. The basic finding is that the Path, or core schema, characteristically appears either in the verb root or in the satellite.

To help correlate these two ways of mapping meaning to form, we can look at some of the same languages treated both in chapter II-1 and here. A language like Spanish immediately fits both perspectives. On the one hand, from the present chapter's perspective, Spanish places its Path component (or core schema) in the verb, not in the satellite. On the other hand, from the perspective of chapter II-1, the verb receives the Path component rather than the Co-event or the Figure.

With respect to other language types, from this chapter's perspective, both English and Atsugewi are alike—and differ typologically from Spanish—in that they place their Path component, or core schema, in the satellite, rather than in the verb. But now chapter II-1's perspective asks: With the Path component tucked away in the satellite, which other semantic component comes to reside in the verb? With respect to that question, the two languages are typologically different. In English, the verb houses the Co-event. In Atsugewi, the verb houses the Figure. And of course, both languages are typologically different from Spanish, whose verb houses the path.

2.5 Aims of This Chapter

The first aim of this chapter is to extend the typology presented in chapter II-1, which dealt only with Motion and some change of state. The present chapter now further demonstrates that, in any language, the syntactic site—verb or satellite—where Path is characteristically expressed is also to a great extent where aspect, state change, action correlation, and realization are characteristically expressed. This typological finding is then prima facie evidence that languages treat these five types of domain schematization—which might otherwise seem to bear little relation to each other—as a single conceptual entity. This entity is the framing event, which this study then further aims to establish as a recognized component of cognitive-linguistic organization. Further observation finds that the framing event is characteristically expressed within a single clause that systematically includes certain additional kinds of content: the co-event and its relation to the framing event. Such single clauses are seen to correspond crosslinguistically in expressing the same type of event complex, namely, a complex event conceptualized as a single event by a process of conceptual integration—here termed the macro-event, which this study then further aims to establish as an additional recognized component of cognitive-linguistic organization.

In this initial brief version, the present study does not treat a number of further important issues. Among such issues are the relations between what serves for language as a single integrated event and the single events of perception or of general cognition; the precise requisite factors that permit conceptual integration of an event complex for linguistic expression; the particular differences between languages as to which types of complex events are amenable to such conceptual fusion; the differences between languages as to which relations the co-event can bear to the framing event; and the competing claims for the presence or absence of consistency in the conceptual organization within any single language, claims that the comparable treatment of the five types of framing event might bear on.

3   A MOTION EVENT AS THE FRAMING EVENT

The first type of framing event we consider—possibly its conceptual prototype—is an event of physical motion or stationariness. We designate this range of motive states with the capitalized term **Motion**.

The general framing event structure that was characterized earlier can be particularized for the Motion event. The figural entity is a physical *object* whose path or site requires characterization and which has the role of **Figure** in relation to the whole event. The ground entity is a second physical *object* functioning as a reference point with respect to which the Figure's path or site is characterized and which bears the role of **Ground** in relation to the whole event. The activating process, when it consists of a transition by the Figure with respect to the Ground, is what is normally understood as translational *motion*. When it consists of the Figure's staying fixed with respect to the Ground, it is *stationariness*. The association function comes out as the (capitalized) **Path**—that is, the *path* followed or the *site* occupied by the Figure with respect to the Ground.

The core schema of the Motion event is generally the Path alone in some languages, such as English. But it is generally the combination of Path + Ground in other languages, such as Atsugewi (see Talmy 1972 and chapter II-1). In accordance with the general mapping typology, the core schema is characteristically expressed by the main verb in verb-framed languages and by the satellite in satellite-framed languages.

For illustration, (5) represents the conceptual structure of four Motion-type macro-events. These vary with respect to the absence or presence of an agentive causal chain and with respect to whether the support relation is Manner or Cause. The concept of motion is represented by the form MOVE or—when this results from an agentive chain—by the form ᴀMOVE. Each macro-event is seen to map in accordance with the two typologically contrasting patterns onto a sentence of Spanish, representing verb-framed languages, and onto a sentence of English, representing satellite-framed languages.

(5) a. *Nonagentive*

    i. *Support relation: Manner*

      [the bottle MOVED in to the cave] WITH-THE-MANNER-OF [it floated]

      English: The bottle floated into the cave.

      Spanish: La botella entró   flotando a la cueva.

           the bottle entered (MOVED-in) floating to the cave

    ii. *Support relation: Cause*

      [the bone MOVED out from its socket] WITH-THE-CAUSE-OF [(something) pulled on it]

      English: The bone pulled out of its socket.

      Spanish: El hueso se salió   de su sitio de un tirón.

           the bone exited (MOVED-out) from its location from a pull

b. *Agentive*

   i. *Support relation: Manner*

   [I $_A$MOVED the keg out of the storeroom] WITH-THE-MANNER-OF [I rolled it]

   English: I rolled the keg out of the storeroom.

   Spanish: Saqué   el barril de   la bodega   rodándolo.
   I extruded ($_A$MOVED-out) the keg   from the storeroom, rolling it

   ii. *Support relation: Cause*

   [I $_A$MOVED the ball in to the box] WITH-THE-CAUSE-OF [I kicked it]

   English: I kicked the ball into the box.

   Spanish: Metí   la pelota a la caja de   una patada.
   I inserted ($_A$MOVED-in) the ball   to the box from (by) a   kick

As the preceding translations show, English often has Path verbs that can directly gloss the Spanish Path verbs, but their use is generally less colloquial and they are largely borrowed from Romance languages, where they are the characteristic type. This is the case, for example, with all the following intransitive Path verbs: *enter, exit, ascend, descend, pass, cross, traverse, circle, return, arrive, advance, join, separate.*

The current examples showcase one of the reasons for considering the main event of a macro-event to be a "framing" event. The main event here represents an event of translational motion—that is, motion in which the Figure object changes its average position in space. Such a translational motion event co-defines a (typically rectilinear) framework in space, within which the activity of a co-event of Manner can come to be anchored. To see this, first note that a class of aspectually unbounded activities that I have called events of "self-contained Motion" is readily able to serve as a Manner-type co-event. Self-contained motion is the Motion of elements that, at a certain larger scope of granularity, do not change their average position in space. This class includes rotation, oscillation, local wander, dilation (expansion/contraction), wiggle, and rest. Such self-contained motion events can be referred to in isolation—for example, in *The ball rolled over and over in the magnetic field* (rotation), or *The ball bounced up and down on one spot* (oscillation). On the other hand, in macro-event sentences like *The ball rolled/bounced down the hall*, we see the self-contained motion occurring concurrently with and as a modifying Manner for an event of translational motion, here, the ball's moving down the hall. Thus, the activity of the self-contained motion has come to be anchored in the framework of translational motion represented by the main event. Hence, this is one justification for calling the main event a "framing" event.

As noted earlier for English, the core schema for a Motion event is usually just the Path alone, but we should present some cases where it is the combination of the Path plus the Ground. This will serve both to illustrate the majority pattern for Motion in languages like Atsugewi, as well as to model the majority pattern for the other framing event types in most languages including English.

Thus, in English, the whole of the Path + Ground concept 'to the home of entity$_1$/entity$_2$' maps onto the satellite *home*. This is seen in *He drove her home*, where it can mean either 'to his home' or 'to her home'.

A comparable case with a more abstract Ground—the Path + Ground combination 'to a position across an opening'—follows our typology. In satellite-framed English, the concept can map onto the satellite *shut*. But in verb-framed Spanish, it must map into the verb together with the 'motion' notion, as in *cerrar* 'to close'. This is shown in (6). Since this example can be interpreted as either motion or change of state or as something in between, it illustrates a relatedness or gradience across these two different framing-event types.

(6) [I $_A$MOVED the door TO POSITION-ACROSS-OPENING]
WITH-THE-CAUSE-OF [I kicked it]

   English: I kicked the door shut.
   Spanish: Cerré   la   puerta de   una patada.
          I closed the door   from (by) a   kick.

The introductory section raised the issue of how an agentive causal chain that precedes a macro-event might relate to the content of that macro-event. This issue matters especially since the macro-event can include a co-event that bears the relation of "Cause" to the framing event. A treatment of this issue is given here for the domain of Motion, but it applies to all the domains, in particular that of state change, as discussed below.

Consider first a co-event that bears the relation of Cause to the framing event within a macro-event proper—that is, one without any Agent. Such a co-event includes an entity that acts on the figural entity of the framing event, causing it to perform its action. Prototypically, the co-event is immediately prior to the framing event (onset causation), but it can also maintain its causal effect coextensively with it (extended causation). Exemplifying this semantic pattern is a complex event that can be represented by the complex sentence *The pen moved across the table from the wind blowing on it*, but that can also be conceptualized as an integrated macro-event and represented monoclausally as *The pen blew across the table from the wind*.

By contrast, a co-event that bears the relation of Manner to the framing event is prototypically a so-conceived additional activity that the figural entity performs concurrently with its framing-event activity. A complex form and an integrated form that exemplify this pattern are *The pen moved across the table, rolling as it went*, and *The pen rolled across the table*.

Now let us add an Agent who initiates a causal chain (which need not be more than one link in length) that affects the macro-event proper. In the case where the co-event bears a Cause relation to the framing event, the Agent's causal chain must indeed lead up to and cause the co-event, which in turn causes the framing event. There is thus here an unbroken causal chain from the Agent through the framing event. Complex and integrated examples of this pattern are *I blew on the pen and made it move across the table*, and *I blew the pen across the table*. This latter mono-clausal form thus represents an Agent-amplified macro-event.

But in the case where the co-event bears a Manner relation to the framing event, the Agent's causal chain must be interpreted as leading to and causing the framing event itself. The co-event is merely a concurrent activity that the figural entity performs while it is being caused to perform the action of the framing event. A complex form of this pattern (stilted in English) is *I acted on the pen and made it move across the table, rolling as it went*. An integrated form is *I rolled the pen across the table*.

In representing this last semantic pattern, some verb-framed languages, like Spanish, use a morphologically agentive form to represent not only the framing verb but also any co-event gerundive that expresses the Manner. This was evident, for example, in (5bi). That example was glossed as "I extruded the keg from the storeroom, *rolling* (trans.) it." But such a grammatical pattern for the co-event verb of Manner does not accurately reflect the semantics, since the figural entity still manifests its ancillary activity on its own.

4   TEMPORAL CONTOURING (ASPECT) AS THE FRAMING EVENT

The second type of framing event we consider is an event of **temporal contouring**. Temporal contouring is linguistic aspect, where such aspect is conceptualized as an event in its own right. The general structure of a framing event can apply to a temporal contouring in either of two ways. In the first way, the figural entity is the **degree of manifestation** of an event. This property refers to whether an event is fully manifested, is not manifested, or has some degree of partial manifestation, as well as to the situation in which this condition changes. Such degrees of manifestation are set into a fixed association with particular points or periods of time that thus function as the ground entity. Thus, if drawn on a graph with time progressing toward the right and degree of manifestation increasing upward, an iterated accomplishment would have the temporal contour of a series of flattened inverted U-shaped curves. Common examples of this degree-of-manifestation type of temporal contouring are 'starting', 'stopping', 'continuing', 'remaining unmanifested', 'iterating', 'intensifying', and 'tapering off'.

There is a second way the structure of a framing event can apply to a temporal contouring. It is where a process affects progressively more of some particular finite quantity, doing so with a certain contour through time. Here, the figural entity is the affected object itself. The activating process is this object's progression through time—represented below as "MOVE," where the quotation marks are to suggest that temporal progression can be conceptualized as an analogue or metaphoric extension of motion through space. The association function indicates the direction of the relationship that the affected object has with the temporal contour (e.g., taking it on or letting it go). And the ground entity is the temporal contour itself. The core schema then consists of these last two components together. The commonest example of this type of temporal contouring is 'finishing'.

This analysis is based on evidence that the organization of conceptualization for linguistic expression sets temporal contouring into analogy with Motion. It does so as part of a broader cognitive analogy by which temporal structuring is conceptualized as paralleling spatial structuring. This conceptual analogy motivates a syntactic and lexical analogy: to a great extent in a language, aspect is expressed in the same constituent type as Path (+Ground), and often by homophonous forms. Thus, in accordance with the general typology, the core schema of an event of temporal contouring appears in the main verb in verb-framed languages, while it appears in the satellite in satellite-framed languages. This is exemplified below respectively by Spanish and by German.

The event of temporal contouring lives up to its name as framing event relative to the whole macro-event in that it determines the overall temporal framework within which the whole has occurrence. The event of temporal contouring also performs a framing function with respect to the co-event in the sense, described earlier, of acting as a shaping structure imposed on a substrate. And, as with the earlier generalization, it has a more abstract character by contrast with the more tangible character of the co-event. Correlatively, the support relation that the co-event bears to the event of temporal contouring is a **constitutive** relation, in effect "filling in" the conceptual region outlined by the temporal contour.

Now, why should the temporal contour of an activity—that is, its sheer envelope of manifestation—be itself treated in conception and in linguistic expression as a separate event or process? That it is so treated is evidenced by the crosslinguistically frequent occurrence, as main verbs, of lexical verb forms comparable to English *begin, end, continue, repeat, finish*. The main cognitive basis may involve force dynamics (see chapter I-7)—that is, the general and language-based conceptual system pertaining to force exertion, opposition, resistance, and overcoming. The particular application of force dynamics here may be that the temporal contouring event, as Antagonist, overcomes the so-conceived intrinsic temporal character of the substrate activity, as Agonist. By this interpretation, for example, a substrate activity conceptualized as having a basic tendency to continue on in a steady state can, by a process of temporal imposition, be overcome so as to yield a cessation or completion of that activity. Or some activity's basic tendency toward termination can be overcome to yield a continuation of the activity. Or an activity's basic tendency to occur once and then cease can be overcome to yield an iteration. Such an imposition to overcome an activity's natural temporal tendency can thus then be conceptualized as a distinct process, separable from an idealized version of the activity itself, and so be amenable to representation by a main verb.

A further cognitive basis for the agentive form of such impositional processes might be an individual's own developmental experience of the exercise of agency. In particular, this could involve one's experience of marshaling one's efforts to effect a desired pattern in an activity, as by speeding up, slowing down, initiating, persevering, or quitting.

But whatever the validity of event status for aspect or of any cognitive bases for such a status, the linguistic facts are that aspect is frequently expressed as the main lexical verb, and often characteristically so in verb-framed languages.

4.1   Spanish/German Aspect Mapping Contrasts

Presented in (7) are a number of different concepts of temporal contouring and of examples showing the mapping of each such concept. They show that the concept is mapped into the main verb in Spanish[2] but in German onto a satellite—a satellite either in the narrower sense or in the broader sense that includes particles and adverbials in construction with the verb. While both these languages, and possibly all languages, express aspectual notions both with the lexical verb and with constituents adjoined to the verb, one or the other of these loci usually tends, as here, to predominate in degree of usage and in colloquiality.

English itself, while perhaps leaning toward the satellite side, does have a fair number of colloquial aspectual verbs—for example, from the set of examples below, *finish, continue, use(d to), wind up, be (-ing)*. But it should be noted that, of these, the first three are borrowings from Romance, where they are the native type, and that this pattern may parallel the borrowing of Path verbs also from Romance, as discussed earlier. Thus, insofar as English presents a mixed typological picture, it does so comparably in both the domains of Motion and temporal contouring.

Representing the temporal contour type in (7a) is a suggested conceptual structure for the macro-event. Here, the core schema consists of a positive direction of association, represented by the form TO, together with a 'terminative' temporal contour, represented by the form COMPLETION. The English construction *to completion*, as in *I wrote the letter to completion*, may be taken to directly reflect the two components making up the core schema, the association function and the ground entity, and so to exhibit syntactically a parallelism between a temporal contour and a Path + Ground. Otherwise, in accordance with the expected typological pattern, German expresses the whole core schema in a framing satellite and the co-event in a verb, while Spanish expresses the whole core schema in a framing verb and the co-event in a verbal complement.[3]

The inclusion of the progressive aspect forms in (7j) is meant to suggest that in Spanish and German the progressive is syntactically treated not as a special form but in accordance with the same pattern as the other forms of temporal contouring. This interpretation is buttressed by the fact that in both languages, unlike English, such progressive forms are optional in the present and exist beside simple present forms: *Escribe una carta*, and *Sie schreibt einen Brief*.

(7) a. 'to finish Ving' / 'to V to a finish/to completion'

Spanish: terminar de V-INF
German: fertig-V

[I "$_A$MOVED" the letter TO COMPLETION]
CONSTITUTED-BY [I was writing it]

Terminé de escribir la carta.
Ich habe den Brief fertiggeschrieben.
"I finished writing the letter." / "I wrote the letter to completion."

b. 'to V again/re-V'

Spanish: volver a V-INF
German: wieder-V/noch mal V

Volví a comer. / Lo volví a ver.
Ich habe noch mal gegessen. / Ich habe ihn wiedergesehen.
"I ate again." / "I saw him again."

c. 'to have just Ved'

Spanish: acabar de V-INF (acabar: imperfective forms)
German: gerade V (perfect forms)

Acabo de comer. / Acababa de comer cuando llegó.
Ich habe gerade gegessen. / Ich hatte gerade gegessen, als er kam.
"I just ate." / "I had just eaten when he arrived."

d. 'to continue to V'/'to still V'

Spanish: seguir V-GER
German: (immer) noch V

Sigue durmiendo. / Seguía durmiendo cuando miré.
Er schläft noch. / Er hat noch geschlafen, als ich nachschaute.
"He's still sleeping." / "He was still sleeping when I looked in."

e. 'to customarily V'

Spanish: soler V-INF
German: normalerweise V (present)/[früher/ . . .] immer V (past)

Suele comer carne. / Solía comer carne.
Normalerweise isst er Fleisch. / Früher hat er immer Fleisch gegessen.
"He eats meat." / "He used to eat meat."

    f. 'to V (NP) one after another cumulatively'

        Spanish: ir V-GER (NP)

        German: (NP) nacheinander/eins nach dem anderen V

        i. Las vacas se fueron muriendo aquel año.

           Die Kühe sind in dem Jahr (kurz) nacheinander gestorben.

           'One after another of the cows died that year [Spanish: not necessarily all].'

           Contrast: Las vacas se estaban muriendo aquel año.

                    "The cows were (all sick and concurrently) dying that year."

        ii. Juan fue aprendiendo las lecciones.

           Johann hat die Lektionen eine nach der anderen gelernt.

           "John learned one after another of the lessons."

    g. 'to finally V' (positive)/'to not quite V' (negative)

        Spanish: llegar a V-INF 'to finally V after all'

                  no llegar a V-INF 'to not quite get so far as to V'

        German: schliesslich/dann doch V

                 nicht ganz/dann doch nicht V

        i. El tiempo llegó a mejorar.

           Das Wetter ist schliesslich/dann doch besser geworden.

           "The weather finally did improve after all."

        ii. La botella no llegó a caer.

           "The bottle never did quite go so far as to actually fall [though teetering]."

           Die Flasche wackelte, aber fiel dann doch nicht um.

           "The bottle teetered, but didn't quite fall."

    h. 'to end up Ving'

        Spanish: acabar V-GER [perf] 'to end/wind up Ving after all'

        German: am Schluss ... dann doch V

        Acabamos yendo a la fiesta.

        Am Schluss sind wir dann doch zur Party gegangen.

        "We wound up going to the party after all (after wavering/ deciding not to go)."

    i. 'to have been Ving (since/for ...)'

        Spanish: llevar V-GER 'to have been Ving'

        German: schon V

Lleva estudiando 8 horas. / Llevaba estudiando 8 horas cuando llegué.
Er studiert schon 8 Stunden lang. / Als ich kam, hatte er schon 8 Stunden studiert.
"He's been studying for 8 hours." / "He had been studying for 8 hours when I arrived."

j. 'to be Ving'

Spanish: estar V-GER
German: gerade V (nonperfect forms)

Está escribiendo una carta. / Estaba escribiendo una carta.
Sie schreibt gerade einen Brief. / Sie schrieb gerade einen Brief.
"She is writing a letter." / "She was writing a letter."

4.2   Treatment of Aspect as Distinct from Other Verbal Categories

While the German examples in (3) are clear evidence that that language uses satellites to express aspect, still, for this to be a distinctive pattern, it must be determined that the satellite is not simply used for nearly any semantic category. On inspection, it can indeed be observed that out of some six verbal categories, aspect is the sole category that receives extensive expression in satellite form, while the other categories are mainly expressed by the main finite-inflected verb. This pattern is even more pronounced in modern spoken German, where earlier inflections, which can be regarded as a type of satellite to the verb stem, have progressively given way to the use of main-verb forms.

Thus, tense is regularly expressed by *haben* 'past' and *werden* 'future' (the present and a residue of past usage are inflectional). Nonactive voice types are indicated by *werden* and *kriegen*. Conditionality is largely expressed by *würden* (though a residue is expressed by subjunctive inflections). Modality is mainly expressed by such modal verbs as *können* 'can', *sollen* 'should', and *müssen* 'must' (though subjunctive inflections can express some modality). And evidentiality, or at least the distinction between deontic and epistemic senses, is largely indicated by the pattern of auxiliary forms, including the main finite-inflected one, as between *Er hat es machen müssen*, 'He had to do it', and *Er muss es gemacht haben*, 'He must have done it' (again, subjunctive inflections can indicate some evidentiality). However, though also expressed by some main-verb forms, aspect is the only one of these verbal categories to receive preponderant expression by satellites, and thus to be placed syntactically in a single class with the expression of Path.

Something of the contrary picture occurs in Spanish. Although in Spanish the distinctness of aspect from the other verbal categories is less pronounced, it can still be noted that, while aspect is extensively expressed by the main verb stem and therein is in the same class with Path, several of the other verbal categories are mostly expressed by non-V-stem constituents, namely, by inflections and clitics to the main V stem. Fitting this description are tense (except for one of the two future forms, "*ir a* V-INF"), conditionality, and passive voice as rendered by the reflexive pronouns.

The explanation for such differential treatment of aspect may lie in the conceptual analogy (cited earlier) that aspect is the temporal structuring of events relative to the ongoing time line and is therefore allied with Path, as the spatial structuring of a progressing line of motion. On the other hand, a comparable conceptual analogy is not readily established for the other verbal categories.

5 STATE CHANGE AS THE FRAMING EVENT

The third type of framing event we consider is an event of **state change**. In the case where it is conceived that a certain property is associated with a particular object or situation, such a framing event consists of a change in, or the unchanging continuation of, that property.

The domain of state change can be structured foundationally in accordance with several different conceptualizations that are prior to the selection of one of these for representation by a framing event. For example, an event involving an association between a property and an object or situation could be conceived and expressed directly in terms of change or stasis in the property itself. A conceptualization of this sort may be reflected by occasional constructions in various languages. And in any case it can be represented by constructed formulations like *Her (state of) health changed from well to ill* (representing change) or *Her (state of) health is illness* (representing stasis).

Alternatively, the property could be conceptualized as a figural entity with respect to the object or situation as a ground entity, as if the property comes to or occurs in the object or situation. This conceptualization is suggested by formulations like *Illness came to him* or *Illness is in him*.

Compare such actually existing expressions as *Death came to him* and *Madness is upon him*).

Or, conversely, the object or situation could be conceptualized as a figural entity with respect to the property as a ground entity, as if coming to or occurring in the property. This conceptualization is suggested by formulations like *She entered (a state of) ill health / She became ill / She sickened* (cf. *She went to sleep*), or *She is in ill health / She is ill / She is ailing*.

While all three of these types of conceptualization, and perhaps still others, may occur in a language or in nonlinguistic cognition, and while no immediately evident factor accounts for any superiority of one type over the others, nevertheless the third type is, with seeming universality, the most basic and preponderant in any language. The framing-event representation for state change should reflect this preferential conceptualization.

Accordingly, in the preferred framing-event representation, the figural entity is the object or situation associated with a property, while the ground entity is the property. The activating process is either the transition of the object or situation with respect to the property (i.e., what is normally understood as **change**), or it is the object or situation's remaining fixed with respect to the property (i.e., **stasis**). And the association function is the direction of the relationship that the object or situation has with respect to the property—what will be termed the **transition type**. The transition type usually involves acquiring the association, represented below as TO, but other possibilities do occur. A property that, as here, is conceptualized as a ground entity can now be called a **state**. In fact, we reserve the term "state" solely for this conceptualization of a property as a Ground entity, and we do not use this term for the alternative conceptualizations of a property outlined above. The core schema of the state change event is generally the combination of the transition type together with the state, and hence is the analog of the Path + Ground of a Motion event.

Thus, we find that the organization of conceptualization for linguistic expression sets state change into analogy with Motion. In particular, change or stasis with respect to states parallels motion or stationariness with respect to objects. And state transition type parallels Path type. This conceptual analogy motivates a syntactic and lexical analogy: to a great extent in a language, state change is expressed in the same constituent type as Path (+ Ground), and often by homophonous forms. Thus, in accordance with the general typology, the core schema of an event of state change appears in the main verb in verb-framed languages but in the satellite in satellite-framed languages, as exemplified below respectively by Spanish and by English or German.

In accordance with the customary properties of a framing event relative to a co-event, an event of state change, as a type of framing event, is largely more abstract in character, often involving change purely in an individual's cognitive state. For instance, state changes from the examples below include 'to become awake/aware/familiar/in possession/existent/ nonexistent/dead'. On the other hand, the co-event is largely concrete and physical, for instance, again from the examples below: 'to battle/play/run/ shake/jerk/rot/boil'.

In the reverse direction, the support relation of a co-event to a framing event of state change can apparently exhibit much the same range of types as in the case of Motion. As with Motion, Manner and Cause are again here the most prevalent types. This can be illustrated for English, first with nonagentive examples. The co-event verbs bear a Manner relation to the framing satellites in *The door swung/creaked/slammed shut* and *He jerked/started awake*. And it bears a Cause relation in *The door blew shut*.

Likewise in agentive constructions, the verb-to-satellite support relation can be one of Manner, as in *I swung/slammed the door shut* and *I eased him awake gently*. Or it can be one of Cause, as in *I kicked the door shut* and *I shook him awake*.

As already discussed for the domain of Motion, in the agentive Manner examples just preceding, the Agent initiates a causal chain of events that culminates in the state-change event and, to this extent, that event is marked as being caused. However, the verb itself names an action that is not one of the chained causal events but rather a process accompanying the state change and qualifying it as Manner. Thus, in *I eased him awake gently*, the process that the verb *ease* refers to is not a link in the causal chain that leads to the awakening but is rather the manner in which one such causal link, or the state change itself, was carried out.

Because the support relation for a state change can consist not only of Cause, but also of Manner, as well as of a range of further types, the traditional terms "result" and "resultative" would be misnomers for the whole state-change category. Within the referential scope of a sentence, a change of state can be a result only if it is conceptually paired with a cause. But this is an arrangement that we have just seen is only one option out of a number. While such a cause-result pairing may predominate in the usage, or in some syntactic circumstances be obligatory, it is not definitional of the entire state-change category. Accordingly, we avoid the terms "result" and "resultative" for referring to the whole category and reserve them only for where they literally apply.

5.1   Forms Suggesting Parallelism with Path + Ground

As before with temporal contouring, the demonstration of state change can be heuristically best begun with an example in which English can represent the core schema—here, the transition type together with the state— part for part by a preposition plus a noun. This would exhibit explicitly the analogy to the usual type of construction that represents the Path plus the Ground of an event of Motion. Thus, as the conceptual structure of the macro-event is schematized in (8), the core schema sequence TO DEATH can be represented in English by the phrase *to death*. This phrase as a whole is perhaps to be interpreted as corresponding to a framing satellite. The Spanish counterpart conflates the core schema together with the activating process, represented by "MOVE" or agentive "$_A$MOVE," with the combination mapping onto the framing verb.

(8) a. *Nonagentive*

[he "MOVED" TO DEATH] WITH-THE-CAUSE-OF
[he choked on a bone]

English: He choked to death on a bone.

Spanish: Murió atragantado por un hueso/porque se atragantó
con un hueso.
'He died choked by a bone/because he choked himself
with a bone.'

b. *Agentive*

[I "$_A$MOVED" him TO DEATH] WITH-THE-CAUSE-OF
[I burned him]

English: I burned him to death.

Spanish: Lo mataron con fuego/quemándolo.
'They killed him with fire/[by] burning him.'

For the domain of Motion, English was earlier seen to exhibit the satellite-framed pattern as its most characteristic type. But in the domain of state change, it exhibits more of a parallel system of conflation (see chapter II-1). In particular, it often has parallel forms, satellite-framed and verb-framed, both of them colloquial. For example, in (8) above, English has ready use of the state-change verbs *die* and *kill*, as in *He died from choking on a bone* and *I killed him by burning him*. Similarly, the earlier-seen constructions with the state-change satellites *shut* and *awake*, as in *I kicked the door shut* and *I shook him awake*, can also be colloquially rendered with state-change verbs, as in *I shut the door with a kick* and *I awoke him with a shake*. In fact, for some state-change notions, English has only the verb-framed construction colloquially available. Thus, English allows only *I broke the window with a kick*, but not **I kicked the window broken*.

By contrast, as discussed below, Mandarin is a far more thoroughgoing examplar of the satellite-framed type. It not only strongly exhibits satellite framing for Motion, as does English, but also for state change. For example, this language does formulate the just-cited 'breakage' example as "I kicked the window broken."

The core schema of the previous illustration, TO DEATH, serves triple duty in that it is further found in German to map as a combination onto a monomorphemic framing satellite, the inseparable verb prefix *er₁-*, as seen in (9). A satellite of this semantic sort thus parallels a Path + Ground-expressing satellite like English *home*. But while such satellites are unusual for Motion in English, they are the norm for state change in English-type languages.

(9) *German:* er₁-V NP-ACC 'V NP to death'/'kill NP by Ving NP'

(er-) drücken/schlagen/würgen/stechen/schiessen
'to squeeze/beat/choke/stab/shoot (to death)'

We can add one further step in this introductory series. To express the meaning of another German satellite, *er₂-* 'into one's possession', English lacks either a satellite or a "P + NP" construction. Instead, it must express the meaning in a verb such as *get/obtain/win*, in just the way typical of a verb-framed language. However, for heuristic purposes, the "P + NP" phrase *into [subject's] possession*, though not used thus in English, does sufficiently follow extant patterns as to be readily pressed into service to render the German construction, as seen in (10). Not all of the state-change concepts treated below will be as amenable in English to this type of suggestive paraphrasing, so that the macro-event representations for such concepts (which here, after all, are indicated with English words) will seem more awkward, but they can still serve as schematics showing the interrelations of the component meanings.

(10) *German:* er$_2$-V NP-ACC (REFL-DAT) "V NP into one's possession"/'obtain NP by Ving'

a. [the army "$_A$MOVED" the peninsula INTO ITS POSSESSION] WITH-THE-CAUSE-OF [it battled]

Die Armee hat (sich) die Halbinsel erkämpft.
"The army gained the peninsula by battling."
As if: "The army battled the peninsula into its possession."

b. Die Arbeiter haben sich eine Lohnerhöhung erstreikt.
"The workers won a pay raise by striking."
As if: "The workers struck a pay raise into their possession."

c. Wir haben uns Öl erbohrt.
"We obtained oil by drilling."
As if: "We drilled oil into our possession."

Note that, in its different usages above, the German prefixal satellite *er-* has been given different subscripts to indicate that it is here regarded as a polysemous morpheme with distinct pockets of meaning, not a morpheme readily fitted with a single abstractionist gloss like 'completive', as is often attempted. This distinctional approach is based on such evidence as the fact that *erdrücken* does not mean 'to squeeze to completion' but rather 'to squeeze to death'. That is, the German notion of 'squeezing' does not have an intrinsic or standardly associated end point that a generic *er-* simply invokes.

5.2   Change in State of Existence

Having introduced the state-change type with examples involving death and possession, we can continue considering the semantic range of state change with an exploration of one domain: change with respect to state of existence. We first consider the transition from an existent to a non-existent state—that is, from presence to absence. This conceptual type is generically expressed in English by the phrases *go/put out of existence*, which directly represent part for part the final three components of the framing event. However, some more particular senses are expressed conflatedly. Our first example exhibits a discrete transition type. The concept of a flame or light becoming extinguished can be expressed in English by the monomorphemic satellite *out*. In Spanish, as per the usual contrast, it is expressed in the verb, as seen in (11).

(11) V out (NP) 'V (NP) to extinguishment'/'extinguish (NP) by Ving'

    a. *Nonagentive with Manner*

    [the candle "MOVED" TO EXTINGUISHMENT] WITH-
THE-MANNER-OF [it flickered/ . . .]

    The candle flickered/sputtered out.

    b. *Nonagentive with Cause*

    [the candle "MOVED" TO EXTINGUISHMENT] WITH-
THE-CAUSE-OF [SOMETHING blew on it]

    The candle blew out.

    c. *Agentive with Cause*

    [I "$_A$MOVED" the candle TO EXTINGUISHMENT] WITH-
THE-CAUSE-OF [I blew on/ . . . it]

    I blew/waved/pinched the candle out.

    Spanish: Apagué la vela soplándola/de un soplido.

                'I extinguished the candle [by] blowing-on it/with a
blow'

The next example has a "bounded gradient" transition type—that is,
the change is a progressive transition through a gradient state that ter-
minates with a final state. The concept of an object's gradual diminish-
ment until final disappearance, through some usually organic process, is
expressed in English by the satellite *away* and, again, in Spanish by a
main verb, as seen in (12).[4] One test for the transition types just adduced
is a form's behavior with different types of temporal expressions. Thus, a
discrete transition type is consonant with a punctual expression, as with
The candle blew out at exactly midnight as against **The meat rotted away
at exactly midnight.* On the other hand, a bounded gradient transition
type is consonant with an expression of bounded temporal extent, as in
The meat rotted away in five days.

(12) V away 'V to gradual disappearance'/'gradually disappear as a
result of Ving'

    [the meat "MOVED" GRADUALLY TO DISAPPEARANCE]
WITH-THE-CAUSE-OF [it rotted]

    The meat rotted away.

    Also: The ice melted away. / The hinge rusted away. /

           The image faded away. / The jacket's elbows have worn away.

English: The leaves withered away.
Spanish: Las hojas se desintegraron al secarse.
      "The leaves disintegrated by withering."

A further case of the bounded gradient transition type is expressed by the English satellite *up* in examples like those of (13). Though needing further elucidation, the semantic difference between *away* and *up* at least involves a conceptual categorization of rate and time scale, with *away* as slow and lengthy and *up* as quick and brief. In addition, these forms with *up* seem to have a particularly aspectual character, and thus point to the likelihood of a conceptual continuum between aspect and state change as opposed to any sharp category division. Accordingly, as noted in the previous section on temporal contouring, much that is traditionally treated as aspect also involves state change, so that a number of the examples appearing there could equally have fit in the present section. It can be further noted that all particular state changes have a specific aspectual contour (or a range of possible contours).

(13) V up 'V to consumedness'/'become consumed in Ving'
      V up NP 'V NP to consumedness'/'consume NP by Ving it'

   a. [the log "MOVED" TO CONSUMEDNESS in 1 hour] WITH-THE-CAUSE-OF [it was burning]

      The log burned up in 1 hour.
      Contrast *burn* alone: The log burned (for 30 minutes before going out by itself).

   b. [I "$_A$MOVED" the popcorn TO CONSUMEDNESS in 10 minutes] WITH-THE-CAUSE-OF [I was eating it]

      I ate up the popcorn in 10 minutes.
      Contrast *eat* alone: I ate the popcorn (for 5 minutes before I stopped myself).

The German prefixal satellite *ver-* also expresses a gradient progression to a final state, indicating that an Agent has exhausted the entirety of some object in acting on it, as illustrated in (10). Here, however, the object itself need not physically disappear and may merely become altered, but what does disappear is the *supply* of the object in its original condition available for the Agent's use in acting on it. Thus, here, the state change from presence to absence pertains not to a first-order object, which instead may continue in existence, but rather to an abstract second-order meta-object, the supply.

(14) *German:* ver-V NP-ACC 'use up/exhaust the supply of NP by Ving (with) the NP'/"V NP to exhaustion"

    a. [I "$_A$MOVED" all the ink TO EXHAUSTION] WITH-THE-CAUSE-OF [I wrote with it]

       Ich habe die ganze Tinte verschrieben.
       'I've written all the ink to exhaustion.'
       "I've used up all the ink in writing."

    b. Ich habe alle Wolle versponnen.
       "I've used up all the wool in spinning."

    c. Ich habe meine ganze Munition verschossen.
       "I've exhausted my ammunition in shooting."

Still in the area of change with respect to state of existence, we now turn to the reverse of the preceding direction of change, hence to the transition from a nonexistent to an existent state—that is, from absence to presence. Again, there are English expressions, *come/bring into existence*, that directly map the final three components of the generic framing event part for part onto syntactic and lexical structure. But in addition, the English satellite *up*—in a different usage than that seen just previously—expresses the same generic concept, as illustrated in (13). Here, the core schema INTO EXISTENCE as a whole maps onto the single morpheme that constitutes the satellite. This satellite covers either a discrete or a bounded-gradient interpretation for the transition type, according to the context, as demonstrated by its equal compatibility with either *at* or *in* type temporal phrases. In its agentive use, the present framing event type—state change from nonexistence to existence—amounts to the traditional notion of "effected object," as contrasted with "affected object." Thus, the English satellite *up* as used here and its counterparts in other languages can be taken as markers of an effected object construction.[5]

(15) V up NP 'V NP into existence'/'make/create NP by Ving'

    a. [I "$_A$MOVED" INTO EXISTENCE three copies of his original letter] WITH-THE-CAUSE-OF [I xeroxed it]

       I xeroxed up (*xeroxed) three copies of his original letter.
       Contrast *xerox* alone: I xeroxed (*up) his original letter.

    b. I boiled up (*boiled) some fresh coffee for breakfast at our campsite.

Contrast *boil* alone (any acceptable use of *up* has a different sense): I boiled (*up) last night's coffee for breakfast/some water at our campsite.

c. [I "$_A$MOVED" INTO EXISTENCE a plan] WITH-THE-CAUSE-OF [I thought (about the issues)]

I thought up (*thought) a plan.
Contrast *think* alone: I thought *up/about the issues.

It was seen above that the German satellite *ver-* expresses the gradual disappearance of an abstract second-order meta-object, namely, a supply. A counterpart for the reverse direction of change exists in English, again represented by the satellite *up*, now used in a third sense. This satellite expresses the gradual appearance of an abstract, second-order meta-object, an 'accumulation', as illustrated in (16). Here, the action specified by the verb affects but does not create the first-order objects named (below: money, property). Rather, the repetition of this action creates an accumulation per se as a higher-level Gestalt entity.

(16) V up NP 'progressively accumulate/amass NP by Ving'

a. [I "$_A$MOVED" INTO AN ACCUMULATION $5,000 in five years] WITH-THE-CAUSE-OF [I saved it]

I saved up $5,000 in five years.
Contrast *save* alone: I saved (*up) (the/my) $1,000 for two years.

b. Jane has bought up beachfront property in the county.—that is, has progressively amassed a good deal of property over time
Contrast: Jane has bought beachfront property in the county.— possibly just a little on one occasion

Two Russian satellites contrast nicely with respect to the conceptual level of the object in reference. The path prefix "s-[V] [NP-pl]-ACC" merely specifies paths of motion that yield a spatial juxtaposition of plural objects, thus corresponding well to English *together*. But the state-change prefix "na-[V] [NP-pl]-GEN" indicates that such a juxtaposition constitutes a higher-level Gestalt, an accumulation, as seen in (17).

(17) *Russian:* na-V NP-GEN 'create an accumulation of NP by Ving NP'

Ona nagrebla orexov v fartuk.
'She accumulation-scraped nuts(GEN) into apron.'

"By scraping them together in her apron, she accumulated (a heap/ pile of) nuts."
Contrast: Ona sgrebla orexi v fartuk.
   'She together-scraped nuts(ACC) into apron.'
   "She scraped together the nuts into her apron."

5.3   Change in Condition

As the introductory examples showed, the state-change type encompasses more than just state of existence, and, for heuristic purposes, we now represent a range of this "change in condition" with examples of both physical and cognitive change, both in the Patient and in the Agent. For a physical case, the concept of changing an object from an intact condition to what can be conceptually categorized as a nonintact condition can be expressed in English again by an *up* satellite, now used in a fourth sense. The same concept is expressed in German more specifically and more productively by the satellite *kaputt-*, and in Spanish, as usual, with a main verb, as seen in (18).

(18) a. *English:* V up NP / *German:* kaputt-V NP-ACC 'make NP nonintact by Ving it'

   [the dog "$_A$MOVED" TO NON-INTACTNESS the shoe in 30 minutes] WITH-THE-CAUSE-OF [he chewed on it]

   The dog chewed the shoe up in 30 minutes.
   Contrast *chew* without *up:* The dog chewed on the shoe (for 15 minutes).

  b. *German:* Der Hund hat den Schuh in 30 Minuten kaputtgebissen.
    'The dog bit the shoe up in 30 minutes.'
   Contrast: Der Hund hat 15 Minuten an dem Schuh gekaut.
    'The dog chewed on the shoe [for] 15 minutes.'

  c. *Spanish:* El perro destrozó el zapato a mordiscos/mordiéndolo en 30 minutos.
    'The dog destroyed the shoe with bites/[by] biting it in 30 minutes.'
   Contrast: El perro mordisqueó el zapato (durante 15 minutos).
    'The dog chewed-on the shoe (for 15 minutes).'

A number of state-change satellites in other languages have no counterpart in English, which must resort to framing verb constructions to render them, and the concepts such satellites express can range quite broadly, more so than English speakers might expect. An example with range of application from the physical to the cognitive is the German satellite construction "ein-V NP/REFL-ACC." The satellite's meaning can be characterized in broad strokes as 'to readiness'. The whole construction's meaning can be more finely characterized as 'to warm (NP) up for Ving by (practicing at) Ving'. Instances of usage include *die Maschine einfahren* 'to warm up the machine for operating it' and *sich ein-laufen/-spielen/ -singen* 'by practicing at the activity itself, to warm up for running/playing/ singing'.

Another German example, possibly in a polysemous chain with the preceding example but semantically distinct enough, is an *ein-* satellite with a solely cognitive meaning that can be characterized broadly as 'to familiarity' and more finely as in (19).

(19) *German:* ein-V REFL-ACC in NP-ACC 'to have gradually managed to become easefully familiar with all the ins and outs of NP in Ving (in/with) NP'

    a. Ich habe mich in das Buch eingelesen.
       'I have read myself into the book.'
       "I've gotten familiarized enough with the book that I can keep all the characters and plot involvements straight."

    b. Der Schauspieler hat sich in seine Rolle eingespielt.
       'The actor has played himself into his role.'
       "The actor has come to know his part with ease in the course of acting in it."

    c. Ich habe mich in meinen Beruf eingearbeitet.
       'I have worked myself into my job.'
       "I know the ropes in my work now."

In these preceding transitive examples, including the reflexive ones, what has manifested the change in condition was the Patient expressed in the direct object NP. But in another transitive example that does not fit this mapping, and so calls for further investigation, the Agent or Experiencer expressed by the subject NP is the entity that manifests the change in condition. In particular, with the German satellite illustrated in (20), the subject Experiencer undergoes a cognitive change, one that can be characterized in broad terms as 'to awareness' and more finely as indicated below.

(20) *German:* heraus-V NP-ACC [V: sensory verb] 'detect and sensorily single out NP among other comparable NPs via the sensory modality of Ving'

Sie hat ihr Kind herausgehört.
'She has heard out her child.'
"She could distinguish her child's voice from among the other children talking."

An inspection of particular satellite-framed languages often yields state-change satellites with meanings that can seem unprecedented from the perspective of other languages. Here are some examples that may seem curious from the English perspective.

(21) a. *Russian:* za-V -s'a (= reflexive) 'become attentionally engrossed/absorbed in the activity of Ving and hence be inattentive to other events of relevance in the context'

where V = čitat' 'read': za-čitat'-s'a 'to get absorbed in what one is reading' (so that, e.g., one misses a remark directed at one)

where V = smotret' 'look': za-smotret'-s'a 'to get absorbed in watching something' (e.g., a person ahead of one as one walks along, so that, e.g., one bypasses one's destination)

b. *Dutch:* bij- V NP 'put the finishing touches on NP in Ving it/execute the few remaining bits of Ving action that will bring NP up to optimal/complete/up-to-date condition' [example from Melissa Bowerman, personal communication]

where V = knippen 'cut with scissors': bij-knippen e.g., 'trim those hairs that have grown out beyond the hairdo'

where V = betalen 'pay': bij-betalen 'pay the additionally necessary increment' (e.g., to correct an error and bring a sum up to the right amount or to upgrade a ticket to the next-higher class)

c. *Yiddish:* tsu-V (NP$_1$) tsu NP$_2$ 'add NP$_1$ by Ving it—or add the (intangible) product of Ving—to the same or comparable material already present in NP$_2$'

Ikh hob tsugegosn milkh tsum teyg.
'I have ADD-poured milk to-the dough.'
"I added milk to the dough by pouring it."
Ikh hob zikh tsugezetst tsu der khevre.

'I have REFL ADD-sat to the group.'

"I pulled up a chair and joined the group."

The present perspective on state-change satellites suggests a pair of worthwhile projects. One project would be to ascertain as exhaustively as possible the set of states represented by the satellites within a single satellite-framed language in order to assess the semantic range that such forms can cover in a language. The other project would be to compare the sets of states represented by satellites across two or more satellite-framed languages. In this regard, a casual look at the state-change satellites in German and Mandarin suggests some similarity of the states represented. Despite the examples of seemingly odd state meanings just presented, a more systematic examination might reveal a universal tendency toward the representation of a certain inventory of state concepts. Such a finding, if true, would contribute much to our understanding of cognitive organization in language.

5.4   Further Construction Types

We have so far seen a state change represented by two different constructions. One construction is the combination of a preposition and a noun, like English *to death*, where the preposition represents the transition type and the noun names a state. The combination here is largely fixed as a collocation with particular lexical forms that cannot vary freely. The other construction is simply a monomorphemic satellite, like German *er-* 'to death', that conflatedly represents both the transition type and the state. We now note the occurrence of further constructions.

In one further state-change construction, the state is represented by a nominal form that now can vary freely. Actually, the NP in this construction is used metanymically to represent 'the state of being an NP'. The transition type is represented by a preposition. This can be accompanied by a satellite whose reference can be construed as qualifying either the transition or the state. The English forms in (22) and (23) exemplify this type of construction.

(22) *English:* V into/to NP 'become NP by Ving'

[the water "MOVED" TO a STATE [BEING a solid block of ice] WITH-THE-CAUSE-OF [it froze]

The water froze into a solid block of ice.

(23) *English:* V down to/into NP 'by Ving, reduce qualitatively (and quantitatively) until becoming NP'

[the wood chips "MOVED" REDUCTIVELY TO a STATE [BEING a pulp]] WITH-THE-CAUSE-OF [they boiled]

The wood chips boiled down to a pulp.

In another state-change construction, an adjective names the state. No further forms are present to represent the transition type, but the constructional meaning is typically that of 'entering' the named state (though another possibility is described below). The construction is illustrated for English in (24).

(24) a. V Adj 'become Adj by Ving'

[the shirt "MOVED" TO a STATE [BEING dry]] WITH-THE-CAUSE-OF [it flapped in the wind]

The shirt flapped dry in the wind.
Contrast: The tinman rusted stiff. / The coat has worn thin in spots.

b. V NP Adj 'make NP Adj by Ving'

[I "_AMOVED" the fence TO a STATE [BEING blue]] WITH-THE-CAUSE-OF [I painted it]

I painted the fence blue.

One justification for treating a bare adjective construction of this sort as representing a "TO" transition type is that it semantically parallels a construction with an overt *to* phrase in the adjective slot. Thus, parallel to *The shirt flapped dry* is the sentence *The man choked to death*.

5.5 Further Transition Types

In all the state-change examples so far, the transition type has been that of 'entry' into a state, which was represented by the deep preposition TO in conjunction with the deep verb "MOVE." But other transition types can be observed or construed.

One further transition type is 'departure' from a state, which can be represented by a deep preposition FROM in conjunction with "MOVE." This type would appear to underlie a combination of preposition plus nominal that explicitly expresses departure from a state. An example of such a combination is *out of existence*, as in *The apparition blinked out of existence*. Further, a state-change satellite like *out*, as in *The candle blew out*—previously construed as representing a concept of state entry, 'to extinguishment'—can alternatively be construed as representing a concept of state departure, 'from ignitedness'.

Other transition types actually involve the lack of transition—that is, they involve fixity or stasis. One such type is 'situatedness' in a state, which can be represented by the deep preposition AT in conjunction with the deep verb BE. Another such type is the continued 'maintenance' of a state, which can be represented by AT in conjunction with the midlevel verb REMAIN or, for the agentive, with the midlevel verb KEEP. An example of this type is shown in (25). Here, the satellite is an adjective, but the constructional meaning is not one of 'state entry', as before, but rather one of 'state-situatedness'. The interpretation of this sentence is that the door was already shut and that I initiated the maintaining of the door in that shut state by driving nails into it. Note that the homologous construction in Mandarin does not permit this 'maintenance of a state' interpretation but only the usual 'change of state' interpretation, so that the sentence corresponding to *I nailed the door shut* could only mean that, by hammering on a nail held against an open door, I moved the door into a shut position.

(25) [I KEPT the door AT a STATE [BEING shut]] WITH-THE-
      CAUSE-OF [I nailed it]

      I nailed the door shut.

At this point, we can present several further English forms that push the envelope of the framework developed so far. These forms, on the one hand, exhibit the satellite-framed type of construction. Their core schema is represented by a satellite and/or preposition, while the co-event is represented by the verb. On the other hand, the concepts represented by the satellite and/or preposition are ongoing processes, rather than fixed states. Perhaps such forms should be treated as representing a sixth type of conceptual domain, one of 'processual progression'. However, we will instead attempt a treatment of these forms as involving the domain of state change, but with their transition type regarded as something like 'traversal' through a state. Such a transition type might be represented by the deep preposition ALONG in conjunction with "MOVE."

One of the new forms involves the preposition *for* in the sense of 'in search of', in conjunction with a verb that expresses the action used to carry out the search. The satellite-framed construction that is the target of this discussion is shown in (26a), while (26b) shows the counterpart verb-framed construction, which in this case also exists in English. The assumption here is that the combination of deep and midlevel morphemes ALONG IN-SEARCH-OF conflates into the preposition *for*.

(26) *English:* V for NP 'V in search of NP/seek NP by Ving'

    a. [I "MOVED" ALONG IN-SEARCH-OF nails on the board]
WITH-THE-MANNER-OF [I felt the board]

    I felt for nails on the board. / I felt the board for nails.
Contrast: I listened to the record for scratches. / I looked all over for the missing button.

    b. I searched for/sought nails on the board by feeling it.
Contrast: I searched for scratches on the record in listening to it. / I sought the missing button by looking all over.

Another English form involves the combination of satellite plus preposition *off with*, which has the sense 'carrying along something that one has stolen', in conjunction with a verb that expresses the Manner in which one moves along as one progressively distances oneself from the site of the theft. As with the previous example, the assumption here is that the combination of the deep and midlevel morphemes ALONG IN-THEFTFUL-POSSESSION-OF gives rise to the surface expression *off with*. This form is illustrated in (27).

(27) *English:* V off with NP 'upon stealing NP, continue in theftful possession of NP while distancing oneself/making one's escape by Ving'

    [I "MOVED" ALONG IN-THEFTFUL-POSSESSION-OF the money] WITH-THE-MANNER-OF [I walked/...]

    I walked/ran/drove/sailed/flew off with the money.

Note that the *off with* in this construction cannot be regarded simply as a path satellite plus a preposition of concomitance that happen to be applied to a motion event in which one can additionally infer theft. The reason is that the same combination of satellite and preposition can be used with two nonmotion verbs—*make off with* and *take off with*—that still have the theft reading (in fact, the form with *make* has only the 'theft' reading).

6   ACTION CORRELATING AS THE FRAMING EVENT

The fourth type of framing event has not to my knowledge been previously recognized. It is part of a much broader linguistic phenomenon—which I propose to call **coactivity**—that has also received scant attention as a consolidated topic. In a case of coactivity, a first agency executing a particular activity is associated with a second agency whose activity is correlated with the first. Typically, the second activity is either comparable to or complementary to the first activity. Prototypically, the first agency is represented by a subject NP and the second agency by an object NP (direct or oblique). Prototypically across languages, such a **coactive** object NP is required by symmetric verbs, comitatives, datives, and certain further syntactic categories. Thus, *I met John/*the mannequin* requires that John also engage in the action of meeting me. The sentence *I ate with Jane/*the mannequin* requires that Jane also engage in eating. The sentence *I threw the ball to John/*the mannequin* or *I threw John/*the mannequin the ball* require that John engage in the action of trying to catch the ball, as an action complementary to my throwing it. And *I ran after Jane/*the building* requires that Jane also engage in swift forward motion.

In the fourth type of framing event, which we term **action correlating**, an intentional Agent effects or maintains a particular correlation between an action performed by herself and an action performed by another Agency, which can be either animate or inanimate. Note that we use the term "Agent" for the first entity and the distinct term "Agency" for the second entity. The framing event consists of the establishment of this correlation per se. The types of such correlation that will be treated below are 'concert', 'accompaniment', 'imitation', 'surpassment', and 'demonstration'. The co-event consists of the specific action performed by the Agent. Except for the 'demonstration' type, this action is either the same as the action performed by the Agency or is in the same category, as understood according to pragmatic norms that will need investigation.

In the way that conceptual structure is organized for linguistic expression, such action correlating appears to be analogized to Motion. Specifically, the correlation of one action with respect to another parallels the path of one object with respect to another. In particular, in the conceptual structuring of the framing event, as schematized in (28), the Agent places his own action as figural entity—generically represented by the term Action—in correlation with an Agency's same-category action as ground entity—generically represented by the term Action'. This structure is thus comparable to that of agentive motion of the type: [Agent $_A$MOVE Figure Path Ground]. The core schema here—the In-Correlation-With component—is then a straightforward Path analogue.

The remainder of the macro-event, also schematized in (28), consists of the co-event, which is the specific action performed by the Agent, here represented as [Agent PERFORM], and the constitutive support relation that this co-event bears to the framing event. This support relation is characterized as "constitutive" because the specific activity of the co-event constitutes the action that the Agent sets in correlation with the Agency's action. It will also constitute the Agency's action in the case where that happens to be identical to the Agent's action rather than just of the same category.

(28) [Agent PUT Agent's Action In-Correlation-With Agency's Action']
    CONSTITUTED-BY [Agent PERFORM]

The macro-event structure as schematized in (28) seems to represent the interrelationships among the conceptual components more closely. But a particular adaptation of this structure, as schematized in (29), seems to be closer to the patterns in which this semantic type is mapped onto occurrent syntactic structures, at least in the languages considered here. Thus, on the basis of (29) and in accordance with the usual typology, in verb-framed languages the core schema maps onto a satellite (plus adposition) and the co-event maps into the main verb. And in verb-framed languages, the combination of the ACT component and the core schema maps onto the main verb (plus adposition) and the co-event maps into an adjunct.

(29) [Agent ACT In-Correlation-With Agency] CONSTITUTED-BY
    [Agent PERFORM]

With respect to the framing event's role in the present type, it clearly provides the overarching framework within which two actions are brought into correlation with each other. In addition, the general pattern is maintained in that the framing event is relatively abstract in character while the co-event is typically concrete. Thus, if an observer were present in the situation referred to by a macro-event of action correlating, that observer would directly perceive the specific co-event activity performed by the Agent and would perceive the same activity or something similar performed by the Agency. For example, as in the illustrations below, these actions could be playing, singing, drinking, and so on. But the observer could generally not perceive the intended relation of the one action to the other, but would rather need to infer it or otherwise know it. For example, the observer would need to infer or know that the Agent performs her action so that it will be in concert with that of the Agency, or in accompaniment to it, or in imitation of it, and so forth.

We now consider the five different cases of action correlating mentioned at the beginning of this section. The first four—'concert', 'accompaniment',

'imitation', and 'surpassment'—have the Agent and the Agency performing the same or same-category actions. The fifth case—'demonstration'—
has the Agent and Agency performing different-category actions.

6.1   The Agency's Action is the Same(-Category) as the Agent's Action

In their semantic distinctions, the first three cases of action correlating—
'concert', 'accompaniment', and 'imitation'—can be taken to form a series
based on an increasing conceptual distance in the correlation of the
Agent's action with that of the Agency. With English and German used as
the languages of illustration, both are needed to represent the series in
terms of expression by satellites, since only English has a satellite proper
for the first case while only German has one for the third.

The conceptual difference between the first two cases of 'concert' and
'accompaniment' is instructive. In the first case, expressed in English by
together (with),[6] as illustrated in (30), the Agent acts in concert with the
Agency. That is, both the Agent's action and the Agency's action are set
in conception as equipotent components of a joint unity, perhaps with
each component as essential for the existence of the whole.

In the second case, expressed in English by *along (with)* and in German
by *mit- (mit-DAT)*, as illustrated in (31), the Agent acts in accompaniment or as an addition or adjunct to the Agency. That is, the Agency's
action, which functions as a ground entity and hence as a conceptual
reference point, is treated as independent or basic and as the essential or
definitional activity of the situation. On the other hand, the Agent's
action as figural entity is treated as an ancillary or incidental aspect of
the total situation. (This second case is one manifestation of an extensive
semantic system in language that distinguishes 'main' from 'ancillary'.)

To contextualize this conceptual difference for the situation of the illustrations, assume that "I" and "he" are each playing a piano on the same
concert stage. Then, in the first case, he and I might be dual pianists,
whereas in the second case, he might be a featured soloist whom I have
joined to assist. Comparably, *I jog together with him* suggests that we
schedule and execute our activity jointly and might not engage in it singly.
However, *I jog along with him* suggests that he has his own regular routine
of jogging independently, whether or not I am present, but where I sometimes accompany him as an addition.

Of note here is the fact that the referent situations for both cases can be
indistinguishably the same physically—for example, as they would appear

on screen if filmed. For this reason, the first two action correlations, 'concert' and 'accompaniment', can be understood to function as conceptual structures overlaid or imposed on a substrate. They thereby constitute excellent examples for cognitive linguistics of conceptual imputation, a mind-to-world direction of fit, as opposed to the often-held notion that only properties in objects "out there" can be reflected in language in a truth-value oriented semantics or by a world-to-mind direction of fit.

The original stipulation that the second participant in an action correlation—which we have distinctively termed the "Agency"—can be either animate or inanimate was made to accommodate the observed linguistic patterns. For instance, in the examples for the first four cases of action correlating below, all three illustrative languages allow replacement of the "him" or its counterpart by "phonograph record" or its counterpart, as in the English *I played along with the phonograph record*. Comparably, the stipulation that the activity of the Agency need only be in the same category as that of the Agent was made to accommodate the English and German satellite usage. For instance, in *Mary sang along with John*, John could be playing an instrument while Mary sings, and rendering a different harmonic part than she. Similarly, the German *Ich trinke mit* "I (will) drink along" can refer to my drinking without eating, after I have joined someone who is eating without drinking.

In accordance with the general typology, the Spanish forms in the examples below express in the main verb the same concept of action correlation for which English and German mostly use satellites. Again, though, English has verbs borrowed from Romance (e.g., *accompany, join, imitate, copy*) with the same mapping pattern as their source language. A further difference can be observed between the two types of languages here, though it is not clear whether it strictly arises from their typological distinction. Specifically, the same-category affordance permitted in German and English does not hold in Spanish. For, in expressing the co-event in an adjunct, Spanish generally must employ different constructions that distinguish between identical actions and same-category but different actions on the part of the Agent and the Agency.

(30) *English:* V together with NP 'act in concert with NP at Ving'

[I ACTed IN-CONCERT-WITH him] CONSTITUTED-BY
[I played the melody]

I played the melody together with him.

(31) *English:* V along (with NP)
German: mit-V (mit NP-DAT)
'act in accompaniment of/as an adjunct to//accompany/join (in with) NP at Ving'
[I ACTed IN-ACCOMPANIMENT-OF him] CONSTITUTED-BY [I played the melody]
English: I played the melody along with him.
German: Ich habe mit ihm die Melodie mitgespielt.
Spanish: Yo lo acompañé cuando tocamos la melodía.
　　　　　 'I accompanied him when we played the melody' (both he and I played).
　　　　　 Yo lo acompañé tocando la melodía.
　　　　　 'I accompanied him [by] playing the melody' (only I played).

Further framing satellites can be observed that refer only to particular portions of the 'accompaniment' concept and so might be thought to add to the number of distinct types of action correlation that must be recognized. Thus, Yiddish has two satellites that, in effect, divide the category of 'accompaniment' in two. Both satellites represent the Agent's action as subsidiary to that of the Agency, but they center on distinct loci within the category. These loci differ as to the Agent's degree of participation in the Agency's action. Thus, one satellite, the prefix *mit-*, centers on a concept of 'contributory accompaniment', in which the Agent's action is understood as adding to the Agency's action so as to form a greater whole. The other satellite, the prefix *tsu-*, centers on a concept of 'peripheral accompaniment', in which the Agent's action is understood as minor or marginal in relation to the whole, and as self-standing, often personal. Though the examples for *tsu-* in (32) could refer to more participatory accompaniment, they are here given contexts that highlight their semantic center further toward the periphery.

(32) *Yiddish:* tsu-V 'V as a peripheral accompaniment to another action'
　　　　 where V = krekhtsn 'to groan, gripe'
　　　　 Er hot tsugekrekhtst.
　　　　 'he has TSU-griped'; for example:
　　　　 "He punctuated his exertions with an undertone of periodic groans." or "He chimed in/piped up in our gripe session with some of his own gripes."

where V = tantsn 'to dance'
Zi hot tsugetantst.
'she has TSU-danced'; for example:
"She did a little dance on the sidelines in time to the music."

English also has a form that can be considered to mark a subtype of 'accompaniment'. It has some similarity to the preceding Yiddish form in that it has a noncontributory, often personal, sense, but it is distinctively narrower in reference. This form is the preposition *to*, as illustrated in (33). In it, the Agency is (the manifestor of) a rhythmic pattern through time, prototypically auditory. The Agent also produces a rhythmic pattern and sets it into some kind of alignment with the Agency's pattern.

(33) *English:* V to NP 'in Ving, set the rhythm of Ving in correlation with the rhythm of NP'

I swayed/tapped my foot/danced/hummed to the rhythm/beat/ music/sound of the waves lapping against the shore.

The third in the series of action correlations, 'imitation', is the case where the Agent directs her own activity so as to be an imitation or copy of the Agency's activity, as illustrated in (34). Here again, the Agency's activity, as ground element, is the reference point in relation to which the Agent endeavors to shape her own activity as a figural entity. In particular, from observing the Agency's activity, the Agent endeavors to make her own activity similar or equivalent to the whole of or to selected structural aspects of the Agency's activity.

Whereas in the first two cases the Agent's activity was concurrent with that of the Agency, here it follows that of the Agency. In this regard, the German *nach-* satellite prototypically suggests that this delay is only a brief part-for-part lagging behind, but the interpretation is also available that the Agent's performance wholly follows the ending of the Agency's performance. Again, the Agency can be an inanimate device like a phonograph, and the Agency's activity can be identical to or only in the same category with the Agent's activity, so that the German sentence in (34) could equally well refer to a recorded vocalist that I imitate on an instrument. And, as before, Spanish employs its main verb to render the action correlation itself, while the adjunct specifies the activities and also distinguishes whether they are the same or different within the same category.

(34) *German:* nach-V (NP-DAT) 'V in imitation of NP'/'imitate/copy NP at Ving'

[I ACTed IN-IMITATION-OF him] CONSTITUTED-BY
[I played the melody]

German: Ich habe ihm die Melodie nachgespielt.
English: I played the melody in imitation of him.
Spanish: Yo lo seguía cuando tocamos la melodía.
　　　　　'I followed him when we played the melody' (both he and
　　　　　I played).
　　　　　Yo lo seguía tocando la melodía.
　　　　　'I followed him [by] playing the melody.' (only I played).

The fourth case of action correlating is that of 'surpassment'. It is illustrated in (35) with the English prefixal satellite *out-*. Here, the Agent either marshals his activity to surpass the Agency's activity, or his activity simply happens to surpass the Agency's activity, which is again used as a reference point. In the specific context of a competition, the Agent thus 'beats' the Agency. As before, the Agency can be inanimate, as in *I outplayed the player piano*, but now the Agency's activity is limited to being the same as that of the Agent, not just to being of the same category, so that there is no **I outplayed the singer* in the sense that I played better than the singer sang. Spanish again can use its main verb to convey the correlation, but this time the gerundive adjunct can be used with the identical-activity interpretation, though apparently a different-activity interpretation is also possible.[7]

(35) *English:* out-V NP 'surpass/best/beat NP at Ving'

　　　　[I ACTed IN-SURPASSMENT-OF him] CONSTITUTED-BY
　　　　[I played (the melody)]

English: I outplayed him.
　　　　　Compare: I outran/outcooked him.
Spanish: Yo le gané tocando la melodía.
　　　　　'I surpassed him playing the melody.'

6.2　The Agency's Action Is Fixed and Distinct from the Agent's Action

The fifth case of action correlating is that of 'demonstration'. It is expressed by the German satellite *vor-*, as illustrated in (36). Here, the Agent executes an activity so that it will function as a demonstration to an Agency that, in turn, will observe the Agent's activity. In the concept of 'demonstration' present here, the Agent has the knowledge and capacity to perform a certain activity that the Agency lacks. The Agent executes this activity so that the Agency can register it either as information about the Agent or as a model for learning to perform the same activity, and the whole situation can have the metaphoric sense of a transfer from the Agent to the Agency. This 'demonstration' case differs from the preceding cases in that the Agency's own activity is fixed, in particular as an activity of observation, and as such it regularly diverges from the Agent's activity. This difference merits a revised schematization of the original macro-event, shown first in (28) and (29). The revised schematization is shown in (36).

Further, this case stretches the preceding notion of correlating, which had been based on the interrelating of comparable activities, to a notion of the coordinating of complementary activities. Specifically, these activities are ones of demonstration and of observation. Still, this case—in common with the others—does relate the activity of one entity to that of another. And the typological mapping patterns are comparable. Thus, German expresses the relationship in the satellite, and Spanish expresses it in the main verb. For this case, though, English lacks a satellite like that of German, and so switches to a verb-framed mapping pattern.

(36) *German:* vor-V NP-DAT 'demonstrate to NP one's Ving'

[Agent PUT Agent's Action IN-DEMONSTRATION-TO Agency's OBSERVATION] CONSTITUTED-BY [Agent PERFORM]

[I ACTed IN-DEMONSTRATION-TO him] CONSTITUTED-BY [I played the melody]

German: Ich habe ihm die Melodie vorgespielt.
        'I played the melody in demonstration to him.'
English: I showed him how I/how to play the melody.
Spanish: Yo le mostré como toco/tocar la melodía (same as English).

7   REALIZATION AS THE FRAMING EVENT

The fifth type of framing event is an event of **realization**. This itself is an encompassive category for a pair of related types that will be termed **fulfillment** and **confirmation**.

7.1   Incremental Semantic Series Containing Realization Types

Since the semantic properties of these types are not very familiar, it may be best to begin by demonstrating them. The demonstration will consist of an incremental series of four verbal patterns into which the two realization types fit. It is presented in (37) in the agentive for a satellite-framed language, English.

For each of the four verbal patterns in the series, the verb is lexicalized to express progressively more kinds of referential material. What is common to all four types of verb is that they represent a particular action that the Agent performs. The scope of the Agent's intention extends at least over the performance of this action. In the first verbal pattern, the scope of intention is coextensive with this action. This intended action thus constitutes the entirety of the verb's reference. In the second verbal pattern, the scope of intention extends beyond the action alone. It now further includes a goal and the intention that the action lead to this goal. The verb is lexicalized to represent only this extent of reference, and so it leaves moot whether or not the intention to attain the goal was fulfilled. In the third verbal pattern, the verb is lexicalized to represent all of the preceding plus the implicature that the intended goal was attained. And in the fourth verbal pattern, the verb refers to all of the preceding, except that it enhances the implicature, in effect, into an assertion that the intended goal was attained. Each different type of verb can enter into construction with a different type of semantically complementary satellite.

(37) a. *Intrinsic-fulfillment verb:* action
        Further-event satellite: the state change resulting from that action

        For example:
        V: *kick* 'propel foot into impact with'
        Sat: *flat:* 'thereby causing to become flat'
        I kicked the hubcap. / I kicked the hubcap flat.

    b. *Moot-fulfillment verb:* action + goal
        Fulfillment satellite: fulfillment of that goal

        For example:
        V: *hunt* 'go about looking with the goal of thereby finding and capturing'
        Sat: *down:* 'with fulfillment of the goal'
        The police hunted the fugitive for/*in three days (but they didn't catch him). The police hunted the fugitive down in/*for five days (*but they didn't catch him).

    c. *Implied-fulfillment verb:* action + goal + implicature of fulfillment of the goal

Confirmation satellite: confirmation of that implicature

For example:

V: *wash* 'immerse and agitate with the goal of cleansing
thereby + the implicature of attaining that goal'
Sat: *clean:* 'with confirmation of the implicature of attaining the
goal of cleansing'
I washed the shirt (but it came out dirty). / I washed the shirt
clean (*but it came out dirty).

  d. *Attained-fulfillment verb:* action + goal + fulfillment of that goal
Pleonastic satellite: fulfillment of the goal (generally avoided in
English)
For example:
V: *drown* 'submerge with the goal of killing
thereby + attainment of that goal'
Sat: *dead/to death:* 'with the attainment of the goal of killing'
I drowned him (*but he wasn't dead). / *I drowned him dead/to
death.

7.1.1   Intrinsic-Fulfillment Verb + Further-Event Satellite   At the semantically simpler end of the series, illustrated in (37a), the verb refers to a situation in which an Agent intends and executes what can be taken as a simplex action. One criterial characteristic of this pattern is that the Agent's scope of intention extends only over the action itself, and no further (i.e., as far as the meaning of the verb per se is concerned). A second characteristic is that the executed action can be conceptualized as a single qualitatively unitary action, as assessed at a certain coarser scale of granularity. Thus, under this conceptualization, the referent of the verb *kick* is regarded as a unitary act consisting of an Agent volitionally thrusting her foot from a more body-proximal location through space into impact with another object, where the Agent has intended this entire sequence but not necessarily any consequences beyond it. A verb with this semantic pattern of lexicalization will be termed an **intrinsic-fulfillment verb.** This term is intended to convey the idea that the Agent's intention for a certain outcome is exactly fulfilled by the action referred to by the verb itself.

With this verbal pattern, the addition of a satellite adds a semantic increment that is wholly extrinsic to the referential content of the verb. For example, adding *flat* to *kick,* as in (37a), simply adds the meanings of the satellite and of the satellite construction to the meaning of the verb. Thus, the same act of kicking is now additionally understood to cause the named state change. A satellite with this semantic relationship to the verb will be termed a **further-event satellite**.

It can be seen that, with respect to the present incremental series, the beginning entry consists of an intrinsic-fulfillment verb paired with a further-event satellite. But, with respect to the categories developed so far in this chapter, these paired constituents are simply a co-event verb that bears the relation of Cause to a framing satellite of the state-change type.

7.1.2 Moot-Fulfillment Verb + Fulfillment Satellite The next verbal pattern involves the fulfillment type of realization. Here, as before, the verb refers to an Agent intending and executing a particular action, the whole of which takes place. But here, in addition, the Agent's scope of intention extends beyond the execution of this action alone. Specifically, the Agent further intends that the action lead to a particular result, one that, within the referential scope of the verb, does not come about and whose eventual success or failure is left moot. A verb with this pattern of lexicalization will be termed a **moot-fulfillment verb**.

With this verbal pattern, the addition of a satellite indicates that this intention to bring about a particular goal has in fact been fulfilled and the goal achieved. Here, the meaning of the satellite's addition is not independent of the meaning of the verb but is sensitive to the internal structure of that semantic complex and complements it. A satellite of this type will be termed a **fulfillment satellite**.

Thus, as illustrated in (37b), the referent of transitive *hunt* consists of an Agent's activity of going about looking, inquiring, tracking, and so on where the Agent has intended this activity, together with the Agent's further intention that this activity will lead to finding and capturing a particular animate entity. When used without a satellite, this verb is moot regarding the outcome. It has unbounded (atelic) aspect—hence, it can take the type of temporal expression that begins with *for*. But the addition of the satellite *down* indicates that the additional intention was fulfilled—that is, that the finding and capturing actually took place. This combined event complex now has bounded (telic) aspect—hence, it can take a temporal expression that begins with *in*.[8]

The fulfillment sense of this type of satellite construction can be regarded as a special kind of state change, one pertaining to ontology. The ontological state of the intended result that is expressed by the verb is originally **potential**, but the satellite indicates the change of this state to **actual**. Thus, when fulfillment is regarded as a kind of state change, one in ontology, it could be equivalently termed **actualization**. In effect, the verb by itself can be considered to express the **schema** for a desired result, while the satellite indicates that this schema has been "filled in," or actualized.

7.1.3 Implied-Fulfillment Verb + Confirmation Satellite   The third verbal pattern involves the confirmation type of realization. In this type, the verb includes the same two components as in the moot-fulfillment type. These two components are an Agent's intended and executed action plus her further intention that this action lead to a certain desired result. But, in addition, the verb conveys a particular implicature: that the intention to bring about the result has been fulfilled. The evidence for the presence of such an implicature is simply that the normal reading of a sentence containing this type of verb, even unaccompanied by a satellite, is that the desired goal is achieved. However, this component of the verb's meaning is merely an implicature, since this reading is defeasible by a disclaiming phrase. A verb with this pattern of lexicalization can more accurately be termed an **implicated-fulfillment verb**. Or it can be more loosely called an **implied-fulfillment verb** for greater brevity.[9]

With the addition of a satellite, though, the attainment of the intended result is now certain and not merely a defeasible implicature. Accordingly, any disclaiming phrase is now unacceptable. That is, the addition of the satellite **confirms** what otherwise is only implicated. A satellite of this type is thus termed a **confirmation satellite**.

Thus, the (37c) sentence *I washed the shirt* not only indicates that I intentionally immersed and agitated the shirt in liquid and had the further intention of getting it clean as a result, but, with nothing more said, also implicates that the shirt in fact got clean. But this implicature can be defeated by adding the clause *... but it came out dirty*. However, the addition of the satellite *clean*, as in *I washed the shirt clean*, certifies that the verb's original implicature has now extended beyond that status to become a claimed fact.

While English is not rich in implied-fulfillment verbs, another example may be the verb *call*. This verb indicates dialing a number with the intention of thereby telephonically connecting with a party, together with the implicature that this connection has occurred. Thus, the sentence *I called her* by itself normally implicates my reaching her. But this implicature is readily defeated, as in *I called her three times but there was no* *answer*. Now, for some speakers at least, the addition of the satellite *up* confirms the connection and thus precludes a disclaimer: *I called her up (*but there was no answer)*. While English has only scattered examples of this verbal pattern, it is a major type in other languages, like Mandarin, as illustrated below.

In both English and Mandarin, the satellites that indicate realization, either fulfillment or confirmation, are of two kinds. The satellite can explicitly name the verb's intended result—as *clean* does in relation to *wash*. Or the satellite can have a meaning not related (unless metaphorically) to the verb's intended result, as is the case with *down* in relation to *hunt* and *up* in relation to *call*. The former kind is a state-change satellite that secondarily indicates fulfillment or confirmation of the verb's intended result by making an independent specification of arrival at the result. But in the latter case, the satellite acts as an abstract marker of the realization factor per se, indicating realization of the verb's intended result, whatever that happens to be. In this way, the second kind of satellite is cleaner evidence of realization as a conceptual category in its own right.

As already seen for a fulfillment satellite, the meaning of the confirmation satellite is—especially for the second kind of satellite—not independent of the verb's meaning, but is sensitive to its internal semantic structure and complements it. In this case, it does so by addressing the verb's incorporated implicature and confirming it, or in effect, upgrading it to the lexical equivalent of an assertion.

And, as before, this confirmation sense of the confirmation type of satellite construction can be regarded as a special kind of state change, one pertaining this time not to ontology but to epistemology. What is basically operative here is the epistemic state of the speaker—and the corresponding epistemic state that the speaker aims to induce in the addressee —with respect to the 'intended result' component of the verb's meaning. With the satellite absent, the speaker is *presumptive* of the occurrence of the intended result. But with the satellite present, the speaker is *certain* of the occurrence of the intended result.

However, by a process that can be termed **objectivization**, these originally epistemic states of the speaker can be converted into so-conceived objective properties of the 'intended result' component itself. Thus, with the satellite absent, the counterpart "objective" state of this component is that it is *apparent*, while with the satellite present, the counterpart "objective" state is that it is *definite*.

To expand on the notion of objectivization, it is a general cognitive process also found in the conceptual organization of language. By this process, an individual's subjective cognitive state regarding some external entity is projected onto that entity, yielding a certain counterpart form. This counterpart is then conceived as an objective property of that entity itself. A ready linguistic example of this process is seen in a formulation like *The cliff is beautiful*, which seems to assert that the cliff has an objective property of 'beauty', in the same way that *The cliff is white* predicates an objective whiteness of the cliff. Alternate constructions like *The cliff is beautiful to me* or *I find the cliff beautiful* directly represent the non-objectivized subjective evaluation or affect of an observing experiencer.

7.1.4 Attained-Fulfillment Verb (+ Pleonastic Satellite)   In the fourth verbal pattern of the incremental series, the verb includes the same two components already seen in the second and third verbal patterns—that is, in verbs of moot fulfillment and of implied fulfillment. These two components, again, are an Agent's intended and executed simplex action plus his intention that this action lead to a certain desired result. However, in addition, the verb indicates neither a moot outcome nor simply an implicature of the fulfillment of the further intention, but rather the actual fulfillment of that intention. A verb of this type cannot add a satellite sensitive to and complementing the verb's internal semantic structure—specifically to indicate the realization of unrealized aspects—since all the conceptual elements referred to by the verb are in fact realized. English, in fact, tends to disfavor even a semantically pleonastic satellite with such a verb.

Thus, as seen in (37d), English *drown* indicates that an Agent intentionally executes the action of submerging an animate entity in liquid, that the Agent further intends that this action will lead to the death of the animate entity, and that this death in fact takes place. This verb, further, does not allow the addition of what would be a redundant satellite constituent such as *dead* or *to death*, as in *I drowned him *dead/*to death*.

Characterized in this way, therefore, the referent of a verb of the fourth pattern is understood as semantically complex, consisting of two qualitatively distinct subevents, one that is earlier than the other and intended to cause it. A verb so conceived can be termed an **attained-fulfillment verb**.

However, it is not clear that this putative attained-fulfillment verb can be systematically distinguished from the putative intrinsic-fulfillment verb described in section 6.1.1, either by formal syntactic criteria or referentially. It may be that the putative intrinsic-fulfillment and attained-fulfillment verbs really comprise only a single referential type on which can be imposed either of two conceptual structures with different granularities.

For example, the referent of *kick*, earlier described as a unitary simplex action of the intrinsic-fulfillment type, could, under a finer-grained conceptualization, be alternatively construed as an attained-fulfillment actional complex in this way: An Agent intentionally executes the action of thrusting her foot forth; she further intends that this action lead to an impact of the foot with a specific object; and this impact takes place (see the comparable Mandarin analysis below). In the other direction, the referent of *drown* could alternatively be construed, under a more coarse-grained conceptualization, as a unitary Gestalt action, and hence be regarded as an intrinsic-fulfillment type of verb.

The intrinsic-fulfillment and the attained-fulfillment types of verbs appear to differ only as to a construal of their granularity. But they share a common factor: their scope of intention matches their extent of fulfillment. Accordingly, we introduce the single term **fulfilled verb** to refer to both types. Correlatively, the moot-fulfillment and the implied-fulfillment types of verbs differ as to their implicatedness of fulfillment. But what they have in common is the fact that their scope of intention overshoots their extent of fulfillment. Accordingly, we introduce the single term **conative verb** to refer to both types. As already seen, the fulfillment and the confirmation types of satellites that can respectively accompany the two verb types are both cases of the single notion of "realization."

7.2   Cline in Strength of Implicature

The implicature associated with the implied-fulfillment type of verb apparently behaves not as a discrete factor that is either present or absent, but as on a cline with different degrees of strength. This might correlate in part with different strengths of the Agent's intention for a further result. Thus, in (38), the first three verbs for some speakers show increasing degrees of implicature of the fulfillment of an intention to kill, while the fourth verb, included as a reference point, no longer implicates but asserts the killing.

(38) The stranger choked/stabbed/strangled/drowned him.

The verb *choke* appears to range from having no implicature of killing for some speakers—referring solely to the action of squeezing in on the neck—to having a slight implicature of killing for other speakers. For the second group of speakers, the example with *choke* in (38) can be fairly felicitously followed by a denial constituent like ... *but he was still alive when the police arrived.*

The verb *stab* seems to implicate killing more strongly, to be felt to do so by more speakers, and to combine well with the same denial clause just cited.

For some speakers, *strangle* entails killing as fully as does *drown*, and if these speakers also sense no implicature of killing in either *choke* or *stab*, the whole series in (38) cannot serve for them as a demonstration of an implicational cline. However, other speakers do find in *strangle* a slight opening for the possibility of unrealized killing and can follow the sentence with the denial clause, as in *The stranger strangled him, but he was still alive when the police arrived.* This is especially the case if these speakers are asked to compare this sentence with one containing *drown* instead, which for them clearly precludes denial. Such speakers thus have in *strangle* an excellent example of very strong implicature that is nonetheless only an implicature and not determinate.

As represented in (39), the increasing degree of implicature of fulfillment across the four example verbs tends to correlate with the verbs' decreasing ability to take a satellite that confirms the fulfillment, perhaps because such confirmation would be increasingly redundant.

(39) The stranger choked/stabbed/?strangled/*drowned him to death.

7.3 Lexicalized Implicature

The implicature of the implied-fulfillment type of verb represents a semantic-syntactic phenomenon that, to be understood adequately, must be narrowed in on through a series of contrasts with related but distinct phenomena. We here take *wash* through this progression of contrasts. We first note that a part of the meaning of *wash* is the Agent's intention to make the Patient clean. This contrasts with the otherwise comparable meaning of *soak*, which lacks such a notion of further intention. Evidence for this is the fact that *soak* but not *wash* can occur felicitously in reference to a situation that precludes cleansing, as in (40).

(40) I soaked/??washed the shirt in dirty ink.

Second, in addition to an Agent's *intention* to make something clean, the use of *wash* as in (41a) implicates that the Patient *becomes* clean, even without any explicit mention of cleanness. This behavior can be contrasted, say, with the use of *soak* as in (41b), whose use makes no such suggestion.

(41) a. I washed the shirt.   Suggestion that Patient becomes clean
                                          as a result of the named process

    b. I soaked the shirt.   No such suggestion

Third, the notion of the Patient's becoming clean is *only* an implicature and not an essential part of the meaning of *wash*, since that notion can be denied, as in (42a). By contrast, in the meaning of the verb *clean* the notion of 'becoming clean' *is* an essential and hence nondeniable part, as seen in (42b) (where *clean* is not used in the sense of sending to the cleaners).

(42) a.   I washed the shirt, but it came out dirty.
    b.   *I cleaned the shirt, but it came out dirty.

Fourth, the notion of 'becoming clean' that we find associated with *wash* cannot be present simply by virtue of being part of some larger metonymic frame. For example, it might be proposed that *wash* refers directly only to the action of immersion with agitation, and that this would act as a metonym for an expanded frame that further included getting clean, drying, and putting away. But there is evidence against such an interpretation. Thus, it is perfectly felicitous to say (43a), thus canceling the 'drying' component of the putative frame, but it is not felicitous to say (43b), which cancels the 'making clean' component, even though by the metonymic interpretation both these components are equally part of the frame.

(43) a.   I washed the shirt and left it wet.
    b.   ??I washed the shirt and left it dirty.

Fifth, while pragmatic theory has a notion of "conventional implicature" that is associated with a lexical item—for example, the implicature of 'contrast' that is associated with the morpheme *but*—this kind of implicature is not defeasible (see Levinson 1983). By contrast, the implicature of 'becoming clean' that is associated with *wash* is indeed defeasible, as in *I washed the shirt, but it came out dirty*, so that this cannot be an instance of conventional implicature.

By zeroing in this way on the implicational phenomena exhibited by a word like *wash*, one must conclude that it is distinct from linguistic phenomena previously described. It is a defeasible implicature associated with a lexical item, and thus presumably part of the lexical content. We propose the term **lexicalized implicature** for this linguistic phenomenon.

7.4   Typological Difference in the Expression of Realization

Languages that systematically express realization appear to divide into the same two typological categories we have seen on the basis of whether the realization is expressed in the main verb or in the satellite, and this assignment appears to align with that of the other framing categories. That is, satellite-framed languages that employ the satellite to express Path, temporal contour, changed state, and action correlation also extend that set to include realization, while verb-framed languages tend to employ the main verb to express the full set of five categories. Apparently, in the organization of conception for linguistic expression, realization is set into analogy with the other framing-event types in something like the following way: As the space domain has motion from elsewhere to a particular location, and as the state domain has change from the absence to the presence of a particular property, so the realization domain has transition from a potential stage to an actualized stage of realization, or from an assumed degree to a definite degree of realization. Reinforcing the analogy, realization can, as we saw, be interpreted as a specialized kind of state change, pertaining to ontological and epistemic states. This analogy can be captured by the conceptual structure assumed for a realization-type macro-event. This is schematized for fulfillment in (44a) and for confirmation in (44b).

(44) a. [Agent "$_A$MOVE" TO FULFILLMENT the INTENTION (to CAUSE X)] WITH-THE-SUBSTRATE-OF [Agent ACT + INTEND to CAUSE X THEREBY]

   b. [Agent "$_A$MOVE" TO CONFIRMATION the IMPLICATURE of the FULFILLMENT of the INTENTION (to CAUSE X)] WITH-THE-SUBSTRATE-OF [Agent ACT + INTEND to CAUSE X THEREBY + IMPLICATURE of the FULFILLMENT of the INTENTION to CAUSE X]

Although the implied-fulfillment type of verb is minimal in English and many other familiar languages, some languages have an extensively developed system of lexicalized implicature and confirmation thereof. Two such languages are Mandarin and Tamil, representing the two typological categories of satellite-framed and verb-framed languages, respectively.

7.5 Mandarin: A Satellite-Framed Language Exhibiting Realization

Mandarin is a strongly satellite-framed language, regularly using its satellites to specify Path, aspect, state change, some action correlation, and much realization. Perhaps the majority of its agentive verbs are of either the moot-fulfillment or the implied-fulfillment types—requiring a satellite for their realization—with the latter apparently the more strongly represented. Some examples appear in (45) to (47).

(45) a. wǒ kāi   le   mén (dàn-shì mén méi   kāi)
        I   open PERF door (but   door not-PAST open)

     b. wǒ kāi   kāi   le   mén
        I   open(V) open(Sat) PERF door

(46) a. wǒ shā le   tā   (dàn-shì méi   shā sǐ)
        I   kill PERF him (but   not-PAST kill dead)

     b. wǒ shā sǐ   le   tā
        I   kill dead PERF him

(47) a. wǒ tī   le   tā   (dàn-shì méi   tī   zháo)
        I   kick PERF him (but   not-PAST kick into-contact)

     b. wǒ tī   zháo   le   tā
        I   kick into-contact PERF him

The semantics of these examples can be explicated as follows. The meaning of (45a) without the parenthetical addition is that I acted on the door in order to open it, with the implicature that the door in fact left the jamb. However, the interpretation that I did not succeed in moving the door from the jamb remains a possibility, one that has greater or lesser prominence in the hearer's attention according to the context. For example, adult speakers report frequent suspicion of their children's implicatures: *Child:* "I opened the door"; *parent:* "Yes, but did you open it open?" With the parenthetical addition, (45a) suggests that I worked at getting the door open—for example, trying to get the key to turn, twisting the doorknob, shoving, and so on—but that the door still never left the jamb. With the confirmational satellite in place in (45b), however, the sentence is now an undeniable assertion that I succeeded in moving the door from the jamb.

Comparably, the first clause in (46a) means that I assaulted a person with the intention of killing him and with the deniable implicature that I succeeded. And the first clause of (47a) means that I kicked my foot out at someone with the intention of connecting and with the deniable implicature that I did make the impact.

7.5.1 Comparison of English and Mandarin Verb Lexicalization
Of course, the English verbs used to gloss the Mandarin verbs here, such as *open, kill, kick*, do not really correspond in meaning, hence they can be misleading. For example, a sentence gloss like "I killed him but he didn't die" is genuinely paradoxical in English but thus incorrectly represents the nonparadoxical Mandarin original. The original would be more closely rendered as "I assaulted him with intent to kill (and with what would otherwise have been the presumption of killing), but he didn't die." The difference is that the English verb is generally construed to refer to a simplex action of the intrinsic-fulfillment type. In particular, it is generally construed to specify the attainment of a certain final state, and to be neutral as to the particular actions that led up to that state. Accordingly, an English verb in the frame cited above leads to a paradox because the follow-up clause contradicts the verb's assertion that its particular final state was attained.

In Mandarin, by contrast, the referential terrain covered by a typical English verb is conceptually divided into two portions, as in the implied-fulfillment pattern. The two portions are as follows: the final outcome, conclusively confirmed by a satellite, and an action performed with the intention that it lead to that outcome, which is indicated by the verb.

Accordingly, the unitary referent of an English verb often has as a counterpart in Mandarin a two-part conceptualization expressed by a verb plus a satellite. We have already seen several examples of this correspondence. Thus, the counterpart of 'kick' is " 'propel the foot so as to impact with' + 'into impact'." The counter part of 'kill' is " 'assault so as to kill' + 'to death'." And the counterpart of 'open' is " 'work on so as to open' + 'ajar'." In the same way, we can observe that the counterpart of 'cure' is " 'treat so as to cure' + 'to health (lit.: good)'." The counterpart of 'break' (e.g., snap a stick) is " 'squeeze circumpivotally in on so as to break' + 'broken'." And the counterpart of 'select' is " 'deliberate over so as to choose among' + 'into choice'."

This contrast between English and Mandarin can be expanded to reveal a complementarity between the two languages. We have just seen that Mandarin verbs are characteristically lexicalized to express either moot fulfillment or implied fulfillment and require additional forms—typically a satellite—to upgrade such a reference to that of attained fulfillment. But we can now note that English verbs work in virtually the opposite way. They are characteristically lexicalized to express attained fulfillment (recall that an intrinsic-fulfillment verb can also be conceptualized as one of attained fulfillment). And they can take additional forms to cut back on the original total reference so as to express moot fulfillment or implied fulfillment. The terms we have used for the typically Mandarin process of filling in the schema of a conative verb have been "fulfillment" and "confirmation"—or, in general, "realization." A term can now be introduced for the English process of cutting back on a verb's basic total reference. It is **resection**, adapted from its usual meaning, the surgical removal of part of an organ.

One linguistic form that performs resection in English is the progressive. Consider the fulfilled verb *open*, say, used in the context of opening a door, as in (48a). If conceptualized as an attained-fulfillment verb, *open* refers to an Agent's acting on the door—for example, by unlocking it, turning the doorknob, and pushing on it—with the intention that that action will lead to the door's moving away from the jamb so as to stand ajar, together with the indication that that intention was fulfilled. But if the verb is in construction with the progressive form *be -ing*, as in (48b), the overall reference is now only to the earlier portion of the verb's meaning—that is, to the Agent's action + goal. In (48b), we do not know whether or not I ultimately moved the door ajar. Thus, the progressive has resected the final portion of the meaning—fulfillment of the goal— and so has cut the verb's reference back to the moot-fulfillment type. (Note that replacing *door* with *wine bottle* in (48b) yields an example that works better for some speakers.)

(48) a. I opened the door.
     b. I was opening the door when I heard a scream.

Another form that performs resection in English is the preposition *at*, sometimes in conjunction with a satellite. Thus, *kick* and *grasp* are normally fulfilled verbs and, specifically, can be conceptualized as attained-fulfillment verbs, as in (49a). Thus, as described earlier, the referent of *kick* can be conceptualized as an Agent's thrusting her foot out with the intention that that action lead to impact with another object, together with the fulfillment of that intention. But the addition of *at*, as in (49b), resects the fulfillment notion, leaving the referent reduced to the status of moot fulfillment.

(49) a. I kicked him. / I grasped the rope.

   b. I kicked (out) at him. / I grasped at the rope.

In fact, English *kick* and Mandarin *tī* may form a nearly perfect complementary pair. Conative *tī* can be closely rendered in English as *kick at*—that is, by a fulfilled verb that has been resected. And fulfilled *kick* can be closely rendered in Mandarin by *tī zháo*, 'kick into-contact'—that is, by a conative verb that has been realized.

7.5.2 Further Semantic Verb-Satellite Relationships in Mandarin   The semantics of the Mandarin verb-satellite system ranges more widely than in English. It includes relationships beyond those described in the incremental series in section 6.1. In particular, Mandarin conative verbs can enter into construction not only with satellites expressing fulfillment or confirmation, but also with ones that express 'underfulfillment', 'overfulfillment', 'antifulfillment', and 'other-event'. We sketch these further relationships here.

We first introduce two Mandarin implied-fulfillment verbs. These verbs refer, respectively, to the breaking (specifically, snapping in two) of a somewhat resistant linear object, like a stick, and to the bending of such an object. The first of these verbs, *zhé*, can be glossed as 'to squeeze circumpivotally in on [a linear object] with the intention of thereby breaking [it], with the implicature that [it] gets broken'. The second verb, *wān*, can be glossed in the same way, except with the notion of 'bending' replacing that of 'breaking'. Each of these verbs can take a confirmation satellite that confirms the implicature, as seen in (50a).

(50) a. wǒ bǎ   gùn-zi zhé   shé/   duàn   le
      I   OBJ stick   break broken/ snapped PERF
      'I broke the stick broken/snapped.'
      "I broke the stick."

   b. wǒ bǎ   gùn-zi wān   wān le
      I   OBJ stick   bend bent PERF
      'I bent the stick bent.'
      "I bent the stick."

But the verb for 'break' can alternatively take a state-change satellite that refers to a 'bent' state, as in (50b). One reading of such a sentence is that I had squeezed in on the stick with the intention of breaking it, but that I only got as far as bending it (perhaps because the stick was too strong).[10] Note that in the usual course of executing the intention expressed by *zhé*, a bent state for the Patient is on the way to a broken state. Thus, the satellite marks an insufficient fulfillment of the full scope of intention. Accordingly, the satellite can be aptly termed an **under-fulfillment satellite**.

(51) wǒ bǎ gùn-zi zhé   wān le
     I   OBJ stick   break bent PERF
     'I broke the stick bent.'
     "I squeezed in on the stick to break it, but only managed to bend it."

In a complementary way, the verb for 'bend' can take a state-change satellite that refers to a 'broken' state, as in (52). This sentence means that I pressed in on a piece of bamboo bark with the intention of getting it into a bent shape but that I overshot the mark and wound up breaking it (perhaps because the bark was too brittle). Since the concept of 'breaking' is here on a continuum with that of 'bending' and conceived as lying beyond it, the satellite that marks this excess is aptly termed an **over-fulfillment satellite**.

(52) wǒ wān shé   le   zhú   pī
     I   bend broken PERF bamboo skin
     'I bent the bamboo bark broken.'
     "I pressed in on the bamboo bark to bend it but wound up breaking it."

Mandarin also allows a conative verb—that is, one expressing an action that is intended to lead to a particular result—to take a satellite that indicates that the reverse of the intended result is what actually occurs. Thus, the implied-fulfillment verb *xǐ* 'wash' has much the same meaning as English *wash*, namely, 'immerse and agitate with the goal of cleansing thereby'. But, as illustrated in (53), this verb can take the state-change satellite *zāng* 'dirty' to yield the following combined meaning: 'immerse and agitate [an object] with the intention of making [it] clean thereby, but actually making [it] dirtier than before'. A satellite for this semantic effect on the verb can be termed an **antifulfillment satellite**.

(53) wǒ bǎ chèn-yī xǐ   zāng le
     I   OBJ shirt   wash dirty PERF
     'I washed the shirt dirty.'
     "I washed the shirt (e.g., in the river), but it came out dirtier than before."

Note that Mandarin does not have a 'nonfulfillment' satellite construction indicating that an intended result was not reached. If it did, the previous example might have a second meaning: "I washed the shirt, but it came out just as dirty as when I started." This meaning is instead expressed by the type of construction in "I washed the shirt not clean," which explicitly represents the failure of fulfillment.

Note that in all the preceding new verb-satellite relations, the state expressed by the satellite fell somewhere along the conceptual axis leading to the verb's represented goal. Thus, the state expressed by the satellite was either before the starting point, at the starting point, almost at the goal, or past the goal. But a Mandarin satellite can also express a state that results from the action of a conative verb but that does not lie on the axis leading to the intended goal. For example, the verb for 'wash' could take a satellite with the meaning 'torn', as illustrated in (54). This sentence means that I performed the action of immersing and agitating or rubbing the shirt with the intention of getting it clean, but, unintendedly, this action led to the shirt's becoming torn. Perhaps such a satellite can simply be said to act as a further-event satellite, as described in section 6.1.1. But there the verb was an intrinsic-fulfillment verb and here it is an implied-fulfillment verb. This fact may entail enough of a different verb-satellite relationship to merit giving the satellite a new term: an **other-event satellite**.

(54) wǒ xī   può le   cheǹ-yī
     I   wash torn PERF shirt
     'I washed the shirt torn.'
     "I washed the shirt, and it got torn in the process."

7.6   Tamil: A Verb-Framed Language Exhibiting Realization

Tamil is a language that systematically expresses realization, but is the typological complement of Mandarin. Tamil is a verb-framed language using its finite-inflected verb for the expression of at least Path and aspect, as well as for the expression of realization. Unlike Mandarin, in which confirmation is indicated by any one of numerous satellites determined by the particular lexical verb present, Tamil uses a single specific verb to express confirmation per se (although apparently other verbs, mainly serving other functions, do also express confirmation). The examples in (55) illustrate.

(55) a. Nāṉ avaṉai koṉrēṉ.
        I   he-ACC kill(FINITE)-PAST-1S
        'I "killed" him.'

Āṉāl avaṉ cāka-villai.
but   he   die-NEG
'But he didn't die.'

  b. Nāṉ avaṉai koṉru-(vi)ṭṭēṉ.
       I   he-ACC kill(NON-FINITE)-leave(FINITE)-PAST-1S
       'I killed him.'
    *Āṉāl avaṉ cāka-villai.
    but   he   die-NEG
    *'But he didn't die.'

8   EVIDENCE THAT THE FRAMING SATELLITE EXPRESSES THE MAIN EVENT

At the conceptual level, the framing event has been shown to be determinative in various respects within the macro-event that contains it—for example, by providing an overarching framework, or by anchoring, or by imposing structure. But, at the level of expression, it remains to demonstrate that what has been called the framing constituent—whether verb or satellite—in fact represents the framing event, as evidenced by its being determinative of a corresponding set of semantic and syntactic factors within the clause that contains it. Such a demonstration is presented in this section. Since the idea that the satellite should have this determinative role is more controversial, the demonstration concentrates on the satellite constituent. However, almost all the same arguments could apply to a framing verb as well.

8.1   Determining Complement Structure and the Semantic Character of Arguments

A framing satellite determines most or all of the complement structure of its clause as well as the semantic character of the arguments represented in these complements. This observation can be demonstrated with a series of paired examples in which the satellite is first absent, then present.

In the initial example, the addition of a framing satellite does not change the semantic character of the arguments, but shifts the clause from an intransitive to a transitive-type complement structure—as well as changing the aspectual properties. With no satellite present, *blow* is inherently an intransitive activity verb able to occur in construction with an oblique constituent with *on*, as in *I blew on the flame*. But, if added, the state-change satellite *out*, 'to extinction', requires a direct object complement for the clause, as in *I blew the flame out* (the conflated counterpart of

I extinguished the flame by blowing on it). Both constructions here can take an object of the same semantic character, like a flame. But the differences are that the construction that lacks a satellite is intransitive, is aspectually unbounded, and refers to a steady-state activity, while the construction with the satellite is transitive, is aspectually punctual, and refers to a transition into a particular state.

A second case is comparable except for also having semantically different objects. The verb *run* refers to an unbounded steady-state activity and is an intransitive form regularly taking an oblique object, as in *I ran along the street*. But the addition of the prefixal action-correlating satellite *out-*, 'into surpassment', changes the reference to a bounded accomplishment and now requires a direct object, as in *I outran him*. Semantically, further, the oblique object with *run* alone refers to a Path and names a Ground object, thus indicating the course followed. But the direct object with *out-* refers to an animate Patient that constitutes the coactive entity surpassed.

Our third example shows that the satellite can determine not only the intrinsic semantic character of an object but also an incidental property—in this case, that of 'definiteness'. Thus, the German verb *schreiben*, 'write', can take an oblique phrase indicating an Instrument or Medium that may be either definite or indefinite, as in *mit (der) Tinte schreiben*, 'write with (the) ink'. But, when added, the state-change satellite *ver-*, 'to exhaustion', now not only requires a direct object, but also requires that this direct object be definite. Thus, it is acceptable to say *die (ganze) Tinte verschreiben* 'exhaust (all) the ink in writing'. But it is unacceptable to say **Tinte verschreiben*, '*exhaust ink in writing'.

Finally, a framing satellite can determine the syntactic realization of not just one argument, as in the preceding examples, but of two arguments, and, further, can determine their relative standing in the complement hierarchy (as treated at length in chapter II-1). For example, in construction with *pour* as a Manner verb, each Path satellite that requires both a Figure argument and a Ground argument also determines the particular complements in which these arguments are expressed. Thus, the Path satellite *in*, in conjunction with the preposition *to*, calls for the Figure to be expressed as the direct object and the Ground as an oblique object, as in *I poured the water [Figure] into the glass [Ground]*. However, the Path satellite *full*, in conjunction with the preposition *of*, has the Ground as direct object and the Figure as oblique, as in *I poured the glass [Ground] full of water [Figure]*.

We have just seen that the framing satellite transfers certain features of the framing event into the argument and complement structure of the whole clause that represents the entire macro-event. But we must note that the framing satellite does not always determine all such features. Specifically, the co-event verb in some cases can transfer particular features of the co-event into the clause. Such transfers are determined by a complex of constraints pertaining to the particular language, construction, satellite, and verb, as well as the interactional effects among these. For one illustration, the English action-correlating satellite *along*, 'in accompaniment', permits the Patient in the co-event to be expressed as a direct object within the full clause, as in *I played the melody along with him*. But the action-correlating satellite *out-*, 'in surpassment', does not permit this: *I outplayed him *the melody*.

Comparably, of course, the framing satellite is typically not determinative of features of complement structure that arise outside the macro-event proper. For example, an external agentive causal chain, and not the framing event, is typically responsible for getting an Agent represented as the subject of the clause and the Figure as direct object.

8.2 Determining Overall Aspect

When appearing in its basic use without a framing satellite, a lexical verb typically exhibits a particular type of inherent aspect (*Aktionsart*). Regardless of this, a framing satellite occurring with that verb is the constituent that determines the aspect for the clausal reference as a whole. The inherent aspect of verbs found in a co-event function is generally of the unbounded steady-state type—either a stative or an activity—though other aspect types do occur. And the aspect type of a framing satellite is perhaps most often that of a bounded extent, but punctual and unbounded types also readily occur. Our demonstration of the aspectual determinativeness of the framing satellite will proceed through the different framing event domains from Motion through realization. The terms for aspect types and the tests with *in* and *for* phrases are described in chapter I-1. (Such aspect terminology as "bounded," "unbounded," "steady-state," and so on is explicated in that chapter and is used instead of terminology based on Vendler 1968.)

Consider first the Motion domain. The inherent aspect of the verb *float*, which can be observed in a clause representing a simplex event, is of the unbounded type, as in *The bottle floated on the water for an hour/*in an* *hour (before finally sinking)*. But when *float* functions as a co-event verb, it is the Path satellite's associated temporal contour that determines the aspect for the full macro-event referent of a clause. Thus, the bounded-extent aspect that can be associated with the Path satellite *across* is determinative in the sentence *The bottle floated across (the entire canal) in 10 minutes/*for 10 minutes*. The punctual aspect of *in* or *past* determines the overall aspect in *The bottle floated in (-to the cleft)/past (the rock) at exactly 3:00/*for an hour*. And the unbounded aspect of *along* appears overall in *The bottle floated along (the canal) for one hour/*in an hour*— where, now, the aspectual unboundedness is due to the satellite, not to the verb's inherent aspectual character.

In the domain of temporal contouring, a framing satellite by definition determines the aspect, as all the pertinent examples in section 3 illustrate. Here, we can illustrate the change in aspect when the satellite is added to the verb. Thus, the English verb *sigh* is inherently of punctual aspect, as shown by its compatibility with a punctual phrase—for example, *She sighed at exactly 3:00*. But the addition of the satellite complex *on and on*, of unbounded aspect, precludes an overall punctual aspect for the clause and permits only unboundedness: *She sighed on and on *at exactly 3:00/ for hours*.

Framing satellites that, as noted earlier, seem to be transitional between the domains of temporal contouring and of state change also exhibit aspectual determinativeness. Thus, the addition of *up* to indicate 'consumption' or 'loss of intactness' introduces bounded aspect where the verb alone has unbounded aspect. This is seen in *The log burned for hours/ ?in one hour* versus *The log burned up in one hour/*for hours*. And it is also seen in *The dog chewed on the shoe for hours/*in one hour* versus *The dog chewed the shoe up in one hour/*for hours*.

Examples fully within the domain of state change exhibit similar contrasts. Thus, *flicker* alone can have either unbounded or punctual aspect but not bounded-extent aspect, as seen in *The candle flickered for minutes/ at exactly midnight/*in 5 minutes*. However, the state-change satellite *out* 'to extinction' calls for either of the latter two aspect types, as seen in *The candle flickered out *for minutes/at exactly midnight/in 5 minutes*.

Comparably, transitive *boil* alone is of unbounded aspect, while the addition of an *up* signaling an effected object requires bounded-extent aspect, as seen in *I boiled some coffee for 10 minutes/*in 10 minutes* versus *I boiled up some coffee in 20 minutes/*for 10 minutes*.

In the domain of action correlating, the 'surpass' satellite *out-* can show the imposition of bounded-extent aspect on an unbounded-aspect verb. An example is *I sawed wood for hours/*in 15 minutes* as contrasted with *He had a head start in the wood-sawing contest, but I outsawed him in just 15 minutes.*

Finally, in the domain of realization, the transitive verb *hunt* alone refers to an unbounded activity, but the addition of the fulfillment satellite *down* introduces an overlay of bounded-extent aspect, as seen in *The police hunted the fugitive for days/*in one week* versus *The police hunted the fugitive down in one week/*for days.*

As with an earlier aviso, we must note that the framing satellite does not determine features of aspect that arise outside its scope. Thus, the state-change satellite *out*, as in *The candle blew out*, may fix the aspect as punctual or bounded within the scope of a single event of candle extinguishment. But it gives way before the usual superordinate aspect-influencing phenomena like those depending on plural subjects or extrinsic iterativity, as seen in *Candles blew out for hours.*

8.3   Determining the Auxiliary in German

In conjunction with its determination of both argument structure and aspect, the framing satellite in German also determines the auxiliary required to mark the past tense, *haben* 'have' or *sein* 'be'. For example, when unaccompanied by a framing satellite, the verb *laufen* 'run' is perhaps basically an intransitive verb with unbounded aspect and a directional complement that requires the *sein* auxiliary, as in (56a). But the addition of the state-change satellite *wund* 'to soreness' converts the sentence into a transitive construction with bounded-extent aspect that requires the *haben* auxiliary, as in (56b).

(56) a. Ich bin/*habe um die ganze Stadt gelaufen.
         'I ran around the whole city.'
     b. Ich habe/*bin die Füsse (*um die ganze Stadt) wundgelaufen.
         'I ran my feet sore (*around the whole city).'
         "I made my feet sore in running."

8.4   Determining the "Upshot"

The framing satellite, in representing the main event, expresses the "upshot" of the whole macro-event. That is (as already indicated in the introduction), it expresses the core of what is asserted in a declarative construction, denied under negation, asked about in an interrogative construction, and demanded in an imperative. When occurring without a framing satellite, the main lexical verb is generally the constituent that focally conveys the upshot, but when a framing satellite is present, it takes over that function.

We illustrate this phenomenon for the upshot of 'negation'. Notice that a negative sentence with the verb *eat* unaccompanied by a framing satellite, as in (57a), indicates that no eating took place. But now consider the sentence in (57b), to which has been added the particle *up*—a state-change framing satellite with aspectual properties that means 'to exhaustion'. The sentence now indicates that eating *did* take place but that the Patient was not exhausted in the process. That is, the negative particle denies the referent of the satellite, in consonance with our claim that this referent is the main framing event of the whole situation, rather than denying the referent of the verb, which we would claim now only represents the co-event.

(57) a. I didn't eat the popcorn.
     b. I didn't eat up the popcorn.

Comparably, a negative with transitive *hunt* alone, a verb of moot fulfillment, as in (58a), indicates that no search took place. But with the fulfillment satellite *down* also present, as in (58b), the search did take place, but there was no finding and no capture. That is, it is the fulfillment meaning of the framing satellite that is denied, here, not the activity referent of what is now only a co-event verb.

(58) a. The police didn't hunt the fugitive.
     b. The police didn't hunt down the fugitive.

A certain type of departure from this pattern as to which constituent is affected by negation does exist. Consider this example. The negative with the verb *run* alone, as in *I didn't run when the alarm sounded*, indicates that no running took place—perhaps I walked or stood still. The additional presence of the Path satellite *out* to yield *I didn't run out when the alarm sounded*, as in the previous pattern, does involve the negation of that satellite's reference. Hence, there was no exiting. But in the previous pattern the positive occurrence of the verb's reference was presupposed. In the present pattern, though, such occurrence is moot. Here, I may or may not have run.

One account for this behavior is that the reading with the positive occurrence of running results in the expected way from the interpretation of *run out* in accordance with the previously discussed pattern. In this pattern, two events are combined: the framing event as upshot, represented by the satellite, and a presupposed co-event represented by the verb. But the reading with the nonoccurrence of running may result from an option available in English to treat a sequence like *run out* as representing a unitary concept. This unitary concept would here comprise an integrated action complex. Under this treatment, negation would deny the whole of the action complex. Such an account gains support in that it is in any case needed for collocations like *turn in* 'go to bed'. Thus, a sentence like *He didn't turn in* has no option to indicate that the reference of *in* is to be denied while that of *turn* is to be maintained. Rather, the denial is of the unitary referent of the lexical complex as a whole.

8.5   Licensing Generic (Dummy) Verbs

In the general pattern for a satellite-framed language, as we have seen, the framing satellite expresses the upshot of the sentence, while the co-event verb refers to some specific ancillary event. Accordingly, the speaker must ascertain within the full referential situation some suitable ancillary event for expression by a lexically specific verb, whether or not that event is especially pertinent in the communicative context. Given this consideration, one might expect a satellite-framed language to develop a system for maintaining the general pattern syntactically while semantically bypassing the expression of an unnecessarily specific ancillary event. And, indeed, serving this function, many such languages have developed a system of **generic** or "dummy" verbs. Such verbs can act, in effect, as syntactic "placeholders" while conveying relatively generic or neutral semantic content and thus permitting the sentence to procede to the satellite, whose semantic content is the relevant factor.

English exhibits a system of this kind, employing such generically functioning verbs as *go, put, do*, and *make*. To illustrate, the specific cause of a flame's extinction is indicated as 'blowing' in the nonagentive sentence *The candle blew out* and in the agentive sentence *I blew the candle out*. But the extinction can be expressed alone, without any indication of a specific cause, through the use of a state-change satellite together with a generic verb, as in nonagentive *The candle went* out, and agentive *I put* the candle out.

Comparably, the temporal contour of 'continuation' can be expressed by the framing satellite *on*. And this satellite can occur with a specific co-event verb, as in *They talked on*, which has the meaning 'They continued talking'. But replacing the specific verb with the generic *go* yields the sentence *They went on*, which now simply means 'They continued'. Similarly, the action correlation of 'surpassment' can be expressed by the framing satellite *out-*. This satellite can occur with a specific co-event verb, as in *I outcooked him*. But it can also occur with the generic verb *do*, as in *I outdid him*, to form a lexical complex that now simply means 'to surpass'. And, in a comparable way, we saw that the combination of satellite plus preposition *off with* represents the core schema for a traversal type of state change, one pertaining to theft and escape. This form can be used with a specific verb, as in *I ran off with the money*, that expresses the locomotive Manner of the escape. But the form can also be used with generic *make*, as in *I made off with the money*, which allows reference to the theft and escape without indication of Manner.

German largely uses *machen* and *gehen* as generic verbs with its extensive system of framing satellites. Examples are *fertigmachen* 'to finish', *weitermachen* 'to continue', *kaputtmachen* 'to destroy', *mitmachen* 'to accompany, join in with', *nachmachen* 'to imitate', and *vormachen* 'to demonstrate'. All these examples employ framing satellites that were discussed earlier in the chapter, though there in construction with specific co-event verbs.

Within a satellite-framed language, the construction consisting of a generic verb and a framing satellite is, in effect, the semantic equivalent of a single framing verb of the kind characteristic of verb-framed languages. In some cases, the analogy can develop still further. In such cases, when some specific co-event does need specification, it can be expressed not only by the verb, in the pattern characteristic of satellite-framed languages, but alternatively by an adjunct, in the pattern characteristic of verb-framed languages. For example, as just noted, the English action-correlating satellite *out-* can occur with the generic verb *do* to yield a resulting unitary meaning equivalent to 'surpass', as in *I outdid him*. The specification of a particular co-event can then be accomplished in the usual pattern through a specific verb substituted for the generic one, as in *I outcooked him*. Or it can be accomplished through the addition of an adjunct, as in *I outdid him at cooking*.

Comparably, the temporal contouring satellite *on*, 'into continuation', can occur with a lexically specific co-event verb, as in *They talked on*. But it can also occur with the generic verb *go* to form a construction meaning 'to continue', and this construction can in turn take a specific co-event complement, as in *They went on talking*.

8.6   Licensing Pleonastic and Extended-Prototype Verbs

We have just seen that satellite-framed languages can use a generic verb to permit expression of the framing event by the satellite without having to express a particular co-event with the verb. But such languages can also use other verb types to accomplish this purpose. One case involves the pleonastic use of a framing verb with a meaning close to that of the framing satellite. Here, the framing event is referred to twice, once by the satellite and once by the verb. The verb is thus removed from service for expression of a co-event. And the combination of verb plus satellite, as in the generic case, can again be treated as a phrasal form of framing verb.

An English example of such a **pleonastic verb** is *search*, when used with the framing preposition *for* 'in search of', in the sequence *search for*. This latter combination of forms can be regarded as a phrasal framing verb equivalent to 'seek'. Such a phrasal form would then require a further adjunct to express the co-event, as in *I searched for nails on the board by feeling it*, by contrast with the original example in the text, *I felt for nails on the board*. Comparably, the 'as an addition' sense of the Yiddish satellite *tsu-* is matched somewhat compatibly in its use with the verb *gebn* 'to give', so that the combined form *tsugebn* can be glossed rather straightforwardly as 'to add'. The 'to exhaustion' sense of the German satellite *ver-* can be paired with the semantically comparable verb *brauchen* 'to use', so that the combination *verbrauchen* can now be glossed as 'to exhaust (use up)'.

A still further device that satellite-framed languages exhibit is to generalize the use of an originally specific co-event verb. The co-event expressed by this verb is usually the prototypical action undertaken to carry out the framing event expressed by the satellite. This arrangement is evident in an English case. The framing-event activity of 'seeking' can be represented by the framing preposition *for* 'in search of'. Seeking is prototypically conducted visually, hence the frequent combination of *for* with the specific co-event verb *look*, to yield the combination *look for*. But this phrasal combination has come to be used to refer to any kind of seeking, whether conducted visually or not. Thus, the sentence *I looked for nails on the board by feeling it* has just about the same meaning as *I felt for nails on the board*. Accordingly, *look* here can be termed an **extended prototype verb**.

9 CONCLUSION

Much material has been left out of this chapter that would extend the theoretical and cognitive framework and provide linguistic demonstration for more of the analysis. However, as it stands, I believe this chapter has shown that there is psychological reality to a certain fundamental conceptual entity with possibly universal linguistic expression. This entity can be conceptualized either as a complex event, consisting in turn of a minor event related to a major event or, alternatively, as a single fused event. The fact that this second alternative is readily expressed by core constructions in any language is evidence for our robust cognitive capacity to integrate certain large amounts and diverse kinds of conceptual material into a single monad. The body of this chapter has primarily been spent documenting the particular patterns and structuring of conceptual material that enter into the present specific process of monad formation. But as a whole, the chapter is intended as a contribution on conceptual integration and unification as a fundament of human thought.

Notes

1. This chapter is a much revised and expanded version of Talmy (1991).

   With my thanks to them, the sources of the non-English forms cited are, for German, Elisabeth Kuhn, Luise Hathaway, and Wolfgang Wölck; for Mandarin, Jian-Sheng Guo; for Spanish, Jon Aske, Guillermina Nuñez, and Jaime Ramos; and for Tamil, Eric Pederson and Susan Herring. In addition, I am indebted to Dan Slobin, Melissa Bowerman, Eric Pederson, Jon Aske, David Wilkins, Patricia Fox, Ruth B. Shields, and Kean Kaufmann for valuable discussions on the material of this chapter.

2. This Spanish type was independently noticed by Jon Aske.

3. It remains to clarify why the syntactic pattern in Spanish for temporal contouring differs from that for Motion as to the constituent in which the co-event's Patient is expressed. For example, the Spanish for (7a) is *not*

(i) *Terminé la carta, escribiéndola.
    "I finished the letter, writing it."

4. For some English speakers, the *away* satellite indicates total disappearance, so that for them, *The meat rotted away* suggests nothing more than a brown stain left on the table. For other speakers, however, the satellite's sense permits a residue.

5. In English, the satellite *out* can, like *up*, also represent the core schema INTO EXISTENCE and, hence, also mark the presence of an effected object:

(i) [I "$_A$MOVED" INTO EXISTENCE a message] WITH-THE-CAUSE-OF
    [I tapped on the radiator pipes]

I tapped out a message on the radiator pipes.

Contrast *tap* alone: ?I tapped a message on the radiator pipes.

Note that the 'into existence' state change does not have to be represented explicitly by a satellite in English, either for the nonagentive or for the agentive, as seen in (ii) and (iii). In such cases, the structure of the macro-event can be assumed to resemble that described in the text. By one interpretation, though, the core schema simply does not show up in a satellite. By another interpretation, the core schema conflates with the basic "MOVE" verb to constitute a "mid-level verb"—"FORM" for the nonagentive, and "MAKE" for the agentive—onto which the co-event then conflates. This is the interpretation adopted in chapter II-1.

(ii) [a hole "MOVED" INTO EXISTENCE in the table] WITH-THE-CAUSE-OF [a cigarette burned the table]

A hole burned in the table.

(iii) [I "$_A$MOVED" a sweater INTO EXISTENCE] WITH-THE-CAUSE-OF [I knitted (yarn)]

I knitted a sweater.

6. The sense of *together* addressed here is that of 'concert' as contrasted with 'accompaniment', not the sense of 'co-location' as contrasted with 'separation'.

7. In this instance, Spanish also has a construction resembling a satellite-framed construction:

(i) Toqué mejor/más que él.

'I-played better/more than he.'

8. Other moot-fulfillment verbs in English are *try* and *urge*, as in *I tried to open the window* and *I urged them to leave*, as well as *beckon* and *wave*, as in *I beckoned to them / I beckoned them toward me / I waved them away from the building*. However, these verbs do not take a fulfillment satellite.

9. This type of verbal pattern was first described by Ikegami (1985) with respect to Japanese and was called to my attention for Mandarin by Jian-Sheng Guo.

10. Beside its implied-fulfillment sense, the verb *zhé* apparently also has an intrinsic-fulfillment sense that consists solely of the action of squeezing in. Based on this sense, an alternative reading of (51) is simply "I bent the stick."

Chapter 4

Borrowing Semantic Space: Diachronic Hybridization

1 INTRODUCTION

This chapter is concerned with the effects on one language's semantic system when it is under the influence of another's, where there is no borrowing of actual morphemic shapes.[1] It is concerned, in particular, with the development of intermediate or hybrid semantic patterns that differ from the influencing language's pattern as well as the borrower's original pattern.

Certain aspects of this investigation are not wholly new. Certainly the particular case to be focused on—Slavic influence on Yiddish verb prefixes —has been long recognized and in certain respects characterized (e.g., U. Weinreich 1952, M. Weinreich 1980:527–530). And the encompassing framework here—the overall semantic organization of a language—is familiar as the major concern of Whorf 1956. But this investigation makes several unique contributions.

First, it aims beyond the pure cataloging of cases of semantic borrowing to the development of an explanatory account. To this end, cases are considered within the general framework of **semantic space**—that is, for any language, the patterns in which semantic domains are subdivided and in which the resulting concepts are represented among the surface morphemes. The characterizing features of semantic space are presented in section 2. Also to this end, the conclusion presents nine principles— generalized from the specific observations of the Yiddish example—that may govern the processes of semantic borrowing in general.

Second, thanks to the larger framework, previously unnoticed forms of semantic borrowing become evident. Several such forms appear among the types of accommodation and nonaccommodation made by Yiddish to Slavic, as set forth in sections 5 and 6.

Third, the overall most contributory finding of this investigation is that the language under study did not simply take on another language's semantic system whole, but creatively adapted it to its own preexisting system, generating hybrid formations, intersections, redistributions of polysemy, extensions, and further forms of novel semantic patterning. This language has thus undergone **diachronic hybridization**. And the conclusion suggests that this process may be quite general for languages in contact.

This chapter's final, but not least, contribution is sheer addition to the relatively small amount in the literature that concerns the borrowing of meanings without adoption of actual morphs. Outside of discussions of calques (loan translations) or the presentation of particular instances, the major offering on the subject has remained chapter 2 of U. Weinreich 1953.

2   THE PARTITIONING OF SEMANTIC SPACE

Before I detail the general features of semantic space, I will illustrate its character with a contrastive example involving two different language groups. Indo-European languages and their neighbors all seem to exhibit a particular semantic pattern. They have a set of verb roots of "object maneuvering" that express an agent's using a body part to move or position an object. Some English examples are shown in (1).

(1) *English verbs of object maneuvering—ones that involve*
   a. positioning: hold/put (in)/take (out)
   b. possession: have/give (to)/take (from)
   c. transport: carry/bring/take (to)
   d. propulsion: throw/kick/bat (away)
   e. steady force: push/pull (along)

In sentences containing such verbs, the agent and object themselves are expressed independently by nominals. The verb root expresses the remainder of the activity. This activity can encompass a number of distinguishable semantic parameters, including those shown in (2).

(2) *Parameters in object maneuvering expressed by verbs*
   a. the type of causality
      e.g., onset (ballistic) causation in *kick*, extended (controlled) causation in *put*

b. the absence or presence of a secondary agent

  e.g., absent in *put*, present in *give*

c. the directional vector of the motion

  e.g., 'to' in *put*, 'from' in *take*

d. deixis

  e.g., 'hither' in *bring*, 'hence' in *take* (to)

e. the type of force exerted

  e.g., compressional in *push*, tractional in *pull*

f. the body part or other object that acts as instrument

  e.g., the arm in *throw*, the leg in *kick*, a rigid linear object in *bat*

Most of these languages in addition have another set of forms—variously known as particles, preverbs, ((in)separable) prefixes, and so on, though I refer to all the different types alike as verb "satellites" (see chapter II-1)—that largely express path configurations in space, such as English *up, out, back, apart*. Further, the languages that have both these morpheme sets—verb roots of object maneuvering and Path satellites—can combine them not only in a compositional construction that expresses the concrete compounded sense of objects maneuvered along paths, but also in a construction with a more abstract, often psychological meaning.

In this context, a notable observation is that particular constructions of this type are often quite parallel across the various languages, comparable in both semantic makeup and resultant meaning, even where their corresponding morphemes are not cognate. Thus, the noncognate verb roots meaning 'hold' in English, Russian, and Latin combine with largely noncognate path satellites to yield forms with very similar abstract and often "psychological" meanings.[2]

(3)	*English*	*Russian*	*Latin*	*Common meaning*
a.	hold	deržat'	tenere	'hold'
b.	hold up	pod-deržat'	sus-tinere	'support'
c.	hold back (tr)	u-deržat'	re-tinere	'restrain'
d.	hold back (intr)	s-deržat'-s'a	abs-tinere	'refrain'
e.	hold out	vy-deržat'	sus-tinere	'endure'

However natural the preceding semantic arrangement may seem to us as speakers of European languages, the fact is that it is far from universal. A wholly distinct semantic landscape appears in America among northern Hokan languages and some of their neighbors—as illustrated by Atsugewi (see chapters II-1 and II-2). To begin with, this language simply lacks verb roots with meanings like 'hold', 'put', 'give', 'throw', and so on. Rather, its roots refer to various kinds of objects or materials as moving or located. Examples include *-qput-* 'for loose dirt to move/be located', *-caq-* 'for a slimy lumpish object (e.g., a toad, cow turd) to move/be located', *-p^{h}up-* 'for a bundle to move/be located'. Forming a second set of forms, some 50 directional suffixes give the combined indication of path or site plus reference object (the Ground). Examples are *-ak·* 'on the ground', *-wam* 'into a gravitic container (e.g., a basket, pocket, cupped hand, lake basin)', *-ta:* 'out of an enclosure', *-wi·s^u* 'over to a neighbor's'. Notably included in this set of suffixes and of the same semantic mold are forms referring to holding: *-ahn* 'in one's grasp', *-ay* 'into someone's grasp', *-tip -ay* 'out of someone's grasp'. Next, in a third set of forms, some two dozen instrumental prefixes indicate the event causing the verb root's action. Examples are *ca-* 'from the wind blowing on (it)', *ru-* 'by pulling on (it)', *ci-* 'by acting on (it) with one's hands', *uh-* 'by acting on (it) with a swinging linear object' (hence, by pounding, batting, or *throwing* [with the arm as linear object]). Finally, a fourth set of forms consists of two deictic suffixes: *-ik·* 'hither' and *-im* 'hence'. Combinations of these four morpheme sets provide the nearest equivalents to the Indo-European-type formulations for putting, giving, and so on. For example:

(4) a. uh-caq-ta:
   Literal: 'by acting on it with a swinging linear object, (cause) a slimy lumpish object to move out of an enclosure'
   Instantiated: "throw a toad out of the house"

   b. ci-p^{h}up-ay
   Literal: 'by acting on it with one's hands, (cause) a bundle to move into someone's grasp'
   Instantiated: "give someone a bundle"

   c. ru-qput-wi·s^u-ik·
   Literal: 'by pulling on it, (cause) dirt to MOVE to a neighbor's hither'
   Instantiated: "drag some dirt over here to a neighbor's"

Thus, the various semantic parameters incorporated within the Indo-European verbs of object maneuvering, or in the nominals they take, are in Atsugewi allocated to different grammatical categories and are conceptualized there in accordance with the way that this language partitions semantic space. The maneuvered object, which is expressed in the direct object nominal in English, is instead expressed in Atsugewi in the verb root, where it is conceptualized less as a static object than as a process involving a moving or located object. The type of force exerted or the action of a body part or other instrument that effects the maneuvering is abstracted off for separate expression in the instrumental prefix set, where it is construed as a distinct causal event giving rise to the main event of object movement/location. Concepts of grasping or possession, or of shifts therein, are expressed by directional suffixes, along with more typical Path + Ground concepts, and are presumably conceptualized there as being kinds of directionals. Deixis is expressed separately by a distinct morpheme pair.

This pattern of semantic structuring in Atsugewi extends to certain further categories of object maneuvering, though with less affixal freedom. Thus, for the category of garments in dressing, distinct verb roots or verbal stems refer to the motion or location of specific garments, while affixes indicate whether one has the garment on, dons it or doffs it, or puts it on or takes it off someone else. For example, the verbal stem *hi-·-pun* 'for an apron to move/be-located with respect to wear' takes the locative suffix *-asẃ* to indicate having an apron on, as in *sẃhe·punásẃa* 'I am wearing the apron'. It takes the prefix *p-* 'back' and the suffix *-ik·* 'hither' to indicate donning an apron, as in *sṗhe·puník·a* 'I put the apron on'. And it takes the suffix *-tip* 'out of liquid/un-' to indicate doffing an apron, as in *sẃhe·púnt^hpa* 'I took the apron off'. Likewise, for the category of locating one's own body parts through internal muscular control, distinct verb roots or verbal stems refer to the motion or location of specific body parts, while the directional and deictic affixes indicate the paths taken or sites occupied by them. For example, the verb root *ismak* 'for a person's ear to move/be-located' can take the suffix *-iḱs* 'laterally onto/into a vertical surface' to refer to placing one's ear against a door (say, to listen to voices on the other side). The verb root *iṗi* 'for a person's tongue to move/be-located' can take the suffix sequence *-hiy -ik·* 'out of moorings' to refer to sticking one's tongue out (say, at someone). The verbal stem *pu-q̇^a* 'for a person's mouth to move/be-located' can take the suffix sequence *-ikn -iw* 'onto/into a mouth' to refer to kissing someone—literally, to 'place-one's-mouth onto-someone's-mouth'. And the verb root *rahẏ* 'for a person's head to move/be-located' can take the suffix *-ay* 'into someone's (or something's) grasp' (the same suffix as for giving someone an object) to refer to laying one's head down on a pillow. Even the concept of 'nothing' to some extent conforms to the Atsugewi organization of semantic space: there is a verb root *raps* 'for nothing to move/be-located' that can take the suffix *-ak·* 'on the ground (in existence)' to refer to the existence of nothing, as in *ẁrapsak·a* 'There is nothing', or the suffix *-ahn* 'in one's grasp (in one's possession)' to refer to having nothing, as in *sẁrapsáhna* 'I have nothing'.

A wider comparison of the different formulations for 'object maneuvering' in the two language groups above reveals that their semantic organizations can differ in a number of respects, as set forth in the following list.

Differences in the Semantic Organization of English and Atsugewi in the Representation of 'Object Maneuvering'
1. Different concepts are expressed—as an example, the Atsugewi notion of a 'gravitic container' has no direct analogue in English.
2. Otherwise corresponding concepts are expressed under different grammatical categories—for instance, 'dirt' is expressed by an English noun but by an Atsugewi verb root.
3. The concepts of otherwise corresponding sets are parceled out in different ways among the grammatical categories—for example, 'giving' and 'throwing' are classed together in English as actions one does to an object, so that both are expressed by verbs, whereas in Atsugewi, 'giving' is classed as a directional concept to be expressed by a directional suffix, while 'throwing' is classed as a precursor causal action to be expressed by an instrumental prefix.
4. Otherwise corresponding concepts are combined with different sister concepts within a morpheme—thus, a path's reference object (Ground) is expressed alone in an English noun (into a *container*) but is combined with indication of the path in an Atsugewi directional suffix (*-wam* 'into a container').
5. Otherwise corresponding concepts have different degrees of inclusiveness—for instance, English *throw* refers to a swinging motion only as made by an arm to propel an object, whereas the Atsugewi instrumental prefix *uh-* can refer to a swinging motion made by any linear object (such as an arm or ax) with any resulting action (such as propelling or chopping).
6. Otherwise corresponding concepts have different obligatoriness of expression—for example, the causal instrumentality within a referent situation must in most cases be indicated in Atsugewi but is largely optional in English.
7. Different morpheme sets are present, having different group meanings —thus, English has a set of verb roots that express the manner of maneuvering; Atsugewi lacks this but has one that expresses the type of object that is in a state of Motion.

8. The morpheme sets come together in different constructions—the English construction that combines a verb, a satellite and/or preposition, and a noun corresponds to the Atsugewi combination of a verb root plus an instrumental prefix and a directional suffix.

9. Otherwise corresponding constructions have some different constructional meanings—for example, while the English and Atsugewi constructions just mentioned correspond in their indication of object maneuvering, the English constructions often extend to indicate abstract and psychological concepts, whereas the Atsugewi ones largely do not (other sets of morphemes that bear such meanings directly are used instead).

Pinker (1994) holds the view that the morphemes of different languages actually express very similar concepts and that this similarity has been obscured by stilted glossings of the morphemes. But the evidence here points toward genuine differences in the semantic organization of language. Poor glossing cannot account for the fact that Atsugewi simply lacks verb roots with meanings like those of the English verbs *have*, *give*, *take*, *hold*, *put*, *carry*, *bring*, *throw*, *kick*, *push*, and *pull*. Nor can it account for any of the other types of language difference just identified.

On the basis of these and additional observations (including ones from Yiddish and Slavic, discussed next), we may compile a number of the factors that can characterize any semantic space. Differences in these factors are a major part of what distinguishes the overall semantic organization of one language from that of another. In the following compilation of factors, the term "meta" indicates the overall concept or meaning associated with the whole of some category or set of morphemes or polysemes.

(5) *Factors that characterize the semantic structure of different semantic spaces*

    a. the particular concepts (with their componential makeup and degree of inclusiveness) expressed by the morphemes—and the metaconcepts expressed by the morpheme sets

    b. in cases of polysemy, the particular set of concepts grouped together under a single morpheme—and the metameaning common to them

    c. the grammatical categories of the individual morphemes and of the morpheme sets[3]

    d. the constructions in which the different morpheme sets come together—and their metameaning

e. the obligatoriness and the frequency of use of each concept and meta-concept

f. the ramifiedness of each metaconcept—that is, its number of distinctions, its complexity of organization, its extent of application . . .

Historically, there may be some diachronic process at work among the cognate languages of each family, such as Indo-European or Atsugewi and its close relatives, acting to maintain a single organization of semantic space. If so, such a process must operate at a linguistic level more abstract than that of particular morphemes, for the parallelisms earlier observed across Indo-European languages largely involved noncognate forms. A process might have to be posited that maintains (among other aspects of pattern) semantic "slots," regardless of the etymologies of the morphemes that come and go to fill them. Such a process can well be imagined, a consequence of a language's high degree of overall structural inter-connection. For example, Atsugewi's expression of 'taking' is perhaps kept suffixal partly because 'having' and 'giving' are also expressed suf-fixally. Further, if a verb root were to take over that meaning, it would have to cede its usual expression of the 'thing taken' to some sentence constituent ill-adapted to it. The sweep of structural readjustments that would be entailed might militate against much of any change at all.

On the other hand, the structure of semantic space can also be observed to be something of an areal phenomenon in that unrelated neighboring languages often share much of their overall semantic organization. On the assumption that such languages typically did not all have the same organization before contact, exposure to outside structure must in some respects be strong enough to overcome resistance to a sweep of changes. The remainder of this chapter sets forth some of the theory and forms of such change under external influence.

What has just been described in terms of diachronic linguistic structures and processes must eventually be explained in terms of ongoing cognitive structures and processes. What can be said in outline now is that, in each individual, the aspects of cognitive organization that support the overall semantic structure of the language he or she has learned are generally more stable—or less responsive to factors for change—than those aspects responsible for the associations between particular morphemes and their referents. However, those further aspects of cognitive organization that process novel forms of semantic structure on exposure to them *can* affect those aspects that otherwise maintain the original semantic structure.

3 THE YIDDISH VERB PREFIXES

Looking now within Indo-European to Germanic and Slavic—whose respective semantic systems do differ, though not as drastically as those above—I turn from comparing two static unconnected systems to observing how one system changes under the influence of another. Yiddish is a particularly appropriate case for such observation because, in migrating, it came under new areal influence. The language developed its initial form beginning around 800 C.E. in the Middle High German–speaking Rhineland and then around 1200 C.E. started extending progressively further into Slavic-speaking territories. Under Slavic influence, the Yiddish semantic system made a number of accommodations, many of which can be observed in the verbal prefix system and its associated constructions.

The main prefixes in this system are listed below, each glossed with only a selection of the senses in its polysemous range. Notice that the originally preposed *hin-/her-* forms have been reduced to an undifferentiated *ar-* and their 'hence'/'hither' meaning distinction eliminated (as colloquial modern German, with forms like *runter-*, is now in the process of doing). There has emerged a group of opposed prefixal doublets, with and without the *ar-*, that now mark a semantic distinction mainly of 'concrete' versus 'abstract'. The prefixes with *ar-* indicate major concrete paths of motion (e.g., *arayn-* 'into'), while their *ar*-less mates indicate some minor concrete paths (e.g., *oyf-* 'to an open position', *ayn-* 'radially inward') and, especially, more abstract and metaphoric path-derived notions.[4]

(6) *Main Yiddish verb prefixes*
    a. Separable [stressed] prefixes
       i. *Doublets*

Long		*Short*	
arayn-	'in'	ayn-	'in', 'radially inward'
aroys-	'out'	oys-	'out', 'to exhaustion'
aroyf-	'up'	oyf-	'open', '⟨perfective⟩'
arop-	'down (from)'	op-	'off', 'in return', 'to a finish'
ariber-	'across/over'	iber-	'in transfer', 'back and forth between',
		unter-	're-', 'overly'
arunter-	'down (through)', 'to underneath'		'up to', 'a bit from time to time'
arum-	'around'	um-	'pivotally over'

ii. *Singlets*

on-	'into an accumula-tion', 'full', 'to capacity'	tsunoyf-	'(severally) together'
durkh-	'through'	tsuzamen-	'(dually) together'
avek-	'away', 'down (upon)'	funander-	'apart'
tsu-	'up to', 'fast', 'additionally'	antkegn-	'opposite', 'counter', 'into encounter'
farbay-	'past'	faroys-	'ahead', 'pre-'
anider-	'down (to)'	mit-	'along (with)'
nokh-	'along after', 'in emulation'	afer-	'forth'
tsurik-	'back'	fir-	'out (from under)'
kapoyer-	'upside down'		

b. *Inseparable [unstressed] prefixes*

tse-	'radially outward'	ba-	'⟨causative⟩'
ant-	'away', 'un-'	far-	'mis-', '⟨causative⟩'
der-	'reaching as far as'	ge-	'—'

4   THE BORROWING PATTERN

To determine higher-level accommodation patterns under semantic influence, one must start by identifying the first-order aspects of another language's semantic space that have transferred over, as well as those that have not. "Aspects" here refers not simply to features like category differences (say, the borrowing of nouns vs. verbs) but to major types of structural phenomena.

4.1   Aspects of Slavic Semantic Space Borrowed by Yiddish

With particular reference to verb prefixes, five aspects of Slavic semantic space can be pointed to as entering the semantic space of Yiddish.

4.1.1   Individual Meanings of Morphemes   One type of semantic borrowing involves the transfer of one meaning of a morpheme in an influencing language into a morpheme of the borrowing language—preferentially into one with similar phonological shape, grammatical category, and prior semantic content. In this way, Yiddish has borrowed a number of individual meanings expressed by Slavic prefixes, using its own prefixes to express them. For example, Russian *na-*, prefixed to a verb V and taking the genitive of a noun N, has the meaning 'create an accumulation of N by Ving'.[5] Thus, with a verb meaning 'tear/pluck' and the noun for

'flowers', *na-rvat' cvetov* means literally 'form an accumulation of flowers in plucking them' and loosely "pick [a bouquet of] flowers."

Yiddish has taken on this exact meaning of *na-* with its phonetically similar and semantically compatible prefix *on-*, otherwise the correlate of German *an-*. It in fact has the analogue of the preceding Russian expression (exact except for the use of accusative for the object noun): *on-raysn blumen* "pick [a bouquet of] flowers." The *on-* prefix in this meaning is now quite freely usable in Yiddish, not tied to the original Slavic models. It appears, for example, in expressions like *Di kats hot ongehat ketslekh*, literally, 'The cat formed an accumulation of kittens by having (giving birth to) them' or, very loosely, "The cat has birthed up quite a batch of kittens in her life."

We can put this prefixal usage in tabular form and add further examples.[6]

(7) | | *Russian* | *Yiddish* | *Common meaning* |
|---|---|---|---|
| a. | na- +GEN | on- +ACC | 'create an accumulation of, Ving' |
| b. | raz- REFL | tse- REFL | 'burst out Ving' |
| c. | pro- +ACC | op- +ACC | 'cover X distance/spend X time, Ving' |
| a'. | na-rvat' | cvetov on-raysn blumen | "pick [a bouquet of] flowers" |
| b'. | ras-plakat'-s'a | tse-veynen zikh | "burst out crying" |
| c'. | pro-žit' god v Moskve | op-voynen a yor tsayt in moskve | "spend a year residing in Moscow" |

4.1.2 The Grouping of Meanings under a Single Morpheme

A language can adopt not only a single meaning from a morpheme of an influencing language into one of its own but also, in a case of polysemy, several meanings from the same morpheme. It might be said that meaning clustering itself is a kind of semantic aspect that can be borrowed. Yiddish shows several prefixal borrowings of this kind from Slavic. Thus, Russian *na-* expresses not only 'accumulate by Ving' but also 'fill by Ving' and, with the reflexive, 'V to one's full capacity'. And Yiddish *on-* has the same three meanings. It should not, however, be assumed that three such meanings simply form a natural set or continuum, so that a morpheme in any language expressing one meaning will also express the others. In fact, in as close a language as German, the three meanings are parceled out for distinct treatments: the 'accumulation' meaning has no prefixal equivalent, the 'fill' meaning is expressed by the prefix *voll-*, and the 'capacity' meaning is taken by the prefix *satt-*.

(8)	*Russian*	*Yiddish*	*German*	*Common meaning*
a.	na- +GEN	on- +ACC		'accumulate Ving'
b.	na- +ACC +INSTR	on- +ACC mit	voll- +ACC mit +DAT	'fill, Ving'
c.	na- REFL +GEN	on- REFL mit	satt- REFL an +DAT	'V to one's capacity'
b'.	na-lit' stakan vodoj	on-gisn a gloz mit vaser	ein Glas mit Wasser voll-giessen	"pour a glass full of water"
c'.	na-smotret'-s'a kartin	on-zen zikh mit bilder	sich an Bildern satt-sehen	"have seen one's fill of pictures"

4.1.3 The Distribution of Usage within a Grouping

Another possible type of borrowing may involve the relative frequencies of occurrence of the different meanings grouped together under a single morpheme. The Yiddish prefixes I have inspected in this regard do not clearly exhibit such a form of borrowing, but I employ a near case to explain the matter for potential application elsewhere. The Russian prefix *raz-*, in combination with various verb roots, exhibits a set of meanings that range from high to low frequency of occurrence in roughly the following order: 'radially outward', 'into dispersal', 'one into many', 'into bits/destruction'. Examples of each meaning are *raz-dut'* 'puff out (as, one's cheeks)', *raz-bežat'-s'a* '(many to) run apart in all directions', *raz-rubit'* 'chop (wood, etc.) into several pieces', *raz-gryzt'* 'gnaw to bits'. The Yiddish prefix *tse-* exhibits the same meanings in just about the same frequency distribution as in the Russian case and participates in quite comparable verbal combinations. The cognate modern German prefix *zer-*, on the other hand, exhibits approximately the opposite distribution, with just one or two cases indicating radial movement (*zer-streuen* 'disperse') and with a majority of cases indicating 'destruction' (e.g., *zer-rühren* 'stir to a pulp'). As it happens, Middle High German *zer-* had a distribution closer to that of Russian, with a number of 'radially outward' and 'dispersal' usages (e.g., *zer-blasen* 'puff out', 'disperse by blowing'), so that Yiddish, coming from this background, had little to change under Slavic influence. It was rather the line leading to modern German that lost most of the 'radial' usages, thus shifting the balance of the distribution. But if we can imagine that Yiddish came from a non-Slavic-type distribution and then changed over, we have a model for a type of semantic borrowing that might come to be observed in other language contact situations.

4.1.4 The Metameaning of a Morpheme Class Another form of semantic borrowing involves the metameaning of a morpheme class. In the present case, Yiddish has borrowed the whole system of using the native set of path prefixes to indicate aspect. That is, it has been influenced to extend metaphorically the class's spatial path reference to cover temporal aspect as well. Actually, since Yiddish, like most languages with path satellites, did already have some instances of aspectual use with them, it would be more accurate to say that what it borrowed was the ramifiedness and obligatoriness of such aspect indication. To characterize it simply for now, the borrowed system consists of the obligatory appending of a prefix, a particular one for each verb, when the aspectual character of the referent situation is perfective. Comparable Russian and Yiddish examples are shown in (9).

(9)   *Russian*   *Yiddish*   *Common meaning*
    a. pro-čitat'   iber-leyenen   'read through ⟨perfective⟩'
    b. na-pisat'   on-shraybn   'write down ⟨perfective⟩'
    c. s-jest'   oyf-esn   'eat up ⟨perfective⟩'
    d. vy-pit'   oys-trinken   'drink up ⟨perfective⟩'
    e. za-platit'   ba-tsoln   'pay ⟨perfective⟩'
    f. raz-rezat'   tse-shnaydn   'cut through ⟨perfective⟩'

4.1.5 The Obligatory Appearance of a Morpheme Class Another form of semantic borrowing is that of the obligatory use of a particular morpheme class in the representation of some metaconcept. The metaconcept of 'Path' is expressed by satellites as well as by prepositions in the Indo-European languages that have both these morpheme classes, and a Path-expressing sentence can often contain the particular combination of a satellite and a preposition together. In some languages, for example in German from Middle High to modern, a satellite is often only optional in a sentence that contains a preposition, and in fact is at times stylistically better omitted. Thus, NHG *Er ging ins Haus*, 'He went into the house', is complete as it stands with only a preposition, but it can also add the correlative satellite *hinein* at the end, though colloquial usage may prefer it absent. In these same circumstances, however, both Yiddish and Russian must include the satellite along with the preposition. Thus, these two languages have no option but to say *Er iz arayn-gegangen in hoyz* and *On vo-šël v dom*, 'He went into the house', with the path prefixes included. This obligatory appearance of the prefix in addition to the preposition is a well-established pattern in Slavic, and it seems that Yiddish must have acquired it under Slavic influence.

4.2   Aspects of Slavic Semantic Space Not Borrowed by Yiddish

An influencing language can include a number of concepts expressed by individual morphemes and metaconcepts expressed by morpheme classes that a borrowing language does not adopt. Some omissions of this sort seem part of a broader pattern of avoidance—perhaps nothing so general as rejection of a whole borrowing "type," on the order of those just preceding, but nonetheless principled. Yiddish exhibits semantic borrowing failures of several kinds with respect to Slavic. I will later suggest a principle that accounts for some of these, but here will simply point them out.

First, Yiddish has not borrowed certain individual concepts expressed by Slavic prefixal constructions—for example, those of Russian *za- za + ACC* 'to beyond/behind' (*za-plyt' za mol* "swim beyond the breakwater"), *s- na + ACC* 'to and back from' (*s-letat' na počtu* "hurry to the post office and back"), *pro- + ACC* 'the length of' (*pro-bežat' vs'u ulicu* "run the whole length of the street").

Second, Yiddish has failed to borrow several Slavic aspectual distinctions. One is the so-called "determinative/indeterminative" distinction marked by most motion verbs, which involves, among other properties, the difference between motion along a single direct path and anything more intricate. Russian marks this distinction either with suppletive verb forms (*idti/xodit'* 'go on foot') or with suffixal material immediately after the root (*let-e-t'/let-a-t'* 'fly')—and Yiddish has copied neither.

Another Slavic aspect is "secondary imperfective," also marked with suffixation, which functions this way: Often the addition of a prefix to a verb root not only renders its meaning perfective, but also adds a nuance or even substantially alters the basic meaning. This novel semantic entity, already a perfective, now needs a sister form for the imperfective, and this is accomplished by the addition of certain stem-forming suffixes—for example, *-yv* in the third form of this Russian series: *pis-at'* 'write (impf.)', *za-pisat'* 'jot down (pf.)', *za-pis-yv-at'* 'jot down (impf.)'. Yiddish exhibits no trace of such forms.

Finally, Slavic languages have suffixation that indicates semelfactive aspect—that is, the single occurrence of a punctual event, such as *-nu* in Russian *čix-nu-t'* 'sneeze once' (vs. *čix-at'* 'sneeze a plurality of times'). However, though Yiddish does indicate semelfactive, and has possibly borrowed the idea of extensively doing so from Slavic, it has not borrowed the idea of using suffixation for the purpose. It uses, instead, a special periphrastic construction (treated below).

5 TYPES OF ACCOMMODATION BY THE BORROWER'S SEMANTIC SYSTEM TO THE DONOR'S

In the preceding, I have presented the cases of borrowing or non-borrowing as if they were more or less insular events that had no moorings within a larger system. In fact, however, every semantic feature that undergoes a transfer is originally situated within an integrated framework and must be adopted into another one. The borrowing language must find creative solutions to the problems that this situation poses. I have identified the following four types of accommodation that Yiddish has made in incorporating features from the noncommensurate semantic space of Slavic: hybrid formation, intersection, depolysemizing, and elaboration.

5.1 Hybrid Formation

One type of accommodation is to borrow only part of some donor semantic system and to incorporate this in a way that it becomes only part of the recipient system. This kind of part-to-part borrowing results in a **hybrid system**, one that is neither wholly like that in the influencing language nor like that originally in the influenced language, but rather a new formation with its own organization of characteristics. I can point to three cases of this sort in Yiddish borrowing from Slavic.

5.1.1 Reduplication in the Prefix-plus-Preposition System Many Slavic prefixes have the same phonological shape as the semantically corresponding prepositions, so that their obligatory use for path indication (section 4.1.5) often results in a kind of **exact reduplication**. Thus Russian has *v- v + ACC* 'into', *na- na + ACC* 'up onto', *s- s + GEN* 'off of', *ot- ot + GEN* 'away from', *iz- iz + GEN* 'emanating from'. Yiddish has borrowed the pattern of obligatory prefix use. But in the case of its prefix doublets, its prior system demanded the use of the long prefix form for the indication of a concrete path. Yet it was only the short prefixes that were phonologically identical to the prepositions. The result was a merely partial overlap of phonological form in a new hybrid system of **inexact reduplication**: *aroyf- oyf + DAT* 'up onto', *ariber- iber + DAT* 'across', *arunter- unter + DAT* 'to under', *farbay- far + DAT* 'past' (this last form is treated further below).

5.1.2 The Polysemous Range of a Prefix and Its Overall Meaning I have shown that a set of meanings under a polysemous morpheme can be

borrowed as a group into a single morpheme of another language, but such borrowing does not have to result in a slavish semantic replica, a morpheme like its model in every detail of meaning. It can happen that only some, not all, of the source morpheme's meanings are borrowed and that the affected morpheme retains some of its own original meanings. The result in such a case is a hybrid polysemy: the range of meanings encompassed by the remodeled morpheme is neither that of the donor nor that of its old self. To the extent that an overall semantic character attaches to a polysemous range, it can be said that because the affected morpheme has added and lost some meanings, its semantic envelope has shifted and also become a hybrid.

Hybrid polysemy seems to be the norm, rather than an exception, in the Yiddish prefixes affected by Slavic. Consider, for example, the same Yiddish *on-* prefix that was earlier seen to have borrowed a group of meanings from, say, Russian *na-*. First, this Yiddish prefix did not borrow all of the Russian prefix's meanings—the others were borrowed by different prefixes. Second, the Yiddish prefix retained some of its original Germanic meanings—which put it in relationship with Russian prefixes other than *na-*. And third, the Yiddish prefix has virtually lost at least one original meaning (the 'initiate' sense seen in German *an-*, as in *anschneiden* 'make the first cut in (a loaf of bread)'), perhaps as a result of semantic "overcrowding" from the newly acquired senses. As a result, the prefixes of Yiddish and Russian (to take one Slavic language) cannot be placed in neat semantic correspondence but rather exhibit a series of overlaps, as seen in (10) (which also lists the origin—"Gmc" or "Slc"—of each meaning of a Yiddish prefix).

(10)

	Russian	*Yiddish*	*Semantic origin of Yiddish form*	*Common meaning*
a.	⌠ ob-V NP + ACC	{ arum-V arum NP	Germanic	'circle NP, Ving'
b.	⌡ ob-V ob NP + ACC	⌐ on-V on/in NP	Germanic	'V to a point against'
c.	{ pri-V k NP + DAT	on-V in/oyf NP	Germanic	'arrive at NP, Ving'
d.	⌐ na-V NP + GEN	on-V NP + ACC	Slavic	'accumulate Ving'
e.	na-V NP + ACC NP +INSTR	on-V NP + ACC mit NP	Slavic	'fill, Ving'
f.	na-V REFL NP +INSTR	on-V REFL mit NP	Slavic	'V to one's capacity'
g.	na-V na NP + ACC	⌠ aroyf-V oyf NP	Slavic	'V upon'
h.	{ voz-V	{ aroyf-V	Germanic	'V upward'

Examples of the forms newly introduced in this table are given in (11).

(11) a′. o-bežat' dom   arum-loyfn arum   "run around a house"
                             a hoyz
     b′. ob-lokotit's'a   on-shparn zikh   "lean against a door"
         o dver'   on a tir
     c′. pri-exat'   on-forn   "arrive in a vehicle"
     g′. na-stupit' na   aroyf-tretn oyf   "step on a snake"
         zmeju   a shlang
     h′. vz-letet'   aroyf-flien   "fly up"

The shifting of semantic envelopes can be more readily characterized for another Yiddish prefix, *op-*, the cognate of MHG *abe/ab/ap* and NHG *ab-*. This prefix has borrowed some, but not all, the meanings of two different Slavic prefixes, while retaining some unique meanings of its own (other original meanings had Slavic counterparts)—as seen in (12).

(12)

	Russian	Yiddish	Semantic origin of Yiddish	Common meaning
a.	pro-V mimo NP +ACC	farbay-V (far) NP + DAT	Germanic	'V past'
b.	pro-V čerez NP +ACC	durkh-V durkh NP	Germanic	'V through (an opening)'
c.	pro-V NP + ACC			'V the whole length of'
d.	pro-V NP + ACC	op-V NP + ACC	Slavic	'cover X distance/ spend X time, Ving'
e.	ot-V	op-V	Slavic	'finish Ving'
f.	ot-V NP + DAT	op-V NP + DAT	Slavic	'V in return/ reciprocation to'
g.	ot-V ot NP + GEN	op-V fun NP	Germanic	'depart from, Ving'
h.	ot-V ot NP + GEN	op-V fun NP	Germanic	'(re)move from a surface, Ving'
i.	ot-V ot NP + GEN	op-V fun NP	Germanic	'disunite one end from the rest, Ving'
j.	ot-V	op-V	Germanic	'repulse, Ving'
k.	ot-V REFL			'get out of (obligation), Ving'
l.		op-V		'arrange/agree to, Ving'

An accurate analysis of a morpheme's polysemous range must include treatment of all the meanings actually occurring (see Lindner 1981 and

Brugman 1988 for some thorough treatments in English)—whereas the above prefixes each have a number of additional meanings not listed. But perhaps something of the following analysis will still stand: The original senses of *op-* in (g) to (j) cluster around a general notion of an object progressively distancing itself from some reference location, as indicated schematically in (13a) (see chapter I-3 for such spatial characterizations). But the meanings that *op-* acquired from *pro-* and *ot-*, (d) to (f), all imply encompassing the whole of some bounded extent, whether each of the end points is definite or merely implicit, as schematized in (13b). Thus, the overall meaning of *op-*, which originally encompassed only motion away from a source point, has expanded to include optionally the trajectory and termination arising from that originating motion. In a way, the original 'depart' sense of *op-*, (g), occupies a pivotal position in this shift. Earlier, it was a suitable member-meaning because of its movement-from-source character, and now it fits because it also implies a destination.

The overall semantic character of Russian *pro-* is quite distinct from that of Yiddish *op-*. It involves movement along a linear path, whether this extends just enough to traverse a reference point or spans the distance between two end points, as suggested in (13c). Thus, the 'distance/time-spanning' sense, (d), common to both *pro-* and *op-*, fits into the larger schema of each of these two morphemes by virtue of two different semantic features. Its feature of 'linear extent' is appropriate to the 'linear path' sense of *pro-*, and its feature of 'boundedness at both ends' is appropriate to the 'bounded-extent encompassing' sense of *op-*. As for Russian *ot-*, its polysemous range mostly fits within that of Yiddish *op-*. But because *op-* additionally includes the 'distance/time-spanning' sense, it fits more centrally within a 'bounded extent' schema than *ot-* does. This allows us to speak of a hybrid character that distinguishes it from its influencing morphemes as well as from its original self.

(13)

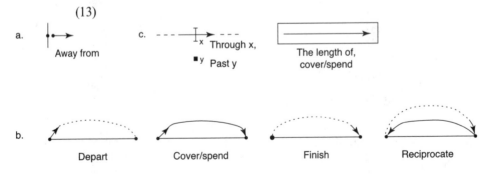

a. Away from

c. Through x, Past y   The length of, cover/spend

b. Depart   Cover/spend   Finish   Reciprocate

5.1.3 The Prefixal Aspect System Yiddish exhibits a further case of hybrid formation in the character of the aspect system manifested by its prefixes. To explain the matter, it is necessary to consider four aspectual notions, those listed in (14), with English sentences for illustration.

(14) a. to completion once   I drank up my milk.
     b. to completion habitually   I drink up my milk every time I'm
                                        given some.
     c. in progress toward   I'm drinking up my milk. / I'm
         completion   getting my milk drunk.
     d. ongoing   I'm drinking my milk.

Slavic and Yiddish verb forms do not distinguish all four aspects but, in different ways, divide them into subgroups. A Russian verb stem that takes a prefix for the perfective but allows no suffixes to indicate a secondary imperfective—for example, *točit'* and *na-točit'* 'sharpen', in the dialect of some speakers—groups the four aspectual notions as shown in (15A). The prefixed form refers solely to an action performed once to completion, such as sharpening a knife to a fine edge—aspect type (a). However, aspect types (b) and (c)—for instance, sharpening a knife to a fine edge every day, or now getting a knife toward full sharpness—have no unique indication and are in fact expressed in the same way as aspect type (d)—ongoingly sharpening away at a knife or knives.

A different grouping pattern is exhibited in Russian by verb stems that can also take suffixes to indicate secondary imperfective—like Russian *uč-it'-s'a* 'learn', which takes prefix *vy-* and suffix *-iv*, as shown in (15B). Here, the form with prefix alone, as before, indicates solely aspect type (a). But now the form that also contains the suffix can refer to either aspect type (b) or aspect type (c), but only to these two, and so distinguishes these two aspect types from aspect type (d). Aspect type (d), as before, is indicated by the unaffixed form.[7]

(15)   A. 'sharpen'   B. 'learn'   C. 'sharpen'
     a.   na-točit'   vy-uč-it'-s'a   on-sharfn
     b.   točit'   vy-uč-iv-at'-s'a   on-sharfn
     c.   točit'   ? vy-uč-iv-at'-s'a   on-sharfn
     d.   točit'   uč-it'-s'a   sharfn

Now, Yiddish verb stems do take prefixes to indicate perfective aspect—as in *sharfn/on-sharfn* 'sharpen'—but they do not take suffixes to indicate a secondary imperfective. Nevertheless, these Yiddish verbs do not behave like the nonsuffixal Russian verb in (15A) but, in a way, more like the suffixal type in (15B). In the Yiddish pattern for grouping the aspect types, shown in (15C), the prefixed form covers the first three types, in effect corresponding to the prefixed Russian verb with or without its suffix. With this seeming parallelism, one might take the more differentiated Russian (15B) pattern as basic, and conclude that the Yiddish prefixed form indicates both the perfective and the secondary imperfective (perhaps with a "zero" derivation for the latter). However, this seems a discordant imposition on Yiddish from an external system, the one found in Russian. For within Yiddish, all three aspectual uses of the prefixed form can be encompassed under a single semantic notion. Whereas the Slavic prefix indicates true perfective—that is, that the end point of a process is actually *reached* (unless countermanded by a secondary suffix) —the Yiddish prefix indicates, rather, that the end point of a process is *in view*. This aspectual arrangement is a hybrid system, the result of differential borrowing of elements from the Slavic system.

5.2   Intersection

In another form of accommodation by one language system to another, the borrowing language maintains all of the distinctions it had originally made in a particular semantic domain while adding on "orthogonal" distinctions made by an influencing language, without either set interfering with the other, and so forms an **intersection** of both distinctional sets. Yiddish exhibits a number of such intersections with Slavic—for example, the following five intersections involving the prefix or the verb.

5.2.1   Separable/Inseparable Distinction + Prefixal Marking of Perfective

Yiddish has maintained the Germanic distinction of separable versus inseparable prefixes, while borrowing from Slavic the use of the prefix to mark perfective aspect. Thus, separable *on-*, requiring a *ge-* in the past participle, and inseparable *tse-*, precluding a *ge-*, both indicate perfective aspect in *Ikh hob ongesharft dem meser* 'I sharpened the knife' and *Ikh hob tserisn mayn hemd* 'I tore my shirt'.

5.2.2   Precedence Marking by Long/Short Prefixes + Prefixal Sense Borrowing

The paired long and short prefixes of Yiddish retain from Germanic their complementary marking of "precedence" for certain nominals in a sentence. Using the term "Figure" for the moving object in a motion event and the term "Ground" for the stationary reference object (see chapter I-5), we can note the following approximate generalization: The long prefix marks the Figure as coming ahead of the Ground on the case hierarchy—for instance, as direct object versus oblique object—while the short prefix marks the reverse precedence. Thus:

(16) a. arayn-shtekhn a nodl (F)   'stick a needle into one's arm'
        in orem (G)
     b. ayn-shtekhn dem orem (G)   'stick (puncture) one's arm
        mit a nodl (F)   with a needle'

By contrast with Yiddish, some Russian verb prefixes permit either of the two Figure/Ground precedences, while some prefixes require either one or the other of the precedences, but they in any case do not exhibit distinct forms that mark their associated precedence. Thus, Yiddish has this feature from its own origins and has not yielded it over to the Russian pattern. Nevertheless, each of the members of the long/short prefix doublets of Yiddish has been free to acquire some of the senses present in the otherwise comparable Slavic prefixes.

5.2.3 Auxiliary Distinction + Construction Borrowing   Without a Slavic parallel, Yiddish maintains its Germanic use of two different auxiliaries for forming the past tense. These are *zayn* 'be' for use with verbs of motion, position, being, and becoming (roughly generalized) and *hobn* 'have' elsewhere. This distinction intersects with constructions otherwise wholly borrowed from Slavic. For example:

(17) a. Oni raz-bežali-s'.   Zey zaynen zikh tse-lofn.
        "They ran off in all directions."
     b. Oni raz-legli-s'.   Zey hobn zikh tse-leygt.
        "Lying there, they stretched out."

5.2.4   Motion Verb Omission + the Reduplicative Satellite Pattern   Yiddish retains from Germanic the option of omitting a nonfinite motion verb from a sentence that contains a path-specifying satellite or prepositional phrase. Omitting the verb in this way is not a Slavic pattern. But Yiddish intersects this pattern with the borrowed Slavic pattern of coupling a reduplicative satellite with a preposition (section 5.1.1). Thus, while German can omit a motion verb in the presence of a path prepositional phrase alone, Yiddish must also include a path satellite there, as in (18).

(18) Bald vi er iz aroyf[getrotn] oyf dem tretar, iz er arayn[gegangen/
     gekumen] in der kretshme.
     "As soon as he stepped onto the sidewalk, he went/came into the
     tavern."

5.2.5 Deixis + Manner   Yiddish has developed a unique construction
that indicates deixis—in particular, motion toward the speaker's perspective point—together with the manner of motion, whether on foot or
in a vehicle, as shown in (19). This construction may have arisen as the
intersection of a Germanic factor with a Slavic one. Germanic frequently
indicates deixis in the verb with its *come/bring*-type forms, which are
largely lacking in Slavic. Slavic, on the other hand, extensively insists on
indicating manner of transit in the verb, a feature that Germanic must
forgo when expressing 'hither'-type deixis in the verb. Yiddish, heir to
both sensibilities, has thus devised a construction that indicates both at
once, as (19) illustrates.

(19) a. kumen tsu geyn/forn   'come walking/riding'
      b. brengen tsu trogn/firn 'bring by carrying/conveying'

5.3   A More Ample Borrower's System Can Depolysemize a Donor System
While Russian has on the order of 22 prefixes, Yiddish has as many as
some 36, and it has put them to good use in taking on Slavic prefixal
meanings. Where a Slavic prefix has several meanings grouped together
under it, Yiddish often splits them up so that they come under distinct
prefixes. This process, moreover, is in large measure semantically principled. Thus, where Yiddish doublet prefixes are involved, the long form
takes on the commoner concrete senses, while the short form takes on the
rarer concrete meanings as well as the more abstract senses, including all
the aspect indications.

For example, Russian uses the same prefix *pod-* to indicate both the
notions 'to underneath' and 'up to', as in *pod-katat'-s'a pod + ACC* 'roll
under' and *pod-exat' k + DAT* 'drive up to'. Yiddish borrowed both these
senses but assigned them to different forms of the same doublet, as in
arunter-kayklen zikh unter 'roll under' and (in some dialect areas) *unter-
forn tsu* 'drive up to'.

Likewise, long prefix *ariber-* acquires any 'across' usages from Russian
pere-, while short *iber-* has taken on the minor motion or metaphoric
senses of *pere-*. One such sense is 'in transfer' as in *iber-shraybn NP* 'copy
NP (something written) in writing' (*pere-pisat'*), or in *iber-ton zikh*

'change clothes' (*pere-odet'-s'a*). Another such sense is 'back and forth between', as in *iber-varfn zikh mit NP* 'throw NP back and forth to each other' (*pere-brosit'-s'a + NP-INSTR*), or in *iber-vinken zikh* 'wink to each other' (*pere-mignut'-s'a*).

With regard to aspect indication, Russian *vy-*, for example, does double duty expressing both spatial 'out' and aspectual 'perfective', as in *vy-bežat'* 'run out', *vy-pit'* 'drink to completion'. Yiddish separates these two senses with its doublet prefixes, as in *aroys-loyfn* 'run out' and *oys-trinken* 'drink to completion'. Likewise, in the other cases of doublet forms indicating aspect, it is always the short prefix that is used, as in these perfective verbs: *iber-leyenen* 'read', *op-vegn* 'weigh (tr.)', *ayn-zinken* 'sink', *oyf-esn* 'eat'.

These Yiddish examples manifest an apparently hitherto unobserved phenomenon. It is the general expectation that a borrowing language will at best be faithful to its influencer's distinctions, but more likely will in part efface them. Here we have instead a case of refinement. The general case can be put this way: One language's subsystem, having more components than the corresponding subsystem in another language, can in a semantically principled way sort out some of the latter's forms of polysemy—or **depolysemize** it—in borrowing from it.

5.4 A Borrower Extending a Borrowed Feature Further Than the Donor

In certain cases of borrowing, a feature of an influencing language so successfully takes root in a borrowing language that it develops there beyond its previous scope. Such seems the case with the semantic notion of semelfactive aspect—that is, singleness of occurrence—in going from Slavic to Yiddish. In Russian, the semelfactive suffix *-nu* is mainly limited to verbs whose imperfective sense involves a sequence of "unit" actions, like jumping or breathing. When *-nu* is added, the resultant reference is to a single such unit—for example, *pryg-at'* 'jump along', *pryg-nu-t'* 'take a jump'. Yiddish, presumably inspired by the Slavic indication of aspect in general and of semelfactive in particular, settled on its occasional inherited semelfactive construction of the type *gebn a kush* 'give a kiss' as a model, and developed an *elaboration* of it into an extensive and sometimes obligatorily used system for indicating single or momentary occurrences of any type. This system's periphrastic construction has basically consisted of a "dummy" verb like *gebn* or *ton* ('give', 'do') plus a nominal form of the contentful verb, but it can now additionally include a satellite and a reflexive, as (20) shows.

(20) a. shmekn   to smell   gebn NP   'to take a sniff/
         NP   NP   a shmek   whiff of NP'
     b. zogn   'to say'   gebn a zog   'to remark'
     c. trakhtn   'to think' gebn a trakht 'to (stop and) think
                                             for a moment'
     d. op-esn NP 'to finish gebn NP   'to finish off (eating)
                   eating NP' an es op   the last remaining
                                             bit of NP'
     e. oyf-efenen 'to open up gebn zikh an 'to suddenly
        zikh   (intr.)'   efn oyf   come open'

It is not clear why Yiddish was so hospitable to the growth of the semelfactive. It is somewhat clearer, though, why the periphrastic construction became its vehicle. First, Yiddish may have generally resisted borrowing verb suffixes from Slavic—as already seen in its failure to adopt the suffixal secondary imperfective—and so also may have avoided the suffixal semelfactive, turning instead to the construction it already possessed with something of this semelfactive meaning. Second, that construction had already gained in currency on another front: it was the main vehicle for the language's incorporation of Hebrew verbs. Examples are *khasene hobn* 'to marry', *moyde zayn zikh* 'to admit'.[8]

Another case of the pupil outstripping the teacher is the use of a reduplicative verb prefix in addition to a preposition (section 5.1.1). Yiddish caught on to the obligatory inclusion of a like-sounding prefix and extended it beyond the cases found in Slavic. Thus, corresponding to nonreduplicative forms in Russian are *durkh*-V *durkh* NP 'through'; *arum*-V *arum* NP 'around'; *nokh*-V *nokh* NP 'along after'; *mit*-V *mit* NP 'in accompaniment with'; *ariber*-V *iber* NP 'over/across'; and *farbay*-V *far* NP 'past'. The last example is noteworthy in that the original and also presently existing form, *farbay*-V NP-*DAT*, gave way to the felt need for some kind of phonological reduplication through the addition, in some dialects, of the semantically unmotivated preposition *far*, presumably because of its phonological character.

6 TYPES OF NONACCOMMODATION BY THE BORROWER TO THE DONOR

The preceding section dealt with cases of actual borrowing of features from one language into another, classing them according to the type of accommodation to them made by the recipient system. But a language that has accepted some features can resist others. Yiddish can be seen to manifest two forms of such nonaccommodation while otherwise under Slavic influence.

6.1 Rejection of Features of an Influencing Language

Much as the instances of borrowing first mentioned in section 4.1 were just now seen to behave as parts of larger systems, in the same way the instances of nonborrowing first mentioned in section 4.2 can now be seen to reflect larger motivating factors. One such factor, stated generally, is that a structure in another language can be incommensurate enough to a potential borrower that neither the structure nor sometimes even the meanings expressed by it will be acceptable. In just this way, Yiddish seems to have an aversion to borrowing inflectional suffixes on the verb to indicate anything but syntactic relations. Only this latter function has been served by its inherited suffixes, which indicate the infinitive, the participles, and person and number agreement. Thus, Yiddish has no precedent for verb inflections that would add meaning, such as notions of aspect,[9] and so has resisted the Slavic inflectional suffixes that do just this. Formally, it has rejected them outright—nothing of them has been borrowed that might appear in the actual form of suffixes. Semantically, Yiddish has also rejected the meaning expressed by one set of Slavic suffixes, those for the determinate/indeterminate distinction of motion verbs (see section 4.2). Yiddish *has* borrowed the function of the suffixes indicating secondary imperfective, but only to the extent that its prefixes have extended their aspectual reference so as to encompass that function. The only strong case of semantic borrowing from a Slavic suffix is the indication of semelfactive, but this, as already seen, is manifested by an entirely distinct construction.

Another factor, possibly widespread, is a language's seeming tendency to ignore an influencing language's relative lack of distinctions. That is, a language otherwise subject to external influence may tend not to lose inherited distinctions just because the influencing language lacks them. Such a factor amounts to a bias in favor of "positive" borrowing—that is, the taking on of novel features and discriminations—rather than "negative" borrowing, the taking on of another system's comparative limitations. An example in our present context is the prefixal indication of the path notion 'down'. Russian has for this only the nonproductive prefix *niz-* and mainly relies on external adverbial expressions to indicate the notion. Yiddish in the face of this prefixal sparseness has maintained its basically four-way distinction: *arop*-V *fun* NP 'down off of', *arunter*-V (*fun/durkh/oyf* NP) 'downward through space', *anider*-V (*oyf* NP) 'down toward/to/onto', *avek*-V *oyf* NP 'down onto'.

6.2 Changes Counter to Influence (and Inheritance as Well)

A language can not only maintain an original structure without assimilation to an influencing language's pattern, but can go so far as to change it in the opposite direction. In the three cases of this type cited next for Yiddish, the avoided Slavic model is largely the same as the inherited Germanic one—Yiddish here flies in the face of both influence and inheritance. To account for such a development, one may have to invoke a notion of strong "drift"-like pressures internal to the system.

6.2.1 Loss of Marking Motion Versus Location by Case One case involves the common Germanic-Slavic use of two different nominal cases, the dative and the accusative, after the same preposition to indicate location and motion, respectively. Counter to both these linguistic inputs, Yiddish has come to use only the dative after all prepositions (except those meaning 'as, like', which take the nominative)—even though it has otherwise largely maintained the dative/accusative distinction in both noun phrases and pronouns. Though Yiddish has thus lost this marking of the motion versus location distinction by case, it can mark it by a novel construction—perhaps one that arose under continuing Slavic pressure for indicating the distinction. In this construction, the path verb prefix is repeated after the object nominal in the case of motion but not of location. Examples are *arayn-krikhn* *in* kastn *arayn* 'crawl *into* the box', versus *zitsn* *in* kastn *(*arayn)* 'sit in the box'.

6.2.2 Loss of Marking Different 'from' Types with Prepositions For a second case, another common Germanic-Slavic feature is the use of different prepositions to distinguish types of 'motion from'—thus, German *aus* + *DAT* 'out of', *von* + *DAT* 'away from', and Russian *iz* + *GEN* 'out of', *s* + *GEN* 'off of', *ot* + *GEN* 'away from'. Yiddish has not maintained such distinctions in its prepositional usage but has gone on to indicate the whole semantic range with the one preposition *fun* 'from'.

6.2.3 Loss of Marking a Bounded Versus Unbounded Path with Satellites
A third Germanic-Slavic shared feature is a certain form of aspect dis-

tinction and the means for indicating it. Traversing the total length of a *bounded* linear path *in* a period of time is indicated in both German and Russian with an accusative and a verbal prefix (inseparable, in the case of German), as in (17a). However, open motion along an *unbounded* path *for* a period of time is indicated with a preposition and no prefix (though German may also include a separable prefix), as in (17b). (The latter construction has become increasingly used in German for the bounded case as well, though the former construction is still not used for the unbounded case.)

(21) a. Der Satellit hat die Erde in 3 Stunden *um*flogen.
Satelit *ob*letel zeml'u v 3 časa.
"The satellite 'circumflew' the earth in 3 hours." (i.e., made one complete circuit)

 b. Der Satellit ist 3 Tage (lang) *um* die Erde geflogen.
Satelit letel *vokrug* zemli 3 dn'a.
"The satellite flew around the earth for 3 days."

Yiddish, preceded and surrounded with this common semanto-syntactic feature, has nevertheless gone on to lose it. It expresses both cases in the same way: *Der satelit iz arumgefloygn arum der erd in 3 sho/3 teg.* The loss is possibly due to the decline of the (a)-type construction in Yiddish. And this decline is itself perhaps the result of Yiddish dropping the inseparable use and retaining only the separable use of such originally dual-functioning prefixes as *um-, durkh-, iber-*.

7   GENERAL PRINCIPLES THAT GOVERN SEMANTIC BORROWING

In this concluding section, I want to abstract and condense into a single set of principles the properties of semantic change that Yiddish prefixes have here been seen to exhibit under Slavic influence. These properties may well apply more generally to other cases where one language adapts its partitioning of semantic space to that of another. Accordingly, the principles below are formulated in a generic phrasing, with "D," for "donor," referring to any influencing language and "B," for "borrower," to any corresponding influenced language. Such phrasing is not intended as a claim that all languages in fact behave according to the principles. It is meant, rather, as a suggestion that some languages might do so, and as a framework for investigating other language-contact situations with an eye toward working out a fully secure set of principles for semantic influence.

(22) *Factors for Semantic-Space Borrowing from a D(onor) Language into a B(orrower) Language*

   a. A metameaning generally transfers from a morpheme-class of D to a *similar* morpheme class of B—that is, to a morpheme class of comparable syntactic category and with some semantic instances already consonant with the metameaning of D's morpheme class.

> Thus, aspect indication by the Slavic verb-prefix category was borrowed by the Yiddish verb-prefix category, in which a few instances of prefix use had already indicated aspect.

   b. Within such corresponding morpheme classes, a meaning generally transfers from a morpheme of D to a *similar* morpheme of B—that is, to a morpheme of comparable phonological shape and with some meanings already consonant with the Donor morpheme's meaning range.

> Thus, Yiddish *op-* sounded like Russian *ot-* and already had certain 'off from' meanings in common with it, before borrowing others of its meanings.

   c. With such corresponding D and B morphemes, *several* meanings tend to transfer over, so that a partial identification grows between the two morphemes.

> Thus, Yiddish *op-* borrowed both the 'finish' and the 'reciprocate' meanings from Slavic (Russian) *ot-*, and Yiddish *on-* borrowed the 'accumulate', 'fill', and 'sate' meanings from Slavic (Russian) *na-*.

   d. As a corollary of (a), B generally borrows neither syntactic category nor meanings from a D morpheme class to which it has no parallel, seeming to treat it, rather, as incommensurate or alien.

> Thus, in Slavic verbs, certain inflectional suffixes add semantic content, whereas Yiddish ones only indicate syntactic relations. Yiddish has developed no suffixes akin to this novelty and, moreover, has largely avoided even the meanings they express.

   e. If B does borrow from an unparalleled D morpheme class, it generally takes on not the syntactic category of the class, but only its metameaning or member meanings, and B expresses these meanings with a preexisting native construction that is already semantically consonant with those meanings.

Thus, Yiddish did borrow the Slavic suffixally indicated semelfactive, but expressed it with its native periphrastic construction, which already had some instances of such meaning.

f. B tends to maintain the properties of its original semantic space—that is, all its inherited semantic and syntactic features and distinctions. Thus, B generally does not replace its original features when borrowing from D. Rather, it adds the novel features to its own features, making various kinds of accommodation between the two patterns. Such accommodations include hybrid formation, intersection, depolysemizing, and extension.

See section 5 for examples.

g. Similarly, due to such retention, B generally does not drop its original features just because D lacks parallels.

Thus, Yiddish kept its four-way prefixally indicated 'down' distinctions and also most original meanings of prefixes like *on-*, even though Slavic lacked these.

h. B does not borrow *all* of D's semantic system but only portions of it. Thus, some original B features continue unchallenged within the B system, or even develop in a direction counter to the D model.

Thus, Yiddish has not borrowed certain Slavic prefixal meanings such as the Russian *pro-* sense 'the whole length of' and has neutralized its inherited accusative/dative 'motion/ location' distinction, counter both to its origins and to the Slavic model.

i. All the preceding factors that govern borrowing probably continue to recycle at successive stages as B remains under D's influence. That is, B, rather than taking over D semantic space at the outset, makes a continuing sequence of "creative" adaptations and accommodations, most of which take it ever closer to the D system. This process might go on until an end point of complete homology between the B and D semantic spaces, with only the morphemes' shapes differing.

Several of the last principles can benefit from further comment. Principle (f) raises the question of how languages resist an overload of features if they tend to preserve old ones while adding new ones. I suspect that a language does not so much replace old features with new ones in direct response to an influencer as that—secondarily in its own time and way—it cuts down on original, borrowed, and hybrid features alike through internal processes of pruning, reshuffling, and so on that operate on the new configurations of material as a whole.

Regarding principle (h)'s assertion that not *all* of an influencer's features are borrowed, it is not clear what factors—outside of principle (d)—might determine the pattern of what is and what is not borrowed. But we can at least be sure of this much: Undoubtedly involved is the integrated sense that native speakers have for their language's overall organization of lexical items and grammatical features—and hence, for what of another language might fit in more felicitously and what less so.

As for principle (i)'s notion of ultimate homology between two contacting languages, Gumperz and Wilson (1971) describe just such an end state for a Dravidian language under Aryan influence in one Indian community. It seems quite possible, however, that a language could continue indefinitely without arriving at such total homology. Yiddish might well have turned out to be such a case if it had continued in Slavic territories, because it had two external connections: continuing associations with the German-speaking world, and its special connection with the Hebrew of religious writings, whose vocabulary and structure exerted a continuing influence on the language.

In conclusion, it appears that the factors presented in section 2 for the partitioning of semantic space in general, and the principles in section 7 for the ways that one such semantic space can affect another—together with the earlier detailing of Yiddish under Slavic influence, a case that instantiates both these sets of factors and principles—provide a framework for understanding the structured interaction of semantic systems.

Notes

1. This chapter is a moderately revised version of Talmy 1982. For their contribution to the preparation of the original paper, I am grateful to several friends and colleagues—to Anna Schwartz, Malka Tussman, and Rose Cohen for their native linguistic expertise in Yiddish, Simon Karlinsky and Esther Talmy in Russian, Karin Vanderspek in German, and Henryka Yakushev in Polish; to Dan Brink and Tom Shannon for their proficiency with Middle High German and to Martin Schwartz for his with the Hebrew component in Yiddish; to Yakov Malkiel and Elizabeth Traugott for their special knowledge of the relevant literature; and to Jennifer Lowood for her editorial acumen. In addition, the following reference works proved of great value: U. Weinreich 1968 for Yiddish, Ozhegov 1968 for

Russian, and Lexers 1966 for Middle High German. Needless to say, these kind folk and worthy volumes are to be held innocent of any misfeasances in presentation, analysis, or assertion of fact that follow. It is my observation, over a variety of Yiddish speakers and writings, that the phenomena reported on here are rather sensitive to differences of dialect. In fact, since the observations below on Slavic-influenced features in Yiddish were gathered from different dialect representatives, it is possible that some dialect might not have them all.

2. Johanna Nichols has pointed out to me that some of the Russian forms—likeliest *pod-deržat'* and possibly also *u-deržat'*—may well be calques based, in fact, on Latin forms. While such a fact would detract from the present tabular demonstration, the general phenomenon of wholly parallel constructions must still be seen to hold.

3. It may at first seem odd to include "grammatical category" among semantic factors, but each grammatical category actually imposes its own semantic "impress" on any concept expressed in it. Thus, the action of telephoning when expressed as a noun instead of a verb (He called me/He gave me a *call*) acquires some sense of reification into a delimited "thing." And a material like blood when expressed by a verb (I'm *bleeding*) seems to lose some of its sense of materiality and become "actionalized" (see chapter I-1).

4. The orthography used here and throughout to represent Yiddish (normally written with Hebrew letters) is the one approved by the YIVO Institute for Jewish Research and adopted by the standard-setting Yiddish and English dictionary of U. Weinreich (1968). It uses "kh," "sh," "ts," and "ch" instead of the more usual linguistic notations "x," "š," "c," and "č."

5. As M. Weinreich (1980: 539) points out, the various Slavic languages are so close that for most phenomena dealt with here they can be regarded as having exerted an undifferentiated Slavic influence on Yiddish. Russian is used as the Slavic language of reference throughout the chapter (though a spot-check of Polish suggested that this language, too, was consonant with the borrowing pattern observed). The term "Germanic" is used differently below. It does not refer to a whole linguistic family, but only to features common to the transmitted Germanic component of Yiddish, the MHG of the Rhineland, and in a number of instances also modern standard German.

6. In the examples cited hereafter, the abbreviations REFL, GEN, ACC, etc., stand for "reflexive," "genitive," "accusative," and so on. After Yiddish prepositions, no case indication is given because they all take the dative (ones meaning 'as' or the like take nominative but do not appear here). The *-it'*, *-et'*, and *-at'* endings on Russian verbs are infinitive suffixes, and *-s'a* is the reflexive. The Yiddish equivalents are *-n* and *zikh*.

7. Depending on the verb and on the speaker, aspect type (c) might not be expressible at all in one word. For example, *pro-čit-yv-at'* can be used for aspect type (b), 'read a newspaper through to the end every day', but not for aspect type (c), 'now be reading a newspaper until the end be reached'. Where this last aspectual

notion would otherwise be called for, aspect type (d) can be used as a near substitute, with the unaffixed verb form used to express it.

8. Martin Schwartz has suggested to me that the conjugational complexities of the Hebrew verb favored its incorporation in a selected frozen form within a periphrastic construction.

9. While it rejects such suffixes for inflections, Yiddish *has* borrowed *derivational* suffixes that add meaning—for example, *-eve* (cf. Russian *-ov-a*), conferring a pejorative sense, as in *shraybeven* 'write in an inferior manner' (M. Weinreich 1980:531).

PART 2

SEMANTIC INTERACTION

Chapter 5

Semantic Conflict and Resolution

1 INTRODUCTION

This chapter concerns the regular linguistic situation in which a portion of discourse received by an addressee provides two or more specifications for the same referent.[1] These specifications can be in accord or in conflict. In the latter case, a range of cognitive operations for resolution of the conflict can come into play in the addressee.

More specifically, the term **multiple specification** is applied to the situation where a sentence, or other portion of discourse, provides two or more specifications of the characteristics of the same referent. We mainly treat the case where two such specifications are made by a closed-class form and an open-class form in a sentence. But we will also consider cases in which they are made by two closed-class forms, by two open-class forms, or by one of these and the overall reference of the whole sentence. In all these cases, both of the forms specify values for a single parameter, or property of the referent. The possibilities for either compatibility or conflict thus exist for the different specifications. In this latter case of **semantic conflict**, various processes of conceptual reconciliation can come into play in an addressee under a general cognitive procedure of **semantic resolution**.

Though there are many more, we will look at five of these processes here. One process involves a "shift" in one specification of one of the forms that brings it into accord with the other form (section 2). Another process involves a "blend" of the two specifications of both the forms (section 3). A third process involves the "juxtaposition" of the two specifications (section 4). In a fourth process, the two specifications are not obviously reconcilable and so are "juggled" to find their best fit, while in a fifth process, the two specifications are so incompatible that any resolution is "blocked" (section 5). One of the resolution processes, that of shift, crucially involves the concept of linguistic basicness, and this concept will be discussed in section 6. It is assumed that any particular conflicting specifications do not necessarily admit to only one of the resolution processes, but rather that an addressee can in general apply any of a range of alternative processes.

This chapter forms a pair with the chapter that follows. That chapter, II-6, concerns the online cognitive processing that takes place in the producer of a discourse to resolve the conflicts among competing communicative goals and available expressive means for the representation of a concept. In a complementary way, the present chapter concerns the online cognitive processing that takes place in the recipient of such a discourse to resolve the conflicts among competing representations of a concept.

2 SHIFTS

When the specifications of two forms in a sentence are in conflict, one kind of reconciliation is for the specification of one of the forms to change so as to come into accord with the other form. This change type of accommodation is termed a **shift**. Several types of shifts are sketched below. In the first two types, a closed-class form exhibits the shift. Here, a component of the basic schema represented by the closed-class form either stretches or is canceled. Such shifts bring the closed-class specification into accord either with the specifications of an accompanying open-class form or with the referent context. The third type of shift is by far the commonest. In it, a basic specification of an open-class form is replaced so that it comes into accord with the specification of an accompanying closed-class form.

2.1   Stretching of a Component of a Closed-Class Schema

The schema represented by the closed-class English preposition *across* has a feature pertaining to the relative lengths of two linear elements. Specifically, this preposition requires that the length of the Figure's path be the same or less than the length of the axis of the Ground object perpendicular to that path. Thus, if I walk *across* a pier having distinct width and length axes, I must traverse the width axis of the pier, because then my path is shorter than the axis of the pier running perpendicularly to my path, namely, its length axis. If I did traverse the length axis, my path would be much longer than the now perpendicular width axis, and in fact *across* could not be used. Rather, the case where the path is longer than the perpendicular axis generally falls into the schematic venue of the preposition *along*, so that I might now say that I was walking *along* the pier.

But now consider the use of *across* with a certain succession of Ground objects. In this succession, the axis of the Ground object that the figure traverses progresses by stages from being shorter to being longer than the Ground axis perpendicular to it, as illustrated in (1).

(1) I swam/walked across the
    a.   river.
    b.   square field.
    c. ?rectangular swimming pool.
    d. *pier.
    ⟨where my path is from one narrow end to the other of the pool/ pier⟩

The partial acceptability of (1c), for which the path is only moderately longer than the perpendicular axis, suggests that the 'relative length' feature of the *across* schema permits some "stretching" of its basic specification. But the unacceptability of (1d) shows that it cannot be stretched too far.

2.2   Cancelation of a Component of a Closed-Class Schema

To take the *across* schema again, it can be considered to include as a basic feature the following relationship between the Figure's path and the Ground's planar geometry: The Figure's path begins at one edge, lies on the surface, and ends at the farther edge of the Ground's bounded plane. This feature is present in the usual understanding of sentences like *The shopping cart rolled across the street* and *The tumbleweed rolled across the field in one hour*. But one or more components of this schematic feature can be suspended or canceled when they conflict with other specifications in the sentence. Such specifications can either be supplied by particular lexical forms or by the overall reference of the sentence.

Thus, in (2), the overall reference of the sentence makes it clear that the cart did not make it all the way to the other side of the street. Accordingly, there is a suspension or cancelation of one component of the cited *across* feature, namely, the final component: '[the Figure's path] ends at the farther edge'. The noteworthy linguistic principle in operation here is that a word—here, *across*—does not have to be dropped just because its basic referent does not perfectly fit the context. Rather, it can continue in use with most of its specifications still intact but made serviceable again by cognitive processes that shift just one or a few of its specifications.

(2) The shopping cart rolled across the street and was hit by an
    oncoming car.

Comparably in (3), the double-boundedness of the *across* schema conflicts with the open-endedness indicated by other elements of the sentence. In particular, this open-endedness is indicated by the *for* of *for one hour* (by contrast with *in*) together with the fact that a prairie's great size places its boundaries outside of a tumbleweed's hour-long trek. Accordingly, there is a cancelation of the first and last components of the cited *across* feature, namely, of the components 'begins at one edge' and 'ends at the farther edge'.

(3) The tumbleweed rolled across the prairie for an hour.

2.3 Replacement of a Component of an Open-Class Specification

Together with its more contentful specifications, an open-class form often includes certain structural specifications of the kind principally represented by closed-class forms. Such structural specifications can conflict in a sentence with those of an accompanying closed-class form. In that case, the open-class form usually replaces its original structural specifications with the specifications of the closed-class form. In this way, the two forms come into semantic accord. This process is exemplified below for two different categories of specifications.

2.3.1 Extension and Distribution

Both closed-class forms and open-class forms can make specifications as to a quantity's "degree of extension" or its "pattern of distribution"—two conceptual categories that were discussed in sections 4.5 and 4.6 in chapter I-1. To consider degree of extension just for the temporal domain, an event can be "point durational" (idealizable as occurring at only a point of time), or "extent durational" (occurring over an extent of time). And as to its pattern of distribution, an event can, for instance, be "one-way" if it involves a transition from one condition to another without a return, or can be "full-cycle" if it does include such a return.

Now, the open-class verb *hit* may be taken to refer most basically to a point-durational full-cycle action that involves a (propelled) object sailing toward another object, impacting with it, and rebounding. In (4a), these basic temporal specifications are consonant with the closed-class forms. Thus, the point duration of *hit* is consonant with the *at* temporal phrase, as well as with the *and . . . again* construction. The fact that a clause like *removed the mallet from the gong* cannot be felicitously included indicates that *hit* is understood here as already being full-cycle, hence as already covering the moving object's departure from the impacted object. By contrast, the sentence in (4b)—which in one reading might be uttered while watching a slow-motion film of the event—has a closed-class form, the progressive construction *be -ing*, whose 'extent-durational' and 'one-way' reading is in conflict with the original temporal structure of *hit*. This latter, accordingly, here shifts into accord with the closed-class specification. In particular, the verb replaces its point-durational extension with an extent-durational extension, and its full-cycle pattern with a one-way pattern. The verb now refers to an extent-durational one-way action that involves a (propelled) object sailing toward an object on a trajectory that will likely lead to its impact with it.

(4) a. She hit the gong with the mallet at exactly 3:00, (*removed the mallet from the gong,) and hit it again five seconds later.
    b. And now she's hitting the gong with the mallet.

2.3.2 Associated Attributes   A survey of comfortably reading sentences with intransitive *bend* as the verb and various nominals as subject—(5) is an example—would show the nominals' referents to be, grosso modo, linear or planar stiff objects. It can be concluded that the verb *bend* itself makes this specification about the character of the involved object, in addition to the specifications that the verb makes as to the action the object undergoes. This object thus has characteristics specified for it by two open-class forms, the subject nominal and the verb. This is therefore a case of multiple specification.

(5) a. The cardboard bent in two.
    b. The handkerchief bent in two.

However, consider the sentence in (5b) and what an addressee's sequence of responses to it might be. The sentence contains a specificational clash: a 'handkerchief' is normally soft, but 'bending' is normally done by something stiff, characteristics mutually incompatible for a single object. An addressee's initial reaction may indeed involve surprise or perplexity, affect often attendant on cognitive incongruity. This may be succeeded, though, by a conceptual resolution. This resolution could involve a blend or juxtaposition of the two specifications (see below). Or it could involve the imagining of some such circumstance as the handkerchief's having previously been dipped into liquid nitrogen. This last form of resolution —in which, as here, an addressee comes up with a context that eliminates the prior incongruity—involves a shift. The attribute of 'softness' normally associated with a 'handkerchief' is replaced by 'stiffness' and thus comes to be in accord with the verb's specification thereof. The cognitive parameter involved here is that of **associated attributes**—the incidental attributes typically associated with one's concept of some entity. Though not discussed further here, more investigation will be needed into the so-conceivedly essential versus incidental characteristics of an entity— along the lines of Fillmore's (1975) analysis of forms like *real/fake gun, real/imitation coffee*.

Here are two further examples of shift with respect to associated attributes. In (6), *home* functions as a closed-class form, specifically as a verb satellite (see chapter II-1), specifying a combination of Path plus Ground-object, in particular 'to one's/ . . . home'. The Ground-object is specified as well by the open-class prepositional object in (a) and (b). In the former case, the double specification is harmonious in terms of normal expectations. But in the latter case, the two specifications are in conflict. A 'hotel room' usually suggests a 'temporary guest lodging', whereas a 'home' usually suggests a 'permanent residence'. One resolution that an addressee could make here, though, is to shift the associated attribute of the open-class form, *hotel room*, to that of the closed-class form *home*. Thus, finally, the place that John goes to is understood both as his home and as a hotel room, where the latter is apparently used for long-term dwelling.

(6) John went home
    a. to his cottage in the suburbs.
    b. to his hotel room.

Comparably, the two alternatives in (7) respectively exhibit concord and conflict between a closed-class specification and an open-class specification with respect to associated attributes. The closed-class form here, a construction that could be called one of "counterpart matching," indicates that the time of day expressed at the end of the sentence is to be understood as being 'on time'. The actual time expression is an open-class form. The 9:00 of (7a) has the associated attribute in this society of being 'on time' for the start of a usual workday. But the *noon* of (7b) would normally be taken as late. This latter attribute is therefore in conflict with the constructional indication. An addressee might at first experience surprise or puzzlement on hearing *noon*, but might then shift its associated attribute of being 'late' to one of being 'on time' by imagining some unusual job situation that begins its day at noon. Once again, then, the open-class form will have shifted so as to accommodate the closed-class form through a process of replacing one of its associated attributes.

(7) Jane got to work late, and Bill didn't get there at
   a. 9:00,
   b. noon,
   either.

3   BLENDS

Where two specifications are disconsonant, a shift brings about a semantic resolution by altering one of the specifications so that it comes into accord with the other. But an alternative cognitive process is a **blend**. Here, the addressee comes up with an amplified cognitive representation that can accommodate both of the specifications. Typically, this representation is an imaginative hybrid that the addressee herself might consider not to correspond to her more objective representations. Thus, in a blend, both of the original specifications are retained in some form. We consider two types of blends, "superimposition" and "introjection."

3.1   Superimposition

Consider the sentence in (8).

(8) My sister wafted through the party.

There is a conflict here between two sets of specifications. On the one hand, the verb *waft* suggests a perhaps leaflike object moving gently to and fro in an irregular pattern through the air. On the other hand, the remaining forms in the sentence specify a person (moving) through a group of other people. These two sets of specifications are apparently too disparate to be reconciled through a shift-type process, as in the "bent handkerchief" example above. Thus, there is no obvious context in which a woman could be a leaf, or a leaf a woman, nor is there one in which a party could be the wind, or the wind a party. Nevertheless, this disparity does not cause any blockage to further conceptual processing. Rather, a conceptual blend or hybrid that is compounded out of the two sets of specified characteristics becomes evoked in the addressee. To me, for example, the sentence evokes the conceptualization of my sister wandering aimlessly through the party, somewhat unconscious of the events around her, and of the party somehow suffused with a slight rushing sound of air. There is, however, some structure to this blend. Of the two sets of specifications, it is my sister walking through the party that emerges as the essential referent of the sentence, while that of something leaflike wafting through air winds up functioning solely as a kind of suggestive coloration that gets blended into the essential referent. The two sets of specifications can be aligned part for part as in (9). Here, the elements actually appearing in the sentence are lowercase, while the suggested elements are in capitals. Still, it is the elements of (9b), both explicit and implicit, that are understood as the essential referent. But the fact that the tinge-imbuing elements of (9a) can be aligned with the essential elements suggests the term **superimposition** for this type of blend.

(9) a. THE LEAF wafted through THE AIR.
    b. My sister WALKED through the party.

The prototype circumstance to which the traditional notion of "metaphor" has been applied is indeed this one of a superimposed blend. But it should be kept in mind that—in the terms of this chapter's analytic framework—such metaphor is only one subtype of a much more general process of resolution of conflict between multiple specifications.

3.2   Introjection

Assume that the two sentences in (10) are descriptions of scenes to be filmed. If the actors are dressed in a nondistinguishing way, a shot could be taken that would look the same for both scenes, one consisting of a hand patting a knee. At least to this extent, accordingly the presence of the reflexive pronoun in (10b) does not alter the basics of the action specified. It merely indicates that of the two impacting objects specified in both scenes, the hand and the knee, both are parts of the same body rather than of two different bodies.

(10) a. As the soldier and the sailor sat talking, the soldier patted the sailor on the knee.
     b. As the soldier and the sailor sat talking, the soldier patted himself on the knee.

But no single camera shot could be found for scenes acted according to the two sentences of (11). The sentence of (11a) involves two people, one of whom lifts and throws the other one forth while himself remaining in place. But the sentence in (11b) involves one person who springs forth. And the movements of this single person in the latter scene do not resemble the movements of either of the persons in the former scene. The presence of the reflexive pronoun in (11b) has this time altered the nature of the action considerably. It seems, in fact, to have altered it in the direction of the action specified by *jump*. Thus, if we were now to film scenes on the basis of (11b) and (11c), we would find the results indistinguishable.

(11) As a military training exercise,
     a. the soldier threw the sailor off the cliff into the ocean below.
     b. the soldier threw himself off the cliff into the ocean below.
     c. the soldier jumped off the cliff into the ocean below.

The conceptual category involved here can be called that of **scene partitioning**. In its basic reference, the open-class verb *throw* specifies a dyadic scene partitioning—that is, one with two major role-playing entities, a 'thrower' and a 'thrown object'. In (11a), this dyadic specification of *throw* is consonant with the occurrence of the two distinct referents specified by the subject and the object nominals. But in (11b), this dyadic verb occurs together with a monadic closed-class form, the construction of subject + reflexive, which specifies just a single referent. Thus, there is a semantic clash between the dyadic specification of the open-class verb *throw* and the monadic specification of the closed-class reflexive construction.

Now, at least one type of semantic resolution takes place here, that of a shift. The dyadic specification of *throw* gives way to the monadic specification of the reflexive, so that the sentence overall now unmistakably refers to just a single referent entity. But the cognitive matter does not appear to rest there. If such a cognitive shift were all that takes place, the newly monadic sentence of (11b) ought to be semantically indistinguishable from the basically monadic sentence of (11c) with respect to the issue of scene partitioning. But for all the cinematic equivalence of the two sentences, they still seem to evoke different cognitive representations. In contrast with (11c), (11b) seems still to be specifying some form of two-roledness—one, in fact, somehow blended in with a basically one-roled occurrence. Such a form of two-into-one blend may accordingly be termed **introjection**. To me, in particular, the sentence in (11b) evokes a sense that the single personhood of the soldier is somehow subdivided into two fractions: His will, jumping musculature, and force exertion is somehow sensed as a thrower, while the rest of his personality and body is sensed as the thrown object.

All the same conclusions seem to hold for the example in (12). The two roles, 'host' and 'guest,' of the basically dyadic social scene specified by *serve* in (12a) are compressed and superimposed on—that is, introjected into—the single actor of (12b). These metaphorically blended-in attributes are all that distinguish the scene here from the cinematically identical scene of (12c).[2]

(12) a. The host served me some dessert from the kitchen.
  b. I served myself some dessert from the kitchen.
  c. I went and got some dessert from the kitchen.

4 JUXTAPOSITIONS

Where two sentence specifications are in conflict, the cognitive process of **juxtaposition** places them side by side for simultaneous consideration within a larger cognitive context. In the cognitive process of blending just discussed, the specificational inputs to the blend seem in general to lose their original individuality in the new conceptual hybrid that emerges. And the semantic conflict that the separate specifications originally represented disappears within the new imaginative blend. But under juxtaposition, the original specifications retain their individuality as well as the conceptual conflict they produce together. In fact, the point of juxtaposition is precisely to foreground or employ this conflict. In particular, the process of juxtaposition draws a perimeter around the disparate specifications and establishes a higher-level perspective point from which to direct attention over them all at once. This attention over incompatible specifications generates the experience of what can be called **incongruity effects**. Included among such effects are surprise, oddity, irony, and humor. We present several instances of the humor type of incongruity to exemplify the process of juxtaposition.

Consider the sentence in (13). There is here a specificational conflict between two of the words: *slightly* indicates a point along a gradient, while *pregnant* has the sense of 'all or none' as a basic structural component. One type of resolution that an addressee might effect on this conflict is a shift. He could alter the 'all or none' component of *pregnant* to one of gradience, so that the resulting reference is now to a stage of gestation.

Alternatively, though, he could employ the process of juxtaposition to comical effect. In particular, the categorical fact of pregnancy appears to be understood as having a negative association that the speaker attempts to underplay by suggesting that the woman has only a modest case of it.

(13) She's slightly pregnant.

A juxtaposition can also be made across two sentences, like those of the interchange in (14). Here, person A's remark would normally be understood with a sense of introjection, as this was discussed in the preceding section. That is, the sentence refers to a single person, but a person into whom is metaphorically blended the suggestion of a dyad. But now a person B might respond as in (14b), using an expression that refers to a plurality of distinct individuals. The effect of this second utterance is to raise the dyadic coloration of the first remark to a suggested level of actuality, to be placed in attention beside the already cognized monadic actuality. The effect is comic absurdity.

(14) A: John likes himself.
     B: Yes, well, birds of a feather flock together.

Incongruous juxtapositions can be made not only of words and expressions, but also of stylistics and delivery. For example, the phraseology of the street person quoted in (15) manifests a semantic and grammatical complexity that suggest an educated articulateness. But the delivery suggests a streetworn nonchalance. The two sets of traits considered together can give a comically inconsistent impression of the speaker's character.

(15) You couldn't help us out with any part of 22 cents ...?
     (spoken with a monotoned rapid slur)

5 JUGGLING AND BLOCKING

On hearing a portion of discourse with conflicting specifications, an addressee might be able to apply one of the preceding types of semantic resolution so quickly and automatically that the cognitive processes involved would normally be difficult to access consciously. But some cases of conflict seem to be novel or problematic enough that an addressee must proceed through a succession of attempts at resolution that can more readily become conscious.

One form of such a succession of attempts can be called **schema juggling**. Consider the sentence in (16). The problem here is that the *across* schema, which prototypically refers to a straight path between two parallel boundaries, cannot obviously be matched to any contextually relevant portion of the complex geometry of a car. Respondents to whom I have uttered this sentence generally report that they quickly go through several ways to place an 'across' path on a car so as to end up with the least poor fit, and that they were readily able to bring this succession into awareness once asked about it.

(16) The snail crawled across the car.

We might note that the respondents' final solutions were varied. Some had the snail crawling over the roof of the car from one side to the other. The difficulty with this solution is that the path is curved and on top—properties better suited to the preposition *over* than to *across*. Some respondents had the snail crawling over the hood of the car from one side to the other. This solution improves over the roof solution in that the path is mid-height and perhaps not so curved, but it has the disadvantage of being located at a peripheral part of the car rather than at the central body of the car. One respondent had the snail crawling in through one open back window, along the back seat, and out the window on the other side. The advantages of this solution are that the path is central and flat, but the disadvantage is that it is interior, hence, better suited to the preposition *through*.

Finally, some cases of discrepancy between two specifications might strike the linguistic faculty of an addressee in such a way that it does not come up with any resolution. In such cases, one may speak of **blockage**. Consider, for example, the sentence in (17). Here, the disparity is between the schema of the preposition *through*, in which the path occurs within a three-dimensional surrounding medium, and the fact that *plateau*, especially in conjunction with *walk*, suggests a two-dimensional top planar surface. If the addressee cannot find a way to shift, blend, or juxtapose these two schematic specifications, she may simply leave the utterance as is, unable to semantically process it further. This would then not be an instance of semantic resolution at all, but rather a form of nonresolution.

(17) *Jane walked through the plateau.

6   THE CONCEPT OF BASICNESS IN SEMANTIC RESOLUTION

One of the processes of semantic resolution—that of shift—criterially depends on the concept of "basicness." Without that concept, another cognitive process would have to be invoked, that of "selection."

Central to the concept of basicness is that of the forms that make up some set, one of those forms is privileged, and that the remaining forms represent a deviation from the privileged one. The concept of privilege has variations, such as that the privileged form is the original one, the commonest one, the structurally simplest one, or the most independent one. And the concept of deviation from the basic can involve an actual change through time from the basic as starting point, or some more static sense of abstract divergence. This concept of a domain's organization can be called the **basic-divergent** model. Many theoretical formulations in linguistics have been based on this model. They include the concepts of word derivation, markedness theory, transformational grammar, prototype theory, and metaphoric mapping.

The main alternative concept of organization of a domain can be called the **even-array** model (see Hockett's (1954) "item and process" model and "item and arrangement" model, respectively). The even-array model is a static form of organization in which the forms of a domain are understood as conjunctions of properties having equal privilege, and/or in which the components of an expression are taken to be simultaneously co-present in a static pattern of interrelationships. Theoretical formulations in linguistics that have been based on this model include paradigms, monostratal grammars, and polysemy (without radiality).

Of these two models, the basic-divergent model is relevant here because only by having the concept that a linguistic form can have a basic meaning can a process of shift be conceived to operate on it to alter that meaning to some nonbasic meaning. Thus, this chapter's original examples with *across* were based on the proposition that this preposition has a basic meaning. Specifically, this basic meaning includes the conditions that the Figure's path fully traverses one axis of the Ground object and that it is not longer than the transverse axis of that object. Accordingly, the cases in which *across* held other meanings were considered to result by processes of deviation from the basic meaning, specifically, by the processes of stretching and cancelation. Under the even-array model, though, these various senses of *across* would all be held to be of equal status, simply alternatives selected from a polysemous range. No process of shift—that is, of alteration—would have taken place, but simply a process of selection.

Notes

1. This chapter is a much-redone version of Talmy 1977. Many portions of that original paper presented in their earliest form some of the ideas that now appear in

chapter I-1 in a more developed form. To avoid repetition, those portions of the original paper have been omitted here. The remainder of the original paper dealt with semantic conflict and processes for its resolution. That portion, moderately revised and expanded, is what appears here. One of the types of semantic resolution treated in the original paper (as well as here), that of "shifts," bears much resemblance to Pustejovsky's (1993) concept of "coercion," while another of the types, that of "blends," bears much resemblance to Fauconnier and Turner's (1998) concept by the same name of "blends."

2. The unusual sentence in (i) shows that not all sensible introjections have become standardized.

(i) ?I'll drop myself off and then let *you* have the car.

Chapter 6

Communicative Goals and Means: Their Cognitive Interaction

1 INTRODUCTION

The present study considers communication from the perspective of the psychological situation at each moment within the producer of a communication.[1] The production of a particular communication at any given moment is seen as the "vector resultant" of a set of simultaneous conditions within the producer: her communicative goals in correlation with the availability of suitable expressive means.

The communication-producing system of the brain does not seem to require precision consistency to function, for goals are often in conflict and every means has gaps and limitations. Rather, the system has structural properties that enable it to handle such internal "contradictions": priorities are set and balances struck among conflicting goals, while all the means are drawn on in various proportions as needed to piece together an adequate realization of the moment's goals. With respect to this last point, in fact, the distinctions between the various expressive means lose much of their usually assumed significance from the present psychological/functionalist perspective.

The perspective just outlined is taken to be relevant to all modes of communicating—including speaking, signing, gesturing, and writing—and so the analysis below is carried out in concepts and terms neutral to such distinctions of mode. Thus, instead of terms like "speaker," "utterance," "listener," and "language," this study uses "communicator," "a communication," "addressee" or "intended recipient," and "communication system." In the case of speech, "addressee" has the further advantage over "listener" of adopting the internal perspective of the communicator and implying nothing about that of the collocutor (such as where the collocutor's attention may be at a given moment).

As already noted there, the preceding chapter, II-5, forms a pair with the present one. The present chapter concerns the online cognitive processing that takes place in the producer of a discourse to resolve the conflicts among competing communicative goals and available expressive means for the representation of a concept. The preceding chapter concerned the online cognitive processing that takes place in the recipient of such a discourse to resolve the conflicts among competing representations of a concept. As with some efforts elsewhere, the aim of the two chapters together is to ground linguistic material in the ongoing cognitive processing that underlies both its production and its comprehension, as a complement to the usual treatment of such material as a decoupled pattern of elements and structures.

1.1   The Nature of Communication

Anything that may at first be seen as an isolable portion of human mental activity, to which a term like "communication" is then applied, ultimately cannot be treated as a watertight compartment, for it inevitably consists of psychological processes that do not relate exclusively to each other but are embedded amidst a continuum of psychological functioning. Accordingly, the issue of communication is addressed here at three levels of inclusivity: a narrowly conceived core, the larger context in which this is situated, and the still more general modificational processes of subportioning, transforming, subsuming, nullifying, embedding, and the like, to which these are subject.

1.1.1   The Communicative Core   There is perhaps a certain psychological process operating as a core to what is generally understood by "communication," one experienced as a need or desire, present in the individual from an early age. This is the urge that certain phenomenological content within oneself—whatever is experienced, whether by apprehending, conceiving, feeling, or the like—become replicated within a certain other or others. Bringing about such a replication entails, for a given content, its encoding, transmission, receipt, and comprehension. These issues are exemplified in section 6 mainly under the discussion of goals (a) through (k).

1.1.2   The Larger Context   The preceding core of communication does not often go on in a self-contained closed circuit but is usually conditioned by one's awareness of further circumstances about oneself and the addressee as well as of the remaining total situation. Moreover, one's intentions for one's communication are often not limited solely to its successful comprehension but extend to its having further interpersonal effects or an avoidance of certain effects. That is, the basic core of communicative functioning is both responsive to and creative of—or in short, is integrated within—the larger context. These matters are further treated in section 6 mainly under the discussion of goals (l) through (p) as well as in chapter II-8—for example, in sections 3.1.3 and 4.4.3.

1.1.3 Modificational Processes The components of the putative "core" of the communicative process can be seen not to enjoy an inviolate collective unity together, for everyday human behavior can be observed that omits some while keeping the rest, transforms some, subsumes them all in a larger system, or even nullifies or appropriates certain of them in the service of some other function. These can be called **modificational processes**. We briefly discuss each of the processes just mentioned.

Omission of a Component. One standard component of the core of communication is intention: One intends to be communicating certain contents. But generally accompanying such intended contents is the information that one conveys about oneself and one's thoughts and feelings through largely unconscious bodily and vocal behavior, as well as through unintended aspects of the message itself. In this form of communication, all the components of the core system minus that of intention are in operation.

Transformation of a Component. One component of core communication may be the proviso that the communicator must actually experience the contents expressed by the communiqué. But such a proviso would then often undergo a transformation—for example, when an adult addresses a child. For the adult may attempt, on the basis of biographical equivalences, to communicate the emotional essence of an experience of his to the child, but to do so he will translate its constituent specifics into ones within the child's ken.

Subsumption in a Larger System. Conceivable as a broader (and perhaps more basic) form of human activity, in which strict communication would be subsumed only as a component, is general interpersonal attunement, responsivity, and communion. This is evident, say, in two people sharing the activity of walking through a park, an activity within which the occasional exchange of utterances forms only one component.

Nullification/Appropriation of a Component by Another Function. Basic communicative functions can be co-opted in the service of another goal, with its constituent components seemingly left intact but in fact partly nullified. For example, in the service of wanting an addressee to form a certain impression of one's self and thought, one may try to project a tailored image, to make this appear like a communication of what is actually in oneself, even when it is not.

The general case of this seems to be that virtually any psychological faculty can, in the service of its own functioning, more or less harmoniously appropriate other psychological faculties with originally different functions. It appears that this process can repeat in a virtually unlimited reflexive capacity of the mind, giving rise to intricate embeddings of intentions and of original-into-transferred functions. To illustrate, in their basic function, "repairs" are a variety of linguistic devices that a speaker uses to remedy hitches in her expression. But in (1)—excerpted from an example in Sacks, Schegloff, and Jefferson 1974—these devices appear to be appropriated and employed in profusion by the speaker as a means of showing embarrassed concern for the addressee's feelings. And built in turn on that function is the further function of the speaker's signaling to the addressee that she has his feelings in mind.

(1) ((pause)) I don' know of anybody—that—'cause anybody that I really didn't *di:g* I wouldn't have the *time*, uh: a:n: to waste I would say, unh if I didn' (   )

By contrast, a speaker who wished to hurt the addressee's feelings might make use of a sure, unbroken delivery style, something like that in "I wouldn't want to waste any time on anybody I didn't really dig."

1.2   Associated Factors

The cognitive system of communication necessarily involves other factors, including evolution, impairment, cultural differences, development, individual differences, and language typology and diachrony. Of these, the last three are now briefly considered.

1.2.1   Child Development   Much more observation is needed, but it seems probable that the course of children's communicative development roughly follows something like the preceding outline of increasing inclusivity and complexity. There are no doubt some generalities and some individualities as to the sequence in which the various goals, means, contextual sensitivities, and manipulations come into operation and are integrated in a child, but they clearly do not all enter at once, and even those

that are singly functional at a particular stage cannot all be juggled together simultaneously by the child.

One example of a child manifesting a hierarchically not-high-enough level of communicative awareness involves a mother talking with her 4;3-year-old daughter (taken from *Tea Party*; Ervin-Tripp 1975).

(2) Mother: Do you think that was a good idea? [spilling out the milk]
      Daughter: Yeah.

Here, the daughter apparently catches only the mild tone imparted by the question form and explicit content of the mother's utterance, but not the mother's use of that form and content as a higher-level device for couching a lesson-administering disapproval.

Another example is of the child who starts telling a stranger about recent events but has not taken into account the stranger's unfamiliarity with the characters, setting, and background of the story. Here, the child can control the content of the story but not the larger discourse context.

1.2.2 Individual Differences   The whole pattern of balances in the communication system outlined above shifts in accordance with differences in the goals, means, and capabilities that occur in different individuals.

Thus, people differ as to the strengths and priorities of their goals. For example, a person with a strong need to express what is at this moment on his mind (goal (a) below) and with this in priority over his desire to attend to others' communicative needs (goal (m)) may be seen as conversationally pushy by a person with a different balance.

Further, one person differs from another not only in the strengths and priorities she accords to various goals, but also in the facility she has in realizing those different goals. Such facility could pertain, for example, to the extent to which she can hold in mind the whole content of a discourse, take an interlocutor's feelings into account, or press her communicative wishes (relevant, respectively, to goals (l), (m), (o) below). For example, in the goal of conveying an extensive idea, a person who counts among her reliable facilities an ability not to lose track of earlier points and to hear another's words during her own will be more willing to accept a give-and-take interchange as a context in which to fulfill her goal than a person without these facilities, who might instead require an assured period without interruption.[2]

Comparably, one individual can differ from another in her facility with the various expressive means. For instance, in the goal of expressing her ideas in speech, one kind of person might not have quick access to the most apt vocabulary items (means (c) below) but might have a ready facility for forming complex constructions out of common words (means (f)). Such a person will usually compensate for the former with the latter, contributing a major component to her characteristic speaking style. This style might be regarded as wordy, without any compelling bon mots, but still able to convey the ideas overall. By contrast, an individual with the reverse facilities is able to express his ideas through an apt selection of just the right words, while placing these within a rather terse matrix.

1.2.3   Language Comparison, Language Change, and Observational Adequacy   The differential availability of expressive means is not only a psychological issue for the communicator, one perhaps best studied by the psychologist of communication, but also a universalist comparative issue across the world's various languages for the descriptive linguist to treat. In addition, the integratedness of language as a system within a broader communicative, and then psychological/sociocultural, system affects a particular language's pattern of change in the course of time—a matter for the diachronic linguist. These issues will be discussed more fully in section 7.

Though based on a fair amount of observation (including the cited examples), this chapter's discussion of communication points to the need for much more data, testing, and experimentation, on which the validity of any analysis ultimately rests. The present study is offered largely as a contribution to the kind of organizational thought that can help direct a fuller program of observation.

2   COMMUNICATIVE GOALS

Below, grouped in accordance with the earlier analysis of communicative functioning, individual communicative goals are listed. It is not assumed that any goal as listed has any psychological reality as a discrete unit. Nor is it assumed that the list of goals taken together constitutes a non-overlapping, gapless, and exhaustive coverage of purposive communication. Rather, the list is basically heuristic, intended to help map out the extent and contour of the domain of purposive communication. The psychological organizational realities for this domain may turn out to be quite different, involving subdivisions, hierarchicizations, and relationships barely considered in this study.

A few distinctions relevant to the domain can be noted here, however. Different portions of communicative functioning differ in the degree to which at any moment they are, or can become, conscious in the individual and, correlatively, in the degree to which they afford her volitional control over the manipulation of means. To the extent that any function is unconscious, the more appropriate a term like "process" and the less so a term like "goal" is for it.

Second, the goals as listed differ greatly as to their variability or constancy during a communication. It is surely not the case that at each instant a communicator reassembles his configuration of goals from scratch. Rather, while some goals fluctuate swiftly (e.g., those pertaining to advancing a local idea), others remain relatively constant through long stretches and so have the same pertinence in each moment's combination of goals (e.g., goals pertaining to communicating one's mood or attitude).

The goals identified next will be discussed and exemplified in section 6.

(3) *Communication per se*

To get certain phenomenological content existing within oneself (ideas, feelings, perceptions, and so on) replicated within certain addressees

Goals Pertaining to the Content of a Communication

a. To convey a particular propositional content or component notion

b. To set the degree of specificity and salience of a whole proposition or component notion

c. To organize the sequentiality of the contents (so as to direct how the ideational whole develops temporally in the addressee)

d. To manifest (or project an image of) one's character, mood, or attitude (toward the topic, addressee, situation, and so on)

e. To signal the nature/type of the present communication

Goals Pertaining to the Structure of a Communication

f. To conform to "grammaticality": a communication system's structural "design" properties

g. To conform to "felicity": a communication system's preferences among expressive means (relative to a particular style)

h. To conform to "aesthetics": one's own sense, or canons, of what is pleasing in a communication's form

Goals Pertaining to the Transmission, Reception, and Comprehension of a Communication

     i. To accommodate a communication's temporal/physical manifestation to external temporal/physical exigencies, or vice versa

     j. To accommodate one's communication to the characteristics of the addressee's receptivity

     k. To ease (or, more generally, to control) the addressee's processing task

(3′) *Communication in a Larger Context*

To condition the nature of one's communication, before and during its production, on the basis of one's assessments of one's self, one's addressee(s), and the remaining total context; and

To have, with one's communication, certain further interpersonal effects and noneffects

     l. To make a communication's content appropriate to the immediate or long-range context (and to the "metacommunication")

     m. To make one's communication satisfy some more general interpersonal intention or program pertaining to the addressee

     n. To adjust one's communication with attention to its potential effect outside the direct communicator-addressee linkage

     o. To initiate/maintain/terminate/avoid communication or some aspect thereof (such as topic)

     p. To engender, via one's communication, certain actions/states in the addressee (or others)

(3″) *Master Control*

Goals Pertaining to Generativity

     q. To conform to each moment's schema for the realization of one's communicative goals that arises in one by unconscious processes

Evaluative and Remedial Goals

     r. To maintain/repair one's communication on the basis of an ongoing monitoring of its adequacy in realizing one's communicative goals

Though these goals are treated further below, (q) deserves immediate attention since it involves a substantial addition to our notion of communicative functioning.

From the author's introspective observation, the production of a communication usually seems to be a two-staged process. In the first stage, a not-fully-specified schema for a communication's overall formal and contentful structure arises in the individual. This schema is generated by unconscious processes that do most of the work of integrating the moment's communicative goals and conditions. Their work in finding an appropriate schema is perhaps eased by an initial check through a smallish set of "target structures," learned as the preferred or most common of the particular communication system being used.[3] The conscious experience of the schema's emergence, impressionistically, can be a sudden knowing in general what one is going to say and how to say it.

In the next stage, the actual communication is produced by following the schematic outline and particularizing its general/vague aspects with choices as to lexical items, "local syntax," and so on. No doubt, at times—varying with the person and the occasion—many "second stage"-type specifics arise as part of the schema itself or are filled in before the communication's actual production. But the majority of the processing for specifics would seem to take place at this second stage.

After one has progressed along a first-stage schema for a short while, or even before its implementation, the schema is apparently often scrapped and replaced by a new one as the result of a quick reassessment of its adequacy in realizing one's communicative goals (by the operation of process (r)). Such a phenomenon seems at work, for example, in a speaker's false starts, which perhaps reflect the successive arising and dropping of different schemas, or in a sudden shift of direction or a semi-independent section in an utterance. Schema formation, insofar as it yields speech-based structures, would seem to operate equally for the processes of speaking and writing. Whether it, or something comparable, operates as well for bodily expressivity, or for signing and writing by the congenitally deaf, remains to be explored.

3   COMMUNICATIVE MEANS

Some formal expressive means are listed below. They are given in some cases because of their relevance to later examples. There is in any case no assumption about them of natural entityhood or exhaustiveness—that is, similar avisos apply here as earlier to the list of goals. Various communication-systemic dimensions have been set up as rubrics and each means is placed under the most relevant one, although, as the divisional lines are drawn, many means partake of more than one dimension.

One's communicative goals, thus, are realized through choices among the expressive means in (4).

(4) *Systemic*
    a. the particular language/communication system
    Ideational
    b. phraseology
    c. lexical items/other morphemes/lexicalization
    d. lexical-derivation processes
    e. omission/deletion
    Structural and relational
    f. the syntactic structure of a constituent or sentence
    g. order (of words/phrases/propositions)
    h. repetition
    i. the verb's case-frame setup
    j. a nominal's grammatical relation
    Sonic or other physical medium
    k. segmental "phon"ology
    l. suprasegmental "phon"ology
    m. other nonsegmental characteristics
    Temporal
    n. flow management
    o. other temporal characteristics
    Kinesic
    p. (nonsystemic) gesture
    q. physical action

Some of the means listed here require a bit of characterization.

(b) refers to how an idea is put or cast. This involves both the way a total ideational content is divided up and the way the particular subset of component notions is selected for explicit expression.

(h) refers to cross-referential relationships through text, including repetition of words as a grammatical or semantic means, repetition of sounds in poetry, and nonrepetition of words in certain literary styles.

(k) and (l) refer to the systematically organized aspects of any communication system's physical medium. "Phonology," as contrasted with "phonetics," refers to this component in spoken language; "emics" may be the only general term that would apply as well—for example, to signing. For speech, (l) here has its traditional reference to intonation, stress, and tone, but for signing, it is questionable that any (k)–(l) distinction should be seen exactly between the manual and the nonmanual (as argued by Baker (1976)).

(m) includes reference to voice quality, pitch register, intonational spread, volume, volume spread, and enunciation (slurred $\leftrightarrow$ precise) in the case of speech, and to comparable characteristics in the case of signing, such as the size, energy, and clarity of the motion. This as well as (o) may be classed together with (p) as a general kinesic component of communication, a highly expressive one operating parallel to the more strictly systemic one.

(n) includes stopping, backtracking, hesitating, restarting, iterating, and stretching.

(o) includes reference to speed and rhythmic patterns.

(p) refers to facial, manual, and general bodily positions and movements.

In the case of signing there may be no distinction between (m) and (p).

4 THE CONCORD AND CONFLICT OF GOALS

On occasion, perhaps, all of a moment's communicative goals are in harmonious concord, with the resultant communication satisfying them all. More often, two or more goals held simultaneously are in conflict, requiring inconsistent or incompatible means for their realization.

An example of inconsistency is in the following communication by a young street person.

(5) You couldn't help us out with any part of 22 cents . . .
     ((spoken with a monotoned rapid slur))

Here, the style of delivery (means (m) and (o)) seemed on the one hand to indicate that the speaker wanted to convey an attitude of a streetworn aloof nonchalance (goal (d)), while the semantic and grammatical complexity of the utterance (means (b) and (f)) seemed on the other hand to indicate a desire to manifest high ideational articulateness (goal (b)), perhaps for the pleasure of exercising a native talent. While the means that realize these goals can in this case co-occur, together they gave incongruously—and comically—opposite impressions of the speaker's character.

In the case of incompatibility, a communicator must decide in favor of one goal over the other (often, presumably, in accordance with their relative importance to him), or else manage to strike some other balance. As an example for both live and written discourse, a communicator with only one especially gripping item in his whole message has to choose between maximizing its dramatic impact by saving it for last (goal (c)) and gaining the addressee's attention in the first place (goal (j)). This is because satisfying both goals would place the impossible demand on surface ordering (means (g)) that an item appear both exclusively at the beginning and exclusively at the end. Sometimes the communicator can effect a balance, putting part of the item first (the "teaser") and the best part last.

By contrast with most writing, where there is time to find just the right means to satisfy such goals as notional accuracy (a), logical sequencing (c), and satisfying style (h), in most live communicating the operation of the timing goal (i) often demands compromises from one's other goals in a continuing speed-versus-quality conflict. For example, if one has already paused too long looking for just the right word, one may have to grab at its nearest forthcoming neighbor, being ready at this point to pay the price of representing one's idea grossly in the interests of keeping one's turn or the addressee's attention. In this same interest, a person who has already made several false starts by discarding schemas may stick with the next one that arises and look to following it with emendations for any inadequacies it may have. Here, it is the monitoring and remedial process (r) that, as the deciseconds tick away, reevaluates priorities in the shifting balance of factors.

5 THE LIMITATIONS OF MEANS

Every expressive means of a communicative system has arbitrary gaps and limitations. The communicator, consequently, must draw in various proportions on them all to piece together an adequate realization of his goals.

To take an example (comparable to the "commercial scene" in Fillmore 1977), for English speakers to express any particular combination of the elements of a theft scene in different degrees of salience, they must select from the set of forms in (6) (T = thief, G = goods, V = victim). These forms draw in an irregular fashion on the use of three or four means: different lexical verbs (means (c)), different omission/deletion patterns or case frames (means (l), (i)), and different syntactic constructions (active/passive: means (f)).

(6)	T steal	T rob V	G be stolen	V be robbed
	T steal G	T rob V of G	G be stolen by T	V be robbed by T
	T steal from V		G be stolen from V	V be robbed of G
	T steal G from V		G be stolen from V by T	V be robbed of G by T

In the "steal" column's middle two forms, omission/deletion is the means used to pare down the number of elements explicitly mentioned. But, apart from the column's top form, one cannot carry through with this same means to get all the one-element forms

(7) Sam stole (again tonight). / *Stole a necklace. / *Stole from a dowager.

but rather must switch to the use of different verbs and voices (*A necklace was stolen. The dowager was robbed*).

The process of working around gaps in the means is so integral to the communication-producing system that, from its perspective, the means' lack of thoroughgoingness, as in the preceding example, largely does not matter. Nor, from the perspective of conveying a message, are the differences between the means important. In the preceding, for instance, as (8) suggests, one can even draw on gesture (means (p)) as an equivalent of a spoken constituent, making up the full message complement in that way.

(8) She got robbed $\begin{Bmatrix} \text{of her necklace} \\ ((+\text{a gesture to one's neck as if grasping a necklace})) \end{Bmatrix}$ on the street.

A problem involving the limitations of means often arises in conjunction with the operation of the schema-forming process (q). For example, a speaker wanting to convey that she likes a man because he is charming and observant (goal (a)) and wanting to foreground the presence of these qualities at the beginning of her utterance (goal (b)), while wanting to name these qualities explicitly only at the end of her utterance (goal (c)), may come up with a first-stage schema for a pseudocleft equational sentence with final nominal slots. But as she proceeds through the production of an utterance in accordance with the schema, as in (9a), she runs up at the end against a lexical gap—a gap in means (c)): there is no noun for being observant. If she had foreseen that at the beginning, she might have come up with a different schema, but now, short of starting afresh, she is stuck with making some form of local accommodation by appeal to other means. One solution, as in (9b), would be the creative use of lexical derivation processes (means (d)) (at the expense of conforming to grammaticality—goal (f)). Another solution, as in (9c), would be to draw on the availability of other lexical items (means (c)) (though at the expense of fidelity to the original notion—goal (a)). A third solution, as in (9d), could be to form a noun phrase (means (f)), though this might render the predicate too vernacular for the speaker's projection of self-image (goal (d)) or too asymmetrical for her aesthetics (goal (h)).

(9) a. What I like about him is his charm and
   b. ... his *observance/observantness.
   c. ... his perceptiveness.
   d. ... how he's observant.

6   DISCUSSION AND EXAMPLES OF PARTICULAR GOALS AND MEANS

Most of the goals listed in section 2 (all except (h) and (o), here treated as self-explanatory) are discussed and/or exemplified below under separate headings. Their original phrasing should be reconsulted, since the headings are merely intended as reminders. The "subgoals" that appear under some headings are simply particular forms of the more generic goal named in the heading. The examples are not of any single kind but touch on the diverse range of communicative issues brought forth in section 1. Often, a particular example involves several different goals, so that its placement below is partly arbitrary.

6.1   Propositional Content (Goal a)

The conveying of propositional content or of a particular component notion is perhaps the aspect of communication most familiar in the study of language. Within that, though, the following cases explore some less noted phenomena.

Example: One linguist, during a lecture, got tongue-tripped in trying to say the phrase shown below with its 10 assorted sibilants (in italics). After several attempts at repair work, he stopped cold and then repeated the whole phrase in the manner indicated in (10).

(10) *c*ertain *s*pe*c*ific a*s*pect*s* of the *s*pee*ch* *s*i*t*ua*t*ion
     ((spoken in stressed rhythm with large sharp downward bends of the torso at each stress while the eyes are screwed shut))

In this finally successful production, the fact of repetition (means (h)), verbal qualities and rhythms (means (m), (o)), and body movements (means (p)) together seemed to convey the compound message in (11). The point here is that a form of propositional content is conveyed through communicative means other than those involving standard morphemes.

(11) This phrase is a tough one, but I'm going to get it right this time.
I'm having to work my way effortfully through an impedimentary
medium.
Let me turn my slight embarrassment over muffing it into the
humor of an exaggerated conquest over a worthy opponent.

Subgoal: To indicate one's perspective point: where one places one's
mental eyes to look out over the rest of the scene.

Example: The difference in perspective between a smoker and a potential tobacconist in talking to a neighborhood resident—quoted in (12) and
(13), respectively—is indicated by the choice between the two generic
pronouns in English, *you* and *they* (means (c)).

(12) Where can you buy cigarettes around here?
or: Where do they sell cigarettes around here?

(13) Where do they buy cigarettes around here?
or: Where can you sell cigarettes around here?

Example: The difference in case-frame setup (means (i)) between (14a)
and (14b) can reflect a difference in a speaker's imagistic perspective of either
riding the crest of an advancing smoke wave out into a room or stationarily
watching the wave approach from a position one has at the room's rear.

(14) a. Smoke slowly filled the room.
     b. The room slowly filled with smoke.

Subgoal: To indicate a particular element as the topic (about which
there is comment).

Example: The preferred English means for marking a referent as topical
is to get the form that refers to it in sentence-initial position and as the
grammatical subject (means (g), (j)). This preferred type of marking takes
place for the form that refers to 'the pen' in (15a) in a sentence referring
to an event of location. But where such marking is not possible for some
sentence type—for example, for a sentence referring to an event of
possession—an alternative means is used, that of a special intonation
pattern (means (l)), as in (15b).

(15) *In answer to:* Where's the pen?
     a. (It's) on the table.

     b. JOHN has it.
        ⟨with a heavy stress and high pitch on *John* and with an extra
        low pitch on *has it*⟩

6.2 Degree of Specificity and Salience (Goal b)

Subgoal: To avoid explicit mention of an involved element because it is too emotion-laden, direct, hand-tipping, and so on.

Example: A Yiddish story in which a boy invites a girl to the woods has her answer, not with embarrassingly direct I/You, as in (16a), but with the special nonspecific pronoun (means (c)), as in (16b).

(16) a. I can't go with you. You'll want to kiss me.
     b. Me tor nisht geyn ahin. Me vet zikh veln kushn.
        (One mustn't go there. One will want to kiss another
        [= reflexive].)

Example: The two Danish words for addressing a single person as "you" have interpersonal connotations that one graduate student felt were both inappropriate—too formal or too informal—in addressing her professor. So she reformulated (means (b)) any sentence that would have included a "you" form if spoken spontaneously, like that in (17a), into a sentence lacking a "you" form, as in (17b).

(17) a. Where are you going now?
     b. Is there a class to go to now?

Example: On being asked by his visiting mother where he'd gotten his new mattress, a student—who'd spotted it in a "free box," where articles no longer wanted by their original owners are left for others—answered as in (18a). Such a dissemblance makes no explicit false statement like (18b), but omits (means (e)) embarrassing elements from a fuller truth, like that in (18c), in such a way that the addressee is led toward the false picture.

(18) a. Somebody didn't want it, so *I* took it.
     b. Somebody I know didn't need it any more, so I took it from
        him.
     c. Somebody or other threw it away in the free box, and I found it
        and took it.

Subgoal: To avoid or background the mention of an involved element because it is less important, irrelevant, or already known about.

Example: In English, omission or deletion as a means (e) for avoiding an unnecessary element must occur in conjunction with getting the right case-frame setup (means (i)). This is because such omission can take place very rarely for a subject (as seen in (18)), and only sometimes for a direct object, but is generally quite grammatically feasible for an oblique object,[4] as exemplified in (19).

(19) a. *Figure = direct object | Ground = oblique: only Ground omittable*
    i.   I sprinkled flour over the pan.
    ii. Then I sprinkled sugar.
        (understood as: Then I sprinkled sugar over the pan.)
    iii. *Then I sprinkled over the board.
        (intended meaning: Then I sprinkled flour over the board.)
  b. *Ground = direct object | Figure = oblique: only Figure omittable*
    i.   I sprinkled the pan with flour.
    ii. Then I sprinkled the board.
        (understood as: Then I sprinkled the board with flour.)
    iii. *Then I sprinkled with sugar.
        (intended meaning: Then I sprinkled the pan with sugar.)

Example: The fact of air transit, salient in (20a), can be backgrounded, as in (20b), by its conflation with the verb (means (c)); = lexicalization, as treated in Talmy 1975b: GO + by-plane = *fly*.

(20) a. I went to Hawaii last month by plane.
    b. I flew to Hawaii last month.

6.3 Sequencing (Goal c)

Example: For the propositional content that the communicator wants to convey in (21), the sentence in (21a) probably has the smoothest phrasing, thus satisfying goals (g) and (h). But the communicator may consider it more important that the notion with the most wallop appear at the end for the greatest dramatic effect (goal (c)), and so will recast the way the idea is put (means (b)) to get it there, as in (21b).

(21) a. You're really a thief disguised as a philanthropist.
    b. You act like a philanthropist, but you're really a thief.

Example: Where Event 1 occurs before Event 2, a communicator who refers to these events may want her addressee to cognize them in the same order that they occurred in and, hence, want to avoid a formulation like that in (22a). Ways for realizing this goal in English include the use of a different lexical form for the subordinating conjunction (means (c)), as in (22b); preposing the subordinate clause (means (g)), as in (22c); and the use of the "copy-cleft" construction (discussed in chapter I-6)—means (f))—as in (22d).

(22) a. E2 after E1: She went home after she stopped at the store.
   b. E1 before E2: She stopped at the store before she went home.
   c. After E1, E2: After she stopped at the store, she went home.
   d. E1, and then E2: She stopped at the store, and then she went home.

6.4   One's Character, Mood, and Attitude (Goal d)

Goal (d) is realized largely by one's (momentary) "style," which comprises selections as to the dialect or language used (means (a)) and as to elements of vocabulary, syntax, delivery, and kinesics (means (c), (d), (m)/(o), (p)). Via style, one can, for example, express one's character as macho or upper class, one's mood/state as excited or vulnerable, and one's attitude toward the topic as approving or disapproving, toward the addressee as friendly, deferential, or disdainful, and toward the situation as formal or informal. One example was already discussed in connection with (5). The following additional examples show that one's character can be projected as well by selection as to the propositional content expressed, and one's mood by the use of special morphemes.

Example: On his professor's clarifying an earlier point, one graduate student responded as in (23).

(23) That's what I misunderst- had in mind as a question.

The student's mid-utterance correction might have been undertaken solely in the goal of propositional accuracy. But it might also have resulted from a desire to be regarded one way as against another—say, as comprehensionally skillful rather than as easily confused.

Example: While riding through the countryside, a mother might speak to her child in Yiddish as in (24a), or as in (24b) using the so-called "diminutive" noun endings.

(24) a. Gib a kuk oyf di ki.
       'Give a look at the cows.'
   b. Gib a kuk oyf di kielekh.
       'Give a look at the cows-diminutive.'

In the former, the mother simply directs her child's attention to a sight. But in the latter, parallel to this, she expresses warm affection for the animals, or for her child, or in empathy with her child's potential enjoyment of the animals. The diminutive morphemes do not affect the propositional content, for there is no implication that the cows are small, young, or even intrinsically cute—merely that the speaker feels "cutely" toward them or something else in the situation.[5]

6.5   The Type of a Communication (Goal e)

There is an extensive range—greater than normally recognized and not at all cataloged—of intonational effects and delivery styles (means (l), (m), (o)) that signal how the segmental content of an utterance is to be taken— its illocutionary force, role in the ongoing interaction, and so on.

Example: Cook-Gumperz and Gumperz (1976) cite a teacher addressing her class, in part as in (25).

(25) a. At ten o'clock we'll have assembly. We'll all go out together and go to the auditorium.... When he [the principal] comes in, sit quietly and listen carefully.

b. Don't wiggle your legs. Pay attention to what I'm saying.

They characterize the differences in her delivery style for (25a), signaling this as instructions for later to the group, and for (25b), signaling this as an immediate order to an individual.

Example: Aside from the fact that the content gives it away, the utterance by the 4;7-year-old boy quoted in (26b) (taken from the videotape *Making Cookies*; Ervin-Tripp 1975)

(26) a. Woman investigator: No, you know what his name is [speaking of cameraman].
Boy: What?
Woman: Don't you remember?

b. Boy: His name is poopoo kaka. ((spoken with exaggerated enunciation, special melody, more chantlike rhythm, and laughing-sarcastic voice quality))

is clearly signaled by its delivery as intended as a teasing invitation to playful engagement with the man, rather than, say, a factual assertion of belief.

In general, a content and delivery that leave some doubt as to how a remark is intended (e.g., "You're really dumb!" said without a clear burlesque or laughing tone) often prompt an addressee to check the speaker's facial expression more closely for further cues, and have led to such culturally familiar expressions as "I can't tell if you're serious or joking" and "Smile when you say that!"[6]

6.6   Grammaticality (Goal f)

"Grammaticality" is intended here in a broad sense to refer to all of a communication system's structural canons of well-formedness—for example, for a language, its lexical and phonological, as well as syntactic, particulars. Cognitively, adherence to grammaticality is a possibly distinct function that maintains itself against such other possible cognitive functions as a drive toward regularity of pattern. This may explain the perseveration through generations of otherwise easily closed gaps or of otherwise easily regularized pattern irregularities in a language. An example of such a persistent gap is the lexicosyntactic gap of the *say to* locution, which can occur in the passive, as in (27a), but not in the active, as in (27b). An additional example is the lexicoparadigmatic gap of some perhaps two score Russian verbs—used beside otherwise comparable gapless verbs—which lack a first-person singular present form, as in (28a), and require a circumlocution there, as in (28b) (as discussed in Hetzron 1975). A final example is the lexicoderivational gap of *observant* lacking a noun form, as already discussed in (9).

(27) a.   He is said to have once been a sailor.
      b.   *They say him to have once been a sailor.

(28) a.   *Pobežu. / *Pobeždu.
           'I (will) win.'
      b.   Oderžu pobedu.
           'I (will) sustain victory.'

The drive to adhere to grammaticality can be seen in further ways. For example, consider a Russian speaker who has already uttered a string of adjectives with masculine agreement in anticipation of an upcoming masculine noun head but who then decides to switch to a different noun, one now with feminine gender. Often, such a speaker will start the phrase all over again to say the adjectives now with feminine endings, doing so even at the cost of other communicative goals, such as that of not disrupting the communicative flow. Or, again, consider the speaker cited in Jefferson 1972 who—after the other collocutor had mispronounced the Mona Lisa as the "Mama Lisa"—exclaims: "The *Ma*ma Lisa?" in sarcastic imitation. One may imagine that—even though the intended target form was clear enough from context—this speaker's sense of well-formedness was disrupted by the collocutor's mispronunciation, and was experienced strongly enough to prompt the exclamation, again even at the expense of the communicative flow.

Of course, other communicative goals sometimes win out over that of grammaticality. For example, in the preceding Russian example, some speakers might in fact just go ahead with the new feminine noun head, even though this engenders a break in concord. And we might also consider the following example.

Example: A bank customer who had asked the teller to check her savings balance spoke as in (29a). The first-stage schema that she had come up with to respond to the teller led her—as she realizes at her brief hesitation—to a grammatical blind alley. Her decision at this point is to just go ahead and complete the utterance ungrammatically rather than to start afresh with some new formulation such as that in (29b).

(29) a. Teller: Oh, if you have an automatic deposit...!
      Customer: Yeah, that's what I wanted to see ... if it happened.
   b. What I wanted was to see if that happened.

As emphasized by the functionalist perspective, many aspects of language are to varying degrees on a flexible continuum regulated solely by what, communicatively, "works," yet language seems mostly constructed on a two-tier plan of a "correct" fixed structure and the possibility of stretching or deviating from that. There appears to be a strong drive in the language learner to ascertain, and in the language user to adhere to, this "correct" structure, and it appears to have an innate psychological existence independent of the urge to communicate per se. The intuitively isolated sense for such a natively inbuilt drive is perhaps one of the factors that have led linguists through a history of paradigm and rule abstraction and to a notion of "competence" as opposed to "performance."

6.7 Felicity (Goal g)

Words and constructions are not entered in a language user's mind like items in a dictionary or reference grammar, solely with their "absolute" values (as a textbook language learner or machine-translation programmer finds out), but are instinct with various additional qualities and relative weightings. It is discriminations among these latter—that is, the operation of goal (g)—that keep colloquial words and constructions out of written prose, those of written prose out of colloquy, and obsolescent forms out of both. Within the realm of the constructionally possible—which includes, for example, multiple center embedding—they distinguish the awkward from the smooth. In general, they constitute an intrapreferential dimension among the means of a communication system.

Example: In spoken Italian, a verbal that takes a preposition, like "have need of," which is perfectly colloquial in a main clause as in (30a), gives rise in a relative clause to a sense of awkwardness over the pied-piped constituent "of which," as in (30b). To avoid this awkwardness, a speaker will often prefer to use an altogether different verbal with a different case-frame setup (means (c)), like "be of use" as in (30c).

(30) a. Ho bisogno del denaro.
     'I have need of the money.'
   b. Il denaro, di cui ho bisogno ...
     'The money, of which I have need ...'
   c. Il denaro, che mi serve ...
     'The money that is of use to me ...'

Example: In the discussion of (15), it was said that for expressing an element as topic, the preferred means in spoken English is to get it as initial subject, but a special intonational means is used when this is blocked. The fact of preference is demonstrated in (31) with an example where a lack of blockage permits the use of either means.

(31) *In answer to:* Where's the pen?
   a. It's beside the ashtray.   Preferred
   b. The ASHTRAY is beside it.   Dispreferred

6.8   Timing and Physics (Goal i)

The concern of this goal is to get one's communication to reach the addressee by adjusting its temporal and physical execution so that it will pass through the "windows" open in the temporophysical transmissional medium, or else by adjusting the medium so that it will accommodate the communication.

This includes the following: starting one's communication during another's pause so as to gain the floor, not pausing too long so as to keep the floor, and aborting an already-begun communication if another communicator has not relented first (all involve means (n)).

In the case of speech, the adjustment can also include waiting until a fire engine has passed (means (n)), talking louder when there is heavy background noise (means (m)), and turning down a too-loud radio (means (q)).

In the case of signing, it can include waiting until someone walking between oneself and the addressee has passed (means (n)), and moving to a lighter area when it is too dark to see easily (means (q)).

6.9 The Addressee's Receptivity (Goal j)

Here are understood all the characteristics of the addressee that must be taken into account in forming one's communication to ensure the addressee's comprehensional reception. This includes:

• *The addressee's receptive capacity with respect to content and signal.* Thus, one reduces the level of semantic complexity for a child or a newcomer to one's communication system (means (b)). And one signs to a deaf signer and speaks more clearly to the nonnative and the hearing-impaired (means (a), (m)).

• *The addressee's openness to receiving a communication.* One has to gauge the addressee's focus of attention, attention span, and interest. Thus, to get an idea across within the narrow slot allowed by an impatient collocutor, one may have to speak fast, sacrifice specificity for brevity (such as *might be able to* for *could*) and generally consolidate one's message (means (o), (c), (b)).

• *The addressee's background knowledge.* Since an addressee has to have enough background information to be able to interpret a communication as intended, one must assess its amount and, if too low, either tailor one's message down to it or supply the missing information. The following example illustrates these points.

Example: A host said first (32a) and then, after a moment's pause, (32b) to a visiting friend.

(32) a. Would you like some music on?

b. ... because I'm going to the bathroom.

Only after saying (32a) did the speaker realize that the listener could not have shared his own implicit background assumptions for the remark and therefore could not understand its intended meaning—namely, that the guest would be left alone during his imminent absence, perhaps in need of entertainment—and so he undertook with (32b) to correct that lack (means (b)).

6.10 The Processing Task (Goal k)

Efforts to ease the addressee's processing task can include circumventing a looming ambiguity, positioning related constituents into adjacency, and breaking up complex constructions.

Example of avoiding a possible ambiguity: *Denying* in (33a) could mean 'disclaiming facts' or 'begrudging possessions.' The verb in each sense has some distinctive case frames. These can be evoked (means (i)) with "placeholding" nonspecific nominals, eliminating ambiguity, as in (33b) and (33c).

(33) a. Then the child went through an imperious period of denying.
    b. ... denying things.
    c. ... denying people things.

Examples of breaking up a construction: Such an operation applies where there is a complicated constituent requiring much linguistic processing embedded in a complicated construction also requiring much processing. Without a breaking-up operation, the processing of the former must take place amidst the processing of the latter in what may be too cumbersome a performance task. One form of breakup is left dislocation—or, its generalization, "copy clefting," as described in chapter I-6 (also the source of the examples below). This operation provides for the processing of the formerly embedded constituent separately and beforehand. And it leaves a placeholding proform that represents the Gestalt resultant of this latter processing in the matrix construction for the processing to occur there next, which is therefore also simplified.

Thus, the breakup process applied to the presumably more basic (a) forms below converts them into the (b) forms. The process applies in (34) within an English nominal constituent, in (35) to the nouns of a signed sentence (italicized words indicate the signs actually made), and in (36) to a whole clause of an English complex sentence.

(34) a. Now we'll investigate the more general process of population stabilization.
    b. Now we'll investigate *a more general process, that of population stabilization.*

(35) a. Hank went-to Fresno.
    b. You know *Hank*? You know *Fresno*? Well, *he-went-there.*

(36) a. We stayed home because it was raining.
    b. It was raining, so (< and because of that) we stayed home.

6.11   The Semantic Context (Goal l)

Subgoal: To make the content of a communication appropriate to the "metacommunication."

For the most part, the content explicitly expressed by the actual words, phrases, and sentences of a communication, whether from a single source or in an interchange, constitutes a dotting of disconnected islets of information from the perspective of a seamless logical continuum. A fuller, more continuous conceptualization exists in the minds of the intercommunicators as a skein of knowledge and familiarities, presuppositions and expectations, presumptions and deductions. The interactional relation between the manifest communication and this metalevel is that the former have interpretable significance only within the context of the latter, while the latter emerges, shifts, and undergoes emendation from the input of the former.[7]

The metalevel can be seen as a generalization of the notion of the "speech act" (e.g., an assertion, order, request—as in Searle 1969) or of the "adjacency pair" (e.g., question/answer, request/compliance, warning/heeding—as in Sacks, Schegloff, and Jefferson 1974). These notions isolate out a singular or binomial superordinate communicative significance that holds over a short stretch. The metacommunicative level is, rather, a skein interwoven of these along with further elements.

Example: The *because* back in (32b) has no parsable meaning within the manifest communication of (32) taken by itself. It is pragmatically present, rather, as a connective to an implicit—certainly unspoken—metacommunication something like the explanation in (37).

(37) "I ask you that not because, as you might at first have thought, I felt you might like some background music as we talk, but because I'm going to the bathroom and you'll be left alone, possibly in need of entertainment."

Example: On a hot day, a customer interacted with the cashier in a drugstore as in (38).

(38) a. Customer: Are you aware that these are melting? ((putting some candy bars on the counter))
b. Checker: There's nothing we can do about it.
c. Customer: No, I mean ... hh ((breaking into a smile))
d. Checker: Oh, they really are! ((feeling a candy bar))

The checker's response in (38b) shows that she had taken the customer's metacommunication in (38a) to have been

"I want to complain about the poor quality you personnel keep your merchandise in."

The customer, realizing this meta-miscommunication, seeks in (38c) to explicitly repair it:

"*No*, I didn't mean that the way you took it, *I mean* that the melting is funny and I wanted to share the humor of it with you."

The checker in (38d) seems then to metacommunicate:

"*Oh*, now I see what you meant. I'm sorry I reacted as if you were being surly, and let me make amends with a heightened response now to your original intent."

6.12   The Interpersonal Context (Goal m)

The use of a communication system (say, speech) between people is certainly not the starting point of interpersonal relations—not phylogenetically, developmentally, or in terms of present psychological functioning—but it, rather, fits in as a component within the context of these latter phenomena.

Thus, politeness in verbal behavior is in basis the counterpart of a general predisposition of consideration toward another—that is, courtesy in speech is a particular manifestation of a general program of doing that which makes someone feel good and avoiding doing that which makes him feel bad. Likewise, curtness in one's verbal interactions with another is likely one manifestation of a general feeling toward him, such as aversion.

Example: The same boy quoted in (26) at another time has the following interaction with his father.

(39)   Boy: Daddy, how come you're here? ((father has just come in))
         Father: Well, this is where I live.
         Boy: Uh-uh. You live someplace else. ((pulls on father's shirt))
         Father: Where?
         Boy: You live in Colorado. ((said in teaseful singsong))

The boy and his father have a warm rapport based on teaseful play. On the boy's part, this latter is realized both nonverbally—here with a mildly provocative physical encroachment (the shirt tug)—and verbally with joking of the form: asserting the opposite of a known characteristic of the addressee.

6.13   Heed to Outside Effects (Goal n)

Aside from its intended purpose as a transmission from a communicator to an addressee, a communication is a physical entity that exists in the world and that therefore exerts possible effects on it. A communicator can be cognizant of these possible effects, have certain desires with regard to them, and want to adjust the characteristics of the communication accordingly.

Such adjustments can include speaking softer (means (m)) so that others around will not be bothered; communicating one's message obliquely (means (b)) or in another code (means (a)) so that others around will not understand; speaking or signing gently (means (m)) so as not to tax oneself when one is ill.

6.14 Intent for Further Effects (Goal p)

One often intends consequences and effects for one's communication beyond its bare comprehension by the addressee. One kind of intended effect is to induce the addressee to perform a certain action, such as to answer a question or carry out a request or order. It is in fact such an intention for further action that turns an otherwise plain communication into a question, request, or order. Another kind is to induce the addressee into a certain state or mood—for example, to cheer someone up by recounting pleasant or diverting matters.

One may also intend effects on others around one outside of the explicit addressee. Thus, while manifestly addressing the addressee, one can introduce elements into the message that are intended for the others—for instance, information one wants them to have or hints one wants them to take (such as to let oneself and one's addressee be alone).[8]

6.15 Monitoring and Repair (Goal r)

It can be theorized that the faculty of assessing heard speech is (developmentally prior to and) partially distinct from that of producing speech, and that it comes to operate on the latter's output in a feedback loop that constitutes the initial linguistic self-monitoring system in the individual.[9] Subsequent development, as the theory might continue, involves the internalization of the monitoring process to progressively earlier stages in the preexpressional formation of an utterance. When such monitoring is conscious, one in effect "hears" with the "mind's ear" how an utterance will sound if produced. It is on the basis of monitoring, whether preproductional or postproductional, that an utterance, or any communication, is assessed for its level of adequacy in realizing the moment's communicative goals.

A communication that continues on unemended is usually to be taken as having passed the monitoring system's adequacy requirements of the moment (unless the system is not operating, as happens no doubt at many moments of, e.g., play speech and language pathology). Otherwise, the operation of the system includes the following measures.

1. indicating the cancelation of an earlier ill-formed element, and replacing it with a well-formed one, in satisfying the goals for grammaticality, felicity, or aesthetics (f, g, h)
2. for an earlier propositional element, canceling and replacing it, qualifying it, emending it, or elaborating it, in satisfaction of the goal (a) of expressing certain ideational content accurately
3. halting the immediate topic and in its place giving auxiliary information, realized as needed for the addressee's comprehension (goal (j))

Example of (2): To a playmate, a 4;3-year-old girl says (from the video *Playing Doctor*; Ervin-Tripp 1975):

(40) When I lie down—When I bend over my back hurts.

The girl's original schema for her utterance seems to have had only loose control over ideational content, selecting a more common locution, "lie down," in the generally appropriate semantic area rather than the more accurate locution, "bend over." The girl corrects this, though, after hearing it.

Example of (3): A girl recounts a story to a friend as follows (taken from Keenan and Schieffelin, 1975):

(41) My sister, when we were up in camp, when she was 12, and all the guys were 16, ((pause)) and 15, they don' wanna go out with 12-year-olds. So I told everyone that she was 13 1/2, almost 14.

More than likely, this episode exists in the girl's memory in two tiers: a less accessible body of background context and specifics, and a readily accessible upshot. The upshot here might be something like "My sister wanted the guys to go out with her, so I told them she was 14." In her own reminiscences, the girl might well become fully conscious only of the upshot and experience the remainder as an implicit background that lends sense to it. And she may rely on the upshot as a handle by which to draw the background tier explicitly forth into consciousness if necessary. In starting to tell the story, her first impulse, it seems, is to express the upshot. She immediately realizes, however, that she must first backtrack to prepare the ground for the addressee. In the present example, in fact, she makes a succession of such corrections, at each going back to a further point of background.

7   LANGUAGE COMPARISON AND CHANGE

The goals and means outlined to this point can vary in their combinations and strengths across languages or diachronically within a single language while retaining their character as an integrated system.

7.1   Language Comparison

Cultures and subcultures have different (constellations of) communicative goals and realize them with different (combinations of) expressive means, as investigated in works in the tradition of Gumperz and Hymes (1972). We address a more specifically linguistic issue within this: that languages have different means available for realizing the same communicative purpose, sometimes with typological/universalist implications.

Example: Returning to the example of answers to the question "Where's the pen?", first discussed in connection with (15), we notice that marking the topic element by getting it in initial position as sentence subject is the means used, in the case of simple location, in Spanish and Russian as well as English. Illustrations are provided by (42a) to (42c).

(42) *English:*   a. (It's) on the table.   d. JOHN has it.
     Spanish: b. (Está) en la mesa.   e. Lo tiene Juan.
     Russian: c. (Ono) na stole.   f. (Ono) u Ivana.

But where, as in the case of possession, English is blocked from using this means because the topic must be expressed as the direct object in a rigid SVO system—and so must resort to the means of special stress and intonation, as in (42d)—the other languages proceed differently. Spanish, in (42e), still gets the topic in initial position, even though as direct object, because it has the availability of flexible word order (means (g)). And Russian, in (42f), continues to use the original preferred means—getting the topic element to be sentence initial as the subject—because of the availability of lexical means (c), namely, its preposition *u* 'in the possession of'—which permits this formulation. Thus, the sentence in (42f) can be rendered as "(It) [is] in-the-possession of-John.

Example: With regard to marking an utterance for the way in which it is to be taken, discussed above in connection with examples (25) and (26), English speakers may employ the special intonation and delivery style (means (l), (m)) available in their language to mark the message in (43a) as a playful warning. But Atsugewi (a Hokan Indian language) has a special verb-inflectional mode (means c)—which I have termed the "admonitive" and which is usually translatable as 'I/you/he ... better watch out lest ...'—that exactly expresses a warning, often playful, as in (43b).

(43) *English*:   a. I'm going to tickle you!
     Atsugewi: b. Tamlawilcahki.
                    "You-better-watch-out-or-I'll-tickle-you."

Example: The preferences among alternative means that constitute felicity vary from language to language. Thus, the use of the passive (means (f)) to background a human subject is fairly natural in English, as in (44a), but is quite forced in Yiddish, as in (44b). In Yiddish, the use of the nonspecific-human pronoun (means (c)) is preferred, and when this is combined with the use of direct object fronting (means (g)), as in (44c), the resultant effect is virtually identical to that of the English passive.

(44) *English*:   a. That claim wasn't believed.
     Yiddish: b. Di tayne iz nisht gegleybt gevorn.
                       'That claim was not believed.'   Forced
                    c. Di tayne hot men nisht gegleybt.
                       'That claim one did not believe.'   Natural

Example: Certain preferences among alternative means may be universal. But they can be exercised only in those languages with the availability of the preferred alternative and not in those that lack it.

Thus, there may well be a universal dispreference of pied-piping. As seen in (30), this means can be avoided in Italian relative clauses only by a shift to a different lexical verb. By contrast, English speakers have no problem: they can avoid a construction like (45a) because they can dangle their prepositions, as in (45b).

(45) a. Any book on which I can get my hands ...
     b. Any book I can get my hands on ...

Comparably, one means, as against others, may be universally easier in its processing requirements but be enjoyed only in those languages in which it is available. This would seem to be the case for a ready derivational means by which a notion lexicalized in one part of speech can be equivalently expressed in another, as *-ness* acts in English to convert an adjective into a noun. But English has no such means for converting other parts of speech into an adjective—as Yiddish does with its *-(d)ik* ending

—and usually must resort to the construction of a whole adjective phrase or to an altogether different lexical item.

(46) *English*   *Yiddish*

Other	*Adjective*	*Other*	*Adjective*
uncle	av-uncular	feter	feterdik
now	current	itst	itstik
enough	sufficient	genug	genugik
soon	that will come soon	bald	baldik
this year	for this year	di yor	di-yorik

(e.g., a calendar for this year/*a this year('s) calendar: a di-yoriker kalendar)

Example: In (42) and (43), the means for marking an element as topic and for marking an utterance as a warning were compared for a two- and three-language sample. In a like way, any single factor—structural, semantic, or otherwise communicational—can be checked through the panoply of communication systems for the scope and configuration of its possible manifestational range (a method that Greenberg (e.g., 1961) helped perfect within spoken languages).

Thus, the means for expressing modality (possibility, necessity, and so on) include the following: specific verb inflectional modes, like the subjunctive and optative in classical Greek; auxiliary verbs, like *can* and *might* in English; independent (adverbial) particles and phrases, like *perhaps* and *in all likelihood* in English; and a specifically modal sentence constituent, recognizable as a new grammatical category, as noted by Susan Steele for Luiseño and Aztec. Other means for expressing modality include an embedding matrix sentence, like French's *il faut que* 'it is necessary that ...'; a special syntactic construction, "periphrasis," like that for necessity in Latin (e.g., where "I must go" is expressed as "[it]-is to-be-gone to-me"); and, in signing, certain head and facial gestures (e.g., where "I should have gone to the party" can be expressed by signing "I went to the party" while shaking the head with a grimace of displeasure, this having the meaning "It's unfortunate that (I) didn't").

7.2 Language Change

At every point in the history of its usage, a language is a comprehensive system whose available means together must handle all that needs expressing. Changes through time might accordingly be expected to show correlations between the dropping out of some means and the development of others, as the pattern of available means maintains a shifting-balance level of adequacy. Li and Thompson (1976) have considered the expression of causation through the history of Mandarin from this systems perspective (as is also touched on in chapter I-8).

Consideration in this same light is provoked, as a possible further example, by three universalistically unusual syntactic means that coexist in present-day Tagalog (as treated in Schachter and Otanes 1972). The first is an elaborate system of verb voices—a lexical verb can be morphologically marked to fit into many alternate case-frame setups. The second is indication of a nominal's (in)definiteness by its surface case, accordingly mediated by the first system. The third is the relativization of a clause by the participialization of its verb; again, the first system permits the general applicability of this means by allowing a nominal of almost any underlying case to become subject. One may speculate that these three means developed in correlation with each other. If, for example, for other reasons Tagalog's precursor had lost, or been blocked from developing, independent morphemes to mark definiteness and relativity—as English, for one, has in its *a/the* and *which/that*—that condition might have spurred the development of the more unusual means and the elaboration of the voice system to undergird them.

Notes

1. This chapter is a moderately revised version of Talmy 1976a.

2. The individual's pattern of balances does not, of course, stop within the confines of his communicative system, but extends into the rest of the personality. For example, a person with a great need to express himself but with a low degree of verbal facility may need to accommodate to the resultant standstill with the rest of his psychological system. (This could include a solution—e.g., possibly, going out dancing more often and putting more expression in the dance movements.)

3. Such structures, again, are understood to consist not only of a syntactic framework, but also of the pattern in which semantic content is distributed over that framework. Their familiarity is what enables an interlocutor, in the case of conversation, to project the arrival of a suitable entry point (as discussed in Sacks, Schegloff, and Jefferson 1974).

4. Here, it can be said that the whole oblique constituent undergoes "pied-piping deletion," for the preposition follows its nominal into extinction.

5. This last matter—that the diminutive morphemes often express a more global feeling, though attaching to the nearest noun—is clearer in the example of a speaker fondly urging his cat *Es fun dayn shisele* "Eat from your bowl-diminutive!") though feeling nothing for the cat's everyday bowl.

6. A metalinguistic awareness of this distinction between the propositional content of the segmental forms of an utterance and the discourse purpose of the utterance's delivery can be seen in a certain form of wordplay once current among schoolchildren. In this wordplay, a speaker follows his own or another's remark with a quotative aside, of the kind found in written prose, that specifies the style and intent of the remark. An example is the following: " 'We could go to the movies,' he suggested tentatively."

7. Garfinkel (1972:78) sees the same two levels—referring to them as "documentary evidences" and the "underlying pattern"—and the same interrelation between them: "The underlying pattern was not only derived from a course of individual documentary evidences but the documentary evidences in their turn were interpreted on the basis of 'what was known' and anticipatorily knowable about the underlying patterns."

Fillmore (1975:136–137), using the terms "text" and "image," clearly has a comparable notion: "A text induces its interpreter to construct an image.... The image the interpreter creates early in the text guides his interpretation of successive portions of text."

Cook-Gumperz and Gumperz (1976) speak in a comparable way of "conversational communication" generating "context" and of the latter's helping the interpretation of the former.

8. It may be alternatively interpreted that the fraction of one's message that is directed obliquely is in its own right a communication to an addressee, here a covert one, perhaps better referred to as the "intended recipient."

9. In this vein, Zakharova (1958:283–284) notes from her investigations of Russian preschoolers' language acquisition: "In the process of constructing case forms of unfamiliar words, children often pronounce them aloud with different endings, as if deciding in this manner which form would be the correct one in the given case, correcting themselves and deciding on the ending only after that."

She goes on to speculate: "The choice of the correct endings through oral repetition of some of them can probably be explained by the fact that the additional sound and kinesthetic signals from the speech organs, entering the cerebral cortex during the process of repetition, facilitate control over the speech activity of the child. . . ."

PART 3
OTHER COGNITIVE SYSTEMS

Chapter 7

The Cognitive Culture System

1 INTRODUCTION

This chapter outlines a cognitivist analysis of the transmission and maintenance of culture.[1] **Cognitivism** indicates that cultural patterns exist primarily because of the cognitive organization in each of the individuals collectively making up a society. This analysis arrives at particular positions on the issues of what is universal across cultures and what varies, of what is innate and what is learned, and of how the individual and the group are related. This cognitivist view of culture disputes several other theoretical positions, such as the position that culture has mainly or solely an autonomous existence beyond the cognition of individual humans. Our aim here has been, first, to array arguments and evidence for an individual-based cultural cognitivism in a way that consolidates this position, and, second, to lay out a framework in which further research could amplify, complement, or emend this position.

1.1 Overview of Cultural Cognitivism

Our general perspective is that there has evolved in the human species an innately determined brain system whose principal function is the acquisition, exercise, and imparting of culture. This system for cultural cognition encompasses a number of cognitive capacities and functions, most of which are either weak or absent in other species. This system does not operate solely through a few simple forms of algorithmic processing applied broadly and iteratively. Rather, it processes culture as a highly differentiated, systematic, and structured complex that includes certain categories of phenomena but not others. The content of this structured cultural complex pertains both to conceptual-affective patterns and to behavior patterns. Aspects of the cognitive culture system's functioning are accessible to consciousness, but it seems probable that consciousness is not a necessary or automatic concomitant of many operations of the system.

This view that a cognitive system specific to culture has evolved contrasts with a generally held assumption—itself not always articulated—that human culture occurs simply as a concomitant of other cognitive faculties, such as general intelligence or perhaps language. Some assume further that culture is not an especially coherent structure but a collection of particulars arising as a by-product of more basic cognitive operations. The view advanced here, however, is that culture is a highly organized cognitive construction, and that little in cognition of such a complex and systematic character "just happens" without specific neural provision for it.

The cognitive culture system operates in each individual in accordance with its innately structured program. As stated above, the functions of this system are the acquisition, exercise, and imparting of culture. These three functions can be given the following introductory sketch.

In its acquisition function, the cognitive culture system within an individual assesses the conceptual-affective and behavioral patterns that it sees others exhibit, as well as attending to instruction on such patterns, and internalizes what it has abstracted from this assessment and instruction. It performs the process of assessment in a highly structured way. The process includes determination of the outside groups most relevant to the self, abstraction across the members of each such group, attention to only certain categories of phenomena manifested by those members, and resolution of conflicts among the patterns of different groups. While this acquisition function may operate most extensively and internalize patterns most deeply during the individual's childhood, it can remain in operation throughout the individual's lifetime, processing cultural changes or transpositions to new cultures.

In its second function of exercising culture, the cognitive culture system implements the cultural patterns it has acquired, both to produce them and to comprehend new instances of their production by others. In the case of production, the system generates a conceptual-affective pattern in the individual and directs the individual in the performance of behavioral practices in accordance with the cultural structure it has acquired. In the case of comprehension, the system guides the individual in the perception and interpretation of ongoing cultural manifestations by others, also in accordance with the cultural structure it has acquired.

Third, in its imparting function, the cognitive culture system can direct the individual in the performance of certain practices, such as teaching, that facilitate the acquisition of culture by others.

The issue of cultural universals—as well as of cultural differences—must in our view be approached within the perspective of a theory of cultural cognition. One factor that, with certain qualifications, is universal is the innately determined processing program of the cognitive culture system itself (as this will be characterized below). This system does exhibit some range of variation across individuals, for example, as to the particulars of the processing program, the system's accessibility to consciousness, or the system's degree of adaptability. But in the main, the functioning of the cognitive culture system is uniform. Accordingly, while cultures differ in many respects, they appear to have a commonality in the way they are structured and in the types of phenomena involved in this structuring, a commonality that can in our view be traced to the inherited uniformity of the cognitive culture system in the brain. To be sure, some universals of cultural patterning may be due to common conditions affecting human groups or to the operations of innate cognitive systems other than that of cultural cognition. Still, the proposal here is that the cognitive culture system accounts for much of what is universal across cultures. And, in a complementary fashion, much of what varies across cultures involves phenomena with respect to which the cognitive culture system is not constrained.

To provide an orientation to cultural universality at the outset, we offer Murdock's (1965) list of 72 cultural universals—that is, of phenomena present in all the cultures of which he had knowledge. Though much of Murdock's work is now considered outdated by many anthropologists, the investigation of cultural universals has on the other hand not been an active agenda in anthropology in the intervening years, so that it is appropriate to reconnect with that older work here as a renewed starting point. As we noted, cultural universality can arise from a number of causes and is not ipso facto proof that a phenomenon plays a structural role in culture. Accordingly, without further evidence, we accord no significance for cognitive structure to any particular items on the list. Nevertheless, it is likely that enough items on the list tend in the direction of having structural status to serve as an indicator of what universals of cultural structure might consist of. In addition, this list will serve as the basis for a subsequent contrast with universals of linguistic structure (see section 3.5.1). Here then, in its original alphabetical order, is Murdock's list (1965:89).

age-grading, athletic sports, bodily adornment, calendar, cleanliness training, community organization, cooking, cooperative labor, cosmology, courtship, dancing, decorative art, divination, division of labor, dream interpretation, education, eschatology, ethics, ethnobotany, etiquette, faith healing, family, feasting, fire-making, folklore, food taboos, funeral rites, games, gestures, gift-giving, government, greetings, hair-styles, hospitality, housing, hygiene, incest taboos, inheritance rules, joking, kin groups, kinship nomenclature, language, law, luck superstitions, magic, marriage, meal times, medicine, modesty concerning natural functions, mourning, music, mythology, numerals, obstetrics, penal sanctions, personal names, population policy, postnatal care, pregnancy usages, property rights, propitiation of supernatural beings, puberty customs, religious ritual, residence rules, sexual restrictions, soul concepts, status differentiation, surgery, tool making, trade visiting, weaning, weather control

1.2   Parallelisms between Cultural Cognition and Linguistic Cognition

Many of the characteristics here proposed for the cognitive culture system evidently parallel characteristics of the cognitive language system as this was posited in the Chomskyan tradition—the so-called "language acquisition device" or "LAD" (Chomsky 1965). The parallelisms include the following. In the Chomskyan conception, the language system, too, is believed to be an innately determined brain system that has evolved to its present state in the human species. It directs the acquisition of language, the production and comprehension of language, and some might say also the facilitation of language acquisition by others. It also includes "universal grammar"—that is, the complex of requirements, constraints, and parameters that underlie most of the structural commonalities present across languages.

However, in pointing to a parallelism, we do not mean to imply that all the assumptions in the Chomskyan tradition pertaining to the LAD apply as well to the culture system, or even that they are all true of the language system either. There is much to challenge in the autonomous modularity that the Chomskyan and Fodorian traditions ascribe to the language system, and any extension of this attribution to the putative culture system would require even greater challenge. In fact, it is assumed here that both the language system and the culture system are much more greatly integrated and interpenetrated with connections from other cognitive systems than is envisioned by the strict modularity notion generally associated with the LAD concept (as in Fodor 1983). Thus, to express its distinctive conception, cultural cognition is here termed the cognitive culture system, rather than, say, the "culture acquisition device"—or, presumably, the "CAD."

Some of the parallelisms between the linguistic and the cultural cognitive systems may arise from their evolutionary history. Our assumption is that the cognitive systems underlying language and culture were the last two cognitive systems to have evolved in the lineage leading to humans. In both cases, the characteristics they developed were presumably conditioned by the other cognitive systems already in place, systems such as perception in different modalities, motor control, memory, attention, and inferencing. Further, the two cognitive systems presumably evolved over much the same time period, hence, coevolved, developing their properties interactively. In addition to the language-culture parallelisms cited just above as well as throughout the chapter, we can note here that, of all the cognitive systems, only language and culture extensively exhibit the pattern of a universal abstract structure underlying a variability of instantiation determined by the social group (i.e., various particular languages and cultures). Despite such parallelisms, though, language and culture have evolved as distinct cognitive systems, as section 3.5 argues.

1.3   The "Overlapping Systems" Model of Cognitive Organization

In contrast with the modularity model, converging lines of evidence in the author's research point to the following picture of human cognitive organization. Human cognition comprehends a certain number of relatively distinguishable cognitive systems of fairly extensive scope. This research has considered similarities and dissimilarities of structure—in particular of conceptual structure—between language and each of these other cognitive systems: (visual and kinesthetic) perception, reasoning, affect, attention, memory, planning, and cultural structure. The general finding is that each cognitive system has some structural properties that may be uniquely its own, some further structural properties that it shares with only one or a few other cognitive systems, and some fundamental structural properties that it has in common with all the cognitive systems. We term this view the **overlapping systems** model of cognitive organization (see the introduction to this volume for further details).

In this chapter, to make the case for a distinct cognitive culture system, we emphasize the factors that tend to distinguish cultural cognition from other types of psychological functioning. However, we also identify a number of similarities between cultural cognition and other cognitive systems, especially noting repeated parallelisms between the culture system and the language system.

2 CHARACTERISTICS OF THE COGNITIVE CULTURE SYSTEM

In this section, we examine more closely the functioning of the cognitive culture system within the individual in the acquisition, exercise, and imparting of culture. We then examine what is universal and what is variable in these functions. Finally, we examine how the operation of these functions within the individual can account for patterns at the group level.

2.1 The Acquisition and Exercise of Culture

In its acquisition and exercise functions, the cognitive culture system within an individual either includes or helps orchestrate several different clusters of cognitive processing. The cluster largely emphasized in this chapter might be generally termed that of the **assessment** forms of processing. In this section, we go into assessment processes and then briefly discuss other clusters.

We can give a summary overview of the assessment processes. In general, in its range of operations, this cluster directs the attention of the self in a systematically differentiated way to the surrounding individuals. Specifically, it assesses the surrounding society for the groups that make it up. It concludes which of these groups the self is a member of. In accordance with certain structural criteria, it abstracts a schematic pattern from across the behaviors manifested by the members of each group. It reconciles any conflicts among such schemas. It internalizes the results of these operations as the major part of the individual's understanding of the social world. And it helps shape the individual's own practices and conceptual/affective manifestations in relatively close accord with the schemas abstracted from the self-identified groups.

2.1.1 Ascertaining Groups Relevant to the Self and Assessing Their Patterns To recapitulate, the present analysis posits that there is a specific cognitive system innate in humans that is involved with the acquisition and maintenance of culture and that functions in the following way: It directs the individual, particularly the developing child, to preferentially attend to and observe certain aspects of the behavior of the people most directly interacting with that individual, and to assess these observations

for certain kinds of regularities, patterns, and norms. The behavior observed in this way includes not only others' overt physical actions but, crucially, also the referential and psychological content—the ideas, affect, and so on—that they select for expression or otherwise manifest. The term "behavior" throughout this chapter will be used in this broad sense to cover both practice and discourse, including all the thought and affect thus manifested or represented. Our use of the term "behavior" is specifically not intended to evoke any associations with the tradition or descendants of behaviorism.

As already noted, this cognitive system for assessing group behavior concomitantly assesses which groups of people around the individual are the relevant ones across which it will abstract its generalizations. Thus, exposed to a complex enough society, the cognitive culture system may partition its surroundings into what it will see as several distinct groups of relevance to it, say, a family group, a gender group, a peer group, an ethnic group, a religious group, a group based on class or other social status, and a national group (and at the broadest level, as will be discussed below, an "entity" group, namely, that of humans as against animals or objects).

For example, in a boy from a Chinese family recently emigrated to America, the operation of his cognitive culture system can assess as relevant to him such groups as his immediate kinsfolk for his family, males for his gender, youngsters of roughly his age for his peer group, Chinese people for his ethnicity, Buddhists for his religion, working people for his class, and Americans for his nationality.

Given the appropriate circumstances, the cognitive culture system can conclude that several groups at the same level of organization, such as two ethnic or peer groups, are relevant to the self. For example, the daughter of a Jewish father and an African-American mother can feel herself to belong to two ethnic groups, both among Jews and among African-Americans, while a high school boy who is on the football team and in the science club can feel himself to be a member of both those two different peer groups.

The cognitive culture system can generate certain identity-related experiential categories built on its assessment that a particular group of individuals—call them Xs—is relevant to the self. Thus, the culture system can generate the experience that the self is a "member" of the Xs. Further, it can generate the experience that, as part of its identity, the self "is" an X. And perhaps still further, it can generate the sense that there is an abstractable essence of *X*ness that the self "incorporates" as a characteristic.

It is likely that the culture system in an individual also attends to and abstracts patterns across other groups in his surroundings that the system assesses as groups to which the individual does not belong. These assessments, however, are not made with any design for their eventual execution by the self. Rather, the functions served by such assessments are the increase of knowledge about the surrounding social structure, and the refinement of the patterns of behavior involved in membership in his own groups in accordance with the encounters that these do or will have with the other groups. Such assessments may also serve the function of clarifying other group behaviors as a "negative model" for what the self will strive to avoid resembling, so as to more clearly consolidate and signal his own group memberships. On identifying the groups to which the self belongs, the cognitive culture system probably causes the individual's attention to be directed more intensely and minutely to the patterns of behavior exhibited by the members of these groups—given that the self will need to emulate them closely—than to the non-self-identified groups. There may even be some active disattention to such other groups, perhaps with a concomitant experience in consciousness to the effect of "I need not or should not know about that group because I am not one of them."[2]

We have so far discussed two of the processes in the assessment cluster within the cognitive culture system: ascertaining the particular groups relevant to the self and ascertaining the particular patterns of behavior manifested across each such group. But these forms of processing cannot operate independently of each other or in strict sequence. Rather, as with much else in the organizing of cognition, they interact and co-determine each other.

2.1.2 Types of Accommodation to Incompatible Patterns The cognitive culture system can conclude that there are incompatibilities or conflicts between the patterns it detects in two or more different groups assessed as relevant to the self, whether these groups are at the same or different levels of organization. For example, the boy in the earlier immigrant family can experience a conflict between the patterns of his family's Chinese culture and those of the surrounding American culture. The girl may experience incompatibilities arising from her mixed ethnic parentage, and the high school boy from his dual social affiliation. In such circumstances, the culture system can adopt one out of a set of available accommodations or resolutions to the incompatibilities. Accommodations of this sort can include focusing on one pattern to the relative exclusion of the other patterns, developing a distinctive blend of two or more of the patterns, and developing psychologically compartmentalized forms of each of the patterns. Each of these types of accommodation is next considered more closely. We can here note in addition that the cognitive culture system can also address conflicts through various combinations of these accommodation types applied in various proportions.

2.1.2.1 Accommodation by Selecting One of the Incompatible Patterns over the Others   One type of accommodation—what could be termed the **selection** type of resolution—consists of a focus on and the adoption of one of the competing patterns to the relative exclusion of the others. A culture system may settle on this form of resolution because it is more consonant with the individual's other cognitive traits, giving it preferential attention as well as a greater sense of relevance and meaningfulness to the individual.

For example, the immigrant boy might settle on adopting the Chinese cultural patterns of his family—perhaps because he associates it with warmth and intimacy, which figure importantly in his particular cognitive configuration—and take the home worldview, values, behaviors, and even language into his dealings with the macro-culture. Alternatively, he might adopt the patterns of the surrounding American culture—perhaps because the need for acceptance by his peers and a desire to move freely in the larger world figure more importantly in his cognitive configuration— so that he brings the new worldview, values, behaviors, and language into his family home.

2.1.2.2 Accommodation by Blending the Incompatible Patterns   Another form of accommodation to assessed incompatibilities—what can be termed the **blending** type of resolution—consists of the development or construction in the individual of a distinctive hybrid mixture of components from two or more of the conflicting cultural patterns, or indeed the creation of some novel fusions. For example, the immigrant boy might develop a single, approximately homogeneous personal pattern manifested equally in the home and outside, but a pattern that blends together aspects of both the Chinese and the American worldview, values, behavior, and so on.

2.1.2.3 Accommodation by Separately Compartmentalizing Each Incompatible Pattern
A third form of accommodation—what can be termed the **compartmentalization** type—involves the individual's acquisition of both or all of the conflicting patterns, but with each pattern maintained separately in a relatively intact form close to its source character, and manifested mainly in its corresponding context. The individual switches back and forth between the different cultural patterns in the course of shifting between contexts. This accommodation rests on our more general psychological capacity to compartmentalize, maintaining alternative patterns side by side.

In the case of the immigrant boy, an accommodation of this type would entail his experiencing and manifesting Chinese worldview, values, behavior, and so forth when at home or in other Chinese contexts, while switching to the American pattern when in a macro-cultural context.

2.1.2.4 Linguistic Parallels to Cultural Accommodation Types
Linguistic parallels to these different accommodations to cultural conflict can appear in an individual exposed to two or more distinct languages or dialects. For example, paralleling accommodation by selection, a young woman who moves from Texas to New York may retain her original dialect intact—or, alternatively, she may acquire the new New York dialect rather fully and retain it even when visiting Texas. Or, as with the blending accommodation, she may develop a distinctive blend of the two dialects that she uses both when visiting her Texas relatives (who think she has lost her Texas accent) and when she is with her New York friends (who think she still retains her original Texas accent). Or, as with the compartmentalizing accommodation, she may learn to control both dialects and switch between them as she shifts between the corresponding contexts.

2.1.3 The Structural Character of Cultural Cognition
To set up foils for comparison so as to put the actual properties of the system into greater relief, we note that the operation of the cognitive culture system in assessing groups and their behavior is not comparable to setting up video-audio recording equipment in the midst of a group setting. Nor can the cultural patterns of behaving and cognizing that a child develops be explained solely as resulting from some relatively simple algorithmic process of averaging or of norm formation across some undifferentiated body of percepts. Rather, such patterns show dependence on organized structure that governs both the observations made and the cognitive forma-

tions created. The culture system is innately configured in such a way as to analyze out only certain aspects of behavioral phenomena, and to process these aspects not simply to produce statistical norms but also to generate conceptual structures that are articulated and compounded in specific innately determined ways.

Presumably as functions of its innate design, the cognitive culture system imputes or discerns a particular structure in externally observable phenomena and selects certain aspects of that structure for internalization and reproduction. This structure includes the categorization of surrounding entities at different levels of granularity for the purpose of selective modeling, the differentiation of distinct behavior patterns within any such category, the schema-based abstraction of a behavior pattern from across a range of exemplars of the pattern by different individuals, and the distinguishing of a behavior pattern from the personal mannerisms of its execution by any one individual. We next examine these forms of structuring in order. The existence of such complex and extensive structure is one of the arguments for the existence of a specialized cognitive system that is tailored to it.

2.1.3.1 *Categorization of Surrounding Entities for Selective Modeling*
Beginning with the individual's categorization of external entities and looking first at a coarser level of granularity, we note that the child will form the cognitive categories of people, animals, and inanimate objects (among others). He will select the behaviors exhibited by people for acquisition but will ignore the activities of the other two categories for this purpose.

For example, the child will pick up on the movement patterns of the people around him with respect to the way they get food into their mouth, perform toilet functions, keep clean, and get from one room into another. But the culture-acquiring child does not internalize and reproduce the movement patterns of, say, the family's dog or cow performing these same activities (unless imitating them for humor or the like). Thus, the child does not lap up water or move his mouth to where the food is instead of bringing it to his mouth with his hands, he does not lift one leg to urinate against a tree, he does not lick himself to get clean or rapidly twirl his torso left and right after immersion in water to dry off, and he does not trot on all fours to get to the next room.

Comparably, the child does not internalize and reproduce the movement patterns of inanimate objects in their manifestation of analogous functions (again, except as imitation for humor or the like). Thus, the child does not imitate the patterns of a grinder receiving meat in its hopper, of a sponge when it is squeezed and liquid emerges from it, of a shirt in a washing machine or of the washing machine itself, or of a ball rolling from one location to another. However apparent, observations like these cannot be taken for granted if the aim is to limn out the foundational structural properties of cultural cognition.

The process of categorization at a finer level of granularity has already been discussed. Thus, in addition to selecting one out of the preceding three broad categories, the child differentially selects for cultural acquisition from among various more finely delimited categorial alternatives, such as those pertaining to gender, peer group, ethnic group, and social status. The main point earlier was that the cognitive culture system assesses which groups (coarse or fine) the individual belongs to. The point here is that, on the basis of this structured assessment, the cognitive culture system largely sets these groups as the domains over which to exercise its processes of abstraction for behavioral patterns.

2.1.3.2 *Differentiation of Distinct Behavior Patterns*   Each category of individuals that the cognitive culture system of the child establishes manifests a great range of behaviors. If the culture system functioned by assessing across this full range without first differentiating them, the result would be a blur of superimposed movements. Instead, the culture system distinguishes particular behavior patterns at all levels of granularity and determines the ways these patterns nest one within another or otherwise relate.

For example, at their headquarters in Jerusalem, the Gerer sect of Hassidim perform a number of distinct rituals during Sabbath day observances. In one ritual, the Rebe—spiritual leader of the sect—sits against one wall, and the men and boys form a large circle that moves clockwise in front of him. The greater part of the circle away from the Rebe's location is tight, pressed, and slow moving, whereas along the stretch of the circle before the Rebe, the members suddenly space out and move very rapidly. In another ritual, the Rebe sits at a table behind a stout banister. The men and boys exchange the fresh outer garments they had been wearing for old worn ones and suddenly gather in a large group pressing up against the banister with great physical exertion. Some individuals not in this press pass water bottles forward into the group for the participants to drink from in their exertions, while other previously free individuals run with some force into the outer boundary of the group and penetrate into it a short distance before their momentum is absorbed. The concept in both rituals is that the expression of a straining to reach the Rebe is a representation of striving toward God. In a third ceremonial activity, a small group of men forms into a choir to sing part of the liturgy.

Our point here is that the cognitive culture system of a child in this setting would have to perform operations of segmentation on the continuum of activity so as to emerge with separate schemas for the different rituals, as well as for the component parts of each ritual. That is, the culture system has to analyze the flow of occurrence with great sensitivity to its structure. If it were otherwise, a child's cultural learning might emerge not with differentiated rituals, but with an amalgam or mélange—in this case, maybe the conception of a dense pack of people singing and wearing both old and new garments that rotates clockwise and through which a sparser pocket moves.

2.1.3.3 Schematic Abstraction across Exemplars of a Behavior Pattern

The preceding subsection dealt with the structural nature of the cognitive culture system in its segmentation of the flow of activity into behavioral units. But each such behavior pattern is manifested in different ways by different members of the culture, or even by a single member of the culture on different occasions. Thus, the cognitive culture system here must further assess the culturally relevant structure embedded in these differing manifestations—that is, determine what the underlying schema is—and abstract only that as its model.

To illustrate, consider a Sabbath service in an orthodox synagogue of the East European Ashkenazic Yiddish-speaking tradition (see Zborowski and Herzog 1952). In the course of conducting their prayer activity—*davenen*—the men exhibit certain variations. While reading from the prayer book, all sway rhythmically (*shoklen zikh*), but some bend their torsos forward and back, some rotate their torsos right and left, and some alternate between the two. Some limit the forward-back swaying to a slight head nod, while others bend energetically at the waist. All utter the words of the prayers, but some mumble with barely moving lips, while others speak out loudly. Some sit, while others stand or alternate between the two. Though most orient their bodies roughly toward the front, different individuals face different directions. Some locate themselves in particular spots within the synagogue on a regular basis, while others move about, praying as they walk.

In observing this variety of manifestations of the behavioral unit known as *davenen*, the child must abstract the structural delineations that are criterial for the davening activity as culturally recognized. The child cannot "average" across all this variety without emerging with a blur. What, after all, is the average of walking, sitting, and standing? To be sure, certain averaging processes must go on and have their proper place. For example, each synagogue may have its own range in the magnitude of the swaying movements, and the child will assimilate this range and remain within it. Even here, though, the child might observe structural correlations between different degrees of swaying and, say, categories of age and personality type. Thus what the cognitive culture system of the child is mainly involved in here is the determination of structural schemas and their abstraction from across a variety of executions.

2.1.3.4   The Distinguishing of a Behavior Pattern from Personal Mannerisms of Its Execution   Any adult's execution of a cultural behavior pattern is inevitably enmeshed within and shaped by the personal mannerisms of that individual. Such mannerisms include the physical and nervous control characteristics of the individual's body, her personality and idiosyncrasies, and her shifting moods. In assessing the behavior of another individual, part of the structural functioning of the cognitive culture system in someone acquiring a culture is to discriminate the abstract schema of the behavior pattern from personal mannerisms in order to select the one but not the other for internalization and reproduction.

For example, a Mexican child will learn to tear off a piece of tortilla, fold it into a particular configuration, and use it to scoop food off her plate and carry it to her mouth. But she will not adopt the slow, awkward, and jerky movements of her arthritic grandmother as she eats her food with tortilla pieces. Nor will she adopt the crude quick ripping movement that her mother uses to remove a piece from a tortilla when she is angry. Comparably, she will not adopt her father's limp and stoop as he comes to the dinner table to eat.

2.1.3.5   Structural Selectivity   Obvious as the preceding series of observations may be, they should not be taken for granted. Presenting them together like this forces one to ask why they are as they are. Evidently, the cognitive culture system assesses the surrounding environment for its structural characteristics and selects certain aspects of this structure for assimilation while rejecting other aspects. This characteristic of the system can be termed its **structural selectivity**.

Thus, in particular, the cognitive culture system is geared to assess the category of entities relevant to it—humans, rather than animals or objects—as the model for its behavioral abstraction. Within this category of people, it discriminates different groups and selects those of relevance to it for modeling. Among all the behaviors manifested by any such group, it segments out the patterns relevant to the culture, keeps these patterns sorted out for separate internalization, and disregards the rest of the behavior for any assimilation. Across a variety of individual exemplars of any particular behavior pattern, it discerns an abstract schematic formation that it selects for assimilation. And the cognitive system recognizes aspects of behavior that can be attributed to an individual's personal or idiosyncratic characteristics so as to reject them as material appropriate for imitation. Instead, it seeks only the abstraction embedded within the complex of that individual's total behavior that could represent a metapersonal cultural pattern.

2.1.4 Further Clusters of Cognitive Cultural Processes This discussion of the individual's acquisition and exercise of culture has so far dealt only with the cluster of cognitive processes termed the assessment type. But the cognitive culture system includes or helps orchestrate some further clusters of processes.

2.1.4.1 Learning from Teaching A further possible cluster of cognitive cultural processes would seem to comprise an active response to teaching from others. This is not simply "learning," a term that too generally refers to all forms of change in an individual's cognition due to encounter with the environment. Rather, it is specifically **learning from teaching by others**. Such teaching may be explicit, as in formal instruction, or inexplicit, as in the narration of tales with moral or informational implications.

Further, on hearing the content of such recitations, the developing child does not simply catalog the concepts in some intellective memory store— as an adult might do on hearing comparable recitations from a member of another culture. What is noteworthy in the cognitive processing of the developing child, rather, is that it will largely direct the processed conceptual contents of the recitations further on to the child's deeply internalized store of conceptual-affective patterns and practices, where they will be assimilated as part of the child's cognitive cultural structure.

These processes may have little linguistic parallel. Though adults in many cultures try to give their children instruction and correction on the adult use of the native language, such efforts appear to have little effect—outside of a few pockets of usage—on what the children would do.

2.1.4.2   The Approval/Disapproval Response   A further probable cluster of cognitive cultural processes could be termed the **approval/disapproval response**. The child is largely pleased by approval and pained by disapproval from most adults and especially from the adults that it is close to. This cluster essentially amounts to a feedback system. In its developmental phases, the child manifests certain behaviors in accordance with the cognitive culture structure that it has assembled to that point. Approval by others will generally work to fix a particular behavior pattern in the child's cognitive culture structure, whereas disapproval will work to eliminate the pattern and to send the cognitive culture system in search of a more adequate pattern.

2.1.5   Interaction of the Acquisition and the Exercise of Culture   The cognitive culture system assesses group behavior patterns not solely for the purpose, say, of enabling the self to subsequently recognize those patterns in others. Rather, it does so as well for the purpose of enabling the self in turn to produce these very same behavior patterns—or else to produce the accommodations settled on to resolve conflicting patterns.

Further, these two cognitive processes—the assessment and the production of cultural patterns—take place neither independently of each other nor in strict sequence, but rather interact. Thus, during a child's development, both functions of the culture system presumably become progressively more elaborated and refined, with each function contributing to and partially determining the changes in the other. Thus, the pattern-assessment function must progressively inform the behavior-producing function with its updates. At the same time, the succession of behavior patterns that the developing individual comes to execute improves the individual's culturally relevant cognitive skills, and this sensitizes the ascertainment function for further and finer determinations. These manifested behaviors also evoke reactions from other group members that are used by the assessment function to refine its schemas.

2.2   The Imparting of Culture

The functions of the cognitive culture system pertaining to the acquisition and exercise of culture that have been the topic of the discussion so far have necessarily been in operation in every unimpaired individual, and robustly so. But the cognitive culture system may also have a third function, that of imparting culture to others. This imparting function facilitates the acquisition of culture by others through any of several processes, including clarification, exposure, and implicit or explicit instruction. The imparting function—though probably also innately provided for—can perhaps lie relatively dormant in some individuals or may vary more greatly from weak to robust operation.

Perhaps the predominant means by which culture is transmitted is simply by virtue of adults going about the business of exercising their cultural patterns and of children using their cluster of assessment processes to abstract these patterns from observation. But the adults may also employ their culture-imparting capabilities in ways that will abet the children's cognitive culture system in its acquisition function. In several of these forms, a co-evolution of the imparting and acquisition functions of the human cognitive culture system may have taken place, so that the operations of the two functions are well tailored to each other. We next characterize the several forms of the imparting function noted above and the ways these might dovetail with different forms of the acquisition function. Though further attention and research will need to be directed to the issue, it may be that most of the forms described either do not appear in nonhuman primates or appear in weak or precursor forms.

First, the imparter can execute his cultural behavior more slowly, more distinctly, in a simplified form, and with repetition in interaction with a child. The greater distinctness can involve spacing out the components of the behavior, demarcating them more crisply, and performing them more exaggeratedly. The simplification can consist of the omission of the subtler or less basic components. This **clarification** form of the culture-imparting function operates both in physical practices and in the contents of communication. This particular form of the imparting function may have no specific counterpart in the child's acquisition function. The child still uses her usual cluster of assessment processes, but now they simply have an easier time of performing their assessments.

There may be a linguistic parallel to this clarification form of the culture-imparting function. Our language system seems to be innately programmed to execute certain different "registers" of communication that ease the task of an imperfect language user. "Parentese" is the collection of language shifts that an adult makes in addressing a child (see Gallaway and Richards 1994). It includes all the same properties as just presented for cultural imparting. Thus, the adult speaks more slowly, with words pronounced more distinctly, with exaggerated intonation patterns, with simplified syntax, lexicon, and overall content, and with repetitions (plus additionally raising the pitch level). Similar shifts are often made in adopting a register for talking with adult nonnatives. Again, it seems likely that we come to this mode of speaking innately, triggered by the knowledge that we are interacting with a child or less competent adult.[3]

Another form of the imparting function is to take actions that ensure that the child will be exposed to behaviors it will need to acquire. Examples might be an adult taking a child along in hunting or fishing, or seating the child alongside while weaving. The child can be engaged as a helpful participant in these activities. Often undertaken without explicit instruction, this **exposure** form of imparting again may have no specific counterpart in the acquisition function, but it does feed directly into the standard cluster of assessment processes.

Further, though, the imparter can instruct, whether through implicational narrative or through explicit explanation. This **instruction** form of the imparting function would seem to correspond directly to the form of the child's acquisition function described earlier as "learning from teaching" and presumably co-evolved with it.

Finally, an adult can show approval or disapproval to a child in a way that helps shape the child's behavior. This **approval/disapproval** form of the imparting function clearly corresponds to the "approval/disapproval response" form of the acquisition function in the child, as described earlier, and presumably also co-evolved with it.

2.3   Universality and Variation in the Cognitive Culture System

Cultural universals have two main sources: the innately determined cross-individual commonalities of the cognitive culture system, and the commonalities of environmental circumstances that all cultures must accommodate. The environmental exigencies may account for most of the substantive cultural universals—that is, those that are more perceptually palpable or conceptually contentful—such as the ones enumerated by Murdock (1965) (see above). The cognitive culture system may also be responsible for some substantive universals. But, for the most part, we see the universality in this system as functional, consisting of an abstract program of procedures for certain forms and targets of observation and for certain forms of assessing and processing the results of this observation. This universalist functioning of the cognitive culture system, then, leads not so much to explicit universals of substantive cultural practices.

It leads more to implicit universals of abstract cultural structuring, a "scaffolding" that runs in common across cultures.

This characterization of the cognitive culture system may largely parallel the nature of universality in language. Linguistic universals are rarely substantive particulars—they are usually abstract patterns and relationships, procedures and processes, principles and constraints. In fact, the history of universalist studies of language has included many cases of a certain theoretical sequence. In this sequence, researchers first posit a substantive universal, then are alerted to a language that disobeys the posited formulation, and consequently change their theory by positing a more abstract principle or relationship. Continued investigation of cultural universality may follow the same theoretical sequence. As it stands, though, we would hold that many of the structural properties that appear to run in common across cultures can be traced to the characteristics of a cognitive culture system along the lines laid out in this chapter.

Outside of these forms of universality, everything else about culture can vary. We can divide this variation into two types. One type is the cultural variation that the standard operation of the cognitive culture system allows or promotes. The other type is cross-individual variation of the cognitive culture system itself—that is, forms of variability outside its relatively stable core characteristics that are the result of genetic as well as environmentally caused differences across individuals.

2.3.1   Variation Countenanced by the Standard Operation of the Cognitive Culture System   The standard operation of the cognitive culture system can be seen to function in two ways with respect to cultural variation: ascertaining it and promoting it. In its ascertainment function, it is precisely the differences of the cultures in which children develop that constitute the subject matter of observation by the cognitive culture system in the first place, and the assessments of which continue differentially through the systems processing. Such differences between cultures can be large, can affect virtually every domain of behavior, and can involve the finest filigree of conceptual-affective structure and physical practice. The assessment processes and other processing clusters of the cognitive culture system allow the child to acquire the particular form that his surrounding culture takes amidst the great range of possible variation.

The engagement of the cognitive culture system's ascertainment function with such cross-cultural differences may have a significant consequence: a differential effect on the neurophysiology, as well as on the somatic physiology, of the individuals in a culture. The reason for such an effect would be that the greater quantity or elaboration of a behavior in one culture relative to another may engage the capacities for plasticity in the brain and the body to accommodate to the greater demand. The possible effects of behavior on somatic physiology are no doubt more amenable to investigation. For example, it might turn out, and instrumentation may exist to show, that the anatomy of the knees of individuals in a culture with the practice of sitting on one's legs folded under one differs on the average from that of individuals in a culture with the practice of sitting on chairs.

In a similar way, if a culture emphasizes certain forms of cognition through its discourse and practices, it may be that the systems of the brain that most deal with those forms of cognition will develop more greatly (say, will develop a greater density and intricacy of neural connections) and will become more determinative relative to other brain systems than in the case of cultures without such emphases. The forms of cognition whose emphasis may lead to an increased development of brain systems can be perception based, as perhaps in cultures with a practice of hunting prey that is difficult to spot, or with a practice of maintaining awareness of one's orientation relative to compass points. Or such forms of cognition may involve affect or values and lead to the elaboration of the brain systems that undergird those forms. Examples of such forms of affect and values that cultures can emphasize to different degrees include a sense of personal honor and the value of revenge as against a laissez-faire attitude; neighborliness and friendliness as against suspicion and hostility; a sense for the easy expression of anger as against the valuing of civility; the valuing of intelligence and knowledge as against disregard or suspicion of them; and a sense of communalism as against a sense of individualism. Thus, with respect to such cultural differences, the thesis here is that the cognitive culture system of an individual ascertains the emphases of its culture, and, as the result of its directing the individual to behave in accordance with these emphases, the brain and somatic systems of the individual that underlie such behavior increase in capacity, elaboration, and determinative power within the total ecology of the individual's brain and body.

As noted, the standard operation of the cognitive culture system not only ascertains cultural variation but also promotes it. The nature of the cognitive culture system's operation and of the recycling phenomenon (see below) promotes a certain degree of variation in the course of cultural acquisition and may have so evolved to facilitate cultural accommodation to changing circumstances. The explanation is that the behavioral manifestations generated by an individual's culture system are not in lockstep with the behavior patterns observed in others. One reason for this variation is that the behavior-assessing system in the individual does not have sole control over all the individual's behavior but, rather, interacts with other cognitive systems in the same individual, including systems involved with individual personality. A second reason for variation is that the assessing system's abstractions and generalizations were made across people who themselves already differed from each other in various respects as the very result of their own intracognitive interactions.

2.3.2 Variation in the Cognitive Culture System Itself   Another locus of variation in the process of culture acquisition is the genetic blueprint for the cognitive culture system itself, which, like all genetically controlled structures, exhibits some individual variation. But it seems that different brain systems admit different degrees of variability across individuals. Some systems have a high degree of consistency—that is, have very similar characteristics—from individual to individual. Examples might be visual processing in humans or control of flight in a bird species. While our supposition is that the characteristics of visual perception vary across individuals more than is generally recognized, systems like perception and flight presumably must operate within relatively narrow tolerances to function well enough to confer a selective advantage. Other cognitive systems, however, may not be under such tight tolerances and would then be more subject to the selective pressures for variation across a population. Perhaps examples of this sort in humans are the cognitive systems for affect, memory, and general motor control. It seems probable that the cognitive system for assessing and executing cultural patterns similarly exhibits substantial variation across individuals.

The parameters of genetic variation in the cognitive culture system can involve the accuracy of its assessments as well as the fidelity of its executions. They can also involve the strength or dominance of this system relative to other cognitive systems performing different kinds of assessments in the same individual. In addition to these, the parameters of variation that we will treat next are the accessibility of the system to consciousness, the system's propensity to generate an overall integration, and the system's adaptability to new cultural conditions.

2.3.2.1 Access to Consciousness   One can observe differences between individuals in their metalinguistic or metacultural capabilities that can be attributed to differences in the degree to which the processing products of their cognitive culture or linguistic system are accessible to their consciousness, and how actively they have employed that access in the course of their lives. Thus, field linguists and anthropologists find that contacted individuals range from being poor consultants to being excellent ones, able to indicate the structure of their language or to articulate the structure of their culture. In my own linguistic field experience with Atsugewi, a California polysynthetic language (i.e., one with an extreme degree of affixation), the first speaker I worked with was unable to identify any of the component morphemes or meanings within the multiaffixal verb. But the second speaker, on being asked how to say a particular phrase in her language, spontaneously volunteered a series of utterances that varied in just a single morpheme slot of the verb. She thus revealed a segment of the verb's semantic and grammatical structure in an analyzed array. It is a possible explanation that in the second speaker, or in a comparably adept informant for cultural descriptions, the cognitive systems for linguistic or for cultural analysis have in the course of their lives functioned more actively and with greater accessibility to consciousness than in the general population.

Similarly, it seems further possible that the linguists and cultural anthropologists with a gift for their disciplines are individuals in whom these cognitive systems are innately more active and accessible to consciousness —as well as being individuals who live in a culture that has permitted or fostered the development and exercise of these systems as a professional specialization. (Thus, given the opportunity, the second Atsugewi speaker might have made a good linguist.) It is further possible that the very disciplines of linguistics and cultural anthropology have developed into societal institutions as a cumulative large-scale expression of the activity of the language- and culture-analyzing brain systems in individuals, especially those in whom these systems are particularly dominant.

2.3.2.2 Integration   The cognitive culture system may exhibit genetic variation across individuals in several further respects. One is the degree to which the system functions to integrate the various aspects of its assessments of the surrounding culture into a single coherent conceptual structure. It appears that the cognitive culture systems in different individuals can vary over a range. At one end of the range, the system easily allows the co-presence of disparate compartmentalized chunks consisting of the separate analyses of different aspects of the surrounding culture. At the other end of the range, the system labors to accommodate as many as possible of the various aspects of analysis to each other and to reconcile conflicting analyses so as to form an overarching conceptual framework. In the individuals that have a cognitive culture system of the latter sort, the affect experienced in consciousness in relation to this aspect of processing may be a sense of striving to achieve an integration and a sense of pain insofar as it is not achieved.

Whole cultures appear to differ in the degree to which their patterns are integrated, thus achieving a coherent system of symbolism, value, practice, and so on. Many historical factors may account for the rise of inconsistent patterns within a formerly integrated culture. But a subsequent trend toward a new integration is probably the large-scale result of the drive toward integration present in the cognitive culture systems of a critical mass of the members of the culture.

2.3.2.3 Adaptability and Affective Attachment Another respect in which the cognitive culture system may vary genetically is adaptability. This pertains to the period through the individual's life during which the system remains able to process and accommodate to ongoing changes in the surrounding culture, and the magnitude of the changes that it can thus respond to. The system is clearly most ready to take on new configurations during the individual's youth and would seem to decline afterward. But individuals differ as to whether this decline is early and precipitous or late and gradual. And they vary as to whether the decline precludes only radical transpositions to a new culture or also the ongoing shifts within the native culture (see section 3.2).

A related variable factor is the strength of affect that attaches to the products of the cognitive culture system's processing. Thus, some individuals are motivated to defend to the death their way of life against external threat to its continuation. Other individuals have little emotional attachment to their familiar way of life and are content to have a new cultural surrounding.

2.4   The Relationship between Individual and Group

Given our perspective that culture is foundationally represented in the cognition of the individual, an account must be given for the cultural patterns manifested by groups larger than a single individual. This task is particularly important, since many theories of culture are wholly based at the level of the group, which they treat solely as a suprapersonal emergent phenomenon. In this section, we outline four processes by which an individual-based cognitive culture system can account for the existence of group-level patterns. These processes are the following: each individual acquiring roughly the same first-order pattern, which thus then appears in the aggregate; each individual acquiring schemas for the structure of complex group events; each individual acquiring a metaschema for the unequal presentation of first-order cultural material to developing individuals; and each individual that is acquiring culture belonging to a group of individuals that are doing the same.

While genuine emergent characteristics may exist at a societal level, it is necessary to distinguish them from those large-scale or group-level patterns that can be traced directly to individually based cognitive structure.

2.4.1 Individuals' Shared Schema Summated over the Group For the kind of group pattern in which all the individuals making up the group exhibit approximately the same behavior—for example, all the members of a society using their eating utensils in roughly the same way—there is little difficulty in tracing the relationship between the individual and the group. Each individual simply acquires the behavior, which is then manifested in the aggregate. This form of individual-group relation can be called the **summary aggregate** form, or the form with an **individually shared schema summated over the group**.

2.4.2 Individuals' Shared Schema for Group Cooperation More is required, though, to explain the kind of group pattern in which different individuals manifest different behaviors that complement each other and together constitute an integral pattern, as in the case of a wedding or a war.

The cognitivist account here too, though, is still rather straightforward. The cognitive culture system of the developing individual is built with the following two properties (the first of which is simply a further form of the assessment function). It can learn about or observe in the group around it a pattern composed of complementary behaviors by different individuals, and internalize this as an abstract conceptual structure or schema. And it has the concept of itself performing a particular one of these behaviors in interaction with others performing the remaining behaviors in accordance with the schema. Each individual in the society will have acquired approximately the same schema and can adopt one or more of the roles in it. Thus, a number of such individuals can together enact the full complex of the pattern, because each shares with the others the same overall schema and performs one part of the schema in cooperation with others performing the complementary parts. Each individual may have different degrees of familiarity with any particular role within the schema, from detailed knowledge of its performance, to familiarity with its performance by others, to simple awareness that this particular category of role exists. There may even be some roles in a cultural pattern—which will come to be performed by other members of the society—that the individual is unaware of. But, taken together, this understanding in the individual limns out a relatively complete sketch of the overall schema. This form of individual-group relation can be called the form with an **individually shared schema for group cooperation**.

To illustrate, for a wedding to take place, each participant will generally have a preexisting conceptual schema of the roles and behaviors of all the distinct types of participants. Thus, in a traditional wedding of East European Yiddish-speaking Ashkenazic Jews (see Zborowski and Herzog 1952), the groom will know the roles of himself as groom (*khosn*); of the bride (*kale*); of those who escort the bride and groom to the wedding canopy, usually their parents (*unterfirer*); of the performer of the marriage ceremony, usually the rabbi (*mesader kedushin*); of the four men holding up the ends of the wedding canopy (no special designation); and of the witnesses who sign the wedding contract (*eydes*). The groom will also know the roles of the special figure that combines the functions of master of ceremonies, orchestrator of emotions, and poignant jester (*batkhn*); of the ritual guard who watches over the room in which the newly married couple sit alone together to break their fast (*shoymer*); and of the musicians (*klezmoyrim*). Of these roles, the groom may himself have detailed knowledge of several of them, say, of canopy bearer and of musician, having performed those functions previously; have familiarity with several other roles because he had previously witnessed them, say, with the roles of the rabbi and the batkhn; be aware of the category and outline character of certain other roles because of having heard them described or referred to, say, of the witnesses to the contract; and be unfamiliar with the role of the ritual guard.

Our view here thus opposes the view largely maintained in "practice theory" (see Lave 1988). The structure and pattern of progression of a culturally based multi-individual activity is not an emergent phenomenon arising solely in the process of interaction and whose nature could not be seen or grasped before its actual unfolding. On the contrary, its structure, the pattern of its progression, the types of roles played by participants in it, and the contents of these roles are largely understood beforehand and exist as a conceptual schema in the cognition of each individual who will take part in or witness the event. A participant or witness may be surprised by some novel effects that inevitably arise during interaction, but he cannot be startled at some fresh emergence of an entire complex event, as the characterizations of practice theory might lead one to imagine. Even some role or factor wholly unexpected by a society member would likely not throw that person's understanding or performance into chaos, since the new factor would enter into an already richly furnished conceptual structure. We would maintain that a cooperative and coordinated activity could not otherwise take place.

Similarly, while studies of distributed cognition (e.g., Hutchins 1993) emphasize the distinctness and partiality of the knowledge of any one participant in a collective activity (and analyze these aspects correctly, in our view), we here emphasize the complementary idea that such coordination could not occur if the participants did not already largely share a common conceptual template of the overall activity. However sketchily, such a template delineates the overarching structure of the activity, its constituent parts and processes, and the way these are to relate to each other.

This idea of individual internalization of a cultural schema for cooperative activity has a linguistic parallel in the area of discourse. Each party in a conversation understands both the role of the speaker and the role of the listener, as well as how these two roles are to interact cooperatively. This turn-taking structure of discourse, as described by conversation analysts (e.g., Sacks, Schegloff, and Jefferson 1974), is not an emergent phenomenon whose nature each interlocutor had no inkling of before starting to speak and is amazed to see emerge. On the contrary, each participant can, in full consciousness, understand and manipulate the two roles.

2.4.3 Individuals' Shared Metaschema of Group Differentiation We have so far presented the operation of a developing individual's cognitive culture system as if it had open access to all the patterns of behavior present in the whole society around it. In fact, however, adults, both singly and as groups, can to various degrees control the particular cultural patterns that a developing individual is exposed to. For example, men may present male cultural patterns to a boy that they do not present to a girl. Adult members of a particular totemic affiliation may exhibit their rituals to a youngster of the same affiliation but not to one outside it. In a culture with an apprenticeship system in which specialized knowledge is transmitted to particular individuals, a child apprenticed, say, to a master of canoe building will acquire the detailed lore of this craft, but an unapprenticed child will not. In a society with classes, a higher class will provide a child with more elaborate forms of education and technology, as well as lore in the maintenance of power, that are generally not available to the child of a lower class.

In all such cases, the cognitive culture system of the developing individual still functions as described until now, cross-assessing and abstracting patterns from the behaviors that it observes. The only difference is that the behaviors it is able to observe are partly determined by a cultural **metapattern** that establishes the parceling out of exposure. Further, the approximate overall structure of such a metapattern is itself acquired in a roughly comparable form as a **metaschema** by most children, in a manner similar to that described in the preceding section for the acquisition of a cooperative schema. That is, a child, in addition to acquiring the particular portions of his culture that the adults differentially expose him to, also acquires in schematic form the cultural metapattern that establishes which groups of adults present which categories of first-order cultural patterning to which children. For example, both boys and girls in the gender-differentiated society mentioned above acquire the cultural metaschema that certain practices exist that will be shown to the boys and not to the girls. And the children of both the rich and the poor in the society with classes may acquire the cultural metaknowledge that certain first-order forms of knowledge will be passed on to the children of the rich but not to the children of the poor. In turn, of course, a child grows up and becomes one of the adults that together institute the metaschema in accordance with their own acquisition of it. This form of individual-group relation can be called the form with an **individually shared metaschema of group differentiation**.

2.4.4 Individuals' Shared Schema Acquisition from a Group   Several forms of cultural transmission described earlier—clarification, individual exposure, and implicit or explicit instruction—can take place on a one-on-one basis, from single imparter to single acquirer. But the main form of cultural transmission that this chapter has treated is cognitively a many-one relation: the partially differing behaviors of many adults are cross-assessed by the cognition of each single developing child. A structural issue, then, is how such a group-dependent process can persist over time if its end product is a matter of individual cognition. The many-one relationship renews itself through the generations in an evident way: Although cultural acquisition is accomplished singly by each developing individual, there are of course many such developing individuals performing the same process of acquisition at the same time. In addition, since they realize this process in partially different ways, they internalize partially different cultural behavioral patterns. In turn, then, these individuals will become the group of adults with partially differing behavioral patterns that will be cross-assessed by the cultural cognition within each individual of a new round of developing children. This form of individual-group relation can be called the form with **individually shared schema acquisition from a group**. The process that takes place in this form—presumably the main process in cultural transmission—can also be termed the **recycling of culture**. This process allows for internal cultural change because of all the previously described forms of variation and of departure or slippage from uniformity that occur in the process.

3   EVIDENCE FOR A COGNITIVELY DISTINCT CULTURE SYSTEM

If the cognitive culture system that has been posited here is indeed a distinguishable cognitive system based on a distinct neural system, it is likely to exhibit certain characteristics that other such entities have shown. Thus, it might exhibit developmental phases, sensitive periods, system-specific impairments due to brain lesions or other malfunctions, a weaker form or a precursor or an absence in other species, and relatively little overlap with other cognitive systems that might otherwise have seemed to be closely related. In this section, for each of these categories in turn, we cite existing evidence or suggest kinds of evidence to be looked for in further research. The more such evidence becomes consolidated, the more compelling the argument for a neurally based distinct cognitive culture system appears.

3.1   Developmental Phases in Culture Acquisition

Determining the pattern in which a child acquires his culture can help select among alternative theories as to the cognitive undergirding of culture. One possibility is that children acquire culture in the same way as used to be believed was the case for their acquisition of language. Namely, they manifest a relatively continuous gradient of learning until achieving the adult form. This learning proceeds mainly by a generic process of imitation, perhaps abetted by some explicit instruction. The child begins by making many random shifting mistakes due to an imperfect ability to imitate and grasp the adult forms, but gradually hones its productions through ever finer imitation until it reaches the adult target.

But several decades of research in child language acquisition (e.g., Slobin 1985) have shown that a child's acquisition of a language occurs in quite another way. It proceeds in a succession of incremental phases, with each phase characterized by its own distinctive "grammar" that remains relatively consistent throughout that phase and that the child persists in despite outside attempts at correction. The phases emerge through the successive introduction of general principles of structure. Each such introduction can entail a general reorganization of the interim grammar to maintain the overall coherence of the system. Further, certain aspects of the phases that a child progresses through seem to be universal, whether they are so because they are dependent on certain other aspects of cognitive development that are themselves universal or because they are the result of innate properties of the language system.

In a parallel way, attention must be given to whether culture acquisition proceeds as a continuum of mistake-correcting imitation or, instead, as a lawful succession of coherent organized structures. And, if the latter, it must be seen whether any aspects of the succession follow universals of structural change. Minoura (1992) presents evidence for the existence of a phase roughly between the ages of 9 and 15 during which an individual interiorizes his culture's pattern for peer relationships. But there is little research of this kind. If further research confirms culture-acquiring phases of this sort, that will constitute further evidence for the thesis that humans have a distinct cognitive culture system.

3.2 Sensitive Period for Culture Acquisition

Something like a sensitive or critical period may exist for cultural acquisition. This possibility is raised not with any thought of a child who grows up in a culture-free environment and is subsequently unable to acquire any culture—an unfortunate situation that could arise only under the most unusual circumstances. Rather, at issue is an individual who has acquired a first cultural pattern as a child but who, on later exposure to a second culture, is less able or unable to acquire certain of its features. With the sensitive-period notion applied in this way, then, an individual would need to be exposed to certain cultural phenomena, and perhaps also to have the opportunity to put them into practice, within a particular early period of his life for those phenomena to be acquired and remain available throughout life.

An individual's acquisition of particular cultural phenomena is understood here to include at least the following: her ability to recognize the phenomena when manifested by others in the culture and to respond accordingly to them, to think and feel in terms of the phenomena, and to manifest them herself. Such acquisition can be understood as occurring at two degrees of depth: whether a particular cultural feature is acquired at all, or whether it is acquired in its full subtlety, elaboration, and integration with other features. Accordingly, an individual who first encounters such phenomena later in life might be able to discern, comprehend, and respond with some appropriateness to them, perhaps mostly by using her intellectual capacities. But under the sensitive-period notion, she would have had to experience those phenomena during an earlier stage of life for them to have become internalized and interconnected at a more foundational level of cognitive organization.

The posited sensitive period is probably subject to much variation across different individuals and different cultural features or domains with respect to its onset, duration, contour, and severity. Here, "contour" refers to such dynamics as whether the period's onset or cessation is relatively gradual or abrupt, and "severity" pertains to the degree to which a cultural feature or domain might be internalizable outside the sensitive period, from not at all to fairly extensively. Other cognitive systems, perhaps visual perception, appear to have a more clear-cut and severe sensitive period for particular visual phenomena (such as the perception of horizontal stripes). But for the cognitive culture system, the acquisition period for many phenomena may not be so much a matter of all-or-none criticality as of facilitation or enhancement.

For a cross-cultural example, one can consider one's experience with some long-term immigrants to one's country who, though they have learned the new language well enough to get along in it, nevertheless behave, interact, and manifest concepts and emotions in ways that strike one as nonnative. To be sure, some such immigrants recognize certain of the cultural differences and have consciously chosen to retain original customs and values. But immigrants to whom the notion of a cultural sensitive period would most clearly apply are those who, it appears, have genuinely wanted to assimilate, yet end up not fully able to do so—whether or not they are themselves aware of the cultural shortfall.

Relevant here is Minoura's (1992) study of Japanese children who moved to the United States at various ages and subsequently returned to Japan. Her finding is that the period between ages 9 and 15 is a sensitive period for "the interiorization of cultural meaning systems about interpersonal relationships" (Minoura 1992:333). Children who return to Japan before this period readily readjust to their original culture, but children who return after this period have interiorized the American conceptual and affective patterns of peer relationships to an extent that they have difficulty adjusting to the Japanese pattern on their return.

Another type of example involves a quickly changing single culture. An older member of such a society may well retain various practices, values, and aspects of worldview that were prevalent when she was young—that is, during her sensitive period—but that are no longer broadly manifested. Both she and younger members of the culture may be conscious of the disparity. In accordance with their valuation of the change leading to the disparity, the young might variously see the woman as, say, superior or old-fashioned, while she might see the behavior of the young as a sign of societal advance or decline. The woman can of course have used aspects of cognition outside the cognitive culture system to establish individual practices, values, and beliefs (see section 3.6) and on the basis of these rejected certain potential revisions of her early pattern—in the same way that some young individuals might reject aspects of their contemporary pattern and try to follow the older pattern. Apart from this, though, this woman has not changed her earlier cultural pattern to the new pattern in the respects at issue. The sensitive period theory would explain this fact by holding that, with respect to certain aspects of such patterns, the woman is largely unable to shift because her cognitive culture system is already set for the pattern that it became attuned to during its sensitive period.

The existence of a sensitive period can support the hypothesis of a cognitive culture system given that sensitive periods have elsewhere been found to apply to distinguishable cognitive systems, such as visual perception and language. Consider the linguistic parallels to the cultural sensitive-period notion. An individual acquires certain features and categories of features of his first language, learned during his linguistic sensitive period, whose counterparts he may be unable to acquire at all, or to acquire in full depth, in a second language.

Such failures of acquisition can involve phonology, grammar, or semantics. Phonological examples are the native French speaker who cannot pronounce the English "th" or "r" sounds, and who cannot seem to grasp the relevance of syllabic stress, or the native English speaker who seems unable to appreciate the phenomenon of tone in Chinese. That is, some individuals not exposed to stress or tone in their critical period may emerge, in effect, "stress-deaf" and "tone-deaf" in second-language acquisition. An example for grammar is the native English speaker who cannot later deeply internalize grammatical gender and case in Russian. Rather than fluently producing the appropriate noun and adjective suffixes, such an individual might at best be able to generate them by calculation from memorized textbook tables. Semantically, a native German speaker may never be able to master the English distinction between the simple and the progressive present (*I teach here* vs. *I'm teaching here*).

3.3 Cultural Impairments

The hypothesis of a cognitive culture system rooted in some specific neurophysiological system requires investigation into whether any impairments to the culture system exist that can be traced to dysfunctions of the neural system. Considering again the linguistic parallels, the fact that there are various forms of neuronally based language impairments—aphasias and dysphasias—leads one to explore whether any neuronally based impairments exist in an individual's capacities for cultural acquisition or maintenance, what might be termed "anethnias" and "dysethnias."

One study that bears on this possibility is Goffman's (1956) analysis of a culture's rules of conduct and their abrogation in varying respects and to varying degrees by institutionalized patients on psychiatric wards. The more disturbed patients under his observation would ignore or transgress this culture's rules of deferential avoidance (to use Goffman's terminology). They would state their unfavorable views of others' appearance or dress openly to them; accost any attending doctor for his attention; grab food for themselves in a way that disregarded others' reaching for food or take the food off another's plate; curse at others; and touch, grab, hit, or throw feces at another person. Such patients ignored or transgressed the norms of personal demeanor by variously exhibiting slovenly dress and unclean hygiene, emitting loud belches and flatulence in public, and abruptly lurching to and from the dinner table.

Although Goffman did not explicitly address the matter, it appears from his descriptions that many of these patients did not suffer from wholly general cognitive incapacities of knowledge and attention that simply affected cultural maintenance along with other manifestations across the board. Rather, some functions seemed to be spared while others were disturbed. Although the disturbance presumably did not affect the patient's cultural manifestations alone but at least included their emotional and conceptual systems, the fact that their cultural functioning was selectively disrupted could be part of an argument for the presence of a distinct culture system.

While psychiatric patients of the above degree of disturbedness presumably have some form of neurophysiological impairment (rather than, say, what may simply be associative neural interconnections that lie within standard variation in the case of neurotic behavior), it remains to be determined whether documentable brain lesions can have selective effect on an individual's cultural structure.

3.4   Culture Acquisition by Nonhuman Primates

If a child's acquisition of his surrounding culture were simply a matter of learning to imitate the visually evident patterns of behavior around him, we should expect that any animal capable of and motivated toward such imitation and reared in the same cultural surrounding would emerge with a behavior pattern similar to that of the human child, if somewhat coarser or slower. On the other hand, human culture acquisition may be a species-specific process orchestrated by an innate cognitive system that includes the specific capabilities to attend to and incorporate certain species-relevant and structurally distinguishable categories of behavior. In that case, we should expect to find that nonhuman animals with some capacity for imitation would be able to exercise that capacity unequally on only some aspects of the behaviors manifested around it, rather than at roughly the same level of competence across the board.

Tomasello, Kruger, and Ratner (1993) have argued for just such a disparity in the chimpanzee Kanzi, reared by humans and taught the use of signs. Kanzi successfully acquired many of the behaviors around him such as drinking from a cup, stirring a pot with a cooking spoon, cutting vegetables with a knife, lighting a fire with a lighter, and loading his backpack to go outside. But Kanzi used the signs he had learned preponderantly in an "imperative mode" to give directives to others to do things that he wanted. He almost never used the signs in a "declarative mode" to show a new object to someone or to direct someone's attention to an object that he had noticed, as if to share the experience. The most that Kanzi did in this regard was, for example, to press the "ball" button on seeing a ball on television. He did not perform the declarative actions that even very young human children perform, such as holding up an object, alternating gaze between this object and the intended viewer, and exhibiting positive affect. Yet just such behavior was amply manifested by the people around him and presumably was as visually evident as the imperatives given by those people. Nevertheless, Kanzi did not acquire that category of symbolic use.

It could be argued either that Kanzi could not recognize that form of expression or that he could do so but was not interested in producing it. In either case, though, the part of Kanzi's cognition that directed his communicative interactions clearly differed structurally from the communicative system of humans, since Kanzi's performance was not simply reduced equally across all categories of human communication but showed qualitatively distinct highs and lows. On the assumption that the cognitive subsystem for communication in humans is part of or at least partially shaped and directed by the cognitive culture system, the specific communicative shortfall evident in a chimpanzee suggests that the cognitive culture system of a human child is so built as to perform the specific functions that the chimp is unable or unmotivated to perform.

Further, Tomasello, Kruger, and Ratner argue that even the forms of imitation that Kanzi did exhibit were amplified from a naturally lower readiness to imitate by contact with humans. Thus, he argues that in its natural social environment, a chimpanzee is little motivated to imitate the behavior of the other chimpanzees around it. What it mostly appears to do is to become attentionally drawn to a desirable circumstance produced by another chimp, and either to employ familiar behaviors already in its repertoire to bring that circumstance about, or to engage in nonorganized behaviors that might happen to lead to the desired circumstance. It seems minimally to observe the behaviors that another individual has used to attain that outcome and to imitate that behavior. Thus, the proposed human cognitive system for culture acquisition may also include an evolutionarily increased capacity and motivation for imitation.

As before, there is a linguistic parallel to this species difference in cultural cognition. Humans appear to be innately wired to acquire a language in its full-blown structural complexity. Of this complex, chimpanzees appear able to perform only certain aspects easily or at all. One interpretation of the human language research with animals is that a chimp has concepts perhaps much like those that humans have. And it can associate a particular symbol with each such concept—especially visual symbols—so that seeing the symbol evokes the concept, and having the concept can motivate the production of the symbol. It seems further likely that a chimp can manipulate its concepts in forms of understanding and reasoning that may resemble that of humans. But chimps seem unable in anything beyond a rudimentary fashion to manipulate the symbols within structured complexes in a way that could correspond to the formation and manipulation of conceptual complexes of human linguistic structure.

3.5   The Independence of the Culture System from Other Cognitive Systems: Language

Further evidence for the distinctness of a cognitive culture system would be provided by a demonstration of its difference from other cognitive systems that might otherwise have been expected to form a continuum with cultural knowledge and behavior. We can provide such a demonstration with the cognitive system of language.

Developing further a traditional linguistic distinction, chapter I-1 presents evidence that the task of conceptual representation by language is functionally divided between two types of linguistic forms, the open-class forms (primarily the roots of nouns, verbs, and adjectives) and the closed-class forms (including inflectional and derivational affixes; unbound forms like prepositions, conjunctions, and determiners; word order; grammatical categories and grammatical relations; and grammatical constructions). These two types of forms perform complementary functions, respectively, that of expressing conceptual content and that of assigning conceptual structure. Thus, in the total conception evoked by any single sentence of a language, the majority of its content is contributed by the open-class forms, while the majority of its structure is determined by the closed-class forms.

Further, the meanings represented by all the closed-class forms of all languages are highly constrained, both as to the conceptual categories and as to the member concepts within a category that they can ever express. For example, although many languages have noun endings that indicate the number of the noun's referent, no language has noun endings indicating the color of the noun's referent. Thus, the conceptual category of 'number' is among the categories that closed-class forms can express, but the category of 'color' is universally excluded from closed-class expression. Further, with respect to the member concepts within the category of

number, many of the languages that do have number on their nouns have
endings for notions like 'singular', 'dual', and 'plural', but no such language has endings that indicate 'even', 'odd', 'dozen', or 'numerable'.

Taking together all the conceptual categories and member concepts
that are ever expressed by closed-class forms under their severe semantic
limitations, this totality of all closed-class meanings can be understood to
constitute the fundamental conceptual structuring system of language. If
this system in language is now compared with what can be taken as the
conceptual structuring system of culture, only a few correspondences and
many differences are found. This fact can serve as a testimony to the distinctness of language and culture as separate cognitive systems.

Two types of comparison of this sort will be used to demonstrate this
distinctness, a transverse type and a longitudinal type.

**3.5.1 Cross-Cultural and Crosslinguistic Comparison of Conceptual
Structure** For the first demonstration, we make use of Murdock's (1965)
list of cultural universals, already enumerated in section 1.1. The noteworthy observation about this list is that out of its 72 apparently universal
cultural categories, only eight have any representation in the closed-class
conceptual structuring system of language, and of these eight, only some
three or four have extensive representation. One of the most extensively
represented categories is "status differentiation," which, for example, is
represented in the familiar versus the formal forms of the second person
in many European languages, as well as in the elaborate pronominal
and inflectional forms of Japanese. Related is the Murdock category of
"etiquette," which is grammatically represented by various markers and
constructions for requesting as against commanding (*Could you please
speak up?* vs. *Speak up!*), for suggesting as against directing (*Why not go
abroad?* vs. *You should go abroad*), and for many other forms of politeness (see Brown and Levinson 1987). "Property rights" is perhaps linguistically represented by those closed-class forms that express ownership and
transfer of possession. "Personal names," as a subset of proper nouns,
have somewhat distinctive syntactic characteristics in some languages.
Comparably, a few languages have somewhat special syntax for "kinship
nomenclature." And perhaps most, if not all, languages accord special
syntax to "greetings," to "numerals," and to "calendar" designations.
But aside from these several relatively modest forms of intersection between the conceptual structuring system of language and that of culture,
there is remarkably little correspondence between these two systems. This

finding is an argument for the status of culture and of language as distinct cognitive systems.

3.5.2 Single-Culture and Single-Language Comparison of Conceptual Structure This same line of argument can be pursued for the language and culture of a single people. A comparison here falls in the domain of the Sapir-Whorf hypothesis. This hypothesis proposes that much parallelism exists between the conceptual structure manifest in the grammatical system of a language and that in the culture of the people who speak the language. In his work on the language and culture of the Mparntwe Arrernte, an Australian Aboriginal group, Wilkins (1988, 1989, 1993) has gathered together all that he could discern of the grammatical forms in the language that seem to reflect aspects of cultural structure. There are several such forms, almost all of them involving kinship relations and totemic affiliations for both people and places, intense cultural preoccupations in Aboriginal Australia, as documented by Heath, Merlan, and Rumsey (1982). Nevertheless, the number and extent of these forms is minute compared to the entire grammatical system of the language. And even here, several of these cases involve no novel grammatical categories but only certain special applications of familiar categories. We describe most of the six or so cases that Wilkins has found for Mparntwe Arrernte. This demonstration is significant—and thus accorded some space—because of its challenge to the prominent Sapir-Whorf hypothesis and its relevance to cognitive theory pertaining to culture and language.[4]

Mparntwe Arrernte has a "switch-reference" system—common enough in languages around the world—by which the verb in a dependent clause takes inflections that indicate whether its subject is the same as or different from the subject of the main clause verb. For example, consider a sentence referring to two geographically distinct locations: *Location A became defiled, when location B broke apart.* Usually the verb for *broke apart* would be inflected for 'different subject'. But if the two locations have the same totemic affiliation, and this fact is pertinent to the meaning of the sentence, and the speaker wishes to foreground the fact, the verb can be marked with the 'same subject' inflection.

For a further example of the same phenomenon, consider the sentence that can be translated as *The little boy cried, as they walked along.* In general, the speaker can inflect the *walk along* verb for either 'same subject' or 'different subject' depending on whether the boy is considered part of the group or distinct from it. But, to take the latter case, if the grounds for considering the boy distinct from the group pertain to their social relations, the only permissible interpretation is that the boy is of a different "harmonic generation" from that of the rest of the group. (Ego and Ego's grandparents and grandchildren are in the same harmonic generation; Ego's parents and children are in a different one.) Thus, it is not a permissible interpretation that the boy is of a different family or friendship circle. While a switch-reference grammatical system per se reflects no cultural patterns, therefore, its application in this language does reflect the culture's emphasis on and specifics of totem and kinship.

For another case, in Mparntwe Arrernte all dual and plural pronouns in all three persons come in three distinct forms. One form refers to two or more people who are members of different patrimoieties. A second form refers to people of the same patrimoiety but of different generations, while the third form refers to people of the same patrimoiety and of the same generation. Thus, where English would just use *we, you*, and *they* without regard to any characteristics of the groups referred to by these pronouns, this Aboriginal language pronominally distinguishes such groups with respect to kinship relations of relevance to the culture.

For a third case, Mparntwe Arrernte has two distinct sets of singular possessive pronominal suffixes to express meanings like 'my', 'your', and so on. Most nouns can take the general set, but all kinship terms take only the second set. Thus, this second set indicates not only that one individual bears a relation of 'possession' to another, but that this is a kinship relationship. By itself this grammatical phenomenon may reflect the cultural salience of kinship. In addition, though, this second set of suffixes can be used with two further nouns in a way that shows the cultural identification between kinship, land, and totem. The noun *pmere* has a meaning range that covers the senses 'place', 'camp', 'home', 'country', 'land', 'shelter', and 'Dreaming site'. But with a second-set suffix, it can only refer to land one is responsible for and bound to by Dreamtime law. Comparably, the noun *altyerre* includes the senses 'a dream', 'Dreamtime', 'Dreaming country', 'a totemic ancestor', and 'the law'. But with a second-set suffix, it can only refer to a person's Dreaming country, or a person's totem. Thus, the application of this special set of grammatical inflections reflects the cultural importance of kinship and of its identification with land and totem.

Finally, Mparntwe Arrernte has three sets of grammatically distinct noun classifiers. One set consists of four classifiers with the meanings 'man', 'woman', 'child', and 'place'. Each of these four can, for example, be put in construction with the noun for 'kangaroo' to refer to a man, woman, child, or place of the kangaroo totemic affiliation. The fact that place is grouped formally with people here again reflects the cultural association that brings kinship, land, and totemism together.

While the above examples and perhaps several further cases do seem to reflect a cultural penetration into the grammar of Mparntwe Arrernte, these few cases represent the full extent of such penetration. The vast remainder of the language's grammatical system manifests conceptual categories widely represented among the languages of the world, regardless of their cultural contexts. It might have been expected that progressively more of a culture's conceptual structure would enter into the conceptual structuring system of the language the longer that continuous forms of the language and the culture coexisted for a single people. Certainly, this Australian group is an instance of such a people. Nevertheless, their language and culture reflect little of each other. Apparently, each of these two cognitive systems follows principles of organization that, presumably due to their innate determinedness, remain largely independent of each other. Thus, the Sapir-Whorf hypothesis, at least in this site of its testing, seems not to be borne out.

3.6   The Independence of the Culture System from Other Cognitive Systems: Personality

The collective profile of individual psychological characteristics that vary from person to person within an otherwise culturally or subculturally coherent group is what is generally understood under the notions of "temperament" or "personality." As suggested by growing research, including studies on separated identical twins, much of personality evidently has an innate basis in an individual's neurophysiology. Whether or not it should be concluded that personality constitutes a distinct cognitive system, it seems necessary to distinguish aspects of individual personality in a person from the functioning of that person's cognitive culture system. One may observe apparent disparities between an individual's personal propensities and the cultural patterns of the society that the individual is in. The existence of such disparities is further evidence of the distinctness of the cognitive culture system within an individual's total cognitive organization.

Disparities of this sort seem to be at work in the following three cases of different types. First, the legal systems apparently possessed by all societies take sanctions at least in part against an individual's transgressions against cultural patterns. But if an individual's behavior were solely determined by the predominant cultural patterns, no deviations from those patterns could ever arise. The mere fact that such deviations do occur—deviations that in fact are recognized as such by the local culture and against which the culture includes a system of legal sanctions—is evidence that an individual's behavior can be governed by forms of cognitive organization outside that of the cognitive culture system.

For a second kind of disparity, we note that there may be a number of periods in an individual's lifetime during which he experiences himself at variance with his surrounding cultural or familial expectations. The concept of the "midlife crisis" current in our own culture rests on an understanding of a conflict of this sort. In this concept, a midlife crisis is typically the culmination of a situation in which a person has had individual characteristics different from those valued by the culture but who, throughout his earlier years, tried to mold himself in accordance with the external precepts. The idea is that gradually, his own individual characteristics incrementally grew and came unto their own until they finally challenged the outside expectations. This semifolk concept may well reflect a genuine phenomenon of cognitive structure and process, though we suspect that such conflicts between personal characteristics and internalized cultural expectations can manifest during many periods in an individual's life (not just during midlife) and do so with a range of intensities (not just as a crisis).

For a third kind of personality/culture disparity, we note that interviews with different members of a single subcultural group often reveal different attitudes toward the patterns of that subculture. For example, some of the women sequestered in some Muslim cultures will personally enjoy this practice, perhaps feeling that they are being especially cared for, while other women will experience the practice as a constraining barrier to their desire for social mobility.

This last kind of disparity pertained to different personality types having different degrees of fit within a single culture. Its corollary is that the same personality type would have different degrees of fit within different cultures. For example, an individual with an introspective bent might well have a generally happy life if born into a culture with respect and institutions for an introspective lifestyle, while that same individual might lead a troubled life if born into a culture that valued active outgoing behavior and denigrated internality. Or a very aggressive individual might be esteemed in a culture with a concept of boldness and bravery in battle but might be regarded as a pariah in a pacific culture.

Patterns like the ones just cited distinguish cultural cognition as a system relatively separate from other individually based cognitive activity.

However, these two portions of cognition may also interact. Consider first that, as in the preceding discussion, a culture may hold up one particular personality type as an ideal. Or it may set up a different ideal type for each of several categories within the culture, say, one for men and another for women. But a culture can also recognize a certain set of different personality types as alternative models for individuals to adopt. Such a set of models can either replace an ideal or be ranked next below it (whether a whole-culture or a category ideal). Such personality models might include a forceful type and an easygoing type, an outgoing type and an inward type. Cultures differ from each other in the set of personality models they recognize, as well as in their particular realizations of an otherwise shared model. Thus, the concept of a tranquil balanced type of person might be accorded a standard niche in one culture but not even be recognized in another. And while the concept of an inward type of personality might be equally recognized in two different cultures, it might be associated with introspective wisdom in one of the cultures but with an unsociable withdrawn character in the other. A child growing up in a culture with such a range of available personality models may tend to adopt for himself the model with the fit closest to his own experience of himself. Now this arrangement points to an interaction between the two cognitive components—the cognitive culture system and the individual personality—whose independence this section has otherwise argued for. This interaction has two main opposite directions. On the one hand, the personality models that a culture recognizes ultimately derive from actual personality tendencies that individuals exhibit. On the other hand, a child growing up in a particular culture may tend to shape her personality predisposition in accordance with the closest specific model presented by the culture.

4   COGNITIVISM CONTRASTED WITH OTHER VIEWS OF CULTURE

The cognitivist position on culture that has been outlined in this chapter is often at variance both with beliefs that form part of a culture's own lore, and with beliefs that form part of the theoretical structure of some academic disciplines. Such beliefs often view the nature of culture as a quiddity that is transpersonal and pervasively resident in the group. (A culture's lore may go on to view this quiddity as pervasive throughout the space of the group's territory and as integrated into still more encompassive beliefs about deity and cosmos.) For example, to a great extent, sociology in general and ethnomethodology (e.g., Garfinkel 1967) as well as conversation analysis (e.g., Sacks, Schegloff, and Jefferson 1974) in particular maintain the view that the structure and principles of culture and communication reside not in separate individuals concurrently but pervasively over a group as a whole or, seemingly, in the interstitial space between the members of the group. Thus, works in the tradition of conversation analysis give the impression of holding that the principles of conversational structure exist in the space between the interlocutors, as if the latter were mere secondary elements that plugged into receptor sites in the interstitial medium. Holding a related version of such views, the "culturology" or "cultural criticism" in some European thought maintains an ontology in which a culture exists autonomously in the form of an abstracted structure, perhaps as a kind of Platonic ideal.

The cognitivist perspective faults the preceding views on the grounds that there is no substantive reality to their extrapersonal, interstitial, or Platonic-type conceptions of causal efficacy, whereas there is substantive reality to neurophysiology and neural activity, together with a presumptive causal link between these and the contents of consciousness. This cognitivist basis does not deny the existence of emergent effects arising from the interaction of a number of distinct nervous systems with each other and with environmental events. In fact, an expanded version of this chapter would directly characterize such emergent effects so as to distinguish them from large-scale cultural patterns that can be traced to the activity of individual cognitive culture systems. The emphasis of the present chapter, though, is on the great extent to which such cultural patterns can in fact be traced to a cognitive culture system resident in the individual.

Notes

1. This chapter is a substantially revised and expanded version of Talmy 1995a.

An early version of this chapter was prepared for a May 1991 workshop on the topic of "Rethinking Linguistic Relativity," organized by John Gumperz and Stephen Levinson and sponsored by the Wenner-Gren Foundation.

For discussions that helped in the development of the present version of the chapter I am grateful to Patricia Fox, Janet Keller, Donald Pollack, Naomi

Quinn, Barry Smith, Claudia Strauss, Michael Tomasello, and David Wilkins. Much of the view set forth here may have been inspired by the thought of the psychologist Theodore Kompanetz (*olev hasholem*).

The framework outlined in this chapter seems largely consonant with a developing cluster of views in anthropology, psychology, and linguistics, such as those put forward by Boyer (1994), Hamill (1990), Jackendoff (1992), Keller and Lehman (1991), Minoura (1992), Quinn and Strauss (1993), and Tomasello, Kruger, and Ratner (1993).

2. In some circumstances, it may be that the possibly more crude, spotty, or distorted assessments that the self has made of some nonself group can nevertheless subsequently be tapped into for a more or less clumsy enactment. For example, a widowed father of a young daughter may tap into his memories of how his own mother attended to his sister when they were children so as now to enact such behavior to his daughter.

3. Parentese seems to be used to little or no extent in some cultures (see Schieffelin 1979, Heath 1983). But since its characteristics are largely similar in the cultures where it does appear, one may conclude that parentese is at least in part innately determined and is suppressed in the exceptional cultures rather than formed afresh in each culture that possesses it.

4. This demonstration was not the aim of the Wilkins papers but our use of his findings.

Chapter 8

A Cognitive Framework for Narrative Structure

1 INTRODUCTION

This chapter lays out a framework of factors and relationships intended to represent the structure of narrative and its context.[1] Here, narrative is understood to encompass productions of a certain kind, whether these are conversational, written, theatrical, filmic, or pictorial. More broadly construed, narrative can be understood to encompass nonproduced entities of a certain kind, such as history or an individual's life. The ultimate goal is to develop a comprehensive framework for ascertaining and characterizing the structure of all existing and potential forms of narrative, as well as the larger context within which narrative is situated. Such a comprehensive framework would include provision for the points of articulation around which narratives and contexts of any kind can vary.

The specific framework set out in this chapter is a step in that direction. This framework was constructed as a working grid for heuristic purposes—much will need to be added to it, and no doubt much of it will need to be revised. The goal here was not to analyze some smaller circumscribed area exhaustively, nor to include all the categories relevant to the final analysis. Rather it was to discern a number of the main structural articulations in their distribution over a broader and, in some respects, perhaps unbounded domain. By presenting a distributed selection of such structures, we aim to initiate the process of limning out the comprehensive framework.[2]

1.1 The Cognitive Approach to the Analysis of Narrative

Our treatment of narrative adopts the presuppositions of cognitive science, cognitive psychology, and cognitive linguistics in assuming the existence of a mind that has produced the narrative as well as of a mind that is cognizing the narrative. Unlike some approaches that limit their scope of attention to the confines of the narrative alone or that deny the existence of individual minds, the approach here describes a wealth of structural interrelationships that could be observed only by the adoption of a wider scope that includes the existence of both generative and interpretative mental activity. Thus, in our theoretical framework, a particular portion of space-time can be a narrative "work" only insofar as there is a mind that has assembled it and a mind that perceives and cognizes it as such. Otherwise, it is merely some physical pattern.

More accurately, this last statement applies only to more narrowly construed narrative—that is, to our usual idea of narrative. But it needs to be amended in two ways to cover narrative more broadly construed. First, the perceiver of a narrative need not be an entity separate from its producer. Thus, a producer can create a narrative without any separate sentient entity to perceive it. But that producer will function as perceiver as well, even if only in the course of production.

Second, an intentional sentient producer is not strictly necessary for the construal of something as a narrative. A perceiving mind by itself is capable of experiencing some naturally occurring formation or some unintended formation by a sentient entity, as being a narrative work. More systematically, a perceiver regularly construes the external events she has witnessed over a period of time as narrative—a type that might be termed "history." And a perceiver regularly construes the sequence of personal experiences he has had over time—both interior and externally based experiences—as constituting a narrative, that of his "life." Thus, for there to be a narrative, there must at least be a cognizant perceiver, while narrowly construed narrative also requires a cognizant producer.

Broadly construed, narrative can be placed within a larger cognitive context by bringing in the notion of **cognitive systems** (which can themselves be posited as a part of overall psychological functioning). A cognitive system consists of a set of mental capacities that interact with each other to perform a particular integrated and coherent function. Cognitive systems, which can range from small to large, are assumed not to be wholly autonomous, like Fodor's (1983) concept of modules. A putative cognitive system for interconnecting an assembly of mental experiences so as to form a single overall pattern is relevant here. This can be called the **pattern-forming cognitive system**. This general system, then, has a specialized application to a sequence of experiences that are cognized over time. It integrates them into a single pattern understood as a story, a history, or a life. This functioning of the pattern-forming cognitive system with respect to sequences experienced through time will be called the **narrative cognitive system** here.

Thus, we posit that the mental faculty for the generation and experiencing of broadly construed narrative constitutes a specific cognitive system in its own right. This narrative cognitive system would generally function to connect and integrate certain components of conscious content over time into a coherent ideational structure. More specifically, as detailed in section 4.4.1, this is a system that ascribes entityhood to some sequential portion of experienced phenomena, that imputes continuity of identity to that entity, that integrates contents associated with that continuing identity into an ideational whole, and that fixes a feeling of attachment to that complex. As noted, we posit that this cognitive system functions in approximately the same way to generate in consciousness the experience of a time-based pattern that constitutes a story one has heard, or a history one has witnessed, or the life one has lived.

It appears that the narrative cognitive system is typically a robustly active system and so can commandeer much of an individual's attentional resources. This system is thus responsible for the sense that an individual often has of being gripped by a story and of being unwilling to disrupt it until its conclusion. This operation of the system must be in place rather early in development, since stories typically absorb young children.

The pattern-forming cognitive system and its application to temporal sequence in the narrative cognitive system presumably evolved through selective pressure into their present form of having great scope and attentional attraction. The advantage in the increase of scope was that it made possible the cognizing of larger patterns and longer-range plans. To the extent that such patterns and plans corresponded accurately to actual conditions, the increase was adaptive.

The fact that the human mental faculty for narrative may constitute a particular cognitive system has led to a principal feature of the present analysis: an endeavor to relate the narrative system to other cognitive systems. As background, we note that a principal direction of the author's work has been to determine the properties of conceptual structuring that apply in common across many or all the major cognitive systems that constitute human mental functioning insofar as these are accessible to consciousness. As presented in the introduction and in a number of the chapters in this volume, this line of research has so far examined structural properties in common between language and such other major cognitive systems as perception, reasoning, affect, memory, anticipatory projection, and cultural structure. And to these cognitive systems can now be added the putative cognitive system for pattern formation and its temporal specialization, the narrative cognitive system, dedicated to the formation of narrative structure broadly construed.

As part of our "overlapping systems model" of cognitive organization, a comparison of these cognitive systems has provisionally yielded the general finding that each system has certain structural properties that are uniquely its own, certain structural properties that it shares with only one or a few other systems, and certain structural properties that it shares with most or all the other systems. These last properties would constitute the most fundamental properties of conceptual structuring in human cognition. Certain aspects of this fundamental structure were described in chapter I-1. But their greatest expansion and detailing to date appears in section 4 of the present chapter. The parameters described in that section are the factors that to this point in the present line of research seem the most general and common across the range of cognitive systems. Because they have been included in the present treatment of narrative, most of the examples used to illustrate the parameters pertain to narrative structure. But their cognitive generality is nevertheless intended.

To sum up our cognitive approach, we see narrative as something that by necessity is cognitively produced or experienced, rather than as anything that could exist autonomously in its own right. We believe that it represents the operation of a cognitive system and that its characteristics share the properties that are common across cognitive systems generally, so that it can, in turn, be used to better understand the nature of those properties. This particular cognitive perspective distinguishes the present analysis from most other treatments of narrative.[3]

1.2 The Cognitive Approach to the Narrative Context

As indicated above, narratives per se are understood as necessarily situated within a larger context. Heuristically partitioned, this context encompasses —in addition to the narratives proper—their producers, experiencers, containing societies, and the surrounding world. Since our analytic framework is cognitively based, we must address the ways that its factors and constructs apply to the divisions of this context.

First, as already discussed, this cognitively based framework will apply directly to the cognition of the producer of a narrative, both generally and in the course of producing the narrative, as well as to the cognition of the experiencer of a narrative, both generally and in the process of experiencing the narrative.

In addition, the cultures and subcultures in which the producers and experiencers of narratives cognitively participate can constitute a largely coherent cognitive system that informs much of the conceptual structure, affective structure, presuppositions, values, and, in general, the "worldview" of those individuals. This culturally based cognitive system within the psychological organization of these individuals can affect or determine a set of narrative characteristics, and so it is an additionally appropriate target for the kind of analytic framework proposed here.

Finally, the surrounding physical world for humans is seldom—perhaps it intrinsically cannot be—simply a matter of autonomous physics. It can be argued, rather, that the characteristics that are attributed to it, at any level of organization, are entirely determined by the individual's cognitive processing of the stimuli impinging on her and by the cognitively generated schemas that she imputes to it. To be sure, the ways that human cognition performs this processing and imputation reflect a biological evolution in which the organisms that preceded humans interacted with their environments. But, regardless of its origins, human cognition presently has a set of characteristics that shape everything pertaining to mind and behavior. To characterize the ways in which the surrounding world is represented in narrative (as well as in much else of human concern), we must look to the ways human cognition structures such representations, aside from whatever independent examinations we may make of the surrounding world in accordance with a notion of an autonomous reality. Thus, the "surrounding world" can now be understood more broadly to comprise not just the physical world, but also the conceptualization of it that arises from the cultural, producer, and experiencer portions of the full narrative context. Thus, once again, a cognitively based framework of analysis is called for.

1.3   Organization of the Framework

The present heuristic framework treats the narrative context in three divisions. These are the **domains**, the **strata**, and the **parameters**—presented in that order in sections 2, 3, and 4. In brief, the parameters are very general organizing principles, the strata are structural properties that pertain to narrative, and the domains are different areas within the total narrative context to which the first two sets of analytic categories can apply.

More specifically, some of the same analytic categories pertain to what can be heuristically treated as five areas within the total narrative context, as discussed earlier. Here termed "domains," these are a narrative itself, the producer of a narrative, the experiencer of a narrative, the culture in which the narrative and its producer and experiencer are situated, and the surrounding spatiotemporal world. More accurately, such categories apply not only to the cognitive representations in a narrative, but also to the psychology of its producer and experiencer, as well as to our conceptual representation of the culture and the surrounding world.

The "strata" are the basic structuring subsystems of narrative. These subsystems progress concurrently in a coordinated way through the course of a narrative. One image for their operation might be the working of a polygraph machine in which separate styluses trace the concurrent functioning of several different coordinated subsystems of a single body's physiology. The strata presented in section 3 are temporal structure, spatial structure, causal structure, and psychological structure. The term "strata" has been chosen for these structuring subsystems to suggest their parallel alignment but not to suggest any "vertical" ranking among them.

Certain general organizing principles can be observed to apply in common across the structural properties of the strata. These are here termed "parameters." The following parameters are presented in section 4: the relating of one structure to another, relative quantity, degree of differentiation, combinatory structure, and assessment. Further, these parameters, together with others not addressed, appear to constitute the set of organizing principles that apply in common across all the major cognitive systems. As noted, these parameters are the author's most elaborated account to date of such fundamental organizing principles. Though these principles are mostly exemplified with illustrations from narrative, the exposition of them is intended to be fully general. The reader less interested in narrative than in general cognitive properties may prefer to proceed directly to section 4.

Criteria are needed to help determine whether a particular analytic category should be understood as a stratum or as a parameter. Two criteria for assignment as a stratum are as follows: (1) The phenomenon fluctuates at the microlocal or local level of granularity in the temporal progression of a narrative, it is expected to vary in this way as an intrinsic characteristic of the nature of narrative, and the producer of the narrative intentionally controls for this variation. And (2), this phenomenon varies in correlation with other comparably varying phenomena in an integrated way through the progression of the narrative.

Thus, "psychological structure" is treated below as a stratum because a producer typically varies such phenomena as a character's mood or a tonal atmosphere in the course of a narrative. On the other hand, the category of, say, "aesthetics" would not generally count as a stratum, even though an experiencer can feel the beauty of a narrative to fluctuate rapidly as the narrative progresses. This is because a producer rarely induces successive portions of a narrative to vary as to their beauty—in general, he would probably wish it to be of uniformly great beauty. Accordingly, the category of aesthetics is understood as a parameter, not a stratum. However, such divisions cannot be rigid in a framework intended to accommodate changes and ranges of narrative practice. Thus, insofar as a producer intentionally varies the beauty of her narrative for the effects that that would have on the experiencer, to that extent the category of aesthetics would be functioning as an additional stratum.

Of course, a category's assignment could be unclear or dual. For example, below, the category of "significance," which includes the function served by a narrative element, is presented as a parameter because it is a type of organizing principle. But this category could alternatively or additionally have been presented as a stratum because such functions vary in the course of a narrative.

2   DOMAINS

The entire context in which a narrative can exist includes not only the narrative itself, but also the sentience that creates and experiences the narrative and that manifests the culture and appreciates the world in which the narrative is situated. As previously noted, this total context can be heuristically divided up into some five portions, here termed "domains." These are the spatiotemporal physical world with all its (so-conceived) characteristics and properties; the culture or society with its presuppositions, conceptual and affective structuring, values, norms, and so on; the producer or producers of a narrative; the experiencer or experiencers of a narrative; and the narrative itself.

In the rest of this chapter, we will use terms for these domains that are general enough not to suggest solely written narrative. Thus, we refer to a **narrative** or a **work**, instead of, say, to a "book." We refer to an

experiencer or an **addressee** of a narrative, instead of to a "reader." And we call the creator of a narrative either its **producer** or its **author**, since the latter term already applies more generally than just to writers. Several of these terms, like "work" and "author," do suggest narrowly construed narrative, but their intended reference is to broadly construed narrative.

Each of the five domains deserves extensive investigation. Here, though, we only sketch properties of the work itself, then proceed to consider selected interrelations between two or more of the domains.

2.1   The Domain of the Work

First, with respect to its composition, a work comprises both its physical characteristics and its contents. The work's physical characteristics mostly involve aspects of its medium—for example, voices in air, print arrayed over the pages of a book, film projected onto a screen, or the performers and scenery on a stage for a play. The contents of a work are its cognition-related characteristics, encompassing both the affective and intellective, and including the implicit/inferable as well as the explicit/overt. In a narrative, such contents comprise what is called the **story world**.

Next, through an assessment of different genres, we consider the factors that make a work a prototypical narrative. Narrative can be treated as a prototype phenomenon with a core that trails off in various directions. Three factors relevant to characterizing narratives are presented below. A particular value for each of these factors must be present for a narrative to be prototypical.

2.1.1   The Main Cognitive System Engaged

The first factor is the particular type of cognitive system that is primarily engaged by the work. Most prototypical narratives involve the **ideational** system in the cognition of the experiencer. This is the system that establishes "concepts"—ideational, denotative components with referential content—and organizes them in a "conceptual structure." Less prototypical are works that primarily address or engage other cognitive systems, such as a musical work that induces a sequence of moods or affective states in the listener, or a painting that induces in the viewer the class of responses associated with the perception of visual form.

The designation of the ideational system as primary for narrative is not intended to deny the incidental or even systematic evocation of emotion by works basically focused on ideation. Nor, on the other hand, should we underestimate the degree of narrativity in nonprototypical works. For example, a symphony that progresses through a sequence of energetic and calm passages can evoke in the listener a sense of the unfolding of a coherent and meaningful succession of exciting and tranquil events. Nevertheless, ideation appears central for the prototype.

2.1.2 The Degree of Progression   The second factor relevant to characterizing narrative is that of the Degree of Progression. We are probably innately built to have the experience about the world that it can consist of "events" that "occur" in "succession" through "time." These, taken together, are what is here termed **progression**. This is not the only experience we can have about the world, but it is a fundamental one, and a work can evoke this particular category of experience. The more a work evokes this experience of progression, the closer it is to the narrative prototype.

The evocation of progression does not require the conveying of an actual succession of distinct events. The depiction of a single event—or even of a static scene—can serve as long as it is (designed to be) experienced as an excerpt from a progression, where a prior and/or subsequent sequence of events is implied or can be inferred.

A look at forms of nonprogression in a work can help set off the nature of progression. One prominent type of nonprogression involves the consideration of, or the evocation of, the constant characteristics that are present in some situation. This type can be in effect, for example, in a physics textbook describing the principles of magnetism, in a painting of still life, or in a section within a narrative that portrays a static scene.

A nonprogressional aspect of a work can be coupled with a progressional aspect. Consider, for example, a rhetorical political work that characterizes some societal situation. Here, what is nonprogressional is the synchronic situation that the work characterizes. But the progressional is the marshaling of emotions and the "and therefore" quality of the call to action arising from the description of the disliked state of affairs.

There is a certain property a work can have that primarily, if not determinately, evokes an experience of progression. A work with this property is so organized that the experiencer will cognize different parts out of the totality of the work at different times. This part-at-a-time effect can be achieved in two main ways, either or both of which may be operative: the work reveals different parts of itself through time, or the experiencer directs her attention to different parts of the work through time.

A work that reveals different parts of itself through time can be considered intrinsically **dynamic**. Examples of genres of this type are conversation, storytelling, a play, a film, a comedy routine, an improvisational theater performance, a mime performance, a religious ceremony, a dance performance, music, video art, and kinetic sculpture.[4]

Other works are intrinsically **static**, but the experiencer can interact with them by successively directing his attention to different parts of the whole. Static works may be classed into two groups on the basis of whether or not there is a cultural convention that prescribes a particular sequence in which attention is to be directed (even though it would be physically possible to direct one's attention elsewhere). Works that involve such a convention include a book, a cartoon strip, a sequential fresco, and an Australian aboriginal sand tracing depicting mythic treks.

Other types of static work are designed for random access by the experiencer's focus of attention. Examples of such works are a painting or tapestry with a number of different depicted components; a sculpture designed for viewing from different angles; an architectural structure that one can view from different interior and exterior points; and a geographic-sized art work, as by Cristo.

An interesting observation emerges from this analysis. Any old tapestry or painting that in effect depicts a story by showing a number of figures and activities together suggesting a succession of events, but one that the viewer must piece together through her own self-determined sequence of visual fixations, is as much an example of interactive fiction as any modern computer-based form.

The prototype requirement for narrative that it be progressional is abetted to the extent that a genre exhibits a certain one of the characteristics outlined above. This characteristic is that the genre's partwise succession is determined—whether by physical shifts of exposure or by conventions for directing attention—rather than being open to attentional random access.

2.1.3 The Degree of Coherence and Significance   The third and final factor considered here is that of Coherence and Significance. A high degree of coherence and significance are required for the narrative prototype. Coherence is the property that the parts of the work fit together into a sensible whole. That is, relative to the average human conceptual system, the parts of the work can be cognized together in a way that they constitute a higher-level entity that can be assessed as a unity. A work loses coherence to the extent that parts of the work are experienced as contradictory, irrelevant, or random with respect to each other. Significance (in its nonneutral sense) is the property that the parts and the whole of a work can be experienced as fulfilling some purpose or mission on the part of the author.

It can be seen why a prototypical narrative requires that the factor of coherence and significance be added to the previous two factors, and that all three factors have positive values. A "work" could be prototypical in being ideational and progressional but, without coherence and significance, it would hardly qualify as a narrative. An example of this combination of values is a diary or a chronicle, which recounts a succession of ideational events but lacks story character to the extent that the entries do not cohere. A collection of references to a succession of unrelated events—whose juxtaposition would thus not only lack coherence but also significance—would be even less of a narrative. On the other hand, to the extent that a diary is seen as someone's personal history or "story," or that a chronicle is seen as the history or "story" of, say, a kingdom, the recounted succession of events would be accorded a sense of coherence and purpose and so come closer to being experienced as a narrative.

2.2   Relations between the Domain of the Work and the Domains of the Culture and the World

The relation of the surrounding sociophysical world to the story world of a work—as we understand these—offers many research possibilities. One major issue is the particular aspects of the sociophysical world that are represented in, or imputed to, the story world, as against those aspects that are negated or changed. The narrative cognitive system appears to project much of the familiar world into a story world. Perhaps a fundamental projection is to treat a story world as if it were a real and exhaustive world in its own right, in the same way we conceptualize the familiar world around us. Further, we seem to systematically project most of the structures and particulars that we take to inform the surrounding world into the story world. Thus, most readers of Sherlock Holmes would imagine that time in Holmes' world progressed unidirectionally at the same rate as in our world, and that Holmes used the toilet, even though such ideas are not directly represented in the stories.

In fact, an author can exploit this projection process in the addressee to engender certain effects. For example, the space-exploring narrator in a science fiction story might describe the strange inhabitants of a planet he has visited and how they destroyed themselves, where only the last lines in the story make it clear that those inhabitants were humans and the narrator is extraterrestrial. Here, the author relies on an addressee's propensity to project the familiar—in this case, our space exploration—into a story. The author then reverses these projections to bring about in the addressee the surprise of a shifted perspective, the shock of recognition, and the experience of ideational reorientation (see section 2.5 for author-addressee relations).

2.3 Relations between the Domains of the Work and of the Addressee

Another type of interrelationship is that between the domain of the work and the domain of the addressee. One relationship within this type consists of the degree of separation or intermingling of the two domains. In Western works, the norm is a lack of interaction or exchange between individuals in the story world and individual addressees. But some authors play around with the usually impermeable boundary between the story world and the addressee's world—for instance, by having characters in a play address audience members or by bringing audience members onto the stage. Some genres intrinsically bridge the two domains; an example would be the genre of the interactive street mime, who develops his or her brief narrative episodes in the course of interacting with individuals gathered around or passing by.

A further type of relationship across the domains of the work and the addressee involves the balance in the basis for comprehension. This balance occurs along a continuum that runs between the work and the addressee. On one end of this continuum, some narratives are assumed to be self-contained and self-explanatory. That is, all that the experiencer has to do is to progress through the narrative and all its relevant contents will be conveyed (if we presuppose the addressee's general prior familiarity with the form and medium of the narrative's genre). But other narrative types are assumed not to be sufficient in themselves and, rather, to rely on the addressee's prior familiarity with some portion of the story or story world. For example, the story of a classical ballet would generally be inaccessible to a naive viewer. Such a viewer would no doubt pick up on some aspects of the story but generally could not get the whole plot.

For this, the viewer must have knowledge of the story from outside the presentation of the work itself.

2.4   Relations between the Domains of the Author and of the Work

A further type of domain interrelationship is that between the author and the work. If the performers of an enacted work can be considered part of the domain of the work, those performers can be thought to bridge the domains by being co-authorial with the work's main author with respect to certain aspects of the work. These aspects are the ones determined by the performers' intonational emphases, timing, accompanying affect of the delivery, and so on—in short, the **interpretation**. Such aspects can be considered authorial because they affect the meaning and import of the work.

2.5   Relations between the Domains of the Author and of the Addressee

An author composes her narrative and sets its structural features largely on the basis of her assumptions about the way the addressee processes incoming content. For example, an author can set the rate at which story events take place relative to her assumptions about the effects that different rates will have on the average addressee. An author may slow the rate of events to engender a sense of calm in the addressee, or quicken the pace to engender a sense of excitement.

To have the intended effect, these authorial choices must be based on an assumed baseline for rate in the addressee. It is relative to such a baseline that deviations, such as "slow" or "fast" rate, are defined. Of course, such baselines differ across cultures and subcultures. If we are to correctly judge the intentions of an author from another culture or period, we must first assess the likely baseline of the intended addressees.

The author-addressee relation for narrative in general is often assimilated to a "conduit" model of communication. By this model, an author transmits a body of his ideational content to the addressee. By a related model that avoids the concept of transference, the author acts to evoke or replicate in the addressee a body of ideational and other phenomenological content equivalent to his own. This latter model is presented in section 1.1.1 of chapter II-6 as the core form of communication. But as section 1.1.2 of that chapter goes on to show, neither model—however well it may capture our naive or core sense of communication—adequately characterizes the narrative process. This is because an author often wants to engender in the addressee certain conceptual or emotional responses that the author does not himself currently experience. Examples are suspense, surprise, interest, or hurt. To accomplish this, the author must orchestrate the selection, sequencing, and pacing of material in a way that is likely to cause the desired effects, given his understanding of the addressee's psychology.

2.6   Relations across the Domains of the Author, the Work, and the Addressee

We finally consider a type of interrelationship involving three domains, those of the author, the work, and the addressee. One relationship of this type pertains to the timing in which these domains come into play. To a large extent in the Western tradition, the author composes the work first and then the addressee experiences the work. This is the case with all precomposed writing, painting, dance, music, film, and so on. But other forms are composed "online" as the addressee is experiencing the work. This type of work is generally called **improvisational**. Examples occur in music (e.g., some jazz recently in the West, or classical Indian music as a whole), improvisational dance, and improvisational theater performances.

In another relationship of the current three-domain type, the addressees are co-authorial with the main author(s) of the work. For one example, if the performers of an improvisational comedy act are now considered to be the main authors of the work, then the addressees—that is, the audience members—become co-authorial when the performers ask them for suggestions on aspects of the piece to be improvised. Similarly, in some traditional storytelling or puppet shows for children, the children are asked to choose the way the story will end, or are told that they can demand a return to some point in the story to change certain events. More subtly and indirectly, one way that the audience-addressees can become co-authorial is where their online reactions to an ongoing performance influence the performers to alter their delivery, whether these performers are the main authors (as in improvisational comedy) or are themselves, in our sense, co-authorial with the playwright by virtue of their interpretations.

More recent forms of co-authoriality and co-composition include interactive forms in which the addressee makes choices with respect to the progression of the work. An example is interactive video, in which the work is composed with multiple alternatives at various nexuses. Here, the user can choose the particular alternative that gets realized. Comparably, some modern books are written so as to allow the reader alternative routes for flipping back and forth within the text.

3 STRATA

We now turn to the next division of the narrative context: the **strata** that operate within and across domains. The strata can be thought of as the basic, or "ground-level," structuring systems of a domain, prototypically so of the domain of the narrative work, but perhaps as readily so in the other domains of the total narrative context. The several strata are understood as being in effect coextensively. Thus, in the domain of the work, one can track several different strata of a narrative as one progresses through the narrative, noting the concurrence and correlations across these several systems. As noted earlier, an apt metaphor here is that of the polygraph, where each line represents one mode of activity taking place as the narrative progresses.

3.1 Temporal Structure

The stratum of **temporal structure**—that is, the dimension of time—uniquely has the property of "progression." It has internal structure in the form of "events" and "textures." It has contents such as "processes" and "activities" or "situations" and "circumstances." And it has systematic correspondences with other narrative structures, as discussed in the following subsections.

3.1.1 Events One form of structure that can be applied to the temporal stratum is **conceptual partitioning**. By the operation of this cognitive process together with that of the **ascription of entityhood**, the human mind in perception or conception can extend a boundary around a portion of what would otherwise be a continuum of time, and ascribe to the excerpted contents within the boundary the property of being a single-unit entity. One category of such an entity is perceived or conceptualized as an **event**. This is a type of entity that includes within its boundary a continuous correlation between at least some portion of its identifying qualitative domain and some portion of the so-conceived temporal continuum—that is, of the progression of time. Such a correlation may rest on a primitive phenomenological experience that can be characterized as **dynamism**—that is, a fundamental property or principle of activeness in the world. This experience is probably both foundational and universal in human cognition.

An event can vary with respect to a number of parameters, including many of those described in section 4. Thus, an event may be discrete, with a clear beginning and ending point, or it can be continuous, experienced as unbounded within the scope of attention that has been partitioned off by the cognitive processes of event formation. The contents of an event may change over the span of the event, in which case the event is active, constituting a process or activity. Or the contents of the event can remain unchanged over its span, in which case the event is static, constituting a situation or circumstance. An event can be global, spanning, for example, the full length of a narrative, or local, or even microlocal, thought of as covering just a point of time (e.g., a flash of light plus burst of sound that a story could present as a point-durational event). Further, one event could relate to another event along any of the relationship parameters described in section 4—for example, be embedded in it, alternate on a par with it, concurrently overlay it, or exhibit part-for-part correlations with it.

3.1.2 Temporal Textures A perhaps second-order aspect of temporal structure can be termed its **texture**. This consists of the patterns that various events show relative to the overall temporal progression and to each other. In our experience with the world around us, different temporal textures are exhibited. Thus, one kind of temporal texture is exhibited by a waterfall in which a myriad of quick minievents that involve gushing, cascading, spouting, streaming, and dripping merge into and emerge from each other. Another type of texture is exhibited by the gradual slow increase and differentiating change of a flower bud unfolding into full blossom (as we assemble this event in our memory from periodic viewings). And a third type of texture is exhibited by the medium-slow evenly pulsing rhythm of a throbbing headache. Similarly, a person can experience her whole life to have had one or another temporal texture, such as a stately cadence of successive discrete phases, or a helter-skelter jumble of overlapping events impinging on her. Comparably, a narrative can assert or describe a similar variety of temporal textures for any structure within the story world, or can itself exhibit them in its own pacing, or can evoke them in the addressee.[5]

3.1.3 The Relations of Narrative Time to Addressee Time Temporal

structures can also be related across domains—for example, between a work and an addressee. A narrative work has the following two forms of temporal structure. **Story-world time** is the temporal progression that is attributed to the world that the narrative depicts and within which it sets its particular story. This progression through time is generally taken and supposed to be taken as the same as that of our everyday world, though some works play with that assumption. On the other hand, **story time** is the temporal character of what is selected for explicit depiction or implicit allusion to constitute the narrated story. **Addressee time** is the progression of the addressee's life in the course of the everyday world.

As a comparand against which to observe relevant deviations, we must establish a baseline relationship between story time and addressee time. Here, this baseline will be exact continuously coextensive, forwardly directed, same-rate progression. That is, for this baseline, time and events in the story progress with exactly the same continuity, direction/sequence, and rate as they do in the addressee's world as the addressee attends to the progression of the narrative. This set of correspondences can be termed **co-progression**. Although useful as a baseline, such co-progression is not the norm, and works that aim to achieve it are generally deemed experimental. Examples include quasi-documentary-style films that purport simply to leave the camera on as events before it unfold in their natural way. Such works include, for instance, Andy Warhol's (1969) film of a couple having sex and, perhaps more challenging to the viewer's attention, his (1964) film showing a stationary building through the course of a full day.

There are two main types of deviation from this baseline. In one type, story time deviates from co-progression with the addressee, who is directing steady attention at a conventional rate to the work. In the second type, the addressee deviates from this steady-paced processing.

Under the former type (with the addressee attending in the conventional way), story time can deviate in several ways. First, the story may present only certain discontinuous excerpts selected from the presumed continuous progression of events in the story world. Here, the addressee still progresses forward in story time, but only certain moments and scenes are selected for presentation, with the intervening periods gapped.

Another deviation from the baseline is when story time is out of sequence relative to addressee time. This would include backward jumps in the tale, as for flashbacks or returns from flash-forwards. As noted in section 4, such temporal jumps can themselves form a higher-level pattern. An example from the story "A Free Night" (Costello et al. 1995) is the pattern of flashbacks that progressively zero in on a particular temporal point and the dread event that occupied it, where the flashbacks alternately over-shoot and fall short of that point.

Still another series of narrative temporal characteristics can be attrib-uted to deviations of the rate of story time from the baseline. First, a rate deviation can be steady, so that the rate of the narrative's progression is, by some constant degree, slow or fast relative to the addressee's experi-ence of the rate of events in the everyday world around him. Second, the rate of story time can change, either slowing down or speeding up. Hill (1991) has observed that story time tends to slow down (and the density of detailing tends to increase) as the story approaches a critical or emotion-ally charged point. Third, story time can exhibit different rates at which this change in rate takes place—that is, it can be gradual or abrupt (or somewhere in between) in its slowing down or speeding up. An author can use a story's abrupt shift from a slow to a fast pace to intensify in the addressee certain emotional responses, such as fright or excitement. This abrupt change in pace may be a recurrent component of certain other emotions, such as surprise.

Next we turn to situations where the addressee deviates from the base-line, in particular, from the baseline at which she directs steady attention in a forward progression and at a normative rate to the work. One cate-gory of deviation involves a discontinuity of attending. For example, a reader can put a book down and pick it up later. In this way, forms of discontinuity are introduced into the consciousness of the experiencer that have nothing to do with any discontinuities in the temporal progression of the story. Some works are intentionally constructed to involve addressee discontinuities. An example is the movie adventure **serial**. The very con-cept of a **cliff-hanger** at the end of one episode of a serial depends on the notion of addressee discontinuity.

Another category of addressee deviation pertains to forward sequenc-ing. As an example of this, a reader may choose to skip around in a book rather than read it in the canonical sequence of the printed format. Some recent works directly address the reader's ability to re-sequentialize the print by explicitly suggesting paths for skipping around.

A third category of addressee deviation involves the rate of attending. Thus, a reader can choose to read a written work faster or slower relative to some norm of processing the text. Or a viewer could intentionally run a film faster or slower than its canonical speed.

One motivation for an addressee to undertake deviations from the baseline is to introduce certain additional controls over the effects that the work will have on his cognition. For example, by setting a book down, a reader can give himself a chance to digest and think over some events in a novel before reading on to the next events. By skipping around in a book, a reader could give herself a sense of the story's overall design and character. Or, by playing a video in slow motion, a viewer could give himself greater opportunity to process the details of the scenes.

It should be noted that many of the same relations just described between story time and addressee time can also occur within the story itself. For example, they can occur between the time characteristics of one part of the story and the time characteristics of the consciousness of a character or of the viewpoint of a deictic center. An interesting example is the science fiction story by Zelazny (1971) where the protagonist starts going backward in time through the last portion of his life before that "rewind" process stops and he resumes living forward in time. As this character rewinds, some aspect of his psyche is aware of this backward rewind, noting it as it happens. The viewpoint is located at that aspect of his psyche, and we, the reader, are watching through that viewpoint. From the perspective of this viewpoint, we are really moving forward in its own time awareness, even though the contents of what appears in that awareness is a rewind of what had once been forward progression. Further, that temporal advance of the viewpoint's time awareness itself has a second-order availability of all the deviations described above—it too can skip, think back and forth, and so on.

3.1.4 Relations of the Temporal Stratum to Other Narrative Structures

Only the stratum of time has the intrinsic property of "progression." But for any other structure within the total narrative context, particular related instantiations of that structure can be correlated with different points of the temporal stratum. Where such instantiations are different from each other, that structure has undergone **change**, and where they are the same, it has exhibited **stasis**.

Changes through time can involve the structure of space. In particular, changes in the location of material objects over time constitute the concept of **motion**. Changes through time can also involve psychological structure. This includes changes in the cognition of a character or the atmosphere of the narrative over time. Some structural units must, by definition, change with time. Plot structure is one example.

Change through time is also particularly relevant in the domain of the addressee, in whom the progression of a narrative engenders a continually updated model of the narrative's content and a succession of psychological states consequent on the updates.

3.2 Spatial Structure

The stratum of **spatial structure** exhibits two main subsystems. One subsystem consists of all the schematic delineations that can be conceptualized as existing in any volume of space. This subsystem can be thought of as a matrix or framework that contains and localizes. Static concepts relevant to it include **region** and **location**, and dynamic concepts include **path** and **placement**.

The second subsystem consists of the configurations and interrelationships of material occupying a volume of the first subsystem. The second subsystem is thought of more as the contents of space. Such contents can constitute an **object**—a portion of material conceptualized as having a boundary around it as an intrinsic aspect of its identity and makeup—or a **mass**, conceptualized as having no boundaries intrinsic to its identity and makeup. An analogy may exist conceptually between material as the contents of spatial structure and events as the contents of temporal structure. Both types of contents exhibit a similar array of structural properties, such as being either bounded or unbounded.

The material subsystem of space can bear certain static relations to the matrix subsystem of space. With respect to relations that it can exhibit directly, material can, for example, **occupy** a region and be **situated** at a location.

Spatial properties that material entities exhibit in themselves or with respect to each other can also be related to schematic delineations of the containing framework. We can see three forms of this. First are the spatial properties that a single object or mass of material exhibits in itself. Examples are the contour of the entity's external boundary that determines its shape, like the shape of a doughnut or a skyline, and its internal structure—for instance, the interior disposition of a solid or a latticework. Second are the spatial properties that one material entity can have with respect to another. These include geometric relations, such as those specified by English prepositions like the ones in *X is near/in/on Y*, as well as ones specified more elaborately. And third are the spatial properties that a set of material entities can exhibit as an ensemble. These include their "arrangement," potentially to be conceptualized as a Gestalt of geometric patterning—for example, as in a cluster or a sheaf. (An ensemble whose multiplex composition has been backgrounded can be conceptualized spatially in the same way as a single object or mass.)

The material subsystem of space can also bear certain dynamic relations to the matrix subsystem of space. With respect to relations that it can exhibit directly, material can, for example, **move** through a region or along a path, or exhibit a **transposition** from one location to another. Spatial properties that material entities exhibit in themselves or with respect to each other can also be related to schematic delineations of the containing framework in the same three ways as before. Thus, first, a single material entity can exhibit dynamic spatial properties in itself. Examples include change of shape, like twisting or swelling. Second, one entity can execute various paths relative to another entity. Examples are the paths represented by the English prepositions in *X moved toward/past/ through Y*. Third, a set or ensemble of entities can alter their arrangement. Examples of this are scattering and converging.[6]

As we conceptualize it, the second subsystem, the contents of spatial structure, need not be limited to physical matter but can generalize to more abstract forms. For example, in a narrative, we can apply all our usual conceptions of spatial relations to understanding the location and motion of a viewpoint, the angle and direction of our sighting from that viewpoint to an entity to which we are attending, and the size and shape of the zone of this attentional projection.

Spatial structure can also vary along most of the parameters outlined in section 4. For example, it can exhibit hierarchical embedding, as when we see, or when a narrative describes, a restaurant as a containing structure within which are situated in a particular pattern of arrangement a set of tables, chairs, and people, each of which exhibits its own shape and internal disposition. And the properties of spatial structure can pertain to scope of magnitude from the microlocal to the global—for instance, from a ladybug on the palm of a character in a story, to that character's geographic-scale travels.

This last case can be given an extended illustration. The O. Henry (1903) story about a safecracker at one point has this character look and move about his old apartment within local scope. But it also globally depicts this character first as localized in prison, then leaving there and going to a nearby restaurant, then traveling to another town to get to his old apartment, then traveling to some relatively distant town where he settles down and remains for the rest of his life. The geometric pattern of this trek is significant to the import of the story, metaphorically correlating with phases of the character's psychological development. These correlations appear to be between the prison and his old way of life; the restaurant and his transition to independence and autonomy, where his actions are determined by his choices, not by orders given to him; the old apartment and his closing out his previous life (except that he retrieves his old safe-cracking tools); and, finally the new town and his new life, where the town is distant in the same way that his new way of life is distant from his old one.

Spatial structure can also pertain to cross-domain relations. One such relation is a discorrespondence between the familiar physical world and the story world, as where narrative objects and characters exhibit novel sizes, size changes, or embedding relations. Examples are seen in *Alice in Wonderland* or the film *Fantastic Voyage* (Fleischer 1966) with its miniaturized humans sailing through the bloodstream of a normal-sized person.

One may also wish to extend the stratum of spatial structure to the domain of the addressee. Thus, a playwright or director may aim to evoke a particular effect in the addressees by arranging the audience in one configuration or another relative to the performance area, as with theater in the round. Or he may partially merge the domains of the work and of the audience, as by having the actors pass through the audience.

3.3   Causal Structure

The stratum of **causal structure** can in the first instance be understood to include any so-conceived physics of matter and energy in space and time. The stratum is thus intended to cover any conceptual system of principles that govern or of patterns that characterize the behavior of entities. This stratum therefore applies not only to modern scientific physics, but also to the physics of classical and medieval science, to the physical lore of traditional cultures, to the naive physics in the mental models of untutored individuals, to "cartoon physics," to science fiction story physics, and to the causal conditions set up in stories in the fantasy and magic genre.

In addition to such nonsentient causal properties, the present stratum can be understood to extend as well to those aspects of the psychological stratum that have causal effect. Such aspects include motivation, desire, volition, and intention.

Systems of causal structure may thus address purely material issues, such as whether matter has spatiotemporal continuity or can instead appear, disappear, and translocate; or whether one entity can pass through another entity or occupy its location at the same time. Or these systems may address psychomaterial issues such as whether a sentient entity's volitional will can directly affect the course of events; or whether some supernatural power can exercise this form of will. Or the systems can address purely psychological issues, such as whether a particular psychological state in one individual can engender another particular state in another individual (e.g., self-pity arousing disgust). Narrative traditions can differ as to what they accept as causal agencies—for example, whether a ghost or a deity can affect the course of events.

One system that plays a great role in conceptions of both physical and psychological causality is that of force dynamics (see chapter I-7). This is a system of concepts pertaining to an entity's intrinsic tendency toward rest or activity, another entity's opposition to that tendency, resistance to such opposition, and the overcoming of such resistance. This system further organizes the concepts of forcing, preventing, and letting, as well as of helping, hindering, and acting in vain.

Via force dynamics, we can see that the stratum of causal structure can extend as well to ideational structure—for example, that of a narrative's plot. The force-dynamic system can characterize such relationships as two entities opposing each other, a shift in the balance of strength between the entities, and an eventual overcoming of one entity by the other. This system can then apply as well to such plot patterns as a conflict between any two factors and an eventual resolution of the conflict.

3.4 Psychological Structure

Much that is psychological can have particular associations with elements in—or particular distributions over—the spatial, temporal, and causal strata. Nevertheless, psychology can be regarded as constituting a distinct stratum by itself, with its own essential quiddity and governing principles. We consider this stratum of **psychological structure** in two ways: with respect to the categories of its organization and with respect to the levels of its organization.

3.4.1 Categories of Psychological Structure

The psychological stratum encompasses all the possible contents of cognition. Though cognition as yet has no definitive divisions, some heuristic categories can be ascribed to it. We next suggest six such categories, as well as a sizable sampling of cognitive phenomena included within the categories, to underscore the variety. Each cognitive phenomenon listed is intended to cover the range from good to poor functioning. For example, "accessibility to consciousness" also includes poor access, thus covering additional phenomena such as preconsciousness, repression, and so on, while "memory" also includes forgetting. These categories and their members pertain to the psychological structure of any so-conceived cognitive entity, a typology of which is presented below in section 3.4.2. The relationship of any of these categories or their members to the "cognitive systems" adduced in the introduction is a heuristic matter to be worked on in the course of time.

The first heuristic psychological category includes the "foundational" cognitive systems that underlie or mediate the other psychological functions. It includes consciousness and the accessibility of other cognitive systems to consciousness, attention, perspective, perception, memory, and motor control.

What may be considered a category of "executive" functions includes agency, intention, volition, goal pursuit, planning, and decision.

A third category consisting of the "ideational" or "intellective" functions and systems would include thought, concepts, and conceptualizations; beliefs, knowledge, and explanatory understanding; presuppositions and unnoticed assumptions; opinion and attitude; worldview; the assessment of familiarity, normativity, probability, and veridicality; and reasoning, inferencing, and a sense of logic.

A further "affective" category would include emotions and mood states, motivations and drives, desires and wishes, and aesthetic responses.

An additional category of "values" would include ethics, morals, and priorities—in general, ascriptions along the dimensions of goodness and importance.

Finally, a category of "composite" or "overall" psychological phenomena would include personality, temperament, and character.

These suggestive categories are not mutually exclusive—but largely combine—comparable features. For example, regret and worry are fully emotive but are based on an often-detailed intellective assessment of circumstances.

Perspective Point   We single out one member of a psychological category, that of **perspective point**, for special attention because of its central role in narrative. Perspective point is treated here for its substance, later for its function as a kind of individual, and still later for the properties governing its behavior through time.

We adopt a notion of perspective point that involves both location and assessment. A perspective point has a location either in physical space and time or in some conceptual model of space and time. A conceptual model of this sort is not limited just to an imagistic representation of physical space and time, but can be any form of "abstract space and time." Examples of the latter might be "knowledge space" or "taste space"—the experiential and conceptual domain of all the flavors that an individual can cognize—together with the kinds of timelike progressions that such spaces can exhibit.

In addition, some assessing faculty of some sentient entity is situated at the location understood as a perspective point. This assessing faculty is typically a perceptual system, especially that of vision, but can also comprise a sentient entity's system of beliefs and opinions, among various possibilities. The assessment system situated at the perspective point location assesses properties of phenomena situated at other locations within the same space. The criterial factor in the notion of perspective point is that this assessment is based on the particular characteristics and patterns of characteristics of the external phenomena that are able to arrive at the assessing system's location—or that the assessing system can access—because of their relative positioning within the space.

There is no intrinsic psychological requirement that a perspectival location constitute a minimal "point." In principle, it might be a region, or indeed a set of points or regions. Though the single point is no doubt the prototypical case, the other possibilities need exploration.

It should be noted that the entire characterization here in terms of a perspective point location in a space is inevitably founded on our visual experience. In this experience, our eyes occupy one location and are felt either to look out over the surrounding physical space from that location or, conversely, to receive stimuli from the surrounding physical space that converge on the location of our eyes. This perceptual experience proves a powerful model that structures our experience also with nonperceptual cognitive systems. Consider, for example, such non-perception-based forms of cognition as having an opinion or holding a particular ideological belief. Close analysis may show that the cognitive structure and process exhibited by such forms are not analogous to the ones just associated with perception. In particular, they may not involve features from external phenomena converging on a perspective point location or, conversely, probes projecting out from such a location. Opinion and ideology may involve structure and process other than such convergence or projection —for example, an interactive network of interrelations, or a "filter" that allows some concepts but not others to pass, and so on. Nevertheless, much of our phenomenology—including that pertaining to having an opinion or an ideology—can be experienced as involving locatedness at some point of a space from which one assesses external phenomena. This experience thus presumably underlies expressions referring to opinion such as *from my point of view* and *in my view*.

3.4.2   Levels of Psychological Structure   Our objective judgment may hold that all psychological phenomena are necessarily wedded only to individual sentient biological organisms. But our spontaneous conceptions about psychological phenomena are less limited. In fact, we typically seem to attribute psychological phenomena to three main levels of organization. These are the individual, the group or society, and the atmosphere. We consider each of these in turn.

3.4.2.1   The Individual   The level of organization of the **individual** is presumably the most prototypical for psychological structure. An individual is what can be conceptualized as a sentient, cognitive entity in which all or some of the set of psychological phenomena outlined above are localized together. The crucial notions for the concept of "individual" are the sentience of the entity and the co-localization of the psychological phenomena in that entity. In addition, the psychological characteristics localized within a single individual are also usually interrelated with each other so as to constitute a form of Gestalt unity. However, this property of integrated psychological unity is subject to variation, as in the presentation of an individual as having incompatible attitudes, or even distinct "selves" in the case of "split" or "multiple" personalities."

The prototypical individual is any human and, secondarily, any sentient animal. Within the immediate narrative context, the prototype individuals are the author and the addressee outside the story world, and the narrator and characters inside the story world. An individual, of course, need not be a human or animal, or even a biological organism. Any so-posited entity treated as if psychological properties are concentrated within it can serve the function, including inanimate objects, ghosts, extraterrestrials, and so on, as well as such abstractions as the perspective point of the deictic center.

Individual psychological structure can exhibit most of the parameters of section 4. Thus, a character's conception or mood can be explicit or implicit, clear or vague. It can embed within, alternate with, overlay, or correlate with another conception or mood. It can extend globally or locally. And it can change through time (for example, a character in a novel can evolve). As an example of local changes of psychological state through time that variously involve alternation, overlap, and so forth, we can track the protagonist in "A Free Night" through her evening at home as her thoughts and feelings variously comprise terror, regret, relief, reverie, and here-and-now awareness (Costello et al. 1995).

Narrative Perspective Point as a Type of Individual   As indicated above, a narrative perspective point may be understood as a kind of individual with psychological structure—that is, as a sentient cognitive entity with characterological/personality, psychoaffective, and worldview characteristics, among other psychological properties. It may be that a perspective point typically is defective, at least in some works, as to the psychological properties that appear in it, perhaps evincing primarily the property of perception. But, in some works, or by other analyses, the viewpoint will also include attitude and affect.

For example, consider a line like the following, which might come from a story when it is depicting an ocean scene with no story characters present: "Its body glistening, the porpoise leapt gracefully out of the water, rose majestically into the air, executed a beautiful somersault at the top of its arc, and dove back into the water barely perturbing the surface." Such a scene is presumably being viewed from the vantage of a perspective point located above the ocean surface and near the porpoise. This perspective does include perception, as in the characterization of the events that took place and in the use of the word "glistening." But it also includes evaluation, as in the use of the word "gracefully," it includes attitude and affect in the use of the words "majestically" and "beautiful," and it exhibits expectations in its use of the word "barely," which alludes to a deviation from norms. These additional inclusions are all elements of psychological structure beyond the merely perceptual, and the perspective point is exhibiting them here.

3.4.2.2   *The Group/Society*   Another level of organization to which psychological structure can be attributed is that of the group or of a society composed of first-level individuals. There is a principal division between concepts of group psychology. In one class of concepts, the group is a single superorganism, a metaentity existing in its own right at an emergent level, whose psychological manifestations exist only at that higher level. A second class of concepts regards a group as a collectivity whose psychological characteristics are based on the cognition of its individual members and their interrelations. Concepts of these interrelationships themselves fall into several types. In one type, the psychologies of the individuals in a group are **in concert**. That is, they are the same in some relevant respect, so that the comparable psychological characteristic of the whole group is in this respect simply an aggregation of the individual manifestations. In another type, the individuals' psychological characteristics are **complementary** in some respect, and the individuals may **cooperate** in regard to their differences for a groupwide effect that none of the individuals could exhibit alone. In a third type, the psychological characteristics of the individuals are **in conflict** in some respect, so that the psychological pattern at the group level can include contradictions or reflect conquests, defeats, and resolutions across individuals.

These various concepts about psychology at the group level can be found among the views of laypeople as well as of specialists. Thus, many in the public regularly make characterological attributions of the metaentity type or of the in-concert type to various sociological categories, such as those of gender, race, ethnic group, class, or nation. Comparably, some sociologists and anthropologists with theories of the metaentity type ascribe such properties as worldview and affect style to a culture as a whole or to the conceptually abstracted medium within which individuals interact. Examples are "practice theory" and "conversational analysis." On the other hand, work on "distributed cognition" (e.g., Hutchins 1991) adopts the complementary and cooperative concept, where various members of a team or of a society have partially complementary forms of expertise, all needed in interaction for overall goals to succeed.

Narrative exhibits much group-level psychology, including certain special forms. One such form is the classical Greek chorus, often understood to express the collective moral position of the society, the normative questions of the average member of the society, and the like. Another example is the presentation of a succession of viewpoints expressed by individuals that make up some group, as a device to show the variety or the uniformity of the views of that portion of society. A version of this is seen in Thornton Wilder's play "Our Town."[7]

Note that a plural number of individuals need not necessarily be treated as a group but can also be treated at the level of the individual. Thus, the psychological manifestations of the individuals in any portion of a narrative, including the whole story, can be regarded either at the group level as a collective interaction, or at the individual level as a distribution and succession of separate individuals.

3.4.2.3 *The Atmosphere*   Finally, we consider the third level of psychological structure, that of **atmosphere**. Atmosphere is the experience we can have that certain psychological characteristics pervade some portion of ambient space, or some physically defined region, or some event. Such an experience is thus different from the experience that psychological characteristics are localized within a particular material object at the individual level or associated with a set of such objects at the group level.

Now, our objective judgment may hold that any atmosphere felt as associated with some region or event is merely a projection of feelings that arise in ourselves on perceiving or considering that region or event. Nevertheless, some part of our cognition seems spontaneously to attribute such an atmosphere to that region or event as an intrinsic property of it or as inhering in it.

The psychological character of an atmosphere generally involves the ideational category of psychological structure—with such properties as thoughts, opinions, choice, and the like—less than it involves the affective category. And within the affective category the psychological character of atmosphere mainly involves mood states. Examples of such mood states that might be experienced in association with a region or event are menace, light cheeriness, horror, coziness, protective security, disgusting squalor, luxurious opulence, and numinous spirituality.

Our cognitive capacity to experience atmospheric characteristics in relation to our surroundings is probably innate and largely automatic. Accordingly, the occurrence and product of its functioning within us is barely amenable to internal conscious control. Hence, atmosphere is experienced as a regular concomitant of our environment as we move through it or look about it. In a sense, everything contributes to our current sense of atmosphere. It thus seems to be unavoidable that particular combinations of our sensory surroundings will be processed by the atmosphere-related portions of our cognition so as to generate some affective complex in association with those surroundings.[8]

Given this view of atmosphere, we can note that those in charge of particular venues often employ their understanding—whether intuitive or theoretical—of the ways physical arrangements affect people's experience of atmosphere. They regularly orchestrate and outfit their domains with care so as to engender particular desired senses of atmosphere in other people. Thus, city officials may outfit parks, streets, and buildings to engender a certain sense of atmosphere in the citizenry; shopkeepers establish the decor of their stores in this way for their clientele; and householders arrange their homes in this way for themselves and their families. Hence, a proprietor opening a tea salon and a proprietor opening a sports bar will make very different choices as to furniture, spatial arrangement, color, music, servers, the manner that the servers are required to affect, neighborhood location, and so on.

Authors regularly take pains to orchestrate the operations of our innate capacity so that we will experience particular atmospheres in association with a work. Films, for example, not only shape their visual material to this end, but also regularly use background music to engender the experience of a certain atmosphere as pervading a scene. Hence, the same scene could be apprehended in two different ways with different accompanying music—for instance, as eerily threatening or as lightly humorous. A written work can accomplish similar atmospheric effects by the choice of language and the orchestration of ideas. For example, Kahane (1996) shows how Woolf (1948) establishes an atmosphere of sanity-threatening fractionation through the use of periodic, almost subliminal allusions to menace (e.g., one reference to Bluebeard) and of startling, seemingly disjunct jumps in topic and scene.

4   PARAMETERS

The five **general parameters** presented below, as well as the **particular parameters** that they include, are generic cognitive organizing principles that apply across all the strata. And, as noted earlier, these organizing principles appear to apply not only to such narrative structures, but also to structures across a range of cognitive systems. The parameters presented here can be augmented by a number of those presented in chapter I-1, as well as in other chapters. Together, all these parameters constitute our initial outline of conceptual structure in human cognition in general.

4.1   The Relating of One Structure to Another

The wholes or parts of strata, as well as of domains, can bear certain relations to each other. The relation of one such structure to another structure can fall along certain parameters. A selection of such parameters are considered in this section.

One parameter of this sort is that of **mereology**, which involves the mereological relationship of one structure to another. This parameter is named for the mathematical theory most simply characterized as treating part-whole relationships, but the concepts and terminology presented below were developed separately in a way deemed relevant to language structure. For simple purposes, four mereological relationships should be distinguished. One relationship is **inclusion**, where one structure is wholly located inside a second structure. Another relationship is **coextension**, where one structure occupies the same region as a second structure. A further relationship is **partial overlap**, where part of one structure is coextensive with part of a second structure but where the rest of the two structures occupy different regions. And the final relationship is **separation**, where one structure is wholly located outside a second structure. Below, we consider the relationships of inclusion and coextension in greater detail.

One structure can be related to another structure by means of further parameters. One is the parameter of **parity**. In accordance with this parameter, two structures are conceptualized either as representing two different entities or as representing the same entity. This parameter can be applied, for example, to the first-mentioned mereological relation of inclusion, in which one structure is included within another structure. Under the dual-entity conceptualization, the first structure is separately inserted or embedded within the second structure. Under the single-entity conceptualization, the first structure is a proper part of the second structure, which is the whole. Comparably, the parameter of parity can be applied to the mereological relation of coextension, in which two structures, with respect to some characteristic of theirs, occupy the same region. Here, under the dual-entity conceptualization, the two structures can be understood to interpenetrate or to co-occur, while under the single-entity conceptualization, the two structures are understood as being equal or identical. In a similar way, the parameter of parity can be applied to the fourth-mentioned mereological relation of separation, in which two structures stand wholly apart. Here, under the dual-entity conceptualization, the two structures are two distinct entities, whereas under the single-entity conceptualization, they together constitute a single discontinuous entity. The parameter of parity figures prominently in the analysis below.

One further parameter is that of **equipotence**. In accordance with this parameter, one structure can either be equivalent in priority or privilege to another structure or, alternatively, one structure can be the main one while another structure is ancillary to it. The parameter of equipotence appears below in conjunction with coextension.

4.1.1 Inclusion The relation of inclusion holds between structure A and structure B if A occurs wholly within the region occupied by B. This inclusion relation has two forms, that of **embedding** and that of a **part-whole** relationship, in accordance with whether A and B are understood in terms of the dual-entity conceptualization of parity or of the single-entity conceptualization. Thus, if A and B are held to constitute two different entities, then A is embedded within B. But if A and B are held to comprise a single entity, then A is a part of B. However, it is not always clear which of these two forms is in effect.

An inclusion relationship is often evident between two structures within a particular stratum in narratives. Thus, within the stratum of spatial structure, an obvious example of multiple inclusions in a story is where a character's location is understood as involving a particular city within the nation, a particular street in the city, a particular house on the street, and a particular room in the house. A similar form of inclusion is found within the stratum of temporal structure. In fact, the traditional organization of plays is built around such concentric inclusions, where each particular incident occurs within a particular "scene," which takes place within a certain "act," which in turn occurs within the overall temporal scope of the play as a whole.

Though less clearcut, inclusions can occur not only within a stratum, but also across strata. For example, a reader's attention could first be within the physical spatial structure of the story world, and then enter psychological structure by entering the mental world of one of the characters who is located at some point within that space. This mental world will have its own structure including aspects of space, but it is still understood as embedded within the spatial structure of the story world as a whole. Such an entrance into a mental world is not understood in the same way as, say, a shift to some new location or scene that is otherwise part of the spatial structure of the story world. The mental world the reader has entered is more like some subrealm opened up at a particular location within the main fabric of story space.

An inclusion relation can also be found within a domain. For example, within the domain of the work, one story can be embedded within another as when Shakespeare's Hamlet embeds a play within itself, each with its own story world. Multiple inclusions of this sort are exhibited by the film *Saragossa Manuscript* (Has 1965). The main organizing principle of this film is the repeated nesting of one story within another. In the first and largest portion of the film, each story includes a mysterious incident or aspect that unfolds out into another story that seemingly provides some background to the prior story. By the time the experiencer is wondering if this procedure will continue indefinitely and whether he can keep track of all the unfolding mysteries, the end portion of the film arrives, which zips back through all the nested stories in reverse order, revealing the mysterious events to have all had pedestrian explanations.

Abstraction   The "part-whole" form of the inclusion relation is central to the relation of **abstraction**. One structure bears the relation of abstraction to a second structure within the narrative context if it is a copy of a relevant selection of parts of the second structure.

Perhaps the main manifestation of this relation is the way the contents of a story within the domain of the work can be understood as abstracted from the far richer particulars of the sociocultural and physical domains, including the human psyche and human behavior. Hence, a story typically does not act like a video camera set up to record all the particulars occurring within its frame and span of operation. Moreover, the abstraction process is prototypically not haphazard but selects relevant aspects—ones understood as structural and of concern.

The process of relevant part selection is a regular aspect of our cognitive activity, quite apart from the authorial process of copying such a selection for presentation in a work. This is seen in the fact that the cognitive structures in terms of which we experience and categorize do not much correspond to the texture of everyday life. Consider, for example, such conceptual/affective/actional constructs as jealousy, bravery, and child-rearing. In the everyday world, the components out of which such constructs are built are dispersed through time and space, there is much intervening material of no direct relevance, typical components of the construct may be absent and atypical ones present, and so on. Yet our cognitive processing succeeds in forming the constructs out of the raw experiential material by culling the relevant components, gathering them together, and organizing them into the target patterns. An author may tap into such cognitive constructs as these for use as structures in the narrative. That is, the abstractions incorporated in a story generally correspond to conceptual abstractions already present and regularly generated in our cognition.

The same process of relevant part selection can be observed in the visual medium. For example, cartoons and caricatures are abstractions from the full detail of the physical objects that they represent. Further, in certain respects, the features that they abstract may well bear some of the same relationships to the original as just discussed. Thus, those features tend to comprise the visual structure of aspects of the original that are of concern to us.

It should be noted that abstraction is not the only cognitive operation that we perform on observed phenomena and then replicate for a literary or iconographic work. A complementary cognitive process is that of imposition. We often impose a preconceived schema onto our understanding of the world by deforming otherwise observable phenomena so that they fit the schema. Such cognitive constructs are also copied for representation in a work.

4.1.2   Coextension   Two structures are coextensive with each other if they are manifested over the same region of some stratum.

Dual-Entity Type: Concurrence (with Respect to Time)   We first consider such coextension under the dual-entity conceptualization of parity—that is, where the two structures are considered distinct from each other. Where the stratum in which the two structures relate is that of temporal structure, coextension has the specific designation of **concurrence**.

One structure that is concurrent with another can be taken to be equipotent with it or, instead, to relate to it as an ancillary form to a main form. When coextension is combined in this way with nonequipotence, such a structure can be termed an **overlay**. To illustrate, the work may have an overall atmosphere of, say, menace or inexorable doom, while subparts of the story will be light. This lightness can be experienced as an overlay on a subterranean impending menace whose presence does not fully disappear during the light interlude. Other examples of overlay are where a narrative section is intended to be taken as telling two or more stories at once on different levels, as, say, a parable with its metaphoric interpretation resting on its literal interpretation, or where the author has two concurrent purposes, say, to educate while entertaining. Often, perhaps, an overlay structure is more abstract, while the substrate structure is more concrete.

Single-Entity Type: Equality   We next consider coextension under the single-entity conceptualization of parity—that is, where the two structures are considered identical to each other. This form of coextension will be termed **equality**. Thus, two structures are in a relation of equality if they are considered to be two manifestations of a single entity in different venues.

Several forms of equality are well recognized where such a single entity is an individual within the domains of the work, the author, and/or the addressee. To discuss this, some distinctions need to be established. We can say that the author of a narrative work, at a first level, typically creates an **outer story world**. This outer story world, in turn, consists of a **narrator**, a **narratee**, and an **inner story world**. The narrator is an apparent individual that does the storytelling. The narratee is an apparent individual to whom the narrator recounts the story. And the inner story world is the story that the narrator recounts.

Forms of equality, then, include the following: Where the author is equated with the narrator, the inner story is understood to represent events that the author has witnessed or believes. Where the narrator is overtly equated with one of the characters in the inner story world, the narrator is a **participant** in the inner story. In that case, nonquoted commentaries may include the pronoun *I*. If there is no such identification, the pronoun *I* typically does not appear outside of quotes, and the narrator is understood as a causally noninvolved observer. Where there is a triune identification of the author, the narrator, and a character of the inner story, the work is understood to be **autobiographical** to the extent that the author is not thought to be dissembling. Where the narratee within the outer story world is intended to be overtly equated with the addressee outside the work, the nonquoted commentary may include the pronoun *you* (or such formulations as *The reader may now be thinking that* ...). Otherwise, this pronoun, or comparable formulations, are typically not used, and the outer addressee can have the experience of listening in as the narrator recounts the story to the fictional narratee (although the reader may also feel that the narrator is telling the story directly to her, even without the use of forms of direct address).

The relation of equality also applies to structures across the domain of the work and the domain of the surrounding world. We first look at the case where such structures comprise individuals and events. To the extent that a character of the inner story is equated with an individual in the domain of the external world other than the author, the work is understood to be **biographical**. To the extent that the events as well as the individuals depicted in a work are identified with events and individuals in the external world, that work is considered to be **historical** or **documentary**. Conversely, to the extent that it is assumed that there is no such equivalence, the work is considered to be **fiction**. Works can exhibit various mixtures of equatability and nonequatability of events and individuals between the story world and the external world, yielding such hybrids as historical novels and docudramas.

We next consider equality between the attitudes or worldview that an author expresses in a work and the history of attitudes or worldview in the surrounding world. A work whose worldview coincides with that of its contemporary culture is understood as **modern** for its time, or, if the work appears in the present day, it is simply "modern." A work whose worldview coincides not with that of its contemporary culture but with that of a later period is understood to be **ahead of its time**, while a work whose worldview coincides with that of an earlier period is judged to be conservative or **backward-looking** for its time. To the extent that the worldview of an earlier work coincides solely with that of its contemporary period, it is said to be **dated**, whereas to the extent that its worldview coincides with aspects of the worldview found at other periods and the present, it is considered **timeless** or **universal**.

We next consider equality between the era represented in the story world of a work and the history of different eras in the surrounding world. If the era represented in a work coincides with the era during which it was created, the work is **contemporary** with its time, or, if appearing in the present day, it is simply "contemporary." If the represented era is coincident with an earlier era, the work is a **period** piece or a **historical** work (using a second sense of the word "history"). And if coincident with a relatively subsequent time, the work is **futurist**.

The conceptual equating of entities is a well-studied issue in linguistics. Thus, "co-reference" is the mention of the same entity in two different locations in a discourse. And "deixis" is the equating of an entity being referred to and an entity taking part in the speech event. We can elaborate on one way to regard deixis. Consider the sentence *I ate snails for breakfast* with its deictic pronoun *I*. The utterance of this sentence can be viewed as representing two distinct events separated in time. One event comprises a particular person executing the current speech act and can in effect be expressed as *A speaker is uttering this sentence*. The other is an earlier event comprising a particular person having breakfast that can be expressed as *A person ate snails for breakfast*. Separate filmstrips could record these two events, each of which includes a person who engages in its activity. By its use of the form *I*, the example sentence indicates that the person engaged in the utterance event is to be equated with the person engaged in the breakfast event. That is, they are separate instantiations of the same individual. Deixis is thus an equality relation between two narrative structural units.

4.1.3 Multipart Relations So far in this section, we have presented ways one structure as a whole can relate to another structure as a whole. In addition, though, the parts of one structure can be related severally to the parts of another structure. In one such relation, that of **correlation**, the two sets of parts are aligned in correspondence. In another such relation, that of **interlocking**, the two sets of parts interdigitate.

Correlation One example of correlation is the existence of corresponding points across a set of different strata in a narrative. This form of correlation is in fact the same as the foundational basis of the present analytic system, namely, the polygraph notion in which the different strata of a narrative are linked in their progression. Another example of correlation is that of different media or genres. This occurs, for example, in the synchronizing of dialogue, image, and music in a film or in a multimedia presentation. Another example might be the correlation of the progression in the contents of a story world with the succession of components of the physical medium of the work, as where a story is told by a series of poems with each poem appearing self-contained on each successive page of a book.

Interlocking The main form of interlocking evident in narrative is manifested over a temporal progression. This form can be termed **alternation**. In this form, the "parts" of each related structure are separate instantiations of that structure. The instantiations of each structure do not occur together, but one at a time, and by alternate turns.

Alternation can occur over any scope or scale. Thus, an alternation between the points of view of two different characters in a narrative can take place every other sentence, as in an exchange of dialogue, or every other chapter, as when a narrative presents the progress of a story by turns from the perspectives of the different characters. Other structures frequently alternated in a narrative are different spatial locations, different points in time (as with recurrent flashbacks), and different subplots or side stories.

The following is an example of sentence-scope alternation within the story "It Had Wings," by Gurganus (1991). What alternates is the location of the perspective point and the direction of the gaze from it that is adopted by a single character. The character is an angel addressing an old woman into whose garden he has fallen. First shown are the lines he speaks, indented by different amounts depending on the viewpoint and the view that he adopts. Next shown is a summary of the viewpoints and views adopted in the lines.

(a) We're just another army. We all look alike.
  (b) We didn't before.
    (c) It's not what you expect.
  (d) We miss this other.
    (e) Don't count on the next.
      (f) Notice things here.
(g) We are just another army.

(a) & (g): His viewpoint is in his current celestial existence; he looks around within that.

(b) & (d): His viewpoint is in his current celestial existence; he looks from there back to his former earthly existence.

(c) & (e): His viewpoint is in the woman's current earthly existence; he looks forward from there to her upcoming celestial existence.

(f): His viewpoint is in the woman's current earthly existence; he looks around within that.

4.1.4 Higher-Level Structure   Virtually any structural factor in narrative can be so organized as to exhibit a second-order structural pattern, and that, in turn, to exhibit a third-order pattern, and so on. An example is shown by Costello et al. (1995) in their analysis of the temporal structure of their included story. The first-order structure, comprising the relations of certain out-of-sequence story events to the reader's unidirectional temporal progression, was itself shown to be further orchestrated in the story. It was shown to exhibit a pattern of flashbacks that progressively zero in on a central temporal point (the death of a son), alternately overshooting and undershooting it.

4.2   Relative Quantity

The general parameter called **relative quantity** here is basically realized at three levels, with each larger level serving to embed the next smaller level. From larger to smaller, this general parameter includes **scope**—the relative amount of some structure within the narrative context being considered; **granularity**—the relative size of the subdivisions into which this amount is internally partitioned in one's attention; and **density**—the relative number of elements within any such subdivision that enter into consideration. We discuss these three levels in turn.

4.2.1   Scope   Scope refers to the relative quantity of some structure within the narrative context that is being considered over the full extent of that quantity for the structural properties that exist at that choice of quantity. The narrative structure could be, for example, a whole domain such as the work with its story world, or one or more strata such as the temporal, spatial, or psychological. Then, one can, for example, adopt full scope over a story's temporal and spatial structure so as to track the large-distance geographic movements of a character over the whole period covered in the work. Or one could pick the relatively small temporal and spatial scope of a character moving about in a room in the course of a half hour.

There are several ways of reckoning different magnitudes of scope. One reckoning simply involves the proportion out of the total entity at issue that is excerpted for consideration. This type of reckoning has two main levels of magnitude: **global** (with consideration of the entire entity at issue) and **local**, (with consideration of only a normatively small portion of the whole). But a narrative could make relevant various magnitudes of scope between global and local or could distinguish magnitudes finer than "average local" down to **microlocal**.

Another way of reckoning is based on cognitive capabilities and would yield the following two main sizes of scope: (1) what can be experienced within a single scope of perception and span of attention, and (2) what must be assembled in memory because it is larger than scope size 1. For example, in nonnarrative everyday experience, one can consider an ant crawling across one's palm within a single scope of perception and span of attention. But one can consider a bus trip that one has taken across the country only by assembling aspects of the total experience within one's memory, since the experience is of scope size 2.

Comparably, within a story of sufficient length, certain structural features of the story will lie within one's span of attention and other features will exceed that span. Scope of perception may apply little to written prose (though it may do so to poetry that depends in part on the visual arrangement of the words on the page). But scope of perception can pertain to the sensory input from dynamic works.

4.2.2 Granularity The parameter of granularity applies relative to a particular level of scope. Granularity is the coarseness or fineness of the grid with which one attends to the contents within the chosen scope. That is, it is the general relative magnitude of the subdivisions that result from the further partitioning of the chosen scope of material.

For example, we could select from a narrative a spatial structure of local scope, perhaps a room in which our perspective point is located. Within this scope the narrative might present its material at these two different levels of granularity: One level could constitute a yards-sized metric, a level at which might appear such objects as furniture and people or such features as the room's architectural design. A finer level of granularity could be measured in inches, a level at which might appear such entities as details of wallpaper design, ashtray locations, and facial features. Comparably, over a global scope, in a narrative whose story spans geographic distances, a coarser granularity might pick up national regions, while a finer granularity could present towns.

4.2.3 Density Relative to a particular granularity, the parameter of density is the relative number of elements extant at that particular granularity that are selected for attention or mention. Thus, to continue the previous example with local scope of spatial structure, a sparse description at the yard-type level of granularity might mention, with respect to furniture, only a sofa and a TV, while a denser description could also mention the armchair, floor lamp, coffee table, and so on. Likewise, at the inch-type level of granularity, a sparser level of density might only mention a few items, like the wallpaper design feature and the ashtray location, but a denser description might also include the crack in the ceiling, the sunbeam hitting the family portrait, and the stain on the butler's tie.

Genres as a whole can differ greatly in the general level of their density. Thus, a story presented in a film is enormously denser in the detailing of the material objects and physical features that occupy and characterize the spatial structure than the same story written in prose. Across visual genres, a printed or filmic cartoon version of a story will have much sparser physical detailing than a standard film version. Further, within a single genre, authors often differ as to the level of density they select. Some give innumerable details at a particular level of granularity while others do not. Finally, the level of detailing can also be varied purposively and in correlation with other factors within a single narrative. For example, Hill (1991) notes that, as a narrative approaches a crucial dramatic point, the story time generally slows down relative to reader time and detailedness generally increases.

4.3   Degree of Differentiation

The general parameter **degree of differentiation** encompasses a number of simpler parameters, seven of which are presented in the subsections that follow. These parameters pertain to various ways in which any entity or structure within the total narrative context can be more or less speciated, articulated, distinguished, defined, or determined. As characterized here, these parameters may not be wholly autonomous. They may in part overlap, and many tend to correlate. And some may pertain to certain types of narrative structures more than to other types. Still, at core, they seem to be largely independent and distinct. In the following subsections, the parameters are named with their less differentiated pole first and their more differentiated pole second. Although it is mainly the poles that are named and discussed, these parameters largely exhibit gradient characteristics.

4.3.1   The Continuous-Discrete Parameter

This parameter is the axis that runs from the continuous to the discrete, where the latter is the more differentiated property. This parameter pertains to any structure within the narrative context. At the continuous end of the parameter, that structure is understood as comprising a single unified continuum or gradient that may manifest some progressive transition. At the other extreme, the structure comprises two or more entities that are separate from each other, with clear boundary lines between the entities, and with each entity bearing a distinct relation to the others.

When applied to the domain of a narrative work, this parameter can pertain, for example, to the stratum of spatial structure. Thus, with respect to scene shifting, a character can be presented as jumping from being in one location to being in another, or as progressively executing the transition. Or the parameter can pertain to the stratum of psychological structure. Thus, an author could transpose a reader from the viewpoint of one character to that of another, or instead have the reader transit imperceptibly from the thoughts of one character to those of another. As an example of a work that emphasizes the continuous pole for transitions, the short story "The Haunted House" by Virginia Woolf (1944) sets it as a deliberate design feature of the narrative to shift gradually in many categories of structure. The author does this, for example, with the current narrative location within the house, the identity of the current character, and the time of the events being portrayed.

The parameter applies not only to dynamic shifts, but also to static characterizations. Thus, the psyche of a character can be represented as a unitary entity whose otherwise distinguishable components are smoothly integrated. Or it can be represented as composite—in the extreme case, composed of discrete "selves" in a multiple personality.

The present parameter applies as well across domains. For example, where an audience is involved with an author in the co-creation of a work (several forms of which were described in section 2), the structure consisting jointly of the author and addressee domains can exhibit various degrees along the axis from a discrete separation to a melded gradient across the two contributory domains.

4.3.2 The Uniplex-Multiplex Parameter For any particular type of structure in a narrative context, the parameter of **plexity** (see chapter I-1) pertains to the number of instantiations of that structure. The structure is **uniplex** if there is a single entity manifesting it, and **multiplex** if there are two or more entities manifesting it. This latter case would then represent the more differentiated pole of the parameter. The multiplex case, further, involves the nature of the interrelationships among the plural elements. Thus, they may function jointly, independently, interactively, or in a state of conflict.

The parameter of plexity is pertinent, for example, where a body of phenomena is conceptualized as having changed in the number of distinct entities that make it up, as with splits and mergers (see section 4.4.1). Thus, cell mitosis can be regarded as a process in which the cessation of one entity turns into the start of two new entities. Conversely, the fusion of a sperm and an egg can be regarded as a process in which the cessation of two distinct entities becomes the start of a single new entity.

Comparable forms are evident in narrative. Thus, a shift in the number of entities present—coupled with a shift in perspective point—appears in the story "Reassurance" by Gurganus (1991). The initial representation in this story is of two characters, a soldier lying wounded in a hospital and his mother back home. The reader's perspective point is first located at the soldier apparently writing to his mother about his circumstances. By turns, it becomes clearer that this scene is actually the contents of a dream that the mother has been having. The son has already died, the mother alone remains, and the reader's perspective comes to shift to her location. Thus, the two characters originally in the reader's imagination have gradually melded into a single character. Perhaps more than splitting and merging, the plexity-related processes at work here can be considered ones of "extrusion" and "resorption." Once one guesses that the events presented in the story must be routed through the mother's psyche, one now imagines that the mother's personal identity has extruded a portion of itself. This portion has speciated or budded off and takes on the semblance of a separate identity, that of her son. This "homunculus" is then the quasi-entity that seems to speak in its own voice in addressing the mother. One then conceptualizes the temporary homunculus as becoming resorbed again into the mother's psyche.

4.3.3   The Distributed-Concentrated Parameter   This parameter pertains to whether some single entity is spread out over a larger area or is localized within a small area. More precisely, this parameter constitutes the degree to which some entity within the narrative context, on the one hand, is **distributed** over the next larger structure with which it is associated or within which it manifests itself, or, on the other hand, is **concentrated** or **focused** relative to that structure.

The parameter of section 4.3.1 can intersect the present parameter. That is, the single entity of the current parameter can be internally continuous or discrete. The discrete case allows additional terms for the poles of the parameter. With the single entity thought to be composed of constituents, then, this parameter involves the degree to which the constituents are **dispersed** over a larger area or **gathered together** within a smaller area.[9]

The pole of the parameter that should be taken as the more differentiated one would seem to be the pole of concentration. The reason is that a quantity is generally more amorphous when it is more distributed, but it is more "crystallized"—that is, closer to an ideal notion of well-defined entityhood—when it is more concentrated.

Although this parameter can apply to physical material, as in a description of cosmic dust coalescing over time into a star, in narrative we find it applying most often to concepts and themes. To illustrate, the movie *Schindler's List* (Spielberg 1993) shows the trajectory of Schindler's ever-closer involvement with the Jews he deals with. This progresses from seeing them as useful for his business, to maintaining them against Nazi removals for the sake of his business, to protecting them against Nazi assault out of sympathy for them, to a desperately felt cause to preserve them. The progression along this trajectory is subtle, and, while watching the later stages spanning most of the latter portion of the movie, the viewer might regard them as still involving only pragmatic business concerns plus an increasing sympathy. It is only near the end of the movie in the scene where Schindler breaks down, weeping, obsessed over how he might have saved yet one more Jew, that the audience realizes the actual emotional state of desperate empathy that Schindler had been feeling in those later stages. In this scene, Schindler's emotional state is presented in a concentrated, well-defined, acute form. The viewer then realizes that this same emotional state must also have been present throughout the later stages but distributed there in a more diffuse form.

4.3.4 The Approximate-Precise Parameter The contrast between **approximateness** and **precision** is the difference between a broadband (or rough-and-ready) characterization of any entity and a fine-structural characterization of that entity. An example of this distinction can be seen for motor-visual behavior in regard to gestures. To show someone the outline of some object that is oval, one could make a quick roughly ovoid sweep of the whole hand, or instead one could move one's forefinger slowly and with tightened muscular tension to describe a fine-lined ellipse. It may be that this type of gestural difference is a cross-cultural universal and is innate. An example of the present parameter in narrative could be the depiction of the personality of a character either with broad brush strokes or with a fine-etched articulation.

It might at first seem that the present parameter in the domain of the work correlates with certain psychological characteristics in the domain of the author. Thus, approximateness in a work might be thought to correlate with indifference and carelessness in an author, while precision correlates with care and carefulness. While this association may be common, it does not seem necessary. Thus, care and carefulness can also accompany the appearance of approximateness, as seems, for example, to be the regular association for some schools of Japanese art.

4.3.5   The Vague-Clear Parameter   This parameter pertains to whether the author's or addressee's understanding of some conceptual entity—or whether the narrative presentation that manifests or mediates such understanding—is **vague** or **clear**. On the vague end, this understanding or presentation is murky, where whatever components it may have and their interrelationships are poorly worked out. On the other end, the understanding or presentation is well-developed in its clarity, with its components and their interrelationships well worked out. The pole of clarity, of course, is the more differentiated end of the parameter. One may readily associate with conceptual contents at the clarity pole the notion that they are comprehended intellectively, but at the murky pole the notion is more that they are sensed or apprehended viscerally. Contents at the clarity pole are identified; those at the vague pole are more pregnant with the potential of discovery or of being figured out.

4.3.6   The Sketchy-Elaborated Parameter   This parameter pertains to the extent to which some conceptual structure is addressed and dealt with. A conceptual entity can be less extensively addressed, in which case it is **sketchy** or **schematic**. Or it can be more extensively dealt with, in which case it is more **elaborated** or **specified**. The latter is, of course, the more differentiated pole. It is necessary to distinguish this parameter from the preceding one, since the qualities of sketchiness and elaboration can intersect those of vagueness and clarity. Thus, a matter that is clearly understood and worked out need not exist or be presented with full elaboration but can be sketched out. Contrariwise, a matter only vaguely understood need not exist or be presented sketchily but can get highly elaborated. Accordingly, one can write much and with great elaboration about amorphous murk. Likewise, one can write tersely about a subject one understands clearly.

4.3.7   The Implicit-Explicit Parameter   This parameter pertains to the degree to which any factor or system is **implicit** or **explicit**. At the implicit end, the factor or system is effectively present, as judged by an addressee's cognitive response to a work and perhaps by an assessment of the author's intent, but is not in its own right directly apparent. At the explicit end, the factor or system is perceptibly manifest or is expressed overtly and directly in its own right. Implicit content comes to be present in the addressee's cognition through various processes: It can be presupposed, perhaps as part of the cultural or physical world context. It can be inferred from the explicit content via conventional reasoning processes acting in accordance with background knowledge. It can be inferred on the basis of what was not included amidst the explicit material relative to some baseline of expectations. Or it can exist in the form of second-order patterns in the explicit material that then have to be discerned. The explicitness pole of the present parameter is assumed to be the more differentiated one because the conceptual content of explicit material is more certain and univocal, whereas implicit conceptual content is generally more ambiguous.

Note that although the poles of the present implicit-explicit parameter tend to align with the respective poles of the preceding two parameters— that is, the vague-clear and the sketchy-elaborated parameters—it is in principle distinct from those parameters. Thus, with respect to the vague-clear parameter, a narrative can be quite explicit about vague material, while an implicit suggestion or innuendo can be quite clear and unmistakable. Comparably, with respect to the sketchy-elaborated parameter, explicit material can be quite sketchy, while an author can take pains to arrange for the implicit evocation of a particular elaborate pattern of presuppositions and inferences in the addressee.

An author who intends that certain conceptual content be evoked in the addressee may purposely choose to make it implicit so that it will be less accessible for observation, or for placement within a comparative framework, or for questioning, and thus be outside the conscious awareness or control of the addressee. The aims of such a choice could be to abet persuasion, or the subliminal dramatic effect, or the shock and impact of discovery when the addressee herself pieces together what had been unstated.

Note that there appears to exist a class of affective categories—ones an author may want to evoke—that actually are at their strongest when they are solely implicit. A common denominator of such forms of affect may be that their object is understood as hidden or elusive. Affective categories of this sort would seem to include menace, eeriness, and mystery—to use terms that characterize the stimulus—or foreboding, disquiet, and wonder —corresponding terms that characterize the experience. The existence of such phenomena in our experience seems to depend on their remaining murky or being merely hinted at. When fully explicit or clear, they can lose their intrinsic character and their concomitant emotional impact. Such phenomena would then come under the aegis of other forms of cognition or emotion, such as curiosity, scrutiny, anger, or open fright. Speculatively, our capacity for such affective categories may have evolved in response to the kinds of phenomena in nature that have a hidden character. This would include, for example, stalking predators that employ stealth. There would accordingly have been a selective advantage to the evolution of a cognitive system that would detect and integrate sparse hints (e.g., the snap of a twig, a slight movement) into a suspicion of a causal agency behind them. The physiological hair-raising response, which now seems typically to accompany an inkling of menace, eeriness, or mystery, apparently in fact had its origin as a protective response to threat from another creature.

4.4   Combinatory Structure

Implemented by the pattern-forming cognitive system (described in section 1.1), the general parameter of **combinatory structure** pertains to the pattern in which elements are joined together to constitute a larger whole. Such combinatory structure can consist either of an atemporal or simultaneous association of the elements, or, instead, of a temporal sequencing of the elements. An example of simultaneous association of elements is an atmosphere, as discussed in section 3.4.2.3. An example of temporal sequencing is the plot of a story.

Various systems exist that prescribe certain forms of **well-formedness** of combinatory structure. Such a system can be, for example, culturally or authorially or innately based. The system can be a body of principles that govern, or patterns that characterize, or factors that constrain the combinations that are well formed. Different systems can be applied side by side to different structures within a total narrative context. Among the extant concepts of well-formedness, general forms of it include "consistency" and "coherence" for atemporal combination, and "cohesion" for sequential combination.

In the following subsections, though some cases of simultaneous association are included, we concentrate on temporal succession. We will use the term **sequential structure** to refer to the patterns in which a number of elements of some category combine in a sequence through time, whether these patterns conform to particular principles of well-formedness or, on the contrary, break them.

4.4.1   The Sequential Structure of Identity   A fundamental conceptual construct is the **sequential structure of identity**. One of our cognitive capacities is the ability to draw a conceptual boundary around some portion of the contents of consciousness (including what is perceived or conceived) and to ascribe unitary entityhood to the material within that boundary. Such an **entity** could be a physical inanimate or animate object, an event, an institution, a personality, a trend, and so on. Our cognition can further operate to ascribe to such an entity a distinctive **identity**, so that it is conceptualized as unique and distinguishable from other entities.

The sequential structure of identity has a number of properties. One of them is that the identity of an entity can be conceptualized as maintaining continuity through time regardless of any other changes that the entity may undergo. For example, in the transformation of Kafka's (1936) character Gregor Samsa into an insect, the reader readily accepts the idea that the personal identity of Samsa continues on despite the physical change. In this instance, the personality of the original entity is understood as the essential component of the entity's identity, while its form is understood as incidental. Likewise, with little question we attribute a single continuous identity spanning decades to, say, the General Electric corporation despite what may have been complete or near complete changes in personnel, physical plant, and product.

This form of sequential structure, namely, continuity of identity despite changes, has a synchronic analog, namely, sameness of identity despite differences. Thus, the same property that is considered definitional of a particular entity's identity can be ascribed to a number of concurrent instantiations that differ in other properties. Such separate instantiations are understood as **versions** or **variants** of the same entity. What can be considered the "same story" can be told in book and film versions (where it differs as to the medium), or in short story and novel versions (where it differs in length and detail), or as the related folk tales of two different cultures (where it differs in certain aspects of content).

Another form of continuity of identity through time is the maintenance of identity across temporal gaps. Consider personal relationships. One's sense of another person's continuity of identity can hold across gaps, even long ones, as with a colleague that one sees only every four years at a conference but with whom one feels an unbroken friendship. In such cases, one may be performing an operation of **cognitive splicing**, where one joins one's experience of the various periods one spends with another person into a seemingly seamless continuum from which the intervening periods have been excised. From one perspective, this cognitive phenomenon is merely a correlate of Piaget's object constancy. But it takes on special significance when we realize one of its consequences. Our sense of continuity of identity across gaps allows us to maintain cognizance of an enormous number of separate identities concurrently. Thus, with respect to acquaintanceships, we can conceptually maintain numerous continuing relationships interwoven through the single timeline of our life.

This temporal form of splicing across a gap to maintain identity also has a synchronic spatial analog. Consider sentences like *The park lies in the middle of Fifth St.*, or *Fifth St. extends on either side of the park.* Such sentences represent a conceptualization in which there is a single entity (Fifth St.) that spans a gap, rather than two separated entities.

The concept of identity discussed so far has been its continuation while other factors change. But there is also the concept of a change in identity. This new concept rests on a more complex basis than might at first be thought. Thus, to eliminate one possibility, no change of identity is experienced as taking place simply as a result of a person's first perceiving or conceiving one entity and then shifting her attention to another entity. For example, a person does not experience that an identity has changed when she first looks at a pen in her hand and then at a cloud in the sky, even though the percept or concept of the one entity has in sequence been supplanted by that of the other entity in her mind. Rather, our usual concept of change of identity entails a change in the identity of *something*. Hence, as before, there is a something that has maintained its continuity through time, even if its identity has changed. This situation differs from the preceding one in that here the something that persists is not treated as definitional for an ascription of identity, whereas before it was so treated. However, because of its conceptual underpinning, a conceptualization in terms of change of identity might always be open to a reconceptualization in terms of continuity of identity, namely, that of the "something" that does persist.

This may be illustrated with a type of example introduced by Postal (1976: 211–212). Consider a lizard that had previously lost its tail. One can then say of it either *The lizard grew another tail*, or *The lizard grew back its tail*. The former sentence represents a conceptualization in terms of change of identity. Here, entityhood is associated with a particular quantity of matter that formed the original tail, and since the quantity of matter forming the new tail is different, it is a different tail with its own distinct identity. But the second sentence represents the alternative conceptualization, that of the continuing identity of a persistent something. Here, the concept of a tail is associated with a particular spatio-temporal form bearing a particular relation to the rest of the lizard's body. This form can persist or recur through time regardless of the particular material instantiating it. Such material is thus, as in the earlier discussion, an incidental property that can change without effect on the concept of identity.

Similarly, the sentence *Five windows have broken in this frame* refers to five distinct panes of glass, each with its own unique identity. But *The window in this frame has broken five times* refers to the more abstract entity of the form that fills the frame, which maintains its identity across five material instantiations of it.

In the preceding two example pairs, the conceptualization in terms of change of identity pertained to the concrete material, while the abiding factor was the form. But the reverse can also be observed. For instance, consider a story in which a craftsman has carved a tree into a canoe. Here, even though the concrete material, the wood, has persisted through time, one would usually regard the form as definitional of identity, so that where there had been a tree, there now was a canoe. Here a change of identity is exhibited by the form, whereas the material is abiding.

Even a change of identity of this type too, though, is open to a reconceptualization in terms of continuity of identity. Thus, if the story presents the tree as having a spirit, one would now associate identity with the persisting material and its indwelling spirit, so that the change in form from that of a tree to that of a canoe is merely incidental and no longer constitutes a change of identity.

This sequential change in identity also has a synchronic analog. Consider a courseway for cars that has two different names over different stretches. One can think of this as two separate streets that meet up (perhaps historically, in fact, two separate streets were later joined). This conceptualization, then, involves two distinct identities. Alternatively, as in the sequential case, the other conceptualization in terms of a single identity is also available. Thus, one could think of the courseway as a single street with a single identity that is simply called by different names over different portions of itself.

As another of its sequential properties, an identity can not only remain constant or change, but it can also begin or cease to exist. Both these processes can be conceptualized together as a pair. Thus, we have the cognitive capacity to monitor a sequence of phenomena, to draw a closed boundary around a portion of it, and to ascribe entityhood to that portion, so that phenomena preceding the earlier boundary and phenomena following the later boundary are excluded from that entity. That entity is thus conceived as beginning at the earlier boundary and ending at the later one. This characteristic is exhibited by any so-conceived bounded event, wherein some finite quantity is progressively acted on to exhaustion. English can typically mark such an event with a temporal phrase beginning with *in*, as in *The log burned up in 10 minutes* or *I swept the floor in 10 minutes*. Conceptions can differ as to where to draw a boundary in a principled way. Thus, with regard to an initial boundary, views differ as to whether the identity of a human individual begins, for example, at conception, at the start of fetal brain function, or at birth. And with regard to a terminal boundary, views differ as to whether an individual's life ends at the cessation of brain function, at the cessation of general body functions, or at the point where no revival can be effected.

The conceptualization of an identity as having a finite span or a cessation point can lead to further cognitive formations. If one has an an affective response of attachment to a particular entity, one generally feels a desire to prolong the existence of the entity and to preserve it against threats to its continued existence. Then the entity's ceasing to exist generally evokes an experience of loss and an accompanying feeling of sadness. Such feelings are prototypically associated with the life of another person dear to one. But they can also attach to any liked entity, of whatever nature or degree of abstraction. Thus, readers can experience them over the death of a fictional character—as they did when Arthur Conan Doyle tried to kill off Sherlock Holmes and had to bring him back to life due to public reaction. And one can feel them over the discontinuation of a program or the end of an era.

The cognitive processes that ascribe entityhood to some portion of phenomena, that impute continuity of identity to that entity despite changes in other factors, and that fix a feeling of attachment to that continuity may engender a further cognitive effect. They might produce the conceptualization that the identity continues past a boundary that would otherwise be associated with the cessation of the entity. In particular, we find many traditional concepts of the continuation of an individual's identity beyond the death of his physical body. Such concepts include life after death, the eternality of a soul, and the transmigration of souls.

The sequential properties for identity discussed so far have held constant the number of identities involved at any particular time, and have in fact held this number constant at "one." But some properties also address a change in the number of identities extant. Such properties include splits and mergers. For example, a single bacterium with its own specific identity can divide into two "daughter" bacteria, each with its own particular identity. And, conversely, two streams, each with its own name and identity, can flow together into a single river that bears its own distinct name and identity. As before, this sequential pattern has a synchronic analog. A spatial example is a street that forks into two—or, conversely, two streets that merge into one—with each of the three segments bearing its own name and identity.

Our conceptual ascriptions of entityhood are often challenged by such patterns. Thus, in the bacteria case, one might feel that the "mother" bacterium ceased to exist as an entity on splitting and that two new entities came into existence. Or, one could feel that the original bacterium somehow continues on in a distributed fashion in the two daughter cells. For a comparable example in the reverse direction, we are often unclear whether to regard a case of close symbiosis as two organisms in association or as a third organism with components.

Identity structure can exhibit most of the other parameters discussed in section 4. For example, the parameter of inclusion of the part-whole type is exhibited by an anthology. The whole of an anthology has its own name and identity, while it encompasses a set of separate contributions, each with its own title and identity. Or two entities with distinct identities could exhibit partial overlap. This relationship is often exhibited with respect to geographic distribution—for example, by nations and tribes in Africa, or by county divisions and electoral districts in the United States.

In fact, examples similar to the last one can illustrate a parameter of **accord** or **discord** between two structures. First, note that the cognitive process of drawing a boundary around a portion of phenomena for an ascription of entityhood can be founded on different bases. Thus, establishing the entity of an electoral district over a contiguous potion of territory can be based on a pattern of population density or, alternatively, on a pattern of likely party affiliation. If these two bases are discrepant, a district formed on the latter basis is said to be "gerrymandered." Thus, the concept of gerrymandering is based on the cognitive principles that govern the ascription of entityhood and identity.

The conceptual construct of a particular continuing identity generally has a secondary property: Other phenomena conceptually associated with that identity also become associated with each other. Such other phenomena, further, undergo cognitive processes that select elements from among them and integrate those elements into what can be experienced as a single ideational whole. Even where such elements might seem a disparate collection on other grounds, or as assessed by other cognitive faculties, they can be united into a complex here that seems to accord with well-formedness principles for ideational sequential structure.

A principal type of entity that functions in this way is the conceptual construct of one's self. Under the aegis of this single identity, the experiences that one has had can be conceptually united so as to constitute the ideational entity thought of as one's "life." The cognitive processes that perform this integration can base it on different selections from among the experiences, and can thread the selected components together in different ways to yield different conceptions of one's life. Such alternatives of conception can arise in the same individual at different moments or in association with particular moods, or they can vary across individuals in accordance with their cognitive style and personality (see Linde 1993). Of course, one exercises the same cognitive processes on one's perception of another human, to yield a conceptualization of that person's "life."[10]

Where the entity that serves as the organizing aegis is not a human individual but a nonsentient construct like a work of fiction, the same cognitive process of selection and ideational integration that one exercises yield not a "life" but a "story." And where the entity is a construct like an institution or nation, they yield a "history." The concept of the will of God as having acted purposefully through history may arise as a projection of this cognitive system for weaving a selection of events together into what is then experienced as a well-formed ideational sequence.

Strong cognitive tendencies govern the type of entity that can function in this way as an aegis or venue for the integration of secondary phenomena associated with it. In general, such an entity seems to be conceived of as a contiguous portion of space-time. Thus, a person typically limits this integration to the experiences directly associable with his biological self to form his conception of a single life, rather than mixing together excerpts from his self and from other people into that conception. Comparably, a person for the most part does not cobble together bits and pieces out of various books lying before her from which to fashion a story, but rather limits herself to the confines of a single physical book to integrate its contents into a story.

As they have been described in this section, the cognitive processes for integrating conceptual components into an entity with an identity are a specific application of the pattern-forming cognitive system described in section 1.1. The comment in that section on the evolution of this system can be augmented here. It would presumably have been a selective advantage for an organism to have an increase in its capacity to integrate its experiences over time. Such a development would permit the accumulation, comparison, and conflict resolution of a larger set of experiences in the world, to constitute a reference body of individual lore for an organism. But further, then, this level of experiential integration may have depended on the evolution of the capacity in the pattern-forming cognitive system to form a construct of the "self" as a substrate on which the experiences could be interwoven.

4.4.2 Ideational Sequential Structure Another parameter of sequential structure pertains to ideational or conceptual content and so can be termed **ideational sequential structure**. On the one hand, a particular concept can be represented or experienced at a particular point in time. On the other hand, a number of such concepts can also be combined within a single conceptual structure manifesting through time. Such an ideational structure can range indefinitely upward in scope, embeddedness, or intricacy—with respect to language, say, from a phrase to Proust's *À la Recherche du Temps Perdu*.

Various systems of well-formedness can be applied to such an ideational sequence. Two related systems of this sort that apply within language, mostly over a local scope, are syntax and discourse factors. Another system of well-formedness, one that operates at any scope size, though perhaps typically at a mid-range, is that of "logic," understood in its broad sense. This includes assessments as to whether a current idea follows logically and reasonably from what has preceded, or whether there has been sufficient preparation for it, so that it is not a nonsequitur. Yet a further system, one that realizes its fullest integration over a global scope, is any set of canons or norms of plot development or of story cohesion. A system of this sort would thus comprise a body of principles and normative expectations that pertain to the sequencing of ideas over a broad scope. Accordingly, the concept of **plot** can be located within the present category of ideational sequential structure. Thus, for a narrative work, one notion of plot is that it is basically a form of abstraction from the overall ideational sequential structure of the work. This abstraction is based on some system of evaluation for structural relevance, but it typically concentrates on individuals, events of mid-sized scope, and psychological import. Of course, different sets of canons or norms pertaining to plot development and story cohesion can disagree in their principles of well-formedness. For example, one set will accept an unforeshadowed agency appearing so as to resolve a plot dilemma, while another set will dub such an agency a contrived "deus ex machina."

The ideational structure of a work, as described in the preceding, as well as the character of its ideational content, may tend to reside in the background of an addressee's attention relative, for example, to the ideational content itself. But a work can also make the structure and character of its ideational content the object of the addressee's attention. One form of this is the "Rashomon" effect, where events that one might have thought had an objective character to their contents are instead presented from the perspective points of different individuals. These individuals abstract different aspects from the ideational complex and process those aspects in different ways, or they project different aspects of their own affect or cognition onto the complex, thus leaving the addressee wondering if there is such a thing as objective reality or whether all is instead only subjective interpretation. Alternatively, a work can intentionally leave unclear what has actually happened, or it can present discrepant and contradictory descriptions of what has happened. In all these ways, the character of ideational content and its sequential structure is made an issue of in its own right and is thus foregrounded.

The remainder of this section concerns addressee and authorial assessments of well-formedness in the sequential structure of ideation. An addressee has a cognitive system for assessing the well-formedness of an ideational sequence, for example, of a book he is reading or a film he is watching. Correlatively, an author typically thinks through her body of material for its logical interconnections, so she can shape the work to have the desired effect on the addressee's cognitive system for assessing sequential well-formedness.

Now, authors often intentionally formulate their productions in a way designed not to accord with the addressee's cognitive system for assessing well-formedness in ideational sequence, but rather to tamper with it. One reason an author may have for structuring a work in this way is—as the author might conceive it—to disrupt the addressee's habitual attention to superficial forms of well-formedness in order to urge their attention toward deeper forms. A literary example of this might be absurdist plays, as by Ionesco or Genet. And if sequential well-formedness can be extended from a work of language to one of dance, so as to cover not only a smooth flow of ideas but also a graceful flow of movement, then an example of intentional disruption of traditional norms of well-formedness might be a modern dance performance, as one by Martha Graham (relative to the classical ballet that preceded it). The introduction of random elements, as in some musical forms by John Cage, may be intended to serve a similar function.

Another reason for an author to tamper with—in fact, to subvert—the addressee's systems for assessing logical well-formedness might be to persuade, as with propaganda or courtroom presentations. To induce the addressees' pattern-forming system to proceed in certain directions, an author here may foreground or select certain aspects of a full account; background or omit certain other aspects; distort still other aspects; present certain aspects in a suggestive way that would invoke the addressee's processes for forming inferences but do so in an incorrect direction desired by the author; disrupt the addressee's capacities for forming logical inferences through the use of factors that evoke strong emotions; and the like.

Yet another source of discord with assessments of well-formedness is simply authorial omission. Here, an author fails to work out the ideational content of his production so that it is conceptually integrated and has its components fit sensibly together, where this might otherwise be deemed desirable. An example might be movies that rely on special effects.

Productions stamped with such authorial inability or disregard might still be well received because, in a complementary fashion, enough addressees may not require well-formed ideational structure, especially under certain cognitive circumstances. Thus, the well-formedness system of an individual such as an addressee seems generally to be readily subject to diminution or disruption in its functioning by certain intense-level activity of other cognitive systems. Such activity might consist of the perception of powerful sensory stimuli or the experience of strong emotion. Accordingly, films that have striking visual effects or that rouse intense emotions such as excitement can get away with having plots that are relatively less cohesive than in other films and still be successful.

On this interaction between authorial and addressee attention to well-formedness, it may be further observed that, in some measure, the typical degree to which a narrative is integrated correlates with the typical degree to which the average experiencer is integrative. The scope over which an experiencer is readily able or eager to integrate an ideational sequence and to assess it for well-formedness varies across individuals and across cultures. In fact, it may alter in the course of cultural change. In this regard, some claim, for example, that forces are at work in American culture toward the reduction of an experiencer's integrative attention span down to the scope of a story segment between commercials or of a soundbite.

4.4.3 Epistemic Sequential Structure Another form of sequential structure pertains to epistemology and so can be called **epistemic sequential structure**. This is the structure of "who knows what when." More precisely, for any narrative-related domain, this is the cross-sectional and longitudinal profile of what each individual and group knows and when they know it. Broadly construed, epistemic structure also includes mistaken beliefs as well as beliefs held under various assessments of certainty and quality, as in the case of a hunch or a suspicion.

In a mystery novel, epistemic structure can be the main engine of plot progression for the characters in the story as well as for the author and reader. Thus, to look first within the story alone, epistemic sequential structure provides the rationale for such activities as a character's covering up, throwing a detective off the track, and spying, or a detective's investigating, giving a false sense of security to or decoying a suspect, and tricking the truth out of the real murderer.

And within the authorial domain for a mystery novel, epistemic sequential structure is the system by which the author undertakes such narrative actions as setting up a mystery, leaving clues as well as false trails, introducing a succession of seeming explanations that do not prove out, and delaying explanations until the final resolution at the end.

Accordingly, within the experiencer's domain, epistemic structure can engender in the addressee such experiences as suspense, puzzlement, hunches as to the truth, increases and decreases in her sense of certainty, a sense of letdown over her previous explanatory picture falling apart, and the gratification that she can feel over the consistency and coherence of all the pieces finally fitting together.

Apart from mystery stories, epistemic structure can be seen at work in many respects. For example, it can pertain to the creative style of the author. Thus, an author may be the type that fully plots out the work before composing it, or instead the type that begins the work and "does not know" where the story will go but lets the logic of the story and the psychology of the characters unfold in their own way.

4.4.4 Perspectival Sequential Structure   A perspective point has its own principles of sequential structure, here termed **perspectival sequential structure**. In significant ways, a perspective point is not constrained by or subject to the same principles of standard physics as a material entity, although it does follow them in some respects. For example, "perspective point physics" diverges from material physics with respect to certain aspects of spatial, temporal, and causal structure. Thus, the perspective point can jump about in story-world space, not subject to the usual principles of physical continuity. And, if need be, it can pass through or appear amidst otherwise solid objects, hence not subject to the usual material principle against colocation. Comparably, it can first appear at one story-world time and then jump to another, shifting either forward or backward, thus not subject either to a principle of temporal continuity or to a principle of unidirectional progression. The perspective point has no causal effect on the story world. That is, it can appear anywhere without any consequences to what would otherwise be taking place there.

Related to these physical freedoms, the perspective point is also free to appear in a range of structures across the narrative context. For example, it can appear not only among the material objects of the spatial stratum, but also in the minds of various characters in the psychological stratum. And the perspective point can appear in or jump across domains. This occurs, for example, when a work suddenly redirects the addressee's attention to the author or to the addressee himself, perhaps with the use of the pronouns "I" or "you" in the text. Or it takes place when the text calls attention to itself qua text, entailing that the addressee redirect her attention away from the contents of the text, through herself, and back to the text again. Few other entities have such freedom.

But perspective point physics is also consonant with material physics in a number of ways. Although the perspective point does not affect its surroundings, it can be affected by them, at least insofar as the perspective point's "decisions" as to how long to stay, what to observe, where to go next are concerned. Further, although the perspective point ignores some properties of spatial structure, (e.g., its ability to exhibit path discontinuities and to occupy the same location as another object), it does obey other aspects of spatial structure. For example, it generally remains for some duration of time within the confines of a designated spatial region and abides by the spatial structure of that region. Further, with regard to temporal structure, the perspective point has its own ticking clock that, from its own viewpoint, does determine a forward-progressing timeline.

Thus, although the perspective point may flit backward and forward in story-world time, the resulting observations are registered on the timeline of the perspective point itself as onto a steadily forward-progressing tape.

4.4.5 Motivational Sequential Structure   As a member of the psychological category of "affect" (see section 3.4.1), **motivation** consists of the tendencies toward particular types of action undertaken by a sentient entity that are thought to be associated with or caused by particular psychological states within that entity. In their most schematic prototype, the following might be examples of such tendencies: fear with respect to an object makes one tend to distance oneself from that object; anger, to approach the object so as to hurt or repel it; desire, to approach the object so as to acquire it; interest, to attend to the object; and boredom, to attend to something other than the object. Comparably, desire for a state of affairs—that is, having a goal—tends to make one undertake a sequence of actions that one thinks will culminate in that state of affairs.

With respect now to sequential structure, it is the multiple concatenating, embedding, overlapping, and opposing of motivations on the part of various individuals or groups over various degrees of scope that can constitute an important—often the main—cohesive structure of a narrative. The principles governing such phenomena are called **motivational sequential structure** here.

4.4.6 Psychological Sequential Structure   Recall that, in section 3.4, psychological structure was presented as a stratum—that is, as a type of phenomenon that can assume different values at different loci within the narrative context. It was found to be organized at three levels: the individual, the group, and the atmosphere. Here, we observe that an entity at any of these three levels can exhibit a succession of psychological forms and thus exhibit various patterns of **psychological sequential structure**. The forms of sequential structure presented in the preceding subsections also belong to the psychological stratum, but there they represent "categories" of psychological structure, as these were presented in section 3.4.1. Here, attention is on the "levels" of psychological structure, as these were presented in section 3.4.2.

Thus, at the individual level, an individual can exhibit patterns of psychological sequence like the following: a marshaled progression of rational thought; the gradual coalescence of an amorphous apprehension into a crystallized idea; a stream-of-consciousness type of succession of thoughts, each related to the last by perhaps little more than a shared conceptual component and a similar affective vector; or, indeed, abrupt shifts of ideas and feelings.

At the next level, a group might be thought to be subject to principles that govern psychological sequences like the following: a spread of mass hysteria; the progressive manufacture of public consent through control of media; the slide of a society from vigor to malaise.

And atmospheric transitions could include a shift from a tone of optimism to one of inexorable doom, or a shift from a sense of menace to one of warmth.

In much the same way that science fiction as a genre includes much deliberate play with the canonical principles of physical sequential structure, it also plays with the usual expectations for psychological sequential structure. It does so at the individual level—for example, in representing an alien with inexplicable motivations seeming to govern its course of behavior. It does so at the group level—for instance, in representing an extraterrestrial collective with a partly communal mind abetted by extrasensory communication, or a society with an unfathomable worldview that guides its actions. And it does so at the atmospheric level—for example, in representing a planet that engenders in a human observer uncanny feelings that follow no familiar pattern.

4.5   Evaluation

A psychological entity can perform the cognitive operation of **evaluating** a phenomenon for its standing with respect to some system of properties. A system of properties of this sort is typically understood as being scalar, running from a negative to a positive. Such systems of properties include veridicality, function, importance, value, aesthetic quality, and prototypicality. Thus, a cognitive entity can assess some phenomenon at the positive pole of these scales as being true, purposeful, important, good, beautiful, and standard. All these systems, except that of aesthetics, are addressed in the subsections below.

4.5.1   Veridicality   The parameter of **veridicality** pertains to the closeness of correspondence that some representational structure in a narrative has to some aspects of the "real world," in accordance with the way some cognitive entity assesses such closeness and conceives of such a world. Such a cognitive entity might be an outside analyst, an author, an addressee, or a performer of a work.

To illustrate, a work of fiction generally achieves the status of a **classic** because the experience of a critical mass of critics and the lay readership has been that the author has correctly captured certain truths about the nature of the human psyche or of society and has incorporated them in the story. Or, for an example from the perspective of a performer, an actor that experiences a play as generally nonveridical may find that he cannot believe in his role, perhaps that his character's lines or personality ring false, and consequently may deliver a poorer performance for not being able to get into the part.

Different degrees of veridicality are generally required for different genres of narrative. Thus, nonfiction—say, a history—generally has a higher requirement for a veridical correspondence of the textual descriptions to the external world than does fiction. And the genre of science fiction is generally distinguished from that of science fantasy on the basis of a story's scientific plausibility (as projected from contemporary understanding).

Different degrees of veridicality also occur within a single work in connection with different forms of representation in the work. In fact, some may hold that some divergence from veridicality is necessary for certain other truths to be represented. In this view, a narrative can, for example, exhibit noncorrespondence to superficial probabilities of occurrence that are customarily attributed to the external world, in exchange for greater veridicality in the abstracted representation of certain deeper psychological or societal structures. An example might be a film that is unrealistic about everyday life in a neighborhood but that portrays the behavior of the characters so as to represent certain abstract ideals or hopes about human relations that audience members might actually harbor.

The traditional concept of an addressee's "willing suspension of disbelief" falls directly under the aegis of the present parameter of veridicality. The concept refers to an addressee's acceptance of certain forms and amounts of nonveridicality in a story in exchange for certain other aspects of the narrative—for instance, its affect on the addressee's emotions. By one interpretation of the concept, the addressee prefers veridicality, so that there is a cost for her in a work's divergence from it, even as she enjoys the other aspects of the work that emerge in compensation. By another interpretation, the addressee actually prefers certain forms and amounts of divergence from veridicality because it permits the depiction of a world more enjoyable than that of her everyday life. When an addressee actively seeks such nonveridical narrative as a relief, it is understood as **escapist** literature.

It can be posited that a person's assessments as to degree of veridicality are due to the operation of a cognitive brain system whose function is to perform such assessments. Among its various operations, this cognitive system for veridicality would normally apply to the operations of the pattern-forming cognitive system, specifically with respect to its function of weaving conceptual components into a sequential narrative. The confabulation that some brain-lesion patients exhibit, then, might be attributed to a failed connection between the cognitive system for veridicality and the cognitive system for narrative construction.

4.5.2 Function An author can assess any structure that she considers placing in her work with respect to its relevance and efficacy for her communicative intentions. We can say that the author has a particular **purpose** in placing that specific structure in the work, or—equivalently— that the author intends that the structure serve a specific **function**. All the choices that the author makes in assembling the narrative can be guided by this factor of intended function.

For examples with local scope, an author's purpose for a particular paragraph, sentence, or even word could be to establish particular information or a mood needed for subsequent narrative developments; to keep the addressee's interest and attention active by changing the pace; or to induce in the addressee some particular affect, such as puzzlement.

At the global level, one preponderant intention of an author for her work is to have certain overall psychological effects on the addressee. What differs from work to work is what this effect is to be. Generally, this matter is the purview of the field of "rhetoric." Examples of intended psychological effects for the work as a whole are to make the addressee wiser or morally better, to orchestrate certain sequences and waves of emotion in the addressee that should (as the author's conceptualization may have it) cleanse him or refresh him, or to rouse the addressee to certain actions.

A narrative type can play with the parameter of function. To consider humor in this regard, a standard joke does not play with this parameter, since the elements presented along the way function as background or as lead-ups to the punchline. By contrast, a shaggy-dog story only parasitically mimics this narrative form. The elements in the lengthy body of the story turn out to have no functional relation to the punchline beyond affording the occasion for a pun. At a metalevel, thus, the point of the shaggy-dog genre is its pointlessness.

4.5.3 Importance   A phenomenon has **importance** for a sentient entity to the degree to which it pertains to or can affect—positively or negatively—any preference system held by that entity. A preference system is a system in accordance with which the sentient entity has different degrees of liking for various target elements. Such a system could be the values, desires, aesthetics, or interests of the sentient entity. In the context of this study, the most relevant phenomenon that can have importance is any representational structure within a narrative work—for example, a paragraph or the whole work itself. The sentient entity that experiences or assesses the importance of a phenomenon can be an addressee, an author, or a societal group (or, of course, any character or group represented within a narrative).

4.5.4 Value   A sentient entity can evaluate a phenomenon with respect to some system of values so as to assess it as relatively good or bad. While the parameter of importance addresses the degree to which a phenomenon *pertains* to a preference system such as that of one's values, whether positively or negatively, the parameter of **value** addresses the degree of positivity or negativity along that preference system of values. What seems universal in this parameter is that every familiar sentient entity appears to evaluate phenomena in terms of good and bad. What notoriously differs across sentient entities is which phenomena they assess as good and which as bad. And, of course, a single cognitive entity can hold two inconsistent evaluations of the same phenomenon. In the narrative context, for example, an addressee might consider a didactic aspect of some work both ethically uplifting and presumptuously moralistic.

Assessments along the parameter of value largely align with assessments along the other parameters in this section. For example, a critic will generally evaluate a work as good in correlation with the degree to which he assesses it as important, true to some aspects of the world (such as psychological or social structure), and beautiful, and to the degree to which it achieves the author's purposes through the choices she made in it.

4.5.5 Prototypicality   Any structure within the total narrative context is generally subject to assessments as to its **prototypicality**. That is, an author, an addressee, or members of the culture at large will generally have certain norms, expectations, and forms of familiarity pertaining to that structure as a result of experiences with the historical tradition or with other exposure to narrative contexts. By the nature of this characterization, such norms can be expected to vary for different structures in different genres, for different individuals or groups within a culture, for different periods within a single cultural tradition, and for different cultures.

Authors, or movements of authors, that compose their works to deviate substantially from the current norms may be considered by contemporaries to be **avant-garde** and their works to be **experimental**. Cultural traditions can exhibit a second-order difference in the degree to which they exert pressure on authors to maintain the inherited norms or, on the contrary, to challenge them. Thus, it appears that certain long periods in Chinese art and literature maintained themselves with great conservatism, while this century in the West has rewarded authorial experimentation.

Within the domain of the experiencer, the addressee of a work with prototype divergence will generally experience surprise over the novelty. Such experiences can become affectively tinged in a negative direction, for example, as shock, or in a positive direction—as exhilaration, for instance. In fact, a principal reason for including the parameter of prototypicality in the framework of the present analysis is the necessity, as we see it, of tracking the cognitive effect of an ongoing narrative on an addressee. After all, that profile of responses is something an author generally takes great pains to engineer, and the breaking of norms is a major vehicle for engendering certain desired responses in the addressee.

4.6   Interrelations between Different Parameters

As with domains, the various general and particular parameters presented in this section can interrelate with each other. For example, the parameter pertaining to alternation could apply to the parameter of scope: Two structures in a text could alternate either locally or globally. Or the continuous-discrete parameter could apply to the granularity parameter. For example, a narrative could address an issue from two distinct levels of granularity—say, a fine-grained and a broad-brush treatment of the issue (perhaps alternating between the two). Or it could instead address the issue along a continuous range of granularities. Or, again, the veridicality parameter could apply to the parameter pertaining to abstraction. This combination could pertain, in the judgment of the addressee or of some analyst, to whether the author has correctly captured something

about the nature of the human psyche in the abstractions from his understanding of it that he incorporates into the narrative.

Another way that different parameters may interrelate is as alternatives
shifting in their prominence in accordance with the weighting or interpretation they are given. Thus, depending on particulars of their treatment or of their interpretation by an experiencer, two structures may, in
the course of a narrative, be able to bear to each other all the relationships
of "embedding," "alternation," "concurrence," and "correlation," as
these were discussed in section 4.1. For example, a love story that unfolds
against the backdrop of a nation at war may at times seem to be a small
event **embedded** within a larger historical epic. Or it may seem to be a
drama as intense for its interiority as the social events are for their external power, so that scenes of the one appear to **alternate** on a par with
scenes of the other. Or it may seem like a desperate attempt to wrest a
normal life out of the pervading horrors, hence to appear as a **concurrent**
overlay on the upheaval, one that might even have depended on the
turmoil for its occurrence. Or it may seem to consist of stages whose
unfolding **correlates** with the developments in the war.

5   CONCLUSION

This chapter has presented the beginnings of a framework that will lay
out the main structural delineations of narrative and of the larger narrative context. The framework can be used to guide the analysis of particular narrative works. But it also links up with endeavors in other fields in
cognitive science and the humanities (including the author's own work in
linguistics) to contribute to progress toward an integrated understanding
of conceptual structure in human cognition.

Notes

1. This chapter is a greatly revised and expanded version of Talmy 1995b.

For our discussions on the material of this chapter, I am especially indebted to
the editors of the volume in which the original version appeared—Gail Bruder,
Judy Duchan, and Lynne Hewitt—as well as to the other members of the narrative research group at SUNY Buffalo, including Bill Rapaport, Erwin Segal, Stuart
Shapiro, and David Zubin. My thanks as well to Emmy Goldknopf for her com-
ments on later drafts.

2. This framework can also characterize a diachronic change of structure in the
narrative context, but this aspect is not developed here. We might simply note
that, with respect to narrative structure, within any one historical tradition the

general tendency seems to be for new points of articulation to gradually develop. That is, some set of elements that had previously appeared together to constitute a single packet can in time be broken up into component parts by innovative producers of narrative. It further seems that an articulation of this sort that can show up late in one tradition may have been present early in some other tradition. Thus, some articulations that have appeared only recently in the history of Western literature have long been present in the narrative of some traditional folk cultures.

3. There is much overlap between the work of Genette (1980) and other structuralist narratologists, and the approach put forward here. But our approach is based on a cognitivist perspective, and our framework is based on an assessment of cognitive structure and process.

4. Kinetic sculpture is the only item on this list that does not strictly conform to the aegis of successively revealing different parts of itself, since the whole of the sculpture can be seen at all times. But it could be argued that its different states of conformation constitute different "parts" of the sculpture's totality.

5. While a wide variety of temporal textures may structure our experience and narrative works, the grammatical (closed-class) forms of languages are limited to the expression of only a small subset of these textures, with such typical meanings as 'durative', 'punctual', 'iterative', and 'telic'—collectively termed "aspect."

6. Detailed linguistic treatments of these spatial properties can be found in other chapters of this volume, as well as in a number of works by other authors, such as Herskovits (1986).

7. If group-level psychological factors may be adduced outside the narrative proper, they can be seen at work in collaborating coauthors, a live audience, or the cast of a play.

8. It is possible that we have two different cognitive subsystems for psychological ascriptions. One subsystem would ascribe individual personal psychology to a material entity, while the other ascribes an atmosphere to a region. Accordingly, something that could be conceptualized as belonging to either category could be amenable to either type of ascription. For example, in a story, a house in which strange bad things happen could be presented either as an evil entity in its own right (or one controlled by an evil spirit), or as a venue that an eerie atmosphere pervades.

9. Note that this parameter is readily distinguished from the earlier parameter of density. That parameter pertained to a fixed region and the number of elements densely or sparsely dispersed throughout it. The present parameter, in its discrete usage, pertains to a fixed number of elements and whether they are scattered throughout a particular region or drawn together within it.

10. It is possible that the cognitive construct that is most salient in consciousness in the individual in some cultures tends not to be the set of experiences that he associates with the sequential continuity of his own personal identity, but rather a set of experiences that he associates with the larger group or with his role in the group.

References

Aoki, Haruo. 1970. *Nez Perce grammar*. University of California Publications in Linguistics, no. 62. Berkeley: University of California Press.

Aske, Jon. 1989. Path predicates in English and Spanish: A closer look. In *Proceedings of the 15th Annual Meeting of the Berkeley Linguistics Society*. Berkeley, Calif.: Berkeley Linguistics Society.

Baker, Charlotte. 1976. Eye-openers in ASL. Paper delivered at the California Linguistics Association Conference, San Diego State University, San Diego.

Berman, Ruth, and Dan Slobin. 1994. *Relating events in narrative: A cross-linguistic developmental study*. Hillsdale, N.J.: Erlbaum.

Bowerman, Melissa. 1981. Beyond communicative adequacy: From piecemeal knowledge to an integrated system in the child's acquisition of language. In *Papers and Reports on Child Language Development*, no. 20. Stanford, Calif.: Stanford University Press.

Boyer, Pascal. 1994. Cognitive constraints on cultural representations: Natural ontologies and religious ideas. In *Mapping the mind: Domain specificity in cognition and culture*, edited by Lawrence Hirschfeld and Susan Gelman. New York: Cambridge University Press.

Brown, Penelope, and Stephen C. Levinson. 1987. *Politeness: Some universals in language usage*. New York: Cambridge University Press.

Brugman, Claudia. 1988. *The story of* over: *Polysemy, semantics, and the structure of the lexicon*. New York: Garland.

Bybee, Joan. 1980. What's a possible inflectional category? Unpublished paper.

———. 1985. *Morphology: A study of the relation between meaning and form*. Amsterdam: Benjamins.

Chafe, Wallace. 1970. *Meaning and the structure of language*. Chicago: University of Chicago Press.

Choi, Soonja, and Melissa Bowerman. 1991. Learning to express motion events in English and Korean: The influence of language-specific lexicalization patterns. *Cognition* 41: 83–121.

Chomsky, Noam. 1965. *Aspects of the theory of syntax*. Cambridge, Mass.: MIT Press.

Cook-Gumperz, Jenny, and John Gumperz. 1976. Context in children's speech. Unpublished paper, University of California, Berkeley.

Costello, Anne M., Gail Bruder, Carol Hosenfeld, and Judith Duchan. 1995. A structural analysis of a fictional narrative: "A Free Night." In *Deixis in narrative: A cognitive science perspective*, edited by Judith Duchan, Gail Bruder, and Lynne Hewitt. Hillsdale, N.J.: Erlbaum.

Dennett, Daniel C. 1991. *Consciousness explained*. Boston: Little, Brown.

Dixon, Robert M. W. 1972. *The Dyirbal language of North Queensland*. London: Cambridge University Press.

Ervin-Tripp, Susan. 1975. *Making cookies, Playing doctor, Teaparty*. Videotapes shot for the project *Development of Communicative Strategies in Children*. Berkeley: University of California at Berkeley.

Fauconnier, Gilles, and Mark Turner. 1998. Blends. In *Discourse and cognition: Bridging the gap*, edited by Jean-Pierre Koenig. Stanford, Calif.: CSLI Publications.

Fillmore, Charles. 1975. The future of semantics. In *The Scope of American Linguistics: Papers of the First Golden Anniversary Symposium of the Linguistic Society of America*, edited by Robert Austerlitz et al. Lisse: De Ridder.

————. 1977. The case for case reopened. In *Syntax and semantics* (vol. 8): *Grammatical relations*, edited by Peter Cole and Jerrold Sadock. New York: Academic Press.

Fillmore, Charles, and Paul Kay. Forthcoming. *Construction grammar*. Stanford, Calif.: CSLI Publications.

Fleischer, Richard (director). 1966. *Fantastic voyage*. Screenplay by Harry Kleiner, from a story by Otto Klement and Jay Lewis Bixby, novelized by Isaac Asimov. Hollywood, Calif.: 20th Century Fox.

Fodor, Jerry. 1983. *Modularity of mind: An essay on faculty psychology*. Cambridge, Mass.: MIT Press.

Fraser, Bruce. 1976. *The verb-particle combination in English*. New York: Academic Press.

Gallaway, Clare, and Brian Richards, eds. 1994. *Input and interaction in language acquisition*. New York: Cambridge University Press.

Garfinkel, Harold. 1967. *Studies in ethnomethodology*. Englewood Cliffs, N.J.: Prentice Hall.

————. 1972. Studies of the routine grounds of everyday activities. In *Studies in social interaction*, edited by David Sudnow. New York: Free Press.

Genette, Gerard. 1980. *Narrative discourse: An essay in method*, translated by Jane E. Lewin. Ithaca, N.Y.: Cornell University Press.

Gerdts, Donna B. 1988. *Object and absolutive in Halkomelem Salish*. New York: Garland.

Goffman, Erving. 1956. The nature of deference and demeanor. *American Anthropologist* 58: 473–502.

Goldberg, Adele. 1995. *Constructions: A construction grammar approach to argument structure*. Chicago: University of Chicago Press.

Greenberg, Joseph. 1961. Some universals of grammar with particular reference to the order of meaningful elements. In *Universals of language*, edited by Joseph Greenberg. Cambridge, Mass.: MIT Press.

Gruber, Jeffrey S. 1965. *Studies in lexical relations*. Doctoral dissertation, MIT. Reprinted as part of *Lexical structures in syntax and semantics*, 1976. Amsterdam: North-Holland.

Gumperz, John, and Dell Hymes, eds. 1972. *Directions in sociolinguistics: The ethnography of communication*. New York: Holt, Rinehart and Winston.

Gumperz, John, and Robert Wilson. 1971. Convergence and creolization: A case from the Indo-Aryan border. In *Pidginization and creolization of languages*, edited by Dell Hymes. Cambridge, England: Cambridge University Press.

Gurganus, Alan. 1991. *White people*. New York: Knopf.

Hamill, James F. 1990. *Ethno-logic: The anthropology of human reasoning*. Urbana: University of Illinois Press.

Has, Wojciech J. (director). 1965. *Rekopis Znaleziony W Saragossie* (The Saragossa manuscript). Polski State Film release of a Kamera production.

Heath, Jeffrey, Francesca Merlan, and Alan Rumsey, eds. 1982. *The language of kinship in Aboriginal Australia*. Sydney: Oceania Linguistics Monographs.

Heath, Shirley Brice. 1983. *Ways with words: Language, life, and work in communities and classrooms*. New York: Cambridge University Press.

Henry, O. 1903. A retrieved reformation. In *Roads of destiny*, 134–143. Garden City, N.Y.: Doubleday, Page & Co.

Herskovits, Annette. 1986. *Language and spatial cognition: An interdisciplinary study of the prepositions in English*. Cambridge, England: Cambridge University Press.

Hetzron, Robert. 1975. Where the grammar fails. *Language* 51(4): 859–872.

Hill, Jane. 1991. The production of self in narrative. Paper presented at the Second Bi-Annual Conference on Current Thinking and Research of the Society for Psychological Anthropology, October 11–13, Chicago.

Hockett, Charles. 1954. Two models of grammatical description. *Word* 10: 210–231.

Hook, Peter. 1983. The English abstrument and rocking case relations. In *Papers from the 19th Regional Meeting of the Chicago Linguistic Society*. Chicago: Chicago Linguistic Society.

Hutchins, Edwin. 1991. The social organization of distributed cognition. In *Perspectives on socially shared cognition*, edited by Lauren B. Resnick, John M. Levine, and Stephanie D. Teasley. Washington, D.C.: American Psychological Association.

————. 1993. Learning to navigate. In *Understanding practice: Perspectives on activity in context*, edited by Seth Chaiklin and Jean Lave. New York: Cambridge University Press.

Ikegami, Yoshihiko. 1985. 'Activity'-'Accomplishment'-'Achievement'—a language that can't say 'I burned it, but it didn't burn' and one that can. In *Linguistics and philosophy: Essays in honor of Rulon S. Wells*, edited by Adam Makkai and Alan K. Melby. Amsterdam: Benjamins.

Jackendoff, Ray. 1992. Is there a faculty of social cognition? In *Languages of the mind: Essays on mental representation*. Cambridge, Mass.: MIT Press.

Jefferson, Gail. 1972. Side sequences. In *Studies in social interaction*, edited by David Sudnow. New York: Free Press.

Kafka, Franz. 1936. The metamorphosis. In *Selected short stories of Franz Kafka*, translated by Willa and Edwin Muir, 19–89. New York: Random House.

Kahane, Claire. 1996. *The passions of the voice: Hysteria, narrative, and the figure of the speaking woman, 1850–1915*. Baltimore: Johns Hopkins University Press.

Keenan, Elinor, and Bambi Schieffelin. 1975. Foregrounding referents: A reconsideration of left-dislocation in discourse. In *Proceedings of the Second Annual Meeting of the Berkeley Linguistics Society*. Berkeley, Calif: Berkeley Linguistics Society.

Keller, J. D., and F. K. Lehman. 1991. Complex categories. *Cognitive Science* 15(2): 271–291.

Langacker, Ronald W. 1987. *Foundations of cognitive grammar*. 2 vols. Stanford, Calif.: Stanford University Press.

Lave, Jean. 1988 *Cognition in practice: Mind, mathematics, and culture in everyday life*. New York: Cambridge University Press.

Levinson, Stephen C. 1983. *Pragmatics*. Cambridge, England: Cambridge University Press.

Lexer, Matthias. 1966. *Matthias Lexers Mittelhochdeutsches Taschenworterbuch*. Stuttgart: S. Hirzel Verlag.

Li, Charles, and Sandra Thompson. 1976. Development of the causative in Mandarin Chinese: Interaction of diachronic processes in syntax. In *The grammar of causative constructions*, edited by Masayoshi Shibatani. New York: Academic Press.

Li, Fengxiang. 1993. *A diachronic study of V-V compounds in Chinese*. Unpublished doctoral dissertation, State University of New York at Buffalo.

Linde, Charlotte. 1993. *Life stories: The creation of coherence*. New York: Oxford University Press.

Lindner, Susan. 1981. *A lexico-semantic analysis of English verb particle constructions with* out *and* up. Unpublished doctoral dissertation, University of California, San Diego.

Matisoff, James A. 1973. *The grammar of Lahu*. University of California Publications in Linguistics, no. 75. Berkeley: University of California Press.

Matsumoto, Yo. 1991. On the lexical nature of purposive and participial complex motion predicates in Japanese. In *Proceedings of the 17th Annual Meeting of the Berkeley Linguistics Society*. Berkeley, Calif.: Berkeley Linguistics Society.

McCawley, James. 1968. Lexical insertion in a transformational grammar without deep structure. In *Papers from the Fourth Regional Meeting of the Chicago Linguistic Society*. Chicago: Department of Linguistics, University of Chicago.

————. 1971. Prelexical syntax. In *Monograph Series on Languages and Linguistics*. 22nd Annual Roundtable. Washington, D.C.: Georgetown University Press.

Minoura, Yasuko. 1992. A sensitive period for the incorporation of a cultural meaning system: A study of Japanese children growing up in the United States. *Ethos* 20(3): 304–339.

Murdock, George Peter. 1965. The common denominator of cultures. In *Culture and society*. Pittsburgh: University of Pittsburgh Press.

Ozhegov, Sergei. 1968. Slovar' russkovo jazyka. Sovetskaja Enciklopedia, pub.

Pinker, Steven. 1994. *The language instinct*. New York: Morrow.

Postal, Paul. 1976. Linguistic anarchy notes. In *Notes from the Linguistic Underground (Syntax and Semantics* vol. 7*)*, edited by James D. McCawley. New York: Academic Press.

Pustejovsky, James. 1993. Type coercion and lexical selection. In *Semantics and the lexicon*. Dordrecht: Kluwer.

Quinn, Naomi, and Claudia Strauss. 1993. A cognitive framework for a unified theory of culture. Unpublished manuscript.

Sacks, Harvey, Emanuel Schegloff, and Gail Jefferson. 1974. A simplest systematics for the organization of turn-taking for conversation. *Language* 50(4): 696–735.

Schachter, Paul, and Fe T. Otanes. 1972. *Tagalog reference grammar*. Berkeley: University of California Press.

Schaefer, Ronald. 1988. Typological mixture in the lexicalization of manner and cause in Emai. In *Current approaches to African linguistics* (vol. 5), edited by Paul Newman and Robert Botne. New York: Foris Publications.

————. In press. Talmy's schematic core and verb serialization in Emai: An initial sketch. In *Proceedings of the First World Congress on African Linguistics*, edited by R. K. Herbert and E. G. L. Kunene. Johannesburg: University of Witwatersrand.

Schieffelin, Bambi. 1979. *How Kaluli children learn what to say, what to do, and how to feel: An ethnographic study of the development of communicative competence*. Unpublished doctoral dissertation, Columbia University.

Schlicter, Alice. 1986. The origins and deictic nature of Wintu evidentials. In *Evidentiality: The linguistic coding of epistemology*, edited by Wallace Chafe and Johanna Nichols. Norwood, N.J.: Ablex.

Searle, John. 1969. *Speech acts: An essay in the philosophy of language*. London: Cambridge University Press.

Slobin, Dan I. 1985. Crosslinguistic evidence for the language-making capacity. In *The crosslinguistic study of language acquisition: Theoretical issues* (vol. 2), edited by Dan I. Slobin. Hillsdale, N.J.: Erlbaum.

———. 1996. The universal, the typological, and the particular in acquisition. In *The crosslinguistic study of language acquisition* (vol. 5): *Expanding the contexts*, edited by Dan I. Slobin. Mahwah, N.J.: Erlbaum.

———. 1997. Mind, code and text. In *Essays on language function and language type: Dedicated to T. Givon*, edited by J. Bybee, J. Haiman, and S. A. Thompson. Amsterdam: Benjamins.

Slobin, Dan I., and N. Hoiting. 1994. Reference to movement in spoken and signed languages: Typological considerations. In *Proceedings of the 20th Annual Meeting of the Berkeley Linguistics Society*. Berkeley, Calif.: Berkeley Linguistics Society.

Spielberg, Stephen (director). 1993. *Schindler's list*. Hollywood, Calif.: Universal Pictures.

Supalla, Ted. 1982. *Structure and acquisition of verbs of motion and location in American Sign Language*. Unpublished doctoral dissertation, University of California, San Diego.

Talmy, Leonard. 1972. *Semantic structures in English and Atsugewi*. Doctoral dissertation, University of California, Berkeley.

———. 1975a. Figure and ground in complex sentences. In *Proceedings of the First Annual Meeting of the Berkeley Linguistics Society*. Berkeley, Calif.: Berkeley Linguistics Society.

———. 1975b. Semantics and syntax of motion. In *Syntax and semantics* (vol. 4), edited by John P. Kimball. New York: Academic Press.

———. 1976a. Communicative aims and means—a synopsis. *Working Papers on Language Universals* 20: 153–185. Stanford, Calif.: Stanford University.

———. 1976b. Semantic causative types. In *Syntax and semantics* (vol. 6): *The grammar of causative constructions*, edited by Masayoshi Shibatani. New York: Academic Press.

———. 1977. Rubber-sheet cognition in language. In *Papers from the 13th Regional Meeting of the Chicago Linguistic Society*. Chicago: Chicago Linguistic Society.

———. 1978a. Figure and ground in complex sentences. In *Universals of human language* (vol. 4): *Syntax*, edited by Joseph H. Greenberg. Stanford, Calif.: Stanford University Press.

————. 1978b. Relations between subordination and coordination. In *Universals of human language* (vol. 4): *Syntax*, edited by Joseph H. Greenberg. Stanford, Calif.: Stanford University Press.

————. 1978c. The relation of grammar to cognition—a synopsis. In *Proceedings of TINLAP-2*, edited by David Waltz. New York: Association for Computing Machinery.

————. 1982. Borrowing semantic space: Yiddish verb prefixes between Germanic and Slavic. In *Proceedings of the Eighth Annual Meeting of the Berkeley Linguistics Society*. Berkeley, Calif.: Berkeley Linguistics Society.

————. 1983. How language structures space. In *Spatial orientation: Theory, research, and application*, edited by Herbert L. Pick, Jr., and Linda P. Acredolo, 225–282. New York: Plenum Press.

————. 1985a. Force dynamics in language and thought. In *Papers from the 21st Regional Meeting of the Chicago Linguistic Society*. Chicago: Chicago Linguistic Society.

————. 1985b. Lexicalization patterns: Semantic structure in lexical forms. In *Language typology and syntactic description* (vol. 3): *Grammatical categories and the lexicon*, edited by Timothy Shopen. Cambridge, England: Cambridge University Press.

————. 1987. Lexicalization patterns: Typologies and universals. Berkeley Cognitive Science Report 47. Berkeley: Cognitive Science Program, University of California.

————. 1988a. Force dynamics in language and cognition. *Cognitive Science* 12: 49–100.

————. 1988b. The relation of grammar to cognition. In *Topics in cognitive linguistics*, edited by Brygida Rudzka-Ostyn. Amsterdam: Benjamins.

————. 1991. Path to realization: A typology of event conflation. In *Proceedings of the 17th Annual Meeting of the Berkeley Linguistics Society*. Berkeley, Calif.: Berkeley Linguistics Society.

————. 1995a. The cognitive culture system. *The Monist* 78: 80–116.

————. 1995b. Narrative structure in a cognitive framework. In *Deixis in narrative: A cognitive science Perspective*, edited by Gail Bruder, Judy Duchan, and Lynne Hewitt. Hillsdale, N.J.: Erlbaum.

————. 1996a. Fictive motion in language and "ception." In *Language and space*, edited by Paul Bloom, Mary Peterson, Lynn Nadel, and Merrill Garrett. Cambridge, Mass.: MIT Press.

————. 1996b. The windowing of attention in language. In *Grammatical constructions: Their form and meaning*, edited by Masayoshi Shibatani and Sandra Thompson. Oxford: Oxford University Press.

————. In press. Lexicalization patterns. In *Language typology and syntactic description*, 2nd ed., edited by Timothy Shopen. Cambridge, England: Cambridge University Press.

Tomasello, Michael, Ann Cale Kruger, and Hillary Horn Ratner. 1993. Cultural learning. *Behavioral and Brain Sciences* 16(3): 495–552.

Vendler, Zeno. 1967. *Linguistics and philosophy*. Ithaca, N.Y.: Cornell University Press.

Warhol, Andy (director). 1964. *Empire*. New York: Andy Warhol Films.

———. 1969. *Blue movie*. New York: Andy Warhol Films.

Weinreich, Max. 1980. *History of the Yiddish language*. Chicago: University of Chicago Press.

Weinreich, Uriel. 1952. Tsurik tsu aspektn. *Yidishe Shprakh* 12: 97–103.

———. 1953. *Languages in contact*. New York: Linguistic Circle of New York.

———. 1968. *Modern English-Yiddish Yiddish-English dictionary*. New York: YIVO Institute for Jewish Research.

Whorf, Benjamin Lee. 1956. *Language, thought, and reality*. Cambridge, Mass.: MIT Press.

Wilkins, David P. 1988. Switch-reference in Mparntwe Arrernte: Form, function, and problems of identity. In *Complex sentence constructions in Australian languages*, edited by P. Austin. Amsterdam: Benjamins.

———. 1989. *Mparntwe Arrernte: Studies in the structure and semantics of grammar*. Unpublished doctoral dissertation, Australian National University, Canberra.

———. 1991. The semantics, pragmatics, and diachronic development of 'associated motion' in Mparntwe Arrernte. *Buffalo Papers in Linguistics* 91(1): 207–257. State University of New York at Buffalo.

———. 1993. Linguistic evidence in support of a holistic approach to traditional ecological knowledge: Linguistic manifestations of the bond between kinship, land, and totemism in Mparntwe Arrernte. In *Traditional ecological knowledge: Wisdom for sustainable development*, edited by N. Williams and G. Baines. Canberra: CRES Publications.

Wolkonsky, Catherine, and Marianne Poltoratzky. 1961. *Handbook of Russian roots*. New York: Columbia University Press.

Woolf, Virginia. 1944. *A haunted house and other short stories*. New York: Harcourt, Brace.

Woolf, Virginia. 1948. *The voyage out*. New York: Harcourt, Brace & World.

Zakharova, A. V. 1958. Acquisition of forms of grammatical case by preschool children. In *Studies of child language development*, edited by Charles Ferguson and Dan I. Slobin. New York: Holt, Rinehart and Winston.

Zborowski, Mark, and Elizabeth Herzog. 1952. *Life is with people: The Jewish little-town of Eastern Europe*. New York: International Universities Press.

Zelazny, Roger. 1971. *The doors of his face, the lamps of his mouth and other stories*. Garden City, N.Y.: Doubleday.

Index